PRINCIPLES OF
Microeconomics

About the Authors

John B. Taylor is one of the field's most inspiring teachers. As the Raymond Professor of Economics at Stanford University, his distinctive instructional methods have made him a legend among introductory economics students and have won him both the Hoagland and Rhodes prizes for teaching excellence. As described by the *Wall Street Journal,* Taylor's "sober appearance . . . belies a somewhat zany teaching style." Few of his students forget how he first illustrated a shift of the demand curve (by dressing up as a California raisin and dancing to "Heard It Through the Grapevine"), or how he proved that the supply and demand model actually works (by having student buyers and sellers call out live bids to him in the classroom). It is this gift for clear explanations and memorable illustrations that makes his textbook so useful to students around the country.

Professor Taylor is also widely recognized for his research on the foundations of modern monetary theory and policy. One of his well-known research contributions is a rule—now widely called the Taylor Rule—used at central banks around the world. *U.S. News and World Report* wrote about his rule, "Amaze Your Friends! Predict the Fed's Next Move!" His latest research focuses on international monetary policy.

Taylor has had an active career in public service, recently completing a four-year stint as the head of the International Affairs division at the United States Treasury, where he had responsibility for currency policy, international debt, and oversight of the International Monetary Fund and the World Bank and worked closely with leaders and policymakers from countries throughout the world. He has also served as economic adviser to the governor of his state (California), to the U.S. Congressional Budget Office, and to the President of the United States and has served on several boards and as a consultant to private industry.

Professor Taylor began his career at Princeton, where he graduated with highest honors in economics. He then received his Ph.D. from Stanford and taught at Columbia, Yale, and Princeton before returning to Stanford.

Akila Weerapana is an Associate Professor of Economics at Wellesley College. He was born and raised in Sri Lanka and came to the United States to do his undergraduate work at Oberlin College, where he earned a B.A. with highest honors in Economics and Computer Science in 1994. Inspired by his professors at Oberlin, he went on to graduate school at Stanford University. He received his Ph.D. in Economics from Stanford in 1999, writing his dissertation on monetary economics under the mentorship of John Taylor. Having taught several classes at Stanford while he was a graduate student, Akila was determined to pursue a career as a liberal arts college professor, combining his research interests with the opportunity to teach economics to gifted college students. Since 1999, Akila has taught more than 800 students in the Economics Department at Wellesley College.

Akila's teaching interests span all levels of the department's curriculum, including introductory and intermediate macroeconomics, international finance, monetary economics, and mathematical economics. He was awarded Wellesley's Pinanski Prize for Excellence in Teaching in 2002. He also enjoys working with thesis students, having advised more than a dozen of these students at Wellesley. The projects that these students have worked on range from a study of the economic benefits of eradication of river blindness in Ghana to the impact of joining the European Union on the Spanish economy to analyzing the determinants of enterprise performance in Russia. He has advised many students who have pursued graduate study in economics or have gone on to work in economic research at the Federal Reserve.

In addition to teaching, Akila has research interests in macroeconomics, specifically in the areas of monetary economics, international finance, and political economy. In the area of monetary economics, his work focuses on the international dimensions of monetary policy, including the potential for gains from coordination and the importance of asymmetric relationships between countries. On the political economy side, his work examines the macroeconomic implications of political institutions and policy stances; examples include how the South African government's attitude towards the AIDS pandemic may affect exchange rates, how domestic economic growth responds to political institutions such as redistricting mechanisms and voter initiatives, and how political and economic variables can increase or decrease violent conflict.

PRINCIPLES OF
Microeconomics

JOHN B. TAYLOR

AKILA WEERAPANA

Houghton Mifflin Company
Boston   New York

Executive Publisher: George Hoffman
Executive Editor: Lisé Johnson
Sponsoring Editor: Kathleen Swanson
Senior Marketing Manager: Nicole Hamm
Associate Editor: Megan Hoar
Senior Project Editor: Carol Merrigan
Art and Design Manager: Jill Haber
Cover Design Director: Tony Saizon
Senior Photo Editor: Jennifer Meyer Dare
Senior Composition Buyer: Chuck Dutton
New Title Project Manager: James Lonergan
Editorial Assistant: Angela Lang
Marketing Assistant: Lauren Foye

Cover photography: Harold Burch, New York City

Printed in the U.S.A.

Library of Congress Control Number: 2007934819

Instructor's examination copy:
   ISBN-10: 0-547-00478-8
   ISBN-13: 978-0-547-00478-5

For orders, use student text ISBNs:
   ISBN-10: 0-618-96765-6
   ISBN-13: 978-0-618-96765-0

1 2 3 4 5 6 7 8 9-VH-11 10 09 08 07

Brief Contents

Contents

PART 2   Principles of Microeconomics   115

CHAPTER 5   The Demand Curve and the Behavior of Consumers   116

CHAPTER 6   The Supply Curve and the Behavior of Firms   148

CHAPTER 7   The Interaction of People in Markets   176

PART 3   The Economics of the Firm   203

CHAPTER 8   Costs and the Changes at Firms over Time   204

CHAPTER 9   The Rise and Fall of Industries   244

CHAPTER 10   Monopoly   268

CHAPTER 11   Product Differentiation, Monopolistic Competition, and Oligopoly   298

PART 4   Markets, Income Distribution, and Public Goods   349

CHAPTER 16   Capital Markets   460

PART 5   Trade and Global Markets   489

CHAPTER 17   The Gains from International Trade   490

Preface

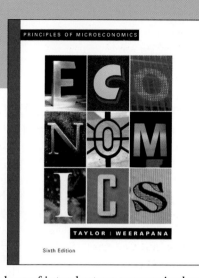

Our goal in this book is to present modern economics in a form that is intuitive, relevant, and memorable to students who have had no prior exposure to the subject. We enjoy teaching introductory economics, and we have enjoyed working on this book. Other teachers of introductory economics have added to our enjoyment by their enthusiastic responses to our approach. Students in our classes, and also email messages from other students around the country and around the world, have rewarded us with their interesting questions and comments. We aim for clarity and for a one-on-one teacher-student focus in the writing, often imagining that we are talking with students as we write.

THE NEW ECONOMICS FROM GENERATION TO GENERATION

We both took introductory economics ourselves—one of us in the 1960s, and the other in the 1990s. People called 1960s-vintage economics the "new economics," because many new ideas, including those put forth by John Maynard Keynes, were being applied to public policy for the first time. But by the 1990s there was a "new" new economics, stressing incentives, expectations, long-run fundamentals, institutions, and the importance of stable, predictable economic policies, that another generation of economists used to improve on the earlier tradition. Now, as we near the end of the first decade of the twenty-first century, there are even newer ideas, many of them dealing with globalization, that are rightfully part of modern economics.

The world economy has also changed radically. The United States and many other countries have experienced far fewer recessions in recent years, and those recessions have been relatively short and mild. The recession in 2001 was one of the shortest recessions on record in the United States. Market economies are now the preferred choice of virtually all countries around the world. The two most populous countries of the world, India and China, have opened up their economies and are experiencing rapid economic growth. Billions of people are linked together through international trade in this new economy. These changes have made economics more fascinating and more relevant than ever.

In this book, we give these recent developments a prominent, clearly explained place within the basic tradition of economics. We emphasize the central idea of economics: that people make purposeful choices with scarce resources and interact with other people when they make these choices. We explain this idea using examples of choices that students actually face. We give real-world examples of how markets work, and we explain why markets are efficient when the incentives are right and inefficient when the incentives are wrong. We know from our teaching experience that examples of how economic ideas are used in practice make economics more interesting to students, thereby making learning economics easier.

CHANGES TO THE SIXTH EDITION

The Sixth Edition has been thoroughly revised, streamlined, and simplified. Introductions, data, case studies, newspaper articles, and boxes discussing academic research have been updated to keep the book topical. Over 75 percent of the articles included in the retitled Economics in the News feature are new and more attention is given to the explanations within each news feature. Many of the Economics in Action boxes are new, providing both instructors and students with fresh applications to discuss. Our hallmark, yellow "conversation boxes" have been retained and extended throughout the text to enhance students' understanding of the material. The Case Study and Point/Counterpoint features from the Fifth Edition have either been removed or incorporated into the text as new features.

In addition to reworking pedagogical elements, many of the more difficult topics have been revised to help make the text more student-friendly. These changes are outlined below.

Content Changes

A detailed account of the chapter-by-chapter changes in the text can be found in the Transition Guide available in the *Instructor's Resource Manual* or on the instructor website. Here are just a few highlights:

- The gasoline market is used as a new example to illustrate the discussion in Chapter 2, "Observing and Explaining the Economy." Attention is also focused on the research work of young economists in the news, to provide students with a glimpse of the possibilities that await someone with a good grasp of economic concepts.

- Chapter 3, "The Supply and Demand Model," now focuses purely on the basics of the supply and demand model, while Chapter 4 has been retitled "Subtleties of the Supply and Demand Model" and now tackles subtler extensions such as price ceilings, price floors, and elasticity.

- Chapter 5, "The Demand Curve and the Behavior of Consumers," now includes a more detailed discussion on some important properties of utility, including its ordinal nature, its reflection of individual preferences, the concept of diminishing marginal utility, and the property of nonsatiation.

- Chapter 7, "The Interaction of People in Markets," no longer includes a discussion of double auction markets. Those who would like to continue covering this section can find it on the course website.

- The discussion of the efficiency of competitive markets in Chapter 7 has been enhanced by explicit analysis of the deadweight loss associated with price ceilings and floors as well as that associated with taxation.

- Chapter 16 has been retitled "Capital Markets," and the discussion of physical and financial capital markets has been expanded to cover corporate governance issues. The discussion of foreign exchange markets has been removed to keep the focus on capital markets.

- Chapter 19, "Transition Economies," has been removed from the Sixth Edition, and Chapter 18, "International Trade Policy," has been updated to function as the new capstone chapter.
- The end-of-chapter questions for each chapter have been thoroughly revised and updated with new figures, data, and examples.

A BRIEF TOUR

Principles of Microeconomics is designed for a one-semester course. Recognizing that teachers use a wide variety of sequences and syllabi, the text allows for alternative plans of coverage. International economic issues are considered throughout the text, with separate chapters on international economic policy.

The text provides a complete, self-contained analysis of competitive markets in the first seven chapters (Parts One and Two) before going on to develop more difficult concepts, such as long-run versus short-run cost curves or monopolistic competition. This approach enables the student to learn, appreciate, and use important concepts such as efficiency and deadweight loss early in the course.

The basic workings of markets and the reasons they improve people's lives are the subjects of Part One. Chapter 1 outlines the unifying themes of economics: scarcity, choice, and economic interaction. The role of prices, the inherent international aspect of economics, the importance of property rights and incentives, and the difference between central planning and markets are some of the key ideas in this chapter. Chapter 2 introduces the field of economics through a case study showing how economists observe and explain economic puzzles. Chapters 3 and 4 cover the basic supply and demand model and elasticity. Here, the goal is to show how to use the supply and demand model to make sense of the world—and to learn how to "think like an economist." The concept of elasticity is now wholly contained in Chapter 4. A trio of chapters—5, 6, and 7—explains why competitive markets are efficient, perhaps the most important idea in economics. The parallel exposition of utility maximization (Chapter 5) and profit maximization (Chapter 6) culminates in a detailed description of why competitive markets are efficient (Chapter 7). The inclusion of interesting results from experimental economics plays a dual role: to illustrate how well models work, and to make the discussion of these important topics less abstract.

A modern market economy is not static; rather, it grows and changes over time as firms add new and better machines and as people add to their skills and training. Chapters 8 and 9 describe how firms and markets grow and change over time. Chapters 10 and 11 demonstrate how economists model the behavior of firms that are not perfectly competitive, such as monopolies. The models of dynamic behavior and imperfect competition developed here are used to explain the rise and fall of real-world firms and industries. Chapter 12 reviews the policy implications.

Chapter 13 considers labor markets. Chapters 14 and 15 are devoted to the role of government in the economy. Tax policy, welfare reform, environmental policy, and the role of government in producing public goods are analyzed. Different countries have taken widely different approaches to the economy. The policy of some countries has been to intervene directly in virtually every economic decision; other countries have followed more hands-off policies. The problem of government failure is analyzed using models of government behavior. Chapter 16 discusses capital markets.

Ever-increasing global economic linkages will be one of the hallmarks of the world that today's students of economics will grow up to live in. Part Five (Chapters 17 through 18) aims to equip students with a better understanding of the economic relationships among countries. With issues about which there are many differing opinions, the text tries to explain these opinions as clearly and as objectively as possible; it also stresses the areas of agreement.

PEDAGOGICAL FEATURES

The following pedagogical features are designed to help students learn economics.

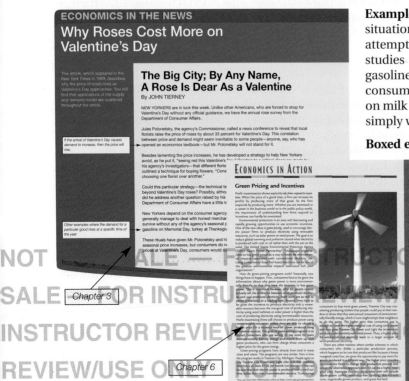

Chapter 3

Chapter 6

Examples within the text. Illustrations of real-world situations help explain economic ideas and models. We have attempted to include a wide variety of brief examples and case studies throughout the text. Examples include a look at the gasoline market in Chapter 2, an article about creating consumer surplus for the poor in Chapter 5, and a case study on milk price supports in Chapter 7. Many other examples are simply woven into the text.

Boxed examples to give real-life perspectives. Economics in the News boxes explain how to decipher recent news stories about economic activities and policy, such as "Why Roses Cost More on Valentine's Day" in Chapter 3 and "Price Fixing in the Ivy League" in Chapter 12. Economics in Action boxes discuss notable current issues and debates, such as "Green Pricing and Incentives" in Chapter 6 and "How Best to Ensure Access to Clean Water in Developing Countries" in Chapter 10.

Stimulating vignettes at the beginning of each chapter. Examples of opening vignettes include the opportunity costs of college for Tiger Woods in Chapter 1 and debates over minimum-wage increases and rising oil prices in Chapter 4. Chapter 10 discusses the antitrust allegations brought against Apple's iTunes by many European countries.

Functional use of full color. Color is used to distinguish between curves and to show how the curves shift dynamically over time. An example of the effective use of multiple colors can be found in the equilibrium price and equilibrium quantity figure in Chapter 3 (Figure 8).

Chapter 3, Figure 8

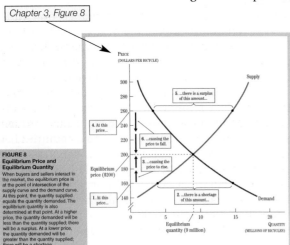

FIGURE 8
Equilibrium Price and Equilibrium Quantity
When buyers and sellers interact in the market, the equilibrium price is at the point of intersection of the supply curve and the demand curve. At this point, the quantity supplied equals the quantity demanded. The equilibrium quantity is also determined at that point. At a higher price, the quantity demanded will be less than the quantity supplied; there will be a surplus. At a lower price, the quantity demanded will be greater than the quantity supplied; there will be a shortage.

Complete captions and small conversation boxes in graphs. The captions and small yellow-shaded conversation boxes make many of the figures completely self-contained. In some graphs, sequential numbering of these conversation boxes stresses the dynamic nature of the curves. Again, Figure 8 in Chapter 3 provides a good example.

Conversation boxes in text margins. These appear when an additional explanation or reminder might help students grasp a new concept more easily.

Use of photos and cartoons to illustrate abstract ideas. Special care has gone into the search for and selection of photos and cartoons to illustrate difficult economic ideas, such as inelastic supply curves or opportunity costs. Many text photos or photo spreads have short titles and captions to explain their relevance to the text discussion.

Key term definitions. Definitions of key terms appear in the margins and in the alphabetized glossary at the end of the book. The key terms are listed at the end of every chapter and appendix.

Brief reviews at the end of each major section. These reviews summarize the key points in abbreviated form as the chapter evolves; they are useful for preliminary skim reading as well as for review.

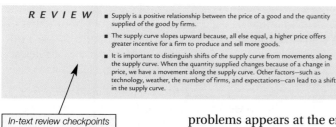

R E V I E W
- Supply is a positive relationship between the price of a good and the quantity supplied of the good by firms.
- The supply curve slopes upward because, all else equal, a higher price offers greater incentive for a firm to produce and sell more goods.
- It is important to distinguish shifts of the supply curve from movements along the supply curve. When the quantity supplied changes because of a change in price, we have a movement along the supply curve. Other factors—such as technology, weather, the number of firms, and expectations—can lead to a shift in the supply curve.

In-text review checkpoints

Questions for review at the end of every chapter. These are tests of recall and require only short answers; they can be used for oral review or as a quick self-check.

Problems. An essential tool in learning economics, the problems have been carefully selected, revised, and tested for this edition. An ample supply of these problems appears at the end of every chapter and appendix. Some of the problems ask the reader to work out examples that are slightly different from the ones given in the text; others require a more critical thinking approach. A second set of problems that parallel those in the textbook has been included in our course management systems.

ENHANCED TEACHING AND LEARNING PACKAGE FOR STUDENTS AND INSTRUCTORS

The highly effective teaching and learning package prepared to accompany this text has been completely revised, updated, and expanded to provide a full range of support for students and instructors. It includes several new options for instructors who wish to take full advantage of the online environment in managing their courses. Students, too, will derive great benefit from the newly revised online tutorials and quizzing that will help walk them through the main concepts from each chapter.

Student Resources

Micro and Macro Study Guides. Revised and updated by David Papell of the University of Houston, Wm. Stewart Mounts, Jr., of Mercer University, and John Solow of the University of Iowa, these study guides provide a wonderful learning opportunity that many students will value. Each chapter contains an overview, an informal chapter review, and a section called Zeroing In that harnesses students' intuition to explain the chapter's most important concepts. The study guides also provide ample means for practice in using the economic ideas and graphs introduced in each text chapter and address a variety of learning needs through graph-based questions and problems as well as multiple-choice practice tests. A section called Working It Out provides worked problems that take the student step-by-step through the analytical process needed for real-world application of the core concepts covered in the chapter. These are followed by practice problems that require students to use the same analytical tools on their own. Detailed answers are provided for all review and practice questions. End-of-part quizzes offer students yet another chance to test their retention of material before taking in-class exams.

Check out the Internet Exercises, Economics W.I.R.E.D., Parallel Problems, and HM NewsNow news feeds and videos powered by the Associated Press to practice and apply economic concepts.

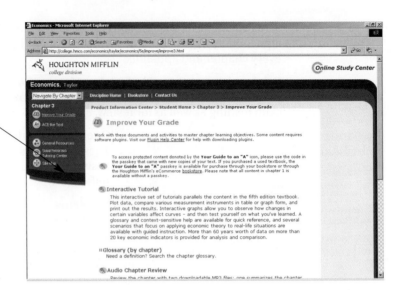

HM EconSpace™ Student Website. The student website (found at college.hmco.com/pic/taylor6e) provides an extended learning environment for students where materials are carefully developed to complement and supplement each chapter. Students will find key economic links as well as numerous opportunities to test their mastery of chapter content—including glossary terms; brief, objective-type quizzes (ACE); and extended Web-based assignments developed by John Kane of State University of New York, Oswego, and John Min of Northern Virginia Community College.

Students who purchase the text package that includes a passkey for accompanying course management or premium content on the student website will receive an additional set of resources developed to reinforce the chapter concepts for students with a variety of learning styles. Included here are step-by-step online tutorials with interactive graphs, audio summary and quiz MP3 files for downloading, and additional online (ACE+) practice quizzes. Students can also utilize electronic flashcards, hangman games, and crossword puzzles to test their knowledge of key terms and definitions.

Instructor Resources

Aplia. Founded in 2000 by economist and professor Paul Romer in an effort to improve his own economics courses at Stanford, Aplia is the leading online learning platform for economics. Houghton Mifflin has partnered with Aplia to provide a rich online experiencethat gets students involved and gives instructors the tools and support they need. The integrated Aplia courses offered for Taylor/Weerapana include math reviews/tutorials, news analyses, and online homework assignments correlated with the relevant Taylor/Weerapana text. In addition, a digital version of the text is embedded in the course, to make it easy for students to access the text when completing assignments. Instructors should consult

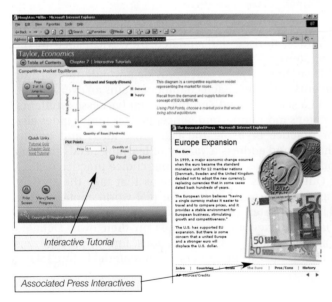

Interactive Tutorial

Associated Press Interactives

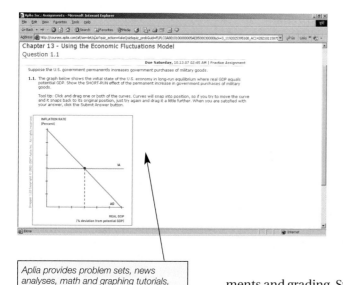

Aplia provides problem sets, news analyses, math and graphing tutorials, experiments, assessment and grading functionality and more.

their Houghton Mifflin sales representative for more information on how to use Aplia with this text.

Course Management Systems. The content found on the Eduspace online learning tool is also available on Blackboard course cartridges and WebCT ePacks for instructors who wish to use these systems to create distance-learning or hybrid courses.

Eduspace®. One of the most challenging aspects of teaching a Principles course is providing students with ample opportunity for practice and review. The Eduspace online learning tool pairs the widely recognized resources of Blackboard with high-quality, text-specific content from Houghton Mifflin. Auto-graded homework problems that parallel the text and multimedia homework exercises come ready to use for online assignments and grading. Students will find a wealth of chapter review material as well, including tutorials with interactive graphs developed for each chapter.

Smarthinking™ Online Tutoring Service. Students who need more individualized, one-on-one tutorial help will have access to the Smarthinking Online Tutoring Service. This live tutoring service allows students to interact online with an experienced Smarthinking e-structor (online tutor) between 3:00 P.M. and 1:00 A.M. ET every Sunday through Thursday and between 12:00 P.M. and 6:00 P.M. ET every Friday and Saturday. Smarthinking provides state-of-the-art communication tools, such as chat technology and virtual whiteboards designed for easy rendering of economic formulas and graphs, to help students absorb key concepts and learn to think economically.

NEW!
eBooks
Digital Textbook Solutions

Multimedia eBook. In addition, a multimedia eBook combines the text with interactive elements such as Houghton Mifflin videos, Associated Press Interactive clips, audio chapter reviews, tutorials, and more, to go beyond the typical learning experience. Content is correlated with the Table of Contents so that students can use a particular asset to enhance their understanding as they read. For example, students can listen to chapter-specific summaries when they read the end-of-chapter conclusion and key points. Students can also highlight text and take virtual notes to help them internalize key concepts.

Micro and Macro Test Banks. A reliable test bank is the most important resource for efficient and effective teaching and learning. The Micro and Macro Test Banks for the Sixth Edition have been revised and prepared by Jim Lee of Texas A&M, Corpus Christi, and Eugenio D. Suarez of Trinity University. They contain more than 5,000 test questions—including multiple-choice, true/false, and short answer problems—many of which are based on graphs. The questions are coded for correct answer, question type, level of difficulty, and text topic. The test banks also include a set of parallel problems that match the end-of-chapter problems from the text. Printed test banks are available on demand; please contact your Houghton Mifflin sales representative for more information on how to obtain a printed copy.

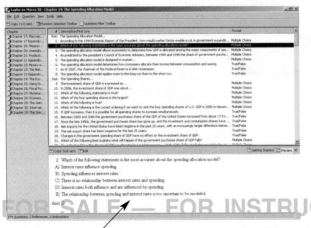

With HMTesting, instructors can scramble the questions and answer choices, edit questions, add their own questions to the pool, and customize their exams in various other ways.

HMTesting CD, powered by Diploma. HM Testing allows instructors to generate and edit tests easily. The program includes an online testing feature that instructors can use to administer tests via their local area network or over the Web. It also has a gradebook feature that lets users set up classes, record and track grades from tests or assignments, analyze grades, and produce class and individual statistics. The program prints graphs and tables in addition to the text part of each question. HMTesting provides a complete testing solution, including classroom administration and online testing features in addition to test generation.

Instructor's Resource Manual. Prepared and revised by John Taylor, Wm. Stewart Mounts, Jr., of Mercer University, and Sarah E. Culver of the University of Alabama at Birmingham, the *Instructor's Resource Manual* provides both first-time and experienced instructors with a variety of additional resources for use with the text. Each chapter contains a brief overview, teaching objectives, key terms from the text, a section that orients instructors to the text's unique approach, and a suggested lecture outline with teaching tips that provide both additional examples not found in the text and hints for teaching more difficult material. Discussion topics and solutions to end-of-chapter text problems are also provided.

PowerPoint Slides. Created by Brian Rosario of the University of California, Davis, the Premium PowerPoint Lecture Slides provide a complete lecture for each chapter, including animations and key figures and tables from the text. Both these presentations and slides of the Main Text Figures and Tables are available to download through the instructor website or through our course management systems. Instructors can use these presentations as is or can delete from and add to them to suit specific class needs.

Overhead Transparencies. Overhead transparencies of the Premium PowerPoint Lecture Slides and the Main Text Figures and Tables are available to adopters of *Economics, Principles of Microeconomics,* and *Principles of Macroeconomics.*

Check out the PowerPoint Slides that accompany HM NewsNow news feeds and videos from the Associated Press on the instructor website.

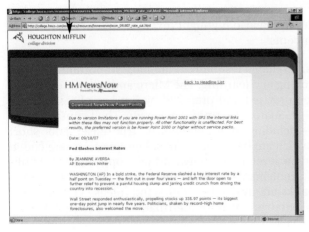

Classroom Response System (CRS). Using state-of-the art wireless technology and text-specific content, a Classroom Response System provides a convenient way to gauge student comprehension, deliver quizzes or exams, and provide "on-the-spot" assessment. Various answering modes, question types, and display options mean that the CRS is as functional as you want it to be. The content is customizable and available on the instructor website or through our course management systems.

HM EconSpace™ Instructor Website. The instructor website (found at college.hmco.com/pic/taylor6e) provides guided Web activities related to the key concepts of each chapter of the textbook. These include, among other materials, Internet Assignments (with solutions) prepared by John Kane of SUNY, Oswego, and Economics W.I.R.E.D. Web links developed by John S. Min of Northern Virginia

Community College. Brief tips to the instructor on how the material might best be used in the classroom along with discussion questions or exercises for assessing student learning accompany the W.I.R.E.D. exercises. The instructor website also contains all of the instructor materials found in the *Instructor's Resource Manual* and a complete set of parallel questions (and solutions) that match the end-of-chapter problems from the text. Additionally, we offer HM NewsNow news feeds and videos from the Associated Press with PowerPoints that include discussion, polling, and multiple-choice questions.

ACKNOWLEDGMENTS

Completing a project like this is a team effort, and we both have been blessed with good students and colleagues who have given us advice and encouragement.

John B. Taylor. I am grateful to my colleagues at Stanford, whom I have consulted hundreds of times over the years, including Don Brown, Tim Breshanan, Anne Kreuger, Tom McCurdy, Paul Milgrom, Roger Noll, John Pencavel, Paul Romer, Nate Rosenberg, and Frank Wolak. I must acknowledge with very special gratitude Akila's willingness to join this project. Akila first demonstrated his extraordinary teaching and writing skills even before completing his Ph.D. at Stanford. After receiving his Ph.D., Akila joined the faculty at Wellesley College, where he has taught the Principles course for many semesters and further established his reputation for teaching excellence, and where, in 2002, he received the Anna and Samuel Pinanski Teaching Award. His ability to get complex topics across to his students and his enthusiasm for bringing policy implications alive is clearly reflected in our new coauthored book.

Akila Weerapana. I am exceedingly grateful to John for giving me the opportunity to communicate my enthusiasm for teaching economics to a broader audience than the students in my classes at Wellesley. My passion for economics stems from the inspiration I received from my economics professors: Barbara Craig and Peter Montiel at the undergraduate level, and John Taylor, Frank Wolak, and Chad Jones at the graduate level. I too have benefited immensely from working with my colleagues. The faculty members in the Economics Department at Wellesley live up to the liberal arts ideal that I aspire to, combining excellent teaching with active research. Special thanks are owed to Courtney Coile and David Lindauer for the time they spent helping me understand how best to pitch topics in microeconomics that I am less familiar with teaching than they are. The real inspirations for this book, however, are the students that I have taught over the past decade—two years at Stanford, but especially, the last eight years at Wellesley. Without their enthusiasm for economics, their willingness to be continually challenged, and their need to better understand an ever-changing world, none of this would be possible. My contributions to this book are shaped by countless hours spent talking economics with my students. Through this book, I hope that this conversation extends to many others. Along these lines, special thanks go to Helena Steinberg, Class of 2008 at Wellesley. She served as an invaluable and patient resource for how students would react to and understand economic concepts, examples, newspaper articles, photographs, cartoons, and study questions.

We would also like to thank William B. Stronge of Florida Atlantic University, who provided wonderful end-of-chapter problems that are conceptually challenging and require students to think more deeply about the concepts. Bill's efforts helped us meet an incredibly demanding schedule, and we are grateful for his contributions.

Numerous reviewers provided insights, suggestions, and feedback along the way—often at critical points in product and supplement development. These individuals include Mohsen Bahmani-Oskooee, University of Wisconsin, Milwaukee; Erik Craft, University of Richmond; David H. Eaton, Murray State University; Lewis Freiberg, Northeastern Illinois University; Wang Fuzhong, Beijing University of Aeronautics & Astronautics; Janet Gerson, University of Michigan; Lisa Grobar, California State University, Long Beach; Ritika Gugnani, Jaipuria Institute of Management (Noida); Gautam Hazarika, University of Texas, Brownsville; Aaron Johnson, Missouri State University; Jacob Kurien, Rockhurst University; Babu Nahata, University of Louisville; Soloman Namala, Cerritos College; Sebastien Oleas, University of Minnesota, Duluth; Greg Pratt, Mesa Community College; Virginia Reilly, Ocean County College; Brian Rosario, University of California, Davis; William B. Stronge, Florida Atlantic University; Della Lee Sue, Marist College; J. S. Uppal, State University of New York, Albany; Michele T. Villinski, DePauw University; and Laura Wolff, Southern Illinois University, Edwardsville.

We are grateful to Sarah L. Stafford of the College of William and Mary and Robert J. Rossana of Wayne State University for their detailed and timely accuracy checks of the main texts and several key supplements.

We are especially appreciative of the contributions of the Sixth Edition supplements authors for their creativity, dedication, and careful coordination of content; this group includes Sarah E. Culver, University of Alabama, Birmingham; David H. Eaton, Murray State University; John Kane, State University of New York, Oswego; Jim Lee, Texas A&M University, Corpus Christi; John S. Min, Northern Virginia Community College; Wm. Stewart Mounts, Jr., Mercer University; David H. Papell, University of Houston; Virginia Reilly, Ocean County College Center for Economic Education; Brian Rosario, University of California, Davis; John Solow, University of Iowa; William B. Stronge, Florida Atlantic University; Eugenio D. Suarez, Trinity University; and Laura Wolff, Southern Illinois University, Edwardsville. We would also like to thank Edward Gullason of Dowling College for reviewing many of these supplements and Matthew Berg and Julia Ong for copyediting them.

Finally, we would like to thank the team at Houghton Mifflin who labored over this Sixth Edition, including Ann West, Kathleen Swanson, Carol Merrigan, James Hamilton, Angela Lang, and Megan Hoar.

Reviewers

This book would not exist without the help of all the reviewers and readers who have provided suggestions incorporated into each revision.

Mark D. Agee
Pennsylvania State University, Altoona

James Alm
University of Colorado, Boulder

Lee J. Alston
University of Illinois

Christine Amsler
Michigan State University

Lisa Anderson
College of William and Mary

Charles Andrews
Mercer University

Mohsen Bahmani-Oskooee
University of Wisconsin, Milwaukee

Dean Baim
Pepperdine University

R.J. Ballman, Jr.
Augustana College

Samiran Banerjee
Georgia Institute of Technology

Raymond S. Barnstone
Northeastern University and Lesley College

Laurie Bates
Bryant College

Kari Battaglia
University of North Texas

Klaus G. Becker
Texas Tech University

Valerie R. Bencivenga
Cornell University

Sidney M. Blumner
California Polytechnic University

William M. Boal
Drake University

Brian Boike
Boston University

Roger Bowels
University of Bath

Paula Bracy
University of Toledo

Jozell Brister
Abilene Christian University

Robert Brown
Texas Tech University

Robert Buchele
Smith College

Mark L. Burkey
North Carolina A&T State University

Michael R. Butler
Texas Christian University

Richard Call
American River College

Leonard A. Carlson
Emory University

Michael J. Carter
University of Massachusetts, Lowell

William F. Chapel
University of Mississippi

Chiuping Chen
American River College

Kenneth Chinn
Southeastern Oklahoma State University

Marcelo Clerici-Arias
Stanford University

Stephen L. Cobb
University of North Texas

Mike Cohick
Collin County Community College

Kathy L. Combs
California State University, Los Angeles

Joyce Cooper
Boston University

Erik Craft
University of Richmond

Steven Craig
University of Houston

Sarah Culver
University of Alabama, Birmingham

Michael A. Curme
Miami University

Ward S. Curran
Trinity College

Joseph Daniels
Marquette University

Audrey Davidson
University of Louisville

Gregg Davis
Marshall University

Gregory E. DeFreitas
Hofstra University

Mary E. Deily
Lehigh University

David N. DeJong
University of Pittsburgh

David Denslow
University of Florida

Enrica Detragiache
Johns Hopkins University

Michael Devereux
University of British Columbia

Michael Dowd
University of Toledo

Douglas Downing
Seattle Pacific University

Dean Dudley
United States Military Academy

David H. Eaton
Murray State University

Mary E. Edwards
St. Cloud State University

Ken Farr
Georgia College

David Figlio
University of Oregon

Lewis Freiberg
Northeastern Illinois University

Gerald Friedman
University of Massachusetts, Amherst

Edwin T. Fujii
University of Hawaii

Wang Fuzhong
Beijing University of Aeronautics & Astronautics

Mary Gade
Oklahoma State University

Charles Geiss
University of Missouri

Janet Gerson
University of Michigan

J. Robert Gillette
University of Kentucky

Donna Ginther
Southern Methodist College

David Gleicher
Adelphi University

Mark Glick
University of Utah

Stuart M. Glosser
University of Wisconsin, Whitewater

Abbas Grammy
California State University

Phil Graves
University of Colorado, Boulder

Gregory Green
Idaho State University

Paul W. Grimes
Mississippi State University

Lisa Grobar
California State University, Long Beach

Lorna S. Gross
Worcester State College

Shoshana Grossbard-Shechtamn
San Diego State University

Ritika Gugnani
Jaipuria Institute of Management (Noida)

Robin Hahnel
American University

Alan Haight
Bowling Green State University

David R. Hakes
Linfield College

Greg Hamilton
Marist College

Mehidi Harian
Bloomsburg University

Richard Harper
University of West Florida

Mitchell Harwitz
State University of New York, Buffalo

Gautam Hazarika
University of Texas, Brownsville

Mary Ann Hendryson
Western Washington University

James B. Herendeen
University of Texas, El Paso

Pershing J. Hill
University of Alaska, Anchorage

Denise Hixson
Midlands Technical College

Gail Mitchell Hoyt
University of Richmond

James M. Hvidding
Kutztown University

Beth Ingram
University of Iowa

Murat F. Iyigun
University of Colorado, Boulder

Joyce Jacobsen
Wesleyan University

Syed Jafri
Tarleton State University

David Jaques
California Polytech University, Pomona

John Jascot
Capital Community College

Allan Jenkins
University of Nebraska at Kearney

Aaron Johnson
Missouri State University

David Johnson
Wilfred Laurier University

Charles W. Johnston
University of Michigan, Flint

Nake Kamrany
University of Southern California

John Kane
State University of New York, Oswego

Manfred Keil
Claremont McKenna College

Kristen Keith
University of Alaska

Elizabeth Kelly
University of Wisconsin, Madison

Jongsung Kim
Bryant University

John Klein
Georgia State University

Harry T. Kolendrianos
Danville Community College

Jacob Kurien
Rockhurst University

Margaret Landman
Bridgewater State College

Phillip J. Lane
Fairfield University

William Lang
Rutgers University

William D. Lastrapes
University of Georgia

Lawernce A. Leger
Loughborough University

David Li
University of Michigan

Susan Linz
Michigan State University

John K. Lodewijks
University of New South Wales

R. Ashley Lyman
University of Idaho

Bridget Lyons
Sacred Heart University

Craig MacPhee
University of Nebraska, Lincoln

Michael Magura
University of Toledo

Robert A. Margo
Vanderbilt University

John D. Mason
Gordon College

Robert McAuliffe
Babson College

Henry N. McCarl
University of Alabama, Birmingham

Laurence C. McCulloch
Ohio State University

Rob Roy McGregor
University of North Carolina, Charlotte

Richard McIntyre
University of Rhode Island

Mark McLeod
Virginia Tech

Gaminie Meepagala
Howard University

Frederick Menz
Clarkson University

Micke Meurs
American University

Khan A. Mohabbat
Northern Illinois University

Norma Morgan
Curry College

Peter Morgan
State University of New York, Buffalo

W. Douglas Morgan
University of California, Santa Barbara

Wm. Stuart Mounts
Mercer University

Vai-Lam Mui
University of Southern California

David C. Murphy
Boston College

Babu Nahata
University of Louisville

Soloman Namala
Cerritos College

Andrew Narwold
University of San Diego

Ronald C. Necoechea
Ball State University

John Neri
University of Maryland

Rebecca Neumann
University of Colorado, Boulder

Hong V. Nguyen
University of Scranton

Edd Noell
Westmont College

Lou Noyd
Northern Kentucky University

Rachel Nugent
Pacific Lutheran University

Anthony Patrick O'Brien
Lehigh University

William C. O'Connor
Western Montana College

Sebastien Oleas
University of Minnesota, Duluth

Eliot S. Orton
New Mexico State University

Jan Palmer
Ohio University

David Papell
University of Houston

Walter Park
American University

Charles Parker
Wayne State College

A. Cristina Cunha Parsons
Trinity College, Washington, D.C.

James Payne
Eastern Kentucky University

David Petersen
American River College, Sacramento

E. Charles Pflanz
Scottsdale Community College

William A. Phillips
University of Southern Maine

Glenn J. Platt
Miami University

Charles Plott
California Institute of Technology

Lidija Polutnik
Babson College

Salena Porca
University of South Carolina

Greg Pratt
Mesa Community College

David L. Prychitko
State University of New York, Oswego

Salim Rashid
*University of Illinois, Urbana-
Champaign*

Margaret A. Ray
Mary Washington College

Virginia Reilly
Ocean County College

Geoffrey Renshaw
University of Warwick

John Ridpath
York University

Brian Rosario
University of California, Davis

B. Peter Rosendorff
University of Southern California

Robert J. Rossana
Wayne State University

Greg Rose
Sacramento City College

Marina Rosser
James Madison University

Kartic C. Roy
University of Queensland

Daniel Rubenson
Southern Oregon State College

Jeffrey Rubin
Rutgers University

Robert S. Rycoft
Mary Washington College

Jonathan Sandy
University of San Diego

Jeff Sarbaum
*State University of New York,
Binghamton*

Gary Saxonhouse
University of Michigan

Edward Scahill
University of Scranton

James Byron Schlomach
Texas A&M University

Torsten Schmidt
University of New Hampshire

Thomas J. Shea
Springfield College

William J. Simeone
Providence College

Michael Smitka
Washington & Lee University

Ronald Soligo
Rice University

John Solow
University of Iowa

Clifford Sowell
Berea College

Michael Spagat
Brown University

David Spencer
Brigham Young University

Sarah L. Stafford
College of William and Mary

J.R. Stanfield
Colorado State University

Ann B. Sternlicht
University of Richmond

Richard Stevenson
Liverpool University

James Stodder
Rensselaer Polytechnic Institute

Leslie S. Stratton
University of Arizona

William B. Stronge
Florida Atlantic University

Robert Stuart
Rutgers University

Della Lee Sue
Marist College

Dave Surdam
Loyola University, Chicago

James Swoffard
University of South Alabama

Bette Lewis Tokar
Holy Family College

Paul Turner
University of Leeds

J. S. Uppal
State University of New York, Albany

Lee J. Vanscyoc
University of Wisconsin, Oshkosh

Michele T. Villinski
DePauw University

Gerald R. Visgilio
Connecticut College

Manhar Vyas
University of Pittsburgh

Shaianne T.O. Warner
Ithaca College

William V. Weber
Eastern Illinois University

Karl Wesolowski
Salem State College

Jospeh Wesson
State University of New York, Potsdam

Geoff Whittam
University of Glasglow

Kenneth P. Wickman
State University of New York, Cortland

Catherine Winnett
University of Bath

Jennifer P. Wissink
Cornell University

Laura Wolff
Southern Illinois University, Edwardsville

Simon Wren-Lewis
University of Strathclyde

Peter R. Wyman
Spokane Falls Community College

Yung Y. Yang
California State University, Sacramento

Ali Zaker Shahrak
University of Santa Clara

PRINCIPLES OF
Microeconomics

Part 1

Introduction to Economics

1

The Central Idea

This is a true story. In the spring of 1996, a 19-year-old college sophomore who had just finished taking introductory economics was faced with a *choice:* to continue college for an additional two years or to leave college and begin devoting all his time to a job. The job was being a professional golfer on the PGA Tour—a job for which that sophomore was uniquely qualified, having already won three U.S. amateur titles. Doing both college and the PGA Tour was not an option because time is *scarce.* Since there are only 24 hours in a day, that sophomore simply did not have the time for both activities, so he had to make a choice. But in choosing one activity, he would incur a cost by giving up the other activity. Choosing golf would mean passing up the job opportunities that would inundate a college senior who was well trained in economics; choosing college would mean passing up the potential tournament winnings and the guarantees of advertising endorsements that awaited a professional golfer. The golfer—a young guy named Tiger Woods—had to make a choice, and he did. He became a professional golfer.

A decade later, it seems that Tiger Woods made the right choice. He was selected to be the Sportsman of the Year in 1996, he won the venerable Masters Tournament in 1997, and by the end of 2006 he had won 54 tournaments, 12 major championships, and almost $65 million in prize money. His endorsement income was even greater; he had earned almost $500 million over his first decade of play and was predicted to be the first athlete to make over a billion dollars in endorsement income.

Tiger Woods was able to reap such rich rewards from his golf talents because of the opportunities he had to *interact with people.* Golf fans enjoyed watching him play. They were willing to pay money to interact with him by sitting in the gallery as he played in tournaments. Executives who ran companies like Nike, American Express, and General Motors interacted with him and paid him to endorse their products. And Tiger's family, friends, and teachers interacted with him, conveying basic skills, enhancing his confidence, and helping him remain cool under pressure. Tiger gained from these interactions with different groups of people, and they gained from interacting with Tiger, too.

The story of Tiger Woods is a story about economics, and not simply because of all the money that he has earned. His story illustrates the idea that lies at the center of economics: that people make *purposeful choices* with *scarce resources* and *interact with others* when they make these choices. More than anything else, **economics** is the study of how people deal with scarcity.

Scarcity is a situation in which people's resources are limited. People always face a scarcity of something—even someone as rich as Tiger Woods faces a scarcity of time. Scarcity implies that people must make a **choice** to forgo, or give up, one thing in favor of another. Most of the time the choices are far more difficult than the one Tiger Woods faced: A student may have to find a job to support her family instead of going to college; a worker may have to delay his retirement to hold on to a job that has health benefits; a parent may have to decide between staying at home with a child and working. As you read this, you may find yourself reflecting on decisions that you have had to make in your life—which college to attend, whether to take economics or biology, whether you should take all your classes after 10 A.M. or try to have them all done before noon.

Economic interactions between people occur every time they trade or exchange goods with each other. For example, a college student will buy education services from a university in exchange for tuition. A teenager may sell labor services to Taco Bell in exchange for cash. Within a household, one member may agree to cook dinner in exchange for the other person agreeing to wash the dishes. Economic interactions typically take place in a **market.** A market is simply an arrangement by which buyers and sellers can interact and exchange goods and services with each other. There are many markets in the United States, ranging from the New York stock market to a local flea market. Interactions do not have to take place with the buyer and seller in close physical proximity to each other; the telephone, radio, television, and the Internet all help enhance the opportunities for economic interactions to take place.

The purpose of this book is to introduce you to the field of economics, to provide you with the knowledge that will help you understand how so much of what happens in the world today is shaped by the actions of people who had to make choices when confronted by scarcity. A better understanding of economics will equip you to understand the opportunities and challenges that you face as an individual—should you take out a student loan to continue your studies in graduate school? It will also

economics: the study of how people deal with scarcity.

scarcity: the situation in which the quantity of resources is insufficient to meet all wants.

choice: a selection among alternative goods, services, or actions.

economic interactions: exchanges of goods and services between people.

market: an arrangement by which economic exchanges between people take place.

The choice was to continue college or join the Pro Tour. What would you have done?

leave you better able to be a more informed citizen about the challenges that the nation faces—should the government provide affordable health care for everyone in the economy? Soon you will find yourself viewing the world through the lens of economics. Your friends may tell you that you are "thinking like an economist." You should take that as a compliment!

The first step toward this goal is for you to get an intuitive feel for how pervasive scarcity, choice, and economic interactions are in the real world. That is the purpose of this chapter.

SCARCITY AND CHOICE FOR INDIVIDUALS

It is easy to find everyday examples of how people make purposeful choices when they are confronted with a scarcity of time or resources. A choice that may be on your mind when you study economics is how much time to spend on it versus other activities. If you spend all your time on economics, you may get a 100 on the final exam, but that might mean you get a zero in biology. If you spend all your time on biology, then you may get a 100 in biology and a zero in economics. Most people resolve the choice by *balancing* out their time to get a decent grade in both subjects. If you are premed, then biology will probably get more time. If you are interested in business, then more time on economics might be appropriate.

Now let us apply this basic principle to two fundamental economic problems: individual choices about what to *consume* and what to *produce*. For each type of economic problem, we first show how scarcity forces one to make a choice, then show how people gain from interacting with other people.

Consumer Decisions

Consider Maria, who is going for a walk in a park on a sunny day. Maria would love to wear a hat (baseball style with her school logo) and sunglasses on the hike, but she has brought neither with her. Maria has brought $20 with her, however, and there is a store in the park that is having a "two for one" sale. She can buy two hats for $20 or two pairs of sunglasses for $20. She would prefer to buy one hat and one pair of sunglasses, but that is not possible. Her scarcity of funds causes her to make a choice. The $20 limit on her spending is an example of a *budget constraint*, a scarcity of funds that limits her to spending no more than this amount. Her choice will depend on her tastes. Let us assume that when she is forced by scarcity to make a choice, she will choose the sunglasses.

opportunity cost: the value of the next-best forgone alternative that was not chosen because something else was chosen.

■ **Opportunity Cost.** Maria's decision is an example of an economic problem that all people face: A budget constraint forces them to make a choice between different items that they want. Choosing one item means that you have to give up other items. The **opportunity cost** of a choice is the value of the next-best forgone alternative that was not chosen. The opportunity cost of the hats is the loss from not being able to wear the sunglasses. An opportunity cost occurs every time there is a choice. For example, the opportunity cost of going to an 8 A.M. class rather than sleeping in is the sleep you lose when you get up early. The opportunity cost of Tiger Woods's staying in college was millions of dollars in prize money and endorsement income. In many cases involving choice and scarcity, there are many more than two things to choose from. If you choose vanilla ice cream out of a list of many possible flavors, then the opportunity cost is the loss from not being able to consume the *next-best* flavor, perhaps strawberry.

Now, suppose Maria is not the only hiker. Also in the park is Adam, who also has $20 to spend. Adam also loves both hats and sunglasses, but he likes hats more than sunglasses. When forced to make a choice, he buys the hats. His decision is shaped by scarcity just as Maria's is: Scarcity comes from the budget constraint. He must make a choice, and there is an opportunity cost for each choice.

■ **Gains from Trade: A Better Allocation.** Now suppose that Adam and Maria meet each other in the park. Let's consider the possibility of economic interaction between them. Maria has two pairs of sunglasses and Adam has two hats, so Maria and Adam can trade with each other. Maria can trade one of her pairs of sunglasses for one of Adam's hats, as shown in Figure 1. Through such a trade, both Maria and Adam can improve their situation. There are **gains from trade** because the trade reallocates goods between the two individuals in a way that they both prefer. Trade occurs because Maria is willing to exchange one pair of sunglasses for one hat, and Adam is willing to exchange one hat for one pair of sunglasses. Because trade is mutually advantageous for both Maria and Adam, they will voluntarily engage in it if they are able to. In fact, if they do not gain from the trade, then neither will bother to make the trade.

gains from trade: improvements in income, production, or satisfaction owing to the exchange of goods or services.

This trade is an example of an economic interaction in which a reallocation of goods through trade makes both people better off. There is no change in the total quantity of goods produced. The number of hats and sunglasses has remained the same. Trade simply reallocates existing goods.

The trade between Maria and Adam is typical of many economic interactions that we will study in this book. Thinking like an economist in this example means recognizing that a voluntary exchange of goods between people must make them better off. Many economic exchanges are like this, even though they are more complicated than the exchange of hats and sunglasses.

Producer Decisions

Now consider two producers—Emily, a poet, and Johann, a printer. Both face scarcity and must make choices. Because of differences in training, abilities, or inclination, Emily is much better at writing poetry than Johann is, but Johann is much better at printing greeting cards than Emily is.

If Emily writes poetry full time, she can produce 10 poems in a day; but if she wants to make and sell greeting cards with her poems in them, she must spend some time printing cards and thereby spend less time writing poems. However, Emily is not very good at printing cards; it takes her so much time to do so that if she prints 1 card, she has time to write only 1 poem rather than 10 poems during the day.

If Johann prints full time, he can produce 10 different greeting cards in a day. However, if he wants to sell greeting cards, he must write poems to put inside them. Johann is so poor at writing poems that if he writes only 1 poem a day, his production of greeting cards drops from 10 to 1 per day.

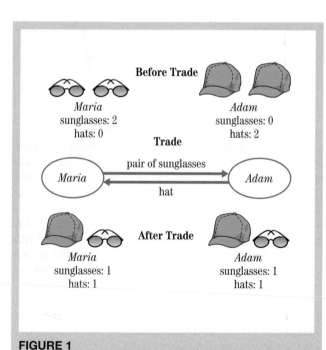

FIGURE 1
Gains from Trade Through a Better Allocation of Goods
Without trade, Maria has more pairs of sunglasses than she would like, and Adam has more hats than he would like. By trading a hat for a pair of sunglasses, they both gain.

The following is a summary of the choices Emily and Johann face because of a scarcity of time and resources.

	Emily, the Poet		Johann, the Printer	
	Write Full Time	*Write and Print*	*Print Full Time*	*Write and Print*
Cards	0	1	10	1
Poems	10	1	0	1

If Emily and Johann cannot interact, then each can produce only 1 greeting card with a poem on the inside in a day. Alternatively, Emily could produce 10 poems without the cards and Johann could produce 10 cards without the poems, but then neither would earn anything. We therefore assume that when confronted with this choice, both Emily and Johann will each choose to produce 1 greeting card with a poem inside. In total, they produce 2 greeting cards.

■ **Gains from Trade: Greater Production.**   Now consider the possibility of economic interaction. Suppose that Emily and Johann can trade. Johann could sell his printing services to Emily, agreeing to print her poems on nice greeting cards. Then Emily could sell the greeting cards to people. Under this arrangement, Emily could spend all day writing poetry, and Johann could spend all day printing. In total, they could produce 10 different greeting cards together, expending the same time and effort it took to produce 2 greeting cards when they could not trade.

Note that in this example the interaction took place in a market: Johann sold his print jobs to Emily. Another approach would be for Emily and Johann to go into business together, forming a firm, Dickinson and Gutenberg Greetings, Inc. Then their economic interaction would occur within the firm, without buying or selling in the market.

Whether in a market or within a firm, the gains from trade in this example are huge. By trading, Emily and Johann can increase their production of greeting cards fivefold, from 2 cards to 10 cards.

■ **Specialization, Division of Labor, and Comparative Advantage.**   This example illustrates another way in which economic interaction improves people's lives. Economic interaction allows for **specialization:** people concentrating their production efforts on what they are good at. Emily specializes in poetry, and Johann specializes in printing. The specialization creates a division of labor. A **division of labor** occurs when some workers specialize in one task while others specialize in another task. They divide the overall production into parts, with some workers concentrating on one part (printing) and other workers concentrating on another part (writing).

The poetry/printing example of Emily and Johann also illustrates another economic concept, **comparative advantage.** In general, a person or group of people has a comparative advantage in producing one good relative to another good if that person or group can produce that good with comparatively less time, effort, or resources than another person or group can produce that good. For example, compared with Johann, Emily has a comparative advantage in writing relative to printing. And compared with Emily, Johann has a comparative advantage in printing relative to writing. As this example shows, production can be increased if people specialize in the skill in which they have a comparative advantage[1]—that is, if Emily specializes in writing and Johann in printing.

specialization: a concentration of production effort on a single specific task.

division of labor: the division of production into various parts in which different groups of workers specialize.

comparative advantage: a situation in which a person or group can produce one good at a lower opportunity cost than another person or group.

---

[1] Other examples are explored in Chapter 29, where you can see that comparative advantage can also occur when one person is absolutely better at both activities.

ECONOMICS IN ACTION

Gains from Trade on the Internet

The Internet has created many new opportunities for gains from trade. Internet auction sites like eBay allow sellers a way to offer their goods for sale and buyers a way to make bids on sale items. The gains are similar to those of Maria and Adam as they trade sunglasses for hats. Hundreds of different types of sunglasses and baseball hats (and millions of other things) can be bought and sold on eBay—nearly 39,000 types of sunglasses and 5,900 types of baseball hats were for sale at last count.

If you—like Maria—want to sell a pair of sunglasses and buy a baseball hat, you can simply go to www.ebay.com, offer a pair of sunglasses to sell, and search for the hat you would like to buy. The computer screen will show photos of some of the sunglasses and baseball hats that are offered. You may also find yourself looking through other categories, like baseball cards or beachwear, and decide to enter into another economic transaction, simply because eBay is an extremely large marketplace that lets you interact with more individuals than you had intended to when you first decided to look for a baseball hat.

Even though many of the Internet-related businesses that started in the mid-1990s failed to make it through the tech implosion of the early part of this decade, eBay has remained hugely successful—it is a $40 billion company with offshoots, imitators, and competitors all over the world. Today there are nearly 100 million registered users, with millions of sales of items, ranging from sunglasses and baseball hats to antiques and cars, transacted in a single day.

Another site that has been phenomenally successful at bringing individuals together to gain from trade is Craigslist. Craig Newmark, the founder of Craigslist, saw the power of the Internet for bringing together buyers and sellers who previously had typically interacted through classified advertisements in the back pages of newspapers. Craigslist has become one of the first places that people go when they are looking for an apartment to rent or a used car to buy (or, for that matter, looking to rent out their apartment or to sell their used car). Furthermore, Craigslist was quick to exploit the fact that for certain goods and services (apartment sublets, secondhand furniture, used cars), it was more important to reach a group of buyers and sellers who lived in geographical proximity to the person initiating the transaction than it was to reach millions of people all over the world, as eBay did. The success of Craigslist has been such that a 2005 article in *SF Weekly* estimated that Bay Area newspapers were losing more than $50 million a year in classified advertising revenue as a result of economic transactions switching over to Craigslist.

Perhaps the main reason for the success of these online marketplaces is their underlying simplicity. They provide information and a means for buyers and sellers to interact with each other, just as markets have done throughout history, but the scale of these virtual flea markets dwarfs what was possible before the Internet. The Internet will only continue to grow as a technology that enhances economic interactions. Social networking sites like Facebook and MySpace are already extremely popular with young people today. The vast sums of money that companies are prepared to pay to own these sites indicates that they too will become important online locations for economic interactions to take place in the future.

QUESTIONS TO PONDER

1. Can you think of potential gains from trade for you (or for a friend or a family member) that can be realized by using eBay or Craigslist?

2. Craigslist was able to successfully distinguish itself from eBay in the types of transactions that took place on it. How can social networking sites like Facebook or Myspace best distinguish themselves from other Internet trading sites?

International Trade

Thus far, we have said nothing about where Emily and Johann live or work. They could reside in the same country, but they could also reside in different countries. Emily could live in the United States; Johann, in Germany. If this is so, when Emily purchases Johann's printing service, **international trade** will take place because the trade is between people in two different countries.

The gains from international trade are thus of the same kind as the gains from trade within a country. By trading, people can better satisfy their preferences for goods (as in the case of Maria and Adam), or they can better utilize their comparative advantage (as in the case of Emily and Johann). In either situation, there is a gain to both participants from trade.

international trade: the exchange of goods and services between people or firms in different nations.

R E V I E W

- All individuals face scarcity in one form or another. Scarcity forces people to make choices. When a choice is made, there is also an opportunity cost of not doing one thing because another thing has been chosen.

- People benefit from economic interactions—trading goods and services—with other people.

- Gains from trade occur because goods and services can be allocated in ways that are more satisfactory to people.

- Gains from trade also occur because trade permits specialization through the division of labor. People should specialize in the production of goods in which they have a comparative advantage.

SCARCITY AND CHOICE FOR THE ECONOMY AS A WHOLE

Just as individuals face scarcity and choice, so does the economy as a whole. The total amount of resources in an economy—workers, land, machinery, factories—is limited. Thus, the economy cannot produce all the health care, crime prevention, education, or entertainment that people want. A choice must be made. Let us first consider how to represent scarcity and choice in the whole economy and then consider alternative ways to make the choices.

Production Possibilities

To simplify things, let us suppose that production in the economy can be divided into two broad categories. Suppose the economy can produce either computers (laptops, desktops, servers) or movies (thrillers, love stories, mysteries, musicals). The choice between computers and movies is symbolic of one of the most fundamental choices individuals in any society must face: how much to invest in order to produce more or better goods in the future versus how much to consume in the present. Computers help people produce more or better goods. Movies are a form of consumption. Other pairs of goods could also be used in our example. Another popular example is guns versus butter, representing defense goods versus non-defense goods.

ECONOMICS IN ACTION

Teaching Jobs and Graduate School Applications—Two Sides of the Same Coin

Dozens of new teachers join schools in Silicon Valley, California. Applications to MBA programs at Chicago and MIT soar. Do these two seemingly unrelated events have anything in common? Actually, they do. Behind them we find the same economic phenomenon at work: opportunity costs.

For years, California and other parts of the United States have experienced teacher shortages. During the economic boom of the 1990s, college graduates who might have been interested in teaching had better-paying alternatives in the private sector. In 2000, a teaching job in Silicon Valley paid an average salary of $50,000, while a job in the computer industry paid an average of $80,000, not counting possible gains from stock options—at least a $30,000 differential.

At the same time, college graduates who were considering advancing their education faced a similar decision: "Should I get an MBA and improve my career and future salaries, or should I accept an immediate, high-paying job at a start-up or consulting firm?"

As the recession hit the United States in 2001, many workers were laid off, and others saw their salaries reduced.

The U.S. unemployment rate grew from 4.7 percent in January 2001 to 5.6 percent in January 2002, and in Santa Clara County—the heart of Silicon Valley—the increase in the unemployment rate was more dramatic: from 1.7 percent to 7.7 percent. Hewlett-Packard, for example, laid off 6,000 workers—almost 7 percent of its work force—while one of its spinoffs, Agilent, reduced salaries 10 percent for all its 48,000 employees in 2001.

With lower salaries and fewer jobs in the private sector, the opportunity cost of teaching and studying fell. Business schools reported a barrage of applications, with increases of between 50 and 100 percent over the previous year. School districts witnessed a sharp decrease in the number of vacancies available, with many new teachers willing to undergo months of training and substantial pay cuts relative to their old high-tech jobs.

Think of the options you will be facing when you graduate. Given the jobs and salaries currently available, what career do you think you would like to pursue? What would your opportunity cost be?

With a scarcity of resources such as labor and capital, there is a choice between producing some goods, such as computers, versus other goods, such as movies. If the economy produces more of one, then it must produce less of the other. Table 1 gives an example of the alternative choices, or the **production possibilities,** for computers and movies. Observe that there are six different choices, some with more computers and fewer movies, others with fewer computers and more movies.

Table 1 tells us what happens as available resources in the economy are moved from movie production to computer production or vice versa. If resources move from producing movies to producing computers, then fewer movies are produced. For example, if all resources are used to produce computers, then 25,000 computers and zero movies can be produced, according to the table. If all resources are used to produce movies, then no computers can be produced. These are two extremes, of course. If 100 movies are produced, then we can produce 24,000 computers rather than 25,000 computers. If 200 movies are produced, then computer production must fall to 22,000.

production possibilities: alternative combinations of production of various goods that are possible, given the economy's resources.

TABLE 1
Production Possibilities

	Movies	Computers
A	0	25,000
B	100	24,000
C	200	22,000
D	300	18,000
E	400	13,000
F	500	0

Increasing Opportunity Costs

The production possibilities in Table 1 illustrate the concept of opportunity cost for the economy as a whole. The opportunity cost of producing more movies is the value of the forgone computers. For example, the opportunity cost of producing 200 movies rather than 100 movies is 2,000 computers.

An important economic idea about opportunity costs is demonstrated in Table 1. Observe that movie production increases as we move down the table. As we move from row to row, movie production increases by the same number: 100 movies. The decline in computer production between the first and second rows—from 25,000 to 24,000 computers—is 1,000 computers. The decline between the second and third rows—from 24,000 to 22,000 computers—is 2,000 computers. Thus, the decline in computer production gets greater as we produce more movies. As we move from 400 movies to 500 movies, we lose 13,000 computers. In other words, the opportunity cost, in terms of computers, of producing more movies increases as we produce more movies. Each extra movie requires a loss of more and more computers. What we have just described is called **increasing opportunity costs,** with emphasis on the word *increasing*.

Why do opportunity costs increase? You can think about it in the following way. Some of the available resources are better suited for movie production than for computer production, and vice versa. Workers who are good at building computers might not be so good at acting, for example, or moviemaking may require an area with a dry, sunny climate. As more and more resources go into making movies, we are forced to take resources that are much better at computer making and use them for moviemaking. Thus, more and more computer production must be lost to increase movie production by a given amount. Adding specialized computer designers to a movie cast would be very costly in terms of lost computers, and it might add little to movie production.

increasing opportunity cost: a situation in which producing more of one good requires giving up an increasing amount of production of another good.

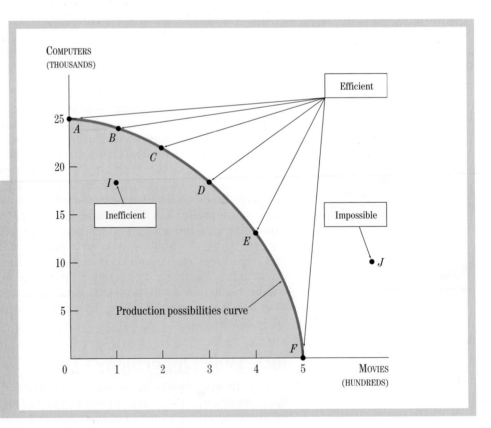

FIGURE 2
The Production Possibilities Curve

Each point on the curve shows the maximum number of computers that can be produced when a given amount of movies is produced. The points with letters are the same as those in Table 1 and are connected by smooth lines. Points in the shaded area inside the curve are inefficient. Points outside the curve are impossible. For the efficient points on the curve, the more movies that are produced, the fewer computers that are produced. The curve is bowed out because of increasing opportunity costs.

The Production Possibilities Curve

Figure 2 is a graphical representation of the production possibilities in Table 1 that nicely illustrates increasing opportunity costs. We put movies on the horizontal axis and computers on the vertical axis of the figure. Each pair of numbers in a row of the table becomes a point on the graph. For example, point *A* on the graph is from row A of the table. Point *B* is from row B, and so on.

production possibilities curve: a curve showing the maximum combinations of production of two goods that are possible, given the economy's resources.

When we connect the points in Figure 2, we obtain the **production possibilities curve.** It shows the maximum number of computers that can be produced for each quantity of movies produced. Note that the curve in Figure 2 slopes downward and is bowed out from the origin. That the curve is bowed out indicates that the opportunity cost of producing movies increases as more movies are produced. As resources move from computer making to moviemaking, each additional movie means a greater loss of computer production.

■ **Inefficient, Efficient, or Impossible?** The production possibilities curve shows the effects of scarcity and choice in the economy as a whole. Three situations can be distinguished in Figure 2, depending on whether production is in the shaded area, on the curve, or outside the curve.

First, imagine production at point *I*. This point, with 100 movies and 18,000 computers, is inside the curve. But the production possibilities curve tells us that it is possible to produce more computers, more movies, or both with the same amount of resources. For some reason, the economy is not working well at point *I*. For example, a talented movie director may be working on a computer assembly line because her short film was not yet been seen by studio executives, or perhaps frequent power outages have disrupted all production of computer chips. Points inside the curve, like point *I*, are *inefficient* because the economy could produce a larger number of movies, as at point *D*, or a larger number of computers, as at point *B*. Points inside the production possibilities curve are possible, but they are inefficient.

Second, consider points on the production possibilities curve. These points are *efficient*. They represent the maximum amount that can be produced with available resources. The only way to raise production of one good is to lower production of the other good. Thus, points on the curve show a *tradeoff* between one good and another.

Third, consider points to the right and above the production possibilities curve, like point *J* in Figure 2. These points are *impossible*. The economy does not have the resources to produce those quantities.

■ **Shifts in the Production Possibilities Curve.** The production possibilities curve is not immovable. It can *shift* out or in. For example, the curve is shown to shift out in Figure 3. More resources—more workers, for example, or more cameras, lights, and studios—would shift the production possibilities curve out. A technological innovation that allowed one to edit movies faster would also shift the curve outward. When the production possibilities curve shifts out, the economy grows because more goods and services can be produced. The production possibilities curve need not shift outward by the same amount in all directions. There can be more movement up than to the right, for example.

As the production possibilities curve shifts out, impossibilities are converted into possibilities. Some of what was impossible for the U.S. economy in 1975 is possible now. Some of what is impossible now will be possible in 2035. Hence, the economists' notion of possibilities is a temporary one. When we say that a certain

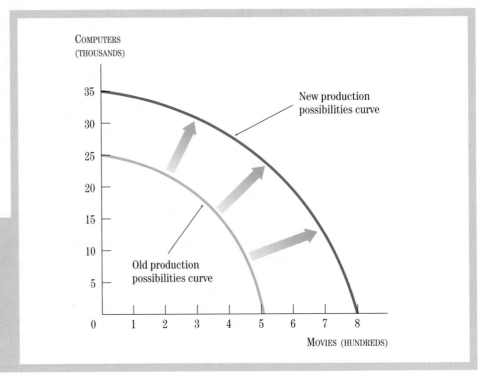

FIGURE 3
Shifts in the Production Possibilities Curve
The production possibilities curve shifts out as the economy grows. The maximum numbers of movies and computers that can be produced increase. Improvements in technology, more machines, or more labor permit the economy to produce more.

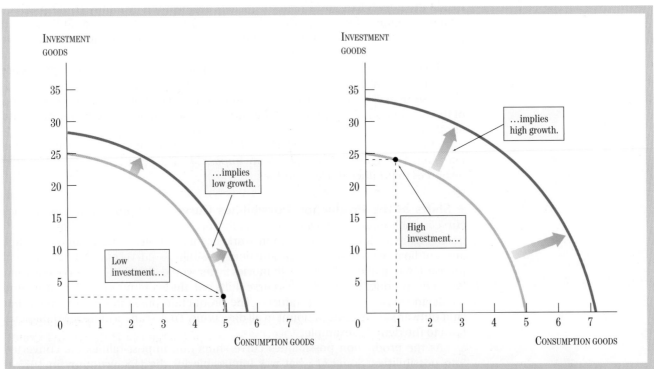

FIGURE 4
Shifts in the Production Possibilities Curve Depend on Choices
On the left, few resources are devoted to investment for the future; hence, the production possibilities curve shifts only a little over time. On the right, more resources are devoted to investment and less to consumption; hence, the production possibilities curve shifts out by a larger amount over time.

combination of computers and movies is impossible, we do not mean "forever impossible," we only mean "currently impossible."

■ **Scarcity, Choice, and Economic Progress.** However, the conversion of impossibilities into possibilities is also an economic problem of choice and scarcity: If we invest less now—in machines, in education, in children, in technology—and consume more now, then we will have less available in the future. If we take computers and movies as symbolic of investment and consumption, then choosing more investment will result in a larger outward shift of the production possibilities curve, as illustrated in Figure 4. More investment enables the economy to produce more in the future.

The production possibilities curve represents a *tradeoff,* but it does not mean that some people win only if others lose. First, it is not necessary for someone to lose in order for the production possibilities curve to shift out. When the curve shifts out, the production of both items increases. Although some people may fare better than others as the production possibilities curve is pushed out, no one necessarily loses. In principle, everyone can gain. Second, if the economy is at an inefficient point (like point *I* in Figure 2), then production of both goods can be increased with no tradeoff. In general, therefore, the economy is more like a win-win situation, where everyone can achieve a gain.

R E V I E W

- The production possibilities curve represents the choices open to a whole economy when it is confronted with a scarcity of resources. As more of one item is produced, less of another item must be produced. The opportunity cost of producing more of one item is the reduced production of another item.

- The production possibilities curve is bowed out because of increasing opportunity costs.

- Points inside the curve are inefficient. Points on the curve are efficient. Points outside the curve are impossible.

- The production possibilities curve shifts out as resources increase.

- Outward shifts of the production possibilities curve or moves from inefficient to efficient points are the reasons why the economy is not a zero-sum game, despite the existence of scarcity and choice.

MARKET ECONOMIES AND THE PRICE SYSTEM

There are three essential questions or problems that every economy must find a way to solve, whether it is a small island economy or a large economy like the United States.

- *What* is to be produced: movies, computers, guns, butter, greeting cards, Rollerblades, health care, or something else? In other words, where on the production possibilities curve should an economy be?

What? How? For Whom?

The Three Fundamental Economic Questions

Any economic system has to answer three questions: What goods and services should be produced—cars, televisions, or something else? How should these goods or services be produced—in what type of factory, and with how much equipment and labor? And for whom should these goods be produced?

- *How* are these goods to be produced? In other words, how can an economy use the available resources so that it is not at an inefficient point inside the production possibilities curve?
- *For whom* are the goods to be produced? We know from the hat/sunglasses example that the allocation of goods in an economy affects people's well-being. An economy in which Maria could not trade her sunglasses for a hat would not work as well as one in which such trades and reallocations are possible. Moreover, an economy in which some people get everything and others get virtually nothing is also not working well.

market economy: an economy characterized by freely determined prices and the free exchange of goods and services in markets.

command economy: an economy in which the government determines prices and production; also called a centrally planned economy.

Broadly speaking, the **market economy** and the **command economy** are two alternative approaches to answering these questions. In a market economy, most decisions about what, how, and for whom to produce are made by individual consumers, firms, governments, and other organizations interacting in markets. In a command, or centrally planned, economy, most decisions about what, how, and for whom to produce are made by those who control the government, which, through a central plan, commands and controls what people do.

Command economies are much less common today than they were in the mid-twentieth century, when nearly half the world's population, including the residents of Eastern Europe, the Soviet Union, and China, lived in centrally planned economies. After many decades of struggling to make this system work, leaders of the command economies gradually grew disillusioned with the high degree of inefficiency resulting from the planned approach, which required that the state, or central planners, make critical detailed production decisions; this often resulted in shortages or surplus of products and, as a by-product, in political unrest. Since

1990, most command economies have, with varying degrees of success, tried to convert from a command to a market system. The difficulties are partly due to the fact that these economies had none or few of the social, legal, or political fixtures critical to the market system. China has been by far the most successful of these economies at making the transition, developing a model that the Chinese term "socialism with Chinese characteristics." Beginning in the 1970s, elements of both the command and market economies coexisted in China; in the mid-1990s, market mechanisms grew more dominant. Today, while its political system is still highly centralized, China's economy is much more decentralized. Many people credit China's rapid economic growth in recent years to its successful transition away from a decentralized economic system.

Key Elements of a Market Economy

Let's take a closer look at some of the ingredients critical to a market economy.

■ **Freely Determined Prices.** In a market economy, most prices—such as the price of computers—are freely determined by individuals and firms interacting in markets. These **freely determined prices** are an essential characteristic of a market economy. In a command economy, most prices are set by government, and this leads to inefficiencies in the economy. For example, in the Soviet Union, the price of bread was set so low that farmers fed bread to the cows. Feeding bread to livestock is an enormous waste of resources. Livestock could eat plain grain. By feeding the cows bread, farmers added the cost of the labor to bake the bread and the fuel to heat the bread ovens to the cost of livestock feed. This is inefficient, like point *I* in Figure 2.

freely determined prices: prices that are determined by the individuals and firms interacting in markets.

In practice, not all prices in market economies are freely determined. For example, some cities control the price of rental apartments. We will look at these exceptions later. But the vast majority of prices are free to vary.

property rights: rights over the use, sale, and proceeds from a good or resource.

■ **Property Rights and Incentives.** Property rights are another key element of a market economy. **Property rights** give individuals the legal authority to keep or sell property, whether land or other resources. Property rights are needed for a market economy because they give people the ability to buy and sell goods. Without property rights, people could take whatever they wanted without paying. People would have to devote time and resources to protecting their earnings or goods.

Moreover, by giving people the rights to the earnings from their work, as well as letting them suffer some of the consequences or losses from their mistakes, property rights provide an **incentive.** For example, if an inventor could not get the property rights to an invention, then the incentive to produce the invention would be low or even nonexistent. Hence there would be few inventions, and we would all be worse off. If there were no property rights, people would not have incentives to specialize and reap the gains from the division of labor. Any extra earnings from specialization could be taken away.

incentive: a device that motivates people to take action, usually so as to increase economic efficiency.

■ **Freedom to Trade at Home and Abroad.** Economic interaction is a way to improve economic outcomes, as the examples in this chapter indicate. Allowing people to interact freely is thus another necessary ingredient of a market economy. Freedom to trade can be extended beyond national borders to other economies.

International trade increases the opportunities to gain from trade. This is especially important in small countries, where it is impossible to produce everything. But the gains from exchange and comparative advantage also exist for larger countries.

■ **A Role for Government.** Just because prices are freely determined and people are free to trade in a market economy does not mean that there is no role for government. For example, in virtually all market economies, the government provides defense and police protection. The government also helps establish property rights. But how far beyond that should it go? Should the government also address the "for whom" question by providing a safety net—a mechanism to deal with the individuals in the economy who are poor, who go bankrupt, who remain unemployed? Most would say yes, but what should the government's role be? Economics provides an analytical framework to answer such questions. In certain circumstances—called **market failure**—the market economy does not provide good enough answers to the "what, how, and for whom" questions, and the government has a role to play in improving on the market. However, the government, even in the case of market failure, may do worse than the market, in which case economists say there is **government failure.**

market failure: any situation in which the market does not lead to an efficient economic outcome and in which there is a potential role for government.

government failure: the situation where the government fails to improve on the market or even makes things worse .

■ **The Role of Private Organizations.** It is an interesting feature of market economies that many economic interactions between people take place in organizations—firms, families, charitable organizations—rather than in markets. Some economic interactions that take place in an organization also take place in a market. For example, many large firms employ lawyers as part of their permanent staff. Other firms simply purchase the services of such lawyers in the market; if the firm wants to sue someone or is being sued by someone, it hires an outside lawyer to represent it.

Economic interactions in firms differ from those in the market. Staff lawyers inside large firms are usually paid annual salaries that do not depend directly on the number of hours worked or their success in the lawsuits. In contrast, outside lawyers are paid an hourly fee and a contingency fee based on the number of hours worked and how successful they are.

Incentives within an organization are as important as incentives in markets. If the lawyers on a firm's legal staff get to keep some of the damages the firm wins in a lawsuit, they will have more incentive to do a good job. Some firms even try to create marketlike competition between departments or workers in order to give more incentives.

Why do some economic interactions occur in markets and others in organizations? Ronald Coase of the University of Chicago won the Nobel Prize for showing that organizations such as firms are created to reduce market *transaction costs*, the costs of buying and selling, which include finding a buyer or a seller and reaching agreement on a price. When market transaction costs are high, we see more transactions taking place within organizations. For example, a firm might have a legal staff rather than outside lawyers because searching for a good lawyer every time there is a lawsuit is too costly. In a crisis, a good lawyer may not be available.

The Price System

The previous discussion indicates that in market economies, freely determined prices are essential for determining what is produced, how, and for whom. For this reason, a market economy is said to use *the price system* to solve these problems. In this section, we show that prices do a surprising amount of work: (1) Prices serve as *signals* about what should be produced and consumed when there are changes in tastes or changes in technology, (2) prices provide *incentives* to people to alter their production or consumption, and (3) prices affect the *distribution of income*, or who gets what in the economy.

Let's use an example. Suppose that there is a sudden new trend for college students to ride bicycles more and drive cars less. How do prices help people in the economy decide what to do in response to this new trend?

■ **Signals.** First, consider how the information about the change in tastes is signaled to the producers of bicycles and cars. As students buy more bicycles, the price of bicycles rises. A higher price will signal that it is more profitable for firms to produce more bicycles. In addition, some bicycle components, like lightweight metal, will also increase in price. Increased lightweight metal prices signal that production of lightweight metal should increase. As the price of metal rises, wages for metalworkers may increase. Thus, prices are a signal all the way from the consumer to the metalworkers that more bicycles should be produced. This is what is meant by the expression "prices are a signal."

It is important to note that no single individual knows the information that is transmitted by prices. Any economy is characterized by limited information, where people cannot know the exact reasons why prices for certain goods rise or fall. Hence, it is rather amazing that prices can signal this information.

■ **Incentives.** Now let's use this example to consider how prices provide incentives. A higher price for bicycles will increase the incentives for firms to produce bicycles. Because they receive more for each bicycle, they produce more. If there is a large price increase that is not merely temporary, new firms may enter the bicycle business. In contrast, the reduced prices for cars signal to car producers that production should decrease.

■ **Distribution.** How do prices affect the distribution of income? On the one hand, workers who find the production of the good they make increasing because of the higher demand for bicycles will earn more. On the other hand, income will be reduced for those who make cars or who have to pay more for bicycles. Local delivery services that use bicycles will see their costs increase.

R E V I E W

- The market economy and the command economy are two alternative systems for addressing the questions any economy must face: what to produce, how to produce, and for whom to produce.

- A market economy is characterized by several key elements, such as freely determined prices, property rights, and freedom to trade at home and abroad.

- For a market economy to work well, markets should be competitive and the government should play a role.

- Prices are signals, they provide incentives, and they affect the distribution of income.

Gains from Trade on the Radio

Even in today's Internet-connected world, economic interactions that use older technologies like the radio are very common. Tradio helps potential buyers and sellers learn about each other in a virtual market, realizing gains from trade that would not be possible without the exchange of information. All you need is someone who wants to sell something and someone else who wants to buy. Even though radio stations do not charge buyers and sellers, you will notice that tradio is not just a public service. Tradio is very low-cost programming that attracts a large audience and many paid ads from local businesses—a win-win situation for individual buyers and sellers, radio stations, and local businesses. Gains from trade in action!

Who Needs eBay? For Towns Across U.S., Tradio Is Real Deal

By REID J. EPSTEIN, Staff Reporter | The Wall Street Journal
September 11, 2002

GLASGOW, Mont.—It was a little after nine one recent morning, and local residents were already on the line to Lori Mason's radio show.

One caller wanted to unload a riding lawnmower ($500). Another tried to sell an irrigation pump ($100), and four offered up washing machines, including one that "leaks a little bit" ($10). Others still were looking to buy eight bales of straw, fresh dill and a large dog house.

When one young woman phoned in to put her '79 GMC pickup on the block, the 54-year-old Ms. Mason not only recognized her voice but urged her to loosen up.

"Oh, sorry," said the caller, 23-year-old day-care provider Jamie Seyfert. "We're willing to trade for guns, jet skis or anything fun."

This is the sound of "tradio" (pronounced TRADE-ee-o), a kind of on-air swap meet that has been a fixture of small-town stations from Florida to Alaska for decades. Far from being rendered obsolete by the Internet, many tradio shows are doing surprisingly well these days. They are the top moneymakers for some stations, often commanding a premium from local advertisers. And the format may be pushing into bigger markets. In April, WCCO in Minneapolis introduced "The WCCO Great Garage Sale" and saw its ratings jump 29% in the time slot.

Three-Stoplight Town

Here in Glasgow, a three-stoplight railroad town of 3,253 people on the lonely plains of northeastern Montana, the half-hour show is simulcast three mornings a week from the second-floor studio of locally owned stations KLTZ and KLAN. Virtually everyone in town, from the mayor to the editor of the weekly paper, has bought or sold something on the show.

Here's how it works: Callers announce they're selling something—a gas heater that "would be good in your garage, your huntin' shack or whatever," a "very large collection of Fiestaware dishes in all the new colors" or some "very friendly young goats"—and leave their phone number. Anyone interested calls the seller, and the transaction is negotiated face-to-face.

Internet Connection

While it may sound archaic in the age of eBay, the tradio format seems to be benefiting from the buzz generated by the popular Web auction site. Some tradio shows are using the Internet to their advantage—allowing listeners to submit items for sale via e-mail and posting items called into the show on their Web sites.

The tradio format first took hold in the early 1950s when powerful nationwide radio networks cut back on programming. To fill the void, small-town stations began broadcasting obituaries, birthdays and anniversaries. An appliance-store owner in Seguin is believed by many in the industry to have started the first tradio show. He began buying air time to read notices of items for sale that customers had posted on a bulletin board inside his store.

In small towns that don't have daily newspapers—the closest daily to Glasgow is the *Herald* in Williston, N.D., 144 miles away—tradio takes the place of classifieds and, perhaps more important, gossip. When Ms. Mason heard a caller say he was selling his $100 irrigation pump, she exclaimed, "You're on the new water line!" and quizzed him about the difference that had made in his water supply.

Another big attraction is the price. A classified ad in the weekly *Glasgow Courier* costs $5.25 per column inch, while calls to "Tradio" are free. And eBay, which exacts a sliding fee based on the price of the item sold, also requires a hookup to the Internet.

Alicia Sibley, a 24-year-old hay farmer, is a regular listener to the Glasgow show. She was driving her tractor a few weeks ago when she heard a caller offering to sell a 6-foot freezer. She phoned the seller—who had bought the freezer to stock up on frozen foods for fear of a catastrophe at the turn of the millennium—and made a deal for $200. "It's a real nice one, too," Ms. Sibley said. "I saved around $200."

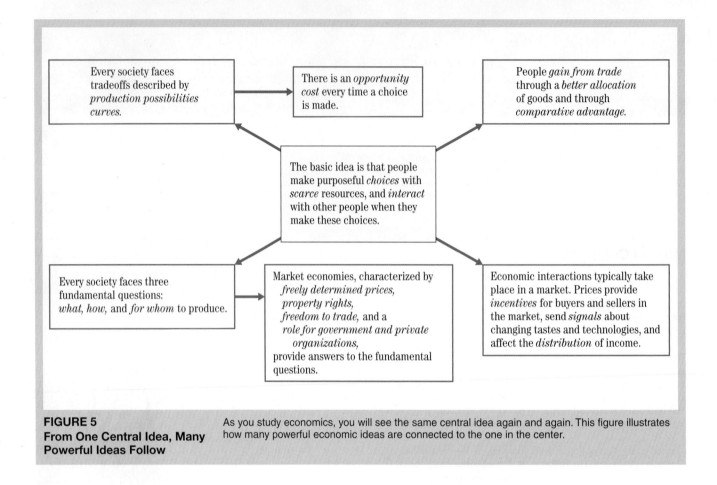

FIGURE 5
From One Central Idea, Many Powerful Ideas Follow

As you study economics, you will see the same central idea again and again. This figure illustrates how many powerful economic ideas are connected to the one in the center.

CONCLUSION

One basic idea lies at the center of economics: People make purposeful choices with scarce resources, and interact with other people when they make these choices.

This introductory chapter illustrates this idea, starting with Tiger Woods's decision whether to leave school and continuing with simple examples of people making choices about what to consume or produce.

From this central idea, many other powerful ideas follow, as summarized visually in Figure 5. There is an *opportunity cost* every time a choice is made. People *gain from trade*, both through a *better allocation* of goods and through *comparative advantage*. Every society faces tradeoffs described by *production possibilities curves*. Every society faces three fundamental questions: *what, how,* and *for whom* to produce. Market economies—characterized by *freely determined prices, property rights, freedom to trade,* and *a role for both government and private organizations*—give an answer to these three questions. The price system helps a market economy work by providing *incentives,* sending *signals,* and affecting the *distribution* of income.

You will see this central idea again and again as you study economics.

KEY POINTS

1. Everyone faces a scarcity of something, usually time or resources.
2. Scarcity leads to choice, and choice leads to opportunity costs.
3. Trade leads to gains because it allows goods and services to be reallocated in a way that improves people's well-being.
4. Trade also leads to gains because it permits people to specialize in what they are relatively good at.
5. The production possibilities curve summarizes the tradeoffs in the whole economy due to scarcity.
6. Economic production is efficient if the economy is on the production possibilities curve. Production is inefficient if the economy is inside the production possibilities curve.
7. Points outside the production possibilities curve are currently impossible. More investment, more workers, or better technology can shift the production possibilities curve out and make the impossible possible.
8. The three basic questions that any economy must face are what, how, and for whom production should take place.
9. A well-functioning market system, involving freely determined prices, property rights, freedom to trade, and a role for government and private organizations, can answer these basic questions.
10. Prices transmit signals, provide incentives, and affect the distribution of income in a market economy. If prices are set at the wrong levels by government, waste and inefficiency—such as feeding bread to livestock—will result.

KEY TERMS

economics
scarcity
choice
economic interactions
market
opportunity cost

gains from trade
specialization
division of labor
comparative advantage
international trade
production possibilities

increasing opportunity cost
production possibilities curve
market economy
command economy

freely determined prices
property rights
incentive
market failure
government failure

QUESTIONS FOR REVIEW

1. What is the basic idea at the center of economics?
2. Why does scarcity imply a choice among alternatives?
3. What is the opportunity cost of making a choice?
4. How can there be gains from trade even when total production of goods and services doesn't change?
5. How can specialization lead to gain from trade?
6. What is the principle of increasing opportunity costs?
7. Why is the production of a combination of goods that is located inside the production possibilities curve considered to be inefficient?
8. What are the key ingredients of a market economy?
9. What are the three basic questions that any economic system must address?
10. What roles do prices play in a market economy?

PROBLEMS

1. Suppose that you are president of the student government, and you have to decide how to allocate a $20,000 fund for guest speakers for the year. Conan O'Brien and Will Ferrell each cost $10,000 per appearance, Stephen Colbert costs $20,000 per appearance, and former economic advisers to the government charge $1,000 per lecture. Explain the economic problem of choice and scarcity in this case. What issues would you consider in arriving at a decision?

2. Michelle Wie, a teenage golf prodigy who earned $16 million in endorsements and $4 million in prize money and appearance fees in 2006, announced that she would enroll as a student at Stanford University in the fall of 2007. What is her opportunity cost of a year of college? How does it compare to your opportunity cost of a year of college?

3. Allison will graduate from high school next June. She has ranked her three possible postgraduation plans in the following order: (1) Work for two years at a consulting job in her hometown paying $20,000 per year, (2) attend a local community college for two years, spending $5,000 per year on tuition and expenses, and (3) travel around the world tutoring a rock star's child for pay of $5,000 per year. What is the opportunity cost of her choice?

4. Suppose you have two boxes of chocolate chip cookies and a friend of yours has two 2 gallons of milk. Explain how you can both gain from trade. Is this a gain from trade through *better allocation* or *greater production*?

5. Suppose Tina and Julia can produce brownies and romantic poems (which can be combined to make a lovely gift) in the following combinations in a given week:

Tina		Julia	
Brownies	*Poems*	*Brownies*	*Poems*
50	0	25	0
40	1	20	1
30	2	15	2
20	3	10	3
10	4	5	4
0	5	0	5

a. If Tina and Julia are each currently producing 2 poems per week, how many brownies are they producing? What is the total production of brownies and poems between them?

b. Is there a possibility for increasing production? Why or why not?

c. Suppose Julia completely specializes in producing poems and Tina completely specializes in producing brownies. What will be their total production of brownies and poems?

6. Suppose you must divide your time between studying for your math final and writing a final paper for your English class. The fraction of time that you spend studying math and its relation to your grade in the two classes is given in the table below.

Fraction of Time Spent on Math	Math Grade	English Grade
0	0	97
20	45	92
40	65	85
60	75	70
80	82	50
100	88	0

a. Draw a tradeoff curve for the math grade versus the English grade.

b. What is the opportunity cost of increasing the time spent on math from 80 to 100 percent? What is the opportunity cost of increasing the time spent on math from 60 to 80 percent?

c. Are there increasing opportunity costs from spending more time on math? Explain.

d. Suppose your parents want you to get a 92 in both subjects. What would you tell them?

7. A small country produces only two goods, cars and cakes. Given its limited resources, this country has the following production possibilities:

Cars	Cakes
0	200
25	180
50	130
75	70
100	0

a. Draw the production possibilities curve.

b. Suppose car production uses mainly machines and cake production uses mainly labor. Show what happens to the curve when the number of machines increases, but the amount of labor remains unchanged.

8. Tracy tells Huey that he can improve his economics grade without sacrificing fun activities or his grades in other courses. Can you imagine ways in which this might be possible? What does that imply about the initial situation? If Huey is taking just two courses and he can improve his economics grade without hurting his math grade, how could you represent this situation graphically?

9. Suppose decreased production of oil in the Middle East causes the price of oil to rise all over the world. Explain how this change in the price signals information to U.S. producers of various goods, provides incentives to U.S. producers of various goods, and affects the distribution of income.

10. "When you look at the economies of the United States, Europe, or Japan, you see most of the ingredients of a market economy. For example, consider bicycles. Prices in the bicycle market are free to vary; people have property rights to the bicycles they buy; many people sell bicycles; many bicycles sold in the United States, Europe, and Japan come from other countries; the government regulates bicycle use (no bicycles on the freeways, for example); and bicycle production takes place within firms with many workers." Replace bicycles with another good or service of your choosing in this quotation and comment on whether the quotation is still true.

Chapter 2

Observing and Explaining the Economy

ark McClellan and Jim Hamilton are two of the best economists in the world. Yet, they are hardly household names here in the United States. It turns out that very few economists are widely known outside the profession; this anonymity was sadly deepened in 2006 with the passing away of Milton Friedman and John Kenneth Galbraith, perhaps the two individuals with the highest public name recognition in the discipline. It is unfortunate that so many people are unfamiliar with the work of Mark McClellan and Jim Hamilton because they are experts at observing and explaining trends in the two markets—health care and oil—whose fluctuations have the biggest impact on the budgets of ordinary individuals. The research and policy work that they do sheds light on why these markets behave as they do, and what kind of policies would be most effective at keeping the costs of health care and the price of gasoline down.

Mark McClellan's economic expertise and insights on health-care policy led him to Washington, D.C., where, in 2001 and 2002, he served as one of the three members of President Bush's Council of Economic Advisers. From 2002 to 2004, Mark served as Commissioner of the Food and Drug Administration before going on to a position as an administrator of the Centers for Medicare and Medicaid Services, where he was instrumental in launching the new prescription drug benefit component of the Medicare program. Jim Hamilton is a prolific economist, currently at the University of California at San Diego, who is well known for his work on oil price shocks and monetary policy. He also disseminates his research to a wider audience using an economics weblog at _www.econbrowser.com_. On a recent day, he had posted on his blog articles and opinions about the rising price of oil, the use of subsidies for ethanol production, the implications of oil prices for the trade deficit of the United States, and the macroeconomic implications of an expansion of the war in Iraq into Iran.

The purpose of this chapter is to give you a broad overview of what economists such as Mark McClellan and Jim Hamilton actually do. Even though you are just beginning your foray into economics, for some of you this may be the first step in a journey to becoming an expert on an important industry in the economy. If you reach that goal, you should follow in the footsteps of Mark McClellan and Jim Hamilton and use your knowledge to design policies that improve people's lives and communicate your ideas to a broader audience so that they can become more informed citizens. Who knows, star economists may one day be as famous as star golfers!

WHAT DO ECONOMISTS DO?

Economics is a way of thinking. It entails accurately *describing* economic events, *explaining* why the events occur, *predicting* under what circumstances such events might take place in the future, and *recommending* appropriate courses of action. To make use of economics, you will want to learn to do the describing, the explaining, and even the predicting and recommending yourself—that is, to reason and think like an economist. By making use of economics in this way, you can better understand the economic challenges and opportunities you face, and thereby make improvements in your own life or the lives of those around you.

Just as physicists try to explain the existence of black holes in outer space and biologists try to explain why dinosaurs became extinct, economists try to explain puzzling observations and facts about the economy. Many of these observations come from everyday life. Are there some economic observations—from your own experience, from recent news stories, or from your history or political science courses—that you find puzzling? Some of your questions might be like these:

- Why is college tuition so high?
- Why have the wages of college graduates increased much more rapidly than the wages of high school dropouts since the 1970s?
- Why are there so many different types of toothpaste?
- Why is the average income of people in the United States about 35 times higher than that of people in China?
- Why is unemployment much higher in Europe than in the United States?
- Why has health-care spending increased faster than the rest of the U.S. economy?
- Will the price of gas reach $4 a gallon before it reaches $2 a gallon?

All these questions are based on observations about the economy. Some, like the question about college tuition, are fairly obvious and are based on casual observation. Others, like the question about the historical trends in the wages of high school and college graduates, would become evident in the course of reading a book or talking to a parent or a relative. In order to answer such questions, economists, like physicists or biologists, need to systematically document and quantify their observations and look for patterns. If we can establish the date when dinosaurs became extinct, then we may be able to test our hunch that a cataclysmic event such as an asteroid hitting the earth caused their extinction. To illustrate how economists document and quantify their observations, let us briefly focus on the last of the preceding questions, the one about the price of a gallon of gasoline.

THE FLUCTUATING PRICE OF GASOLINE

Describing an Economic Event

Few prices affect the lives of as many people as does the price of gasoline. In the summer of 2006, the average price of a gallon of gasoline in the United States reached $3 a gallon, according to data gathered by the Department of Energy. Just a few months later, in early 2007, the average price of a gallon of gasoline was close to $2 a gallon. The difference between $3 a gallon and $2 a gallon has a substantial impact on many people. If you own a car, filling your gas tank at the higher price would cost you $60 instead of $40. The more you spend on gas, the less you have to spend on other things—food at the grocery store, for example. The price of food itself will rise because the cost of transporting food will increase. It will cost you more to fly home to visit your family at Thanksgiving because airlines will raise their ticket prices. And if the reason for the increase in the price of gasoline was an increase in the price of crude oil, then millions of low-income families will face serious financial strain as they pay to heat their homes during the winter. Rising oil prices are always a hot-button issue in congressional and presidential elections. But let's focus first on how an economist would go about understanding fluctuations in the price of gasoline.

> **Observation 1:** The price of gasoline has risen sharply in the past five years compared to the preceding decade.

The first task is to collect some historical data so we understand how gasoline prices have changed over time. With relatively little effort, you can track down an online data series from the Department of Energy that provides month-by-month information on the movement of gasoline prices in the United States since 1990.

Graphs are a helpful way to present data like this series on gasoline prices. Figure 1 plots the average price of a gallon of gasoline in the United States between

FIGURE 1
Retail Price of Gasoline in the United States, 1991–2006

For each month from 1991 to 2006, the average price of a gallon of gasoline in the United States is plotted; the line connects all the points.

Source: Department of Energy: U.S. Retail Gasoline Prices.

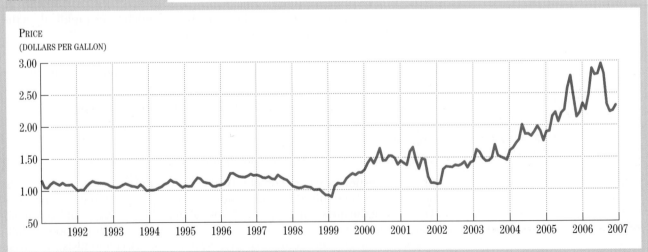

1991 and 2006. The vertical axis is measured in dollars per gallon; the horizontal axis measures the date, in years. How would you characterize the behavior of the average price of gasoline in the United States?

In describing a data series, you should focus on both the long-run movements (any trends you can see in the data) and the short-run movements (how volatile the series is) in the data series. Gasoline prices did not exhibit much of a trend between 1991 and 1998, even though they did fluctuate. Prices were more volatile in the period from 1998 to 2002, first rising smoothly and then dropping sharply. Since mid-2002, gasoline prices show a sharp upward trend, reaching almost $3 in the summers of 2005 and 2006 before cooling off a bit.

relative price: the price of a particular good compared to the price of other things.

To understand how these fluctuations in the price of gasoline affect consumer behavior, economists would be more interested in the **relative price** of gasoline (the price of gasoline compared to the prices all other goods and services in the economy). Even if the $1.10 price of a gallon of gasoline in December of 1991 was similar to the price of gasoline in December 1997, the prices of all other goods and services would have increased between 1991 and 1997. A typical consumer would find it financially less onerous to buy $1.10 gasoline in 1997 than it was for her to buy $1.10 gasoline in 1991; she would have to give up fewer purchases of other goods and services to fill her car's gas tank. In other words, the relative price of gasoline decreased between 1991 and 1997, even though the actual price of gasoline did not. Economists often adjust the price of a good to take into account changes in overall prices before they do comparisons over time.

$$\text{Relative price of gasoline} = \frac{\text{price of gasoline}}{\text{average price of all other goods and services}}$$

The relative price of gasoline is plotted in Figure 2. Observe that the relative price of gasoline fell between 1991 and 1999; it cost less in terms of other goods and services to buy a gallon of gas in 1999. The relative price rose between 2002 and 2006; it cost more in terms of other goods and services to buy a gallon of gas. This indicates that the price of gasoline increased at a faster rate than did the prices of other goods and services. Notice also that the increase in gasoline prices in the last five years is not quite as dramatic when we look at the relative prices. In other words, even though the price of gasoline was rising, the price of other goods and services was rising as well, so $3 per gallon gasoline in 2006 was not as costly in terms of what you had to give up to fill the tank as similarly priced gasoline would have been in the past.

FIGURE 2
Relative Price of Gasoline

Gasoline prices rose by less than did other prices in the early 1990s, and then again in the late 1990s; relative prices fell during this time. Between 2002 and mid-2006, gasoline prices rose much faster than did other prices.

Note: The relative price is a ratio of the price of gasoline to the average price of all goods and services. The ratio is set to 1 in January 2000. This is arbitrary; using another year would not change the conclusions.

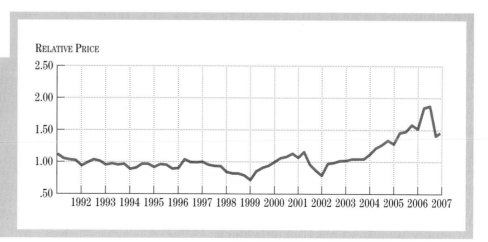

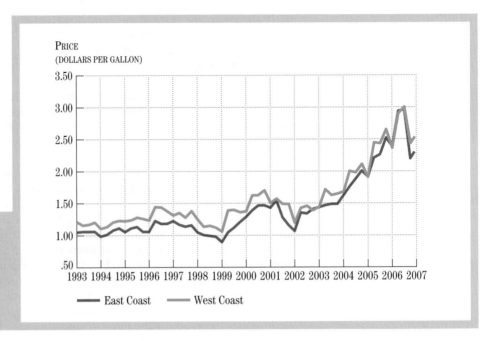

FIGURE 3
Regional Variations in the Retail Price of Gasoline
The two lines show the price of a gallon of gasoline on the East Coast and the West Coast of the United States. The price on the West Coast is typically higher.

■ **Data Limitations.** Economic data are not always accurate. Data that are collected via survey methods can be inaccurate because people sometimes do not understand the survey questions, are too busy to answer them carefully, or do not have the correct information. Sometimes the data may be more aggregated than you would like them to be—the average price of a gallon of gasoline in the United States conceals the substantial regional variation in gasoline prices, as you can see in Figure 3. By not having regional data and focusing only on the national average, you may end up missing a potentially important pattern in the data or fail to identify a potential explanation for the movements in gasoline prices.

R E V I E W

■ Economics is a way of thinking about the world that aims to find the right variables to describe an economic event, to identify what factors may have brought about that event, to predict how changes elsewhere in the economy will affect the variable of interest, and to recommend policies that can improve outcomes.

■ Economists have to think carefully about the limitations of the data they use. For example, when studying changes over time, it is important to correct for changes in the overall price level, which can otherwise lead you to misleading conclusions.

EXPLAINING AN ECONOMIC EVENT

What factors can explain the changes we have observed in the price of gasoline in the United States? If you had read Jim Hamilton's thoughts on the subject on his weblog, you would immediately hone in on the price of a barrel of crude oil in the world market. Gasoline is produced from crude oil in oil refineries; the more expensive crude oil is, the more costly it will be to produce a gallon of gasoline. So, we can use these

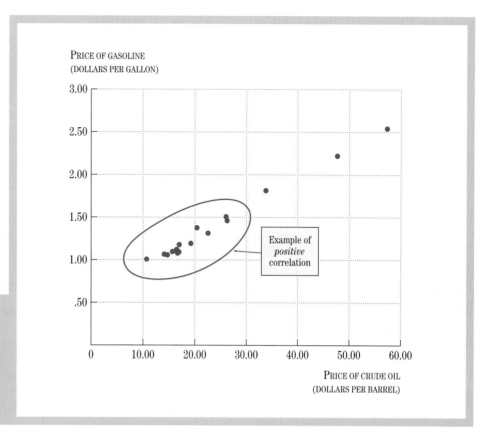

FIGURE 4

Price of Gasoline versus Price of Crude Oil

The figure plots pairs of points: the price of a gallon of gasoline on the vertical axis and the price of a barrel of crude oil on the horizontal axis. These two series show a very strong positive correlation.

economic variable: any economic measure that can vary over a range of values.

two economic variables to quantify our observations about the gasoline market in the United States. An **economic variable** is any economic measure that can vary over a range of values. Are there any obvious patterns in how the prices of these two variables have moved over time?

Figure 4 is useful for determining whether the price of crude oil and the price of gasoline are correlated. Two variables are said to be *correlated* if they tend to move up or down at the same time. There is a *positive correlation* if the two variables move in the same direction—when one goes up, the other goes up. There is a *negative correlation* if the two variables move in opposite directions—when one goes up, the other goes down. Each point in the figure corresponds to the price of crude oil and the price of gasoline in a particular month. The price of gasoline is on the vertical axis, and the price of crude oil is on the horizontal axis.

The points in Figure 4 trace out a very clear pattern: The two variables show a very strong positive correlation. As the price of crude oil rises, the price of gasoline also rises. Conversely, as the price of crude oil falls, the price of gasoline also falls. The price of crude oil will, as you might expect, be an important determinant of gasoline prices. You can already see, though, that the price of crude oil alone will not suffice as an explanation of the price of gasoline because of the differences in gasoline prices between the West Coast and the East Coast of the United States. These regional differences are mostly due to differences in regulations concerning automobile emissions, which mean that the gasoline sold on the West Coast is somewhat different from the gasoline sold elsewhere in terms of the various additives needed to influence how cleanly it burns. The cost of these additives and the presence of state regulations are potential explanatory variables for the regional variation in gasoline prices.

■ **Correlation versus Causation.**   Just because there is a correlation between two variables does not necessarily mean that one caused the other. There is a difference between *causation* and *correlation*. *Correlation* means that one event is usually observed to occur along with another. *Causation* means that one event brings about another event. But correlation does not imply causation. For example, high readings on a thermometer are correlated with hot weather (high readings occur when it is hot outside). But the thermometer readings do not cause the hot weather. In fact, the causation is the other way around: Hot weather causes the reading on the thermometer to be high.

Similarly, in the example we looked at, gasoline prices and crude oil prices are positively correlated. However, gasoline prices do not cause the high crude oil prices. Here too we would have good reason to believe that causation ran from crude oil prices to gasoline prices. In many instances, determining causation is very difficult. For example, spending on health care and the price of health care both rose in the last five years. It's very difficult to conclude whether spending on health care increased because health care was expensive or whether the price of health care was higher because lots of people were spending money on health care and using up scarce medical resources. Economists are often faced with situations where causation is difficult to determine.

■ **The Lack of Controlled Experiments in Economics.**   In many sciences—certainly psychology, medicine, and biology—investigators perform **controlled experiments** to determine whether one event causes another event. An example of a controlled experiment is the clinical trial of a new drug. New drugs are tested by trying them out on two groups of individuals. One group gets the drug; the other group gets a placebo (a pill without the drug). If the experiment results in a significantly greater number of people being cured among the group taking the drug than among the control group not taking the drug, investigators conclude that the drug causes the cure.

controlled experiments: empirical tests of theories in a controlled setting in which particular effects can be isolated.

Unfortunately, such controlled experiments are rare in economics. When faced with a situation with limited data (say, data for one country over a particular time period), causation is hard to determine. In these circumstances, we can try to look at other countries' experience, or we can look at the experience of different states within the United States. But, unfortunately, no two countries or states are alike in all respects. Thus, attempting to control for other factors is not as easy as in the case of clinical trials.

In recent years, economists have adapted some of the methods of experimental science and have begun to conduct economic experiments in laboratory settings that are similar to the real world. These experiments can be repeated, and various effects can be controlled for. **Experimental economics** is a growing area of economics. The findings of experimental economics have affected economists' understanding of how the economy works. Experiments in economics also provide an excellent way to *learn* how the economy works, much as experiments in science courses can help one learn about gravity or the structure of plant cells. But because it is difficult to replicate real-world settings exactly in such experiments, they have not yet been applied as widely as the clinical or laboratory experiments in other sciences.

experimental economics: a branch of economics that uses laboratory experiments to analyze economic behavior.

R E V I E W

- One of the most significant challenges for an economist is to identify whether one variable has a causal impact on another. Even though two variables may be strongly correlated, correlation does not imply causation.

- In the natural sciences, controlled experiments are used to establish causation. Because controlled experiments are rare in economics, establishing causation is more difficult in economics.

ECONOMICS IN ACTION

An Economic Experiment to Study Discrimination

As you know by now, economists are hampered by their inability to run controlled experiments. Without controlled experiments, it is always a challenge to definitively establish whether one variable has a causal impact on another. However, even though good experiments are rare in economics, they are by no means nonexistent. In 2004, economists Marianne Bertrand and Sendhil Mullainathan published a paper[1] that described a labor market experiment they ran to study discrimination patterns in labor markets.

The title of Bertrand and Mullainathan's paper, "Are Emily and Greg More Employable than Lakisha and Jamal?," gives an idea of what their experiment was about. They wanted to test whether résumés that were attached to African American–sounding names (like Lakisha Washington and Jamal Jones) got fewer callbacks for interviews than did identical-quality résumés attached to names that were more typically associated with whites (like Emily Walsh and Greg Baker). This was a controlled experiment in that the only difference between the two résumés was the name of the candidate. If the résumés with African American names got fewer callbacks than the résumés with white names, that would be evidence of differential treatment simply on the basis of race.

A controlled labor market experiment like this is a much better way to test for differential treatment than looking at the observed labor market outcomes of whites and African Americans. After all, in many cases a researcher would not be able to get data on applicants for a position; even if he did get the data, the applicants will have very different profiles and qualifications; and furthermore, it would be very difficult for the researcher to know how to judge whether one candidate was more qualified than another across a variety of job types.

An overview of their project is given here; you can find the complete version of the paper online if you are interested.

- Bertrand and Mullainathan sent out nearly 5,000 résumés in response to 1,300 help wanted advertisements in Boston and Chicago.

- The résumés were of two types: one containing education and work experience for a highly qualified worker, and the other containing information for a less-qualified worker.

- Each position received four résumés, two high-quality ones and two low-quality ones. One résumé of each

type was randomly assigned one of a set of names commonly associated with whites, and the other was assigned a name from a set of names commonly associated with African Americans.

- The results of the experiment showed that applicants with white-sounding names had to send out about 10 résumés before getting a callback, whereas applicants with African American–sounding names had to send out around 15 résumés.

- The researchers found that white names with a higher-quality résumé had a much higher probability of being called back (almost 30 percent) for an interview than whites with a lower-quality résumé. The gap between African Americans with high-quality résumés and African Americans with low quality résumés was smaller, implying that the gap between the races is even wider at the top end of the quality distribution.

- The results held true across different industries and different occupations.

- The researchers also looked at the issue of class by choosing white and African American names that are associated with relatively low levels of parental education and names associated with high levels of education. The differences in perceived class were nowhere near as important as the differences in perceived race.

This paper is an example of how creative, interesting, and influential good economics research can be. The results provided compelling evidence of labor market access differentials across race. Because this was an experiment, we can be much surer that the causal factor behind the differential treatment was the perceived race. Furthermore, the pernicious effect of this lack of equal access is quite substantial: Mullainathan and Bertrand estimate that it takes eight years of extra experience on a résumé to make up for having an African American–sounding name! They also point out that standard policy recommendations for minority unemployment, which include better training and education programs, will not necessarily be the solution here, since the rewards for having more experience and skills seem to be smaller for African American workers than for white workers. While you may be dismayed by the results of the paper, keep in mind that the insights it provides may represent an important step in making people aware of the extent of unequal access to labor markets, and encourage more people to work toward bettering the situation.

---

[1]Marianne Bertrand and Sendhil Mullainathan, "Are Emily and Greg More Employable than Lakisha and Jamal? A Field Experiment on Labor Market Discrimination," *American Economic Review*, 94(4), September 2004.

Predicting the Impact of Future Changes

Having figured out how to describe the economic event, the rise in gasoline prices, and armed with a better understanding of what might explain why gasoline prices have risen, we move on to the next challenge for the economist: predicting what will happen to gasoline prices in the future.

■ **Economic Models.** In order to explain economic facts and observations, one needs an economic theory, or a *model*. An **economic model** is an explanation of how the economy or a part of the economy works. In practice, most economists use the terms *theory* and *model* interchangeably, although sometimes the term *theory* suggests a general explanation and the term *model* suggests a more specific explanation. The term *law* is also typically used interchangeably with the terms *model* and *theory* in economics.

economic model: an explanation of how the economy or part of the economy works.

Economic models are always abstractions, or simplifications, of the real world. They take very complicated phenomena, such as the behavior of people, firms, and governments, and simplify them. Economists like to draw an analogy between a model and a road map—both are abstractions of a much more complex reality. Some maps (like some models) can be very detailed; others are just broad abstractions. There is no single "correct" model, just as there is no single "correct" map. If you wanted to drive from New York to California, you would need an interstate map, one that ignores the details of individual streets within a city to show the main highways. In contrast, if you were headed from one neighborhood of Chicago to another, an interstate map would be of no use; instead, you would need a map that showed city streets in greater detail.

■ **Microeconomic versus Macroeconomic Models.** There are two types of models corresponding to the two main branches of economics: microeconomics and macroeconomics. They each have their purpose.

microeconomics: the branch of economics that examines individual decision-making at firms and households and the way they interact in specific industries and markets.

Microeconomics studies the behavior of individual firms and households or specific markets like the health-care market or the college graduate market. It looks at variables such as the price of a college education or the reason for increased wages of college graduates. Microeconomic models explain why the price of gasoline varies from station to station and why there are discount airfares. The analogy in the map world is to the city street map.

macroeconomics: the branch of economics that examines the workings and problems of the economy as a whole–GDP growth and unemployment.

Macroeconomics focuses on the whole economy—the whole national economy or even the whole world economy. The most comprehensive measure of the size of an economy is the **gross domestic product (GDP).** GDP is the total value of all goods and services made in the country during a specific period of time, such as a year. GDP includes all newly made goods such as cars, shoes, gasoline, airplanes, and houses; it also includes services like health care, education, and auto repair. Macroeconomics tries to explain the changes in GDP over time rather than the changes in a part of the GDP, like health-care spending. It looks at questions such as what causes the GDP to grow and why many more workers are unemployed in Europe than in the United States. The analogy in the map world is to the interstate map.

gross domestic product (GDP): a measure of the value of all the goods and services newly produced in an economy during a specified period of time.

Do not be critical of economic models just because they are simplifications. In every science, models are simplifications of reality. Models are successful if they explain reality reasonably well. In fact, if they were not simplifications, models would be hard to use effectively. Economic models differ from those in the physical sciences because they endeavor to explain human behavior, which is complex and often unpredictable. It is for this reason that the brilliant physicist Max Planck said that economics was harder than physics.

Economic models can be described with words, with numerical tables, with graphs, or with algebra. To use economics, it is important to be able to work with these different descriptions. Figures 5 and 6 show how models can be illustrated with graphs. By looking at a graph, we can see quickly whether the model has an inverse or

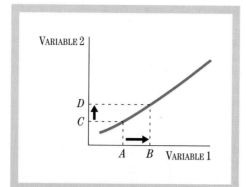

FIGURE 5
A Model with Two Positively Related Variables

The upward-sloping line shows how the variables are related. When one variable increases from *A* to *B*, the other variable increases from *C* to *D*. If one variable declines from *B* to *A*, the other variable declines from *D* to *C*. We say that variable 1 is positively related to variable 2, or that variable 1 varies directly with variable 2.

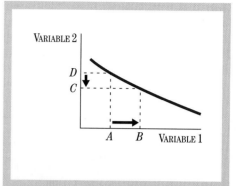

FIGURE 6
A Model with Two Negatively Related Variables

When one variable increases from *A* to *B*, the other variable decreases from *D* to *C*. Likewise, when one variable decreases from *B* to *A*, the other variable increases from *C* to *D*. We say that variable 1 is negatively related to variable 2, or that variable 1 varies inversely with variable 2.

positively related: a situation in which an increase in one variable is associated with an increase in another variable; also called *directly related.*

negatively related: a situation in which an increase in one variable is associated with a decrease in another variable; also called *inversely related.*

a direct relationship. If a model says that one variable varies inversely with the other, this means that if the first variable rises, then the second falls. If a model says that one variable varies directly with another, this means that if one variable rises, the other also rises. In economics, the expression "is positively related to" is frequently used in place of the phrase "varies directly with," which is more common in other sciences. Similarly, the expression "is negatively related to" is frequently used in place of "varies inversely with."

In Figure 5, two variables are shown to be **positively related.** In other words, when variable 1 increases from *A* to *B*, variable 2 increases from *C* to *D* by the specific amount given by the curve. Likewise, when variable 1 decreases from *B* to *A*, variable 2 decreases from *D* to *C*. In Figure 6, a model with two variables that are **negatively related** is shown. Here, when variable 1 increases from *A* to *B*, variable 2 decreases from *D* to *C*. Likewise, when variable 1 decreases from *B* to *A*, variable 2 increases from *C* to *D*. Models have *constants* as well as variables. The constants in the models in Figures 5 and 6 are the positions and shapes of the curves.

■ **An Example: A Model with Two Variables.** Figure 7 shows a model describing how doctors employed in a health maintenance organization provide physical examinations. The model states that the more doctors who are employed at the HMO, the more physical exams can be given. The model is represented in four different ways: (1) with words, (2) with a numerical table, (3) with a graph, and (4) with algebra.

On the lower right of Figure 7, we have the verbal description: more doctors mean more physical exams, but additional doctors increase the number of exams by smaller amounts, presumably because the diagnostic facilities at the HMO are limited; for example, there are only so many rooms available for physical exams.

On the upper left, we have a table with numbers showing how the number of examinations depends on the number of doctors. Exactly how many examinations can be given by each number of doctors is shown in the table. Clearly this table is much more

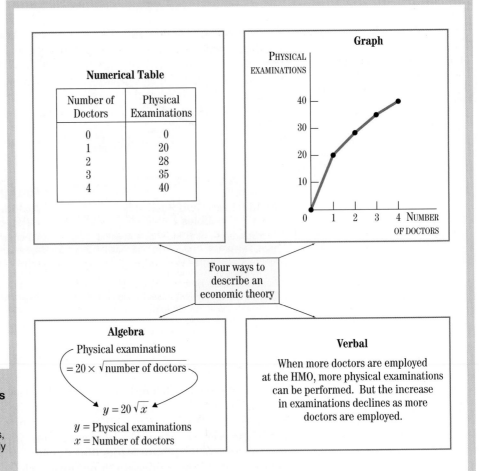

FIGURE 7
Economic Models in Four Ways
Each way has advantages and disadvantages; this book focuses mostly on verbal descriptions, graphs, and numerical tables, but occasionally some algebra will be used to help explain things.

specific than the verbal description. Be sure to distinguish between the meaning of a table that presents a model and a table that presents data. They look similar, but one is a model of the real world and the other represents observations about the real world.

On the upper right, we have a curve showing the relationship between doctors and physical examinations. The curve shows how many exams each number of doctors can perform. The points on the curve are plotted from the information in the table. The vertical axis has the number of examinations; the horizontal axis has the number of doctors. The points are connected with a line to help visualize the curve.

Finally, in the lower left we show the doctor-examination relationship in algebraic form. In this case, the number of exams is equal to the square root of the number of doctors times 20. If we use the symbol y for the number of exams and x for the number of doctors, the model looks a lot like the equations in an algebra course.

All four ways of representing models have advantages and disadvantages. The advantage of the verbal representation is that we usually communicate with people in words, and if we want our economic models to have any use, we need to communicate with people who have not studied economics. However, the verbal representation is not as precise as the other three. In addition to verbal analysis, in this book we will focus on tabular and graphical representations and, when appropriate, algebraic descriptions as well.

The *Ceteris Paribus* Assumption

ceteris paribus: "all other things being equal"; refers to holding all other variables constant or keeping all other things the same when one variable is changed.

In order to use models for prediction, economists use the assumption of **ceteris paribus,** which means "all other things being equal." For example, the prediction that variable 2 will fall from *D* to *C* assumes that the curve in Figure 6 does not shift: The position of the curve when variable 1 is at *A* is *equal* to the position of the curve when variable 1 is at *B*. If other things were not equal—if the curve shifted—then we could not predict that variable 2 would fall from *D* to *C* when variable 1 rose from *A* to *B*. Similarly, predicting that more doctors can produce more physical exams assumes that there is no power outage that would cause the diagnostic equipment to stop operating.

The Use of Existing Models

Because economics has been around for a long time, there are many existing models that can be applied to explain observations or make predictions that are useful to decision-makers. Much of what economists do in practice, whether in government or business or universities, is use models that are already in existence.

The models are used in many different types of applications, from determining the effects of discrimination in the workplace to evaluating the gains from lower health-care prices. Frequently the models are applied in new and clever ways.

The Development of New Models

Like models in other sciences, economic models change and new models are developed. Many of the models in this book are very different from the models in books published 40 years ago. New economic models evolve because some new observations cannot be explained by existing models.

The process of the development of new models or theories in economics proceeds much like that in any other science. First one develops a *hypothesis*, or a hunch, to explain a puzzling observation. Then one tests the hypothesis by seeing if its predictions of other observations are good. If the hypothesis passes this test, then it becomes accepted. In practice, however, this is at best a rough description of the process of scientific discovery in economics. Existing models are constantly being reexamined and tested. Some economists specialize in testing models; others specialize in developing them. There is an ongoing process of creating and testing of models in economics.

In the following chapter, you will be introduced to the supply and demand model, and how it can be applied to understanding the gasoline market.

R E V I E W

■ Economists use models to describe economic phenomena and to understand how changes in some variables affect the variable of interest. Economic models are abstractions, or simplifications, of a more complex reality. They can be extremely detailed or rather abstract, depending on the purpose of use.

■ Economic models are different from models in the physical sciences because they must deal with human behavior. Models can be represented verbally, with numerical tables, with graphs, and with algebra.

■ Economists also have a long-standing interest in improving the economic policy of governments. Economics can be used in a positive sense, to understand why government policies are the way they are, or in a normative sense, to identify what government policies should be enacted.

RECOMMENDING APPROPRIATE POLICIES

Ever since the birth of economics as a field—around 1776, when Adam Smith published the *Wealth of Nations*—economists have been concerned about and motivated by a desire to improve the economic policy of governments. In fact, economics was originally called *political economy*. Much of the *Wealth of Nations* is about what the government should or should not do to affect the domestic and international economy.

Adam Smith argued for a system of *laissez faire*—little government control—where the role of the government is mainly to promote competition, provide for national defense, and reduce restrictions on the exchange of goods and services. One hundred years later, Karl Marx brought a new perspective to Smith's (and other classical economists') view of political economy, arguing against the laissez-faire approach. His analysis of market economies, or **capitalism,** centered on the contradictions that he saw arising out of such a system, particularly the conflict between the owners of production and the laborers. He argued that these contradictions would result in the inevitable collapse of capitalism and the emergence of a new economic system, called **socialism,** in which government would essentially own and control all production. While Marx actually wrote very little about what a socialist or communist economy would look like, the centrally planned economies that arose in the Soviet Union, Eastern Europe, and China in the twentieth century can be traced to Marx's ideas.

Most countries today have rejected the command economy and have moved toward market economies, but the debate about the role of government continues. In many modern market economies, the government plays a large role, and for this reason, such economies are sometimes called **mixed economies.** How great should the role of government be in a market economy? Should the government provide health-care services? Should it try to break up large firms?

capitalism: an economic system based on a market economy in which capital is individually owned, and production and employment decisions are decentralized.

socialism: an economic system in which the government owns and controls all the capital and makes decisions about prices and quantities as part of a central plan.

mixed economy: a market economy in which the government plays a very large role.

Positive versus Normative Economics

In debating the role of government in the economy, economists distinguish between positive and normative economics. **Positive economics** is about what is; **normative economics** is about what should be. For example, positive economics endeavors to explain why health-care spending slowed down in the mid-1990s or why the price of gasoline increased so rapidly in late 2005. Normative economics aims to develop and recommend policies that might prevent health-care spending or gasoline prices from rising rapidly in the future. In general, normative economics is concerned with making recommendations about what the government should do—whether it should control the price of electricity or health care, for example. Economists who advise governments spend much of their time doing normative economics. In the United States, the president's **Council of Economic Advisers** has legal responsibility for advising the president about which economic policies are good and which are bad.

Positive economics can also be used to explain *why* governments do what they do. For example, why did the U.S. government break up AT&T into regional phone companies in 1984? Why were tax rates cut in the 1980s, increased in the 1990s, then cut again in the 2000s? Positive analysis of government policy requires a mixture of both political science and economic science, with a focus on what motivates voters and the politicians they elect.

positive economics: economic analysis that explains what happens in the economy and why, without making recommendations about economic policy.

normative economics: economic analysis that makes recommendations about economic policy.

Council of Economic Advisers: a three-member group of economists appointed by the president of the United States to analyze the economy and make recommendations about economic policy.

Economics as a Science versus a Partisan Policy Tool

Although economics, like any other science, is based on facts and theories, it is not always used in a purely scientific way.

In political campaigns, economists put forth arguments in favor of one candidate, emphasizing the good side of their candidate's ideas and de-emphasizing the

ECONOMICS IN ACTION

Science or Persuasion?

In a recent court case, a grocery store chain, Lucky Stores, was sued for discriminating against female workers. The case illustrates how economics can be used in a partisan as well as a scientific way.

Economists were called as expert witnesses for both sides. Labor economist John Pencavel testified for the plaintiffs, the women who brought the suit. He found that women at Lucky earned between 76 and 82 percent of what Lucky's male workers earned. Pencavel found that women were regularly placed in jobs that paid less than jobs given male coworkers, although there was no significant difference between them in terms of education and experience. There was little difference in the wages of the male and female workers within each type of job, but some jobs paid more than others, and women happened to be assigned to the lower-paying jobs.

Joan Haworth, another labor economist, was an expert witness for the defendant, Lucky Stores. She reported survey evidence showing that Lucky's assignment of women and men to different jobs reflected differences in the work preferences of men and women. Thus, Lucky justified its job assignments by arguing that there was a gender difference in attitudes toward work. Lucky argued that its employment policies were based on observed differences in the career aspirations of male and female employees. For example, one manager at Lucky testified that women were more interested in cash register work and men were more interested in floor work.

After weighing the facts and economic arguments, the judge decided the case in favor of the plaintiffs. Although

You be the judge. Would you have been persuaded by the economic argument used by Lucky Stores or by the defendants?

male and female employees received equal pay for equal work, the judge concluded that Lucky's employment policies involved discrimination. The judge wrote: "The court finds defendant's explanation that the statistical disparities between men and women at Lucky are caused by differences in the work interests of men and women to be unpersuasive."

The decision is a landmark because of the economic analysis that showed that discrimination could exist even if men and women were being paid the same wage for equal work. Of course, not all sex discrimination cases are decided in favor of the plaintiffs. But whoever wins a given case, economics is almost always a key consideration in the judge's decision.

bad side. In a court of law, one economist may help a defendant—making the best case possible—and another economist may help the plaintiff—again, making the best case possible. In other words, economics is not always used objectively. A good reason to learn economics for yourself is to see through fallacious arguments.

But economics is not the only science that is used in these two entirely different modes. For example, there is currently a great controversy about the use of biology and chemistry to make estimates of the costs and benefits of different environmental policies. This is a politically controversial subject, and some on both sides of the controversy have been accused of using science in nonobjective ways.

Economics Is Not the Only Factor in Policy Issues

Although economics can be very useful in policy decisions, it is frequently not the only factor. For example, national security sometimes calls for a recommendation on a policy issue different from one based on a purely economic point of view. Although most economists recommend free exchange of goods between countries, the U.S.

Young Economists at Work

This article which appeared in the *New York Times* describes the work of Emily Oster, one of the young stars in the field of economics. This article appeared just as she embarked on a career as an economics professor. The article also talks about other young economists who are doing important and interesting work. You will be able to easily find most of the work done by Emily and other young economists online.

Emily's research begins with an observation about the economy.

How the scope of economic analysis has expanded in recent years

Emily Oster's explanation for why some African countries had very high rates of HIV

The policy conclusions that follow from Emily Oster's research

The Future of Economics Isn't So Dismal

By DAVID LEONHARDT—Chicago

On a summer day a few years ago, a recent college graduate named Emily Oster was talking to her boyfriend about the research that was, and wasn't, being done on the spread of AIDS. She was an aspiring economist at the time, getting ready to go to graduate school, and she was struck by the fact that her field had little to say about why some countries had such high H.I.V. rates.

To most people, that may not sound like a question an economist needs to be asking. It's more the domain of epidemiologists or public health workers, and they were already doing good work on it.

But economists have been acting a lot like intellectual imperialists in the last decade or so. They have been using their tools—mainly the analysis of enormous piles of data to tease out cause and effect—to examine everything from politics to French wine vintages.

As the daughter of two economists, Ms. Oster probably understood this better than most 22-year-olds. Her father, Ray Fair, invented a semi-famous economic formula that has an impressive track record of predicting presidential elections. Her mother, Sharon Oster, studies business strategy.

So during her time as a Ph.D. student at Harvard, the younger Ms. Oster took on AIDS in Africa. Her most provocative finding was that Africans didn't really behave so differently from people in countries with much lower H.I.V. rates. They did not have many more sexual partners than Americans on average. And, like Americans, Africans had cut back on unsafe sex in response to AIDS—or at least relatively well-off, healthy Africans had.

Poorer Africans, who of course make up the continent's overwhelming majority, had made fewer changes. They had less of an incentive to practice safe sex, Ms. Oster concluded, because many of them could not expect to reach old age, whether or not they contracted H.I.V. Any attack on AIDS should therefore include an attack on poverty.

"This is not the kind of thing epidemiologists would do. It's not the way they would have framed it," Ms. Oster, now 26, said. "It's an idea only an economist would love."

Whatever you think of her conclusions, there's no denying that her subject is more interesting—and, yes, more important—than the esoteric fiscal and monetary models that once dominated economics. Ms. Oster is studying death, not taxes.

Last weekend, hundreds of economists gathered in Chicago for their annual conference, where they interviewed one another for job openings, presented new research papers and had the occasional glass of wine. This was my sixth such conference, and I have often been stunned by how much of the research here, like Ms. Oster's work, would interest non-economists.

As "The Soulful Science," a new book by Diane Coyle, puts it, there has been a "remarkable creative renaissance in how economics is addressing the most fundamental questions—and how it is starting to help solve problems." The reams of data that computers can now crunch have ushered the field into a new golden age, Ms. Coyle writes, yet most of its accomplishments are not widely known.

Other young economists whose work has been deemed interesting by the economics profession

So before this year's conference, I did an informal poll of about 20 senior economists around the country and asked a single question: who are the young (untenured) economists doing work that is both highly respected among experts and relevant to the rest of us? Who, in other words, is the future of economics?

Thirteen names came up more than once, and I'm sure a scientific survey would have produced a longer list. As it is, though, the list is incredibly diverse. It includes Justin Wolfers, who once worked for an Australian bookie and is now an expert on online prediction markets, and Raj Chetty, who grew up in both India and Milwaukee and studies antipoverty policy. ◄

Ms. Oster is on the list, and so is the boyfriend with whom she first discussed her AIDS ideas: Jesse Shapiro, now her husband. He has done innovative work on, among other things, the benefits of television for some toddlers. The two of them are the inaugural fellows at a University of Chicago research center run by Gary Becker (a Nobel laureate), Steven Levitt (co-author of "Freaknomoics") and Kevin Murphy (winner of a MacArthur genius award).

In the end, this new era of economics matters because it has a chance to influence the world that is its subject matter. Ms. Oster, for example, has presented her work to the President's Commission on AIDS and others, and her findings seem to be one small part of the recent push for better H.I.V. prevention measures. ◄

In Massachusetts, a 41-year-old economist named Jonathan Gruber helped design the new state program to provide health insurance for every resident, which is a model for the California plan announced on Monday. The new federal pension law, meanwhile, encourages employers to sign up workers automatically for 401(k) plans largely because academic research has shown just how costly procrastination is.

For all this success, though, there are still two big obstacles holding back the economics revolution. The first is that the field remains too narrow in its approach. As David Colander, an economist at Middlebury College, notes, researchers are rewarded—with job offers, endowed chairs and prizes—for finding statistically significant patterns that can be published in prestigious journals. They're generally not rewarded for collaborating with experts in other fields to put those patterns into better context.

As a result, there is too much "cleverness for cleverness's sake," Mr. Colander says, and not enough "judgment and wisdom."

The second obstacle is that when economists do uncover a nugget of true wisdom, they're often hesitant to follow it to its natural conclusion and to become principled advocates for better policy. Theirs is not to judge, they insist, only to report what they find. Otherwise, they may risk their reputation for impartial research.

Which is a fair point. But it's a risk worth taking, because the alternative is frankly much worse.

When David Hume, the philosopher and friend of Adam Smith, called for the establishment of a "science of human nature" in the 18th century, he helped invent modern economics. The new generation of researchers will probably come closer to realizing his vision, and to making economics a true science, than any of their predecessors.

But think about what scientists do when they uncover a problem: they try to solve it. To do otherwise is to let an impressive piece of research turn into a scientifically rigorous piece of trivia.

Emily Oster, an Assistant Professor at the University of Chicago, is one of a group of young economists whose research has attracted considerable attention.

A reminder about why the study of economics matters

government restricted exports of high-technology goods such as computers during the cold war because defense specialists worried that the technology could help the military in the Soviet Union, and this was viewed as more important than the economic argument. There are still heavy restrictions on trade in nuclear fuels for fear of the proliferation of nuclear weapons.

Disagreement Between Economists

Watching economists debate issues on television or reading their opinions in a newspaper or magazine certainly gives the impression that they rarely agree. There are major controversies in economics, and we will examine them in this book. But when people survey economists' beliefs, they find a surprising amount of agreement.

Why, then, is there the popular impression of disagreement? Because there are many economists, and one can always find some economist with a different viewpoint. When people sue other people in court and economics is an issue, it is always possible to find economists who will testify for each side, even if 99 percent of economists would agree with one side. Similarly, television interviews or news shows want to give both sides of public policy issues. Thus, even if 99 percent of economists agree with one side, the producers are able to find at least one on the other side.

Economists are human beings with varying moral beliefs and different backgrounds and political views that are frequently unrelated to economic models. For example, an economist who is very concerned about the importation of drugs into the United States might appear to be more willing to condone a restriction on coffee exports from Brazil and other coffee-exporting countries in order to give Colombia a higher price for its coffee to offset a loss in revenue from cocaine. Another economist, who felt less strongly about drug imports, might argue strongly against such a restriction on coffee. But if they were asked about restrictions on trade in the abstract, both economists would probably argue for government policies that prevent them.

CONCLUSION: A READER'S GUIDE

In Chapter 1, we explored the central idea of economics: scarcity, choice, and economic interaction. In this chapter, we discussed how economists observe economic events and use economic models to explain these phenomena. It is now time to move on and learn more about the models and application of the central idea. As you study economic models in the following chapters, it will be useful to keep three points in mind. They are implied by the ideas raised in this chapter.

First, *economics—more than other subjects—requires a mixture of verbal and quantitative skills.* Frequently, those who come to economics with a good background in physical science and mathematics find the mix of formal models with more informal verbal descriptions of markets and institutions unusual and perhaps a little difficult. If you are one of these people, you might wish for a more cut-and-dried, or mathematical, approach.

In contrast, those who are good at history or philosophy may find the emphasis on formal models and graphs difficult and might even prefer a more historical approach that looked more at watershed events and famous individuals and less at formal models of how many individuals behave. If you are one of these people, you might wish that economic models were less abstract.

In reality, however, economics is a mixture of formal modeling, historical analysis, and philosophy. If you are very good at math and you think the symbols and graphs of elementary economics are too simple, think of Max Planck's comment about economics and focus on the complexity of the economic phenomena that these simple models and graphs are explaining. Then when you are asked an open-ended question about government policy that does not have a simple yes or no answer, you will not be caught off guard. Or if your advantage is in history or philosophy, you should spend more time honing your skills at using models and graphs. Then when you are asked to solve a cut-and-dried economic problem with an exact answer requiring graphical analysis, you will not be caught off guard.

Second, *economics is a wide-ranging discipline.* When your friends or relatives hear that you are taking economics, they may ask you for advice about what stock to buy. Economists' friends and relatives are always asking them for such advice. Some topics that you study in economics will help you answer questions about whether to invest in the stock market or put your money in a bank or how many stocks to buy. But even these areas of economics will not offer any predictions about the success of particular companies. Rather, what economics gives you is a set of tools that you can use to obtain information about companies, industries, or countries and to analyze them yourself. Furthermore, the scope of economics is vast. Even among the faculty in a small college, you will find economists who study childhood obesity, trade barriers, real estate markets, abortion policy, the formation of American corporations, economic growth, international lending agencies, social security, agricultural pollution, and school choice.

Third, and perhaps most important, *the study of economics is an intellectually fascinating adventure in its own right.* Yes, economics is highly relevant, and it affects people's lives. But once you learn how economic models work, you will find that they are actually fun to use. Every now and then, just after you have learned about a new economic model, put the book down and think of the economic model independent of its message or relevance to society—try to enjoy it the way you would a good movie. In this way, too, you will be learning to think like an economist.

KEY POINTS

1. Economics is a way of thinking that requires observation (describing economic events), explanation (identifying variables that are potential explanatory variables of the event), prediction (building and using economic models to predict future events), and policy recommendations (courses of action for government—and business—to follow, based on these observations and models).

2. Finding the appropriate data series to explain economic events is a challenge because data can often be hard to find or incomplete, or can be misleading if they are not appropriately transformed.

3. Finding explanations for why an economic event occurred is challenging because even if you can find variables that are correlated with the variable you are interested in, correlation does not imply causation. The inability to run controlled experiments also makes it difficult for economists to definitively establish a causal explanation for an economic event.

4. Economists have to explain the complex behavior of humans in economic situations. They often use models that are abstractions, or simplifications, of reality in their work. Economic models, like models in other sciences, can be described with words, with tables, with graphs, or with mathematics. All four ways are important and complement one another.

5. Economists use the tools of economic analysis to come up with policy insights concerning what the government is doing, or what the government should be doing, with regard to the economist's area of interest. Improving economic policy has been a goal of economists since the time of Adam Smith.

6. Economics is a discipline that requires a combination of analytical, mathematical, and verbal skills. You can apply the tools of economics to almost any problem that involves decision-making by individuals. Many students are interested in studying economics because they find it very relevant to events that occur in the world, but the study of economics can be an intellectually stimulating exercise in its own right.

KEY TERMS

relative price
economic variable
controlled experiments
experimental economics
economic model

microeconomics
macroeconomics
gross domestic product
   (GDP)
positively related

negatively related
ceteris paribus
capitalism
socialism
mixed economy

positive economics
normative economics
Council of Economic
   Advisers

QUESTIONS FOR REVIEW

1. How do economists typically approach an economics-related problem?

2. What are the challenges that economists face in trying to describe an economic event?

3. What is meant by a relative price, and why is it important in certain situations to look at the relative price of a good instead of the actual price of that good?

4. What does it mean for two variables to be correlated? What is the difference between positive and negative correlation?

5. Why doesn't correlation imply causation? Can you come up with your own example of why correlation does not imply causation?

6. Why do economists use economic models? Can you come up with some reasons why economists should be careful in using models?

7. What is the *ceteris paribus* assumption? Why is it so important in economics?

8. What is the difference between macroeconomics and microeconomics? Between positive and normative economics?

9. What academic disciplines do you think of as being more scientific than economics? Why do you think so? Which disciplines do you consider to be less scientific, and why?

10. Look through the research and teaching interests of the economics faculty members in your department. Collectively, how wide-ranging are those interests? Are there any areas that you were surprised to find that the tools of economics could be applied to?

PROBLEMS

1. Which of the following variables are studied as part of microeconomics, and which are studied as part of macroeconomics?
   a. The U.S. unemployment rate
   b. The amount of tips earned by a waiter
   c. The national rate of inflation
   d. The number of hours worked by a student
   e. The price paid to obtain this economics textbook

2. Consider the following table, which provides the price of chicken and the price of all foods from 1991 to 2006.
   a. Calculate the relative price of chicken for each year.
   b. Plot the relative price of chicken as in Figure 2.
   c. What can you say about how the price of chicken has varied in comparison to the price of all foods in the decade from 1996 to 2006?

Year	Price of All Foods	Price of Chicken	Relative Price
1996	92	95	
1997	93	98	
1998	96	98	
1999	97	99	
2000	100	100	
2001	103	103	
2002	104	105	
2003	108	106	
2004	111	114	
2005	113	116	
2006	116	114	

3. A change in the relative price of a good matters more than the change in the price of a good in analyzing

the change in spending on that good. Show that the relative price of a good can fall on occasions when the price of that good is rising, falling, or remaining unchanged, using numerical examples from the table in problem 2.

4. Indicate whether you expect positive or negative correlation for the following pairs of variables, labeled X and Y. For each pair, state whether X causes Y, Y causes X, or both.
   a. Sunrise (X) and crowing roosters (Y)
   b. The use of umbrellas (X) and a thunderstorm (Y)
   c. The price of theater tickets (X) and the number of theatergoers (Y)
   d. Weekly earnings of a worker (X) and the number of hours a week she works at her job (Y)
   e. The number of children who were vaccinated against a disease (X) and the number of children who currently suffer from that disease (Y)

5. Consider an economic model of donut production. Show how to represent this model graphically, algebraically, and verbally, as in Figure 6.

Number of Workers	Number of Donuts Produced
0	0
1	100
4	200
9	300
16	400

6. Suppose you decide to build a model to explain why the average worker in a particular occupation works more hours during some weeks than during others.
   a. What data would you collect to describe this phenomenon?
   b. What variable do you believe would supply the major part of the explanation of the variation in hours worked?
   c. If you graph the data with hours worked on the vertical axis and your explanatory variable on the horizontal axis, will the relationship be upward-sloping or downward-sloping?
   d. What does your answer to part c imply for whether the data on hours worked and the data

on your explanatory variable are positively or negatively correlated?

7. Why is it typical for economists to make the *ceteris paribus* assumption when making predictions? Now consider the statement: "If the local McDonald's restaurant reduces the price of a Big Mac hamburger, it will sell a lot more hamburgers." What other variables are most likely being held fixed under the *ceteris paribus* assumption when this statement is being made?

8. Suppose you wanted to modify the Bertrand and Mullainathan study to focus on gender discrimination. Describe the "experiment" that you would run. Also be sure to explain how the *ceteris paribus* assumption is involved in terms of the names you would choose for the men and for the women.

9. Identify whether the following policy statements are positive or normative. Explain.
   a. "The price of gasoline is too high."
   b. "The average price of gasoline rose to a record high of $3.07 in May 2007."
   c. "Forty-four million Americans lack access to health insurance."
   d. "The government needs to provide basic health care to the uninsured."
   e. "The collapse in the real estate market will affect many Americans."

10. Suppose an economic study shows that increasing the tax rate on cigarettes will reduce the amount of smoking. Which of the following statements can be validly made on the basis of the study because they are positive statements, and which cannot be validly made because they are normative statements?
   a. Increasing the cigarette tax rate is a method of reducing smoking.
   b. If the government wishes to reduce smoking, it ought to raise the cigarette tax.
   c. If the government wishes to reduce smoking, it can raise the cigarette tax.
   d. The government ought to reduce smoking by raising the cigarette tax.
   e. The government should not raise the cigarette tax on low-income smokers.

Reading, Understanding, and Creating Graphs

Whether you follow the stock market, the health-care market, or the whole economy, graphs are needed to understand what is going on. That is why the financial pages of newspapers contain so many graphs. Knowing how to read, understand, and even create your own graphs is part of learning to "think like an economist." Graphs help us see correlations, or patterns, in economic observations. Graphs are also useful for understanding economic models. They help us see how variables in the model behave. They help us describe assumptions about what firms and consumers do.

Computer software to create graphs is now widely available. A graphing program with many examples is provided with the software that accompanies this text. To understand how helpful graphs can be, you might want to create a few of your own graphs using the time-series data in the "Explore" section of the software. Here we provide an overview of basic graphing techniques.

Visualizing Observations with Graphs

Most economic graphs are drawn in two dimensions, like the surface of this page, and are constructed using a **Cartesian coordinate system.** The idea of Cartesian coordinates is that pairs of observations on variables can be represented in a plane by designating one axis for one variable and the other axis for the other variable. Each point, or coordinate, on the plane corresponds to a pair of observations.

Time-Series Graphs

In many instances, we want to see how a variable changes over time. Consider the federal debt held by the public—all the outstanding borrowing of the federal government that has not yet been paid back. Table A.1 shows observations of the U.S. federal debt. The observations are for every 10 years. The observations in Table A.1 are graphed in Figure A.1. The graph in Figure A.1 is called a **time-series graph** because it plots a series—that is, several values of the variable—over time.

Observe the scales on the horizontal and vertical axes in Figure A.1. The seven years are put on the horizontal axis, spread evenly from the year 1950 to the year 2010. The last year is a forecast. For the vertical axis,

TABLE A.1
U.S. Federal Government Debt

Year	Debt (billions of dollars)
1950	219
1960	237
1970	283
1980	712
1990	2,412
2000	3,410
2010 (Projected)	5,949

Source: Congressional Budget Office.

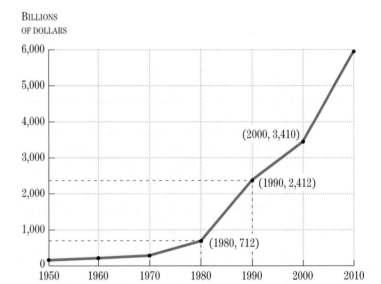

FIGURE A.1
U.S. Federal Debt
Each point corresponds to a pair of observations—the year and the debt—from Table A.1.

FIGURE A.2

Stretching the Debt Story in Two Ways

The points in both graphs are identical to those in Figure A.1, but by stretching or shrinking the scales, the problem can be made to look either less dramatic or more dramatic.

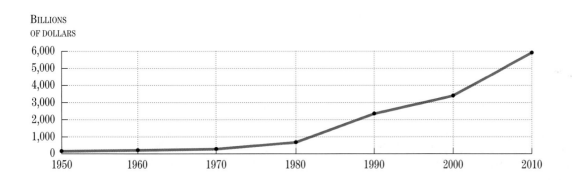

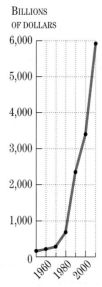

one needs to decide on a scale. The range of variation for the debt in Table A.1 is very wide—from a minimum of $219 billion to a maximum of $5,949 billion. Thus, the range on the vertical axis—from $0 to $6,000 billion in Figure A.1—must be wide enough to contain all these points.

Now observe how each pair of points from Table A.1 is plotted in Figure A.1. The point for the pair of observations for the year 1950 and the debt of $219 billion is found by going over to 1950 on the horizontal axis, then going up to $219 billion and putting a dot there. The point for 1960 and $237 billion and all the other points are found in the same way. In order to better visualize the points, they can be connected with lines. These lines are not part of the observations; they are only a convenience to help in eyeballing the observations. The points for 1980, 1990, and 2000 are labeled with the pairs of observations corresponding to Table A.1, but in general there is no need to put in such labels.

One could choose scales different from those in Figure A.1, and if you plotted your own graph from the data in Table A.1 without looking at Figure A.1, your scales would probably be different. The scales determine how much movement there is in a time-series graph. For example, Figure A.2 shows two ways to stretch the scales to make the increase in the debt look more or less dramatic. So as not to be fooled by graphs, therefore, it is important to look at the scales and think about what they mean.

As an alternative to time-series graphs with dots connected by a line, the observations can be shown on a bar graph, as in Figure A.3. Some people prefer the visual

look of a bar graph, but, as is clear from a comparison of Figures A.1 and A.3, they provide the same information as time-series graphs.

The debt as a percentage of GDP is given in Table A.2 and graphed in Figure A.4. Note that this figure makes the debt look very different from the way it looks in the first one. As a percentage of GDP, the debt fell from the end of

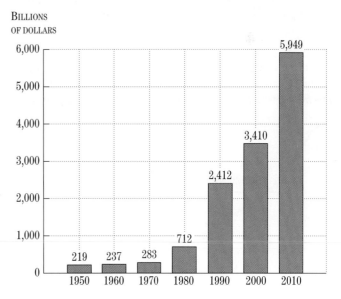

FIGURE A.3

U.S. Federal Debt in Bars

The observations are identical to those in Figure A.1.

TABLE A.2
U.S. Federal Debt as a Percentage of GDP

Year	Debt (percent of GDP)
1950	82.5
1960	46.8
1970	28.2
1980	25.7
1990	42.3
2000	35.9
2010 (Projected)	37.8

Source: U.S. Department of Commerce and Table A.1.

World War II (when it was very large because of the war debt) until around 1980. It increased during the 1980s and declined in the 1990s, but has started to increase again in the 2000s.

Sometimes the data to be graphed have no observations close to 0, in which case including 0 on the vertical axis would leave some wasted space at the bottom of the graph. To eliminate this space and have more room to see the graph itself, we can start the range near the minimum value and end it near the maximum value. This is done in Figure A.5, where the debt as a percentage of GDP is shown up to 1980. Note, however, that cutting off the bottom of the scale could be misleading to people who do not look at the axis. In particular, 0 percent is no longer at the point where the horizontal and vertical axes intersect. To warn people about the missing part of the scale, a little cut is sometimes put on the axis, as is done in Figure A.5, but you have to look carefully at the scale.

PERCENT

FIGURE A.5
A Look at Debt as a Percentage of GDP from 1950 to 1980
(*Note:* To alert the reader that the bottom part of the axis is not shown, a break point is sometimes used, as shown here.)

Time-Series Graphs Showing Two or More Variables

So far, we have shown how a graph can be used to show observations on one variable over time. What if we want to see how two or more variables change over time together? Suppose, for example, we want to look at how observations on debt as a percentage of GDP compare with the interest rate the government must pay on its debt. (The interest rate for 2010 is, of course, a forecast.) The two variables are shown in Table A.3.

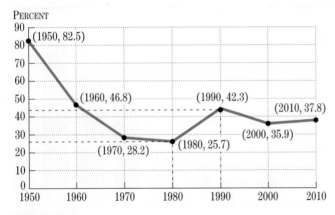

FIGURE A.4
U.S. Federal Debt as a Percentage of GDP
Each point corresponds to a pair of observations from Table A.2.

TABLE A.3
Interest Rate and Federal Debt as a Percentage of GDP

Year	Debt (percent of GDP)	Interest Rate (percent)
1950	82.5	1.2
1960	46.8	2.9
1970	28.2	6.5
1980	25.7	11.5
1990	42.3	7.5
2000	35.9	5.5
2010 (Projected)	37.8	5.5

Source: Federal Reserve Board and Table A.2.

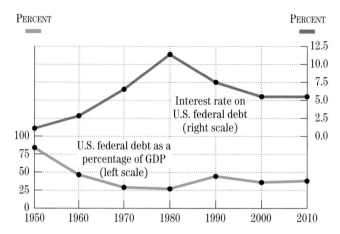

FIGURE A.6
Comparing Two Time Series with a Dual Scale
When two variables have different scales, a dual scale is useful. Here the interest rate and the debt as a percentage of GDP are plotted from Table A.3.

The two sets of observations can easily be placed on the same time-series graph. In other words, we can plot the observations on the debt percentage and connect the dots and then plot the interest rate observations and connect the dots. If the scales of measurement of the two variables are much different, however, it may be hard to see both. For example, the interest rate ranges between 1 and 12 percent; it would not be very visible on a graph going all the way from 0 to 100 percent, a range that is fine for the debt percentage. In this situation, a **dual scale** can be used, as shown in Figure A.6. One scale is put on the left-hand vertical axis, and the other scale is put on the right-hand vertical axis. With a dual-scale diagram, it is very important to be aware of the two scales. In Figure A.6 we emphasize the different axes by the color line segment at the top of each vertical axis. The color line segment corresponds to the color of the curve plotted using that scale.

Scatter Plots

Finally, two variables can be usefully compared with a **scatter plot.** The Cartesian coordinate method is used, as in the time-series graph; however, we do not put the year on one of the axes. Instead, the horizontal axis is used for one of the variables and the vertical axis for the other variable. We do this for the debt percentage and the interest rate in Figure A.7. The interest rate is on the vertical axis, and the debt percentage is on the horizontal axis. For example, the point at the upper left is 25.7 percent for the debt as a percentage of GDP and 11.5 percent for the interest rate.

Pie Charts

Time-series graphs, bar graphs, and scatter plots are not the only visual ways to observe economic data. For example, the *pie chart* in Figure A.8 is useful for

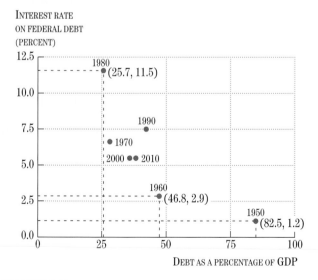

FIGURE A.7
Scatter Plot
Interest rate and debt as a percentage of GDP are shown.

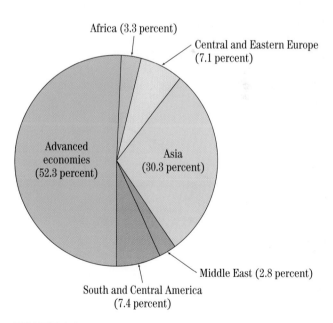

FIGURE A.8
Pie Chart Showing the Shares of the World's GDP
The pie chart shows how the world's GDP in 2005 is divided up into that produced by different groups of countries, including the industrial (advanced) economies, Asia, Africa, South America, Central and Eastern Europe, and the Middle East.

comparing percentage shares for a small number of different groups or a small number of time periods. In this example, the pie chart is a visual representation of how the industrial countries produce more than half of the world's GDP, while the developing countries in Asia, Africa, South and Central America, and the Middle East produce 40 percent and the former communist countries in Eastern Europe and the former Soviet Union, now in transition toward market economies, produce about 7 percent.

Visualizing Models with Graphs

Graphs can also represent models. Like graphs showing observations, graphs showing models are usually restricted to curves in two dimensions.

Slopes of Curves

Does a curve slope up or down? How steep is it? These questions are important in economics, as in other sciences. The **slope** of a curve tells us how much the variable on the vertical axis changes when we change the variable on the horizontal axis by one unit.

The slope is computed as follows:

$$\text{Slope} = \frac{\text{change in variable on vertical axis}}{\text{change in variable on horizontal axis}}$$

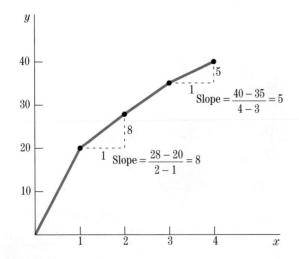

FIGURE A.9
Measuring the Slope

The slope between two points is given by the change along the vertical axis divided by the change along the horizontal axis. In this example, the slope declines as x increases. Since the curve slopes up from left to right, it has a positive slope.

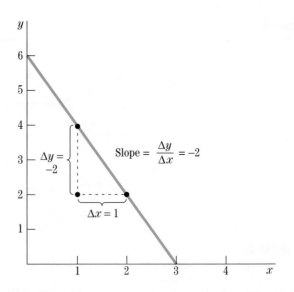

FIGURE A.10
A Relationship with a Negative Slope

Here the slope is negative: $(\Delta y)/(\Delta x) = -2$. As x increases, y falls. The line slopes down from left to right. In this case, y and x are inversely, or negatively, related.

In most algebra courses, the vertical axis is usually called the y-axis and the horizontal axis is called the x-axis. Thus, the slope is sometime described as

$$\text{Slope} = \frac{\text{change in } y}{\text{change in } x} = \frac{\Delta y}{\Delta x}$$

where the Greek letter Δ (delta) means "change in." In other words, the slope is the ratio of the "rise" (vertical change) to the "run" (horizontal change).

Figure A.9 shows how to compute the slope. In this case, the slope declines as the variable on the x-axis increases.

Observe that *the steeper the curve, the larger the slope.* When the curve gets very flat, the slope gets close to zero. Curves can either be upward-sloping or downward-sloping. If the curve slopes up from left to right, as in Figure A.9, it has a **positive slope,** and we say that the two variables are positively related. If the curve slopes down from left to right, it has a **negative slope,** and we say that the two variables are negatively related. Figure A.10 shows a case where the slope is negative. When x increases by 1 unit ($\Delta x = 1$), y declines by 2 units ($\Delta y = -2$). Thus, the slope equals -2; it is negative. Observe how the curve slopes down from left to right.

If the curve is a straight line, then the slope is a constant. Curves that are straight lines—like that in Figure A.10—are called **linear.** But economic relationships do not

Reading, Understanding, and Creating Graphs

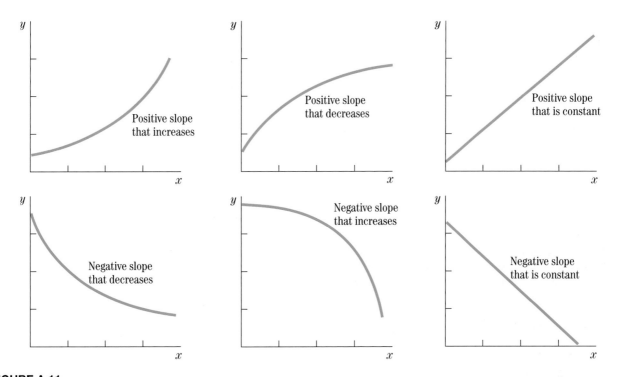

FIGURE A.11
Six Types of Relationships
In the top row, the variables are positively related. In the bottom row, they are negatively related.

need to be linear, as the example in Figure A.9 makes clear. Figure A.11 shows six different examples of curves and indicates how they are described.

Graphs of Models with More than Two Variables

In most cases, economic models involve more than two variables. For example, the number of physical examinations could depend on the number of nurses as well as the number of doctors. Or the amount of lemonade demanded might depend on the weather as well as on the price.

Economists have devised several methods for representing models with more than two variables with two-dimensional graphs. Suppose, for example, that the relationship between y and x in Figure A.10 depends on a third variable z. For a given value of x, larger values of z lead to larger values of y. This example is graphed in Figure A.12. As in Figure A.10, when x increases, y falls. This is a **movement along the curve.** But what if z changes? We represent this as a **shift of the curve.** An increase in z shifts the curve up; a decrease in z shifts the curve down.

Thus, by distinguishing between shifts of and movements along a curve, economists represent models with more than two variables in only two dimensions.

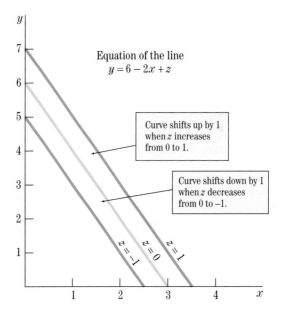

FIGURE A.12
A Third Variable Shifts the Curve
In order to represent models with three variables (x, y, and z) on a two-dimensional graph, economists distinguish between movements along the curve (when x and y change, holding z unchanged) and shifts of the curve (when z changes).

Only two variables (x and y) are shown explicitly on the graph, and when the third (z) is fixed, changes in x and y are movements along the curve. When z changes, the curve shifts. The distinction between "movements along" and "shifts of" curves comes up many times in economics.

KEY TERMS AND DEFINITIONS

Cartesian coordinate system: a graphing system in which ordered pairs of numbers are represented on a plane by the distances from a point to two perpendicular lines, called axes.

time-series graph: a graph that plots a variable over time, usually with time on the horizontal axis.

dual scale: a graph that uses time on the horizontal axis and different scales on the left and right vertical axes to compare the movements of two variables over time.

scatter plot: a graph in which points in a Cartesian coordinate system represent the values of two variables.

slope: a characteristic of a curve that is defined as the change in the variable on the vertical axis divided by the change in the variable on the horizontal axis.

positive slope: a slope of a curve that is greater than zero, representing a positive or direct relationship between two variables.

negative slope: a slope of a curve that is less than zero, representing a negative or inverse relationship between two variables.

linear: a situation in which a curve is straight, with a constant slope.

movement along the curve: a situation in which a change in the variable on one axis causes a change in the variable on the other axis, but the position of the curve is maintained.

shift of the curve: a change in the position of a curve, usually caused by a change in a variable not represented on either axis.

QUESTIONS FOR REVIEW

1. What is the difference between a scatter plot and a time-series graph?

2. Why are dual scales sometimes necessary?

3. What is the advantage of graphs over verbal representations of models?

4. What does a curve with a negative slope look like?

5. What is the difference between a shift in a curve and a movement along a curve?

PROBLEMS

1. The table below presents data on the debt and the debt to GDP ratio predicted by the Congressional Budget Office for the United States for each year through 2015.

Year	Debt	Debt to GDP Ratio
2005	4,656	38.1
2006	4,965	38.5
2007	5,246	38.6
2008	5,506	38.5
2009	5,737	38.2
2010	5,949	37.8
2011	6,054	36.7
2012	6,004	34.8
2013	5,941	33.0
2014	5,847	31.1
2015	5,726	29.1

Source: Congressional Budget Office.

a. Construct a time-series plot of the ratio of government debt to GDP.

b. Construct a time-series plot of the debt.

c. Construct a scatter plot of the debt ratio and the debt.

2. The following table shows the number of physical examinations given by doctors at an HMO with three different-size clinics: small, medium, and large. The larger the clinic, the more patients the doctors can handle.

Exams per Small Clinic	Exams per Medium Clinic	Exams per Large Clinic	Number of Doctors
0	0	0	0
20	30	35	1
28	42	49	2
35	53	62	3
40	60	70	4

a. Show the relationship between doctors and physical exams given with *three* curves, where the number of doctors is on the horizontal axis and the number of examinations is on the vertical axis.

b. Describe how the three relationships compare with one another.

c. Is a change in the number of doctors a shift of or a movement along the curve?

d. Is a change in the size of the clinic a shift of or a movement along the curve?

3. Consider two variables that change over time, which we will denote as Numerator and Denominator. Consider also a combination of the two variables, denoted as Ratio, formed by the formula:

$$\text{Ratio} = \frac{\text{Numerator}}{\text{Denominator}}$$

   a. If both Numerator and Denominator are increasing over time, what must be true if Ratio is to rise over time?
   b. If both Numerator and Denominator are decreasing over time, what must be true if Ratio is to rise over time?
   c. If Ratio is not changing over time, what must be true about the behavior of Numerator and Denominator over time, and relative to each other?

4. A tradeoff is a situation in which more of one variable is obtained along with less of another. Which of the six relationships in Figure A.11 can represent a tradeoff situation?

5. Consider an upward-sloping straight line that has a slope of 1. It bisects the positive xy quadrant. Select any point on the line. What must be true about the distances between the origin and the x coordinate and between the origin and the y coordinate?

Chapter 3

The Supply and Demand Model

I t's called "March Madness" for a reason! Every March, four college basketball teams travel to a neutral city, where they compete in the Final Four, the last round of college basketball's national championship. Each college receives a limited allotment of tickets; if you were a student at one of these colleges, and you were lucky enough to have the opportunity to buy one of these tickets, you would most likely pay about $100 to $200 to get a seat at the game. But when you reached the city where the Final Four is being played, you would find people on the street willing to pay staggering amounts of money for those tickets—as much as $5,000. The temptation to sell the tickets and watch the game on TV would be quite high, even for a fairly devoted fan. On the other hand, if you were a devoted fan of your team, but you did not have the opportunity to buy one of the allotted tickets, then you would find yourself having to pay several thousand dollars for a Final Four ticket, either to an online ticket broker or to a seller on an online auction site or on the street.

Why does a Final Four ticket cost so much? Who decides what price to charge for a Final Four ticket? Why does the college sell its allotment of tickets at a much lower price than that charged by a street seller or by an online ticket broker? How does the college decide who gets its limited allotment of tickets? Who ends up going to the Final Four game, and who ends up selling their ticket and watching the game on television? The purpose of this chapter is to show how to find the answers to such questions using the *supply and demand model.*

Recall from Chapter 2 that a model is a simplified description of a more complex reality. The supply and demand model is what economists use to explain how prices are determined in a market. We can use this model to understand the market for Final Four tickets or Super Bowl tickets, as well in a variety of other settings. What causes the price of gasoline to fluctuate? What causes the price of computers to fall over time, even though the prices of most other goods seem to rise over time? Why do roses cost more on Valentine's Day? Once you understand how the model works, you will find yourself using it over and over again to understand the markets that you come across in your everyday life.

The supply and demand model consists of three elements: *demand*, describing the behavior of consumers in the market; *supply*, describing the behavior of firms in the market; and *market equilibrium*, connecting supply and demand and describing how consumers and firms interact in the market. Economists like to compare the supply and demand model to a pair of scissors. Demand is one blade of the scissors, and supply is the other. Either blade alone is incomplete and virtually useless; but when the two blades of a pair of scissors are connected to form the scissors, they become an amazingly useful, yet simple, tool. So it is with the supply and demand model.

Supply and Demand in the Final Four
The model of supply and demand can explain why tickets to the NCAA Final Four cost so much more in the broader market than what the participating schools charge a few lucky buyers. It also explains more routine buyer and seller interactions, describing the behavior of sellers and buyers and how they connect in markets.

DEMAND

demand: a relationship between **price** and **quantity demanded.**

price: the amount of money or other goods that one must pay to obtain a particular good.

quantity demanded: the quantity of a good that people want to buy at a given price during a specific time period.

To an economist, the term *demand*—whether the demand for tickets or the demand for roses—has a very specific meaning. **Demand** is a relationship between two economic variables: (1) *the price of a particular good* and (2) *the quantity of that good that consumers are willing to buy at that price during a specific time period*, all other things being equal. For short, we call the first variable the **price** and the second variable the **quantity demanded.** The phrase *all other things being equal*, or *ceteris paribus*, is appended to the definition of demand because the quantity that consumers are willing to buy depends on many other things besides the price of the good; we want to hold these other things constant, or equal, while we examine the relationship between price and quantity demanded.

Demand can be represented by a numerical table or by a graph. In either case, demand describes how much of a good consumers will purchase at each price. Consider the demand for bicycles in a particular country, as presented in Table 1. Of course, there are many kinds of bicycles—mountain bikes, racing bikes, children's bikes, and inexpensive one-speed bikes with cruiser brakes—so you need to simplify and think about this table as describing demand for an average, or typical, bike.

Observe that as the price rises, the quantity demanded by consumers goes down. If the price goes up from $180 to $200 per bicycle, for example, the quantity demanded goes down from 11 million to 9 million bicycles. On the other hand, if the price goes down, the quantity demanded goes up. If the price falls from $180 to $160, for example, the quantity demanded rises from 11 million to 14 million bicycles.

demand schedule: a tabular presentation of demand showing the price and quantity demanded for a particular good, all else being equal.

law of demand: the tendency for the quantity demanded of a good in a market to decline as its price rises.

The relationship between price and quantity demanded in Table 1 is called a **demand schedule**. The relationship shows price and quantity demanded moving in opposite directions, and this is an example of the law of demand. The **law of demand** says that the higher the price, the lower the quantity demanded in the market; and the lower the price, the higher the quantity demanded in the market. In other words, the law of demand says that the price and the quantity demanded are negatively related, all other things being equal.

TABLE 1			
Demand Schedule for Bicycles (millions of bicycles per year)			
Price	Quantity Demanded	Price	Quantity Demanded
$140	18	$240	5
$160	14	$260	3
$180	11	$280	2
$200	9	$300	1
$200	7		

The Demand Curve

Figure 1 represents demand graphically. It is a graph with the price of the good on the vertical axis and the quantity demanded of the good on the horizontal axis. It shows the demand for bicycles given in Table 1. Each of the nine rows in Table 1 corresponds to one of the nine points in Figure 1. For example, the point at the lower right part of the graph corresponds to the first row of the table, where the price is $140 and the quantity demanded is 18 million bicycles. The resulting curve showing all the combinations of price and quantity demanded is the **demand curve.** It slopes downward from left to right because the quantity demanded is negatively related to the price.

demand curve: a graph of demand showing the downward-sloping relationship between price and quantity demanded.

Why does the demand curve slope downward? The demand curve tells us the quantity demanded by all consumers. Consumers have scarce resources and need to choose between bicycles and other goods. It is important to remember that when economists draw a demand curve, they hold constant the price of other goods: running shoes, in-line skates, motor scooters, and so on. If the price of bicycles falls, then bicycles become more attractive to people in comparison with these other goods—some consumers who previously found the price of bicycles too high may decide to buy a bicycle rather than buy other goods. Conversely, when the price of bicycles increases, then bicycles become less attractive to people in comparison with other goods—some consumers may decide to buy in-line skates or motor scooters instead of bicycles. As a result, quantity demanded declines when the price rises and vice versa.

There's plenty of evidence in the real world that demand curves are downward-sloping. In June of 2004, vehicle sales at General Motors were slowing. In July, General Motors increased the cash-back offer on most of its trucks and cars. You might (correctly) speculate that this reduction in the price of vehicles was intended to increase vehicle sales. Policies designed to reduce smoking by teenagers or to cut down on drinking on college campuses often aim to do this by raising the price of cigarettes and alcohol. The idea, of course, is that teens would buy fewer cigarettes and students would buy less alcohol if these goods were more expensive.

Shifts in Demand

Price is not the only thing that affects the quantity of a good that people buy. Weather conditions, concerns about the environment, or the availability of bike lanes on roads can influence people's decisions to purchase bicycles, for example. If climate change brought on an extended period of warm weather, people would have more opportunities to ride their bicycles. As a result, more bicycles would be purchased at any given price. Or perhaps increased awareness of the health benefits of exercise might lead people to ride their bicycles to work rather than drive their cars. This would also lead to more purchases of bicycles at any given price. Alternatively, if bike

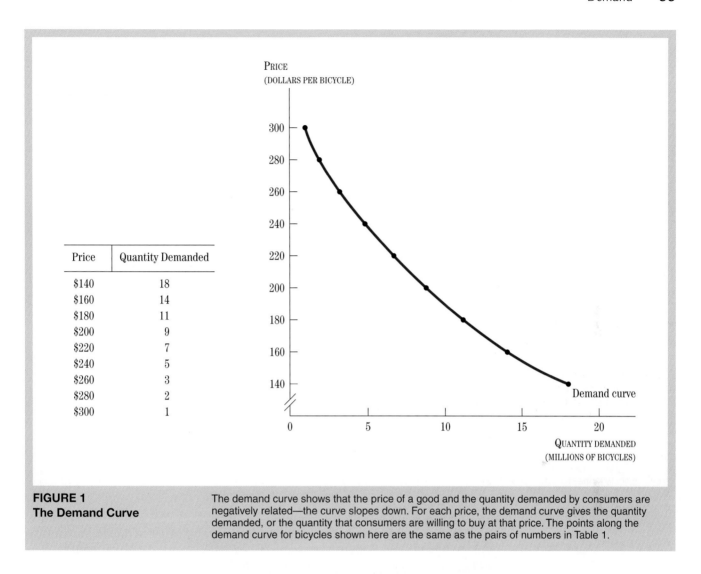

Price	Quantity Demanded
$140	18
$160	14
$180	11
$200	9
$220	7
$240	5
$260	3
$280	2
$300	1

FIGURE 1
The Demand Curve

The demand curve shows that the price of a good and the quantity demanded by consumers are negatively related—the curve slopes down. For each price, the demand curve gives the quantity demanded, or the quantity that consumers are willing to buy at that price. The points along the demand curve for bicycles shown here are the same as the pairs of numbers in Table 1.

lanes are taken away to allow for an extra lane of cars on the road, there will be fewer bicycles purchased at any given price.

The demand curve is drawn assuming that all other things are equal, except the price of the good. A change in any one of these other things, therefore, will shift the demand curve. An increase in demand shifts the demand curve to the right—at every price, quantity demanded will increase. A decrease in demand shifts the demand curve to the left—at every price, quantity demanded will decrease.

An increase in demand is illustrated in Figure 2. The lightly shaded curve labeled "old demand curve" is the same as the demand curve in Figure 1. An extended period of warm weather will increase demand and shift the demand curve to the right. The arrow shows how this curve has shifted to the right to the more darkly shaded curve labeled "new demand curve." When the demand curve shifts to the right, more bicycles are purchased than before at any given price. For example, before the shift in demand, a $200 price led to 9 million bicycles being purchased. But when the demand curve shifts to the right because of warmer weather, that same price leads to 13 million bicycles being purchased. On the other hand, if bicycle lanes were taken away from roads, then the demand curve would shift to the left because people's purchases of bicycles would now be less at any given price.

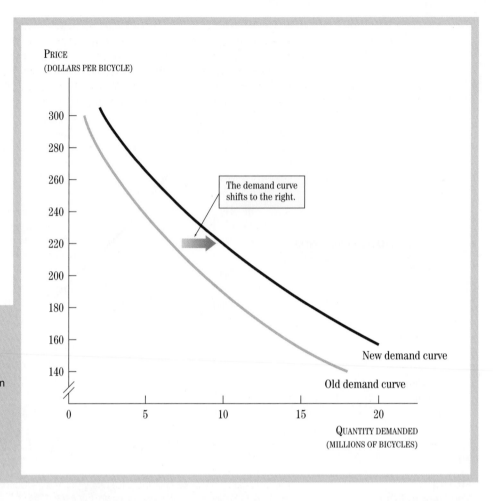

FIGURE 2
A Shift in the Demand Curve
The demand curve shows how the quantity demanded of a good is related to the price of the good, all other things being equal. A change in one of these other things—the weather or people's tastes, for example—will shift the demand curve, as shown in the graph. In this case, the demand for bicycles increases; the demand curve for bicycles shifts to the right.

There are many reasons the demand curve may shift. Most of them can be attributed to one of several sources: *consumers' preferences, consumers' information, consumers' incomes, the number of consumers in the market, consumers' expectations of future prices,* and *the price of related goods.* Let us briefly consider each source of shifts in demand.

■ **Consumers' Preferences.**   In general, a change in people's tastes or preferences for a product compared to other products will change the amount of the product they purchase at any given price. On many college campuses, there has been an increase in demand for clothing that is certified as not having produced in "sweatshops." Also, over the last couple of decades, consumers have shown a great deal of interest in buying "organically grown" fruits and vegetables, which are produced without using artificial pesticides or fertilizers.

■ **Consumers' Information.**   A change in information relating to a product can also cause the demand curve to shift. For example, when people learned about the dangers of smoking, the demand for cigarettes declined. Shortly after an outbreak of *E. coli* in parts of the United States was linked to contaminated spinach, there was a decrease in demand for spinach at grocery stores. After a number of fatal car accidents led to a mass recall of Firestone tires in 2000, the demand for Firestone tires fell fairly dramatically.

normal good: a good for which demand increases when income rises and decreases when income falls.

inferior good: a good for which demand decreases when income rises and increases when income falls.

■ **Consumers' Incomes.** If people's incomes change, then their purchases of goods usually change. An increase in income increases the demand for most goods, while a decline in income reduces the demand for these goods. Goods for which demand increases when income rises and decreases when income falls are called **normal goods** by economists. Many of the goods that people typically purchase—shoes, clothing, jewelry—fall into the category of normal goods.

However, the demand for some goods may decline when income increases. Such goods are called **inferior goods** by economists. The demand for inferior goods declines when people's income increases because they can afford more attractive goods. For example, instant noodles form the basis of many college students' diets. However, after these students leave college and start working and earning a salary, many of them will switch over to eating microwavable meals or to eating out in restaurants. Thus, the demand for instant noodles will fall as income rises. Another example of an inferior good that is familiar to many college students in Boston and New York is the cheap bus service that runs between the "Chinatowns" in the two cities; a bus ticket may cost as little as $10, whereas a plane ticket between the two cities may cost $150. However, as students graduate and start earning money, they often end up buying more of the $150 plane tickets and fewer of the $10 bus tickets. In that case, the plane ticket can be categorized as a normal good, while the bus ticket is categorized as an inferior good.

■ **Number of Consumers in the Market.** Demand is a relationship between price and the quantity demanded by *all* consumers in the market. If the number of consumers increases, then demand will increase. If the number of consumers falls, then demand will decrease. For example, the number of teenagers in the U.S. population expanded sharply in the late 1990s. This increased the demand for *Seventeen* magazine, for Rollerblades, for Clearasil, and for other goods that teenagers tend to buy. As the baby-boom generation in the United States ages, the demand for health care, hair coloring kits and luxury skin care products is increasing.

■ **Consumers' Expectations of Future Prices.** If people expect the price of a good to increase, they will want to buy it before the price increases. Conversely, if people expect the price to decline, they will purchase less and wait for the decline. One sees this effect of expectations of future price changes often. "We'd better buy before the price goes up" is a common reason for purchasing items during a clearance sale. Or, "Let's put off buying that flat-screen TV until the postholiday sales."

In general, it is difficult to forecast the future, but sometimes consumers know quite a bit about whether the price of a good will rise or fall, and they react accordingly. Thus, demand increases if people expect the *future* price of the good to rise. And demand decreases if people expect the *future* price of the good to fall.

In 1995, President Clinton threatened a 100 percent tariff (tax) on some luxury cars produced in Japan. This resulted in an immediate increase in demand for these cars, since buyers were afraid they would become too expensive after the tariff was imposed.

substitute: a good that has many of the same characteristics as, and can be used in place of, another good.

■ **Prices of Closely Related Goods.** A change in the price of a closely related good can increase or decrease demand for another good, depending on whether the good is a substitute or a complement. A **substitute** is a good that provides some of the same uses or enjoyment as another good. Butter and margarine are substitutes. In general, the demand for a good will increase if the price of a substitute for the good rises, and the demand for a good will decrease if the price of a substitute falls. Sales of CDs and downloaded music are substitutes. You would therefore expect a decrease in the price of downloaded music to decrease the demand for CDs. This may help

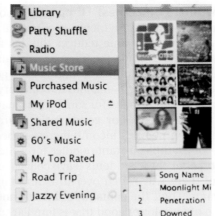

Substitutes and Complements
Music CDs and downloaded music are examples of substitutes; they share similar characteristics. You would expect, therefore, that a rise in the price of CDs would result in an increase in the sale of downloaded music—and vice versa. SUVs and gasoline are examples of complements; they tend to be consumed together. With an increase in gasoline prices in 2004 and 2005, consumers were less eager to purchase SUVs, and their sales declined.

complement: a good that is usually consumed or used together with another good.

explain why the recording industry filed lawsuits against users of online file-sharing software in 2003.

A **complement** is a good that tends to be consumed together with another good. Gasoline and SUVs are complements. The rapid increase in gasoline prices in 2004 and 2005 led to a decrease in demand for SUVs.

Movements Along versus Shifts of the Demand Curve

We have shown that the demand curve can shift, and we have given many possible reasons for such shifts. As you begin to use demand curves, it is very important that you be able to distinguish *shifts* of the demand curve from *movements along* the demand curve. This distinction is illustrated in Figure 3.

A *movement along* the demand curve occurs when the quantity demanded changes as a result of a *change in the price of the good*. For example, if the price of bicycles rises, causing the quantity demanded by consumers to fall, then there is a movement along the demand curve. You can see in Figure 3 that at point *A*, the price is $200 and the quantity demanded is 9 million. Now suppose the price rises to $220. Then the quantity demanded falls from 9 million to 7 million. This can be shown as a movement along the demand curve for bicycles from point *A* to point *B*. Conversely, if the price of a bicycle falls to $180, then the quantity demanded will increase to 11 million bicycles. This can be shown as an increase from point *A* to point *C* in Figure 3. Economists refer to a movement along the demand curve as a *change in the quantity demanded*.

A *shift* of the demand curve, on the other hand, occurs if there is a change that is due to *any source except the price*. Remember, the term *demand* refers to the entire curve or schedule relating price and quantity demanded, while the term *quantity demanded* refers to a single point on the demand curve. As we discussed earlier, if there was an increase in warm weather, people would be more likely to buy bicycles at any given price. This means that the entire demand curve would shift to the right. On the other hand, the elimination of bicycle lanes would make people less likely to buy bicycles at any given price. The entire demand curve would shift to the left. When the demand curve shifts, economists say that there is a *change in demand*.

You should be able to tell whether an economic event causes (1) a change in demand or (2) a change in the quantity demanded; or, equivalently, (1) a shift in the demand curve or (2) a movement along the demand curve. Here's an example to test your understanding of demand shifts and movement along the demand curve. In 2001, Disney's theme park attendance was lower than in previous years as a result of

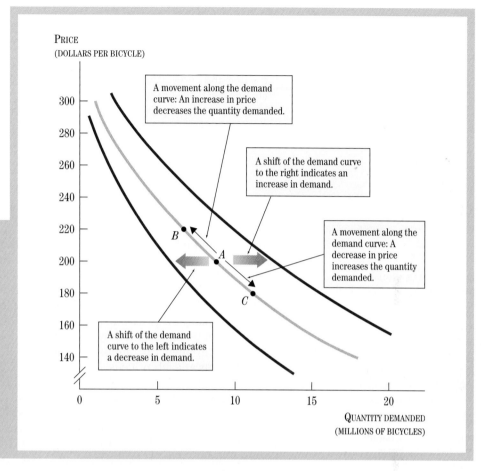

FIGURE 3
Shifts of versus Movements Along the Demand Curve

A *shift* of the demand curve occurs when there is a change in something (other than the good's own price) that affects the quantity of a good that consumers are willing to buy. An increase in demand is a shift to the right of the demand curve. A decrease in demand is a shift to the left of the demand curve. A *movement along* the demand curve occurs when the price of the good changes, causing the quantity demanded to change, as, for example, from point *A* to point *B* or *C*.

the weak economy. Because of the fall in attendance, Disney lowered the adult admission price at its California Adventure park, which helped increase attendance. Which of these was a *change in demand* and which was a *change in the quantity demanded* in the market for theme parks?

The decrease in attendance caused by the weak economy in 2001 was a decrease in demand—fewer people were going to theme parks in 2001 than in prior years for any given ticket price. The demand curve for theme park visits thus shifted to the left. When Disney lowered its admission price, it hoped to entice more people to spend their money on a trip to its California Adventure park instead of on other goods. This is an increase in the quantity demanded—the park management anticipated more attendance at a lower price. This was a movement along the demand curve for theme park visits.

R E V I E W

- Demand is a negative relationship between the price of a good and the quantity demanded, all other things being equal.

- The demand curve slopes down because when the price of a good rises, consumers are less likely to use their scarce resources to buy that good. Conversely, when the price of a good falls, some consumers who previously had not chosen to buy the good because the price was too high may decide to buy the good.

■ It is important to distinguish shifts of the demand curve from movements along the demand curve. When the quantity demanded changes as a result of a price change, we have a movement along the demand curve. When there is a change in demand brought about by something other than a price change, there is a shift in the demand curve.

SUPPLY

supply: a relationship between **price** and **quantity supplied.**

quantity supplied: the quantity of a good that firms are willing to sell at a given price.

Whereas demand refers to the behavior of consumers, supply refers to the behavior of firms. The term *supply*—whether it is the supply of tickets or the supply of computers—has a very specific meaning for economists. **Supply** is a relationship between two variables: (1) *the price of a particular good* and (2) *the quantity of the good that firms are willing to sell at that price,* all other things being the same. For short, we call the first variable the **price** and the second variable the **quantity supplied.**

Supply can be represented by a numerical table or by a graph. An example of the quantity supplied (in millions of bicycles) in the entire market by bicycle-producing firms at each price is shown in Table 2. For example, at a price of $180, the quantity supplied is 7 million bicycles. Observe that as the price increases, the quantity supplied increases, and that as the price decreases, the quantity supplied decreases. For example, if the price rises from $180 to $200, the quantity supplied increases from 7 to 9 million bicycles. The relationship between price and quantity supplied in Table 2 is called a **supply schedule.** The relationship shows price and quantity supplied moving in the same direction, and this is an example of the law of supply. The **law of supply** says that the higher the price, the higher the quantity supplied; and the lower the price, the lower the quantity supplied. In other words, the law of supply says that the price and the quantity supplied are positively related, all other things being equal.

TABLE 2
Supply Schedule for Bicycles (millions of bicycles per year)

Price	Quantity Supplied
$140	1
$160	4
$180	7
$200	9
$220	11
$240	13
$260	15
$280	16
$300	17

supply schedule: a tabular presentation of supply showing the price and quantity supplied of a particular good, all else being equal.

law of supply: the tendency for the quantity supplied of a good in a market to increase as its price rises.

supply curve: a graph of supply showing the upward-sloping relationship between price and quantity supplied.

The Supply Curve

We can represent the supply schedule in Table 2 graphically by plotting the price and quantity supplied on a graph, as shown in Figure 4. The scales of each axis in Figure 4 are exactly the same as those in Figure 1, except that Figure 4 shows the quantity supplied, whereas Figure 1 shows the quantity demanded. Each pair of numbers in Table 2 is plotted as a point in Figure 4. The resulting curve showing all the combinations of prices and quantities supplied is the **supply curve.** Note that the curve slopes upward: At a price of $280, the quantity supplied is high—16 million bicycles. If the price were $160 a bicycle, then firms would be willing to sell only 4 million bicycles.

Why does the supply curve slope upward? Imagine yourself running a firm that produces and sells bicycles. If the price of the bicycles goes up from $180 to $280, then you can earn $100 more for each bicycle you produce and sell. Given your production costs, if you earn more from each bicycle, you will have a greater incentive to produce and sell more bicycles. If producing more bicycles increases the costs of producing each bicycle, perhaps because you must pay the bike assembly workers a higher wage for working overtime, the higher price will give you the incentive to incur these costs. Other bicycle firms will be thinking the same way. Thus, firms are

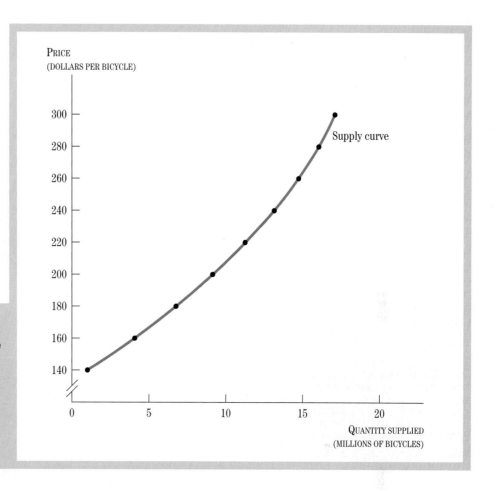

PRICE
(DOLLARS PER BICYCLE)

Supply curve

QUANTITY SUPPLIED
(MILLIONS OF BICYCLES)

FIGURE 4
The Supply Curve
The supply curve shows that the price and the quantity supplied by firms in the market are positively related. The curve slopes up. For each price on the vertical axis, the supply curve shows the quantity that firms are willing to sell along the horizontal axis. The points along the supply curve for bicycles match the pairs of numbers in Table 2.

willing to sell more bicycles as the price rises. Conversely, the incentive for firms to sell bicycles will decline as the price falls. Basically, that is why there is a positive relationship between price and quantity supplied.

When formulating economic policy, it is important to remember this supply relationship. When the price of a good increases, it leads to an increase in the quantity supplied. If U.S. agricultural policy results in the U.S. government offering to pay farmers a higher price for their corn, then the farmers will respond by increasing their production of corn. If there is a collapse in coffee prices on the world market, some coffee farmers in developing countries will switch to producing other crops instead of coffee.

Shifts in Supply

The supply curve is a relationship between price and the quantity supplied drawn on the assumption that all other things are held constant. If any one of these other things changes, then the supply curve shifts. For example, suppose a new machine is invented that makes it possible to produce bicycle frames at less cost; then firms would have more incentive at any given price to produce and sell more bicycles. Supply would increase; the supply curve would shift to the right.

Figure 5 shows that the supply curve for bicycles would shift to the right because of a new cost-reducing machine. The supply curve would shift to the left if there were

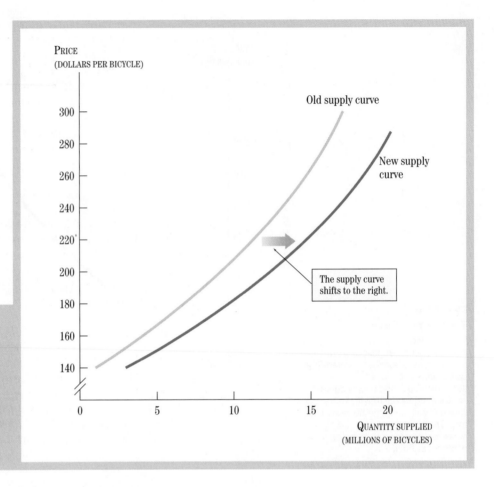

FIGURE 5
A Shift in the Supply Curve
The supply curve is a relationship between the quantity supplied of a good and the price of the good, all other things being equal. A change in one of these other things (other than the good's price) will shift the supply curve, as shown in the graph. In this case, the supply of bicycles increases; the supply curve for bicycles shifts to the right.

a decrease in supply. Supply would decrease, for example, if bicycle-producing firms suddenly found that their existing machines would break down unless they were oiled with an expensive lubricant each time a bicycle was produced. This would raise costs, lower supply, and shift the supply curve to the left.

Many things can cause the supply curve to shift. Most of these can be categorized by the source of the change in supply: *technology, weather conditions, the price of inputs used in production, the number of firms in the market, expectations of future prices*, and *government taxes, subsidies, and regulations*. Let us briefly consider the sources of shifts in supply.

■ **Technology.** Anything that changes the amount a firm can produce with a given amount of inputs to production can be considered a change in technology. The Harbour Report, a study that examines the number of labor hours needed to produce an automobile, calculated that in 2005, General Motors needed 34 hours per vehicle, while Toyota needed only 28 hours per vehicle. Suppose an improvement in technology enabled General Motors to reduce the time it took to produce a car by 6 hours per vehicle. This improvement in technology would correspond to an increase in supply, a shift in the supply curve to the right. Another way of viewing an increase in supply is that producers are willing to sell any given quantity at a lower price than before. This makes sense, since production costs are lower with the improvement in technology.

■ **Weather Conditions.**   Droughts, earthquakes, and hurricanes also affect how much of certain types of goods can be produced with given inputs. A drought can reduce the amount of wheat that can be produced on a farm in the Midwest. An unusually cold winter in 2006 destroyed over a billion dollars worth of citrus fruit in California. Hurricanes Katrina and Rita disrupted oil drilling and refining activities in Texas and Louisiana. Because such events change the amount that can be produced with a given amount of inputs, they are similar to changes in technology. In the examples just given, the supply curve shifted to the left, although you could have favorable weather conditions that would shift the supply curve for a particular good to the right.

■ **The Price of Inputs Used in Production.**   If the prices of the inputs to production—raw materials, labor, and capital—increase, then it becomes more costly to produce goods, and firms will produce less at any given price; the supply curve will shift to the left. When the U.S government imposed trade restrictions that caused the price of imported steel to rise in 2002, firms that used imported steel to produce household appliances were unwilling to produce the same quantity of appliances at existing price levels. So an increase in production costs causes the supply curve to shift to the left, and a decrease in production costs causes the supply curve to shift to the right.

■ **The Number of Firms in the Market.**   Remember that the supply curve refers to *all* the firms producing the product. If the number of firms increases, then more goods will be produced at each price; supply increases, and the supply curve shifts to the right. A decline in the number of firms, on the other hand, would shift the supply curve to the left. For example, if a country removes barriers that prevent foreign car manufacturers from selling cars to the domestic market, then the number of firms producing cars for that country's domestic market will increase, and the supply curve for cars in that economy will shift to the right.

■ **Expectations of Future Prices.**   If firms expect the price of the good they produce to rise in the future, then they will hold off selling at least part of their production until the price rises. For example, farmers in the United States who anticipate an increase in wheat prices because of political turbulence in Russia may decide to store more wheat in silos and sell it later, after the price rises. Thus, expectations of *future* price increases tend to reduce supply. Conversely, expectations of *future* price decreases tend to increase supply.

■ **Government Taxes, Subsidies, and Regulations.**   The government has the ability to affect the supply of particular goods produced by firms. For example, the government imposes taxes on firms to pay for such government services as education, police, and national defense. These taxes increase firms' costs and reduce supply. The supply curve shifts to the left when a tax on what firms sell in the market increases.

The government also makes payments—subsidies—to firms to encourage those firms to produce certain goods. Such subsidies have the opposite effect of taxes on supply. An increase in subsidies reduces firms' costs and increases the supply. If the U.S. government provided subsidies for corn production to encourage the use of ethanol, an alternative fuel for cars that is produced from corn, this would increase the production of corn. On the other hand, when the U.S. government imposes a tax on cigarettes, there will be a decrease in the supply of cigarettes.

Governments also regulate firms. In some cases, such regulations can change the firms' costs of production or their ability to produce goods and thereby affect supply. For example, if a city government decides that only vendors who successfully

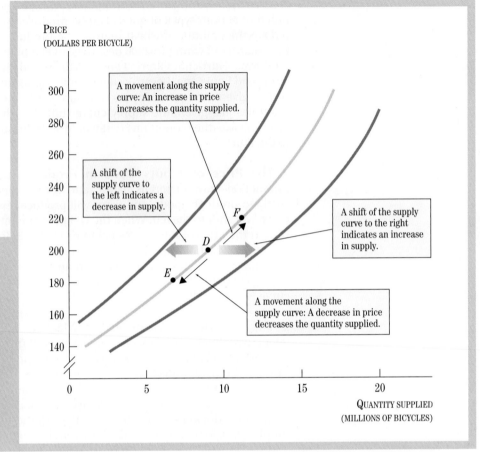

FIGURE 6
Shifts of versus Movements Along the Supply Curve

A *shift* of the supply curve occurs when there is a change in something (other than the price) that affects the amount of a good that firms are willing to supply. An increase in supply is a shift to the right of the supply curve. A decrease in supply is a shift to the left of the supply curve. A movement along the supply curve occurs when the price of the good changes, causing the quantity supplied by firms to change—for example, from point *D* to point *E* or *F*.

pass a health and sanitation inspection are allowed to sell food from street carts, the supply curve for street-vendor food will shift to the left.

Movements Along versus Shifts of the Supply Curve

As with the demand curve, it is very important that you understand how to distinguish between *shifts* of the supply curve and *movements along* the supply curve. This distinction is illustrated in Figure 6.

A *movement along* the supply curve occurs when the quantity supplied changes as a result of a *change in the price of the good*. For example, if a copper mine in Zambia increases its production because the price of copper has increased on the world market, that is a movement along the supply curve. In our bicycle example, an increase in the price of bicycles from $200 to $220 would increase the quantity supplied from 9 million bicycles to 11 million bicycles. This can be shown as a movement along the supply curve for bicycles from point *D* to point *F*. Conversely, if the price of a bicycle were to fall from $200 to $180, then the quantity supplied would decrease to 7 million bicycles. This can be shown as movement from point *D* to point *E* in Figure 6. Economists refer to a movement along the supply curve as a *change in the quantity supplied*.

A *shift* of the supply curve, on the other hand, occurs if there is a change due to *any source except the price*. An unexpected winter freeze in California will mean that farmers will be able to produce fewer oranges at any given price. This means that the supply curve of oranges will shift to the left. When the supply curve shifts, economists say that there is a *change in supply*.

You should be able to tell whether a change in something causes (1) a change in supply or (2) a change in the quantity supplied; or, equivalently, (1) a shift in the supply curve or (2) a movement along the supply curve. Here's an example to test your ability to distinguish between movement along a supply curve and a shift in the supply curve. Suppose that U.S. agricultural policy guarantees farmers a specific price on certain crops. An economist suggested that the government should instead pay farmers to not plant some of their fields. Which policy is describing a *change in supply* and which is describing a *change in the quantity supplied* in the market for corn?

A policy that pays farmers to leave cornfields unplanted describes a decrease in supply. The amount of corn supplied will be lower at any price. When the U.S. government guarantees the price of corn, this describes an increase in the quantity supplied—more corn will be grown in anticipation of the higher price. The increase in price leading to an increase in quantity supplied corresponds to movement along the supply curve.

R E V I E W

- Supply is a positive relationship between the price of a good and the quantity supplied of the good by firms.

- The supply curve slopes upward because, all else equal, a higher price offers greater incentive for a firm to produce and sell more goods.

- It is important to distinguish shifts of the supply curve from movements along the supply curve. When the quantity supplied changes because of a change in price, we have a movement along the supply curve. Other factors—such as technology, weather, the number of firms, and expectations—can lead to a shift in the supply curve.

MARKET EQUILIBRIUM: COMBINING SUPPLY AND DEMAND

Figure 7 summarizes what you have learned thus far about consumers' demand for goods in a market and firms' supply of goods in a market. Now we put supply and demand together to complete the supply and demand model. Consumers who want to buy goods and firms that want to sell goods interact in a market. When consumers and firms interact, a price is determined at which the transaction occurs. Recall that a market does not need to be located at one place; the U.S. bicycle market consists of all the bicycle firms that sell bicycles and all the consumers who buy bicycles.

Fascinatingly, no single person or firm determines the price in the market. Instead, the market determines the price. As buyers and sellers interact, prices may go up for a while and then go down. Alfred Marshall, the economist who did the most to develop the supply and demand model in the late nineteenth century, called this process the "higgling and bargaining" of the market. The assumption underlying the supply and demand model is that, in the give and take of the marketplace, prices adjust until they settle down at a level where the quantity supplied by firms equals the quantity demanded by consumers. Let's see how.

SUPPLY

Supply describes firms.

The supply curve looks like this:

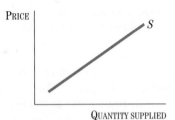

DEMAND

Demand describes consumers.

The demand curve looks like this:

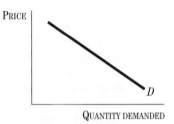

Law of Supply

Price and quantity supplied are positively related.

Law of Demand

Price and quantity demanded are negatively related.

Movements along supply curve occur

when price rises and quantity supplied rises or when price falls and quantity supplied falls.

Movements along demand curve occur

when price rises and quantity demanded falls or when price falls and quantity demanded rises.

Shifts in supply are due to:

Technology (new inventions)

Weather (especially for agricultural products)

Number of firms in market

Price of goods used in production (inputs such as fertilizer, labor)

Expectations of future prices (firms will sell less now if prices are expected to rise; for example, farmers may store goods to sell next year)

Government taxes, subsidies, regulations (commodity taxes, agricultural subsidies, safety regulations)

Shifts in demand are due to:

Preferences (changes in consumers' tastes)

Number of consumers in market

Consumers' information (about smoking, or faulty products, for example)

Consumers' income (normal goods versus inferior goods)

Expectations of future prices (consumers will buy more now if prices are expected to rise in the future)

Price of related goods (both substitutes, like butter and margarine, and complements, like gasoline and SUVs)

FIGURE 7
Overview of Supply and Demand

Determination of the Market Price

To determine the market price, we combine the demand relationship with the supply relationship. We can do this using either a table or a diagram. First consider Table 3, which combines the demand schedule from Table 1 with the supply schedule from Table 2. The price is in the first column, the quantity demanded by consumers is in the second column, and the quantity supplied by firms is in the third column. Observe that the quantity that consumers are willing to buy is shown to decline with the price, while the quantity that firms are willing to sell is shown to increase with the price.

TABLE 3
Finding the Market Equilibrium

Price	Quantity Demanded	Quantity Supplied	Shortage, Surplus, or Equilibrium	Price Rises or Falls
$140	18	1	Shortage = 17	Price rises
$160	14	4	Shortage = 10	Price rises
$180	11	7	Shortage = 4	Price rises
$200	9	9	Equilibrium	No change
$220	7	11	Surplus = 4	Price falls
$240	5	13	Surplus = 8	Price falls
$260	3	15	Surplus = 12	Price falls
$280	2	16	Surplus = 14	Price falls
$300	1	17	Surplus = 16	Price falls

Quantity supplied equals quantity demanded. →

■ Finding the Market Price.   Pick a price in Table 3, any price. Suppose the price you choose is $160. Then the quantity demanded by consumers (14 million bicycles) is greater than the quantity supplied by firms (4 million bicycles). In other words, there is a shortage of 14 − 4 = 10 million bicycles. A **shortage,** or **excess demand,** is a situation in which the quantity demanded is greater than the quantity supplied. With a shortage of bicycles, buyers who really need a bicycle will start to offer to pay more to acquire a bicycle, while firms that are faced with an abundance of potential customers wanting to buy their bicycles will begin to charge higher prices. Thus, $160 cannot last as the market price. Observe that as the price rises above $160, the quantity demanded falls and the quantity supplied rises. Thus, as the price rises, the shortage begins to decrease. Suppose the price increases to $180. At that price, the quantity demanded falls to 11 million bicycles and the quantity supplied rises to 7 million bicycles. There is still a shortage and the price will still rise, but the shortage is now much less, at 11 − 7 = 4 million bicycles. The shortage will disappear only when the price rises to $200, as shown in Table 3.

Suppose instead that you had picked a price above $200, let's say $260. Then the quantity demanded by consumers (3 million bicycles) is less than the quantity supplied by firms (15 million bicycles). In other words, there is a surplus of 12 million bicycles. A **surplus,** or **excess supply,** is a situation in which the quantity supplied is greater than the quantity demanded. With a surplus of bicycles, buyers who really need a bicycle have an abundance of sellers who are eager to sell them a bicycle, while firms have to compete with one another to entice buyers for their products. Therefore, the price of bicycles will fall: Firms that are willing to sell bicycles for less than $260 will offer to sell to consumers at lower prices. Thus, $260 cannot be the market price either. Observe that as the price falls below $260, the quantity demanded rises and the quantity supplied falls. Thus, the surplus decreases. If you choose any price above $200, the same thing will happen: There will be a surplus, and the price will fall. The surplus disappears only when the price falls to $200.

Thus, we have shown that for any price below $200, there is a shortage, and the price rises; while for any price above $200, there is a surplus, and the price falls. What if the market price is $200? Then the quantity supplied equals the quantity demanded; there is neither a shortage nor a surplus, and there is no reason for the price to rise or fall. This price of $200 is called the **equilibrium price** because at this price the quantity supplied equals the quantity demanded, and there is no tendency for the

shortage (excess demand): a situation in which quantity demanded is greater than quantity supplied.

surplus (excess supply): a situation in which quantity supplied is greater than quantity demanded.

equilibrium price: the price at which quantity supplied equals quantity demanded.

Why Roses Cost More on Valentine's Day

This article, which appeared in the *New York Times* in 1999, describes why the price of roses rises as Valentine's Day approaches. You will find that applications of the supply and demand model are scattered throughout the article.

If the arrival of Valentine's Day causes demand to increase, then the price will rise.

Other examples where the demand for a particular good rises at a specific time of the year

The Big City; By Any Name, A Rose Is Dear As a Valentine

By JOHN TIERNEY

NEW YORKERS are in luck this week. Unlike other Americans, who are forced to shop for Valentine's Day without any official guidance, we have the annual rose survey from the Department of Consumer Affairs.

Jules Polonetsky, the agency's Commissioner, called a news conference to reveal that local florists raise the price of roses by about 33 percent for Valentine's Day. This correlation between price and demand might seem inevitable to some people—anyone, say, who has opened an economics textbook—but Mr. Polonetsky will not stand for it.

Besides lamenting the price increases, he has developed a strategy to help New Yorkers avoid, as he put it, "seeing red this Valentine's Day." Pointing to a critical discovery made by his agency's investigators—that different florists in New York charge different prices—he outlined a technique for buying flowers. "Consumers," he explained, "can save significantly by choosing one florist over another."

Could this particular strategy—the technical term is "shopping"—have applications even beyond Valentine's Day roses? Possibly, although the Commissioner did not elaborate. Nor did he address another question raised by his agency's research: do the investigators at the Department of Consumer Affairs have a little too much time on their hands?

New Yorkers depend on the consumer agency to enforce laws against fraud, but they generally manage to deal with honest merchants all by themselves. They could probably survive without any of the agency's seasonal price surveys—roses on Valentine's Day, gasoline on Memorial Day, turkey at Thanksgiving, gefilte fish at Passover.

These rituals have given Mr. Polonetsky and his predecessors publicity as they wail against seasonal price increases, but consumers do not necessarily benefit. If florists didn't raise prices at Valentine's Day, consumers would suffer in two ways.

equilibrium quantity: the quantity traded at the equilibrium price.

market equilibrium: the situation in which the price is equal to the equilibrium price and the quantity traded equals the equilibrium quantity.

price to change. There is no other price for which quantity supplied equals quantity demanded. If you look at all the other prices, you will see that there is either a shortage or a surplus, and thus there is a tendency for the price to either rise or fall.

The quantity bought and sold at the equilibrium price is 9 million bicycles. This is the **equilibrium quantity.** When the price equals the equilibrium price and the quantity bought and sold equals the equilibrium quantity, we say that there is a **market equilibrium.**

First, many cost-conscious New Yorkers who now order other flowers for Valentine's Day—because their partners aren't fanatical about getting roses—would start ordering them, so there wouldn't be enough roses to meet the increased demand. As a result, some rose fanatics would have to do without. ◄

As price rises, the quantity demanded falls. Only those who really value giving roses, instead of other flowers or chocolate, to their Valentine will end up buying roses at the higher price.

Second, the customers who buy roses at other times of the year would end up paying artificially high prices to subsidize the customers on Valentine's Day. There's a good reason that prices are higher this week: the roses cost extra to grow and ship.

To meet this annual peak in demand, growers in the United States, Colombia, Ecuador and Holland must prune their bushes in the late fall to start new growth in time for Valentine's Day. "By pruning, you're cutting off a lot of roses that would have bloomed before Valentine's Day," Jim Lebberes, the president of Kiamos and Tooker, a flower wholesaler in the Bronx, explained. "So you're sacrificing a lot of production, and you need to recover that lost income somehow." ◄

A higher price increases the quantity supplied as growers reorganize their production schedule to get roses to market in early February.

Then there's the cost of shipping. "Let's say there are five regularly scheduled cargo planes that leave Bogota for Miami and New York every night," Mr. Lebberes said. "They fly north with flowers and return south with other cargo. Now suddenly for Valentine's Day you need to charter another 15 planes, and those planes fly back empty, because there's no corresponding increase in demand for southbound cargo. So each one of those roses is costing you a round-trip ticket." ◄

February is not a good time of the year to grow roses in North America—the roses have to be shipped in from South America. The high transportation cost means that supply can't rise to meet all of the increased demand.

When you add these wholesale costs to the extra expenses at the retail level, like overtime pay for employees, the 33-percent increase doesn't sound unreasonable. In fact, it may reflect a phenomenon that economists call the "good-will factor." This phenomenon was demonstrated after Hurricane Andrew hit Miami in 1992 and created a shortage of plywood. Lumber companies refused to raise their prices, forgoing an easy profit because they were afraid they'd offend their long-term customers.

New York's florists presumably show some of the same restraint on Valentine's Day to maintain their customers' good will. With more careful investigation next year, Mr. Polontesky could probably call a press conference the week of Valentine Day's and announce that rose prices are too low. That may not sound immediately appealing to him. But it would definitely be newsworthy.

Our discussion of the determination of the equilibrium price shows how the market price coordinates the buying and selling decisions of many firms and consumers. We see that the price serves a *rationing function*. When there is a shortage, a higher price reduces the quantity demanded and increases the quantity supplied to eliminate the shortage. Similarly, when there is a surplus, a lower price increases the quantity demanded and decreases the quantity supplied to eliminate the surplus. Thus, both shortages and surpluses are eliminated by the forces of supply and demand.

■ **Two Predictions.** By combining supply and demand, we have completed the supply and demand model. The model can be applied to many markets, not just the example of the bicycle market. One prediction of the supply and demand model is that *the equilibrium price in the market will be the price for which the quantity supplied equals the quantity demanded.* Thus, the model provides an answer to the question of what determines the price in the market. Another prediction of the model is that *the equilibrium quantity bought and sold in the market is the quantity for which the quantity supplied equals the quantity demanded.*

Finding the Equilibrium with a Supply and Demand Diagram

The equilibrium price and quantity in a market can also be found with the help of a graph. Figure 8 combines the demand curve from Figure 1 and the supply curve from Figure 4 in the same diagram. Observe that the downward-sloping demand curve intersects the upward-sloping supply curve at a single point. At that point of intersection, the quantity supplied equals the quantity demanded. Hence, the *equilibrium price is at the intersection of the supply curve and the demand curve.* The equilibrium price of $200 is shown in Figure 8. At that price, the quantity demanded is 9 million bicycles, and the quantity supplied is 9 million bicycles. This is the equilibrium quantity.

FIGURE 8
**Equilibrium Price and
Equilibrium Quantity**

When buyers and sellers interact in the market, the equilibrium price is at the point of intersection of the supply curve and the demand curve. At this point, the quantity supplied equals the quantity demanded. The equilibrium quantity is also determined at that point. At a higher price, the quantity demanded will be less than the quantity supplied; there will be a surplus. At a lower price, the quantity demanded will be greater than the quantity supplied; there will be a shortage.

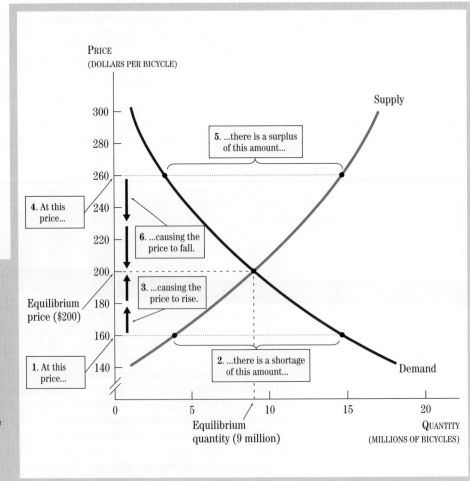

If the price were lower than this equilibrium price, say, $160, then the quantity demanded would be greater than the quantity supplied. There would be a shortage, and there would be pressure on the price to increase, as shown in the graph. The increase in gasoline prices in 2004 and 2005 led to an increase in demand for hybrid automobiles. With a shortage of hybrid vehicles and long waiting lists, some automobile sellers increased the price of the hybrids.

On the other hand, if the price were above the equilibrium price, say, $260, then the quantity supplied would be greater than the quantity demanded. There would be a surplus, and there would be pressure on the price to fall. After September 11, 2001, a large number of vacationers cancelled vacation plans that involved air travel. Caribbean hotels, with a surplus of vacant hotel rooms following this decrease in demand, began to offer big discounts.

Thus, the market price will tend to move toward the equilibrium price at the intersection of the supply curve and the demand curve. We can calculate exactly what the equilibrium price is in Figure 8 by drawing a line over to the vertical axis. And we can calculate the equilibrium quantity by drawing a line down to the horizontal axis.

Market Outcomes When Supply or Demand Changes

Now that you know how to find the equilibrium price and quantity in a market, we can use the supply and demand model to analyze the impact of factors that change supply or demand on equilibrium price and quantity. We first consider a change in demand and then a change in supply.

■ **Effects of a Change in Demand.** Figure 9 shows the effects of a shift in the demand curve for bicycles. Suppose that a shift occurs because of a fitness craze that increases the demand for bicycles. The demand curve shifts to the right, as shown in graph (a) in Figure 9. The demand curve before the shift and the demand curve after the shift are labeled the "old demand curve" and the "new demand curve," respectively.

If you look at the graph, you can see that something must happen to the equilibrium price when the demand curve shifts. The equilibrium price is determined at the intersection of the supply curve and the demand curve. With the new demand curve, there is a new intersection and, therefore, a new equilibrium price. The equilibrium price is no longer $200 in Figure 9(a); it is up to $220 per bicycle. Thus, the supply and demand model predicts that the price in the market will rise if there is an increase in demand. Note also that there is a change in the equilibrium quantity of bicycles. The quantity of bicycles sold and bought has increased from 9 million to 11 million. Thus, the equilibrium quantity has increased along with the equilibrium price. The supply and demand model predicts that an increase in demand will raise both the price and the quantity sold in the market.

We can use the same method to find out what happens if demand decreases, as shown in graph (b) in Figure 9. Suppose that the elimination of dedicated bicycle lanes on roads shifts the demand curve for bicycles to the left. At the new intersection of the supply and demand curves, the equilibrium price is lower, and the quantity sold is also lower. Thus, the supply and demand model predicts that a decrease in demand will both lower the price and lower the quantity sold in the market.

Note in these examples that when the demand curve shifts, it leads to a movement along the supply curve. First, the demand curve shifts to the right or to the left. Then there is movement along the supply curve because the change in the price affects the quantity of bicycles that firms will sell.

■ **Effects of a Change in Supply.** Figure 10 shows what happens when there is a change in the market that shifts the supply curve. Suppose a new technology reduces

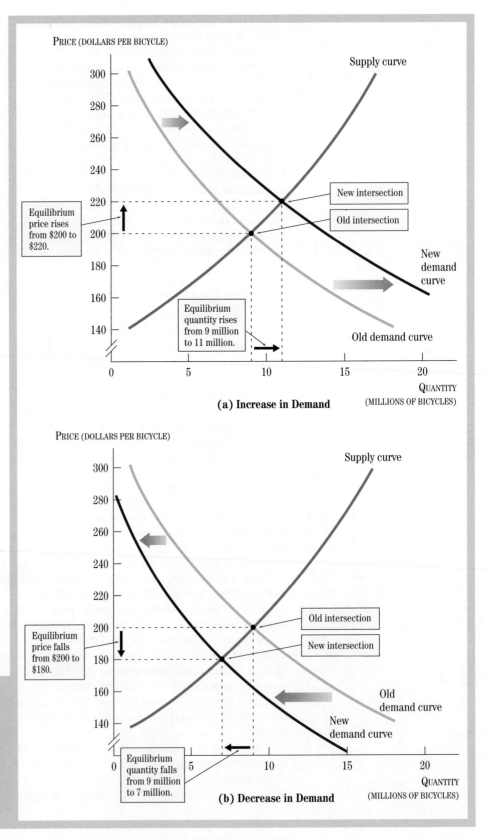

(a) Increase in Demand

(b) Decrease in Demand

FIGURE 9
Effects of a Shift in Demand

When demand increases, as in graph (a), the demand curve shifts to the right. The equilibrium price rises, and the equilibrium quantity also rises. When demand decreases, as in graph (b), the demand curve shifts to the left. The equilibrium price falls, and the equilibrium quantity also falls.

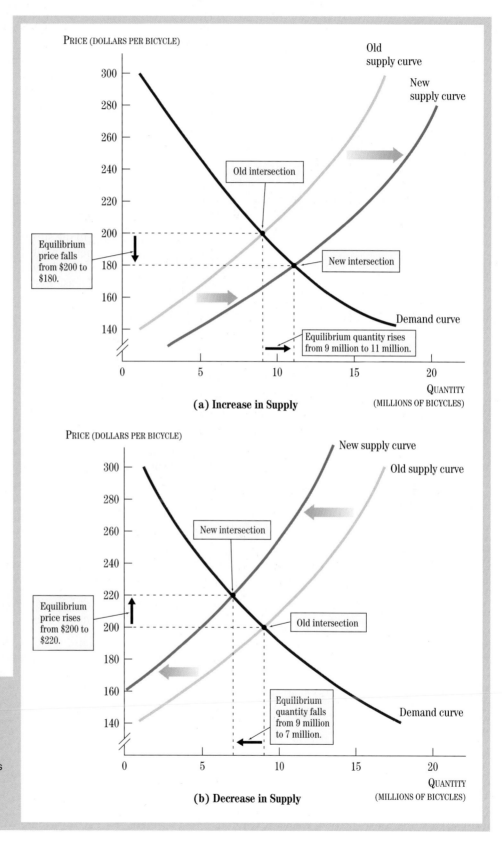

FIGURE 10
Effects of a Shift in Supply
When supply increases, as in graph (a), the supply curve shifts to the right; the equilibrium price falls, and the equilibrium quantity rises. When supply decreases, as in graph (b), the supply curve shifts to the left; the equilibrium price rises, and the equilibrium quantity falls.

TABLE 4
Effects of Shifts in Demand and Supply Curves

Shift	Effect on Equilibrium Price	Effect on Equilibrium Quantity
Increase in demand	Up	Up
Decrease in demand	Down	Down
Increase in supply	Down	Up
Decrease in supply	Up	Down

the cost of producing bicycles, resulting in the supply curve for bicycles shifting to the right. Figure 10(a) shows that there is a new equilibrium price, which is lower than the old equilibrium price. In addition, the equilibrium quantity rises. Thus, the supply and demand model predicts that an increase in the supply of bicycles will lower the price and raise the quantity of bicycles sold.

Suppose instead that an increase in the cost of bicycle tires increases the cost of producing bicycles, resulting in the supply curve for bicycles shifting to the left. Figure 10(b) shows that the equilibrium price rises, and the equilibrium quantity falls. Thus, the model predicts that a decrease in the supply of bicycles will raise the price of bicycles and lower the quantity of bicycles sold.

Table 4 summarizes the results of this analysis of shifts in the supply and demand curves.

■ **When Both Curves Shift.**   The supply and demand model is easiest to use when you are analyzing a factor that shifts either demand or supply, but not both. However, in reality, it is possible for something or several different things to simultaneously shift both supply and demand. To predict whether the price or the quantity rises or falls in such cases, we need to know whether demand or supply shifts by a larger amount. Dealing with the possibility of simultaneous shifts in demand and supply curves is important in practice, as we show in the following example.

R E V I E W

- The supply and demand model is used to predict the price and the quantity that result from interactions of consumers and producers in a market.

- In a market, the price will adjust upward or downward until the quantity supplied equals the quantity demanded. This price is called the equilibrium price, and the corresponding quantity is called the equilibrium quantity.

- Changes in the economy that cause the demand curve to shift to the right will raise both the equilibrium price and the equilibrium quantity. Changes that cause the demand curve to shift to the left will lower both the equilibrium price and the equilibrium quantity.

- Changes in the economy that cause the supply curve to shift to the right will lower the equilibrium price and raise the equilibrium quantity. Changes that cause the supply curve to shift to the left will raise the equilibrium price and lower the equilibrium quantity.

ECONOMICS IN ACTION

Using the Supply and Demand Model to Analyze Real-World Issues

Between January and October of 2005, a period of eight months, the average price of a gallon of gasoline in the United States rose from $1.75 to $2.92 a gallon, an increase of almost 60 percent, according to data gathered by the Department of Energy. Rising gasoline prices are of critical importance to the American people. If you own a car, rising gasoline prices have a direct impact on you—you may have to cut back on driving, or ask your parents for more money to buy gasoline, or spend less on other things because you are spending more on gasoline. Even if you do not own a car yourself, rising gasoline prices can affect you. The prices of goods and services will rise because the cost of transportation increases. Bus fares, taxi fares, and airplane tickets may all rise in price because of the high price of gasoline.

Why did the price of gasoline go up so rapidly in 2005? How long did the high price of gasoline last? What could policymakers do to lower the price of gasoline? The model of supply and demand gives us a tool to model the market for gasoline, to examine the causes of the high price, to understand the impact on the American people and American businesses, and to focus on what policymakers can do to lower the price of gasoline.

One key factor in the rising price of gasoline is that people tend to drive more as the weather gets nicer and winter turns into spring and then into summer. Furthermore, as President Bush pointed out in an April 2005 press conference, "Over the past decade, America's energy consumption has been growing about 40 times faster than our energy production." Demand for gasoline had been increasing, as more Americans were driving gas-guzzling SUVs and people were driving more miles. These factors shifted the demand curve for gasoline to the right.

On the supply side, the destruction caused by Hurricane Katrina disrupted drilling on oil rigs and shut down refineries along the Gulf Coast. This reduction in supply added to a longer-term trend whereby the supply of gasoline was being lowered as a result of a reduction in U.S. refining capacity. In addition, both stricter environmental regulations for refining gasoline and the increasing price of oil led to an increase in production costs for gasoline. All these factors combined to cause the supply of gasoline to shift to the left.

Figure 11 illustrates the events that led to the rapid increase in gasoline prices, using a supply and demand model. The equilibrium price will unambiguously be higher,

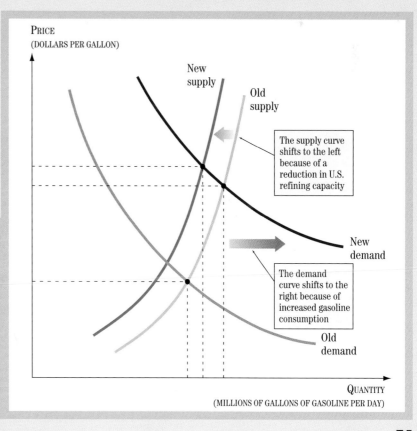

FIGURE 11
Combined Effect of a Simultaneous Increase in Demand and Decrease in Supply of Gasoline

When demand for gasoline increases and, at the same time, the supply of gasoline *decreases* because of decreased refining capacity, the supply curve will shift to the left; the equilibrium price increases, and the equilibrium quantity also increases. In this situation, the increase in demand is larger than the decrease in supply.

75

since the increase in demand and the decrease in supply will both tend to push the price higher. The impact on equilibrium quantity will be ambiguous, since the increase in demand would push the equilibrium quantity higher, but the decrease in supply would push equilibrium quantity lower. Figure 11 illustrates one possible outcome, where the increase in demand is larger than the decrease in supply, leading to a rise in equilibrium quantity.

How did the high price of gasoline hurt American businesses and the American people? Here are a few examples. When its earnings were lower than expected in May 2005, Wal-Mart speculated that its customers had less money to spend because of the high price of gasoline. The rising cost of gasoline caused SUV sales to be lower in 2005. Many Americans had to cut back on their summer travel plans, or cut back their spending on things other than summer travel, because of the rising price of gasoline.

What could policymakers have done to lower the price of gasoline? President Bush stressed in his press conference that Congress needed to pass an energy bill to address the high price of energy. President Bush stated,

"You can't wave a magic wand. I wish I could." A magic wand won't work, but the model of supply and demand can predict what will. Policies that encourage the development of new technologies for conservation of energy and the development of new sources of energy that would reduce the demand for gasoline can help eventually decrease the equilibrium price of oil. President Bush pointed out that the best way to get the price of gasoline to fall quickly would be to encourage oil-producing nations to increase their supply of oil. An increase in the supply of oil would lead to an increase in the supply of gasoline and a reduction in its price.

Figure 12 illustrates the gasoline market with a simultaneous decrease in demand and increase in supply. Both the decrease in the demand for gasoline and the increase in the supply of gasoline would lead to a decrease in the equilibrium price of gasoline. This is a prediction that policymakers could easily make. What if they wanted to also predict the change in the consumption of gasoline resulting from this energy bill? A decrease in demand would decrease equilibrium consumption, while an increase in supply

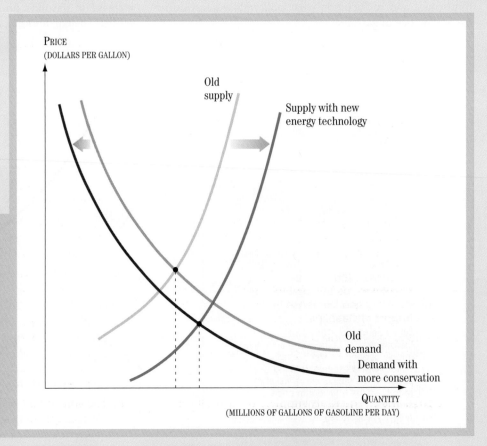

FIGURE 12
Predicted Effects of Energy Policy

The supply and demand model can also be used to predict what would happen with a successful energy policy that promoted the development of new sources of energy and energy conservation. Here, demand decreases slightly due to the effects of energy conservation, and supply increases due to the development of new technology for energy development. When demand decreases and supply increases, the equilibrium price goes down and the equilibrium quantity increases.

would increase equilibrium consumption. Policymakers therefore could not predict whether gasoline consumption would rise or fall without knowing whether demand or supply would shift by a larger amount. Figure 12 shows a resulting increase in the consumption of gasoline because the supply increase is greater in magnitude than the demand decrease.

Draw a graph yourself, but make the demand decrease larger than the supply increase. You will see a resulting decrease in the consumption of gasoline. If policymakers want an energy bill that both reduces the price of gasoline and reduces the quantity of gasoline consumed, they need to be sure that conservation efforts are the primary focus of the plan.

CONCLUSION

This chapter has shown how to use the supply and demand model to find out how equilibrium price and quantity are determined in markets where buyers and sellers interact freely. The supply and demand model is probably the most frequently used model in economics, and it has been in existence for over a hundred years in pretty much the same form as economists use it now. You will come to appreciate it more and more as you study economics.

A key feature of the model is that the equilibrium price and quantity are found at the intersection of the supply and demand curves. We can use the model to analyze how a change in factors that shift either the supply curve or the demand curve (or both) will affect equilibrium price and quantity in the market.

In later chapters we will take a closer look at the supply and demand model to understand issues like by how much equilibrium price or quantity changes when the demand curve or the supply curve shifts. We can also look at whether a market where buyers and sellers interact freely can deliver the best outcomes for society, or if there is some way to improve on those outcomes.

We will also look at the impact of price floors and price ceilings on market outcomes. This will enable you to better understand policy debates about minimum wages and rent controls.

KEY POINTS

1. Demand is a negative relationship between the price of a good and the quantity demanded by consumers. It can be shown graphically by a downward-sloping demand curve.

2. A movement along the demand curve occurs when a higher price reduces the quantity demanded or a lower price increases the quantity demanded.

3. A shift of the demand curve occurs when something besides a change in price changes the quantity of a good that people are willing to buy.

4. Supply is a positive relationship between the price of a good and the quantity supplied by firms. It can be shown graphically by an upward-sloping supply curve.

5. A movement along the supply curve occurs when a higher price increases the quantity supplied or a lower price decreases the quantity supplied.

6. A shift of the supply curve occurs when something besides a change in price changes the quantity of a good that firms are willing to sell.

7. The equilibrium price and equilibrium quantity are determined by the intersection of the supply curve and the demand curve. At this intersection point, the quantity supplied equals the quantity demanded—there are no shortages or surpluses.

8. The adjustment of prices moves the market into equilibrium. In situations where there is a shortage or an excess demand for goods, price will rise,

increasing the quantity supplied and reducing the quantity demanded. In situations where there is a surplus or an excess supply of goods, price will fall, decreasing the quantity supplied and increasing the quantity demanded.

9. We can use the supply and demand model to analyze the impact of changes in factors that move the supply curve or the demand curve or both. By shifting either the supply curve or the demand curve, observations of prices can be explained and predictions about prices can be made.

10. When the demand curve shifts to the right (left), both equilibrium price and equilibrium quantity will increase (decrease). When the supply curve shifts to the right (left), the equilibrium price will fall (rise), and the equilibrium quantity will rise (fall).

KEY TERMS

demand	demand curve	supply	shortage (excess demand)
price	normal good	quantity supplied	surplus (excess supply)
quantity demanded	inferior good	supply schedule	equilibrium price
demand schedule	substitute	law of supply	equilibrium quantity
law of demand	complement	supply curve	market equilibrium

QUESTIONS FOR REVIEW

1. Why does the demand curve slope downward?

2. Why does the supply curve slope upward?

3. What is the difference between a shift in the demand curve and a movement along the demand curve?

4. What are four things that cause a demand curve to shift?

5. What is the difference between a shift in the supply curve and a movement along the supply curve?

6. What are four things that cause a supply curve to shift?

7. How can one find the equilibrium price and equilibrium quantity?

8. What happens to the equilibrium price if the supply curve shifts to the right?

9. What happens to the equilibrium price if the demand curve shifts to the right?

10. If both the supply curve and the demand curve shift to the right, what happens to the equilibrium quantity? What about the equilibrium price?

PROBLEMS

1. For each of the following markets, indicate whether the stated change causes a shift in the supply curve, a shift in the demand curve, a movement along the supply curve, and/or a movement along the demand curve.
   a. The housing market: Consumers' incomes fall.
   b. The tea market: The price of sugar goes down.
   c. The coffee market: There is a freeze in Brazil that severely damages the coffee crop.
   d. The fast-food market: The number of fast-food restaurants in an area decreases.
   e. The peanut market in the U.S. southeast: A drought lowers supply.

2. Determine which of the following four sentences use the terminology of the supply and demand model correctly.
   a. "The price of bicycles rose, and therefore the demand for bicycles went down."
   b. "The demand for bicycles increased, and therefore the price went up."
   c. "The price of bicycles fell, decreasing the supply of bicycles."
   d. "The supply of bicycles increased, and therefore the price of bicycles fell."

3. Use the supply and demand model to explain what happens to the equilibrium price and the

equilibrium quantity for frozen yogurt in the following cases:

a. There is a large expansion in the number of firms producing frozen yogurt.

b. It is widely publicized in the press that frozen yogurt isn't more healthy for you than ice cream.

c. It is widely publicized in the press that people who eat a cup of frozen yogurt a day live to be much happier in their retirement years.

d. There is a sudden increase in the price of milk, which is used to produce frozen yogurt.

e. Frozen yogurt suddenly becomes popular because a movie idol promotes it in television commercials.

4. Suppose a decrease in consumers' incomes causes a decrease in the demand for chicken and an increase in the demand for potatoes. Which good is inferior and which is normal? How will the equilibrium price and quantity change for each good?

5. Consider the following supply and demand model of the world tea market (in billions of pounds).

Price per Pound	Quantity Supplied	Quantity Demanded
$.38	1,500	525
$.37	1,000	600
$.36	700	700
$.35	600	900
$.34	550	1,200

a. Is there a shortage or a surplus when the price is $.38? What about $.34?

b. What are the equilibrium price and the equilibrium quantity?

c. Graph the supply curve and the demand curve.

d. Show how the equilibrium price and quantity can be found on the graph.

e. If there is a shortage or surplus at a price of $.38, calculate its size in billions of pounds and show it on the graph.

6. Consider problem 5. Suppose that there is a drought in Sri Lanka that reduces the supply of tea by 400 billion pounds at every price. Suppose demand does not change.

a. Write down in a table the new supply schedule for tea.

b. Find the new equilibrium price and the new equilibrium quantity. Explain how the market adjusts to the new equilibrium.

c. Graph the new supply curve along with the old supply curve and the demand curve.

d. Show the change in the equilibrium price and the equilibrium quantity on the graph.

e. Did the equilibrium quantity change by more or less than the change in supply? Show how you arrived at your answer using both the table and the supply and demand diagram that you drew.

7. Suppose you notice that the prices of fresh fish have been rising while the amounts sold have been falling in recent years. Which of the following is the best explanation for this?

a. Consumer preferences have shifted in favor of fish because it is healthier than red meat.

b. Fishermen are prevented from using the most advanced equipment because of concerns about overfishing.

c. Consumers' incomes have risen faster than inflation.

d. Consumers have become worried about mercury levels in fish.

8. Suppose the prices of illegal drugs fall in your community at the same time that police drug seizures increase. Which is the best explanation for this?

a. Fewer drugs are being supplied locally.

b. Police arrests are removing more drug dealers.

c. Police arrests are reducing drug consumption sharply.

d. More drugs are being supplied locally.

9. In the United States, corn is often used as an ingredient in animal feed for livestock. Why does an increase in the use of corn to make ethanol, an additive that is used in gasoline, raise the price of meat? Use supply and demand curves for the corn market and the meat market to explain your answer.

10. Using the demand and supply diagrams (one for each market), show what short-run changes in price and quantity would be expected in the following markets if terrorism-related worries about air safety cause travelers to shy away from air travel. Each graph should contain the original and new demand and supply curves, and the original and new equilibrium prices and quantities. For each market, write one sentence explaining why each curve shifts or does not shift.

a. The market for air travel

b. The market for rail travel

c. The market for hotel rooms in Hawaii

d. The market for gasoline

Subtleties of the Supply and Demand Model: Price Floors, Price Ceilings, and Elasticity

When the 110th Congress convened in early January of 2007, one of the first items on the legislative agenda of congressional Democrats was to pass an increase in the minimum wage from $5.15 an hour to $7.25 an hour. Supporters argued that an increase in the legally mandated minimum wage was needed to help low-income workers. Without this intervention, some workers would earn a wage that was "too low"; the higher wage would boost the incomes of these workers and help improve their lives. Opponents of the plan and skeptics argued that intervening in the labor market would not help these workers and might even end up hurting them. They pointed out that raising the minimum wage would result in some low-income workers losing their jobs. They also argued that a minimum-wage increase was a poorly targeted policy—most of the benefits would not in fact accrue to those who were truly in need. Were the supporters of the plan correct in their claim that many poor people's lives could be improved by instituting a higher minimum wage? Or were the opponents correct to claim that a higher minimum wage could end up hurting more people than it helped?

In the run-up to the election that brought the 110th Congress into office, another issue that attracted a lot of attention was the rise in gasoline prices. Oil prices had been rising steadily since 2000 and had reached almost $60 a barrel in September of 2005 in the aftermath of Hurricanes Rita and Katrina. Oil prices had risen sharply several times before—in 1990, in 1980, and in the early 1970s. In the previous chapter, you looked at a case study that examined how rising energy consumption and disruptions in supply can lead to sharp increases in the price of oil. The supply and demand model tells us that an increase in oil supply or a decrease in oil demand will decrease the price of oil. But by how much? For example, by how much would an increase in fuel efficiency standards reduce the price of oil? And how much would the price fall if the U.S. government managed to persuade the oil-producing countries to increase production by 5 percent?

In this chapter, we look at more sophisticated aspects of the supply and demand model that are helpful in understanding policy debates, like the minimum-wage increase or how best to combat the rise in oil prices. We will first look at how to use the supply and demand model in situations where government policies do not allow price to be freely determined in a market. These interventions can take the form of a *price ceiling*, a maximum price imposed by the government when it feels that the equilibrium price is "too high," or a *price floor*, a minimum price imposed by the government when it feels that the equilibrium price is "too low," as in the case of the minimum wage. This extension of the supply and demand model will also be very helpful in solidifying your understanding of the important role played by prices in the allocation of resources.

Then we will move on to discussing an elegant, and remarkably useful, economic concept called *elasticity* that economists use when they work with the supply and demand model. In economics, elasticity is a measure of how sensitive one variable is to another. In the case of the supply and demand model, elasticity measures how sensitive the quantity of a good that people demand, or that firms supply, is to the price of the good. In this chapter we show how the concept of elasticity can be used to answer the questions raised earlier about how changes in the demand for and supply of oil affect the price of oil, and how much unemployment is caused when the minimum wage is raised. You will learn a formula that shows how elasticity is calculated and then learn how to work with and talk about elasticity.

INTERFERENCE WITH MARKET PRICES

price control: a government law or regulation that sets or limits the price to be charged for a particular good.

price ceiling: a government price control that sets the maximum allowable price for a good.

price floor: a government price control that sets the minimum allowable price for a good.

Thus far, we have used the supply and demand model in situations in which the price is freely determined without government control. But at many times throughout history, and around the world today, governments have attempted to control market prices. The usual reasons are that government leaders were not happy with the outcome of the market or were pressured by groups who would benefit from price controls.

Price Ceilings and Price Floors

In general, there are two broad types of government **price controls.** Controls can stipulate either a **price ceiling,** a maximum price at which a good can be bought and sold, or a **price floor,** a minimum price at which a good can be bought and sold. Why would a government choose to intervene in the market and put in a price floor or a price ceiling? What happens when such an intervention is made?

Ostensibly, the primary purpose of a price ceiling is to help consumers in situations where the government thinks that the equilibrium price is "too high" or is inundated with consumer complaints that the equilibrium price is too high. For example, the United States government controlled oil prices in the early 1970s, stipulating that firms could not charge more than a stated maximum price of $5.25 per barrel of crude oil at a time when the equilibrium price was well over $10 per barrel. As another example, some cities in the United States place price controls on rental apartments; landlords are not permitted to charge a rent higher than the maximum stipulated by the **rent control** law in these cities. Tenants living in rent-controlled units pay less than the market equilibrium rent that would prevail in the absence of the price ceiling.

Conversely, price floors are imposed by governments in order to help the suppliers of goods and services in situations where the government feels that the equilibrium price is "too low" or is influenced by complaints from producers that the equilibrium price is too low. For example, the U.S. government requires that the price of sugar in the United States not fall below a certain amount. Another example is in the labor market, where the U.S. government requires that firms pay workers a wage of at least a given level, called the **minimum wage.**

Side Effects of Price Ceilings

Even though price ceilings are typically implemented with the idea of helping consumers, they often end up having harmful side effects that hurt the consumers that the ceiling was put in place to help. If the price ceiling that the government puts in place to prevent firms from charging more than a certain amount for their products is lower than the equilibrium price, then a shortage is likely to result, as illustrated in Figure 1. The situation of a persistent shortage, where sellers are unwilling to supply as much as buyers want to buy, is illustrated for the general case of any good in the top graph in Figure 1 and for the specific case of rent control in the bottom graph.

■ **Dealing with Persistent Shortages.** Because higher prices are not allowed, the shortage must be dealt with in other ways. Sometimes the government issues a limited amount of ration coupons, which do not exceed the quantity supplied at the restricted maximum price, to people to alleviate the shortage. This was done in World War II; people had to present these ration coupons at stores in order to buy certain goods, and only those who had ration coupons could buy those goods. If the price ceiling had not been in place, the shortage would have driven prices higher, and those who were willing and able to pay the higher price would have been able to buy the goods without the need for a ration coupon.

Alternatively, if there are no ration coupons, then the shortage might result in long waiting lines. In the past, in centrally planned economies, long lines for bread were frequently observed because of price controls on bread. Sometimes black markets develop, in which people buy and sell goods outside the watch of the government and charge whatever price they want. In the past, this was typical in command economies. Black markets are also common in less-developed countries today when the governments in these countries impose price controls.

Another effect of price ceilings is a reduction in the quality of the good sold. By lowering the quality of the good, the producer can reduce the costs of producing it. A frequent criticism of rent control is that it can lower the quality of housing—landlords are more reluctant to paint the walls or to repair the elevator since they are prevented from charging a higher price.

rent control: a government price control that sets the maximum allowable rent on a house or apartment.

minimum wage: a wage per hour below which it is illegal to pay workers.

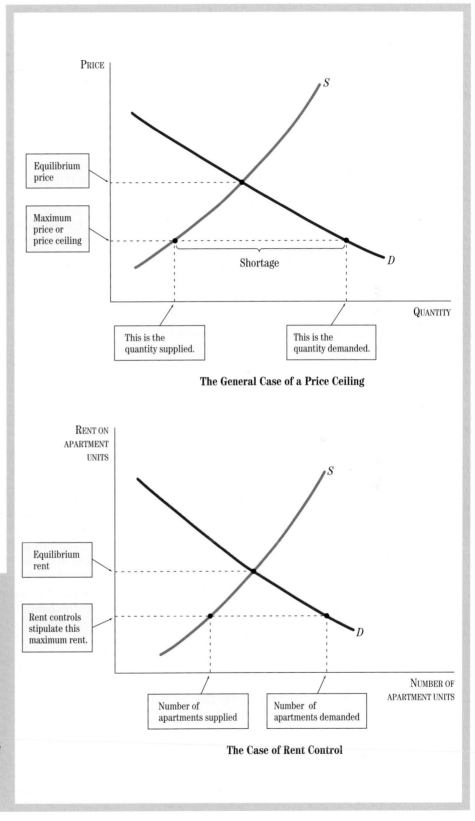

PRICE

Equilibrium price

Maximum price or price ceiling

S

Shortage

D

This is the quantity supplied.

This is the quantity demanded.

QUANTITY

The General Case of a Price Ceiling

RENT ON APARTMENT UNITS

Equilibrium rent

Rent controls stipulate this maximum rent.

S

D

Number of apartments supplied

Number of apartments demanded

NUMBER OF APARTMENT UNITS

The Case of Rent Control

FIGURE 1
Effects of a Maximum-Price Law

The top diagram shows the general case when the government prevents the market price from rising above a particular maximum price, or sets a price ceiling below the equilibrium price. The lower diagram shows a particular example of a price ceiling, rent controls on apartment units. The supply and demand model predicts that there will be a shortage. The shortage occurs because the quantity supplied is less than consumers are willing to buy at that price. The shortage leads to rationing, black markets, or lower product quality.

■ **Making Things Worse.** Although the stated purpose of price ceilings is to help people who have to pay high prices, the preceding examples indicate how price ceilings can make things worse. Issuing ration coupons raises difficult problems about who gets the coupons. In the case of a price ceiling on gasoline, for example, should the government give more coupons to those who commute by car than to those who do not? Rationing by waiting in line is also a poor outcome. People who are waiting in line could be doing more enjoyable or more useful things. Similarly, black markets, being illegal, encourage people to go outside the law. People transacting in black markets may also be more vulnerable to theft or fraud. Lowering the quality of the good is also a bad way to alleviate the problem of a high price. This simply eliminates the higher-quality good from production; both consumers and producers lose. Price ceilings are also not particularly well targeted. Even though the goal of a price ceiling may be to ensure that someone who can't afford to pay the equilibrium price can still end up purchasing the good, there is no way to guarantee that only those who can't afford to pay the equilibrium price end up purchasing the good. For instance, many people who end up living in rent-controlled apartments may not be poor at all.

Side Effects of Price Floors

Like price ceilings, price floors are typically enacted with the goal of helping out producers who are facing low market equilibrium prices, but they often end up having harmful side effects that hurt the people that the floor was put in place to help. If the price floor that the government puts in place exceeds the equilibrium price, then a surplus will occur. The situation of a persistent surplus, where sellers are willing to supply more output than buyers want to buy, is illustrated for the general case of any good in the top graph of Figure 2 and for the specific case of the minimum wage in the bottom graph.

■ **Dealing with Persistent Surpluses.** How is this surplus dealt with in actual markets? In markets for farm products, the government usually has to buy the surplus and, perhaps, put it in storage. Buying farm products above the equilibrium price costs taxpayers money, and the higher price raises costs to consumers. For this reason, economists argue against price floors on agricultural goods. As an alternative, the government sometimes reduces the supply by telling firms to plant fewer acres or to destroy crops. But government requirements that land be kept idle or crops destroyed are particularly repugnant to most people.

As we will see in more detail later in this book, the supply and demand model can also be applied to labor markets. In that case, the price is the price of labor, or the wage. What does the supply and demand model predict about the effects of a minimum wage? In the case of labor markets, a minimum wage can cause unemployment. If the minimum wage exceeds the equilibrium wage, the number of workers demanded at that wage is less than the number of workers who are willing to work. Even though some workers would be willing to work for less than the minimum wage, employers are not permitted to pay them less than the minimum wage. Therefore, there is a surplus of unemployed workers at the minimum wage.

■ **Making Things Worse.** Even though the stated purpose of price floors is to help sellers by paying them a higher price, the preceding examples indicate how price floors can make things worse. The resources allocated to building grain silos to store surplus grain could have been used to hire doctors or teachers or to build low-income houses. The land that farmers are encouraged to keep in an undeveloped, yet unfarmed state could have been used for a housing development or as a high school athletic field. Price floors, like price ceilings, are also not particularly well targeted. Even though the goal of a price floor may be to ensure that a poor farmer does not suffer because crop prices are too low, the benefits of the higher price will typically

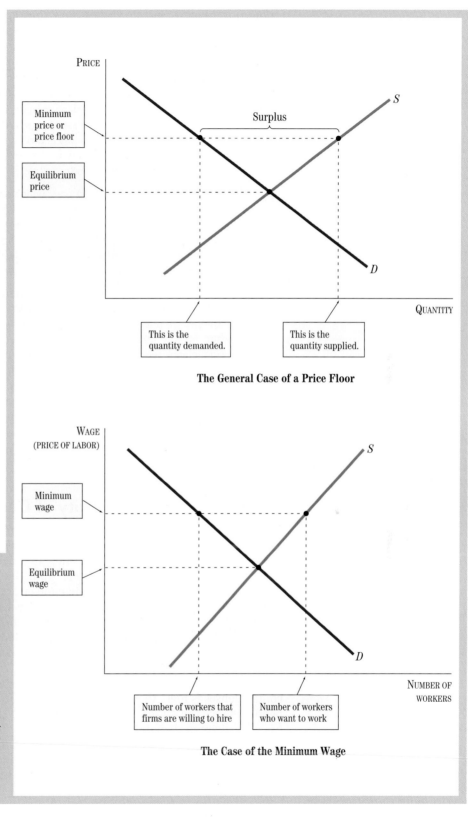

PRICE

Minimum price or price floor

Equilibrium price

Surplus

S

D

QUANTITY

This is the quantity demanded.

This is the quantity supplied.

The General Case of a Price Floor

WAGE
(PRICE OF LABOR)

Minimum wage

Equilibrium wage

S

D

NUMBER OF WORKERS

Number of workers that firms are willing to hire

Number of workers who want to work

The Case of the Minimum Wage

FIGURE 2
Effects of a Minimum-Price Law

The top diagram shows the general case when the government prevents the market price from falling below a particular minimum price, or sets a price floor above the equilibrium price. The lower diagram shows a particular example when the price of labor—the wage—cannot fall below the minimum wage. The supply and demand model predicts that sellers are willing to sell a greater quantity than buyers are willing to buy at that price. Thus, there is a surplus of the good or, in the case of labor, unemployment for some of those who would be hired only at a lower wage.

accrue to extremely wealthy farmers and large agricultural businesses with lots of resources. In the case of the minimum wage, teenagers from relatively well-off families may end up earning a higher salary as a result of the minimum wage, but a poor parent may end up losing his or her job and joining the ranks of the unemployed.

R E V I E W

- Governments will occasionally intervene in markets because they think that the equilibrium price is too high or too low. In some instances where the government thinks the price that buyers have to pay is too high, it may impose a price ceiling. In some instances where the government thinks the price that sellers are receiving is too low, it may impose a price floor.

- Price ceilings cause persistent shortages, which, in turn, cause rationing, black markets, and a reduced quality of goods and services. Price ceilings also may not end up helping the people that the policy was designed to benefit. In the case of rent control, for example, the people who end up in rent-controlled apartments may be more affluent than the individuals who are unable to find an apartment because of the persistent shortages.

- Price floors cause persistent surpluses, which, in turn, result in resources being diverted away from other productive activities. Price floors also may not end up helping the people that the policy was designed to benefit. In the case of a minimum wage, for example, the workers who end up in jobs earning the higher minimum wage may be teenagers from relatively well-off families, while a poor worker may be unable to find a job because of the surplus of unemployed workers.

ELASTICITY OF DEMAND

Defining the Price Elasticity of Demand

The price elasticity of demand is a measure of the sensitivity of the *quantity demanded* of a good to the *price* of the good. "Price elasticity of demand" is sometimes shortened to "elasticity of demand," the "demand elasticity," or even simply "elasticity" when the meaning is clear from the context. The price elasticity of demand always refers to a particular demand curve or demand schedule, such as the world demand for oil or the U.S. demand for bicycles. Since the demand curve slopes downward, as the price increases, the quantity demanded by consumers declines, and as the price decreases, the quantity demanded by consumers increases, all else held equal. The price elasticity of demand is a measure of *how much* the quantity demanded changes when the price changes.

For example, when economists report that the price elasticity of demand for contact lenses is high, they mean that the quantity of contact lenses demanded by people changes by a large amount when the price changes. Or if they report that the price elasticity of demand for bread is low, they mean that the quantity of bread demanded changes by only a small amount when the price of bread changes.

price elasticity of demand: the percentage change in the quantity demanded of a good divided by the percentage change in the price of that good.

We can define the price elasticity of demand clearly with a formula: **Price elasticity of demand** is the percentage change in the quantity demanded divided by the percentage change in the price. That is,

$$\text{Price elasticity of demand} = \frac{\text{percentage change in quantity demanded}}{\text{percentage change in price}}$$

ECONOMICS IN ACTION

How Policymakers Use Price Elasticity of Demand to Discourage Underage Drinking

Policymakers use information about the price elasticity of demand in many ways. Take the government's efforts to reduce underage drinking. In a 2003 study on underage drinking, the National Academy of Sciences recommended that one way to reduce underage drinking would be to increase the tax on alcohol. To implement this policy effectively, it would be important for policymakers to know which demand curve most accurately represents the demand for alcohol by underage drinkers. The amount that a tax would reduce the quantity of alcohol consumed by underage drinkers depends on their price elasticity of demand.

Recall that a new tax is modeled as a decrease in supply. You can see how this works by drawing this supply shift and a demand curve with high price elasticity of demand and then drawing the same supply shift and a demand curve with a low price elasticity of demand, as in Figure 3. Alcohol consumption responds more to the tax when the price elasticity of demand is high. If the price elasticity of demand for alcohol by underage drinkers is low (that is, if the quantity of alcohol demanded by underage drinkers changes by only a small amount when the price of alcohol changes), then a new tax on alcohol must be large to accomplish the goal of a reduction in underage drinking. If the price elasticity of demand for alcohol by underage drinkers is high (that is, if the quantity of alcohol demanded by underage drinkers changes by a large amount when the price of alcohol changes), then the tax might not need to be very big to accomplish the policymakers' goal. Which do you think is more likely?

We emphasize that the price elasticity of demand refers to a particular demand curve; thus, the numerator of this formula is the percentage change in quantity demanded when the price changes by the percentage amount shown in the denominator. All the other factors that affect demand are held constant when we compute the price elasticity of demand.

For example, the price elasticity of demand for gasoline is about .2. Thus, if the price of gasoline increases by 10 percent, the quantity of gasoline demanded will fall by 2 percent ($.2 \times 10$). The price elasticity of demand for alcoholic beverages is about 1.5; thus, if the price of alcoholic beverages rises by 10 percent, the quantity demanded will fall by 15 percent (1.5×10). As you can see from these examples, knowing the elasticity of demand enables us to determine by how much the *quantity demanded* changes when the price changes.

The Size of the Elasticity: High versus Low

There are two graphs in Figure 3, each showing a different possible demand curve for oil in the world. We want to show why it is important to know which of these two demand curves gives a better description of economic behavior in the oil market. Each graph has the price of oil on the vertical axis (in dollars per barrel) and the quantity of oil demanded on the horizontal axis (in millions of barrels of oil a day).

Both of the demand curves pass through the same point *A*, where the price of oil is $20 per barrel and the quantity demanded is 60 million barrels per day. But observe that the two curves show different degrees of sensitivity of the quantity demanded to the price. In the top graph, where the demand curve is relatively flat, the quantity demanded of oil is very sensitive to the price; in other words, the demand curve has a high elasticity. For example, consider a change from point *A* to point *B*: When the price rises by $2, from $20 to $22, the quantity demanded falls by 12 million, from 60 million to 48 million barrels a day. In percentage terms, when the price rises by 10 percent ($2/20 = .10$, or 10 percent), the quantity demanded falls by 20 percent ($12/60 = .20$, or 20 percent).

On the other hand, in the bottom graph, the quantity demanded is not very sensitive to the price; in other words, the demand curve has a low elasticity. It is relatively steep. When the price rises by $2 from point *A* to point *C*, the quantity demanded falls by 3 million barrels. In percentage terms, the same 10 percent increase in price reduces the quantity demanded by only 5 percent (3/60 = .05, or 5 percent). Thus, the sensitivity of the quantity to the price, or the size of the elasticity, is what distinguishes these two graphs.

The Impact of a Change in Supply on the Price of Oil

Now consider what happens when there is a decline in supply in the world oil market. In Figure 4 we combine the supply curve for oil with the two demand curves for oil from Figure 3. Initially the oil market is in equilibrium in Figure 4; in both

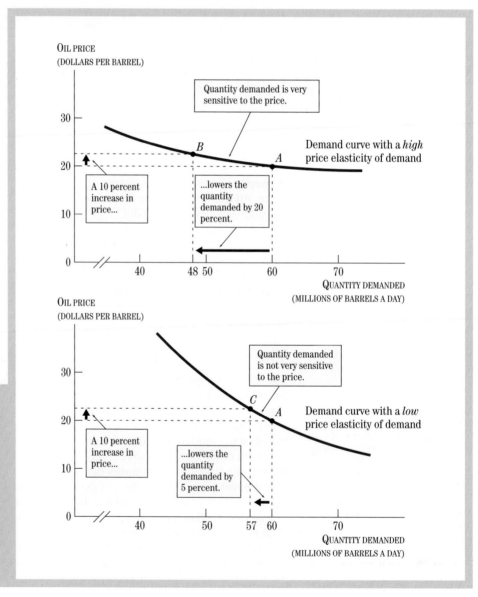

FIGURE 3
Comparing Different Sizes of the Price Elasticity of Demand
Both sets of axes have exactly the same scale. In the top graph, the quantity demanded is very sensitive to the price; the elasticity is high. In the bottom graph, the quantity demanded is not very sensitive to the price; the elasticity is low. Thus, the same increase in price ($2, or 10 percent) reduces the quantity demanded much more when the elasticity is high (top graph) than when it is low (bottom graph).

graphs, the quantity demanded equals the quantity supplied. The equilibrium price is $20 per barrel, and the equilibrium quantity is 60 million barrels a day, just like at point *A* in Figure 3. A reduction in the supply of oil—perhaps because of the reduction in Iraqi oil production or the shutdown of refineries following Hurricane Katrina—is also shown. The exact same leftward shift in supply is shown in the top and bottom graphs of Figure 4.

Now, observe how the equilibrium price changes in the two graphs. Recall that this change is our prediction—using the supply and demand model—of what would happen to the price of oil if the supply declined. We know that a decrease in supply will lead to an increase in the equilibrium price and a decrease in the equilibrium quantity. However, as the two graphs show, there is a huge difference in the size of the predicted price increase. In the top graph, the oil price increases only a little. If the

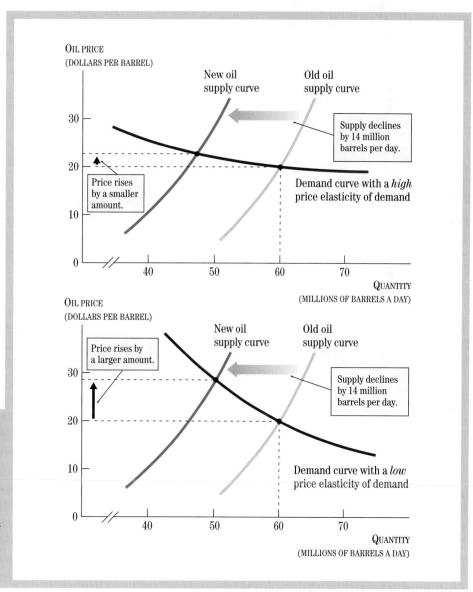

FIGURE 4
The Importance of the Size of the Price Elasticity of Demand
The impact on the oil price of a reduction in oil supply is shown for two different demand curves. The reduction in supply is the same for both graphs. When the price elasticity of demand is high (top graph), there is only a small increase in the price. When the price elasticity of demand is low (bottom graph), the price rises by much more.

Increasing School Enrollment in Africa

The economic weakness of many sub-Saharan African countries can be attributed to myriad factors, including lack of education, civil wars, corruption, resource exploitation, disease, and a lack of adequate institutions. While these problems may seem intractable, sometimes only a small change in policy and a small increase in resources are all it takes, as this article from the *Christian Science Monitor* about how to increase school enrollment shows.

Even though $42 may not seem like a lot to you, this represents about 25% of the average income in some African countries.

For poor families with serious income constraints, the demand for education becomes extremely sensitive to price. Why do you think this effect is especially pronounced for female children?

Lowering the price of education dramatically increased the quantity of students demanding that education. What does that say about the elasticity of demand for education?

Easing the Burden of School Fees in Africa

By STEPHANIE HANES | Correspondent of The Christian Science Monitor

SOWETO, SOUTH AFRICA—Orison Makhaluza leans back on the cracked leather sofa and watches his young grandnieces scurry through the small cement house. They look tiny in their gray school jumpers and knee socks, which they are still wearing, even though school ended hours ago.

Last month, Mr. Makhaluza wasn't sure if the girls would ever wear the uniforms. He wasn't sure if they would go to school at all. The problem, he explains, was school fees. His sister, the girls' grandmother, started taking care of the four children, ages 5 to 11, when their mother died last year. But she couldn't afford to pay the school fees—$42 per student—required by the girls' primary school. So the school told the children they could not attend classes.

"Education, it's the key of the future," says Makhaluza, who has been unemployed for five years and lives at his sister's house. "But our kids, they are told they cannot go to school." Although South African law says that no student should be denied an education and that impoverished students should be exempt from paying fees, children's advocates say that schools often do not understand or follow these regulations. The government pays for teachers' salaries and buildings, but schools need extra money to pay for basics such as water, electricity, and pencils. School officials and education-rights advocates say schools have incentive to take harsh measures, such as keeping a child out of the classroom, to convince parents to pay. Parents, many of whom are uneducated, often don't understand the law well enough to challenge schools. In Makhaluza's case, a grass-roots group called the Education Rights Project talked to the school about his grandnieces, and the girls were admitted. The school said there had been a misunderstanding.

Across Africa and in other developing regions, organizations such as UNICEF and the World Bank, along with children's rights groups, are encouraging countries to provide free education. They worry that school fees are keeping hundreds of thousands of children—particularly girls—from school. Other expenses, such as the cost of books, transportation, and uniforms, can also keep schools out of reach for poor families, many of whom live on less than a dollar a day.

These organizations point to countries like Kenya, where President Mwai Kibaki, fulfilling a campaign promise, declared in 2003 that all primary schools would be free of fees. In just a few months, primary school enrollment increased from about 6 million to 7.2 million. Although the move has put unprecedented strains on Kenya's education system—the government had not budgeted for the huge increase in students—international observers say it proves that fees have kept poor children out of the classroom.

Last year, the United Nations announced that universal free primary education was one of its top priorities. But many countries say they simply cannot afford to lift school fees, adding that parents have a responsibility to contribute to their children's education. About 80 percent of the countries in East Asia and the Pacific have mandatory fees, according to a 2001 World Bank study, as do many Middle Eastern and North African countries, such as Egypt, Jordan, and Tunisia. This year, the Botswana government reintroduced school fees after 20 years of free education, saying it could no longer afford to subsidize schools.

Besides Kenya, a handful of countries in eastern and southern Africa have done away with primary school fees, including Tanzania, Malawi, and Uganda. The efforts are bolstered in part by populist politics and in part by money donated from wealthy countries such as the United States. Yet South Africa, the richest nation in the region, still allows schools to charge. Although South African law says that the government must fund all public schools, the education department says that there is also "a responsibility on all public school governing bodies to do their utmost to improve the quality of education in their schools by raising additional resources to supplement those which the state provides." "All parents," it says, "are thereby encouraged to increase their own direct financial and other contributions." Parents are supposed to vote on the fee level for their children's school. While no school is required to charge fees, in practice, many would go without electricity and water if they did not raise extra funds.

How wealthy countries can assist poor countries to make an important policy change

But school officials say they are getting better at preventing poor children from slipping through the cracks. Regarding fees, the balance of power has shifted to parents, says Rej Brijraj, chief executive officer of the South African Council for Educators, a statutory body charged with maintaining professional standards. The onus is now on schools to prove that parents can pay, rather than parents having to prove to school boards that they cannot afford fees. Last year, the South African Parliament passed the Education Laws Amendment Bill, which makes a certain percentage of South Africa's approximately 28,000 schools "fee free." That bill, however, has not yet been signed into law.

"By and large, I must say that school governing bodies have shown great responsibility in setting school fees, and the state has been very vigilant to make sure that learners are not disadvantaged," Mr. Brijraj says. Recently there have been a number of grass-roots efforts designed to educate both schools and parents about the law and children's rights. But Makhaluza still has concerns. Children who don't pay or can't conform to school rules can face ridicule. His own son was called a "hooligan" by a teacher because he was not wearing a school uniform—a luxury that Makhaluza said he could not afford.

In many African countries, school uniforms are required, which imposes an additional cost.

Sharon September, education project coordinator at South Africa's Alliance for Children's Access to Social Security, says she still hears of schools retaliating against families who cannot pay. "We hear stories where students are refused entry to school," she says. "Or where children attend, and don't get their report at the end of the year because they didn't pay. There have been cases where mothers have been told to clean the toilets to make up for the fact they can't pay." Lerato Mokgadi, a 22-year-old 12th-grader, says her high school in the Soweto township, just outside Johannesburg, refused to release her end-of-year report because her mother had not paid fees. "I never paid the school fees because I wasn't working," says her mother, Maria Mokgadi.

The younger Mokgadi's report was crucial. She knew that she had not passed the countrywide exam necessary for university entrance. But without her report, she didn't know which subject she had failed, so she could not register for additional classes. A local representative of the Education Rights Project spoke with the school on Mokgadi's behalf, and returned with the report card. "If this were an equal society, school fees would be fine," Ms. September says. "Nobody has a problem contributing. But if fees serve as an exclusionary measure, because every child has a right to an education, it should be altered."

ECONOMICS IN ACTION

Predicting the Size of a Price Increase

Economists used a numerical value of elasticity to predict the size of the oil price rise caused by the Iraqi invasion of Kuwait in 1990. Here are the steps they took:

- First, they determined—after looking at historical studies of oil prices and quantities—that the price elasticity of the demand for oil was .1. In other words, $e_d = .1$.

- Second, they calculated—after consulting with oil producers—that the invasion of Kuwait would reduce the world oil supply by 7 percent. They assumed that this 7 percent would also be the percentage decline in the quantity of oil demanded because other sources of oil could not increase in a short period of time. In other words, $\Delta Q_d / Q_d = .07$, or 7 percent.

- Third, they plugged these numbers into the formula for elasticity to calculate that the oil price would rise by 70 percent. Here is the exact calculation behind this step: Rearrange the definition of elasticity, $e_d = (\Delta Q_d / Q_d)/(\Delta P/P)$, to put the percentage change

in the price on the left. That is, $\Delta P/P = (\Delta Q_d / Q_d)/e_d$. Now plug in $\Delta Q_d / Q_d = .07$ and $e_d = .1$ to get $.07/(.1) = .70$, or 70 percent.

The 70 percent price rise predicted might seem large. In fact, the actual rise in the price of oil in 1990 was large, even larger than 70 percent: The price of oil rose from $17 per barrel in July 1990 to $36 in October 1990, or about 112 percent. (The larger-than-predicted price increase may have been due to worries that Iraq would also invade Saudi Arabia and reduce the oil supply even further.)

This type of calculation—showing that a huge oil price increase could be caused by the 7 percent reduction in oil supply—was a factor in the decision by the United States and its allies to send troops to the Middle East to halt the Iraqi invasion of Saudi Arabia and to eventually force Iraq out of Kuwait.

Could you use the same type of reasoning to determine how much the price of oil would fall if oil producers increased supply? Suppose the increase was 4 percent.

elasticity is very high, then only a small increase in the price is enough to get people to reduce their use of oil and thereby bring the quantity demanded down to the lower quantity supplied. On the other hand, in the bottom diagram, the price rises by much more. Here the elasticity is very low, and so a large increase in price is needed to get people to reduce their use of oil and bring the quantity demanded down to the quantity supplied.

Thus, in order to determine how much the price will rise in response to a shift in oil supply, we need to know how sensitive the quantity demanded is to the price, or the size of the elasticity of demand.

REVIEW

- We know that an increase in price will lower the quantity demanded, whereas a decrease in price will increase the quantity demanded. The price elasticity of demand is a number that tells us by how much the quantity demanded changes when the price changes.

- The price elasticity of demand, which we also refer to as "elasticity of demand" or just as "elasticity," is defined as the percentage change in the quantity demanded divided by the percentage change in the price.

- A given change in price has a larger impact on quantity demanded when the elasticity of demand is higher.

- A given shift of the supply curve will have a larger impact on equilibrium quantity (and a smaller impact on equilibrium price) when the elasticity of demand is higher.

WORKING WITH DEMAND ELASTICITIES

Having demonstrated the practical importance of elasticity, let us examine the concept in more detail and show how to use it. Some symbols will be helpful.

If we let the symbol e_d represent the price elasticity of demand, then we can write the definition as

$$e_d = \frac{\Delta Q_d}{Q_d} \div \frac{\Delta P}{P} = \frac{\Delta Q_d / Q_d}{\Delta P / P}$$

where Q_d is the quantity demanded, P is the price, and Δ means "change in." In other words, the elasticity of demand equals the "percentage change in the quantity demanded" divided by the "percentage change in the price." Observe that to compute the percentage change in the numerator and the denominator, we need to divide the change in the variable (ΔP or ΔQ_d) by the variable (P or Q_d).

Because the quantity demanded is negatively related to the price along a demand curve, the elasticity of demand is a negative number: When $\Delta P/P$ is positive, $\Delta Q_d/Q_d$ is negative. But when economists write or talk about elasticity, they usually ignore the negative sign and report the absolute value of the number. Because the demand curve always slopes downward, this nearly universal convention need not cause any confusion, as long as you remember it.

It is easy to do back-of-the-envelope computations of price elasticity of demand. Suppose a study shows that when the price of Australian wine fell by 8 percent, the quantity of Australian wine sold increased by 12 percent. The price elasticity of demand for Australian wine is

$$e_d = \frac{\Delta Q_d / Q_d}{\Delta P / P} = \frac{12}{8} = 1.5$$

Suppose your university raises student season ticket prices from $50 to $60, which results in the quantity of season tickets sold falling from 2,000 to 1,800. The price elasticity of demand for season ticket prices would be

$$e_d = \frac{\Delta Q_d / Q_d}{\Delta P / P} = \frac{200/2,000}{10/50} = \frac{.1}{.2} = .5$$

Notice that measured in percentage changes, the demand for Australian wine is responsive to changes in the price, and the demand for season tickets is not very responsive to changes in the price.

The Advantage of a Unit-Free Measure

An attractive feature of the price elasticity of demand is that it does not depend on the units of measurement of the quantity demanded—whether barrels of oil or pounds of peanuts. It is a **unit-free measure** because it uses percentage changes in price and quantity demanded. Thus, it provides a way to compare the price sensitivity of the demand for many different goods. It even allows us to compare the price sensitivity of less expensive goods—like rice—with that of more expensive goods—like steak.

For example, suppose that when the price of rice rises from 50 cents to 60 cents per pound, the quantity demanded falls from 20 tons to 19 tons: That is a decline of 1 ton for a 10 *cent* price increase.

In contrast, suppose that when the price of steak rises by $1, from $5 to $6 per pound, the quantity demanded falls by 1 ton, from 20 tons to 19 tons of steak. That would be a decline of 1 ton for a 1 *dollar* price increase.

unit-free measure: a measure that does not depend on a unit of measurement.

Using these numbers, the price sensitivity of the demand for steak and the demand for rice might appear to be very different: 10 cents to get a ton of reduced purchases versus $1 to get a ton of reduced purchases. Yet the elasticities are the same. The percentage change in price is 20 percent in each case ($1/$5 = $.10/$.50 = .20, or 20 percent), and the percentage change in quantity is 5 percent in each case: 1 ton of rice/20 tons of rice = 1 ton of steak/20 tons of steak = .05, or 5 percent. Hence, the elasticity is 5/20 = 1/4 in both cases.

Elasticity allows us to compare the price sensitivity of different goods by looking at ratios of percentage changes regardless of the units for measuring either price or quantity. With millions of different goods and hundreds of different units of measurement, this is indeed a major advantage.

Elasticity versus Slope

After looking at Figure 3, you might be tempted to say that demand curves that are very steep have a low elasticity, and demand curves that are very flat have a high elasticity. That turns out not to be the case, so you have to be careful not to simply look at a flat demand curve and say that it has a high elasticity. You need to understand why the *elasticity of the demand curve* is not the same as the *slope of the demand curve*. Remember that the slope of a curve is the change in the y variable over the change in the x variable; in the case of the demand curve, the slope is defined as the change in price divided by the change in quantity demanded. The slope is not a unit-free measure—it depends on how the price and quantity are measured. Elasticity, on the other hand, is a unit-free measure.

To illustrate the difference between slope and elasticity, we show in Figure 5 a demand curve for rice and a demand curve for steak. The two demand curves have different slopes because the prices are so different. When the price of rice increases by 10 cents, the quantity demanded of rice falls by 1 ton; whereas when the price of steak increases by $1 (or 100 cents), the quantity demanded of steak falls by 1 ton. The slope of the steak demand curve is (−100 cents a ton), which is 10 times greater than the slope of the rice demand curve (−10 cents a ton). Yet the elasticity is the same for the change from A to B for both demand curves—the price of rice and the price of steak both increased by 20 percent, while the quantity demanded of rice and the quantity demanded of steak both decreased by 5 percent.

Calculating the Elasticity with a Midpoint Formula

To calculate the elasticity, we need to find the percentage change in the quantity demanded and divide it by the percentage change in the price. As we have already illustrated with examples, to get the percentage change in the price or quantity, we need to divide the change in price (ΔP) by the price (P) or the change in quantity demanded (ΔQ_d) by the quantity demanded (Q_d). But when price and quantity demanded change, there is a question about what to use for P and Q_d. Should we use the old price and the old quantity demanded before the change, or should we use the new price and the new quantity demanded after the change?

The most common convention that economists use is a compromise between these two alternatives. They take the *average,* or the *midpoint,* of the old and new quantities demanded and the old and new prices. That is, they compute the elasticity using the following formula, called the *midpoint formula:*

$$\frac{\text{Price elasticity}}{\text{of demand}} = \frac{\dfrac{\text{change in quantity}}{\text{average of old and new quantities}}}{\div \dfrac{\text{change in price}}{\text{average of old and new prices}}}$$

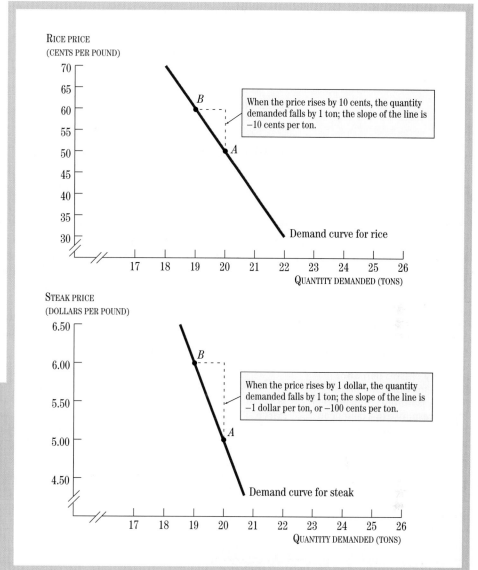

FIGURE 5
Different Slopes and Same Elasticities
The slope of the steak demand curve in the bottom graph is greater than the slope of the rice demand curve in the top graph. The price elasticity of demand for rice and steak from point A to point B is the same, however. From point A to point B, the price rises by 20 percent and the quantity demanded decreases by 5 percent. Thus, the elasticity is 1/4 for both rice and steak at these points.

For example, if we use the midpoint formula to calculate the price elasticity of demand for oil when the price changes from \$20 to \$22 and the quantity demanded changes from 60 million to 48 million barrels a day, we get

$$\left[\frac{12}{(60 + 48)/2}\right] \div \left[\frac{2}{(20 + 22)/2}\right] = 0.2222 \div 0.0952 = 2.33$$

That is, the price elasticity of demand is 2.33 using the midpoint formula. When we originally calculated the elasticity using the old price and the old quantity demanded, we came up with an elasticity of

$$\left[\frac{12}{60}\right] \div \left[\frac{2}{20}\right] = 0.2 \div 0.1 = 2$$

If we had used the new price and the new quantity, we would have calculated the elasticity to be

$$\left[\frac{12}{48}\right] \div \left[\frac{2}{22}\right] = 0.25 \div 0.0909 = 2.75$$

So the elasticity calculated using the midpoint formula turns out to be in between these two values, as you would expect.

Talking about Elasticities

Economists classify demand curves by the size of the price elasticities of demand, and they have developed a very precise terminology for doing so.

elastic demand: demand for which the price elasticity is greater than 1.

inelastic demand: demand for which the price elasticity is less than 1.

perfectly inelastic demand: demand for which the price elasticity is zero, indicating no response to a change in price and therefore a vertical demand curve.

perfectly elastic demand: demand for which the price elasticity is infinite, indicating an infinite response to a change in price and therefore a horizontal demand curve.

■ **Elastic versus Inelastic Demand.** Goods for which the price elasticity is greater than 1 have an **elastic demand.** For example, the quantity of foreign travel demanded decreases by more than 1 percent when the price rises by 1 percent because many people tend to travel at home rather than abroad when the price of foreign travel rises.

Goods for which the price elasticity of demand is less than 1 have an **inelastic demand.** For example, the quantity of eggs demanded decreases by less than 1 percent when the price of eggs rises by 1 percent because many people do not want to substitute other things for eggs at breakfast.

■ **Perfectly Elastic versus Perfectly Inelastic Demand.** A demand curve that is vertical is called **perfectly inelastic.** Figure 6 shows a perfectly inelastic demand curve. The elasticity is zero because when the price changes, the quantity demanded does not change at all. No matter what the price, the same quantity is demanded. People who need insulin have a perfectly inelastic demand for insulin. As long as there are no substitutes for insulin, they will pay whatever they have to in order to get the insulin.

A demand curve that is horizontal is called **perfectly elastic.** Figure 6 also shows a perfectly elastic demand curve. The elasticity is infinite. The perfectly flat demand curve is sometimes hard to imagine because it entails infinitely large movements of quantity for tiny changes in price. In order to better visualize this case, you can imagine that the curve is tilted ever so slightly. Goods that have a lot of comparable substitutes are likely to have high elasticities of demand.

Table 1 summarizes the terminology about elasticities.

FIGURE 6
Perfectly Elastic and Perfectly Inelastic Demand

A perfectly inelastic demand curve is a vertical line at a certain quantity. The quantity demanded is completely insensitive to the price: Whatever happens to the price, the quantity demanded does not change. A perfectly elastic demand curve is a flat line at a certain price. An increase in price reduces the quantity demanded to zero; a small decrease in price raises the quantity demanded by a huge (literally infinite) amount.

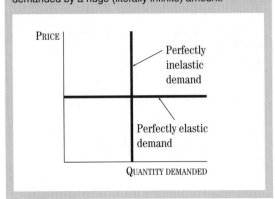

TABLE 1
Terminology for Price Elasticity of Demand

Term	Value of Price Elasticity of Demand (e_d)
Perfectly inelastic	0 (vertical demand curve)
Inelastic	Less than 1
Elastic	Greater than 1
Perfectly elastic	Infinity (horizontal demand curve)

Revenue and the Price Elasticity of Demand

When people purchase 60 million barrels of oil at $20 a barrel, they must pay a total of $1,200 million ($20 × 60 million). This is a payment to the oil producers and is the producers' revenue. In general, revenue is the price (*P*) times the quantity (*Q*), or *P* × *Q*. A change in price will therefore affect revenue. While this seems obvious, it is important that you understand exactly how price affects revenue. In fact, a change in price has two opposite effects on revenue. For instance, when the price increases, people pay more for each item, which increases revenue; but they buy fewer items, which in turn reduces revenue. The price elasticity of demand determines which of these two opposite effects dominates, because elasticity is a measure of how much the quantity demanded changes when price changes.

Figure 7, which is a replica of Figure 3 with the scales changed, illustrates the effects on revenue. In the top graph, revenue went from $1.2 billion (60 million × $20 = $1,200 million) to $1.056 billion (48 million × $22 = $1,056 million). In other

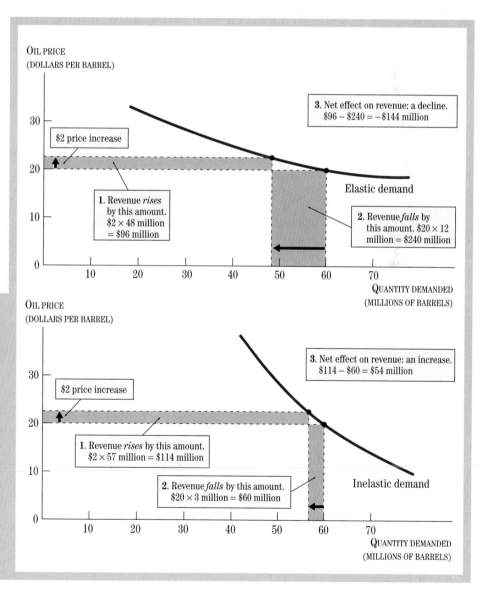

FIGURE 7

Effects of an Increase in the Price of Oil on Revenue

These graphs are replicas of the demand curves for oil shown in Figure 3, with the scale changed to show the change in revenue when the price of oil is increased. An increase in the price has two effects on revenue, as shown by the gray- and pink-shaded rectangles. The increase in revenue (gray rectangle) is due to the higher price. The decrease in revenue (pink rectangle) is due to the decline in the quantity demanded as the price is increased. In the top graph, where elasticity is greater than 1, the net effect is a decline in revenue; in the bottom graph, where elasticity is less than 1, the net effect is an increase in revenue.

words, revenue declined by $144 million even though price increased. Now compare this to the revenue changes in the bottom graph. There revenue went from $1.2 billion to $1.254 billion (57 million × $22 = $1,254 million), an increase of $54 million. Using the old price and the old quantity demanded, you can show that the elasticity of demand in the top graph is 2 while the elasticity of demand in the bottom graph is 0.5. We can see from this example that, following a price increase, revenue fell in the case where the elasticity was greater than 1, and revenue rose when elasticity was less than 1.

Is this always the case? We can illustrate the relationship between elasticity and revenue better by using a simple straight-line demand curve, as shown in Figure 8. Because this is a straight line, the slope is identical at all points on the demand curve—a $1 change in price will change quantity demanded by 2 units.

If you calculate the elasticity of demand at each point along the line, what you will find is that the elasticity of demand is equal to 1 at a price of $5 and a quantity

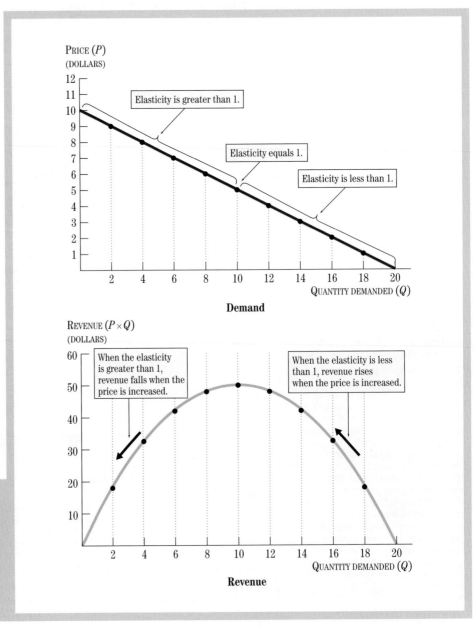

FIGURE 8

Revenue and Elasticity of a Straight-Line Demand Curve

Along the straight-line demand curve at the top, the price elasticity ranges from above 1 (to the left) to below 1 (to the right). When the price elasticity is greater than 1, an increase in the price will reduce revenue, as shown in the lower panel.

demanded of 10. At this point, a $1 change in price (which is equivalent to a 20 percent change in the price) results in a 2-unit change in quantity demanded (which is also equivalent to a 20 percent change in the quantity demanded). To the left of this point, the elasticity of demand is greater than 1. You can see this by considering what happens at a price of $6 and a quantity demanded of 8. A $1 change in price will continue to bring about a 2-unit change in quantity demanded, but the percentage change in price is smaller ($1/$6 = 16.66 percent instead of 20 percent), while the percentage change in quantity is larger (2/8 = 25 percent instead of 20 percent). Thus, the elasticity will now be greater than 1. To the right of this point, the elasticity of demand is less than 1. You can see this by considering what happens at a price of $4 and a quantity demanded of 12. A $1 change in price will continue to bring about a 2-unit change in quantity demanded, but the percentage change in price is larger ($1/$4 = 25 percent instead of 20 percent), while the percentage change in quantity is smaller (2/12 = 16.67 percent instead of 20 percent). Thus, the elasticity will now be less than 1.

For each point along the demand curve, you can calculate revenue by simply multiplying price and quantity. The bottom panel of Figure 8 shows how revenue changes as the quantity demanded changes. Revenue begins at $0 (at a price of $10, quantity demanded is zero), increases for a while as quantity demanded increases, then starts decreasing again, ending up at $0 (because quantity demanded of 20 corresponds to a price of zero). Interestingly, you can see that the range over which revenue is rising with quantity demanded corresponds exactly with the range where the elasticity is greater than 1. Similarly, the range over which revenue is falling corresponds with the region of the demand curve where the elasticity is less than 1. Table 2 summarizes the relationship between revenue and the price elasticity of demand. An increase in price will raise revenue if the elasticity is less than 1 and will lower revenue if the elasticity is greater than 1.

This relationship between the elasticity of demand and the revenue impact of a price change is a very important one. Businesses need to know the price elasticity of demand for their products to understand the implications of raising or lowering prices. For instance, in 2003, United Airlines announced 40 percent cuts in some one-way business fares in the hope of increasing revenue. Would more business travelers decide to fly with lower fares? If so, would the increase in customers lead to an increase or a decrease in United Airlines' revenue? The answer depends on the price elasticity of demand for business air travel. Similarly, the recent increase in the use of wireless phones and prepaid phone cards has resulted in a decrease in the demand for pay phones. In 2001, because of this decrease in demand, SBC Communications Inc. increased the price of a pay phone call. Could this increase in price lead to an increase in revenue? The answer depends on the price elasticity of demand for pay phone calls.

If demand for business air travel is price elastic and demand for pay phones is price inelastic, then both United Airlines and SBC changed prices to increase revenue—United Airlines cut business fares to increase revenue, taking advantage of price-elastic demand, and SBC increased the price of using a pay phone call to increase revenue, taking advantage of price-inelastic demand. How would United or

TABLE 2
Revenue and the Price Elasticity of Demand

Elasticity Is	Effect of a Price Increase on Revenue	Effect of a Price Decrease on Revenue
Less than 1 (< 1)	Revenue increases	Revenue decreases
Equal to 1 (= 1)	No change in revenue	No change in revenue
Greater than 1 (> 1)	Revenue decreases	Revenue increases

TABLE 3 Estimated Price Elasticities of Demand	
Type of Good or Service	Price Elasticity
Jewelry	2.6
Eggs	0.1
Telephone (first line)	0.1
Telephone (second line)	0.4
Foreign travel	1.2
Cigarettes (18–24)	0.6
Cigarettes (25–39)	0.4
Cigarettes (40–older)	0.1
Gasoline (short run)	0.2
Gasoline (long run)	0.7

SBC know whether demand would be elastic or inelastic? The next section discusses the determinants of price elasticity of demand. You should judge as you read this chapter whether demand for business air travel and demand for pay phone calls are likely to be price elastic or price inelastic.

What Determines the Size of the Price Elasticity of Demand?

Table 3 shows price elasticities of demand for several different goods and services. The price elasticity for jewelry, for example, is 2.6. This means that for each percentage increase in the price of jewelry, the quantity demanded will fall by 2.6 percent. Compared with other elasticities, this is large. On the other hand, the price elasticity of eggs is very small. For each percentage increase in the price of eggs, the quantity of eggs demanded falls by only .1 percent.

Why do these elasticities differ in size? Several factors determine a good's elasticity.

■ **The Degree of Substitutability.** A key factor is whether there are good substitutes for the item in question. Can people easily find a substitute when the price goes up? If the answer is yes, then the price elasticity will be high. Foreign travel has a high elasticity because there is a reasonably good substitute: domestic travel.

On the other hand, the low price elasticity for eggs can be explained by the lack of good substitutes. As many fans of eggs know, these items are unique; synthetic eggs are not good substitutes. Hence, the price elasticity of eggs is small. People will continue to buy them even if the price rises a lot.

The degree of substitutability depends in part on whether a good is a necessity or a luxury. There are no good substitutes for a refrigerator if you want to easily preserve food for more than a few hours. However, a fancy refrigerator with an exterior that blends in with the rest of your kitchen is more of a luxury and is likely to have a higher price elasticity.

■ **Big-Ticket versus Little-Ticket Items.** If a good represents a large fraction of people's income, then the price elasticity will be high. If the price of foreign travel doubles, many people will not be able to afford to travel abroad. On the other hand, if the good represents a small fraction of income, the elasticity will be low. For example, if the price of eggs doubles, most people will still be able to afford to buy as many eggs as before the price rise.

■ **Temporary versus Permanent Price Changes.** If a change in price is known to be temporary, the price elasticity of demand will tend to be high because many people can easily shift their purchases either later or earlier. For example, suppose a sewing machine store announces a discount price that will last only one day. Then people will shift their purchase of the sewing machine they were thinking about buying to the sale day.

On the other hand, if the price cut is permanent, the price elasticity will be smaller. People who expect the price decrease to be permanent will not find it advantageous to buy sooner rather than later.

Price Elasticity of Cell Phone Service in the Desert
There's probably not much of a substitute available for long-distance communication in the desert, which would make the price elasticity of the cell phone used here quite low. Do you think the caller in this picture would be equally insensitive to an increase of $.10 per minute in the price of her calls if she were seated in her apartment in Chicago?

■ **Differences in Preferences.** Different groups of consumers may have different levels of elasticity. For example, young cigarette smokers, whose habit of smoking may not be entrenched, are more sensitive to changes in prices than older smokers. Table 3 shows that the price elasticity of demand for cigarettes for young adults between 18 and 24 years old is much higher than the very low price elasticity for people older than 40.

What Is the Price Elasticity of Demand for Star Wars Movies?

For these fans, the prospect of attending the May 2005 opening of *Star Wars: Episode III—Revenge of the Sith* is price inelastic (i.e., they will pay almost anything for a ticket to this opening); but for moviegoers in general, the answer to that question may say a lot about the future of the movie industry. If purchases of movie tickets fall off as the price of a general admission ticket goes up, and at the same time revenue from ticket sales increases, then demand for movie tickets is price inelastic.

■ **Long-Run versus Short-Run Elasticity.** Frequently the price elasticity of demand is low immediately after a price change but then increases after a period of time has passed. In order to analyze these changes, economists distinguish between the *short run* and the *long run*. The short run is simply a period of time before people have made all their adjustments or changed their habits; the long run is a period of time long enough for people to make such adjustments or change their habits.

Many personal adjustments to a change in prices take a long time. For example, when the price of gas increases, people can reduce the quantity demanded in the short run only by driving less and using other forms of transportation more, or by reducing the heating in their homes. This may be inconvenient or impossible. In the long run, however, when it comes time to buy a new car or a new heating system, they can buy a more fuel-efficient one, or one that uses an alternative energy source. Thus, the quantity of gas demanded falls by larger amounts in the long run than in the short run (Table 3).

Habits that are difficult to break also cause differences between short-run and long-run elasticity. Even a large increase in the price of tobacco may have a small effect on the quantity purchased because people cannot break the smoking habit quickly. But after a period of time, the high price of cigarettes may encourage them to break the habit, while discouraging potential new users. Thus, the long-run elasticity for tobacco is higher than the short-run elasticity.

Here are a few examples to test your understanding of the determinants of the price elasticity of demand. The movie industry reported that its summer 2004 revenue was 3 percent higher than the previous year. A closer analysis reveals that ticket sales were down 1 percent. How could ticket revenue increase at the same time that the number of tickets sold decreased? The ticket price must have increased. Demand for movies must also be price inelastic, so that the reduction in ticket sales was more than offset by the increase in the price of the movie tickets. Does this make sense for the movie industry? It is plausible that some people feel that they *must see* the newest release and that the cost of the movie is a little-ticket item for many people who go to the movies. This would make the price elasticity of demand low and demand plausibly price inelastic.

General Motors Corporation reported that in 2002 its revenue rose by 5.4 percent. At the same time, General Motors offered large discounts to customers purchasing cars. How could revenue increase while the price of cars was going down? It must be that more cars were sold at the lower price and that demand for these cars is price elastic. The reduction in price was therefore offset by the increase in cars sold, and revenue increased. Does this make sense for General Motors cars? It is plausible that customers feel there are close substitutes and that this is a big-ticket purchase for many customers. This would make the price elasticity of demand high and demand plausibly price elastic.

Income Elasticity and Cross-Price Elasticity of Demand

Recall that the price elasticity of demand refers to movements along the demand curve. We emphasized in Chapter 3 the difference between a shift in the demand curve and a movement along the demand curve. A *shift* in the demand curve occurs when there is a change in the quantity that people are willing to buy due to a change in anything except the price—for example, a change in income.

The concept of elasticity can be applied to changes in the quantity that consumers are willing to buy caused by changes in income. This elasticity must be distinguished from the price elasticity of demand. The **income elasticity of demand** is

income elasticity of demand: the percentage change in quantity demanded of a good divided by the percentage change in income.

TABLE 4
Estimated Income Elasticities of Demand

Type of Good or Service	Income Elasticity
Food	.58
Clothing/footwear	.88
Transport	1.18
Medical care	1.35
Recreation	1.42

cross-price elasticity of demand: the percentage change in the quantity demanded of one good divided by the percentage change in the price of another good.

the percentage change in the quantity of a good demanded at any given price divided by a percentage change in income. That is,

$$\text{Income elasticity of demand} = \frac{\text{percentage change in quantity demanded}}{\text{percentage change in income}}$$

For example, if incomes rise by 10 percent and, as a result, people purchase 15 percent more health care at a given price, the income elasticity of health care is 1.5. Table 4 lists income elasticities of demand for several different goods and services.

As discussed in Chapter 3, the demand for most goods increases when people's incomes increase. If you have more income, your demand for movies will probably increase at each price. Recall that a normal good is a good or service whose demand increases as income increases. But not every good is a normal good; if the demand for a good declines when income increases, the good is called an inferior good. The income elasticity of demand for an inferior good is negative and is reported as a negative number by economists.

Another type of elasticity relating to shifts in the demand curve is the **cross-price elasticity of demand,** which is defined as the percentage change in the quantity demanded divided by the percentage change in the price of another good. For example, an increase in the price of Rollerblades would *increase* the quantity demanded of bicycles at every price as people shifted away from Rollerblading to bicycle riding. Rollerblades are a substitute for bicycles. A cross-price elasticity can also go in the other direction. An increase in the price of bicycle helmets may *reduce* the demand for bicycles. Bicycle helmets and bicycles are complements. For a complement, the cross-price elasticity of demand is negative.

REVIEW

- The price elasticity of demand, or elasticity, is used to measure how much the quantity demanded changes when the price changes. Elasticity also helps determine how large a price increase will occur as a result of a shift in supply, and by how much revenue will change when the price rises.

- Elasticity is a unit-free measure—it is the ratio of the percentage change in quantity demanded to the percentage change in price. In other words, it measures by what percentage quantity demanded changes when the price changes by 1 percent.

- Horizontal demand curves have infinite price elasticity. Vertical demand curves have zero price elasticity. Most products have a price elasticity between these two extremes. We use the term *elastic demand* to refer to an elasticity of demand that is greater than 1 and *inelastic demand* to refer to an elasticity of demand that is less than 1.

- Other than the horizontal and vertical cases, elasticity is different from the slope of the demand curve, however. A demand curve that is a straight line has a different elasticity of demand at each point.

- The size of the price elasticity of demand depends on the availability of substitutes for the item, whether the item represents a large fraction of income, and whether the price change is temporary or permanent.

- Whereas the price elasticity of demand refers to movements along the demand curve, the income elasticity of demand refers to shifts in the demand curve caused by changes in income. Most goods are normal and have a positive income elasticity of demand. Inferior goods have a negative income elasticity of demand.

- The cross-price elasticity of demand also relates to shifts in the demand curve, in this case, a change in the price of a complement or substitute good.

Economics in Action

Will an Increase in the Minimum Wage Benefit Poor Workers?

When the 110th Congress took office in January 2007, the first bill brought to the floor by the newly elected Democratic majority was an increase in the federal minimum wage from $5.15 to $7.25. The *Washington Post*[1] reported that the plan "could begin the process of ending Congress's longest stretch without a minimum-wage increase since the mandatory minimum was created in 1938. In the past decade, inflation has depleted the value of the minimum wage to the lowest level in more than 50 years." The proponents of the bill argued that a boost in the minimum wage would be an important source of additional income for millions of poor workers (according to the *Washington Post*, almost 6 million workers earning the $5.15 minimum wage and 7 million earning just above that level). Opponents and skeptics argued that the bill would impose too great a burden on employers, would lead to many minimum-wage workers losing their jobs, and would not do as much to help poor people as proponents seemed to claim.

Below, we discuss the policy debate (and provide links to online sources) surrounding the arguments for and against a minimum-wage increase. We also discuss how these arguments relate to the material you have covered, or will cover, in this book.

WHAT IS THE FEDERAL MINIMUM WAGE?

The federal minimum wage is a floor on wages that applies to all "covered non-exempt" workers. In other words, with a few exceptions discussed later, a worker cannot be paid less than the minimum wage—essentially, a floor is placed on the price of labor. If a covered worker resides in a state where the state minimum wage exceeds the federal minimum wage, then the worker has to be paid the higher state minimum. The Department of Labor[2] provides a concise summary of who is a "covered non-exempt worker." Essentially, anyone who works for an enterprise that has more than two employees and does more than $500,000 of business a year is covered. Any individual working in a company that operates interstate is covered, as are domestic workers like nannies and cooks. Exemptions are granted to various categories of workers like farm workers, sailors on non-U.S. registered ships, workers who earn tips (provided tip income + wage income exceeds the minimum wage), teenagers (in the first 90 days of a new job), and workers with disabilities that affect their production.

WHAT ARE THE ARGUMENTS FOR INCREASING THE FEDERAL MINIMUM WAGE?

A nice summary[3] of the arguments in support of an increase in the minimum wage has been provided by the Economic Policy Institute (EPI) a think tank located in Washington, D.C. According to the EPI, an increase in the minimum wage would raise the hourly wage rate of almost 11 percent of the work force, either directly because they earn the minimum wage or indirectly because they earn a wage that is just above the current minimum wage or is tied to the minimum wage. The EPI also argued that the average minimum-wage worker earns more than 50 percent of the family's earnings and that almost 1.5 million single mothers would benefit from the higher minimum wage. The benefits would also accrue more to women, minorities, and working households at the bottom of the income distribution. In addition, because so many years have elapsed since the last minimum-wage increase, even with the benefit of the Earned Income Tax Credit, another program designed to increase the incomes of the working poor, a single parent with two children working 40 hours a week ends up earning below the poverty line. The EPI pointed out that inflation had reduced the real minimum wage—the $5.15 minimum wage that was implemented in 1995 was worth $3.95 in inflation-adjusted terms. Finally, and perhaps most importantly, the EPI argued that there is no evidence of job loss from the last increase in the minimum wage.

To put it simply, the arguments are that the minimum wage has been unchanged for too long, it is now time to increase it to give a boost to the earnings of minimum-wage earners, few workers will lose their jobs because firms will refuse to pay a higher wage, and many minimum-wage workers who will benefit from this increase are extremely dependent on their job to support their families. The EPI also issued a statement of support for increasing the minimum wage signed by 650 leading economists, including five Nobel Prize winners.[4]

WHAT ARE THE ARGUMENTS AGAINST INCREASING THE FEDERAL MINIMUM WAGE?

Not everyone agreed with the arguments made by the proponents of the plan. Opposition in Congress and the Senate-centered around the cost imposed on business

---

[1]"House Passes Increase in Minimum Wage to $7.25," *Washington Post,* January 11, 2007.
[2]http://www.dol.gov/esa/minwage/q-a.htm.

[3]"Minimum Wage, Facts at a Glance," http://www.epi.org/content.cfm/issueguides_minwage_minwage facts.
[4]"Hundreds of Economists Say: Increase the Minimum Wage," http://www.epi.org/content.cfm/minwagestmt2006.

owners who had to pay the salaries. Opponents claimed that the hardships imposed by having to pay $7.25 an hour would force small business owners to lay off workers or even put them out of business. They agreed to be more supportive of the proposal if it was linked with tax relief for business owners to compensate them for the additional costs that were being imposed on them. The general economic arguments against an increase in the minimum wage are nicely summarized by the economist David Neumark.[5] Professor Neumark was not writing about the increase in the federal minimum wage, his focus was on an increase in the minimum wage in the state of Missouri. Nonetheless, the arguments he makes are applicable to this policy as well.

Professor Neumark provides three arguments for why a minimum wage increase may not work the way its proponents intend. First, he points out that in response to a higher price for labor, the quantity demanded of workers (especially low-skilled, low-paid ones) by firms would decrease. In other words, workers making the current minimum wage may lose their jobs and end up earning zero dollars instead of the higher minimum wage. Second, low-income workers losing their jobs would be especially harmful to the poorest families, who depend on these workers' incomes. Third, the higher minimum wage would make it hard for young workers to find jobs, thus denying them the experience and training needed to eventually obtain a higher-paying position. He also points out that many minimum-wage workers are not poor, they are teenagers from relatively well-off families. Hence, he argues, an increase in the minimum wage is not a particularly well-targeted policy in terms of helping the poor.

The Congressional Budget Office (CBO) picked up on this theme of how to best help the poor. The CBO, in a letter dated January 9, 2007, addressed to the outgoing Republican chair of the Senate Finance Committee,[6] pointed out that only 18 percent of minimum-wage workers lived in families who earned an income below the poverty line. Similarly, only 15 percent of the increase in wages would go to families earning below the poverty line. In contrast, the CBO argued, an increase in the Earned Income Tax Credit program, which provides additional income to working poor families through the income tax system, would provide similar amounts of income to poor families for about 20 percent of the cost of the minimum-wage increase.

In essence, the arguments against the minimum-wage increase were that it would lead to job losses, would hurt poor families that were the least able to afford job losses, would benefit mostly workers in families above the poverty line, and was more expensive and less well targeted than other programs designed to boost the incomes of the working poor.

THE KEY ECONOMIC QUESTION

The arguments for and against the minimum-wage increase rest on an economic concept that is familiar to you: the elasticity of demand. If the elasticity of demand for labor is large, then the imposition of a higher minimum wage that increases the price of hiring workers will lead to a substantial decrease in the demand for workers. On the other hand, if the demand for labor is relatively inelastic, then an increase in the price of labor will not lead to much of a decrease in the demand for labor. In essence, you could simplify the argument to say that supporters of the minimum wage increase believed that the demand for labor was not very elastic (more workers would earn a higher wage, and very few would lose their jobs), whereas the skeptics and the opponents believed that the demand was very elastic (many workers would lose their jobs, and only a few would earn the higher wage). How do economists settle disputes like this? Once the theory behind the opposing sides of an argument is understood, the best way to settle the debate is to use data to settle it empirically. In other words, use past experiences with minimum-wage increases, along with the tools of statistical and economic analysis, to estimate the magnitude of the elasticity of demand for minimum-wage labor.

THE EMPIRICAL EVIDENCE

There have been a plethora of empirical studies estimating the impact of a minimum-wage increase on the labor market. Perhaps the work that has had the most impact in recent years is a study by David Card and Alan Krueger,[7] who showed that an increase in the state minimum wage in New Jersey had no impact on the employment of minimum-wage workers in the fast-food industry. Their study surveyed fast-food establishments located along the New Jersey/Pennsylvania border, comparing the response by employers in New Jersey (where wages went up) to the response by employers in Pennsylvania (who did not have to pay higher wages). One interesting explanation for their results was that they found that the price of fast food went up in New Jersey following the change. In other words, employers seemed to be passing on their higher wage costs

[5]David Neumark, "The Economic Effects of Minimum Wages," http://showmeinstitute.org/smi_study_2.pdf
[6]www.cbo.gov/ftpdoc.cfm?index=7721&type=1.

[7]David Card and Alan B. Krueger, "Minimum Wages and Employment: A Case Study of the Fast-Food Industry in New Jersey and Pennsylvania," *American Economic Review*, 84(4), 1994.

to their customers, which in turn would explain why the elasticity of demand was not apparently very high. An earlier, more broad-based study by David Neumark and William Wascher[8] concluded that the elasticity of demand was between −0.1 and −0.2 for teenagers (a 10 percent increase in wages would reduce teenage employment by between 1 and 2 percent).

A more recent paper by the same authors provides a comprehensive survey (more than 150 pages in length) of the empirical literature on the minimum wage.[9] After looking at the evidence for the United States and for other countries, they conclude that recent increases in the minimum wage had indicated an elasticity of demand for teenage labor of between −0.1 and −0.3 and of around −0.1 for workers who made close to the existing minimum wage. They also find generally larger effects on hours (firms are more likely to cut back on the number of hours in response to a higher minimum wage) and more long-term effects (over time, firms are more likely to substitute away from minimum-wage workers to more productive, higher-paid workers or to invest in machines and equipment that do the job that minimum-wage workers do).

---

[8]David Neumark and William Wascher, "Employment Effects of Minimum and Sub-Minimum Wages: Panel Data on State Minimum Wage Laws," *Industrial and Labor Relations Review*, 46(1), 1992.
[9]David Neumark and William Wascher, "Minimum Wages and Employment: A Review of Evidence from the New Minimum Wage Research," *NBER* Working Paper No. 12663, November 2006.

THE DECISION

An increase in the federal minimum wage from $5.15 to $7.25 represents a 40 percent increase in the minimum wage, which, if you go by the estimates above, would reduce teenage employment by between 4 and 12 percent (with higher wages for the remaining 88 to 96 percent of workers) and reduce low-wage employment by between 0 and 4 percent (for the remaining 96 percent of workers). Some questions for you to ponder:

1. If you were in Congress, would you support this increase?

2. Would your answer change if you looked beyond the elasticities and focused on how many minimum-wage workers came from poor households?

3. Is the opportunity cost of implementing a minimum-wage increase, instead of, say, expanding the Earned Income Tax Credit program, worth it?

4. Do you think that legislators who oppose a minimum-wage bill and argue for an expansion of the Earned Income Tax Credit (EITC) program would in fact have supported an EITC program expansion in the absence of the minimum-wage bill?

5. Should Congress continue to have divisive battles over the minimum wage every few years, or should it instead come up with an agreeable number that is automatically indexed to inflation?

ELASTICITY OF SUPPLY

Knowing how sensitive the quantity supplied is to a change in price is just as important as knowing how sensitive the quantity demanded is. The price elasticity of supply measures this sensitivity. "Price elasticity of supply" is sometimes shortened to "supply elasticity" or "elasticity of supply." Supply describes the behavior of firms that produce goods. A high price elasticity of supply means that firms raise their production by a large amount if the price increases. A low price elasticity of supply means that firms raise their production only a little if the price increases.

price elasticity of supply: the percentage change in quantity supplied divided by the percentage change in price.

The **price elasticity of supply** is defined as the percentage change in the quantity supplied divided by the percentage change in the price. That is,

$$\text{Price elasticity of supply} = \frac{\text{percentage change in quantity supplied}}{\text{percentage change in the price}}$$

The price elasticity of supply refers to a particular supply curve, such as the supply curve for gasoline or video games. All other things that affect supply are held constant when we compute the price elasticity of supply. For example, suppose the price elasticity of supply for video games is .5. Then, if the price of video games rises by 10 percent, the quantity of video games supplied will increase by 5 percent (.5 × 10).

Working with Supply Elasticities

All the attractive features of the price elasticity of demand also apply to the price elasticity of supply. To see this, let us first take a look at the definition of the price elasticity of supply using symbols. If we let the symbol e_s be the price elasticity of supply, then it can be written as

$$e_s = \frac{\Delta Q_s}{Q_s} \div \frac{\Delta P}{P} = \frac{\Delta Q_s / Q_s}{\Delta P / P}$$

where Q_s is the quantity supplied and P is the price. In other words, the price elasticity of supply is the percentage change in the quantity supplied divided by the percentage change in price. Observe the similarity of this expression to the analogous expression for the price elasticity of demand on page 93: The only difference is the use of quantity supplied (Q_s) rather than quantity demanded (Q_d). This means that the concepts and terminology for supply elasticity are very similar to those for demand elasticity. For example, if you go to Table 1 and replace "Demand" with "Supply," you have the terminology of price elasticity of supply. Moreover, like the price elasticity of demand, the price elasticity of supply is a unit-free measure, and the elasticity of supply and the slope of the supply curve are not the same thing.

Because of this similarity, our discussion of supply elasticity can be very brief. It is useful to consider the extreme cases of perfectly elastic supply and perfectly inelastic supply, and then to go through an example illustrating the importance of knowing the size of the price elasticity of supply.

Perfectly Inelastic Supply
The paintings of Leonardo da Vinci provide an example of a good with a perfectly inelastic supply. The supply curve is vertical because no matter how high the price, no more *Mona Lisas* can be produced. However, what about the demand to see the *Mona Lisa*? Is it perfectly inelastic? Will raising the price of admission charged by the Louvre Museum in Paris reduce the number of people coming to see the painting?

perfectly elastic supply:
supply for which the price elasticity is infinite, indicating an infinite response of quantity supplied to a change in price and therefore a horizontal supply curve.

perfectly inelastic supply:
supply for which the price elasticity is zero, indicating no response of quantity supplied to a change in price and therefore a vertical supply curve.

■ **Perfectly Elastic and Perfectly Inelastic Supply.**   As in the case of demand, there can be **perfectly elastic supply** or **perfectly inelastic supply,** as shown in Figure 9. The vertical supply curve is perfectly inelastic; it has zero elasticity. Such supply curves are not unusual. For example, there is only one *Mona Lisa.* A higher price cannot bring about a higher quantity supplied, not even one more *Mona Lisa.* But the supply curve for most goods is not vertical. Higher prices will encourage coffee producers to use more fertilizer, hire more workers, and eventually plant more coffee trees. Thus the quantity supplied increases when the price rises.

The horizontal supply curve is perfectly elastic. In this case, the price does not change at all. It is the same regardless of the quantity supplied. It is easier to understand the horizontal supply curve if you view it as an approximation to a supply curve that is *nearly* horizontal, one with a very high elasticity. Then only a small increase in price brings forth a huge increase in the quantity supplied by firms.

■ **Why the Size of the Price Elasticity of Supply Is Important.**   Now let us look at the importance of knowing the size of the supply elasticity even if it is not at one of these two extremes. Figure 10 shows two different supply curves for coffee. The horizontal axis shows the quantity of coffee supplied around the world in billions of pounds; the vertical axis shows the price in dollars per pound of coffee. For the supply curve in the top graph, the quantity supplied is very sensitive to the price; the price elasticity of supply is high. For the supply curve in the bottom graph, the price elasticity of supply is much lower.

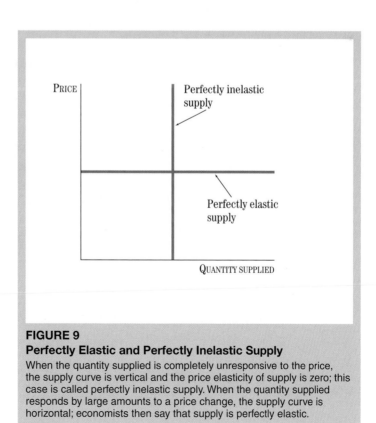

FIGURE 9
Perfectly Elastic and Perfectly Inelastic Supply
When the quantity supplied is completely unresponsive to the price, the supply curve is vertical and the price elasticity of supply is zero; this case is called perfectly inelastic supply. When the quantity supplied responds by large amounts to a price change, the supply curve is horizontal; economists then say that supply is perfectly elastic.

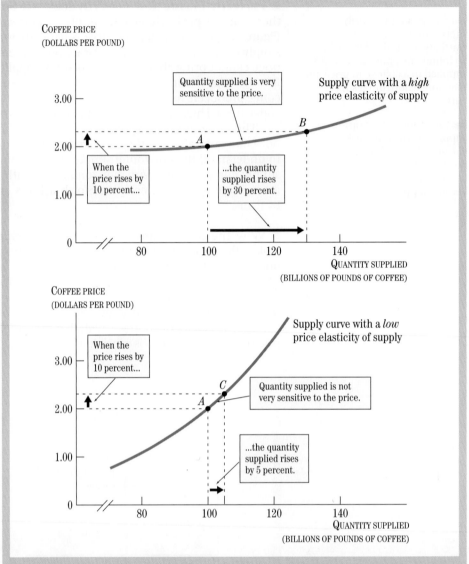

FIGURE 10
Comparing Different Sizes of the Price Elasticities of Supply
In the top graph, the quantity supplied is much more sensitive to price than in the bottom graph. The price elasticity of supply is greater between points *A* and *B* at the top than between points *A* and *C* at the bottom.

The price elasticity of supply is important for finding the response of price to shifts in demand. This is shown in Figure 11, where the demand for coffee declines, perhaps because of concerns about the effect of the caffeine in coffee or because of a decrease in the price of caffeine-free substitutes for coffee. In any case, if the price elasticity of supply is high, as in the top graph, the price does not change as much as when the price elasticity of supply is low, as in the bottom graph. With a high price elasticity, a small change in price is enough to get firms to bring the quantity supplied down to the lower quantity demanded.

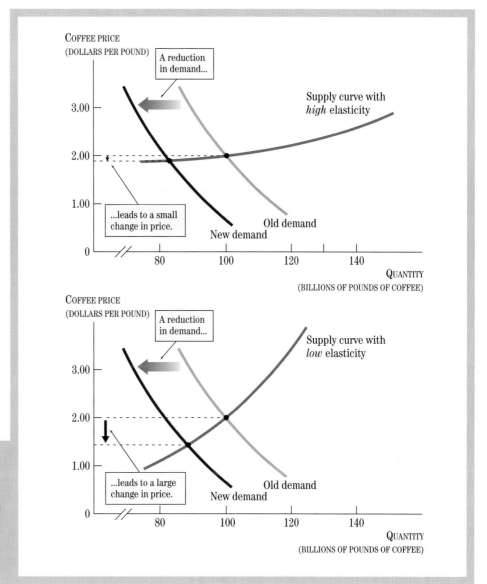

FIGURE 11
Importance of Knowing the Size of the Price Elasticity of Supply
When demand changes, the price will also change. If the price elasticity of supply is high, there will be a small change in price. If the price elasticity of supply is low, there will be a large change in price.

R E V I E W

- The price elasticity of supply is a number that tells us how sensitive the quantity supplied is to the price. It is defined as the percentage change in the quantity supplied divided by the percentage change in the price.

- The attractive features of the price elasticity of demand are also true for the price elasticity of supply. Its size does not depend on the units of measurement of either price or quantity.

- The price elasticity of supply is useful for determining how much prices will change when there is a change in demand.

CONCLUSION

In this chapter, we have extended our analysis of the supply and demand model in two directions. We first learned about what happens when the government intervenes to put a price ceiling or a price floor into the economy. Understanding how to use the supply and demand model with price floors and ceilings enables us to better understand policy debates such as the one surrounding the increase in the minimum wage.

The second extension was to develop an understanding of *how much* the equilibrium price and quantity change in response to changes in supply or demand. The concept of price elasticity of demand helps us understand what happens to the quantity demanded when there is a change in price or when there is a change in the supply of a good. We can also predict whether revenue will increase or decrease when prices are cut or raised. The related concept of the elasticity of supply is also useful in understanding what happens to the quantity supplied when there is a change in price or when there is a change in the demand for a good. We also discussed the concept of an income elasticity of demand, which can help clarify how the quantity demanded for various goods will change as incomes rise, and the cross-price elasticity of demand, which tells us how much the quantity demanded of a good changes as prices for substitute or complementary goods change.

KEY POINTS

1. Governments will occasionally intervene in markets because they think that the equilibrium price is too high or too low. When they act to impose a maximum price on a market, because they think the price that buyers have to pay is too high, they are said to be imposing a price ceiling. When they act to impose a minimum price on a market, because they think the price that sellers are receiving is too low, they are said to be imposing a price floor.

2. Price ceilings cause shortages, with the quantity supplied being less than the quantity demanded. Shortages lead to rationing or black markets. Price floors cause surpluses, with the quantity supplied being greater than the quantity demanded. Surpluses lead to resources being diverted away from other productive activities to deal with the extra output that needs to be stored or disposed of.

3. Rent controls are a classic application of a price ceiling, and minimum wages are a classic application of a price floor. The supply model helps us understand some basic issues related to these policies, which frequently appear in the news today. We will go on to develop the supply and demand model further, which will allow us to do a more

sophisticated analysis of minimum-wage laws, for example, than we have done so far in this chapter.

4. Elasticity is a measure of the sensitivity of one economic variable to another. For example, the price elasticity of demand measures how much the quantity demanded changes when the price changes.

5. Elasticity is a unit-free measure. The price elasticity of demand is the percentage change in the quantity demanded divided by the percentage change in price. It refers to changes in price and quantity demanded along the demand curve, all other things being equal.

6. Demand is said to be elastic if the price elasticity of demand is greater than 1 and inelastic if the price elasticity of demand is less than 1.

7. When the elasticity is greater than 1, an increase in the price reduces the quantity demanded by a percentage greater than the percentage increase in the price, thereby reducing revenue. When the elasticity is less than 1, an increase in the price reduces the quantity demanded by a percentage less than the percentage increase in the price, thereby increasing revenue.

8. The elasticity of demand for a good depends on whether the good has close substitutes, whether its value is a large or a small fraction of total income, and the time period of the change.

9. Whereas the price elasticity of demand refers to movements along the demand curve, the income elasticity of demand refers to shifts in the demand curve caused by changes in income, and the cross-price elasticity of demand refers to shifts in the demand curve caused by changes in the price of other goods. Most goods are normal and have a positive income elasticity of demand. Inferior goods have a negative income elasticity of demand.

10. The price elasticity of supply is defined as the percentage change in the quantity supplied divided by the percentage change in the price. If a good has a high price elasticity of supply, then a change in price will cause a big change in the quantity supplied. Conversely, if a good has a low price elasticity of supply, then a change in price will have only a small impact on the quantity supplied.

KEY TERMS

price control	price elasticity of demand	perfectly elastic demand	price elasticity of supply
price ceiling	unit-free measure	income elasticity of demand	perfectly elastic supply
price floor	elastic demand		perfectly inelastic supply
rent control	inelastic demand	cross-price elasticity of demand	
minimum wage	perfectly inelastic demand		

QUESTIONS FOR REVIEW

1. Why is the price elasticity of demand a unit-free measure of the sensitivity of the quantity demanded to a price change?

2. What factors determine whether the price elasticity of demand is high or low?

3. What is the difference between elastic and inelastic demand?

4. Why is the price elasticity of demand useful for finding the size of the price change that occurs when supply shifts?

5. If the price elasticity of demand for textbooks is 2 and the price of textbooks increases by 10 percent, by how much does the quantity demanded fall?

6. Why is the price elasticity of demand lower in the short run than in the long run?

7. For what values of the price elasticity of demand do increases in the price increase revenue?

8. What is the income elasticity of demand?

9. What is the difference between the price elasticity of demand and the income elasticity of demand?

10. What is the slope of a perfectly elastic supply curve?

PROBLEMS

1. Consider the market for automatic teller machine services in a city. The price is the fee for a cash withdrawal.
   a. Sketch the demand curve and the supply curve for ATM transactions.
   b. How is the equilibrium price determined?
   c. If the town council imposes a ban on ATM fees—equivalent to a price ceiling in this market—what happens to quantity supplied and quantity demanded?
   d. Economists frequently argue against price controls because of the shortages and associated problems that they create. What are some of the potentially negative side effects of interference in the ATM market?

2. In 1991 the price of milk fell 30 percent. Senator Leahy of Vermont, a big milk-producing state, supported a law in the U.S. Congress to put a floor on the price. The floor was $13.09 per hundred pounds of milk. The market price was $11.47.
   a. Draw a supply and demand diagram for milk and show how the equilibrium price and quantity would be determined in the absence of the price floor.
   b. Using the diagram you just drew, explain the effects of the legislation.
   c. The dairy farmers supported the legislation, while consumer groups opposed it. Why?
   d. Economists frequently argue against price floors because of the surpluses and associated problems that they create. What are some of the potentially negative side effects of interference in the milk market?

3. More than twenty states have laws outlawing price gouging during a state of emergency, which might be declared after a hurricane or an earthquake. These laws prohibit price increases on basic necessities, such as gasoline. Which of the arguments against price ceilings might not be very significant during a state of emergency?

4. Donors of organs for transplantation or medical research are prohibited from charging a price for these organs (there is a price ceiling of zero). Will this result in a shortage? How will the market cope with the shortage?

5. Consider the following data for a demand curve:

Price	Quantity
11	10
10	20
9	30
8	40
7	50
6	60
5	70
4	80
3	90

   a. Use the midpoint formula to calculate the elasticity between a price of $10 and $11.
   b. Use the midpoint formula to calculate the elasticity between a price of $3 and $4.
   c. Since this is a linear demand curve, why does the elasticity change?
   d. At what point is price times quantity maximized? What is the elasticity at that point?

6. Consider the following data for a supply curve:

Price	Quantity Supplied
2	10
3	20
4	30
5	40
6	50
7	60
8	70
9	80

   a. Use the midpoint formula to calculate the price elasticity of supply between a price of $7 and $8.
   b. Use the midpoint formula to calculate the price elasticity of supply between a price of $3 and $4.
   c. How does supply elasticity change as you move up the supply curve?
   d. Why does the supply elasticity change even though the slope of the supply curve is unchanged as you move up the supply curve?

7. Given the following income elasticities of demand, would you classify the following goods as normal or inferior goods?
   a. Potatoes: elasticity = 0.5
   b. Pinto beans: elasticity = −0.1
   c. Bottled water: elasticity = 1.1
   d. Video cameras: elasticity = 1.4

8. Calculate the cross-price elasticity for the following goods. Are they substitutes or complements?
   a. The price of movie theater tickets goes up by 10 percent, causing the quantity demanded for video rentals to go up by 4 percent.
   b. The price of computers falls by 20 percent, causing the quantity demanded of software to increase by 15 percent.
   c. The price of apples falls by 5 percent, causing the quantity demanded of pears to fall by 5 percent.
   d. The price of ice cream falls by 6 percent, causing the quantity demanded of frozen yogurt to fall by 1 percent.

9. Food items often have low elasticities of demand. Suppose excellent weather leads to bumper yields of agricultural crops. Why might farmers complain about market conditions?

10. The board of directors of an airline wishes to increase revenue. One group favors cutting airfares, and the other group favors raising airfares. What are the assumptions each group is making about the price elasticity of demand?

11. Compare a market in which supply and demand are very (but not perfectly) inelastic to one in which supply and demand are very (but not perfectly) elastic. Suppose the government decides to impose a price floor $1 above the equilibrium price in each of these markets. Compare, diagrammatically, the surpluses that result. In which market is the surplus larger?

12. In 1992, the federal government placed a tax of 10 percent on goods like luxury automobiles and yachts. The yacht-manufacturing industry had huge declines in orders for yachts and laid off many workers, whereas the reaction in the auto industry was much milder. (The tax on yachts was subsequently removed.) Explain this situation using two supply and demand diagrams. Compare the elasticity of demand for luxury autos with that for yachts based on the experience with the luxury tax.

Principles of Microeconomics

The Demand Curve and the Behavior of Consumers

his is a true story about a college professor who loves to teach introductory economics. The professor is younger than most college professors, but is hard of hearing and wears hearing aids in both ears. The professor teaches one of those large lecture courses, and most students aren't even aware that the professor wears the hearing aids.

In the middle of one of the lectures, the professor simultaneously brings one hand to one ear and the other hand to the other ear and suddenly pulls out both hearing aids, saying, "I can't hear a thing. If it were not for these hearing aids, I wouldn't be here. I couldn't be a teacher. Do you know how much benefit I get from these hearing aids? Certainly more than from my car and maybe even more than from my house. If I had to give you a dollar amount, I would say that the benefit to me is about $60,000. Without the hearing aids, I would probably earn less, and I know my life would not be as enjoyable. Of course, I had to buy these hearing aids, and they are not very cheap. They cost me $500. But, you know, they cost me a lot less than they benefit me. The difference between $60,000 and $500 is $59,500, a huge amount. That difference is a measure of what the hearing aid market delivers to me over and above what I had to pay for the hearing aids. Most people would call that a good deal, but because I am an economics professor, I call it a *consumer surplus*."

In this chapter we show how and why the demand curve for any good—whether hearing aids, MP3 players, grapes, or bananas—can be used to measure the "good deal," or the "consumer surplus," that markets deliver to people.

Figure 1 shows a typical demand curve, with price on the vertical axis and quantity demanded on the horizontal axis. The demand curve is for an entire market, which might consist of millions of consumers. But consumers do not go to the market with a demand curve; they go with certain preferences and objectives. In this

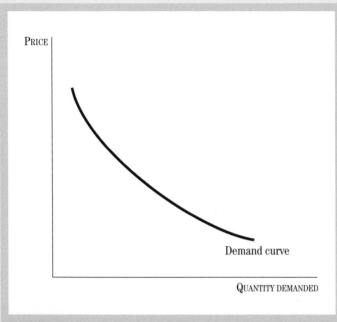

FIGURE 1
A Typical Demand Curve
Demand curves typically slope downward. In this chapter, we examine the behavior of the consumers who underlie the demand curve.

chapter we look under the surface of the demand curve and examine how a consumer's preferences and objectives, combined with the constraints that the consumer faces, determine the demand curve for a particular good for an individual. Then we show how aggregating individual demand curves across millions of consumers generates a demand curve for the entire market for that good.

By the end of this chapter, you should better understand two important concepts. The first is exactly what determines the slope and position of the demand curve—why it slopes downward and why changes in people's preferences or incomes cause it to shift. The second is how to quantify the "good deal," or the consumer surplus, that the market delivers to consumers. Consumer surplus is extremely important for measuring how well a market economy actually works. One of the most important conclusions of the study of economics is that, under certain circumstances, a market economy works better than alternative systems to produce and allocate goods and resources. In order to understand that conclusion—to question it, to criticize it, to prove it, to defend it—we must better understand how much benefit consumers are getting from a market.

UTILITY AND CONSUMER PREFERENCES

Our examination of consumer behavior in this chapter involves constructing a model. The main assumption of the model is that people make purposeful choices with limited resources to increase their satisfaction and better their lives. To make this assumption operational, economists have developed the idea of *utility*, which represents people's preferences for different items (products, jobs, leisure time) among a set of alternatives.

Every person has tastes and preferences for some goods relative to other goods. The millions of people who underlie a typical demand curve do not all have the same tastes and preferences, of course. Some people like Brussels sprouts; some people hate Brussels sprouts. We first focus on how to derive a demand curve for an individual consumer and then show how the behavior of the millions of individuals adds up to generate a market demand curve.

utility: a numerical indicator of a person's preferences in which higher levels of utility indicate a greater preference.

Utility is a numerical indicator of a person's preference for some goods compared to others. If one prefers some activity, such as eating a pizza and drinking two Cokes, to some other activity, such as eating two pizzas and drinking one Coke, then the utility from "one pizza and two Cokes" is greater than the utility from "two pizzas and one Coke." In general, if activity A is preferred to alternative B, then the utility from A is greater than the utility from B.

Be careful not to confuse the economist's definition of utility with the everyday meaning. If you look up *utility* in the dictionary, you will probably see the word *usefulness*, but to an economist, higher *utility* does not mean greater "usefulness"; it simply means that the item is preferred to another item. Watching *Gray's Anatomy* or *Lost* might give you more utility than attending a review session for your economics course, even though it is certainly not as useful for studying for the final.

A Consumer's Utility Depends on the Consumption of Goods

Let us consider an example of utility. Grapes are a product with which we have a lot of experience. They have been around for more than 4,000 years (at least since 2400 B.C. in ancient Egypt), and, in one form or another, they are still consumed around the world. Bananas are another popular fruit, also consumed around the world. Let us use grapes and bananas for our example of utility.

marginal utility: the increase in utility when consumption of a good increases by one unit.

Figure 2 shows an example of the utility that one individual might get from consuming different amounts of grapes and bananas. Remember that every person is different, so the utility shown in Figure 2 is just an example. You might imagine that the person is you, standing in front of a bin of fresh grapes and bananas in a grocery store and deciding what fruit to buy. Or it could be the person in the picture at an open-air market who is deciding how many pounds of grapes and bananas to buy with her money.

Observe how Figure 2 is organized. The number of pounds of grapes is listed vertically on the left outside the box, from 0 up to 5 pounds. The number of pounds of bananas is listed horizontally below the box, from 0 over to 5 pounds. The entries inside the box show the utility from consuming different combinations of grapes and bananas. The box at the intersection of a row and a column shows the utility for the consumption of that specific combination of grapes and bananas. For example, if the individual consumes 2 pounds of grapes and 2 pounds of bananas, then the utility is 27.

Remember that utility is an indicator of people's preferences, with higher utility indicating a stronger preference. As you move up a column or across a row, utility increases. This increase in utility is called **marginal utility.** In general, *marginal utility* is the increase in utility from consuming an additional unit of a good.

For example, consider an individual consuming 2 pounds of grapes and 2 pounds of bananas. For this individual, at that level of consumption, consuming 1 additional pound of grapes (making her consumption 3 pounds of grapes and 2 pounds of bananas) increases utility by 3 (from 27 to 30); the marginal utility of a pound of grapes is 3. Had she instead chosen to consume 1 more pound of bananas (making her consumption 2 pounds of grapes and 3 pounds of bananas), her utility would have increased by 4 (from 27 to 31); the marginal utility of a pound of bananas is 4.

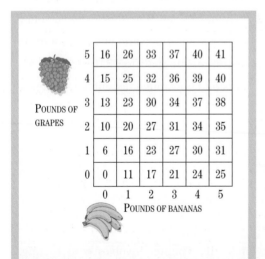

FIGURE 2
Example of Utility from Grapes and Bananas
The numbers inside the box give the utility from consuming the amounts of grapes and the amounts of bananas shown outside the box. For example, utility from 4 pounds of grapes and 3 pounds of bananas is 36. Combinations of grapes and bananas with higher utility are preferred to combinations with lower utility.

"If we buy two at full price, we can buy another six we don't want at half price."

Important Properties of Utility

We can use Figure 2 to illustrate some important assumptions that economists often make about utility.

1. *Utility can be used to rank alternative consumption combinations.* A consumer's utility describes the consumer's preference for one good compared with another. According to Figure 2, the consumer prefers a combination of 4 pounds of grapes and 1 pound of bananas to a combination of 1 pound of grapes and 2 pounds of bananas because the utility of the former (25) is greater than the utility of the latter (23). Other combinations can be ranked similarly. In some cases there are ties; for example, the consumer is *indifferent* as to 2 pounds of grapes and 3 pounds of bananas versus 1 pound of grapes and 5 pounds of bananas because the utility of both is 31.

   Of all possible combinations, the one with the highest (maximum) utility is the one that is preferred to all the others. Thus, by maximizing utility, the consumer is making decisions that lead to the most preferred outcome from her viewpoint. In this way, utility maximization implements the assumption that people make purposeful choices to increase their satisfaction.

2. *Having more of a good never makes an individual worse off.* In Figure 2, as you move across a row or up a column, utility is increasing, which means that marginal utility is a positive value. This implies that this individual would get more utility from 3 pounds of grapes and 2 pounds of bananas (utility = 30) or from 2 pounds of grapes and 3 pounds of bananas (utility = 31) than she would gain from 2 pounds of grapes and 2 pounds of bananas (utility = 27). This seems like a reasonable assumption. On occasion, an individual may derive zero marginal utility from a particular good, although that is not the case in the example in Figure 2. As long as you can freely dispose of goods, adding more of a good should never reduce utility, in other words, marginal utility should never be negative.

   A corollary to this statement is that having more of both goods is always a more preferred option for a consumer, just as having less of both goods is always a less preferred option. For example, consider the choice of 2 pounds of grapes and 2 pounds of bananas for the individual, highlighted in Figure 3. All the bundles that involve the same amount or more of one fruit *and* more of the other (which are the gold-shaded entries to the right and above) are preferred to the combination of 2 pounds each of grapes and bananas. Alternatively, the consumer prefers the 2 pounds of grapes and 2 pounds of bananas combination to all the bundles that involve the same amount or less of one fruit *and* less of the other (which are the blue-shaded entries to the left and below). The consumer would find the remaining combinations (which involve more bananas and fewer grapes or fewer bananas and more grapes) either more preferred or less preferred or would be indifferent between them, depending on what is contained in those combinations.

POUNDS OF GRAPES						
5	16	26	33	37	40	41
4	15	25	32	36	39	40
3	13	23	30	34	37	38
2	10	20	**27**	31	34	35
1	6	16	23	27	30	31
0	0	11	17	21	24	25
	0	1	2	3	4	5
			POUNDS OF BANANAS			

FIGURE 3
Deriving Utility from Grapes and Bananas
Consuming 2 pounds each of grapes and bananas gives a utility level of 27. Combinations that have at least as much of one fruit and more of the other have a higher level of utility (gold-colored region). Combinations that have at least as much of one fruit and less of the other have a lower level of utility (blue-colored region).

diminishing marginal utility:
the tendency for a consumer to derive less additional benefit from adding to the consumption of a good as consumption of that good increases.

3. *Marginal utility decreases as the consumption of a good increases.* If you look at Figure 2, you can see that marginal utility is decreasing as you consume more bananas or more grapes. For example, the marginal utility of a pound of bananas for a consumer who is consuming 2 pounds of bananas and 2 pounds of grapes is 4 (31 − 27 = 4). But the marginal utility of adding 1 more pound of bananas to her new consumption bundle of 3 pounds of bananas and 2 pounds of grapes is only 3 (34 − 31 = 3). Intuitively, what this is showing is that the more an individual is consuming of a good, the less additional benefit she will get from adding to her consumption of that good. This is known as **diminishing marginal utility.**

4. *The units that utility is measured in do not matter.* Utility is a numerical indicator of preferences, but the units used to measure it do not matter. For example, suppose we multiply the utilities from grapes and from bananas in Figure 2 by 10, and then reexamine what utility implies about preferences. Rather than 27 units of utility, we would have 270 units of utility from 2 pounds of grapes and 2 pounds of bananas. Instead of this combination, the consumer would still prefer 3 pounds of grapes and 3 pounds of bananas, which would now have a utility of 340 instead of 30. In fact, you can multiply utility by any positive number—even a billion or a billionth—and still get the same ordering of one combination compared to another.

   The fact that the description of people's preferences does not depend on the units we use to measure utility is very important, because in reality economists have no way to measure utility. That is why Figure 2 does not give units, just a number.

5. *You can't compare utility levels across people.* Because you can multiply the utility of any individual by any number without changing the description of that individual's preferences, the utilities of different people cannot be compared. In other words, we can't say that one person's utility is higher or lower than another person's utility. Only the preferences of a particular person are represented by utility.

REVIEW

- Utility is a numerical indicator of a person's preferences for different goods.

- For each combination of goods, there is a numerical value of utility. Combinations of goods with a higher utility are preferred to combinations of goods with a lower utility.

- The change in utility from consuming one additional unit of a good is known as marginal utility. As long as you can freely dispose of goods, marginal utility will never be negative.

- Marginal utility will typically decrease as the consumption of a good increases—additional units of a good will be more valued when the consumer is not already consuming much of that good.

- The units by which utility is measured do not affect the preference for one combination compared with another.

- Utility levels cannot be compared across people. Utility is an indicator of one individual's preferences.

THE BUDGET CONSTRAINT AND UTILITY MAXIMIZATION

We now know how a consumer's preferences can be described by utility. We also know that the consumer wants to maximize utility—to make a purposeful choice that provides the most satisfaction. Since marginal utility is never negative for a good, you might be wondering how a consumer can ever reach a maximum level of utility. Wouldn't she always want to consume one more unit of a good? Keep in mind that economics is about how people make purposeful choices *using scarce resources*. In other words, the consumer is maximizing utility given some constraints, or limits, on her behavior. Even though she may want one more unit of a good, she may not be able to afford that additional unit. In this section, we will introduce the limits on the consumer's choice and explain how utility maximization works.

The Budget Constraint

budget constraint: an income limitation on a person's expenditure on goods and services.

Consumers are limited in how much they can spend when they choose between grapes and bananas or other goods. For example, suppose the individual choosing between grapes and bananas is limited to spending a total of $8. That is, total spending on grapes plus bananas must be less than or equal to $8. This limit on total spending is called the **budget constraint.** In general, a budget constraint tells us that total expenditures on all goods and services must be less than a certain amount, perhaps the person's income for the year. The budget constraint is what limits the consumer's choices.

Modeling a Consumer's Choice
This consumer, with a limited amount to spend, makes a choice that maximizes her utility. The combination of grapes and bananas that she prefers to other possible combinations of grapes and bananas must have a higher utility for her than the other combinations have.

FIGURE 4
The Budget Constraint and Expenditures at Two Different Prices

The numbers inside the box give the total dollar expenditures on different combinations of grapes and bananas. For example, in the left box, where the price of both bananas and grapes is $1 per pound, the total dollar expenditure would be $7 for 4 pounds of grapes and 3 pounds of bananas. If the price of grapes were $2 per pound and the price of bananas were $1 per pound, as in the right box, that same combination would cost $11. The numbers in the red-shaded area are greater than the $8 budget constraint.

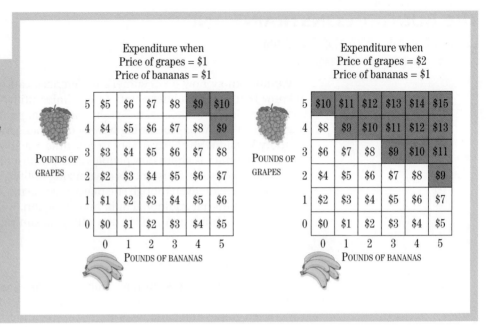

How much a consumer can spend and still remain within the budget constraint depends on the prices of the goods. Suppose the price of a pound of grapes is $1 and the price of a pound of bananas is $1. Her expenditure on a combination of 2 pounds of grapes and 2 pounds of bananas would be $4, well within the budget constraint of $8. But the cost of buying 5 pounds of each would be $10, a sum that exceeds the budget constraint and, therefore, is not possible. So even though 5 pounds of bananas and 5 pounds of grapes have a utility level of 41, compared to a utility level of 27 for the combination of 2 pounds of bananas and 2 pounds of grapes, you will not see the consumer buy that bundle because of her constrained budget.

Figure 4 shows expenditures on grapes and bananas for two different situations. In the box on the left, both the price of bananas and the price of grapes are $1. All the combinations of grapes and bananas from Figure 2 are shown in Figure 4, but several of the combinations are not within the $8 budget constraint; these are in the red-shaded area. What happens if the price of grapes is $2 instead of $1? The resulting expenditure for each combination is listed in the panel on the right. Because the price of grapes has risen from $1 to $2, each bundle is now more expensive than before. As a result, more combinations are outside the budget constraint and fewer are within the budget constraint. In general, a higher price for a good reduces consumption opportunities for the individual.

Maximizing Utility Subject to the Budget Constraint

utility maximization: an assumption that people try to achieve the highest level of utility given their budget constraint.

Given the utility in Figure 2 and the budget constraint in Figure 4, we can now show what happens when the individual maximizes utility subject to the budget constraint. **Utility maximization** means that people choose the highest possible level of utility given their budget constraint. Figure 5 shows the utility combinations from Figure 2, but now we shade in red the combinations for which expenditures are greater than the $8 budget constraint from Figure 4. The budget constraint means that your choices are limited to those combinations that are outside the red area, these are the combinations that do not violate the budget constraint.

FIGURE 5
Maximizing Utility Subject to the Budget Constraint at Two Different Prices

The red-shaded areas represent combinations for which total expenditures would be greater than the $8 budget constraint. The bold number is the maximum level of utility for which spending is less than or equal to $8. In the left box, the maximum utility of 39 represents a choice of 4 pounds of grapes and 4 pounds of bananas. In the right box, with the higher price of grapes, the maximum utility is 34, corresponding to 2 pounds of grapes and 4 pounds of bananas.

Maximum utility subject to budget constraint when Price of grapes = $1 Price of bananas = $1

POUNDS OF GRAPES

	0	1	2	3	4	5
5	16	26	33	37	40	41
4	15	25	32	36	39	40
3	13	23	30	34	37	38
2	10	20	27	31	34	35
1	6	16	23	27	30	31
0	0	11	17	21	24	25

POUNDS OF BANANAS

Maximum utility subject to budget constraint when Price of grapes = $2 Price of bananas = $1

POUNDS OF GRAPES

	0	1	2	3	4	5
5	16	26	33	37	40	41
4	15	25	32	36	39	40
3	13	23	30	34	37	38
2	10	20	27	31	34	35
1	6	16	23	27	30	31
0	0	11	17	21	24	25

POUNDS OF BANANAS

Suppose first that the price of grapes is $1 per pound and the price of bananas is $1 per pound. By looking at the box on the left, you can find the choice that generates the highest level of utility achievable by the consumer with an $8 budget constraint. That combination is 4 pounds of grapes and 4 pounds of bananas (with a utility level of 39). The utility-maximizing choice, and the resulting level of utility, is shown in blue boldface type. This is the most preferred combination that the individual can buy. Even though utility is higher for some combinations that lie in the red-shaded areas, those represent combinations for which total expenditures would be greater than the $8 budget constraint, hence they are not possible choices.

The right-hand box does a similar exercise, but as in the right box of Figure 4, it assumes that the price of grapes is now higher at $2, which increases the number of unaffordable combinations. When there is a price change, individuals will typically end up choosing a different utility-maximizing combination. But the reason for their switch is not because the level of utility for each combination changed; in fact you can clearly see that the utility levels of the different combinations did not change when the price changed. Instead, what changed were the combinations that the consumer could or could not afford. For example, at the new higher price of grapes, the previous utility-maximizing choice of 4 pounds of bananas and 4 pounds of grapes is not affordable; it is in a shaded box. Now the utility-maximizing choice is 4 pounds of bananas and 2 pounds of grapes, corresponding to a utility level of 34.

Deriving the Individual's Demand Curve

We can use the results from the utility maximization to derive the individual's demand curve for grapes. When the price of grapes was $1 (and the price of bananas was also $1), the individual would choose to consume 4 pounds of grapes (and 4 pounds of bananas). Another way of saying this is that at a price of $1 per pound of grapes, the quantity demanded of grapes by this individual would be 4 pounds. But what happened when the price of grapes rose to $2 (with the price of bananas still being $1)? The individual chose to consume only 2 pounds of grapes. At a price of $2, therefore the quantity demanded will now be 2.

Price of Grapes	Quantity of Grapes Demanded by the Consumer
$1	4 pounds
$2	2 pounds

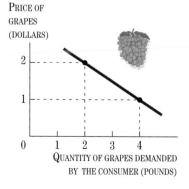

PRICE OF GRAPES (DOLLARS)

QUANTITY OF GRAPES DEMANDED BY THE CONSUMER (POUNDS)

ECONOMICS IN ACTION

Peering Deeper into How Individuals Make Decisions

The basic assumption inherent in the preceding discussion of utility is that people make consumption decisions by first comparing utility levels across different combinations of consumption goods that do not violate the budget constraint, and then choosing the bundle that gives them the highest utility. What economists have not done, until recently, is to try to understand at a deeper level *why* people get a higher level of utility from one activity over another. In essence, the field of economics, which is all about the interactions of human beings who make decisions with scarce resources, has treated the decision-making process itself like a "black box."

The emerging field of neuroeconomics tries to open up this black box. Colin Camerer, a leading economist working in the field, provides a very accessible introduction to the field,[1] which he describes as "[t]he use of data on brain processes to suggest new underpinnings for economic theories, which explain how much people save, why there are strikes, why the stock market fluctuates, the nature of consumer confidence and its effect on the economy, and so forth." The tools that neuroeconomists use are also strikingly different. Instead of the traditional economist's tools of a pencil, a pad of paper, and a computer equipped with various pieces of software, neuroeconomists use brain scanners and neuron-measuring electrodes.

Challenges to the traditional way that economists have modeled the process of decision-making are not new.

Neuroeconomics is simply the most recent manifestation, and the one most rooted in the natural sciences. In 2002, the Nobel Prize in Economics was awarded to Daniel Kahneman of Princeton University and Vernon Smith of George Mason University, pioneers in the field of behavioral economics. Behavioral economics applies tools of psychology to the process of economic decision-making. The contribution of Professors Kahneman and Smith, and others in the field, followed more traditional economists in thinking of individuals as making decisions in the face of constraints to maximize utility, but deviated from traditional economics by also taking into account the fact that people were often making decisions in a world in which emotion, memory, and fear also played a significant role.

In a related paper, Camerer, Loewenstein, and Prelec[2] discuss how brain scans have helped economists understand how people behave in gambling situations. Some individuals are simply unable to generate enough of the chemical dopamine (which is typically released when an individual has had a rewarding experience). These individuals are likely to take far more risky gambles in search of the high rewards that they need in order to feel the same sense of reward that the rest of us get from ordinary activities. They also discuss how economists can understand the behavior of businessmen and entrepreneurs, people who are less afraid of the unknown than ordinary people, by

---

[1]Colin Camerer, "What Is Neuroeconomics?" http://www.hss.caltech.edu/~camerer/web_material/n.html.

[2]Colin F. Camerer, George F. Loewenstein, and Drazen Prelec, "Neuroeconomics: Why Economics Needs Brains," *Scandinavian Journal of Economics*, 106(3), September 2004.

These two points are plotted on the figure in the margin. Notice that what we have derived are two points on a demand curve for the consumer. When the price goes up, the quantity demanded goes down; when the price goes down, the quantity demanded goes up. Thus, we have shown that the assumption that people maximize utility subject to a budget constraint implies that a higher price leads to a reduced quantity demanded. In other words, we have derived two points that lie along a downward-sloping demand curve. Furthermore, we have shown that changes in price lead to a *movement along* a demand curve.

■ **Effect of a Change in Income: A Shift in the Demand Curve.** Now consider the effect of a change in the individual's income on the quantity of grapes that the individual will purchase. Suppose that the individual has only $5 to spend rather than $8; in other words, there is a $3 reduction in the individual's income. What will happen to the quantity of grapes demanded by the consumer? At a price

looking at the activity of a part of the brain called the amygdala, which plays an important role in registering fear.

Other economists applying the tools of neuroeconomics and behavioral economics to better understand economic behavior include Antonio Rangel and Douglas Bernheim, who study addiction. You may not think of addiction as a typical economics problem, but Bernheim and Rangel[3] point out that various types of addiction (alcohol, drugs, tobacco, gambling, pharmaceuticals) carry private and social costs of almost half a trillion dollars a year! Understanding why addictive behavior happens and how best to prevent, treat, or mitigate it can have dramatic economic effects. They model individuals as operating in either a "cold mode," which is similar to our utility-maximizing individual calmly choosing the best feasible option, or a "hot mode," in which decisions are driven not by preferences but by short-term desires to chase pleasure or avoid pain, triggered by the brain. Addictive substances distort these short-term desires, leading the hot mode to overrule the cold mode in the decision-making process. To improve outcomes, policymakers should target people who are trying to stop indulging in the addictive activity and subsidize rehabilitation efforts, such as drug and alcohol rehabilitation programs that are designed to minimize opportunities.

In an article on the field of neuroeconomics, the *Economist* magazine profiled the work of several economists, including David Laibson,[4] who has popularized the idea that individual behavior shows a strong tendency to chase after rewards that are imminent. This theory, known as hyperbolic discounting, can best be summarized by a simple example, as provided in the article in the *Economist*. Offered a choice between $100 now or $115 next week, many individuals will choose the $100 now, even though if they were offered a choice between $100 in one year's time and $115 in one year + one week's time, they would take the latter. Although this theory was initially presented as a behavioral theory, Professor Laibson has used the tools of neuroeconomics to show that the calculation of the short-term option (the today to next week comparison) triggers activity in a different part of the brain from the calculation of the long-term option (the one year to one year plus a week comparison). Hyperbolic discounting has been incorporated into many corporate and government policies, which seek to pass off decision-making to the more calculating part of the brain. For example, the Federal Trade Commission's "cooling-off rule" gives you three days to cancel a purchase of over $25.[5]

The fields of neuroeconomics and behavioral economics are new and important ones, but for now most economists still continue to model decision-making by individuals using the framework we discuss in this chapter. The more you understand about the traditional methods that economists use to model individual preferences and decision-making, the better positioned you will be to come up with richer descriptions that take a look inside the "black box" of the human decision-making process.

[3]B. Douglas Bernheim and Antonio Rangel, "Addiction and Cue-Triggered Decision Processes," *American Economic Review* 94(5), December 2004.
[4]"Can Studying the Human Brain Revolutionise Economics?" *The Economist*, January 13, 2005.
[5]See http://www.ftc.gov/bcp/conline/pubs/buying/cooling.htm.

of $1 per pound of grapes and $1 per pound of bananas (which means that the boxes on the left of Figures 4 and 5 apply), the number of unaffordable combinations has increased, or, equivalently, the number of affordable combinations has shrunk. As an exercise, you should see if you can figure out which combinations need to be shaded because they are no longer affordable, given that expenditure is limited to $5. If expenditures are limited to $5, then the maximum utility occurs when 2 pounds of grapes and 3 pounds of bananas are purchased, resulting in a utility level of 31.

We can also calculate the effects of a similar income change at a different set of prices. If the price is $2 for grapes and $1 for bananas, then the boxes on the right of Figures 4 and 5 apply. (Again, you might want to shade the additional combinations of grapes and bananas that are not feasible with only $5 to spend.) With a limit of $5 to spend, the maximum utility occurs when 1 pound of grapes and 3 pounds of bananas are purchased, resulting in a utility level of 27.

Price of Grapes	Quantity of Grapes Demanded by the Consumer
$1	2 pounds
$2	1 pound

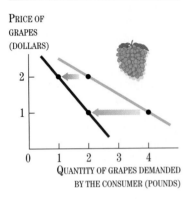

PRICE OF GRAPES (DOLLARS)

QUANTITY OF GRAPES DEMANDED BY THE CONSUMER (POUNDS)

With $8 to spend, the quantity of grapes demanded was 2 (at a price of $2) and 4 (at a price of $1). Now, with only $5 to spend, the quantity of grapes demanded is 1 (when the price is $2) and 2 (when the price is $1). Thus, as shown in the margin, we have derived another demand curve corresponding to the decreased amount of income. Observe that the demand curve with the lower amount of income ($5) is shifted to the left compared with the demand curve with the higher amount of income ($8). Thus, we have shown explicitly that a change in income will *shift* the consumer's demand curve.

■ **Income and Substitution Effects of a Price Change.**   Using the concepts of utility and the budget constraint, economists distinguish between two separate reasons why an increase in the price leads to a decrease in the quantity demanded. When the price of grapes rises from $1 to $2 per pound, there are two ways in which it affects the quantity demanded of grapes.

Manner 1: Certain combinations are no longer within the budget constraint at a grape price of $2 per pound, even though they were within the budget constraint at a grape price of $1 per pound. For instance, a total of 15 options are outside the budget constraint at a grape price of $2 per pound (in the red-shaded area of the right tables of Figures 4 and 5), whereas only 3 are outside the budget constraint at a grape price of $1 per pound (in the red-shaded area of the left tables of Figures 4 and 5). In other words, the purchasing power of the consumer's income is curtailed even though her income was unchanged.

Manner 2: You can now buy 2 pounds of bananas for the same price as a pound of grapes (whereas before you could buy only 1 pound of bananas for the price of a pound of grapes). Because the relative price of grapes has risen, consumers will be more likely to buy bananas than grapes. These are the two ways in which an increase in price affects quantity demanded. The first is known as the income effect, and the second is known as the substitution effect.

income effect: the amount by which the quantity demanded falls because of the decline in real income from a price increase.

The Income Effect of a Change in the Price   The **income effect** is the amount by which quantity demanded falls because of the decline in real income from the price increase. When we say that "real income" has decreased, what we mean is that income measured in terms of what goods we can buy with it has decreased. Another way to think about this is that the rise in the price of grapes reduces the number of affordable combinations; for example, the combinations of grapes and bananas that the consumer can buy have decreased *even though her actual income has not decreased.* The income effect is a general phenomenon that applies to many goods; for example, when the price of gasoline rises, people will spend less on gasoline in part because their real income has declined. With less real income, they will also spend less on most goods and services.

substitution effect: the amount by which quantity demanded falls when the price rises, exclusive of the income effect.

The Substitution Effect of a Change in the Price   An increase in the price of grapes with no change in the price of other goods causes an increase in the relative price of grapes. Because grapes become relatively more expensive, people will switch their purchases away from grapes toward bananas, and would do so even if you were to give them additional income to make up for the income effect. A more technical way to think about this is that at the higher price of $2 per pound of grapes, the opportunity cost of consuming a pound of grapes is 2 pounds of bananas (at $1 per pound), whereas at a price of $1 per pound of grapes, the opportunity cost of consuming a pound of grapes is 1 pound of bananas. Since 2 more pounds of bananas will yield more marginal utility than 1 more pound of bananas, consumers will be more likely to consume less grapes and more bananas *even if you give them additional income to make up for the income effect.* The **substitution effect** is the amount by which the quantity demanded falls when the price rises, exclusive of the income effect.

R E V I E W

- Individuals choose the combination of goods that maximizes utility, but the set of options from which to make that choice is constrained by scarce resources.

- The demand curve for an individual can be derived from the assumption that people maximize utility subject to a budget constraint. Given a certain set of prices for goods and a certain level of income, an individual will choose the combination that gives her the most utility from among the affordable combinations.

- A change in the price of a good changes the number of affordable combinations and thus changes the utility-maximizing quantity demanded. We showed that when the price of grapes rises, the utility-maximizing choice changes to a combination that contains fewer grapes. In other words, a higher price of grapes leads to a lower quantity demanded for grapes, indicating a downward-sloping demand curve.

- A change in income also changes the number of affordable combinations, and thus changes the utility-maximizing quantity demanded. We showed that a reduction in income would reduce the quantity demanded of grapes for any given price of grapes. This represents a shift in of the demand curve. An increase in income would, on the other hand, lead to a shift out of the demand curve.

- The total effect of a change in the price on the quantity demanded can be divided into two parts—an income effect and a substitution effect. The income effect captures the change in demand that is brought about by the change in real income. The substitution effect captures the change in demand that is brought about by the change in relative prices, exclusive of the income effect.

WILLINGNESS TO PAY AND THE DEMAND CURVE

TABLE 1
Willingness to Pay (Benefit) and Marginal Benefit

Quantity of X	Willingness to Pay for X (Benefit from X)	Marginal Benefit from X
0	$0.00	—
1	$5.00	$5.00
2	$8.00	$3.00
3	$9.50	$1.50
4	$10.50	$1.00
5	$11.00	$.50

The connecting lines emphasize how marginal benefit is the change in benefit (or willingness to pay) as one more unit of a good is consumed.

The choice between one good (grapes) and another good (bananas) in the previous section is useful for showing how to derive a demand curve from the basic idea that consumers maximize utility subject to a budget constraint. In this section, we extend the analysis to move beyond the simple choice between one good and another good and consider the choice between one good and all possible other goods.

Measuring Willingness to Pay and Marginal Benefit

Suppose we asked a person who is consuming a zero amount of good X, "How much money would you be willing to pay for one unit of X?" Because the money that the person would pay can be used to buy all goods, not just one good, the question implicitly asks the person to compare X with all other goods. In general, the answer to this question will depend on how much the person's utility would increase with one unit of X and how much the person's utility would decrease because less would be spent on other goods, given the budget constraint. In other words, the answer would depend on the person's preferences for X and all other goods, as represented by utility.

Suppose that the person gives us a truthful answer of $5. Now, we could ask, "How much would you be willing to pay for two units of X?" Suppose the answer is, "I would be willing to pay $8." We could then continue to ask the consumer about more and more units of X. We summarize the hypothetical answers in Table 1. The column labeled "Willingness to Pay for X" tabulates the answers to the question.

marginal benefit: the increase in the benefit from, or the willingness to pay for, one more unit of a good.

Assuming that the answers to the questions are true, willingness to pay measures how much the consumer would *benefit* from different amounts of X. The **marginal benefit** from X is the increase in benefit from one more unit of a good, or the additional willingness to pay. Observe that the marginal benefit in Table 1 diminishes as more is consumed. This implies that as a person consumes more and more of a good, the marginal benefit from additional amounts is likely to diminish.

You can intuitively understand this better if you suppose that X is pizza. Imagine that you are very hungry and there is no food in the house, and you have a craving for pizza. At this point, you might be willing to pay $5.00 for a big, hot slice of pizza. Now suppose that after you have eaten that slice of pizza, you're still a little hungry. You might be willing to pay $3.00 for an additional slice. Now your willingness to pay for a third slice of pizza is going to be even less because you are no longer as hungry and your craving has for the most part been satisfied. So the more slices of pizza you eat, the less you are willing to pay for another slice of pizza.

Graphical Derivation of the Individual Demand Curve

A demand curve can be derived from the information about willingness to pay (benefit) and marginal benefit of X for the person described in Table 1. Suppose that X is chocolate-covered raisins (pizza, ice cream, orange juice, CDs, movies, or any other good will serve just as well as an example). Suppose that the person has $10 to spend on chocolate-covered raisins and other goods. We want to ask how many pounds of chocolate-covered raisins the person would buy at different prices. We imagine different hypothetical prices for chocolate-covered raisins, from astronomical levels like $7 a pound to bargain basement levels like $.50 a pound.

To proceed graphically, we first plot the marginal benefit from Table 1 in Figure 6. Focus first on the black dots in Figure 6; the associated lines will be explained in the

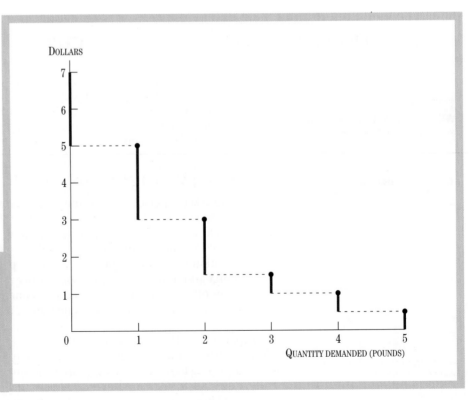

FIGURE 6
Derivation of the Individual Demand Curve

The dots are exactly the same as the marginal benefit in Table 1. At each dot, price equals marginal benefit. The vertical lines indicate how much is demanded at each price if the consumer is restricted to purchasing whole pounds.

next few paragraphs. The horizontal axis in Figure 6 measures the quantity of choco-late-covered raisins. On the vertical axis we want to indicate the price as well as the marginal benefit, so we measure the scale of the vertical axis in dollars. The black dots in Figure 6 represent the marginal benefit that an individual gets from consuming different amounts of chocolate-covered raisins.

How many pounds of chocolate-covered raisins would this person consume at different prices? First, suppose that the price is very high—$7 a pound. We are going to derive a demand curve for this individual by gradually lowering the price from this high value and asking the same question: How many pounds would the person buy at this price? To make things simple at the start, assume that the person buys only whole pounds of chocolate-covered raisins. You might want to imagine that the chocolate-covered raisins come in 1-pound cellophane packages. We consider fractions of pounds later.

Suppose, then, that the price is $7 a pound. The marginal benefit from 1 pound of chocolate-covered raisins is $5. Thus, the price is greater than the marginal benefit. Would the person buy a pound of chocolate-covered raisins at this price? Because the price the person would have to pay is greater than the marginal benefit, *the answer would be no*; the person would not buy a pound of raisins at a price of $7. We have shown, therefore, that the quantity demanded of raisins is *zero* when the price is $7.

Now start to lower the price. As long as the price is more than $5, the person will not buy any chocolate-covered raisins because the most he is willing to pay for that first pound of chocolate-covered raisins is $5. Hence, the quantity demanded at all prices higher than $5 is zero. We indicate this by the red line on the vertical axis above the $5 mark.

When the price drops to $5, the marginal benefit from a pound of chocolate-covered raisins is $5 and the price is $5, so the marginal benefit of the pound of chocolate-covered raisins is sufficient to cover the price. Since the person is willing to pay the $5 to buy 1 pound of chocolate-covered raisins, the person buys 1 pound rather than 0 pounds when the price is $5. This is indicated in Figure 6 by showing that the quantity demanded is given by the black dot at 1 pound when the price equals $5.

Continue lowering the price from $5. Consider, for example, a price of $4. The person has already decided that 1 pound will be bought; the question is whether a second pound of chocolate-covered raisins is worthwhile. Another pound has a marginal benefit of $3 (willingness to pay goes from $5 to $8 as the quantity increases from 1 to 2 pounds). The person has to pay $4, which is more than the marginal benefit. Hence, *the quantity demanded stays at 1 pound when the price is $4*. In fact, the quantity demanded will stay at 1 pound as long as the price remains above the marginal benefit of buying another pound of chocolate-covered raisins, which is $3. However, when the price falls to $3, another pound is purchased. That is, when the price is $3, the quantity demanded is 2 pounds, which is shown graphically by the black dot at 2 pounds.

Now suppose the price falls below $3, perhaps to $2. Is a third pound purchased? The marginal benefit of a third pound is $1.50; is it worth it to buy a third pound at $2 per pound? No. The quantity demanded stays at 2 pounds when the price is between $3 and $1.50, which we denote by extending the red line downward from the black dot at 2 pounds. This story can be continued. As the price continues to fall, more pounds of chocolate-covered raisins are demanded.

By considering various prices from over $5 to under $.50, we have traced out an **individual demand curve** that slopes downward. As the price is lowered, more chocolate-covered raisins are purchased. The demand curve is downward-sloping because of diminishing marginal benefit. At each black dot in the diagram, price equals the marginal benefit.

individual demand curve: a curve showing the relationship between quantity demanded of a good by an individual and the price of the good.

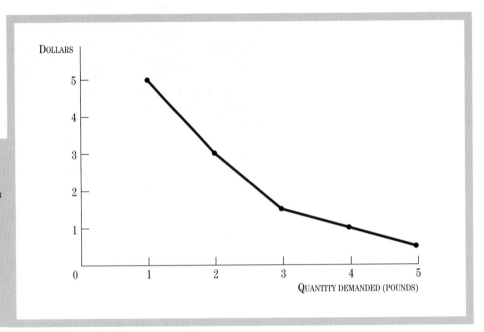

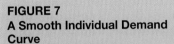

FIGURE 7
A Smooth Individual Demand Curve

If the consumer can buy fractions of a pound and if the marginal benefits of these fractions are between the whole-pound amounts, the demand curve becomes a smooth line, as in the figure, rather than the series of steps in Figure 6. In some cases, such as the demand for cars, we cannot consider fractions, and so these individual demand curves will look like steps.

The jagged shape of the demand curve in Figure 6 may look strange. It is due to the assumption that the consumer can consider only 1-pound packages of chocolate-covered raisins. If it is possible to buy fractions of a pound, and if the marginal benefits of the fractions are between the values for the whole pounds, then the demand curve will be a smooth line, as shown in Figure 7. Then price will equal marginal benefit not only at the black dots but also on the lines connecting the dots. If you are unsure of this, imagine creating a new Table 1 and Figure 6 with *ounces* of raisins. There will be a point at each ounce, and with 16 ounces per pound, there will be so many points that the curve will be as smooth as Figure 7.

The Price Equals Marginal Benefit Rule

We have discovered an important principle of consumer behavior. If the consumer can adjust consumption of a good in small increments—such as fractions of a pound—then the consumer will buy an amount for which the *price equals marginal benefit*. The price equals marginal benefit rule can explain a number of otherwise puzzling observations. For example, consider Adam Smith's diamond-water paradox. As Smith put it, "Nothing is more useful than water: but it will purchase scarce any thing; scarce any thing can be had in exchange for it. A diamond, on the contrary, has scarce any value in use; but a very great quantity of other goods may frequently be had in exchange for it."[6] Why are diamonds expensive and water cheap even though diamonds are less "useful" to the world's population than water?

---

[6]Adam Smith, *Wealth of Nations* (New York: Modern Library Edition, 1994), pp. 31–32.

The price equals marginal benefit rule helps explain the paradox. The price of diamonds will be high if the marginal benefit of diamonds is high. The price of water will be low if the marginal benefit of water is low. As we saw earlier, the marginal benefit of something declines the more people consume of it. Thus, water has relatively low marginal benefit because with water being so plentiful, people consume a lot of it every day. The marginal benefit is low even though the total benefit from water consumption in the world is very high. On the other hand, diamonds have a high marginal benefit because with diamonds being so scarce, people consume relatively little of them. The marginal benefit of diamonds is high even though the total benefit of diamonds may be low. Thus, the price equals marginal benefit rule explains the diamond-water paradox.

REVIEW

- People's preferences are reflected in their willingness to pay for different amounts of a good. Because dollars can be used to buy any good, willingness to pay compares one good with all other goods.

- The marginal benefit from a good is the increase in the benefit from, or the additional willingness to pay for, one more unit of a good.

- The marginal benefit that an individual derives from a good will typically decline as the individual increases consumption of that good.

- An individual demand curve can be traced out by changing the price of a good and looking at how many units consumers are willing to buy at each price.

- When the price of a good exceeds the marginal benefit of the first unit of a good, consumers will not demand any of that good. As the price falls, consumers will demand more and more units of the good as the price of each additional unit becomes equal to the marginal benefit of that unit.

- Hence, the diminishing marginal benefits from consuming more of a good results in a individual demand curve that slopes down.

- If the good is divisible into fractional quantities, the demand curve will become a smooth line instead of a series of discrete steps.

THE MARKET DEMAND CURVE

market demand curve: the horizontal summation of all the individual demand curves for a good; also simply called the demand curve.

Thus far, we have graphically derived the demand curve for an individual. Now we consider the **market demand curve,** which is the sum of the individual demand curves. Figure 8 shows how we do the summing up. The figure shows the demand curves for chocolate-covered raisins for two individuals, Jack and Diane. To get the market demand curve, add up, for each given price, the total amount demanded by both Jack and Diane. For example, at a price of $5, Jack's demand is 1 pound and Diane's demand is 1 pound. The market demand is then 2 pounds. When the price is $3 a pound, the demand is 2 pounds for Jack and 2 pounds for Diane, or 4 pounds for the market as a whole. Obviously, the market for chocolate-covered raisins consists of more than just Jack and Diane. To get the whole market, you would have to sum up the demands for millions of people.

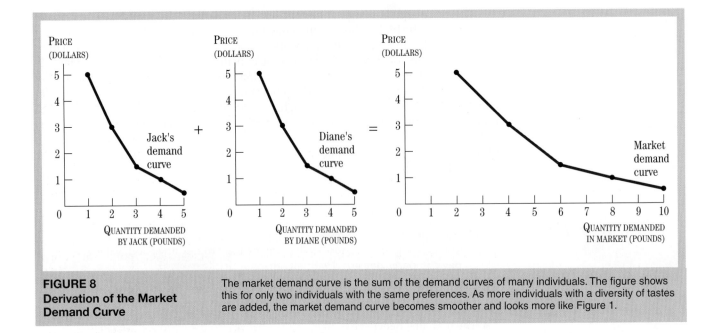

FIGURE 8
Derivation of the Market Demand Curve

The market demand curve is the sum of the demand curves of many individuals. The figure shows this for only two individuals with the same preferences. As more individuals with a diversity of tastes are added, the market demand curve becomes smoother and looks more like Figure 1.

Different Types of Individuals

In Figure 8, Jack's and Diane's demand curves are the same. They do not have to be. In fact, it is most likely that Jack and Diane have different preferences. Jack could be a health-food fan and be willing to pay less for chocolate-covered raisins than Diane would. It is incorrect to assume that everyone will be willing to pay the same amount for any good. There are all kinds of people in the world with different preferences. But you can still add up the demands of all these people at any given price to get the market demand curve. As you add up many individual demand curves for different types of people, the market demand curve gets smoother, even when the product cannot be bought in fractions of a unit. For example, the market demand curve for cars is smooth even though most individuals buy either zero, one, or perhaps two cars. When you add the demand curves for millions of people, the market demand curve for cars looks like the market demand curve (Figure 1) that we typically draw—smooth and downward-sloping. To confirm your understanding of the market demand curve, make sure you work through the problems at the end of the chapter.

REVIEW

- The market demand curve is derived from individual demand curves. At each price, we add up how much is demanded by all individuals; the total is the market demand at that price.

- Even if the individual demand curves are not smooth, the market demand curve will be smooth because people have different tastes and preferences and prefer different benefits.

CONSUMER SURPLUS

consumer surplus: the difference between what a person is willing to pay for an additional unit of a good—the marginal benefit—and the market price of the good; for the market as a whole, it is the sum of all the individual consumer surpluses, or the area below the market demand curve and above the market price.

In many cases, people are willing to pay more for an item consumed than they have to pay for it. For example, you might be willing to pay $40 to see your favorite movie star appear in a new blockbuster movie. But like everyone else in line at the movie theater, you pay only $10, even though it is worth $40 to you. In general, **consumer surplus** is the difference between the willingness to pay for an additional item (say, $40 to see the movie)—its marginal benefit—and the price paid for it ($10 to buy a ticket that let you see the movie). Consumer surplus is $30. The college professor who was willing to pay $60,000 for a $500 hearing aid that enabled him to lecture to a large audience of students would derive a consumer surplus of $59,500 from the hearing aid. If the hearing aid cost $5,000 instead, he would still derive $55,000 in consumer surplus.

A graphical derivation of how to find consumer surplus is shown in Figure 9, which shows the individual demand curve for chocolate-covered raisins that we derived in Figure 6. At a price of $2, the consumer will demand 2 pounds of chocolate-covered raisins. The first pound produced a marginal benefit of $5 and cost $2 to buy, thus the consumer surplus associated with the first pound would be $3. The second pound has a marginal benefit of $3 and cost $2 to buy, so the consumer surplus associated with the second pound would be $1. Overall consumer surplus is $3 + $1 = $4. Consumer surplus can therefore be defined as the sum of the differences between the marginal benefit of each unit and the price paid for the item. Graphically, consumer surplus is the area between the demand curve and the line indicating the price. In Figure 9, the total shaded area is equal to 4, consisting of two rectangular blocks, one with an area of 3 and the other with an area of 1. The area is the extra amount that the consumer is getting because the market price is lower than what the consumer is willing to pay.

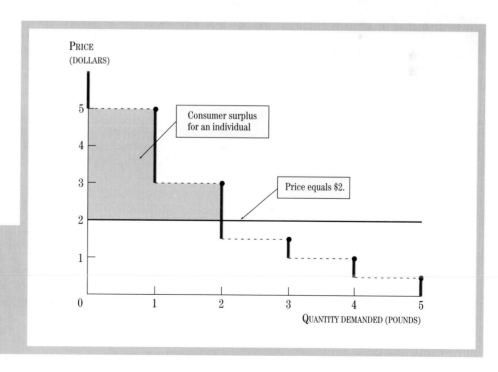

FIGURE 9
Consumer Surplus for an Individual

The consumer surplus is the difference between the marginal benefit that a person gets from consuming a good and the price. It is given by the area between the demand curve and the price.

This article shows how there is a high willingness to pay for certain goods and services even in very poor countries. Entrepreneurs and investors who provide goods that have a high degree as associated consumer surplus can improve the lives of many consumers while making money for themselves.

Power to the People

March 9, 2006—The Economist print edition

Illustrates the consumer surplus associated with a telephone call

Iqbal Quadir pioneered wider access to mobile phones in Bangladesh. Can he do the same for electricity and clean water?

AS A young boy in rural Bangladesh in 1971, Iqbal Quadir walked ten miles to collect some medicine for a sibling who was unwell. But when he arrived at his destination, the medicine man was not there, so he had to walk home empty-handed, having wasted an entire day. Many years later, having moved to America and become an investment banker, Mr. Quadir was reminded of this episode when the network at his New York office stopped working. Without communications, he realised, people are far less productive, whether in a modern office or a rural village; a simple telephone call could have prevented him from making that unnecessary round trip all those years earlier. As he waited for the e-mail to start flowing again, Mr. Quadir was seized by the idea that "a telephone is a weapon against poverty." He decided to dedicate himself to making telephones more widely available to the poor in his homeland. "I didn't know anything about telecoms," he says. "But maybe that was helpful."

It was only after having many fruitless meetings with firms and policymakers that Mr. Quadir finally hit upon the right approach. He was inspired by Grameen Bank, a Bangladeshi organisation well known for supplying "microcredit," or small loans, mainly to the rural poor. In a typical example, a woman borrows enough money to buy a cow, and then repays the loan using the profits that result from selling its milk. The loan is repaid, the woman earns an income from the cow, and her neighbours can buy milk. Mr. Quadir looked at this model and realised that "a cell phone could be a cow." He formed a consortium with Grameen Bank and Telenor, a Norwegian mobile operator that provided the required telecoms expertise. He was then able to secure loans from development banks and aid agencies, and won a licence from the Bangladeshi government. GrameenPhone launched its service in March 1997, and today has more than 6m subscribers, making it the country's largest telecoms operator. Bangladesh now has six mobile operators and more than 9m subscribers in what has become a booming market.

As consumers derive a high marginal benefit from cell phone access, enterprising firms can take advantage of the opportunity to serve this market.

Around 200,000 of GrameenPhone's subscribers are "telephone ladies" who provide access to telephony in more than 50,000 rural villages, with a total population of 80m people. Despite accounting for a small proportion of the mobile phones in circulation, these "village phones" account for one-third of the traffic on the network, since they are shared between a large number of users. By making telephony widely available, says Mr. Quadir, GrameenPhone has increased the country's GDP by a far greater amount than repeated infusions of foreign aid. Mobile phones promote economic activity, prevent wasted journeys, make it easier to look for work, and widen access to markets. GrameenPhone is not a charity, but a profitable venture: it made net profits of $101m in 2004. Its approach is now being replicated in other countries in Asia and sub-Saharan Africa, including Uganda and Rwanda.

GrameenPhone's success is a striking endorsement of Mr. Quadir's unusual approach to promoting economic development. The problem with the traditional top-down approach of supplying developmental aid to governments, he complains, is that it widens the gap between politicians and the people, by increasing the power of central authorities. "The key to economic progress in Bangladesh does not lie in foreign aid, but in the hands and brains of its masses," he says. "We need to find technologies that can activate those hands and brains for productive purposes." Using technology to empower citizens from below, as mobile phones do, is a far better way to promote development, says Mr. Quadir: "Top-down approaches do not work. The bottleneck is at the top of the bottle."

There are historical precedents for this bottom-up approach, notes Mr. Quadir, who lectured in technology and economic development at Harvard University's Kennedy School of Government for four years from 2001 and has recently moved to the Massachusetts Institute of Technology, where he is establishing a new programme in development entrepreneurship. In medieval Europe, innovations such as spectacles, water wheels, clocks and printing had the effect of empowering people from below and stimulating economic development, often in the face of opposition from church and state. Similarly, the industrial revolution was the result of entrepreneurial, bottom-up activity, not government planning. Having proven the effectiveness of his approach with GrameenPhone, Mr. Quadir is now working to apply the same combination of technology and bottom-up entrepreneurship in other areas, starting with the supply of electricity. "I see myself as an entrepreneur between the geek and the meek," he says.

Other examples of goods that have a high degree of consumer surplus associated with them

The aim of his new venture, Emergence Energy, is to establish small, neighbourhood power plants in Bangladesh that can provide electricity to a handful of homes, shops and businesses. This time he has teamed up with Dean Kamen, an American inventor best known for creating the Segway electric scooter. During 2005 they conducted a six-month trial in two rural villages in Bangladesh of prototype generators, created by Mr. Kamen, based on a design called a Stirling engine.

The generators can be powered by biogas extracted from cow manure. The idea is that one entrepreneur, funded by a microcredit loan, sets up a business to turn manure into methane gas and fertiliser; another entrepreneur, also funded by microcredit, buys the methane to power the generator, and sells the resulting electricity. This will, Mr. Quadir hopes, unleash all kinds of economic activity. "Energy gives you the power to empower," he says.

The trial was intended as a test, to find out what people would use electricity for, and whether there was an economically viable business model. The results were promising: the scheme proved to be technically feasible, there was strong demand for electrical power, and consumers were willing to pay for a regular supply. The main use of electricity was for lighting, says Mr. Quadir; using low-power bulbs, each generator, which produces one kilowatt of power, was able to light up 20 households or shops.

Electricity is another good with high consumer surplus, especially in rural villages where there is no electricity. The marginal benefit of that first kilowatt of power is very high.

This allowed shops to stay open later, enabled students to study for longer hours, and let people enjoy television and other forms of entertainment. Surprisingly, Mr. Quadir found that some households already had televisions, powered using car batteries. Such batteries are also used to recharge mobile phones. This suggests that the potential "chicken and egg" problem that there would be no demand for electricity, since nobody owns any electrical appliances, will not arise. Access to a regular supply of electricity should, however, promote the wider adoption of electrical devices of all kinds.

The next step is to mass produce the generators so that the scheme can be launched commercially. Mr. Quadir says he hopes to convince a manufacturing company to license Mr. Kamen's design and set up a factory in Bangladesh to build the generators. This would have several advantages over simply importing the technology (as happened with the mobile phones): it would create jobs, avoid import tariffs that would otherwise make the generators less affordable, and the resulting transfer of technology and skills would ensure that the machines could be fixed by locals, rather than having to rely on foreign technicians.

To finance the purchase of the generators by entrepreneurs, Mr. Quadir is working with BRAC, another microcredit lender. The generators will cost several thousand dollars, far more than a mobile phone. But microloans are already being used to finance larger purchases, such as houses, says Mr. Quadir, so he is confident that the microcredit model can be applied to the new venture. The result, as entrepreneurs start to install generators in villages, will be to produce electricity, fertiliser and jobs.

ECONOMICS IN ACTION

Building Roads and Bridges with Consumer Surplus

You may be surprised to learn that the concept of consumer surplus was not invented by an economist but by an engineer. Jules Dupuit was a civil engineer living in France in the mid-1800s. He wanted to demonstrate that the value of the roads and bridges he was building was much more than what people were willing to pay to use them. Consumer surplus was his idea of a demonstration. If a person paid a toll to cross a bridge, then the price of the toll could be as much of an underestimate of the benefit as the price of hearing aids is to the professor of economics in the introduction to this chapter. Thus, his consumer surplus argument helped persuade people to build more bridges and roads.

Dupuit offered a visual description of consumer surplus: "If society is paying 500 million for the services rendered by the road, that only proves one thing—that [the benefit from the road] is at least 500 million. But it may be a hundred times or a thousand times greater. . . . If you take the [500 million] as the figure . . . you are acting like a man who, wishing to measure the height of a wall in the dark and finding that he cannot reach the top with this raised arm says: 'This wall is two meters high, for if it were not, my hand would reach above it.' In daylight and equipped with a ladder . . . our alleged two-meter wall is fifty meters high."*

Do you think Dupuit's walls are a good analogy? In Dupuit's vision, how many "meters high" is consumer surplus?

---

*English translation of Jules Dupuit, "De la Mesure de l'Utilité des Travaux Publics," translated and reprinted in K. J. Arrow and T. Skitovsky, eds., *Readings in Welfare Economics* (Homewood, Ill.: Irwin, 1969).

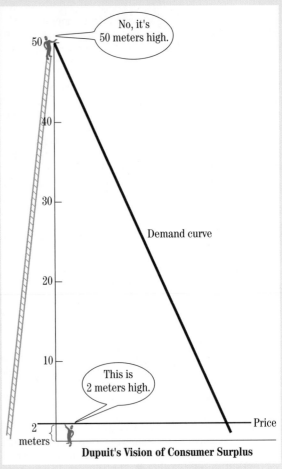

Dupuit's Vision of Consumer Surplus

Consumer surplus for the entire market is the sum of the consumer surpluses of all individuals who have purchased goods in the market. In Figure 10, consumer surplus is the area between the market demand curve and the market price line.

Consumer surplus has many uses in economics. It is a measure of how well off consumers are (because it measures how much they were willing to pay above and beyond the price to acquire the good), and thus it is an important component used to gauge how well the market system works. Consumer surplus can also be used to measure the gains to consumers from an innovation. For example, if a new production technique or a policy change lowers the price of a good and increases the quantity demanded, consumer surplus for the market will increase. Those who had a high willingness to pay will now derive even more consumer surplus as a result of the lower price, and those who had a marginal benefit that was less than the old price will now be demanding more of the good as well. In short, when the market price of a good falls, the area between the demand curve and the market price line increases. This increase is a measure of how much the new technique or the policy change is worth to society.

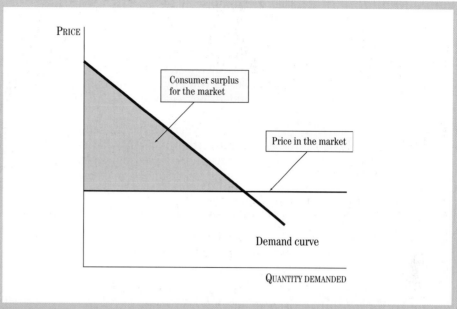

FIGURE 10
Consumer Surplus for the Market
The sum of the consumer surplus for all individuals in the market is the area between the demand curve and the price.

R E V I E W

■ Consumer surplus is the area between the individual demand curve and the market price line. It is a measure of how much the consumer gains from buying goods in the market.

■ The consumer surplus for the market is the sum of the individual consumer surpluses. It can be calculated as the area between the market demand curve and the market price line. It is a measure of how much all the consumers in the economy gain from buying goods in the market.

■ Consumer surplus is an important tool for measuring the performance of an economic system. Changes in consumer surplus can be used to measure the beneficial impact of a technology change or a policy change that changes the market price of a good.

CONCLUSION

This chapter is the first of three that looks at the individual behavior that underlies the economist's demand and supply curves. This chapter focused on consumers, Chapter 6 looks at firms, and Chapter 7 looks at the interaction of consumers and firms in markets. The payoffs in terms of understanding how and how well markets work will not be fully realized until we have completed all three chapters, but we have already derived a number of useful results.

We showed that the idea that people make purposeful choices with limited resources can be made operational with utility. In a two-good setting, we showed that utility maximization can be used to derive an individual demand curve that is downward-sloping, and that individual demand curves can be aggregated to obtain a market demand curve.

In a more general setting, we showed how to derive an individual demand curve from the idea that consumers would buy an additional unit of a good only when the marginal benefit was not less than the price of the good. Because marginal benefit declines as you buy more units of a good, a lower price leads to a higher quantity demanded. Aggregating the individual demand curves would generate a market demand curve.

Finally, we derived the concept of consumer surplus for an individual, the difference between the individual's marginal benefit and the market price. Adding up individual consumer surplus generates the consumer surplus for the entire market, an important measure of how much gain people receive from the market.

KEY POINTS

1. The idea of utility maximization subject to a budget constraint implements the assumption that people make purposeful choices with limited resources.

2. Utility indicates the preferences people have for one activity compared with other activities. The units used to measure utility do not matter, and the utility level of one person can't be compared with the utility level of another person.

3. Economists assume—at least as an approximation—that people maximize their utility subject to a budget constraint that limits how much they can spend. This implies that they choose the feasible combination of goods that delivers the most utility.

4. An individual's demand curve can be derived from utility maximization subject to a budget constraint. Utility maximization implies that a higher price reduces the quantity demanded.

5. A higher price can reduce the quantity demanded in two ways: by reducing the purchasing power of an individual's income (income effect), and by making the relative price of that good more expensive (the substitution effect).

6. In general, the demand curve for an individual can be derived by applying the principle that the individual will demand to buy the number of units for which marginal benefit is equal to price.

7. Market demand curves are derived by adding up the quantity demanded by all individuals at each price.

8. An individual's consumer surplus is the sum of the differences between the marginal benefit the individual receives from each unit and the market price of that unit.

9. An individual's consumer surplus can be calculated as the area between the individual's demand curve and the market price line. Consumer surplus for an individual is a measure of how much benefit an individual gains from buying a product.

10. Overall consumer surplus is the sum of consumer surplus across individuals. It can be calculated as the area between the market demand curve and the market price line. Consumer surplus for a market is a measure of how much all consumers in that market gain from buying a product.

KEY TERMS

utility
marginal utility
diminishing marginal
   utility

budget constraint
utility maximization
income effect

substitution effect
marginal benefit
individual demand curve

market demand curve
consumer surplus

QUESTIONS FOR REVIEW

1. What is the relationship between utility and preferences?

2. Why don't the units by which utility is measured matter?

3. Why are economists typically interested in utility maximization subject to constraints?

4. Why does an increase in the price of a good typically reduce the quantity demanded by a utility-maximizing consumer?

5. Why does a reduction in income typically lead to a reduction in the quantity demanded at each price?

6. Why are market demand curves usually smoother than individual demand curves?

7. What is the relationship between willingness to pay and marginal benefit?

8. Why does marginal benefit decrease as the number of units consumed of a good increases?

9. What does an individual's "consumer surplus" measure? How can you find what the individual's consumer surplus is from the demand curve?

10. What is the relationship between individual consumer surplus and consumer surplus for the market? How can you find what the consumer surplus for the market is from the demand curve?

PROBLEMS

1. Using the example of utility in Figure 2, find the quantity of each good the consumer will purchase in the cases shown in the table below.

Case	Budget	Price of Grapes	Price of Bananas
A	$7	$1	$1
B	$6	$2	$1
C	$8	$1	$2

2. Analyze the following data for Mara's utility from consumption of books and coffee.

4	50	75	81	83	84
3	46	70	76	78	79
QUANTITY 2 OF BOOKS	40	60	66	68	69
1	30	40	46	48	49
0	0	10	16	18	19
	0	1	2	3	4

QUANTITY OF COFFEE

a. Determine how much of each good Mara will consume if she has $20 and if the price of books is $10 and the price of coffee is $3.

b. Suppose the price of coffee goes up to $5. How much coffee will Mara consume now? Why does the amount change?

c. Multiply the utility received from books and coffee by 10. Will your answers to parts (a) and (b) change? Explain.

3. Which of the following statements are true? The income effect of a reduction in the price of gasoline refers to
   a. the reduction of income incurred by gas stations.
   b. the increase in the demand for other products as gasoline buyers experience increased real incomes.
   c. the increase in the quantity demanded of gasoline as gasoline buyers experience increased real incomes.
   d. the increase in the quantity demanded of gasoline as gasoline buyers experience increased nominal incomes.

4. Which of the following statements are true? The substitution effect of a decrease in the price of beef, with no changes in the prices of other goods, refers to
   a. the decrease in the quantity demanded of beef and the increase in the quantity demanded of substitutes such as chicken.
   b. the increase in the quantity demanded of beef and the decrease in the quantity demanded of substitutes such as chicken.
   c. the increase in the quantity demanded of beef and the increase in the quantity demanded of substitutes such as chicken.
   d. the decrease in the quantity demanded of beef and the decrease in the quantity demand for substitutes such as chicken.

5. Consider the example of willingness to pay for X (chocolate-covered raisins) in Table 1. Assume that the price is $.75 and that the person has $10 to spend.
   a. Compute what it costs to pay for different amounts of chocolate-covered raisins from 0 to 5 pounds.

b. For each of the above amounts, calculate how much is left over from the $10 the person started out with.

c. Using the information from Table 1 and your answers above, calculate the sum of the benefit plus the dollars left over for different amounts of chocolate-covered raisins from 0 to 5 pounds.

d. How many pounds of raisins will maximize the sum of the benefit plus the dollars left over? How does the answer compare to that using the price equals marginal benefit condition?

6. Individuals receive diminishing marginal benefits from consuming more of a particular good. Do you think this means that individuals receive diminishing marginal benefits from each extra dollar that they earn? Explain your answer.

7. The following table shows Carl's willingness to pay for clothing.

Quantity of Clothing	Willingness to Pay
1	$35
2	$60
3	$80
4	$97
5	$112
6	$126

a. Calculate Carl's marginal benefit from clothing.

b. Draw Carl's individual demand curve for clothing.

c. Suppose the price of one item of clothing is $17. How much would Carl consume, and what is his consumer surplus? Show your answer graphically as well as numerically.

8. Suppose that the willingness to pay for hearing aids by the economics professor mentioned in the introduction to this chapter was $60,000 for one pair, $60,400 for two pairs, $60,600 for three pairs, and $60,700 for four pairs.

a. Draw the professor's demand curve for hearing aids.

b. If the price of a pair of hearing aids is $500, how many pairs would the professor buy?

c. Now suppose that a technological breakthrough reduces the price of hearing aids to $150 a pair. How many pairs would the professor buy now?

9. The following table shows Margaret's and Dennis's willingness to pay for cookies.

Quantity of Cookies	Margaret	Dennis
1	$7	$15
2	$13	$25
3	$18	$34
4	$21	$42
5	$23	$45

a. Calculate the marginal benefits for both people.

b. Derive Margaret's and Dennis's individual demand curves for cookies. Derive the market demand curve if only Margaret and Dennis are in the market.

c. Suppose that the price of cookies is $4.50. How many cookies will Margaret and Dennis buy? Calculate their consumer surplus. Draw a diagram to show the area representing consumer surplus.

d. Use a diagram to show the consumer surplus for the whole market using the market demand curve.

10. Economics professors like to ask their students about the diamond-water paradox: Why is it that a good that is as essential to human existence as water costs so much less than a good like a diamond that is far less useful? Show that if we use consumer surplus, rather than price, as our measure of how "valuable" a good is to human existence, then there is no paradox—water is valued much more highly than diamonds are.

Consumer Theory with Indifference Curves

Chapter 5 derives the demand curve from the assumption that consumers maximize utility subject to a budget constraint. Here we give a graphical illustration of that derivation.

Consider a single consumer deciding how much of two items to buy. Let one of the items be X and the other be Y. We first show that the consumer's budget constraint can be represented by a budget line, and then we show that the consumer's preferences can be represented by indifference curves.

The Budget Line

Suppose that the consumer has $20 to spend on X and Y, and suppose that the price of X is $2 per unit and the price of Y is $4 per unit. How much of X and Y can the consumer buy? If the consumer spends all $20 on Y, then 5 units of Y and no units of X are consumed. If the consumer buys 4 units of Y at $4 per unit, then $16 will be spent on Y and the remaining $4 can be spent buying 2 units of X. These and several other amounts of X and Y that can be bought with $20 are shown in the following table.

Units of Y	Units of X	Expenditures
5	0	5 × $4 + 0 × $2 = $20
4	2	4 × $4 + 2 × $2 = $20
3	4	3 × $4 + 4 × $2 = $20
2	6	2 × $4 + 6 × $2 = $20
1	8	1 × $4 + 8 × $2 = $20
0	10	0 × $4 + 10 × $2 = $20

These combinations represent the maximum amounts that can be purchased with $20. Note that the amounts are inversely related; as more is spent on X, less must be spent on Y. This inverse relationship is shown graphically in Figure A.1. We put units of Y on the vertical axis and units of X on the horizontal axis, and then plot the pairs of points from the table. The points are then connected. The points trace a downward-sloping line starting at the upper left at $X = 0$ and $Y = 5$ and ending on the right with $X = 10$ and $Y = 0$. All the other combinations of X and Y in the table, such as $X = 4$ and $Y = 3$, are

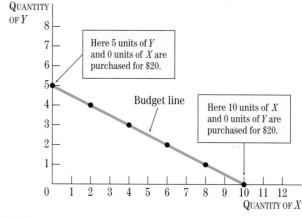

FIGURE A.1
Budget Line for a Consumer
The line shows how much a consumer with $20 can consume of quantity X at a price of $2 per unit and quantity Y at $4 per unit. If $20 is spent on Y and nothing on X, then 5 units of Y can be purchased, as shown on the vertical axis. If $20 is spent on X and nothing on Y, then 10 units of X can be purchased. Other combinations are shown on the line.

shown on the line. If it is possible to consume fractions of X and Y, then all the points on the line between the plotted points can also be purchased with the $20. (For example, 2.5 units of Y and 5 units of X would cost $20: $2.5 \times \$4 + 5 \times \$2 = \$20$.) Because all these pairs of X and Y on this line can be purchased with a $20 budget, we call it the **budget line.** The consumer is constrained to buy combinations of X and Y that are either on or below the budget line. Amounts of X and Y consumed below the budget line cost less than $20. Points above the line require more than $20 and are not feasible.

The budget line will shift out if the consumer has more to spend, as shown in Figure A.2. For example, if the consumer has $24 rather than $20, then the budget line will shift up by 1 unit because the extra $4 permits the consumer to buy 1 more unit of Y. Alternatively, we could say that the budget line shifts to the right by 2 units in this case because the consumer can buy 2 more units of X with $4 more.

141

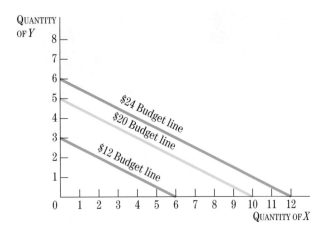

FIGURE A.2
Effect of a Change in Income on the Budget Line
If the consumer has more to spend, then the budget line is farther out. If the consumer has less to spend, then the budget line is farther in. Here a higher and a lower budget line are compared with the $20 budget line in Figure A.1.

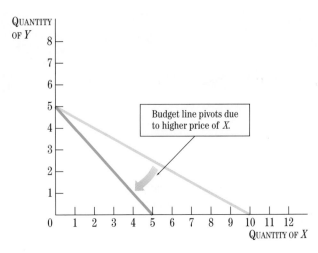

FIGURE A.3
Effect of a Higher Price of X on the Budget Line
The budget line pivots if the price of X changes. Here the price of X rises from $2 to $4 and the budget line twists down.

The steepness of the budget line depends on the prices of X and Y. In particular, the slope of the budget line is equal to -1 times the ratio of the price of X to the price of Y. That is, slope $= -(P_X/P_Y)$, which is $-\frac{1}{2}$ in this example. Why is the slope determined by the price ratio? Recall that the slope is the change in Y divided by the change in X. Along the budget line, as X is increased by 1 unit, Y must fall by $\frac{1}{2}$ unit: Buying 1 more unit of X costs $2 and requires buying $\frac{1}{2}$ unit less of Y. Thus, the slope is $-\frac{1}{2}$.

In order to derive the demand curve for X, we need to find out what happens when the price of X changes. What happens to the budget line when the price of X increases from $2 to $4, for example? The budget line twists down, as shown in Figure A.3. The intuitive rationale for the twist is that the slope steepens to $-(P_X/P_Y) = -\$4/\$4 = -1$, and the position of $X = 0$ and $Y = 5$ on the vertical axis does not change, because 5 units of Y can still be purchased. You can show this by creating a new table with pairs of X and Y that can be purchased with $20 at the new price and then plotting the points.

To summarize, we have shown how a budget line represents the budget constraint for the consumer; now we show how to represent the consumer's preferences.

The Indifference Curve

Utility is an indicator of how a consumer prefers one combination of items in comparison with another. If the level of utility is the same for two combinations of X and Y, then the consumer is *indifferent* between the two com-

binations. Suppose that the utility is the same for the combinations of X and Y that appear below.

Units of Y	Units of X
6	1
4	2
2	6
1	12

The consumer is indifferent among these combinations. Observe that these amounts are inversely related. As consumption of Y declines, the consumer must be compensated with more X if the level of utility is not to decline.

We can plot these different amounts on the same type of graph we used for the budget line, as shown in Figure A.4. The consumer is indifferent among all four points. We have connected the points with a curve to represent other combinations of X and Y about which the consumer is indifferent. The curve is called an **indifference curve** because the consumer is indifferent among all points on the curve. The indifference curve slopes downward from left to right.

The slope of the indifference curve can be found from the marginal utilities of X and Y. Marginal utility is *the increase in utility from consuming an additional unit of a good*. For example, look back at Figure 2 and consider the marginal utility of increasing consumption of grapes by 1 additional pound, from 3 pounds to 4 pounds. You will see that utility increases by 2. Thus, the marginal utility of grapes is 2 at the amount of consumption. Let MU_X

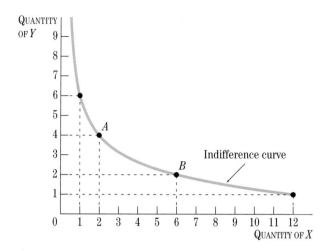

FIGURE A.4

An Indifference Curve for a Consumer

The consumer is indifferent between A and B or any other point on an indifference curve. For example, the consumer is indifferent between consuming 4 units of Y and 2 of X or 2 units of Y and 6 of X.

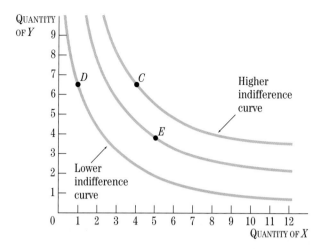

FIGURE A.5

Higher and Lower Indifference Curves

Amounts of X and Y on indifference curves that are higher are preferred to amounts on indifference curves that are lower. Of the three combinations C, D, and E, the combination at D is the least preferred and the combination at C is the most preferred.

be the marginal utility of X, and let MU_Y be the marginal utility of Y.

The slope of the indifference curve is equal to negative 1 times the ratio of the marginal utility of X to the marginal utility of Y; that is, slope = $-(MU_X/MU_Y)$. The reason is that utility is the same for all points on an indifference curve. In other words, the decline in utility as X falls $(-MU_X \times \Delta X)$ must equal the increase in utility as Y rises $(MU_Y \times \Delta Y)$. Thus, $(MU_X \times \Delta X) = (-MU_Y \times \Delta Y)$, or $-MU_X/MU_Y = \Delta Y/\Delta X$, which is the slope of the indifference curve.

The ratio of marginal utilities MU_X/MU_Y is called the **marginal rate of substitution;** it gives the number of units of one good (Y) for which the consumer is willing to trade 1 unit of the other good (X) and have the same amount of utility—or be indifferent. For example, if the marginal rate of substitution is 4, then the consumer is willing to trade 4 units of Y for 1 unit of X with utility remaining the same.

Note that the indifference curve is bowed in toward the origin. That is, the indifference curve is steep when a small amount of X is consumed and flat when a large amount of X is consumed. This curvature is due to the declining marginal rate of substitution. When the consumer is consuming only a little bit of X, a large amount of Y is required as compensation for a reduction in X. As X increases, less of Y is required as compensation.

We can represent higher levels of utility or more preferred combinations of X and Y by higher indifference curves, as shown in Figure A.5. Any point on a higher indifference curve is preferred to any point on a lower indifference curve.

Getting to the Highest Indifference Curve Given the Budget Line

Now we can combine the budget line and the indifference curves on the same diagram to illustrate the model of consumer behavior. Utility maximization subject to the budget constraint means getting to the highest possible indifference curve without going above the budget line. The process is shown in Figure A.6. The budget line from Figure A.1 and the indifference curves from Figure A.5 are shown in the diagram. The consumer cannot go beyond the budget line, and any point inside the budget line is inferior to points on the budget line. Thus the combination of X and Y with the highest utility must be on the budget line. The highest indifference curve with points on the budget line is the one that just touches—is tangent to—the budget line. This occurs at point T in Figure A.6. The **tangency point** is the highest level of utility the consumer can achieve subject to the budget constraint. It is the combination of X and Y that the consumer chooses. Figure A.6 shows that, in this example, the consumer buys $2\frac{1}{4}$ units of Y and $5\frac{1}{2}$ units of X.

The Utility-Maximizing Rule

Observe that at the tangency point, the slope of the budget line is equal to the slope of the indifference curve. That is, $P_X/P_Y = MU_X/MU_Y$. In other words, the ratio of the price of two goods equals the ratio of the marginal utility of the two goods as long as the consumer is maxi-

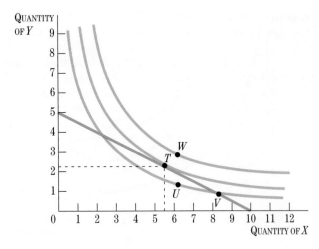

FIGURE A.6
The Best Choice for the Consumer
When the budget line is tangent to the indifference curve, the consumer cannot do any better. The point of tangency is at point *T*. Compare this with the other points. Point *U* is not the best point because it is inside the budget line. Point *V* is not the best point because there are other points on the budget line that are preferred. Point *W* is preferred to point *T*, but it is not feasible.

mizing utility. This equality between the price ratio and the ratio of the marginal utilities, or the marginal rate of substitution, is called the *utility-maximizing rule*.

Effect of a Price Change on the Quantity Demanded

Now suppose that the price of X increases; then the budget line twists down, as shown in the lower panel of Figure A.7. With the new budget line, the old consumer choice of $2\frac{1}{4}$ units of X and $5\frac{1}{2}$ units of Y is no longer feasible: Point T is outside the new budget line. The highest level of utility the consumer can now achieve is at point S in the lower panel of Figure A.7. At point S, the quantity of X has declined. Thus, a higher price of X has reduced the quantity demanded of X.

In the top graph in Figure A.7, we show the relationship between the price of X and the quantity demanded of X. The price of X is put on the vertical axis, and the quantity demanded of X is put on the horizontal axis. The lower quantity demanded at the higher price shows the negative slope of the demand curve.

Effect of an Income Change on Demand

We can also examine what happens when the consumer's income changes but the price remains constant. This is illustrated in Figure A.8, where income declines. The

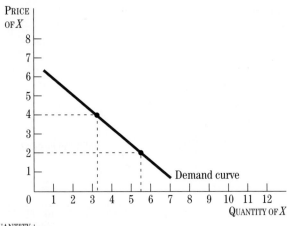

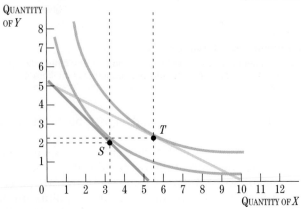

FIGURE A.7
An Increase in the Price of *X*
If the price of *X* rises, the budget line pivots down and the consumer's choice changes from point *T* to point *S* in the lower panel. The quantity of *X* consumed goes down. The price of *X* and the quantity of *X* are plotted in the top panel, showing the negative relationship between price and quantity demanded.

lower income leads to less consumption of both X and Y. In this case, both X and Y are normal goods because consumption goes down when income goes down. If the consumption of X increased as the budget curve shifted in, then X would be an inferior good.

Graphical Illustration of the Income Effect and the Substitution Effect

The effect of a change in the price on the quantity demanded can be divided into an income effect and a substitution effect. These two effects can be represented graphically as shown in Figure A.9.

As in Figure A.7, there is a twist in the budget line due to the higher price of X. But now we draw in another budget line—the dashed line in Figure A.8—correspond-

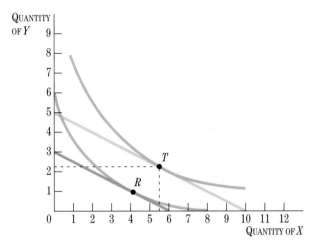

FIGURE A.8
A Decrease in Income
If the consumer's income falls, there is a new point at which utility is maximized: The consumer moves from point *T* to point *R*. In this case, consumption of both *X* and *Y* declines. Neither good is an inferior good in this example.

ing to a lower level of income due to the higher price of *X*, but without twisting the line. This budget line has the same slope as the original line. Thus the dashed budget line shows the reduction in income due to the price increase of *X* but keeps the relative price of *X* to *Y* the same as it was before the price of *X* increased. The dashed line

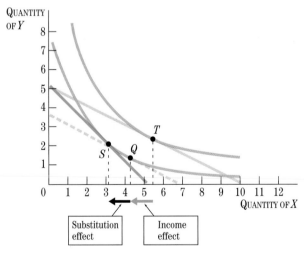

FIGURE A.9
Illustration of Income Effect and Substitution Effect of a Price Change
The dashed budget line has the same slope as the original line and leads to the income effect. The rest of the decline in the quantity of *X* is the substitution effect.

can be used to find the income effect without the substitution effect because it has the same slope as the original budget line.

Observe that the tangency of this dashed budget line with the indifference curve at *Q* gives a lower level of consumption of *X* compared with the original point *T*. The decline of consumption from *T* to *Q* is the income effect. The remaining decline from *Q* to *S* is the substitution effect.

KEY POINTS

1. The budget line represents the consumer's budget constraint in a diagram with the quantity consumed of each of two goods on the axes.

2. The budget line is downward-sloping, with the slope equal to negative 1 times the ratio of the price of the good on the horizontal axis to the price of the good on the vertical axis.

3. A higher price of the good on the horizontal axis twists the budget line down.

4. An indifference curve shows the combinations of goods among which the consumer is indifferent.

5. Combinations of goods on higher indifference curves are preferred to combinations of goods on lower indifference curves.

6. The model of consumer behavior assumes that the consumer tries to get to the highest possible indifference curve without going beyond the budget line.

7. The consumer chooses the combination at the tangency of the budget line and the indifference curve.

8. A higher price of a good lowers the quantity demanded, according to the indifference curve and budget line diagram.

KEY TERMS AND DEFINITIONS

budget line: a line showing the maximum combinations of two goods that it is possible for a consumer to buy, given a budget constraint and the market prices of the two goods.

indifference curve: a curve showing the combinations of two goods that leave the consumer with the same level of utility.

marginal rate of substitution: the amount of one good for which the consumer is willing to trade one unit of another good and still have the same utility.

tangency point: the only point in common for two curves; the point where the two curves just touch.

QUESTIONS FOR REVIEW

1. Why does the budget line slope downward?

2. What determines the slope of the budget line?

3. Why does the indifference curve slope downward?

4. Why does the consumer choose a point where the indifference curve is tangent to the budget line?

PROBLEMS

1. Darnell has $30 to spend on either muffins, which cost $3 each, or cartons of orange juice, which cost $1.50 each.
   a. Graph Darnell's budget line for muffins and orange juice.
   b. What is the maximum quantity of orange juice that Darnell can buy with $30?
   c. Suppose the price of orange juice increases to $2 per carton. Show the change in the budget line.

2. Suppose you are having a party in half an hour and you have two 6-packs of beer in your refrigerator. One is an imported premium beer, and the other is a standard domestic beer. A neighbor comes to you and asks you to trade some imported premium beer for the standard domestic beer, since he is also having a party. You agree to trade 2 premium bottles for 3 standard bottles. Twenty minutes later, the neighbor comes back and asks for 2 more premium bottles. Will you still trade on a 2 premium for 3 standard basis? Suppose you demand 4 standard bottles for two premium bottles. What property of indifference curves is illustrated by this example?

3. Suppose that the prices of two goods consumed by an individual are reduced by the same percentage. What change will happen to the budget line? What change will happen to the consumer's indifference curves? What will happen to the consumption of the two goods? Show each of the above graphically.

4. Sarah has $20 to spend on slices of pizza and cans of diet cola. Pizza costs $1 per slice, and diet cola costs $.50 per can.
   a. Graph Sarah's budget line for pizza and diet cola.
   b. Suppose Sarah's total budget for pizza and diet cola increases to $25. How does her budget line shift?
   c. Draw a set of indifference curves for the situation in which pizza is a normal good, and one for the situation in which pizza is an inferior good.

Chapter 6

The Supply Curve and the Behavior of Firms

Americans love their bumper stickers. They buy tens of thousands of them every year to proclaim their loyalty to movements, political candidates, schools, or a particular way of life. But some people who would like to express their views on their car might hesitate to apply a sticker that could be hard to remove later on. So when yellow-ribbon car magnets proclaiming support for U.S. troops in Iraq showed up in stores in 2003, many people eagerly bought them, paying far more for the magnets (around $5 each) than the pennies it cost to produce them—creating, in economic terminology, a *producer surplus*. Dwain Gullion, who began the whole craze with the casual production of 1,000 magnets that he intended to sell at his Christian bookstore, had to gear up production fast. By the summer of 2004, Gullion's new company, Magnet America, was shipping more than 100,000 magnets a week and employing more than 100 contract workers.

Three years later, in March 2007, an article appeared in the *Financial Times*[1] describing how circumstances had changed for Magnet America. As the war in Iraq became unpopular, people cut back on their magnet purchases. Sales had fallen from over 1 million a month to a mere 4,000 a month, with almost a million magnets that had been produced waiting for buyers. The article described how Magnet America's work force had dwindled to fewer than a dozen workers.

In this chapter we examine how a firm like Magnet America decides how many magnets to produce and how it responds to changing market conditions. The behavior of firms like Magnet America can be described by supply curves like the one in Figure 1, which shows a typical supply curve, with price on the vertical axis and quantity supplied on the horizontal axis. The supply curve is for an entire market; it tells us how much all the firms in the market—not just a single firm like Magnet America—would produce at each price. In this chapter we look under the surface of

---

[1] "Yellow Ribbons Dwindle with War Support," *Financial Times*, March 2, 2007.

the supply curve and examine how the profit-maximizing behavior of a firm determines how much of a good that firm will choose to produce at a given market price. Then we show how aggregating individual firms' supply curves generates a supply curve for the entire market for that good.

As with our study of the consumers who underlie the demand curve in Chapter 5, there are two important reasons to study the firms that underlie the supply curve. First, we want to show why the supply curve has the slope and position it does. Such information enables us to assess how a change in technology or societal trends or a new government policy affects the supply curve. Second, we want to show how and why a supply curve can be used to measure the "producer surplus" of firms. Producer surplus is a measure of how much a producer gains from participating in the market. In conjunction with consumer surplus, producer surplus is extremely useful for measuring how well a market economy actually works, and in explaining why a market economy works better than alternative systems to produce and allocate goods and resources.

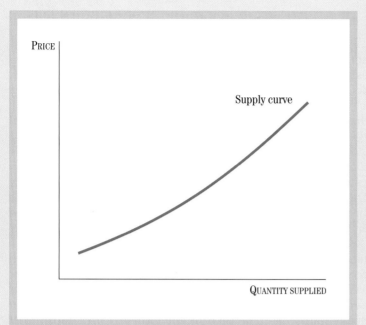

FIGURE 1
A Typical Supply Curve for a Market
Supply curves typically slope upward. In this chapter, we look at the factors that motivate firms in the market to increase the quantity supplied as the price rises.

In 2003, these magnets were extremely popular purchases, but by 2007 demand had waned, leading Magnet America to lay off workers.

Basic Economic Principle	When Applied to the Behavior of Consumers	When Applied to the Behavior of Firms
People...	*Consumers...*	*Firms...*
make purposeful choices...	maximize utility...	maximize profits...
with scarce resources.	subject to a budget constraint relating expenditure to income.	subject to a production function relating output to input.

FIGURE 2
Applying the Central Idea of Economics
People make purposeful choices with scarce resources and interact with other people when they make these choices. In Chapter 5, the people were the consumers. In this chapter, they are the firms. In Chapter 7, the consumers and the firms interact with each other.

DEFINITION OF A FIRM

firm: an organization that produces goods or services.

We start by looking at the behavior of a single firm. A **firm,** by definition, is an organization that produces goods or services. Just as no two consumers are exactly alike, no two firms are exactly alike. A firm can be a small family farm in the country or a grocery store in the city. Bakeries, restaurants, auto dealers, and bicycle shops are all examples of firms that are usually relatively small. Other firms—such as General Motors—are very large, producing many different products in large volume.

The terms *firm, company*, and *business* are used interchangeably. A firm may include several *establishments*, which are separate physical locations, such as an office, a factory, or a store, where work is done. For example, the U.S.-based grocery chain Kroger is a firm with over 2,500 supermarkets (most operating under the Kroger or Ralph's labels), almost 800 convenience stores (including Turkey Hill and Kwik Shop), and over 400 jewelry stores (including Fred Meyer jewelers). Of course, not all firms are like Kroger; most small firms have only one establishment.

In the United States, about 80 percent of all firms are *sole proprietorships*, with one owner, or *partnerships*, with only a few owners, who usually manage the firm. Most of these are very small when compared with corporations like Kroger or General Motors. A *corporation* is unlike a sole proprietorship or partnership in that the managers are usually somewhat removed from the owners. For example, most people who own shares of General Motors never even meet the managers of the firm. This separation of managers and owners means that the managers must be given an incentive to keep the owners' interests in mind. A common incentive is to have managers share in the profits of the firm.

You might expect that the decisions made by the managers of a firm would be more complicated—and consequently more difficult to understand—than the decisions made by consumers. Of course, many more people have had the experience of being a consumer than have had the experience of managing a firm. But if you can picture yourself as the owner/manager of your own firm, you will see that the economics of a firm's decision about how much to sell is analogous to the economics of a consumer's decision about how much to buy. The following example places you in that position.

Your Own Firm: A Pumpkin Patch

Imagine that you are the owner and manager of a firm that grows pumpkins on a pumpkin patch; the patch has good soil and gets plenty of rain. Your firm is one of many specializing in growing and selling pumpkins—in other words, there are many other firms with which you must compete. During the spring and summer you grow the pumpkins, and in the fall you sell them. As owner and manager of the firm, you must pay rent at the start of each growing season to the landlord who owns the pumpkin patch. During the season, you hire workers to tend the patch. The more workers you have tending the pumpkins, the more pumpkins you can grow on the patch.

Your firm is typical of many small firms and has features that apply to larger firms as well. Your firm is one with a single product (pumpkins) and two factors of production—land (the patch) and labor (the workers). One of the factors of production, land, cannot be changed during the season because the rent was paid in advance; this makes land a *fixed factor*. The other factor, labor, can be varied during the season, because you can choose to hire more or fewer workers; this makes labor a *variable factor*.

Many people buy pumpkins in the fall to use as Halloween decorations or for making delicious foods like pumpkin pie or pumpkin soup. As the owner of a small pumpkin firm, you are a price-taker because your pumpkins are like everyone else's pumpkins.

Your Firm as a Price-Taker in a Competitive Market

The first task is to derive the supply curve for your pumpkin firm. *A supply curve for a single firm tells us the quantity of a good that that firm will produce at different prices.* To find the supply curve, we imagine that the firm looks at the price of the good it is

price-taker: any firm that takes the market price as given; this firm cannot affect the market price because the market is competitive.

selling and then decides how much to produce. For example, a baker considers the price of a loaf of bread prevailing in the market when deciding how many loaves of bread to produce. So in this case you must decide how much to produce and sell after looking at the price of pumpkins in the market. In a competitive market, any individual firm will be a **price-taker;** this means that the firm cannot influence the market price but instead has to decide how much to produce and sell at the given market price of the goods. In the case of your pumpkin firm, what this implies is that you cannot affect the price of pumpkins in the market through your decision to produce more or fewer pumpkins.

This description of a firm as a price-taker may seem odd to you. After all, if the firm doesn't set the price, then who does? Of course, in some sense, each firm does. If you go to a bakery for a loaf of bread, a price tag states the price of the loaf, so the baker is clearly determining the price. But this is not the way economists look at it; there is a subtlety here in the way economists describe the market. When there are many bakers selling bread, in an important sense, the individual bakers do not have the ability to affect the price by much. If one baker charges $3 for a loaf of bread, and all the other bakers in the community charge $1.50 for the same loaf, no one will buy bread from the first baker. People will not even go to the store if they know the price is that high. They will go to other bakeries, where bread sells for $1.50 a loaf. Although in principle an individual firm has the ability to set any price it wants, in reality a firm cannot charge a price far from the price that prevails in the market without soon losing all its customers.

A market in which a single firm cannot affect the market price is called a **competitive market.** Because many firms are producing pumpkins along with your pumpkin firm, the pumpkin market is competitive. A competitive market requires that there be at least several firms competing with one another. Exactly how many firms are required to make a market competitive is difficult to say without studying the market carefully—as we do in later chapters. If a market is competitive, so that firms are price-takers, then we can derive a supply curve for the individual firm by asking, "How many pumpkins would the pumpkin firm produce if the price of pumpkins were $35 a crate? $70 a crate?" and so on.

competitive market: a market in which no firm has the power to affect the market price of a good.

Other Types of Markets

Not all markets are as competitive as the fresh bread market or the pumpkin market, and part of our job later in the book is to study these markets. The exact opposite of a competitive market is a market in which there is only one firm, in which case the firm is called a *monopoly*. Strictly speaking, the question "How much does the monopoly produce at a given price?" has no meaning because the monopoly is not a price-taker that has to take the price as given. Instead, it is a price-maker who can dictate the price. We consider monopolies in Chapter 10. For now we focus on the price-taking firms in a competitive market.

In deriving the demand curve in Chapter 5, we assumed that the individual consumer could not affect the price. This seems natural because we do not usually see buyers setting the price for bread or other commodities. As long as there are at least several buyers and several sellers in the market, we can assume that the price is taken as given by both buyers and sellers. In Chapter 7, when we study the interaction of buyers and sellers in markets, we will show how the market price is determined.

R E V I E W

- A firm is an organization that produces goods or services that are sold in a market. There are a great variety of sizes and types of firms.

- In the United States, most firms take the form of sole proprietorships or partnerships, which means that they are owned by either a single owner or very few owners, respectively. Other firms, known as corporations, are owned by many individuals who are typically disconnected from the day-to-day operations of the firm, which is run by the managers of the firm.

- To understand firm behavior, we begin by focusing on a simple case of a single owner of a firm that is operating in a competitive market. A market is said to be competitive if no single firm can affect the market price.

- Not all markets are competitive. The polar opposite of a competitive market is a monopoly market, where there is a single producer who dictates the price that the good sells for in that market. This chapter will focus only on competitive markets.

- In a competitive market with many firms, each firm is a price-taker. The owner of the firm has to decide how much of the good or service to produce at the given price. The supply curve of an individual firm describes how the quantity produced by that firm depends on the price.

THE FIRM'S PROFITS

profits: total revenue received from selling the product minus the total costs of producing the product.

Profits for any firm—a bakery producing bread or a farm producing pumpkins—are defined as the *total revenue* received from selling the product minus the *total costs* of producing the product. That is,

Profits = total revenue − total costs

When profits are negative—total revenue is less than total costs—the firm runs a *loss*. When profits are zero—total revenue is equal to total costs—the firm is *breaking even*.

We assume that the firm *maximizes* profits. That is, the firm decides on the quantity of production that will make profits as high as possible. To see how this is done, we

TABLE 1
Total Revenue from Pumpkin Production at Three Prices

Quantity Produced (crates)	Total Revenue		
	Price = $35/crate	*Price = $70/crate*	*Price = $100/crate*
0	0	0	0
1	35	70	100
2	70	140	200
3	105	210	300
4	140	280	400
5	175	350	500

must examine how profits depend on the quantity produced. To do this, we must consider how total revenue and total costs—the two determinants of profits—depend on the quantity produced. We consider first total revenue and then total costs.

Total Revenue

total revenue: the price per unit times the quantity the firm sells.

Total revenue is the total number of dollars the firm receives from people who buy its product. Total revenue can be computed by multiplying the price of each unit sold by the quantity sold. That is,

$$\text{Total revenue} = \text{price} \times \text{quantity}$$
$$= P \times Q$$

where we use the letter P to stand for price and Q to stand for quantity. Because we are looking at an individual firm and a particular product, P is the price of the particular product the individual firm is selling, and Q is the number of items the firm sells. There are a variety of ways to measure the quantity sold: number of pumpkins, crates of pumpkins, pounds of pumpkins. Any of these measures will suffice for our analysis.

total costs: the sum of all costs incurred in producing goods or services.

Table 1 uses crates of pumpkins as the measure of quantity. Note that total revenue depends both on the price of a crate of pumpkin and on the number of crates of pumpkins sold. Each row of the table shows the total revenue the firm receives from selling a specific amount of pumpkins: 0 crates, 1 crate, and so on. Each column showing total revenue corresponds to a different price: $35 per crate, $70 per crate, and $100 per crate. For example, when the firm can get $70 per crate, it receives $280 for selling 4 crates.

From Table 1, you can see that the more items are sold at a given price, the higher total revenue is. Thus, the firm can increase total revenue by producing and selling more goods. Total revenue therefore increases with the quantity produced for your pumpkin-producing firm.

Reminder: In Chapter 1, we saw that costs include *opportunity costs*. Thus, total costs for your pumpkin firm would include the opportunity cost of any time you spent operating the firm rather than doing something else, like studying for an exam. To emphasize that opportunity costs are included in total costs when computing profits, economists sometimes use the term *economic profits* rather than simply profits.

Production and Costs

Now that we have seen how total revenue depends on the quantity produced, let's examine how total costs depend on the quantity produced. **Total costs** are what the firm has to incur in order to produce the product. For your pumpkin firm, total costs include the workers' salaries and the rent on the land. To see how total costs depend on the quantity produced, we must look at what happens to the quantity of labor and land used by the firm when the quantity produced increases or decreases.

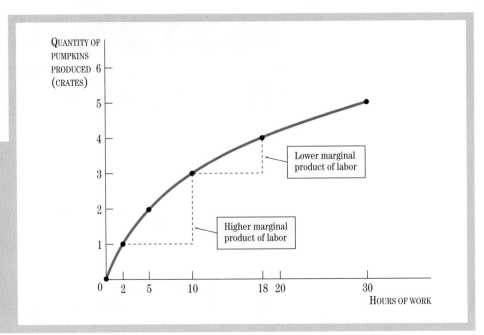

FIGURE 3
A Production Function Relating Output to Labor Input

As more workers are employed, production increases. But the increase in production added by each additional hour of work declines as more workers are hired because the land the workers have to work with does not increase. Thus, there is a decreasing marginal product of labor, or diminishing returns to labor.

■ The Time Period. Here, we are looking at the pumpkin firm's production decisions over a short period of time—such as one growing season—rather than over a long period of time—such as several growing seasons. Because we are focusing on the short run, we assume that only the labor input to production can be varied. Our analysis of the firm in this chapter is called a *short-run* analysis because the time is too short to change the other factors of production, such as land; only labor can be changed. We make this assumption simply because it is easier to examine the firm's decisions when only one factor of production can be changed. It is a simplifying assumption that we will modify. In Chapter 8 we take up the *long run*, in which other factors of production—such as the size of the pumpkin patch—can change as well as labor.

■ The Production Function. Figure 3 plots the relationship between pumpkin production and labor input for a given size of pumpkin patch. The number of hours of work is on the horizontal axis, and the quantity produced is on the vertical axis. Each point in Figure 3 shows the number of hours of work and the quantity of pumpkins produced: To produce 3 crates requires 10 hours of work; to produce 5 crates requires 30 hours of work. Clearly, more pumpkin production requires more labor input. The graph in Figure 3 is called the firm's **production function** because it tells us how much is produced for each amount of labor input, given a fixed amount of land input.

The **marginal product of labor** is defined as the increase in production that comes from an additional unit of labor. Figure 3 shows that, because of the curvature of the production function, the marginal product of labor *declines* as labor input increases. In other words, the same increase in hours of work leads to a smaller increase in production when labor input is large than when labor input is small. In Figure 3, when the hours of work increase from 2 to 10, the quantity of pumpkin crates produced increases by 2 crates, from 1 to 3 crates. However, an increase of labor input of the identical magnitude from 10 to 18 will increase the quantity of pumpkins by only 1 crate, from 3 to 4 crates.

production function: a relationship that shows the quantity of output for any given amount of input.

marginal product of labor: the change in production due to a one-unit increase in labor input.

TABLE 2
Example of Costs for a Single Firm

Quantity Produced (crates)	Hours of Labor Input	Variable Costs at $10 Wage (dollars)	Fixed Costs (dollars)	Total Costs (dollars)
0	0	0	50	50
1	2	20	50	70
2	5	50	50	100
3	10	100	50	150
4	18	180	50	230
5	30	300	50	350

diminishing returns to labor: a situation in which the increase in output due to a unit increase in labor declines with increasing labor input; a decreasing marginal product of labor.

variable costs: costs of production that vary with the quantity of production.

Another term for the phenomenon of declining marginal product of labor is **diminishing returns to labor.** In your pumpkin firm, diminishing returns to labor occur as additional workers are employed. For a given amount of land, hiring more workers is initially very helpful in terms of increasing output, as the workers can water the pumpkins, pull out weeds, and harvest the pumpkins at the appropriate time. But as more and more workers are employed on a given amount of land, there are fewer tasks for each worker to do, and each additional worker adds less and less additional output. Diminishing returns is a general phenomenon that occurs when some inputs to production—such as land or machines—are fixed. Because the size of your pumpkin patch is fixed, additional workers must eventually add less to production. Otherwise a single plot of land could produce all the world's pumpkins by employing huge numbers of workers. Diminishing returns to labor occur in nonagricultural examples as well. Employing more and more workers in an automobile factory without increasing the size of the factory or adding more machines will increase the amount of cars produced by the factory by less and less.

■ **Costs.** Table 2 shows how total costs depend on the quantity of pumpkins produced at your pumpkin firm. The first column shows the quantity of pumpkins produced. The second column shows the labor input required to produce that quantity of pumpkins, using the production function from Figure 3. The third column shows the costs of hiring the labor input at a rate of $10 per hour of work. These costs are called **variable costs** because they vary according to how much is produced; more workers are hired and more wages paid as more pumpkins are produced. We also assume that you have to pay $50 up front for rent on the patch. The fourth column shows the cost of the land. The $50 payment for the land is considered to be a *fixed cost* because it must be paid no matter how many pumpkins

Diminishing Returns to Labor
Adding the second worker to this machine in a French vineyard increased the quantity of grapes produced by much less than the first worker did. Adding a third worker to the machine would increase the quantity of grapes produced by even less than adding the second worker did. Thus, this is an example of a decreasing marginal product of labor, or diminishing returns to labor.

TABLE 3
Total Costs and Marginal Cost

Quantity Produced (crates)	Total Costs (dollars)	Marginal Cost (dollars)
0	50	—
1	70	20
2	100	30
3	150	50
4	230	80
5	350	120

The connecting lines emphasize how marginal cost is the change in total costs as the quantity produced increases by one unit.

fixed costs: costs of production that do not depend on the quantity of production.

are produced or even if you produce no pumpkins at all. By definition, **fixed costs** are the part of total costs that do not depend on how much is produced. Variable costs and fixed costs together constitute all the costs of producing the product. Hence, *the sum of fixed costs and variable costs equals total costs*, as shown in the last column of Table 2.

Each row of Table 2 shows the costs of producing a particular quantity of pumpkins. The first row indicates that even if no pumpkins are produced, the firm will incur the fixed costs of $50. The second row shows the cost of producing 1 crate of pumpkins. Since 2 units of labor are needed for the production of this 1 crate, the total cost of producing 1 crate of pumpkins is $70, the $50 fixed costs plus the $20 in variable costs. The third row of Table 2 shows the costs of producing 2 crates of pumpkins. Since 5 units of labor (at a cost of $10 each) are needed for the production of these 2 crates, the total cost of producing 2 crates of pumpkins is $100, the $50 fixed costs plus the $50 in variable costs.

As more pumpkins are harvested, more workers must be hired, and the total costs increase. The remaining rows of Table 2 show what happens to costs as the quantity produced increases further.

marginal cost: the change in total costs due to a one-unit change in quantity produced.

Marginal cost is defined as the increase in total costs associated with an additional unit of production. Table 3 shows how marginal cost is calculated for the example in Table 2. For example, the marginal cost of increasing production from 1 crate to 2 crates is $30 ($100 − $70 = $30), and the marginal cost of increasing production from 2 crates to 3 crates is $50 ($150 − $100 = $50).

Notice how marginal cost increases as production increases. Marginal cost is greater when we go from 2 crates to 3 crates ($50) than when we go from 1 crate to 2 crates ($30). The pattern of *increasing marginal cost* is apparent throughout the range of production in Table 3.

Observe that *increasing marginal cost is due to the diminishing marginal product of labor:* The marginal cost of going from 2 crates to 3 crates is greater than that of going from 1 crate to 2 crates because more worker hours are required to raise production from 2 crates to 3 crates (5 additional hours of labor) than are required to raise production from 1 crate to 2 crates (3 additional hours of labor).

Increasing marginal cost is a general phenomenon that occurs in many production processes. It is essential for deriving the supply curve. In fact, as we will soon see, increasing marginal cost is the whole reason that the supply curve for an individual firm slopes upward.

There are exceptions to the principle of increasing marginal cost. One important exception is that marginal cost need not be increasing over the entire range of production. For example, there might be a decrease in marginal cost at very low levels of production. If a team of at least two workers is needed to harvest pumpkins, for

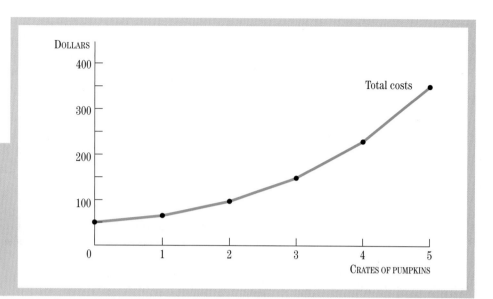

FIGURE 4
Total Costs
In order to produce goods, a firm incurs costs. For example, more workers must be paid to produce more goods. As more goods are produced, the firm's total costs rise, as shown here. At higher levels of production, costs increase by larger amounts for each additional item produced.

example, then the marginal product of a second worker might be greater than the marginal product of a first worker. One worker might add very little, whereas the second might add a lot. But diminishing returns to labor and increasing marginal cost eventually set in as more workers are hired and more pumpkins are produced.

In this chapter, we assume that marginal cost increases over the whole range of production. This is a common assumption used by economists and is a good approximation except for very low levels of production.

■ **Graphical Representation of Total Costs and Marginal Cost.** A better understanding of how a firm's total costs depend on production can be obtained by representing the total costs graphically. Figure 4 plots the pairs of numbers for total

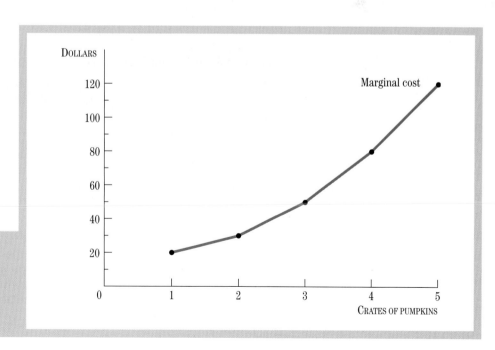

FIGURE 5
Marginal Cost
The change in total costs as more units of the good are produced is called marginal cost. Marginal cost increases as more units are produced, as illustrated here.

costs and quantity produced from the first two columns of Table 3. Dollars are on the vertical axis, and the quantity of pumpkins produced is on the horizontal axis. Note how the total costs curve bends up: As the quantity produced of pumpkins increases, the curve gets steeper, or the slope increases. The marginal cost is the slope of the total costs curve. The increasing slope is a visual way to show the increasing marginal cost.

Figure 5 shows the relationship between marginal cost and number of crates of pumpkins produced. The points in Figure 5 correspond to the pairs of numbers in the first and third columns of Table 3. Note that the marginal cost curve slopes upward, illustrating how marginal cost increases as the quantity of pumpkins produced increases.

R E V I E W

- Profits are defined as the difference between total revenue and total costs. Profits depend on the quantity produced because both total revenue and total costs depend on the quantity produced.

- Total revenue is defined as the price (P) times the quantity (Q) produced and sold. Total revenue increases as the quantity produced increases.

- Total costs are all the costs that the firm has to incur in order to produce its product. The costs that a firm incurs include opportunity costs.

- In this chapter we look at the firm's production decisions over a short period of time. One factor of production, land, has to be held fixed while the other factor of production, labor, can be varied as the quantity produced varies.

- The production function describes how much output can be produced as the quantity of inputs (in this case hours of labor) varies. Typically, the marginal product of labor declines as more and more labor is employed. This phenomenon is also described as diminishing returns to labor.

- Total costs are the sum of fixed costs (which do not vary with the quantity produced) and variable costs (which vary according to how much is produced). In the pumpkin firm example, fixed costs are the cost of renting the pumpkin patch, while variable costs are the costs of hiring workers.

- Variable costs increase with the quantity produced because it takes more inputs—such as workers—to produce more output. As a result, total costs also increase with the quantity produced.

- Marginal cost is defined as the change in total costs associated with an additional unit of production. Marginal cost increases as more is produced because of diminishing returns to labor.

PROFIT MAXIMIZATION AND THE INDIVIDUAL FIRM'S SUPPLY CURVE

profit maximization: an assumption that firms try to achieve the highest possible level of profits—total revenue minus total costs—given their production function.

To derive the firm's supply curve, we assume that the firm chooses a quantity of production that maximizes profits. This is the assumption of **profit maximization.** Now that we have seen how profits depend on the quantity produced, we can proceed to show how the firm chooses a quantity to maximize profits.

An Initial Approach to Derive the Supply Curve

Continuing with our pumpkin firm, we create a table that uses total revenue and total costs to calculate profits. Because total revenue depends on the price, we need a separate panel for each of three possible prices.

■ **A Profit Table.** Table 4 shows profits for your pumpkin firm. It has three panels, one for each of three possible prices. (The prices are the same as in Table 1.) Each panel reports total revenue and total costs for quantities ranging from 0 to 5 crates. The last column of each panel reports profits, which are defined as total revenue less total costs.

Total revenue, shown in the second column, increases with the number of pumpkins sold. Because total revenue depends on the price, we need a separate panel showing total revenue for each price. The third column of Table 4 shows how total costs increase with production. This is the same information already presented in Table 2. We repeat it here so that total costs can easily be compared with total

TABLE 4
Profit Tables Showing Total Costs and Total Revenue at Different Prices

PANEL I
If price equals $35 per crate, then production equals 2 crates.

Crates	Total Revenue	Total Costs	Profits
0	0	50	−50
1	35	70	−35
2	70	100	−30
3	105	150	−45
4	140	230	−90
5	175	350	−175

PANEL II
If price equals $70 per crate, then production equals 3 crates.

Crates	Total Revenue	Total Costs	Profits
0	0	50	−50
1	70	70	0
2	140	100	40
3	210	150	60
4	280	230	50
5	350	350	0

PANEL III
If price equals $100 per crate, then production equals 4 crates.

Crates	Total Revenue	Total Costs	Profits
0	0	50	−50
1	100	70	30
2	200	100	100
3	300	150	150
4	400	230	170
5	500	350	150

revenue to calculate profits. The range of total costs is the same for all these panels because total costs do not depend on the price.

Consider Panel I, where the price of pumpkins is $35 a crate. Total revenue equals the price ($35) times the number of crates sold. If you sell 1 crate, the revenue is $35; if you sell 2 crates, the revenue is $70, and so on. Clearly, if no pumpkins are sold, the total revenue will be zero. Panels II and III show total revenue for two higher prices—$70 per crate and $100 per crate.

The last column of Table 4 shows profits, which equal total revenue minus total costs. Consider the $35 per crate price in panel I first. When no pumpkins are produced, total costs are $50 because $50 is paid for the land. Total revenue is zero. Profits, therefore, are −$50, which implies that the firm loses $50. If you produce 1 crate, the loss is $35; the revenue from 1 crate ($35) minus the total cost of producing 1 crate ($70) equals a profit of −$35. For 2 crates, profits are still negative, at −$30. Total revenue is $70 while total costs are $100, leaving a loss of $30. Three crates of pumpkins yield an even greater loss of $45.

A glance down the last column in panel I shows that profits are negative at all production levels. In this case, any production at all may seem fruitless. But remember that you already paid $50 for the use of the pumpkin patch. Hence, it is best to produce 2 crates and cut your losses to $30. You still lose, but not as much as by producing only zero or 1 crate. Even though it may seem strange because profits are negative, the profit-maximizing level of production is 2 crates. The maximum of profits would be −$30. Stated differently, the minimum loss would be $30.

The same type of profit-maximizing exercise with a different price is illustrated in panel II of Table 4. Here the price of pumpkins is $70, and so the total revenue is higher. If you sell nothing, then total revenue is zero and the loss is $50. If you sell 1 crate, total revenue is $70 and profits are zero. But if you sell 2 crates, total costs are $100 and total revenue is $140. Finally, some positive profit can be seen. Profits can be increased further: The profit-maximizing level of production is 3 crates.

Panel III shows profits for a still higher price, $100 a crate. At this price, you would produce 4 crates. Profits would be $170. More or less production than 4 crates would lower profits.

In these three cases, you maximize profits by adjusting the quantity supplied. As the price rises from $35 to $70 to $100, the profit-maximizing quantity of pumpkins supplied goes from 2 crates to 3 crates to 4 crates. Thus, the price and the quantity supplied are positively related. This is the positively sloped supply curve.

■ **A Profit Graph.** The relationship between profits and production for your pumpkin firm given in Table 4 can be illustrated with a graph that compares total costs and total revenue. This is done in Figure 6. The curved line in the top graph of Figure 6 is the total costs curve. It corresponds to the total costs listed in Table 4 and is the same as the total costs curve in Figure 4. The upward-sloping straight line shows what total revenue would be for a price of $70 per crate. This line corresponds to the total revenue column in panel II of Table 4.

Profits are given by the gap between the total revenue line and the total costs curve. The gap—profits—is plotted in the lower panel of Figure 6. Note how profits first increase and then decrease as more is produced. The profit-maximizing firm chooses the quantity to produce that leads to the biggest gap, or the biggest level of profits. That quantity is 3 crates of pumpkins.

The Marginal Approach to Derive the Supply Curve

The above approach to deriving the supply curve can be very involved because of the need to calculate a separate profit table for each price level. Economists use a different approach to analyzing profit maximization and deriving the supply curve. Once

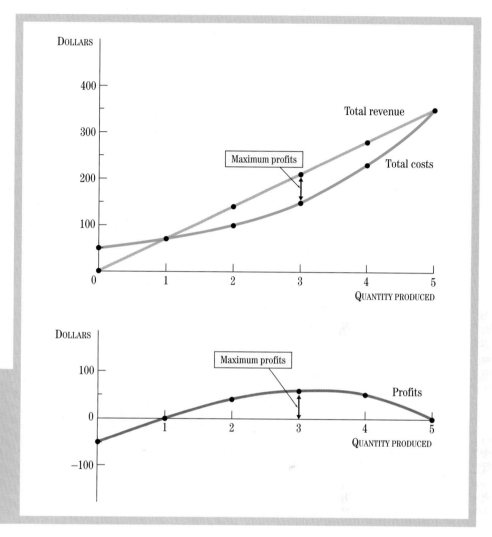

FIGURE 6
An Initial Approach to Profit Maximization

The top panel shows total costs and total revenue for a price of $70 per crate of pumpkins. Profits are the gap between total revenue and total costs. The bottom panel shows explicitly how profits first increase and then decrease as production increases.

you know this approach, you will find it an easier and faster way of deriving the individual firm's supply curve than using total revenue, total costs, and total profits.

Continuing with our pumpkin firm, we first plot the marginal cost from Table 3 in Figure 7. Focus for now on the black dots in Figure 7; we derive the lines in the next few paragraphs. Each dot in Figure 7 represents the marginal cost of producing a crate of pumpkins at a different level of production (the marginal cost when production is 1 crate is $20, the marginal cost when production is 2 crates is $30, etc.).

■ **Finding the Quantity Supplied at Different Prices.** Suppose the price of pumpkins is $10 a crate. At $10, the price is less than the marginal cost of producing 1 unit, which is $20, according to Figure 7. Would it make sense to produce pumpkins at this price? No, because the *additional* revenue that comes from producing one more crate, which is the price of a crate of pumpkins, is $10. Because laying out $20 and getting back $10 reduces profits, you would not bother to produce any pumpkins.

marginal revenue: the change in total revenue due to a one-unit increase in quantity sold.

The additional, or extra, revenue that results from producing and selling one more unit of output is called **marginal revenue.** We can summarize the above conclusion by saying that we do not increase production from 0 to 1 crate because the

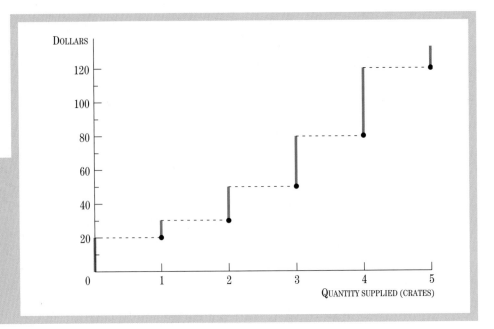

FIGURE 7
Derivation of the Individual Firm's Supply Curve

The dots represent the marginal cost from Table 3. At each dot, price equals marginal cost. These dots and the thick vertical lines indicate the quantity the firm is willing to supply at each price. Along the vertical lines, the firm produces the quantity that keeps marginal cost closest to price without exceeding it.

marginal cost of increasing production would be greater than the marginal revenue. Therefore, producing nothing would be the profit-maximizing thing to do.

Suppose the price of pumpkins rises. As long as the price is below $20, there is no production because marginal costs exceed marginal revenue (which is the price). Thus, the amount supplied at prices from $0 to $20 is given by the thick blue line at the bottom of the vertical axis, indicating that quantity supplied equals zero.

Suppose the price rises to $20. Now the price equals the marginal cost, and the marginal revenue from selling a crate of pumpkins will just cover the marginal cost of producing the crate. You now have sufficient incentive to produce some pumpkins. Strictly speaking, the price would have to be a little bit greater than $20 (say, $20.01) for you to earn more by producing 1 crate rather than 0 crates. At a price of exactly $20, you might be indifferent between producing 0 crates and 1 crate. At a price of $19.99, you would definitely produce nothing. At a price of $20.01, you would definitely produce 1 crate. The price of $20 is right between, but let's assume that you produce 1 crate rather than 0 crates at a price of $20. We indicate this in Figure 7 by showing that the quantity supplied is given by the black dot at 1 crate and $20.

Now consider further increases in the price. At prices above $20 up to $30, you would produce 1 crate because the marginal revenue received for producing an extra crate (which again is the price of a crate of pumpkins) is less than the marginal cost of $30. However, at a price of $30, the quantity supplied increases to 2 crates because price just equals the marginal cost of increasing production from 1 to 2 crates. A supply curve is now beginning to take shape. You can complete the curve by continuing to raise the price and watching what happens.

To shorten the story, let us move toward the other end of the scale. Suppose the price of pumpkins is $100 and you are producing 4 crates of pumpkins. Would it make sense to produce another crate? No, because increasing production from 4 crates to 5 crates has a marginal cost of $120. The marginal revenue that comes from producing one more crate is $100. Because laying out $120 and getting back $100 is a losing proposition, you would not do it. Production would stay at 4 crates. If production went up to 5 crates, profits would go down because the marginal cost of producing the fifth crate is greater than the marginal revenue.

Economics in Action

Green Pricing and Incentives

Profit maximization shows explicitly *why firms respond to incentives*. When the price of a good rises, a firm can increase its profits by producing more of that good. So the firm responds by producing more. Whether you are interested in a career in the business world or in the public policy world, the importance of understanding how firms respond to incentives can hardly be overstated.

Environmental protection is an area with fascinating and rapidly growing opportunities to use economic incentives. One of the new ideas is *green pricing*, used to encourage electric power firms to produce electricity using renewable resources, such as solar power or wind power. The goal is to reduce global warming and pollution caused when electricity is produced with coal or oil rather than with the sun or the wind. The United States Environmental Protection Agency (EPA)'s Green Power Partnership[2] "encourages organizations to buy green power as a way to lessen the environmental impacts associated with conventional electricity use. Using conventional fossil fuel based electricity can be one of the greatest environmental impacts associated with your organization."

How do green-pricing programs work? Essentially, two things have to happen. First, consumers have to be given the information about why green power is more environmentally friendly so that they have the incentive to buy green power. This is important because, after all, people cannot actually tell the difference between wind-produced electricity and coal-produced electricity, both work just as well to power a television or a reading light. Second, firms have to be given the incentive to produce electricity with a renewable resource because the marginal cost of producing electricity using wind turbines or solar power is higher than the cost of producing electricity using nonrenewable resources. Profit-maximizing firms will choose to produce power using nonrenewable resources unless they are able to obtain a higher price for a kilowatt-hour of power produced using renewable sources. The goal of green-pricing programs is to attract consumers who are willing to pay more for more environmentally friendly energy and match them up with green producers, who can then charge those consumers a higher price for the green energy.

Green-pricing programs have already been tried in many cities and states. The programs are very similar. Here is how the program works in Traverse City, Michigan. People agree to pay Traverse City Power and Light (the firm that produces electricity) an extra $7.50 per month (on average) if they can be sure that their electric power is produced with a wind turbine, rather than with a nonrenewable resource. To encourage

consumers to buy more green power, Traverse City was considering producing stickers that people could put in their window to show that they were proud consumers of environmentally friendly energy, which in turn might tempt their neighbors to do the same. The higher price that consumers pay is enough to cover the higher marginal cost of using wind power and thus gives Traverse City Power and Light the incentive to produce more electricity with wind power. Thus, a higher price for wind-produced electricity leads to a larger amount of wind-produced electricity.

There are other markets where similar schemes in which consumers who dislike a particular production process, which happens to be one that producers like because it keeps marginal costs low, are given the opportunity to pay more for goods produced in a different way. The higher price provides incentives for firms to change their production process and adopt the alternative approach even if it carries a higher marginal cost. Examples that you are familiar with will include shade-grown coffee, sweatshop-free clothing, dolphin-safe tuna, organically grown produce, and grass-fed beef.

[2]You can find more information online at http://www.epa.gov/greenpower/.

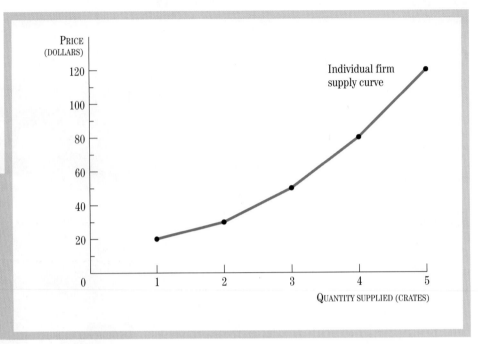

FIGURE 8
A Smooth Individual Supply Curve
If the firm can adjust its production by small amounts, the supply curve becomes a smooth line, as in this figure, rather than a series of steps, as in Figure 7. In some cases, such as the building of an airport, a dam, or a suspension bridge, fractions are not possible, and the supply curves will still have steps.

We have traced out the complete *individual* supply curve for your firm using Figure 7 with the assumption of profit maximization and the concept of marginal cost. The supply curve in Figure 7 is steplike; it consists of small vertical segments shooting up from the dots. At the dots, price equals marginal cost; on the vertical segments above the dots, the price is greater than the marginal cost of production, but the price is not great enough to move on to a higher level of production. What the vertical lines show is that as the price rises, the quantity supplied of pumpkins increases as well.

In reality, for most products it is possible to divide production into smaller units—half crates, quarter crates, even a single pumpkin. As we do so, the jaggedness of the diagram disappears, as shown in Figure 8. In reality, the diagram would consist of hundreds of dots rather than five dots. With hundreds of dots, the vertical segments would be too small to see and the firm's supply curve would be a smooth line. Price would equal marginal cost at every single point.

■ **The Price Equals Marginal Cost Rule.** In deriving the supply curve with Figure 7, we have discovered the key condition for profit maximization for a firm: *The firm will choose a quantity to produce so that marginal revenue equals marginal cost.* This is a general rule that makes intuitive sense for any profit-maximizing firm, whether it is a competitive firm or a monopoly. If the marginal revenue from producing an additional quantity of output is greater than the marginal cost, then the firm should produce that quantity; by doing so, it will increase total revenue by more than it increases total costs, and therefore it will increase profits. However, if the marginal revenue from an additional quantity is less than the marginal cost, then the firm should not produce that quantity. Thus the firm maximizes profits by choosing the quantity of production for which marginal revenue equals marginal cost.

In a competitive market, we can come up with a special case of this rule that makes finding the profit-maximizing quantity even easier. *The firm will choose its quantity such that price equals marginal cost.* You can see that from Figure 7. When the price is $80, the firm chooses a level of production for which the marginal cost equals $80 and produces 4 crates. Why is the price equals marginal cost rule for a competitive firm a special case of the marginal revenue equals marginal cost rule? Because *for the case of a price-taking firm in a competitive market, the marginal revenue is equal to the price.* Changes in the quantity of goods that the firm supplies do not affect the market price, so each additional unit sold brings in the same additional revenue, namely the market price of the good. For example, as we showed above, if the price of pumpkins is $10 per crate, then the marginal, or additional, revenue from producing 1 crate of pumpkins is $10. Later, in Chapter 10, we will show that for a *monopoly*, the marginal revenue does not equal the price, so that even though marginal revenue equals marginal cost, the price does not equal marginal cost.

A Comparison of the Two Approaches to Profit Maximization

We have now considered two different approaches to profit maximization. One approach looks at the explicit relationship between profits and production. The other approach compares the price to the marginal cost. Both approaches give the same answer. How do the approaches compare?

In Table 4 we looked at several prices, and we derived the profit-maximizing level of production by looking at profits for different levels of production at these prices. To do so, we had to create a new table for each price. This is quite time-consuming. In contrast, with the marginal cost approach, we only had to look at marginal cost for each unit of production and compare it with the price. Thus, the price equals marginal cost approach is considerably easier. Moreover, because marginal cost increases as the number of items produced increases, the price equals marginal cost approach tells us why the supply curve slopes upward. It is for these two reasons that economists usually use the price equals marginal cost approach.

R E V I E W

- The supply curve for a firm is derived by assuming that the firm chooses the quantity of production that maximizes profits. Profits are the difference between total revenue and total costs.

- As price changes, the profit-maximizing quantity changes as well. The relationship between price and the profit-maximizing quantity is the firm's supply curve.

- A profit table is an accurate if long-winded way of determining the profit-maximizing quantity produced by a firm for a given price. As the price changes, the profits calculated in the table change, providing a different profit-maximizing quantity.

- For the pumpkin-producing firm, the profit-maximizing quantity increased with price, resulting in an upward-sloping supply curve.

- A less work-intensive way of calculating the profit-maximizing quantity is to consider the marginal revenue and the marginal cost of an additional unit of production. If marginal revenue exceeds marginal cost, then profits would go up with the additional unit of production. If marginal revenue is less than marginal cost, then profits would go down with the additional unit of production.

- A profit-maximizing firm would therefore produce at a quantity such that marginal revenue equaled marginal cost.

■ For a competitive firm, marginal revenue equals the price of the good, since the firm's production decisions do not affect the market price. Therefore, the profit-maximizing quantity can be easily found as the quantity that equates the marginal cost with the price of the good.

■ Marginal cost increases as the quantity produced increases. Therefore, as price rises, the profit-maximizing firm will respond by increasing the quantity it produces. In other words, the upward-sloping marginal cost curve implies an upward-sloping supply curve.

THE MARKET SUPPLY CURVE

The *market* supply curve can be obtained by adding up the supply curves of all the *individual* firms in the market. Figure 9 gives an example in which there are two individual firm supply curves for pumpkins: One curve corresponds to your pumpkin firm, and the other, which is identical to yours, corresponds to the firm of your competitor, Fred, who is growing pumpkins on the other side of town. You and Fred have the same marginal cost for pumpkin growing, so your supply curves are exactly the same. You will both choose to produce the same number of pumpkins if the price is the same.

If only you and Fred are in the market, the market supply curve is the sum of just your two supplies. You get the market curve by adding in the horizontal direction, as shown in Figure 9. For example, if the price is $30, the quantity supplied by Fred will be 2 crates, and the quantity you supply will be 2 crates; thus the quantity supplied in the market at $30 is 4 crates. If the price rises to $50, Fred will produce 3 crates and you will also produce 3 crates; thus the quantity supplied in the market rises to 6 crates.

In reality, of course, there are more than two firms in a competitive market, and the individual supply curves for different firms in the market are usually different. But the concept of deriving the market supply curve is the same whether there are

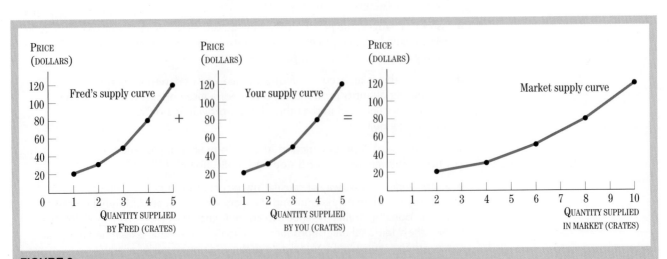

FIGURE 9
Derivation of the Market Supply Curve
The market supply curve is the sum of the individual firms' supply curves for all the firms in the market. The figure shows how the supply curves of two firms—Fred's and yours—sum to a market supply curve.

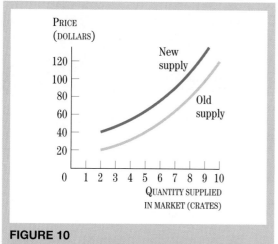

FIGURE 10
Shifts in the Market Supply Curve
An increase in marginal cost would shift the supply curve upward or to the left.

only 2 firms or 2,000 firms, and whether they are all the same or are all different. After adding up the individual supply curves for all the firms in the market, we arrive at a market supply curve like Figure 1. Thus, we have fulfilled one of the objectives of this chapter—deriving the market supply curve.

If there are many different firms in the market, the market supply curve can be much smoother than the individual supply curves. For example, a general contractor may be able to build only one house a year. But the market for new houses in any one year consists of many contractors with many different marginal costs. As the price of new houses rises, more and more contractors will build houses, and the market supply curve for houses will look very smooth.

The Slope of the Supply Curve

We have shown that the slope and position of the individual firms' supply curves depend on the marginal cost at the different firms. If marginal cost rises very sharply with more production, then the supply curve will be very steep. If marginal cost increases more gradually, then the supply curve will be flatter.

Because the market supply curve is the sum of the individual firms' supply curves, its slope will also depend on marginal cost. The market supply curve can get very steep at high levels of production because marginal cost gets very high when production is high.

Shifts in the Supply Curve

Because the supply curve for the individual firm is given by its marginal cost, anything that changes marginal cost will shift the individual supply curves and therefore the market supply curve. For example, a new technology might reduce the marginal cost at every level of production. If this happens, then the marginal cost curve will shift down and the profit-maximizing quantity for each price level will increase. Observe that a downward shift of the marginal cost curve is equivalent to a rightward shift of the supply curve. Similarly, an increase in marginal cost—perhaps because of a disease affecting the pumpkins, so that more labor is required for each crate of pumpkins—would shift the supply curve upward or to the left (see Figure 10).

REVIEW

- The market supply curve is derived by adding up the individual supply curves of all the firms in the market.

- When the price rises, the individual firms in the market increase the quantity supplied. Hence, the market supply curve is upward-sloping.

- The slope of the supply curve depends on how sharply marginal cost increases. If marginal cost rises very sharply with more production, then the supply curve will be steep. If marginal cost does not change very much as production increases, the supply curve will be flat.

- Anything that raises marginal cost will shift the market supply curve upward or to the left. Conversely, anything that lowers marginal cost will shift the market supply curve downward or to the right.

Supply Shifts Caused by Natural Disaster

Marginal cost is defined as the increase in total costs associated with each additional unit of production. Anything that decreases marginal cost will shift the supply curve down (or to the right), and anything that increases marginal cost will shift the supply curve up (or to the left). This article, which appeared in early 2005, discusses how U.S. firms would have to adjust to the effects of the tsunami that hit South and Southeast Asia in December of 2004. Can you identify the firms whose supply curves would have shifted in response to increased marginal costs—and those that would not have experienced such a shift?

After Tsunami, US Firms Adjust

By DIANE E. LEWIS | Global Staff

January 6, 2005

An example of how natural disasters can increase the marginal cost of production by destroying vital infrastructure

US companies whose goods are made in Southeast Asia are shifting production and changing distribution routes in order to limit the commercial impact of the deadly earthquake and tsunami.

Clothing retailer Gap Inc., with more than 700 manufacturing contractors worldwide, sought to minimize disruptions by transferring shipments bound for an Indian port to another site in the country.

"There were problems in southern India," said spokeswoman Kris Marubio. "Roads leading to the major thoroughfare were impacted. So we moved them to other ports in India. We did this over the past few days."

Although Southeast Asia has become a hub for apparel and footwear manufacturers, big US companies have so many contractors that they can readily shift production from one country to another without affecting retail prices, analysts say.

Gourmet coffee roasters, however, don't have that luxury. The natural disaster could limit the supply of coffee grown on the island of Sumatra and drive up already high prices.

Chuck Coffman, president of Armeno Coffee in Northborough, said Sumatran coffee has risen to about $3 per pound, almost double what he had been paying last year. He sells 17 varieties of Indonesian coffee, including Sumatran coffee made from the Arabica bean, prized among gourmands.

But this week, Coffman learned that future supplies could be jeopardized by lack of workers and bad roads.

"No one knows what will happen," said Coffman. "What we are fearing is that the crop will mature, but there will not be enough workers to pick it, and they may not be able to get it down from the mountains."

Before the natural disaster, the price of Sumatran coffee had risen 25 cents a pound last year because of concerns over limited supply. Now consumers will be paying more for Sumatran coffee.

The inward shift of the supply curve will raise prices for consumers.

"Potentially, I think there will be a higher acceptance for the higher price by the consumer," said Thomas Fricke, chief executive and cofounder of organic coffee producer ForesTrade, which gets 60 to 70 percent of its coffee from the Aceh region, one of the hardest-hit areas.

For owners of gourmet coffee stores and bars, the marginal cost of coffee beans has been driven up by the disaster.

Consumers "have the perception that people in Indonesia are having a difficult time and may be willing to accommodate higher prices, regardless whether the impact warrants it or not," he said.

Consumers could also see tuna and other fish prices increase. The tsunami destroyed fishing fleets in Indonesia, India, and Thailand, said John Connelly, president of the National Fisheries Institute in Washington, D.C. "Fishing fleets have been decimated, and that could impact the tuna we get," he said, adding that Thailand is a major exporter of tuna to the United States.

UPS, the global package delivery service, dealt with the disaster by implementing a plan to get relief and commercial goods into parts of Indonesia with smaller aircraft.

"Commerce is pretty much at a standstill in some areas because there is so much congestion due to the aid relief in the airport and ports," said spokesman John Flick. "Before the tsunami, when we flew to Jakarta, we used one aircraft. Now, Jakarta has been taken out of the equation. We're going directly to the smaller islands, and going directly to smaller aircraft to move goods." ◀

Other examples of how marginal costs have been increased by the strains put on infrastructure by a disaster

While many apparel and footwear factories may have escaped damage, distribution problems could arise, analysts say. Footwear companies like Reebok and Nike, which produce a good portion of their shoes in the region, could face some obstacles if they rely on trucks to transport goods along roads uprooted by the earthquake, or use ports glutted with goods from relief efforts.

"The biggest impact may be that some of the trucks that move product from the factory to ports will not be available," said Madison Riley, a principal and national service director for consulting firm Kurt Salmon & Associates Inc.

"Future distribution could be impacted somewhat," he said. "But I don't see prices going up. Instead, if products are delayed retailers might cancel some of it and wholesalers could be stuck with it. But there could be a greater opportunity for lower-cost products."

At Reebok, where about 40 percent of its shoes are made in Thailand and Indonesia, there were no disruptions to the firm's **supply chain** or production, said spokesman Denise Kaigler.

Nike said one of its apparel contractors in Sri Lanka appears to have been damaged by the tsunami, but that would not affect overall production. Five percent of the firm's global apparel production is located in the region, said Caitlin Morrs, Nike's senior manager of global issues management.

As of October, Nike had 42 contractors in Indonesia, including nine footwear producers, 29 apparel makers, and five producers of athletic equipment such as yoga mats and golf bags, she said. Most were based in Jakarta, where there is no damage.

Source: Diane Lewis, "After Tsunami, US Firms Adjust," *Boston Globe,* January 6, 2005. Copyright 2005 by the *Boston Globe.* Reproduced with permission of the *Boston Globe* in the format textbook, conveyed via Copyright Clearance Center, Inc.

PRODUCER SURPLUS

producer surplus: the difference between the price received by a firm for an additional item sold and the marginal cost of the item's production; for the market as a whole, it is the sum of all the individual firms' producer surpluses, or the area above the market supply curve and below the market price.

In Chapter 5, we learned about consumer surplus, the difference between the marginal benefit derived from consuming an additional item and the price paid for it, as a measure of how well off consumers are. We can derive a similar concept for measuring how well off producers are by engaging in the production of goods for the market. **Producer surplus** is defined as the difference between the marginal cost of an item and the price received for it. For example, suppose that the price of pumpkins is $25, at which price you produce 1 crate of pumpkins. Then you get $25 for producing 1 crate and incur $20 in marginal cost. The difference, $5, is your producer surplus for producing that first crate of pumpkins. If the price of pumpkins is $35, you produce 2 crates and your producer surplus is $15 ($35 − $20) for the first crate plus $5 ($35 − $30) for the second crate, for a total of $20 producer surplus.

A Graphical Representation of Producer Surplus

Producer surplus can be represented graphically as the area above the individual firm supply curve and below the price line, as illustrated in Figure 11. Producer surplus in the whole market can be obtained by adding up producer surplus for all producers or by looking at the area above the market supply curve and below the price. This is illustrated in Figure 12. Producer surplus provides a measure of how much a producer gains from the market. The sum of producer surplus plus consumer surplus is a comprehensive measure of how well a market economy works, as we will see in Chapter 7.

What Is the Difference Between Profits and Producer Surplus?

Profits and producer surplus are not the same thing. Profits are the difference between total revenue and total costs, while the producer surplus measures the difference between the price and the marginal cost of every unit. How can we compare these two measures?

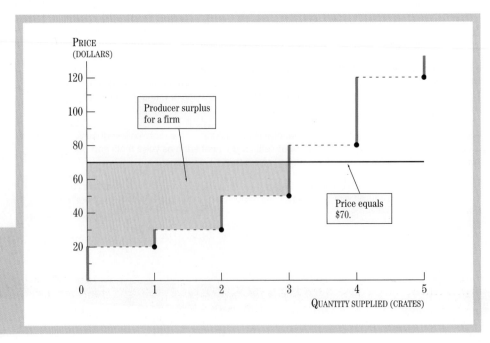

FIGURE 11
Producer Surplus for an Individual Firm
As shown here, for an individual firm, the producer surplus is the area between the price line and the supply curve.

Suppose the price of pumpkins is $70 per crate; then you are willing to produce 3 crates of pumpkins. Total revenue is $210 and total costs are $150; thus, you are making a $60 profit. (See panel II of Table 4.) How much is your producer surplus when 3 crates are sold at $70? As just defined,

$$\text{Producer surplus} = (P - MC_1) + (P - MC_2) + (P - MC_3)$$
$$= (\$70 - \$20) + (\$70 - \$30) + (\$70 - \$50) = \$110$$

where MC_1 is the marginal cost of the first crate, MC_2 is the marginal cost of the second crate, and MC_3 is the marginal cost of the third crate. Thus, profits are $60 and producer surplus is $110.

Notice that there is a difference of $50 between profits and producer surplus. That number happens to be equal to the fixed costs of the firm. Thus, producer surplus equals profit plus fixed costs. Try using the same method for different prices and quantities sold, and you will arrive at the same result: Producer surplus always equals profits plus fixed costs. We now show that this is no coincidence.

When the producer sells a quantity Q, we can say that

$$\text{Producer surplus} = (P - MC_1) + (P - MC_2) + (P - MC_3) + \cdots + (P - MC_Q)$$

The number of terms in this sum is Q. For the example above, $Q = 3$ and there were Q terms in the sum. Thus, we can translate this definition of producer surplus into the price (P) of the good times the quantity (Q) sold minus the sum of the marginal costs of all units. That is,

$$\text{Producer surplus} = (P \times Q) - \text{sum of marginal costs}$$

Since $P \times Q$ is total revenue, we can write the above equation as

$$\text{Producer surplus} = \text{total revenue} - \text{sum of marginal costs}$$

The marginal cost of an additional unit is the additional costs incurred in producing that unit of output. Thus, as we sum up marginal costs for any quantity Q produced, we count all costs associated with increasing production from zero units to Q units. To obtain total costs, we would need to add fixed costs, the cost of producing zero units, to the above sum. In other words,

$$\text{Total costs} = \text{sum of marginal costs} + \text{fixed costs}$$

This can be rearranged to show that

$$\text{Sum of marginal costs} = \text{total costs} - \text{fixed costs}$$

Substituting into the definition of producer surplus, we can see therefore that

$$\text{Producer surplus} = \text{total revenue} - (\text{total costs} - \text{fixed costs})$$

This implies that

$$\text{Producer surplus} = \text{total revenue} - \text{total costs} + \text{fixed costs}$$

which gives us the result we want in order to understand the difference between profits and producer surplus, namely that

$$\text{Producer surplus} = \text{profits} + \text{fixed costs}$$

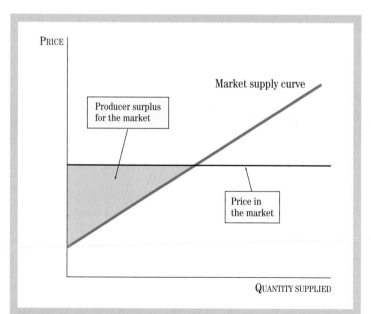

FIGURE 12
Producer Surplus for the Market
If we add up producer surplus for every firm, we get the producer surplus for the whole market. This is given by the area between the price and the market supply curve.

R E V I E W

- Producer surplus associated with an item is the difference between the price a firm receives for selling that item and the marginal cost of producing that item. It is a measure of how well off producers are as a result of their decision to produce that item.

- Graphically, producer surplus for a firm is the area below the price line and above the firm's supply curve.

- For all the firms in a market, the producer surplus is the area below the price line and above the market supply curve.

- Producer surplus is different from profits. Producer surplus is greater than profits by the amount of fixed costs.

CONCLUSION

In this chapter, we derived the supply curve in a competitive market by looking at the behavior of firms. We assumed that a firm decides how much to produce at a given market price by choosing the quantity that maximizes profits. The firm makes this decision taking prices as given and considering its production function, which relates the number of hours of work at the firm to the output of the firm. The production function enters the firm's profit calculations through its effects on the firm's costs. Because the production function has diminishing returns to labor, the firm faces increasing marginal cost.

Profit maximization implies that the firm will produce the quantity where marginal revenue equals marginal cost. In a competitive market, the marginal revenue from selling an additional unit always equals the price. Therefore the profit-maximizing quantity is where price equals marginal cost.

As the price rises, the firm will respond by increasing production until marginal cost and price are equal again. As a result, the supply curve for an individual firm will be upward-sloping. The slope of the supply curve will be steep when marginal cost increases rapidly as more units are produced, and it will be flat when marginal cost does not rise by very much as more units are produced. The supply curve will shift out when marginal cost falls because of some event like a change in technology and shift in when marginal cost rises.

The connection between marginal cost and the supply curve is fundamental to understanding how markets work. We will make use of this connection many times throughout this book, especially when we consider public policy issues, such as the efficiency of markets, taxation, and regulation of firms. When economists see or draw a supply curve, they are usually thinking about the marginal cost of the firms that underlie the supply curve. The supply curve and the marginal cost curve are virtually synonymous for economists.

We have examined firm behavior in this chapter and consumer behavior in Chapter 5. In Chapter 7 we will examine the interactions of these firms and consumers. In Chapters 5 and 6, we derived two rules for characterizing individual and firm behavior: Profit-maximizing firms will produce according to the price equals marginal cost rule, while utility-maximizing consumers will consume according to the price equals marginal benefit rule. In Chapter 7, we will combine these two concepts to point out an attractive feature of competitive markets.

KEY POINTS

1. A firm is an organization that uses inputs to produce goods or services.

2. In a competitive market, no single firm can affect the price.

3. The foundations of supply are found in the profit-maximizing behavior of firms, with each firm's supply curve being derived as the profit-maximizing quantity that corresponds to various possible market prices.

4. Profits are defined as total revenue minus total costs. Total revenue increases as the quantity sold increases. Total costs, which are the sum of fixed costs and variable costs, also increase with production.

5. The change in total costs when production is increased is called marginal cost. How large marginal cost is depends on the production function, which shows how many inputs are needed for producing different quantities of output. Marginal cost increases as more is produced because of diminishing returns to inputs.

6. A firm produces up to the point where marginal revenue equals marginal cost, which is the key rule for profit maximization. In a competitive market, marginal revenue always equals the price of the good. Therefore, the profit-maximizing quantity for a price-taking firm can easily be found as the quantity such that price equals marginal cost.

7. The reason the supply curve slopes upward is that marginal cost is increasing. A higher price enables the firm to produce at higher levels of marginal cost. The marginal cost curve and the supply curve are virtually synonymous.

8. The market supply curve is obtained by adding up the individual supply curves. The market supply curve can be smooth even if the individual supply curves are not.

9. Producer surplus is the difference between the price of a good and its marginal cost of production. Graphically, producer surplus for an individual firm is the area above the individual supply curve and below the price line. The producer surplus for all firms in the market is the area above the market supply curve and below the price line.

10. Producer surplus and profit are not the same thing. Producer surplus equals profits plus fixed costs.

KEY TERMS

firm
price-taker
competitive market
profits

total revenue
total costs
production function
marginal product of labor

diminishing returns to labor
variable costs
fixed costs

marginal cost
profit maximization
marginal revenue
producer surplus

QUESTIONS FOR REVIEW

1. What is a firm?

2. What is the definition of a competitive market?

3. Describe the relationships that exist among total costs, fixed costs, variable costs, and marginal cost.

4. Why does marginal cost increase as more is produced?

5. Why does profit maximization imply that marginal revenue equals marginal cost? Why is it that in a competitive market only, profit maximization implies that price equals marginal cost?

6. What is the relationship between an individual firm's supply curve and its marginal cost curve?

7. How is the market supply curve derived from individual supply curves?

8. Why might the market supply curve be smoother than the individual supply curves?

9. What is producer surplus and how is it calculated?

10. How does producer surplus differ from profits?

PROBLEMS

1. Name three businesses in which firms are price-takers. Name three businesses in which firms are not price-takers. Suppose you set up a business where you tutor students on campus. Would you be a price-taker or a price-maker?

2. Does the assumption that firms are price-takers in a market seem less valid than the assumption that consumers are price-takers in that market? Explain why. Would your answer change if you were told that there were 50 firms and 50 consumers in the market? Explain.

3. Before the Industrial Revolution, people lived in agricultural societies. What are the two primary inputs to production in an agricultural society? Which one of these inputs is variable and which one is fixed? Why is there reason to believe that the rate of growth of the food supply will slow down as the population increases?

4. Consider the example of the cost of pumpkins in Table 4. Compute the total revenue, total costs, and profits when the price of a crate of pumpkins is $60. How many crates of pumpkins will maximize profits? Now find the profit-maximizing quantity by using the marginal cost approach. How do your answers compare? Which approach did you find easier?

5. The following table shows the total costs of producing strawberries on a small plot of land.

Pounds of Strawberries	Total Costs (dollars)
0	10
1	11
2	14
3	18
4	25
5	34

a. Calculate the marginal cost schedule.
b. Draw the farmer's supply curve.
c. Suppose the price of 1 pound of strawberries is $4. How much would this farmer produce? What are profits?
d. Suppose the price of strawberries goes up to $7 per pound. How much will the farmer produce now? What are profits now?

6. Suppose a price-taking producer of barrels for storing wine has the following total costs schedule:

Quantity	Total Costs
0	20
1	30
2	42
3	55
4	75
5	100
6	130

a. Calculate marginal cost. If the price of a barrel in the market is $20, how many barrels will the firm produce?
b. Suppose the price in the market falls to $12 per barrel. How many barrels will this firm produce in order to maximize profits?
c. Suppose there is an improvement in technology that shifts total costs down by $8 at every level of production. How much will the firm produce and what will profits be at a price of $20 and at a price of $12?

7. Consider the following information:

Quantity Produced (dozens of loaves)	Total Costs (dollars)
0	20
1	22
2	26
3	32
4	40
5	50
6	62
7	76

Daily Production and Costs at Jill's Bread Bakers

a. Calculate the marginal cost for Jill's bread production.
b. Draw the supply curve for this firm.
c. Jill can sell as many loaves as she wants in the market at a price of $12 for a dozen loaves. How many loaves will she sell each day? What are her profits?
d. Use your diagram to show how much producer surplus Jill receives.

8. Suppose you are able to mow lawns at $12 per hour. The only cost to you is the opportunity cost of your time. For the first 3 hours, the opportunity cost of your time is $9 per hour. But after 3 hours, the opportunity cost of your time rises to $15 per hour because of other commitments.

   Draw the marginal cost to you of mowing lawns. On that diagram, draw in the price you receive for mowing loans, indicate for how long you will mow lawns, and graphically indicate the area of your producer surplus in addition to calculating the magnitude of your producer surplus.

9. Consider the following information about a firm that sells ice cream–making machines:

Quantity	Total Costs	Total Revenue
0	500	0
1	700	500
2	1,100	1,000
3	1,500	1,500
4	2,300	2,000
5	3,500	2,500

   On the same diagram, plot the total revenues and total costs curves for this firm. What are the maximum profits that this firm can earn? Show this level of profits in the diagram. What is the relationship between the slopes of the two curves at the quantity that maximizes profits?

10. What is the relationship between producer surplus, profits, and fixed costs? In what types of industries would you expect producer surplus to be high while profits are low? Provide one or two examples of such industries.

Chapter 7

The Interaction of People in Markets

This is an old but true story, going back to before the field of economics even existed. It is about an absent-minded philosophy professor who was interested in understanding human interaction. He was particularly fascinated by how the economy, consisting of the interaction of millions of people pursuing their own interests, worked. He did not have much to go on; there were no economics professors at his school or at any other school. So, although he was a gifted teacher, he quit his teaching job at the university and traveled; he interviewed businesspeople; he visited factories; he talked to workers; he watched ships come and go; he studied the economies of other countries and of other times. Amazingly, not only was he able to pull all this material together into a coherent view, but he also managed to get it down on paper for other people to read, learn, and enjoy. By doing so, he invented the field of economics and presented a view of the economy that is still the dominant view today.

The professor's name was Adam Smith, and the book he wrote, called *Wealth of Nations*, was first published in 1776. His deepest insight, among many deep insights, is called the **invisible hand** theorem, best stated using his own words: "It is not from the benevolence of the butcher, the brewer, or the baker that we expect our dinner, but from their regard to their own interest." And whether it is the butcher, the brewer, or the baker, he is "led by an invisible hand to promote an end which was no part of his intention. . . . By pursuing his own interest he frequently promotes that of the society more effectually than when he really intends to promote it." In other words, without any formal coordination, firms (butchers, brewers, bakers, and many others) that are pursuing their own interests interact with consumers who are also pursuing their own interests, and somehow everyone ends up producing and consuming a quantity that is efficient.

The main goal of this chapter is to state clearly and prove the invisible hand theorem. The theorem is not always true, and we want to be clear about the circumstances

invisible hand: the idea that the free interaction of people in a market economy leads to a desirable social outcome; the term was coined by Adam Smith.

Corporate leaders gather in a field outside Darien, Connecticut, where one of them claims to have seen the invisible hand of the marketplace.

competitive equilibrium model: a model that assumes utility maximization on the part of consumers and profit maximization on the part of firms, along with competitive markets and freely determined prices.

in which it is true. We first need to explain what is meant by *efficient* (the modern term for Smith's "effectual"), and then show why and under what circumstances the quantity produced and consumed is efficient. We also show how to measure the economic loss from producing more or less than the efficient quantity.

Chapters 5 and 6 have paved the way for our goal in this chapter. In Chapter 5 we studied the behavior of consumers. We can say that consumers who maximize their utility are pursuing their own interests. In Chapter 6 we studied the behavior of firms. We can say that firms that maximize profits are also pursuing their own interests. Now we study the interactions of firms and consumers in competitive markets. Figure 1 is a schematic illustration of the model we use to explain this interaction and thereby explain the invisible hand theorem. The model, called the **competitive equilibrium model,** is the supply and demand model discussed in Chapter 3, now with the behavior of consumers and firms explicit.

INDIVIDUAL CONSUMERS AND FIRMS IN A MARKET

In our analysis of economic interaction, it is very important to think about what individual consumers and firms are doing. Consider an example of consumers and producers of the same commodity: long-stemmed roses. Maria and Ken are two of many potential rose consumers who are deciding how many roses to buy. Both are willing to pay a certain amount for roses, but not necessarily the same amount. Hugo and Mimi are two of many rose producers who are deciding how many roses to produce in their gardens. They are both willing to sell roses provided the price is right, but they have different marginal costs for producing roses.

The Hard Way to Process Information, Coordinate, and Motivate

The actions of Maria, Ken, Hugo, Mimi, and all the others in the market clearly have an effect on one another. For example, an increase in Hugo's marginal costs—perhaps because of the need to use a new pesticide to ward off an insect infestation—will

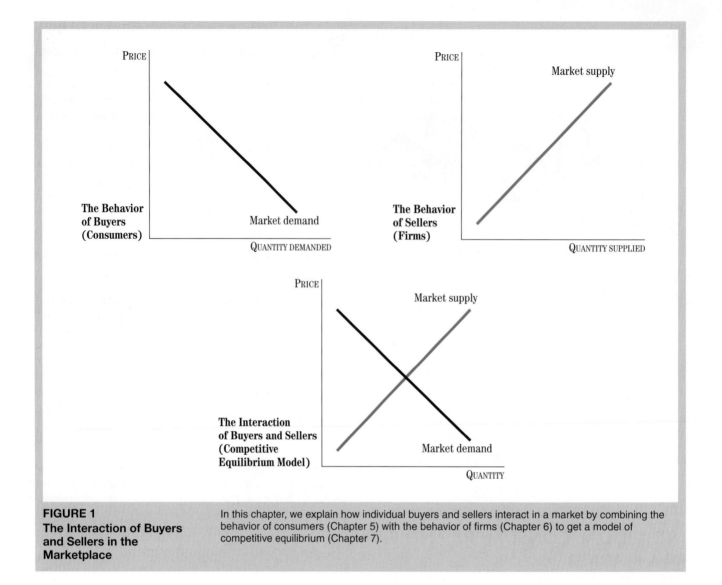

FIGURE 1
The Interaction of Buyers and Sellers in the Marketplace

In this chapter, we explain how individual buyers and sellers interact in a market by combining the behavior of consumers (Chapter 5) with the behavior of firms (Chapter 6) to get a model of competitive equilibrium (Chapter 7).

probably reduce the number of roses he decides to produce; either this means less rose consumption for Ken, Maria, and other consumers, or it means more rose production for Mimi and other producers. Similarly, if Ken finds a new romantic interest and decides to purchase more roses on a weekly basis, someone else must decide to decrease consumption or increase production.

How are all these decisions worked out? What *information* is needed in order to determine that an increase in rose production is needed to meet the additional demand coming from Ken or to cover the shortfall in production coming from Hugo? Who *coordinates* whether the production increases needed to meet Ken's demand comes from Hugo's garden or Mimi's garden? Who decides whether Maria should cut back her consumption or Mimi should increase her production in response to Hugo's production cutbacks? What *motivates* Hugo, Mimi, and others to produce more if consumption rises, or motivates Ken, Maria, and other consumers to consume less if production falls?

Suppose you had to work out all these issues. To make your job easier, suppose that Maria, Ken, Hugo, and Mimi were the whole world as far as roses go. If you and they were all in one place together, you might imagine providing information so that they could adjust their consumption and production activities to respond to changing market conditions. When more production was needed, you would inform Mimi of the problems that Hugo was having and ask her to increase the number of roses she produces to make up for the shortfall. When Ken started buying more roses, you would have to explain to Maria about Ken's new romantic interest and ask her to cut back on her consumption, or you would have to inform Hugo and Mimi that they need to increase production to meet Ken's insatiable demand for roses.

But simply providing information is not enough. You would also have to coordinate the responses of the various consumers and firms. In response to Ken's increased purchases of roses, for example, you would have to determine how much of the extra output was being produced by Mimi and how much was being produced by Hugo. You would also have to make sure that Maria's consumption plans had not changed in the meantime. Coordinating the actions of even two consumers and two firms can be a challenge!

Even if you provided sufficient information, and in spite of your best attempts at coordinating everyone's responses, there would be no guarantee that either the consumers or the producers would change their behavior unless they had a reason for doing so. To provide motivation, you might reason with Mimi that she could sell more now that Hugo had production problems or plead with Maria to cut back on her rose purchases until Ken's romantic fervor cools or cajole Hugo and Mimi to increase production.

If this is not already beginning to sound ridiculously impossible, remember that if you had this job in the real world, you would have to coordinate, motivate, and know intimately millions of consumers and producers. This is an amazingly complex job even for this single, relatively simple commodity.

The Easy Way to Process Information, Coordinate, and Motivate

Fortunately, you do not need to worry about being called upon to perform such an impossible task. What Adam Smith showed was that there is a remarkable device that does the information processing, coordinating, and motivating for us. No one person invented this device; it evolved slowly over thousands of years and is probably still evolving. It is called *the market*. Of course, like many markets, the rose market does not take place in any one location. It consists of all the florists, street carts, and farmers' markets where roses are sold and all the gardens and greenhouses where roses are grown, whether in the United States, Europe, Latin America, Africa, Australia, or Asia. Fortunately, a market can serve as an information-processing, coordinating, and motivating device even if it does not take place at any one location. In fact, buyers and sellers never even have to see one another.

How does the market work? What will be the total quantity of roses consumed? Who will consume what amount? What will be the total quantity of roses produced? Which firm will produce what amount? Let us see how economists answer these questions about how people interact in a market.

Coordination Failure in Responding to a Famine

One of the last remaining centrally planned economies is North Korea, a country where political and economic activity is very tightly controlled by its reclusive leader, Kim Jong-Il. A famine during the 1990s killed hundreds of thousands of people in North Korea; even today a significant proportion of the North Korean population suffers from malnutrition and hunger. Since all economic activity in North Korea is dictated by central government planners, an effective response to this food shortfall requires skillful coordination between farmers, traders, and importers to get goods to the market. Unfortunately, the North Korean government has clearly been incapable of rising to the task. This article, which appeared in early 2007, symbolizes the often farcical attempts of the government to do this.

A government official thinks he has a solution to the challenge of feeding hundreds of thousands of hungry people.

The next step is for the government to step in and set up a breeding program.

Without seeming to recognize that this was hardly a cost-effective solution—it would take food that the country did not have to create food that the country needed.

A Colossal Leap of Faith in Fight Against Famine; North Koreans See Potential in German Breeder's Giants

CRAIG WHITLOCK | Washington Post Foreign Service

Few people raise bigger bunny rabbits than Karl Szmolinsky, who has been producing long-eared whoppers since 1964. His favorite breed, German gray giants, are the size of a full-grown beagle and so fat they can barely hop. Last year, after the retired chauffeur entered some of his monsters in an agricultural fair, word of his breeding skills spread to the North Korean Embassy in Berlin. Diplomats looked past the cute, furry faces with the twitching noses and saw a possible solution to their nation's endemic food shortage: an enormous bunny in every Korean pot.

The North Koreans approached Szmolinsky in November and asked whether he'd advise them on how to start a rabbit breeding program to help "feed the population," the 67-year-old pensioner recalled in an interview at his home in Eberswalde, an eastern German town a few miles from the Polish border. Sympathetic to the Koreans' plight, he agreed to sell some of his best stock at a steep discount and volunteered to travel to the hermetic nation as a consultant. "They liked what they saw, and they liked how big they were," he said, as he showed off other bunnies that he raises in weathered hutches in his back yard. "It's harder than you think to raise them. They need a varied diet, but they have to be fed like pigs, basically, to get that big."

In December, Szmolinsky stuffed six of his rabbits into modified dog carriers and took them to the airport in Berlin, where they boarded a flight for Pyongyang, via Frankfurt, Germany, and Beijing. Robert, a 23-pounder, was the largest of the bunch, which included four female rabbits and one other male carefully selected for their breeding potential.

How, exactly, the Democratic People's Republic of Korea intends to parlay the small herd of German Flopsies into hunger relief for its 23 million citizens is unclear. An official at the

The government plan was to turn 6 rabbits into a hunger relief plan for 23 million people!

North Korean Embassy in Berlin, who would not give his name, confirmed that the Asian nation coveted the German bunnies for their gigantism. But he refused to answer any other questions about the breeding program.

In the hands of a skilled butcher, a German gray giant can yield up to 15 pounds of meat, according to Szmolinsky. "There's not much fat, and it's very tender." Their gray-and-white pelts are soft and supple but are generally worthless on the European market, he said. The breeder said he was notified by an attache at the North Korean Embassy that Robert and the other rabbits from Eberswalde had arrived safely at their destination. But he allowed that he was a little concerned their new masters might not know how to care for them properly. He said he hopes to travel to North Korea in April to inspect their living conditions."If they aren't able to feed them the way I do here, I won't send them any more," he said. "I don't want them to be half-starved."

The Koreans' choice of rabbits has other German breeders scratching their heads. Karl-Heinz Heitz, chairman of the State Association of Rabbit Breeders in Berlin-Brandenburg, said that German gray giants are hard to beat for size but that they aren't cheap to fatten up. It takes wheelbarrow-loads of hay, vegetables and rabbit chow to bring them to maturity. "Let me say this: There are certainly breeds that are more economically profitable; I do not know why the North Koreans wanted this one," said Heitz, who introduced the Korean officials to Szmolinsky.

Breeds such as New Zealand red or big light silver or Vienna blue are only half as big but are more cost-effective to raise. "You do not have to put in as much to get out a fair amount of meat," Heitz said. For whatever reason, the German gray giants appear to hold a special allure in Asia. A North Korean television crew visited Eberswalde last year to film Szmolinsky's rabbits for a children's program. And a couple of Chinese visitors showed up unannounced at his doorstep the other day, asking if they could buy some of his critters." I had to get rid of them," he said of the Chinese. He's not parting with any of his 14 remaining adult rabbits until he can breed some more.

What the lack of a profit incentive has led the North Koreans into. Even for a far-fetched scheme, they seem to have picked the most inefficient version possible.

One-Stop Shopping for Processing Information, Coordinating, and Motivating: The Market
This New York City flower vendor represents just one piece of the huge and multifaceted market for flowers that exists throughout the world.

The Competitive Equilibrium Model

Economists use the *individual* demand curves and the *individual* supply curves derived in Chapters 5 and 6 to describe what happens to consumers and firms when they interact in a market.

Recall that each of the individual demand curves depends on the marginal benefit—the willingness to pay for additional consumption—the individual gets from consuming the goods. Together, these marginal benefits create a market demand curve for roses. The demand curve shows how much consumers in total are willing to buy at each price.

Recall also that individual supply curves depend on the marginal costs of the firms. Together, their marginal costs create a market supply curve for roses. The supply curve shows the total quantity supplied by all firms at each price.

The resulting market demand and supply curves are shown in the center of Figure 2, flanked by Maria's and Ken's individual demand curves and by Hugo's and Mimi's individual supply curves. We continue to assume that Maria, Ken, Hugo, and Mimi are the whole market so that we can show the market in one diagram. A competitive market would typically require more buyers and sellers. The price (*P*, measured in dollars per rose) is on the vertical axis, and the quantity (*Q*, the number of roses) is on the horizontal axis.

We have seen supply and demand curves like those in the center of Figure 2 before in Chapter 3. But now—after Chapters 5 and 6—we know much more about what the demand and supply curves mean. Individual consumer behavior and individual firm behavior are now seen as underlying the supply and demand model. To emphasize that the supply and demand model incorporates utility-maximizing consumers and profit-maximizing firms in competitive markets, we refer to it as the *competitive equilibrium model*. Making the behavior of consumers and firms more explicit implies that we can do more analysis with the competitive equilibrium model than we were previously able to do with the supply and demand model.

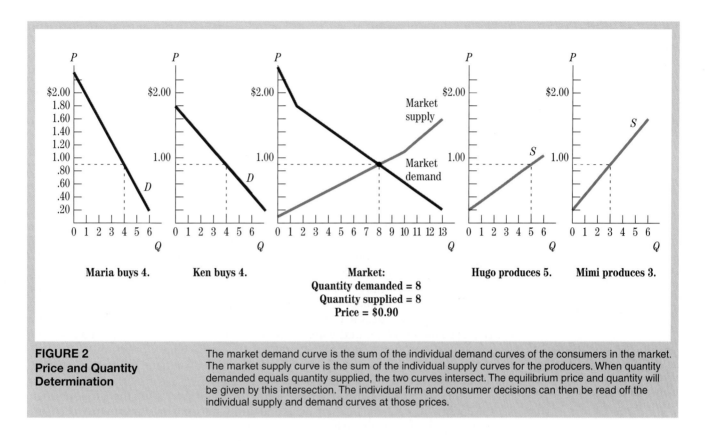

Maria buys 4.   Ken buys 4.   **Market:**
Quantity demanded = 8
Quantity supplied = 8
Price = $0.90   Hugo produces 5.   Mimi produces 3.

FIGURE 2
Price and Quantity
Determination

The market demand curve is the sum of the individual demand curves of the consumers in the market. The market supply curve is the sum of the individual supply curves for the producers. When quantity demanded equals quantity supplied, the two curves intersect. The equilibrium price and quantity will be given by this intersection. The individual firm and consumer decisions can then be read off the individual supply and demand curves at those prices.

■ **Individual Production and Consumption Decisions.** A key prediction of the competitive equilibrium model is that a price will emerge from the interaction of people in the market such that the quantity supplied *equals* the quantity demanded. This is the *equilibrium price*. Graphically, the price is given at the point of intersection of the market supply curve and the market demand curve; here the quantity supplied in the market equals the quantity demanded in the market. For the example shown in Figure 2, the equilibrium price is $.90 a rose.

equilibrium price: the price at which quantity supplied equals quantity demanded. (Ch. 3)

Once we have determined the price in this way, the supply and demand curves tell us how much in total will be consumed and produced at that price. We look at the market demand curve and see how much is demanded at that price, and we look at the market supply curve and see how much is supplied at that price. Because the curves intersect at the market price, the quantity demanded and the quantity supplied are the same. They are at the point on the horizontal axis directly below the intersection. In Figure 2, the quantity bought and sold is 8 roses.

Thus far, we have not done anything more with the competitive equilibrium model than we did with the supply and demand model. But now, armed with the price, we can go to the individual demand curves to see how much Maria and Ken will buy. Look to the left in Figure 2 to find the quantity demanded by Maria and by Ken when the price is $.90 a rose. They each buy 4 roses. Maria and Ken are motivated to buy this amount—without any central coordinator—because, at $.90 a rose, they maximize their respective utilities by consuming this amount. Observe that Maria and Ken do not have the same individual demand curves. Nevertheless, the quantity demanded by each can still be determined from their demand curves, as shown in Figure 2.

The individual supply curves tell us how much Hugo and Mimi will produce. Look to the right in Figure 2 to see how much Hugo and Mimi produce when the price is $.90 a rose. Hugo produces 5 roses, and Mimi produces 3 roses. Hugo and

Mimi are motivated to produce this amount—again without any central coordinator—because, at $.90 a rose, they maximize their profits by producing this amount.

In sum, the competitive equilibrium model, which includes the behavior of the consumers and the firms, not only predicts the equilibrium price and quantity in the market, it also predicts the quantity consumed by each person and the quantity produced by each firm.

▨ **Adjustment to the Equilibrium Price.**   In Figure 2, consider what would happen if the price were higher than the price at the intersection of the supply curve and the demand curve, say $1.20. At that price, utility-maximizing consumers like Maria and Ken would consume 3 units each, so the quantity demanded would be 6 units. However, at the higher price, profit maximizers like Hugo and Mimi would increase their production, with Hugo producing 6 units and Mimi producing 4 units. The quantity supplied would exceed the quantity demanded; there would be a *surplus* in the market. When there is a surplus, the price will fall, resulting in demand increasing and supply decreasing until the surplus disappears.

surplus (excess supply):
a situation in which quantity supplied is greater than quantity demanded. (Ch. 3)

Conversely, suppose the price were lower than the predicted market price, say $.60. At that price, utility-maximizing consumers like Maria and Ken would consume 5 units each, so the quantity demanded would be 10 units. However, at the lower price, profit maximizers like Hugo and Mimi would decrease their production, with Hugo producing 3 units and Mimi producing 2 units. The quantity supplied would be much less than the quantity demanded; there would be a *shortage* in the market. When there is a shortage, the price will rise, resulting in demand decreasing and supply increasing until the shortage disappears

shortage (excess demand):
a situation in which quantity demanded is greater than quantity supplied. (Ch. 3)

Thus, if the price falls when there is a surplus and rises when there is a shortage, the actions of profit-maximizing firms and utility-maximizing consumers will ensure that the price will converge to the equilibrium price.

R E V I E W

- Centrally coordinating and motivating the thousands of consumers and producers of any good would be an amazingly complex task requiring a vast amount of information.

- The market is a device that provides information and coordinates and motivates consumers and producers in a decentralized way. The market does this job in a way that no one individual can.

- Economists describe the interactions of people in the market through the competitive equilibrium model, which is the supply and demand model with consumer and firm behavior made more explicit.

- According to the model, the equilibrium price and quantity are given by the intersection of the market supply and demand curves. At the equilibrium price, we can use the individual demand curves to find out each individual's decisions about consumption and use the individual firms' supply curves to figure out each firm's production decisions.

ARE COMPETITIVE MARKETS EFFICIENT?

We have shown how to use the competitive equilibrium model to explain *how* a market works. Now let's use the competitive equilibrium model to see *how well* the market works. Are the quantities produced and consumed in the market efficient?

The Meaning of Efficient

In general, an inefficient outcome is one that wastes scarce resources, and an efficient outcome is one that does not waste scarce resources. Extremely inefficient economic outcomes are easy to spot. Constructing 300 million new coffeehouses each year in the United States (or approximately one store per person) would obviously be wasteful. The workers building the new stores could be building other things that people wanted. If the U.S. economy produced such an outcome, everyone would say it was inefficient; shifting production to fewer coffeehouses would clearly make many people better off.

An equally inefficient situation would occur if only one new coffeehouse a year was built; at that rate, it would take more than 7,000 years to match the number of Starbucks stores that now exist in the United States. In such a situation, shifting production toward more coffeehouses would clearly make many people better off.

Both these situations are inefficient because a change in production could make people better off. We might, therefore, define an efficient outcome as one that is so good that there is no change that would make people better off.

■ **The Need for a More Precise Definition.**   However, because the economy consists of many different people, we need to be more careful in defining efficiency. For every economic outcome, it is possible to make someone better off at the expense of someone else. If someone takes a long-stemmed rose from Maria and gives it to Ken, then Ken is better off, but Maria is worse off. More generally, the possibility of transferring a good from one person to another, thereby making someone better off at the expense of someone else, is not an indication that an economic situation is inefficient or wasteful.

However, if there were a situation in which it was possible to change consumption or production in a way that would make someone better off without hurting someone else, then that situation would be inefficient. In such a situation, resources are being wasted, because someone, perhaps many people, could have a better life without someone else being harmed.

Pareto efficient: a situation in which it is not possible to make someone better off without making someone else worse off.

Based on such considerations, economists have developed the following definition of efficiency: An outcome is **Pareto efficient** if it is not possible to make someone better off without hurting someone else. The Italian economist Vilfredo Pareto is the person who developed this concept of efficiency. Economists use the term *Pareto* to distinguish this definition of efficiency from other meanings, but unless we say otherwise, when we use the term *efficient* in this chapter, we mean efficient in the sense of Pareto. If a market is not efficient in the sense of Pareto, then there is something wrong with the market.

■ **Three Conditions for Efficient Outcomes.**   There are three conditions that must hold if a market outcome is to be efficient in the sense of Pareto efficient.

First efficiency condition: $MB = MC$ for last item produced.

First, *the marginal benefit* (MB) *must equal the marginal cost* (MC) *of the last item produced.* Why is this condition needed for efficiency? Suppose it did not hold. If the marginal cost of the last item produced is greater than the marginal benefit, then too much is being produced. In the example of producing 300 million coffeehouses a year, the marginal cost of producing the 300 millionth coffeehouse is much greater than the marginal benefit. Reducing production (by a lot) would be appropriate. If the marginal cost of the last item produced is less than the marginal benefit, then too little is being produced. In the example of producing only one coffeehouse a year, the marginal cost is certainly much less than the marginal benefit; more production would be appropriate. Only when marginal benefit is equal to marginal cost is the economic outcome efficient.

One way to better appreciate this condition is to imagine that you grow your own roses in your own garden. Clearly you would never produce more roses if the marginal cost to you was greater than the marginal benefit to you. But you would produce more roses if your marginal benefit from more roses was greater than your marginal cost. Only when marginal benefit equals marginal cost would you stop producing and consuming more.

The second condition for efficiency relates to the production of goods at different firms. It is that *the marginal cost of a good should be equal for every producer.* Again, if this were not the case, then production could be increased without increasing costs. For example, if Hugo's rose garden could produce an extra dozen roses at a marginal cost of $10 and Mimi's rose garden could produce an extra dozen roses at a marginal cost of $50, then it would make sense for Mimi to reduce her production of roses by a dozen, saving her $50, and use that money to pay Hugo to produce two dozen roses that she could then sell on the market. Both Hugo and Mimi would be better off as a result. Only when the marginal costs are the same is there no way to increase production without cost. Note that it is not necessary for Hugo and Mimi or any other producer to be the same or even to have the same total costs; all that we require for efficiency is that the *marginal* costs be the same.

The third condition for efficiency relates to the allocation of goods to different consumers. It is that *the marginal benefit of consuming the same good should be equal for all consumers.* If the marginal benefits were not equal, then there could be a gain for some people with no loss for anyone else. For example, suppose Ken's marginal benefit from a rose was $3 and Maria's was $1; then if Maria sold a rose to Ken for $2, both would be better off. But if their marginal benefits were the same, then no improvement for one without harming the other would be possible.

In sum, there are three conditions for efficiency: (1) the marginal benefit equals the marginal cost for the last item produced; (2) the marginal cost of producing each good is equal for all producers; and (3) the marginal benefit from consuming each good is equal for all consumers.

> Second efficiency condition: Every producer's *MC* is the same.

> Third efficiency condition: Every consumer's *MB* is the same.

Is the Market Efficient?

Now that we know the three conditions for efficiency, can we say that the market is efficient? The competitive equilibrium model provides us with a quick answer to that question.

According to the model of consumer behavior in Chapter 5, an individual consumer chooses a quantity of a good such that *price equals marginal benefit*—that is, $P = MB$. This equality holds for every consumer at every point on the market demand curve. According to the model of firm behavior in Chapter 6, a firm produces a quantity of a good such that *price equals marginal cost.* That is, $P = MC$. This equality holds for every firm at every point on the market supply curve. At a point of intersection of the supply curve and the demand curve, both of these conditions must hold because the point of intersection is on both the supply curve and the demand curve and the price P is the same. That is, $P = MB$ and $P = MC$ simultaneously. This implies that at the quantity produced by the market, *marginal benefit equals marginal cost.* That is, $MB = MC$. This is true of every good.

Thus we have proved that a competitive market satisfies the first condition of efficiency. The marginal cost of producing roses, grapes, bread, peanuts, or automobiles is equal to the marginal benefit that people get from consuming them. This occurs without any person coordinating consumers and producers.

The result is illustrated in Figure 3. At the market equilibrium quantity (point *E*), the marginal cost (the point on the supply curve) is equal to the marginal benefit (the point on the demand curve). At any other point, either marginal benefit will be greater than marginal cost or marginal benefit will be less than marginal cost.

> Here's the reason in a nutshell why the first condition is satisfied:
>
> At a market equilibrium:
>
> $P = MB$ and $P = MC$
>
> Thus since $P = P$, we must have
>
> $MC = MB$

Here's the reason in a nut-
shell why the second condition is satisfied:

Hugo's $MC = P$

Mimi's $MC = P$

Thus

Hugo's $MC =$ Mimi's MC

Here's the reason in a nut-
shell why the third condition is satisfied:

Maria's $MB = P$

Ken's $MB = P$

Thus

Maria's $MB =$ Ken's MB

**first theorem of welfare
economics:**   the conclusion that
a competitive market results in an
efficient outcome; sometimes
called the "invisible hand
theorem"; the definition of
efficiency used in the theorem is
Pareto efficiency.

The other two criteria for efficiency also hold in a competitive market. To see this, it will help to look back at Figure 2. Observe that in a market equilibrium, the marginal cost for the producers is the same, because *they all face the same price;* along each of their individual supply curves, all producers—Hugo, Mimi, and others—set marginal cost equal to the price. Similarly, in a market equilibrium, *all consumers—Maria, Ken, and others—face the same market price.* Hence, their marginal benefits are all equal, because on each of their individual demand curves the marginal benefit equals the price.

In sum, for each good produced in a competitive market, (1) the marginal benefit equals the marginal cost of the last item produced, (2) the marginal cost is equal for all producers in the market, and (3) the marginal benefit is equal for all consumers in the market. Thus, we can say that the competitive market is Pareto efficient. In a competitive market, it is not possible to make one person better off without hurting someone else.

The proposition that competitive markets are efficient is one of the most important in economics, so much so that when it is proven with the mathematics necessary to keep track of many different goods and time periods, it is called the **first theorem of welfare economics.** The word *welfare* means that the theorem is about the overall well-being of people in the economy (the word *welfare* is synonymous with "well-being," not with a transfer payment to a poor person). The word *first* is used to distinguish this theorem from the second theorem of welfare economics, which states the converse of the first: Any Pareto efficient outcome can be obtained via a competitive market.

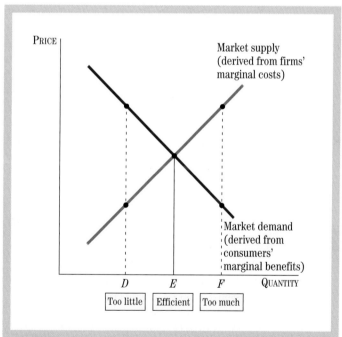

FIGURE 3

The Efficiency of the Market: Marginal Benefit Equals Marginal Cost

Only at quantity *E* is the marginal benefit of an extra unit equal to the marginal cost of an extra unit. Point *D* is not efficient because the marginal benefit of an extra unit is greater than the marginal cost of producing it. Point *F* is also not efficient because the marginal cost of producing an extra unit is greater than the marginal benefit.

Efficiency and Income Inequality

Efficiency is a very important goal of an economic system, but it is not the only goal. Another goal is to avoid outcomes where a few people earn most of the income and do most of the consumption in the economy while the rest of the population falls into dire economic circumstances. Thus, reducing **income inequality** is also a desirable goal in most economic systems.

income inequality: disparity in levels of income among individuals in the economy.

It is important to emphasize that efficiency and income equality are not the same thing. An allocation of bread between Hugo and Mimi is efficient if their marginal benefit of bread is the same and if the marginal benefits equal the marginal cost of bread. Then there is no mutually advantageous trade of bread between Hugo and Mimi that will make one better off without hurting the other.

However, suppose that Hugo has a low income, earning only $7,000 per year, and that Mimi has a high income, earning $70,000 per year. Suppose a severe drought raises the price of wheat and thus the price of bread. If the price of bread in the market gets very high, say, $3 a loaf, then Hugo will be able to buy few loaves of bread and may go hungry, especially if he has a family. In this case, the economy gets good marks on efficiency grounds but fails on income inequality grounds.

To remedy the situation, a common suggestion is to put price controls on bread. For example, to help Hugo and others like him, a law might be passed requiring that bread prices not exceed $.50 a loaf. Although this may help the income inequality problem, it will cause inefficiency because it interferes with the market. At $.50 a loaf, bread producers will not produce very much, and Mimi will probably start buying bread to feed the birds, wasting scarce resources.

The temptation to deal with income inequality problems in ways that interfere with the efficiency of the market is great in all societies. Price ceilings (rent controls) on rental apartments in some U.S. cities, which we examined in Chapter 4, are one example. A better solution to the income inequality problem is to transfer income to Hugo and other low-income people from Mimi and other high-income people. With a transfer of income—say, through an income-support payment to the poor—the market would be able to function and the inefficiencies caused by price controls on bread would not occur. Even at the high price of bread, Hugo will be able to eat, perhaps buying some rice or a bread substitute, and the bread, which is so expensive to produce, will not be wasted on the birds. We will see that such transfers have advantages and disadvantages. Compared to price controls, their main advantage is that they allow the market to operate efficiently. On the other hand, such transfer programs will typically have to be financed through taxes, which are often going to create inefficiencies themselves, as you will see in the next section.

REVIEW

- Economic inefficiency implies a waste of resources. A Pareto efficient outcome is one in which no person's situation can be improved without hurting someone else.

- There are three conditions that must hold if an outcome is to be Pareto efficient. These conditions are that (1) the marginal benefit of the last item produced must equal its marginal cost, (2) the marginal cost of production for all producers must be identical, and (3) the marginal benefit for all consumers must be identical.

- If marginal benefit exceeds marginal cost, then too little of the good is being produced, whereas if marginal cost exceeds marginal benefit, too much of the good is being produced. In both cases, adjusting the quantity being produced would enhance efficiency.

- If the marginal costs of producers were not identical, then it would be possible to increase production without increasing costs, simply by making the producer with the high marginal cost produce less and the producer with the low marginal cost produce more.

- Finally, if marginal benefits are not identical, then having the person with the high marginal benefit buy the item from the person with the low marginal benefit for a price that is in between the two marginal benefits would enhance efficiency by making both parties better off.

- One of the most desirable features of competitive markets is that at the equilibrium level of production, on the demand curve, marginal benefit equals the market price, while on the supply curve, marginal cost equals the market price. Together these imply that marginal benefit equals marginal cost.

- Similarly, since all consumers and all firms face the same market price, the marginal benefits of each consumer will be identical (and equal to the market price), as will the marginal costs of each individual producer.

- Thus competitive markets are efficient. Any change in consumption or production that makes one person better off must make someone else worse off.

- Efficiency is not the same thing as equality. An efficient outcome can coexist with an unequal outcome.

- Attempts to remedy an unequal situation by the use of price ceilings or by rationing lead to inefficiencies in production and consumption. It may be better to redistribute resources from the more affluent to the less well off.

MEASURING WASTE FROM INEFFICIENCY

We know from Chapters 5 and 6 that consumer surplus and producer surplus are measures of how much consumers and producers gain from buying and selling in a market. The larger these two surpluses are, the better off people are.

Maximizing the Sum of Producer Plus Consumer Surplus

An attractive feature of competitive markets is that they maximize the sum of consumer and producer surplus. Producer and consumer surplus are shown in the market supply and market demand diagram in Figure 4. Recall that the producer surplus for all producers is the area above the supply curve and below the market price line, and that the consumer surplus for all consumers is the area below the demand curve and above the market price line. Both the consumer surplus and the producer surplus are shown in Figure 4. The lightly shaded gray area is the sum of consumer surplus plus producer surplus. The equilibrium quantity is at the intersection of the two curves.

Deadweight Loss

We can show that at the equilibrium price and quantity, consumer surplus plus producer surplus is maximized. Figure 4 also shows what happens to consumer surplus plus producer surplus when the efficient level of production does not occur. The middle panel of Figure 4 shows what the sum of consumer surplus and producer surplus is at market equilibrium. The top panel of Figure 4 shows a situation in which the quantity produced is lower than the market equilibrium quantity. Clearly, the

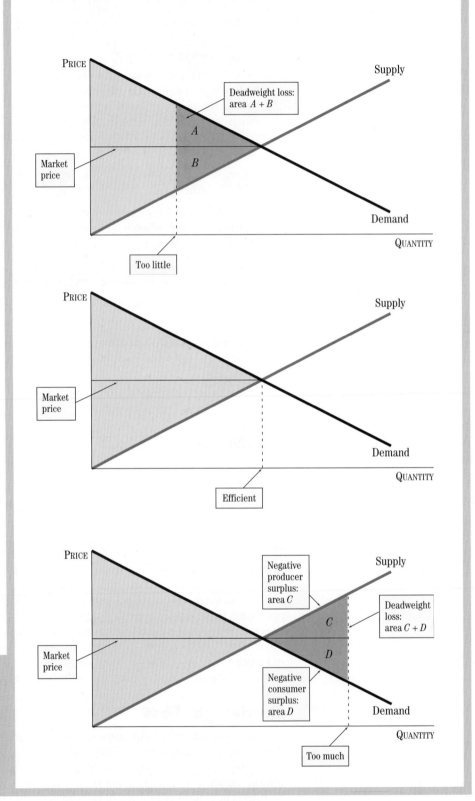

Another way to think about the lightly shaded areas in the graphs: The sum of consumer surplus plus producer surplus is the triangular area between the demand curve and the supply curve—shown by the lightly shaded area in the middle graph of Figure 4. The graph shows another way to think about this sum: The sum of consumer surplus plus producer surplus equals the marginal benefit minus the marginal cost of all the items produced.

FIGURE 4
Measuring Economic Loss

When production is less or more than the market equilibrium amount, the economic loss is measured by the loss of consumer surplus plus producer surplus. In the top diagram, the quantity produced is too small. In the bottom diagram, it is too large. In the middle diagram, it is efficient.

sum of consumer and producer surplus is lower. By producing a smaller quantity, we lose the amount of the consumer and producer surplus in the darkly shaded triangular area $A + B$. The bottom panel of Figure 4 shows the opposite situation, in which the quantity produced is too high. In this case, we have to subtract the triangular area $C + D$ from the lightly shaded area on the left because price is greater than marginal benefit and lower than marginal cost, which means that consumer surplus and producer surplus are negative in the area $C + D$. In both the top and bottom panels of the figure, these darkly shaded triangles are a loss to society from producing more or less than the efficient amount. Economists call the loss in this darkly shaded area the **deadweight loss.** It is a measure of the waste from inefficient production.

deadweight loss: the loss in producer and consumer surplus due to an inefficient level of production.

Deadweight loss is not simply a theoretical curiosity with a morbid name; it is used by economists to measure the size of the waste to society of deviations from the competitive equilibrium. By calculating deadweight loss, economists can estimate the benefits and costs of many government programs. When you hear or read that the cost of U.S. agricultural programs is billions of dollars or that the benefit of a world-trade agreement is trillions of dollars, it is the increase or decrease in deadweight loss that is being referred to. In order to compute the deadweight loss, all we need is the demand curve and the supply curve.

> ### REVIEW
>
> - Consumer surplus and producer surplus are measures of how well off consumers and firms are as a result of buying and selling in the market. The larger the sum of these surpluses, the better off consumers and firms (society as a whole) are.
>
> - Competitive markets maximize producer surplus plus consumer surplus.
>
> - If the quantity produced is either greater or less than the market equilibrium amount, the sum of consumer surplus plus producer surplus is less than at the market equilibrium. The decline in consumer plus producer surplus measures the waste from producing the wrong amount. It is called deadweight loss.

THE DEADWEIGHT LOSS FROM PRICE FLOORS AND CEILINGS

In Chapter 4 we used the supply and demand model to examine situations where governments have attempted to control market prices because they were unhappy with the outcome of the market, or because they were pressured by groups who would benefit from price controls. We examined two broad types of price controls: price ceilings, which specify a maximum price at which a good can be bought or sold, and price floors, which specify a minimum price at which a good can be bought or sold. An example of a price floor was the minimum wage, while an example of a price ceiling was a rent control policy.

Using the supply and demand model, we were able to illustrate some of the problems that stemmed from the imposition of price floors or ceilings. When a price floor that is higher than the equilibrium price is imposed, the result will be persistent surpluses of the good. This situation is illustrated by Figure 5. The surpluses imply that an inefficient allocation of resources is going toward the good whose price has been artificially inflated. Frequently, costly government programs will be created to buy up surplus production. When a price ceiling that is lower than the equilibrium price is imposed on a market, then the result will be persistent shortages of the good. These shortages mean that mechanisms like rationing, waiting lines, or black markets will be used to allocate the now scarce good. This situation is illustrated by Figure 7.

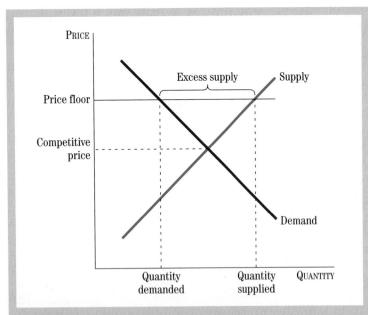

FIGURE 5
Price and Quantity Effects of a Price Floor

If the price floor is set higher than the competitive market price, the quantity demanded by consumers decreases and the quantity supplied by firms increases, creating excess supply.

Now that we understand the concepts of consumer and producer surplus as well as the idea of deadweight loss, we can use these tools to quantify the negative impacts of price ceilings and price floors.

The Deadweight Loss from a Price Floor

Figure 6 shows how consumer and producer surplus are affected by the imposition of a price floor. Prior to the imposition of the price floor, the sum of consumer and producer surplus is given by the area of the triangle *ABC*, of which the area *BCD* denotes consumer surplus and the area *ACD* denotes producer surplus.

Now consider what happens to consumer surplus and producer surplus when a price floor is imposed. The impact on producer surplus is ambiguous. On the one hand, those producers who are fortunate enough to sell at a higher price will obtain more producer surplus. But because the quantity demanded is lower at the higher price, there will be a loss of producer surplus for those producers who were previously able to sell the good but now have no buyers. Producer surplus would be given by the area *AEFG*, which reflects an increase of *DEFI* (shown in blue) and a decrease of *CGI* (shown in shaded green) from the previous level of producer surplus. Consumer surplus is unambiguously reduced by the amount *CDEF* (shown in red). Overall, when we add up the lost consumer and producer surplus and the gained producer surplus, there is a deadweight loss equivalent to the area *CFG* in Figure 6.

FIGURE 6
The Deadweight Loss from a Price Floor

The price floor creates an excess supply of goods at the new higher price. Consumers are unambiguously worse off. Producers may be better off or worse off depending on whether they are able to sell at the higher price. The sum of consumer and producer surplus is lower, indicating a deadweight loss associated with the floor.

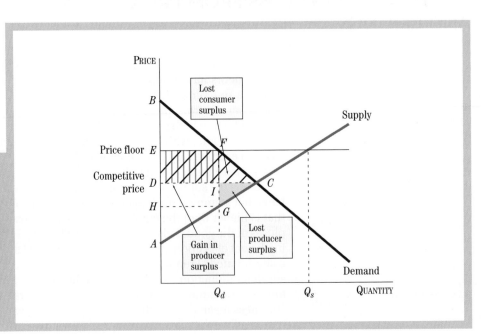

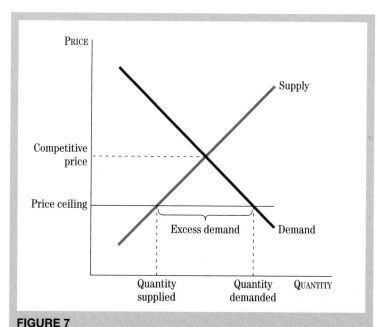

FIGURE 7
Price and Quantity Effects of a Price Ceiling

If the price ceiling is set below the competitive market price, the quantity demanded by consumers increases and the quantity supplied by firms decreases, creating excess demand.

The Deadweight Loss from a Price Ceiling

Figure 8 shows how consumer and producer surplus are affected by the imposition of a price ceiling. As before, prior to the imposition of the price ceiling, the sum of consumer and producer surplus is given by the area of the triangle *ABC*, of which the area *BCD* denotes consumer surplus and the area *ACD* denotes producer surplus.

Now consider what happens to consumer surplus and producer surplus when a price ceiling is imposed. The impact on consumer surplus is ambiguous: On the one hand, those consumers who are able to acquire the good at the lower price will obtain more consumer surplus. But because only a smaller quantity of goods is available for purchase, there will be a loss of consumer surplus for those who were previously able to buy the good but now cannot. Consumer surplus would be given by the area *BFGH*, which reflects an increase of *DHGI* (shown in blue) and a decrease of *CFI* (shown in red) from the previous level of consumer surplus. Producer surplus is unambiguously reduced by the amount *CDHG* (shown by the green shaded area). Overall, when we combine the lost consumer and producer surplus with the gained consumer surplus, there is a deadweight loss equivalent to the area *CFG* in Figure 8.

FIGURE 8
The Deadweight Loss from a Price Ceiling

The price ceiling creates an excess demand for goods at the new lower price. Producers are unambiguously worse off. Consumers may be better or worse off depending on whether they are able to buy at the lower price. The sum of consumer and producer surplus is lower, indicating a deadweight loss associated with the ceiling.

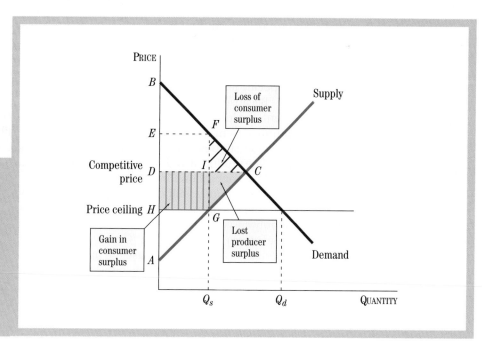

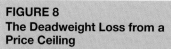

R E V I E W
- Both price floors and price ceilings bring about deadweight loss. Some parties clearly lose; other parties may gain, but overall, the losses exceed the gains.

- In the case of a price floor, consumers unambiguously lose because they buy fewer units at a higher price. Some producers gain because they are able to sell at a higher price than before. Others lose because they are no longer able to sell the good because the government doesn't allow them to lower the price to attract buyers.

- In the case of a price ceiling, producers unambiguously lose because they sell fewer units at a lower price. Some consumers gain because they are able to buy the good at a lower price than before. Others lose because they are no longer able to buy the good, even though they are willing to pay more, because the government doesn't allow firms to raise the price.

THE DEADWEIGHT LOSS FROM TAXATION

Another important application of deadweight loss is in estimating the impact of a tax. To see how, let's examine the impact of a tax on a good. We will see that the tax shifts the supply curve, leads to a reduction in the quantity produced, and reduces the sum of producer surplus plus consumer surplus.

Figure 9 shows a supply and demand diagram for a particular good. In the absence of the tax, the sum of producer and consumer surplus is given by the area of the triangle *ABC*, of which the area *BCD* denotes consumer surplus and the area *ACD* denotes producer surplus.

A Tax Paid by a Producer Shifts the Supply Curve

A tax on sales is a payment that must be made to the government by the seller of a product. The tax may be a percentage of the dollar value spent on the products sold, in which case it is called an *ad valorem tax*. A 6 percent state tax on retail purchases is an ad valorem tax. Or it may be proportional to the number of items sold, in which case the tax is called a *specific tax*. A tax on gasoline of $.50 per gallon is an example of a specific tax.

Because the tax payment is made by the producer or the seller to the government, the immediate impact of the tax is to add to the marginal cost of producing the product. Hence, the immediate impact of the tax will be to shift the supply curve. For example, suppose each producer has to send a certain amount, say, $.50 per gallon of gasoline produced and sold, to the government. Then $.50 must be added to the marginal cost per gallon for each producer.

The resulting shift of the supply curve is shown in Figure 9. The vertical distance between the old and the new supply curves is the size of the sales tax in dollars. The supply curve shifts up by this amount because this is how much is added to the marginal costs of the producer. (Observe that this upward shift can just as accurately be called a leftward shift because the new supply curve is above and to the left of the old curve. Saying that the supply curve shifts up may seem confusing because when we say "up," we seem to be meaning "more supply." But the "up" is along the vertical axis, which has the price on it. The upward, or leftward, movement of the supply curve is in the direction of less supply, not more supply.)

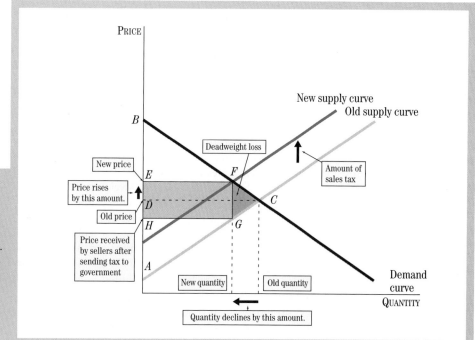

FIGURE 9
Deadweight Loss from a Tax
In this graph the dark triangle represents the deadweight loss and the blue rectangle the amount of tax revenue that goes to the government. The sales tax, which is collected and paid to the government by the seller, adds to the marginal cost of each item the producer sells. Hence, the supply curve shifts up. The price rises, but by less than the tax increase.

A New Equilibrium Price and Quantity

What does the competitive equilibrium model imply about the change in the price and the quantity produced? Observe that there is a new intersection of the supply curve and the demand curve. Thus, the price rises to a new, higher level, and the quantity produced declines.

The price increase, as shown in Figure 9, is not as large as the increase in the tax. The vertical distance between the old and the new supply curves is the amount of the tax, but the price increases by less than this distance. Thus the producers are not able to "pass on" the entire tax to the consumers in the form of higher prices. If the tax increase is $.50, then the price increase is less than $.50, perhaps $.40. The producers have been forced by the market—by the movement along the demand curve—to reduce their production, and by doing so they have absorbed some of the impact of the tax increase.

Deadweight Loss and Tax Revenue

Now consider what happens to consumer surplus and producer surplus with the sales tax. Because the total quantity produced is lower, there is a loss in consumer surplus and producer surplus. The right part of the triangle of consumer plus producer surplus, corresponding to the area *CFG*, has been cut off, and this is the deadweight loss to society, as shown in Figure 9.

Consumer surplus is now given by the triangle *BEF*, while producer surplus is given by the triangle *AGH* (keep in mind that producers do not receive the new price; they only get the new price less the tax). The tax generates revenue for the government that can be used for financing government activity, Some of what was producer surplus and consumer surplus thus goes to the government. If the tax is $1 and 100 items are sold, the tax revenue is $100. This amount is shown by the

ECONOMICS IN ACTION

Price Controls and Deadweight Loss in the Milk Industry

Since the 1930s, the federal government has intervened in the milk market (and other agricultural markets) in order to stabilize farm prices and provide some income protection for U.S. farmers. The government has used a combination of complex regulations that include government purchases and subsequent disposal of dairy products, import restrictions, export subsidies, and pricing mechanisms depending on the location and purpose of the production of milk. We can see how price controls lead to deadweight loss by looking more closely at one of these programs.

The Food and Agriculture Act of 1977 was aimed at sustaining higher prices received by dairy farmers. As we know, the competitive market price occurs when the quantity demanded equals the quantity supplied, but the higher price floor mandated by the government reduced the quantity demanded and gave farmers an incentive to produce more milk, causing excess supply. To support the price floor, the government purchased the excess supply of milk in the form of dry milk, butter, and cheese. Of course, there was a cost to this program: close to $2 billion a year in net government expenditures in the early 1980s.

In 1994 economists Peter Helmberger and Yu-Hui Chen estimated what would happen if the government deregulated the milk market. In the short run, they found that consumer surplus would increase by $3.9 billion a year, producer surplus would decrease by $4 billion, and net government expenditures would decrease by $600 million, eliminating a deadweight loss of $500 million a year. As you can see, the price floor is $500 million more expensive than a simple program in which the government directly transfers $3.9 billion from consumers to farmers and throws in an extra $100 million. Interestingly, though, consumers would be much more likely to protest against such a blatant transfer of income than they are to complain about the much more wasteful and inefficient price support program.

The Federal Agricultural Improvement and Reform (FAIR) Act of 1996 mandated the elimination of the price support program by the end of 1999. However, the dairy subsidies were soon reinstated by the farm bill signed by President Bush in May 2002, which increased total agricultural subsidies from $100 billion to close to $200 billion a year. The current system of dairy subsidies chose the market price of drinking milk in Boston as the standard for the rest of the country. When that price falls below $16.94 per hundred pounds, all U.S. dairy farmers receive a governmental subsidy of 45 percent of the difference between the Boston market price and $16.94. What do you think have been the effects of this legislation on the milk market?

The current system of dairy subsidies will be reexamined by Congress in 2007. Read newspaper articles about the policy debate surrounding the renewal of dairy subsidies and see for yourself how much economic analysis is employed in public policy debates.

blue rectangle *EFGH* on the diagram. Adding up consumer and producer surplus plus the government revenue gives us an area corresponding to *ABFG*, which differs from the original sum of consumer and producer surplus (*ABC*) by the magnitude of the deadweight loss (*CFG*). So even though taxes may be necessary to finance the government, they cause a deadweight loss to society in the form of lost consumer and producer surplus that are not available to anyone in the economy anymore.

R E V I E W

- The impact of a tax on the economy can be analyzed using consumer surplus and producer surplus.

- Taxes are necessary to finance government expenditures, but they lower the production of the item being taxed.

- The loss to society from the decline in production is measured by the reduction in consumer surplus and producer surplus, the deadweight loss due to the tax.

INFORMATIONAL EFFICIENCY

We have shown that a competitive market works well in that the outcome is Pareto efficient. For every good, the sum of consumer surplus and producer surplus is maximized. These are important and attractive characteristics of a competitive market.

Another important and attractive characteristic of a competitive market is that the market processes information very efficiently. For example, in a competitive market, the price reflects the marginal benefit for every buyer and the marginal cost for every seller. If a government official were asked to set the price in a real market, there would be no way that such information could be obtained, especially with millions of buyers and sellers. In other words, the market seems to be informationally efficient. Pareto efficiency is different from this *informational efficiency*.

In the 1930s and 1940s, as the government of the Soviet Union tried to centrally plan production in the entire economy, economists became more interested in the informational efficiency of markets. One of the most outspoken critics of central planning, and a strong advocate of the market system, was Friedrich Hayek, who emphasized the importance of the informational efficiencies of the market. In Hayek's view, a major disadvantage of central planning—where the government sets all the prices and all the quantities—is that it is informationally inefficient.

Coordination Without a Market
Although prices provide a valuable coordination role in a market economy, some activities are better coordinated without the market. It would not be efficient to coordinate each of the hand and foot movements of these 100 skydivers with prices.

If you had all the information about all the buyers and sellers in the market, you could set the price to achieve a Pareto efficient outcome. To see Hayek's point, it is perhaps enough to observe that without private information about every one of the millions of buyers and sellers, you or any government official would not know where to set the price. However, economists do not have results as neat as the first theorem of welfare economics to prove Hayek's point. The reason is that in some situations, the market would be unwieldy, and it is difficult to describe these situations with any generality.

Difficulties arise in using a market system in situations where prices will not bring about a sufficiently precise or speedy response. For example, if demand for furniture made out of mahogany timber rises, it is difficult for producers to meet that demand immediately because it takes several dozen years for a mahogany tree to reach maturity. In such a situation, unscrupulous producers may chop down mahogany trees in a public forest to meet the demand. This implies that we should not rely solely on the competitive market system to motivate producers to increase production in situations where property rights are weak or where there are communal resources that need to be managed. Nevertheless, a competitive market system offers considerable informational advantages over other systems.

R E V I E W

- The market has the ability to process information efficiently. The lack of informational efficiency is a key reason why central planning does not work well in complex and changing environments.

- For some activities, however, the market has few informational advantages. A production process in situations where property rights are weak or where there are communal resources that need to be managed will be poorly coordinated through prices.

CONCLUSION

Adam Smith's idea of the "invisible hand" is perhaps the most important discovery in economics: Individuals, by freely pursuing their own interests in a market economy, are led as if by an invisible hand to an outcome that is best overall. The first theorem of welfare economics is the modern statement of Adam Smith's famous principle; in tribute to Smith's seminal idea, we call it the "invisible hand theorem." Understanding why, and under what circumstances, the invisible hand theorem is true is an important part of thinking like an economist.

Understanding the theorem has required an investment in economic model building: The behavior of consumers and the behavior of firms were combined into a competitive equilibrium model describing how consumers and firms interact in markets. This model is an extension of the supply and demand model we used in Chapters 3 and 4.

Building the competitive equilibrium model has had payoffs beyond understanding this most important theorem in economics. We can use individual demand curves and individual firm supply curves to determine the actions of each individual consumer and each individual producer at the market equilibrium price. Armed with the ideas of consumer surplus and producer surplus, we can measure the costs of deviations from the competitive market equilibrium. Such measures are used by economists to assess the costs and benefits of government programs that interfere, for bad or good, with the market outcomes. Starting with Chapter 10, we will see that deviations from the competitive market equilibrium are caused by monopolies and other factors. But first we will look more closely at how costs and production within individual firms and competitive industries change over time. We do this in Chapters 8 and 9.

KEY POINTS

1. Processing information and coordinating and motivating millions of consumption and production decisions is difficult, but the market is a device that can do the job remarkably well.

2. The interaction of producers and consumers in a market can be explained by the competitive equilibrium model, which is the supply and demand model with consumer and firm behavior made more explicit.

3. Using the competitive equilibrium model, we can not only find the equilibrium price and quantity, but also use each individual's demand curve to find that individual's consumption decision and use each individual firm's supply curve to figure out its production decision.

4. An outcome is Pareto efficient if it is not possible to change production or consumption in a way that will make one person better off without hurting someone else.

5. Pareto efficiency requires three criteria to hold: marginal benefit must equal marginal cost for the last item produced, all producers must have identical marginal costs, and all consumers must have identical marginal benefits.

6. A competitive market is Pareto efficient. In a competitive market, the sum of producer surplus and consumer surplus is maximized.

7. Efficiency is not the same thing as equality. An efficient outcome can coexist with an unequal outcome.

8. Attempts to remedy an unequal situation by the use of price ceilings or floors lead to inefficiencies in production and consumption. Using transfers to redistribute resources from the more affluent to the less well off may be better than imposing price or quantity controls.

9. Such transfers often need to be financed by tax revenue. The imposition of a tax that reduces the quantity produced creates deadweight loss for society. The competitive equilibrium model can be used to calculate the magnitude of this deadweight loss.

10. The market also has the ability to process information much more efficiently than a central planner could do. However, there are no general theorems that prove the informational efficiency of the market.

KEY TERMS

invisible hand	equilibrium price	Pareto efficient	income inequality
competitive equilibrium model	surplus (excess supply)	first theorem of welfare economics	deadweight loss
	shortage (excess demand)		

QUESTIONS FOR REVIEW

1. What are the information-processing, coordination, and motivation functions that arise when buyers and sellers interact?

2. Why is it difficult for one person or group of persons to perform the functions listed in question 1? How does the market perform these functions?

3. What is the relationship between the competitive equilibrium model and the supply and demand model?

4. How does the competitive equilibrium model explain the decisions of individual consumers and producers?

5. What is the meaning of Pareto efficiency?

6. What are the conditions that are needed for Pareto efficiency to hold? Why would the violation of any one of those conditions bring about a situation that is not Pareto efficient?

7. How does a competitive market satisfy the conditions that are needed for Pareto efficiency to hold?

8. Why is the sum of consumer surplus and producer surplus maximized in the competitive market?

9. How does the imposition of a price floor create deadweight loss for the economy?

10. How does the imposition of a tax create deadweight loss for the economy?

PROBLEMS

1. Suppose that in a competitive market for ukuleles, there are three buyers (Peter, Paul, and Mary) with the marginal benefit (MB) schedules below.

Quantity	MB—Peter	MB—Paul	MB—Mary
1	150	140	130
2	120	110	100
3	90	80	70
4	60	50	40
5	30	20	10

If the equilibrium price is $80, calculate the following:
   a. The quantity purchased by each buyer
   b. The consumer surplus for each buyer
   c. The consumer surplus for the market as a whole

2. In the same market, there are three sellers (John, George, and Ringo) with the marginal cost (MC) schedules shown below.

Quantity	MC—John	MC—George	MC—Ringo
1	30	20	10
2	60	50	40
3	90	80	70
4	120	110	100
5	150	140	130

If the equilibrium price is $80, calculate the following:
   a. The quantity produced by each seller
   b. The producer surplus for each seller
   c. The producer surplus for the market as a whole

3. Using the answers you provided above for Problems 1 and 2, verify that the three efficiency conditions are satisfied for the ukulele market.

4. Firm A and firm B both produce the same product with the following total costs:

Firm A		Firm B	
Quantity Produced	Total Costs	Quantity Produced	Total Costs
0	5	0	2
1	6	1	5
2	8	2	9
3	11	3	14
4	15	4	20

Consider a situation in which the market price is $3 and 4 units are produced in total: Firm A produces 2 units, and firm B produces 2 units.
   a. Explain why this situation is not Pareto efficient.
   b. Come up with two different production allocations for the two firms that allow the 4 items to be produced at a lower overall total cost.
   c. Which of these two allocations would be the outcome in a competitive market where both firms maximized profits?
   d. How would the actions of the two firms be coordinated in a competitive market to achieve this outcome?

5. Suppose that in the ukulele market described in Problem 2, the government imposes a $40 sales tax, which causes the equilibrium price to go up to $100. Calculate the following:
   a. The quantity purchased by each buyer, the consumer surplus for each buyer, and the consumer surplus for the market as a whole
   b. The quantity produced by each seller, the producer surplus for each seller, and the producer surplus for the market as a whole

c. The amount of revenue collected by the government

d. The deadweight loss for the economy resulting from the tax

6. Consider the following supply and demand schedule for candy bars:

Price	Supply (millions of candy bars)	Demand (millions of candy bars)
$.25	2	14
$.50	6	12
$.75	10	10
$1.00	14	8
$1.25	18	6
$1.50	22	4
$1.75	26	2

a. Sketch the market supply and demand curves. Show the equilibrium quantity and price.

b. Graphically show the producer surplus and consumer surplus in the market for candy bars.

c. What would happen to the price of this product if a tax of $.75 per candy bar sold were enacted by the government? Show your answer graphically.

d. Show the deadweight loss due to the tax on your diagram.

7. Suppose that an unanticipated bout of good weather results in almost ideal growing conditions, leading to a substantial increase in the supply of wheat in the United States.

a. Draw a supply and demand diagram to show what will happen to the equilibrium price and quantity of wheat in the United States, assuming that the demand curve does not shift.

b. Suppose the U.S. government observes that the price of wheat is likely to fall rapidly and imposes a price floor equal to the original equilibrium price. What effect does the price floor have on the quantity supplied and demanded of wheat?

c. How are consumer and producer surplus affected by the price floor?

d. Graphically show the deadweight loss created by the price floor.

8. High international prices for soybeans in recent years led many Argentinean farmers to switch land that had been used as pasture to raise cattle to soybean production. This resulted in a shortfall in the supply of beef.

a. Draw a supply and demand diagram to show what will happen to the equilibrium price and quantity of beef in Argentina, assuming that the demand curve does not shift.

b. In March of 2007, the Argentinean government, concerned about the rising price of beef, imposed a price ceiling on beef. Assuming that the price ceiling was equal to the original equilibrium price before the supply decreased, what effect does the price ceiling have on the quantity supplied and demanded of beef?

c. How are consumer and producer surplus affected by the price ceiling?

d. Graphically show the deadweight loss created by the price ceiling.

The Economics of the Firm

Chapter 8

Costs and the Changes at Firms over Time

On a cold Saturday morning, a wrenching story appeared on the front page of a California newspaper. It began:

> The end came at precisely 11:46 a.m. Friday. After 82 years, after four generations of toil and take-home pay, with deep roots tapping into two centuries, the end came without frill or fanfare. . . . There were tears. There were handshakes. . . . "Listen. There's a silence. It's like a hush has fallen over the place," said Bob Armstrong, the superintendent of the plant.[1]

The story was an account of a firm—a cannery—shutting down its production facilities. It sounds like something out of a Depression-era Steinbeck novel, but in fact this article was written in 1999, a year when the U.S. economy was enjoying an unprecedented boom. Even in a boom year, many firms, such as this cannery, shut down. But many more firms start up, so that the number of firms in existence continues to increase year after year. In the United States, about 700,000 firms start up each year. Many of these firms are successful and will expand, but others may have to downsize and eventually shut down. The purpose of this chapter is to develop a model for analyzing the changes at firms over time. To do so, we will extend the model of firm behavior developed in Chapter 6.

What we will find in this chapter is that costs are of vital importance to a firm's decision to start up or shut down. Some of the most successful new firms, as well as some of the most rapidly growing older firms, in the United States have prospered because of their ability to use innovative management techniques and new technologies that cut costs. For example, the creation of the World Wide Web enabled Jeffrey

---

[1] Geoffrey Tomb, "As the Final Harvest Ends, a Tech Torture Begins," *San Jose Mercury News*, December 18, 1999, p. 1.

Small businesses make up the largest share of businesses in the United States, employing, on average, half of all private sector employees. There are nearly 23 million small businesses in the United States, and they are opening and closing at a fairly steady rate. At least two-thirds of small businesses survive the first two years; about 50 percent are still open after four years. Small businesses close for a variety of reasons, including lack of adequate capital, but some businesses simply run their course. This storefront sign announces the 2002 closing of Florence Huie's laundry business in Derby, Connecticut—a business Ms. Huie started with her husband in 1960.

Bezos to found Amazon.com, which was able to become one of the largest bookstores in the world by conducting its entire business online on the Web, thus avoiding the "bricks and mortar" costs of building or renting space to sell books in. Conversely, the online grocer Webvan, which wanted to move the grocery purchasing business out of the store and onto the Web, had to fold because the costs of maintaining its own food warehouses and running a distribution business proved to be too great.

Costs also play a vital role in the expansion and contraction of firms. Wal-Mart—a firm that expanded rapidly in the 1990s—developed a system whereby salesclerks electronically scan a bar code on each item purchased and automatically transmit the information back to the manufacturer, who can then immediately begin producing more of that item. This enabled Wal-Mart to reduce costs by minimizing its need to hold lots of unsold goods in inventory. In addition to determining which firms grow and which firms shrink, costs determine how large a firm should be. Differences in the costs of the equipment needed for manufacturing cement and the equipment needed to set up a hair salon, for example, mean that cement firms are usually large and hair salons are usually small.

Costs also determine where firms should expand. For example, when firms choose between expanding their manufacturing facilities in the United States and acquiring another company abroad, they take into account the costs of labor and transportation as well as the effects of government policy toward firms. In recent years, many call centers—places that handle telephone calls and provide customer service for clients—have relocated to India, where educated English-speaking workers can be hired for less money than in the United States. Similarly, car manufacturers in Germany have set up plants in countries like Slovakia because the cost of hiring workers in those countries is considerably cheaper than in Western Europe.

In this chapter we will show how costs are such a crucial determinant of firm behavior. You will learn how economists can capture the whole essence of a firm with a graph of its costs. By looking at such a graph, economists can determine the profitability of a firm and whether it should shut down or expand. This chapter shows how.

COSTS FOR AN INDIVIDUAL FIRM

In this section, we show how to find different types of cost measures for a hypothetical transportation firm. These measures include total costs, average costs, fixed costs, variable costs, and marginal cost. It is important to have a clear and intuitive understanding of each of these concepts and how they relate to one another. We will also look at how the costs of a firm are related to the firm's production function. This will illuminate how changes in the technology used by firms to produce output affects the firm's cost function.

Total Costs, Fixed Costs, Variable Costs, and Marginal Cost

total costs: the sum of all costs incurred in producing goods or services. (Ch. 6)

Total costs (TC) are the sum of all costs incurred by a firm in producing goods or services. The more that is produced, the larger are total costs. Recall from Chapter 6 that *fixed costs* (FC) and *variable costs* (VC) are the two key components of total costs.

fixed costs: costs of production that do not depend on the quantity of production. (Ch. 6)

variable costs: costs of production that vary with the quantity of production. (Ch. 6)

Fixed costs are the part of total costs that do not vary with the amount produced in the short run; they include the cost of the factories, land, machines, and all other things that do not change when production changes in the short run. *Variable costs* are the part of total costs that vary in the short run as production changes. Variable costs include wage payments for workers, gasoline for trucks, fertilizer for crops, and all other things that change when the amount produced changes. By definition, total costs equal fixed costs plus variable costs; or, in symbols, $TC = FC + VC$.

short run: the period of time during which it is not possible to change all inputs to production; only some inputs, such as labor, can be changed.

long run: the minimum period of time during which all inputs to production can be changed.

■ **The Short Run and the Long Run.** Distinguishing the short run from the long run is the key to distinguishing fixed costs from variable costs. The *short run* and the *long run* are two broad categories into which economists parcel time. The **short run** is the period of time during which it is not possible to change all the inputs to production; only some inputs, such as labor, can be changed in the short run. The short run is too short, for example, to build a new factory or apartment building, to lay a fiber-optic cable, to launch a new communications satellite, or to get out of a lease on a storefront. The **long run** is a period of time long enough that all inputs, including capital, can be changed. The cost of each of the items that cannot be changed in the short run—factories, buildings, satellites—can be changed in the long run.

Economists frequently use *capital* as an example of a factor that does not change in the short run and use *labor* as an example of a factor that can change in the short run. In the examples in this chapter, we refer to the cost of labor as the main variable cost and the cost of capital as the main fixed cost.

TABLE 1
Finding Average and Marginal Cost for Melodic Movements
(costs measured in dollars per day)

Quantity (pianos moved per day) (Q)	Total Costs (TC)	Fixed Costs (FC)	Variable Costs (VC)	Marginal Cost (MC)	Average Total Cost (ATC)	Average Fixed Cost (AFC)	Average Variable Cost (AVC)
0	300	300	0	—	—	—	—
1	450	300	150	150	450	300	150
2	570	300	270	120	285	150	135
3	670	300	370	100	223	100	123
4	780	300	480	110	195	75	120
5	900	300	600	120	180	60	120
6	1,040	300	740	140	173	50	123
7	1,200	300	900	160	171	43	128
8	1,390	300	1,090	190	174	38	136
9	1,640	300	1,340	250	182	33	149
10	1,960	300	1,660	320	196	30	166
11	2,460	300	2,160	500	223	27	196

$$TC = FC + VC$$

$$\frac{\text{Change in } TC}{\text{Change in } Q}$$

$$ATC = \frac{TC}{Q}$$

$$AFC = \frac{FC}{Q}$$

$$AVC = \frac{VC}{Q}$$

Table 1 illustrates these definitions with cost data for a hypothetical firm called Melodic Movements. The firm, located in Houston, Texas, specializes in the strenuous but delicate job of moving pianos from one part of Houston to another. We use these hypothetical data rather than actual data to keep the example simple, but it is important to realize that the same analysis can be applied to data from any firm. Roadway Express, an actual moving firm that started in Houston with 16 trucks and has since gone nationwide, is a more complex example illustrating the same point. Table 1 lists the total costs, fixed costs, and variable costs for different levels of output at Melodic Movements. Observe that, consistent with the definition, fixed costs do not change as output changes, but variable costs do increase with output.

The pictographs in Figure 1 show that fixed costs do not change in the short run at Melodic Movements. Fixed costs, or the cost for four trucks and two terminals where the trucks are parked, are $300 per day regardless of how many pianos are moved during the day. Figure 1 also shows that variable costs increase with the amount produced. They increase from $600 to $1,660 as the number of pianos delivered per day rises from 5 to 10. Variable costs are shown in Figure 1 to rise because additional workers are hired to carry the goods and to drive and service the trucks. Thus, total costs rise from $900 to $1,960 as the number of pianos delivered rises from 5 to 10.

Figure 2 shows the same type of information as Figure 1 in graph form. Pairs of numbers on total costs and quantity from Table 1 are plotted in Figure 2. Connecting these dots results in the total costs curve. You can see how the total costs of moving the pianos steadily increase with the number of pianos moved. Fixed costs are shown to be unchanged at all levels of output. Figure 2 shows variable costs by the distance between the total costs curve and the fixed costs curve.

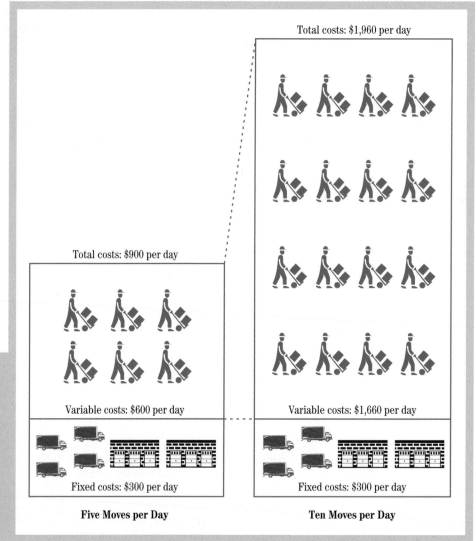

FIGURE 1
Fixed Costs versus Variable Costs

Fixed costs remain constant as the output of the firm increases in the short run. In the example of Melodic Movements, fixed costs are the daily rental or interest costs for trucks and terminals under long-term lease or owned by the firm. Variable costs change with the level of output. In the case of Melodic Movements, more workers must be hired to move more pianos.

marginal cost: the change in total costs due to a one-unit change in quantity produced. (Ch. 6)

■ **Marginal Cost.** Table 1 also shows how the *marginal cost* of Melodic Movements depends on the quantity of services produced (the number of pianos moved). Recall from Chapter 6 that marginal cost is the change in total costs due to a one-unit change in the quantity produced. For example, the marginal cost of increasing production from 5 piano moves to 6 piano moves a day is the change in total costs ($1,040 − $900 = $140) divided by the change in production (6 − 5 = 1). The fifth column of Table 1 shows the marginal cost for each additional piano moved by Melodic Movements, from the first to the eleventh piano.

Observe that in Table 1, marginal cost declines at low levels of production and then begins to increase again. Marginal cost reaches a minimum of $100 when production increases from 2 to 3 units of output. Recall that in the examples in Chapter 6 (Table 4), marginal cost increased throughout the whole range of production. In the example of Melodic Movements, marginal cost declines over part of the range of production. We will explain the reason for the difference later in this chapter.

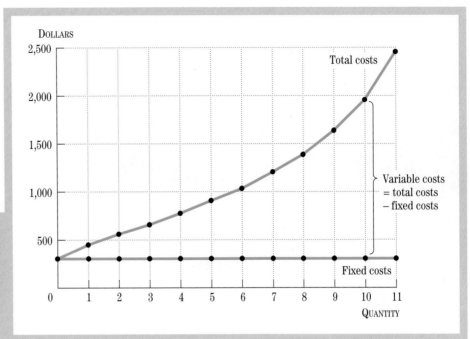

FIGURE 2
Total Costs Minus Fixed Costs Equal Variable Costs
The two lines on the diagram show total costs and fixed costs for Melodic Movements. Variable costs are the difference between the two lines. Variable costs rise with production, but fixed costs are constant.

Average Cost

average total cost (ATC): total costs of production divided by the quantity produced (also called cost per unit).

average variable cost (AVC): variable costs divided by the quantity produced.

average fixed cost (AFC): fixed costs divided by the quantity produced.

Average total cost (ATC) is defined as total costs (TC) of production divided by the quantity (Q) produced; in other words, it is the cost per unit of production. In symbols, $ATC = TC/Q$. For example, if the total costs of producing 4 items are $3,000, then the average total cost is $750 ($3,000/4). We can also define average cost for fixed and variable costs. Thus, **average variable cost (AVC)** is defined as variable costs divided by the quantity produced: $AVC = VC/Q$. **Average fixed cost (AFC)** is defined as fixed costs divided by the quantity produced: $AFC = FC/Q$. Of the three averages, we will use average total cost most frequently. However, the other two averages are important for knowing whether to shut down a firm or keep it open when it is losing money.

Average total cost for Melodic Movements is shown in Table 1. For example, total costs for 2 pianos moved (Q = 2) are $570; dividing $570 by 2 gives an average total cost of $285. For 3 pianos moved (Q = 3), total costs are $670; dividing by 3 gives $223 for average total cost. Notice that, in this example, average total cost initially declines as production increases from low levels. Then average total cost starts to increase once the output level reaches 8 units. That average total cost first decreases and then increases as production rises is a common pattern for most firms.

Average variable cost is also illustrated in Table 1. For 2 pianos moved (Q = 2), for example, average variable cost is $270 divided by 2, or $135. You can see that average variable cost, in this example, first declines and then increases throughout the rest of the range of production. Finally, observe in Table 1 that average fixed cost gets smaller as production rises. Because average fixed cost is calculated by dividing fixed costs (which are by definition fixed) by the quantity produced, average fixed cost must decline as the quantity produced rises.

Inputs and the Production Function
Labor (the two workers) and capital (the truck) are inputs to production (moving the piano).

The Relationship Between a Firm's Costs and the Firm's Production Function

The cost information in Table 1 is determined by how much *input* of labor and capital it takes to produce a given quantity of *output* and by the price of capital and labor. First consider some illustrative calculations of costs as the firm increases production. According to Table 1, it costs Melodic Movements $300 a day for capital, which is 4 trucks and 2 terminals (suppose trucks cost $25 per day and a terminal costs $100 per day). If the trucks and terminals were leased for one year, then the fixed costs would include the rental payment on the lease. If the trucks and the terminals were purchased on credit by Melodic Movements, then the fixed costs would include interest payments on the loans. If the trucks and the terminals were bought outright, then the fixed costs would include the opportunity cost—the forgone interest payments—of the funds used to buy the trucks and the terminals. These fixed costs will be incurred even if zero pianos are moved.

To move pianos, however, Melodic Movements needs labor. To move 1 piano, it might be enough to have 1 driver, 1 mechanic to service the truck, and 1 worker to help carry and load the piano. As production increases from $Q = 0$ to $Q = 1$, variable costs increase from zero to $150 and total costs increase from $300 to $450. Thus, the marginal cost of moving 1 piano rather than zero pianos is $150. If wages are $10 an hour, this implies that 15 hours of work are needed collectively from the 3 employees to move that first piano.

To move to a higher level of production, Melodic Movements requires more hours of work. According to Table 1, if production rises from 1 piano moved to 2 pianos moved, then total costs increase from $450 to $570; marginal cost is $120. With wages of $10 an hour, this marginal cost is the cost of 12 more hours of work. Notice that marginal cost *declines* as production increases from 1 to 2 units of output. Why? Because it takes less additional labor input to move from 1 piano move to 2 piano moves than it did to move from zero piano moves to 1 piano move. For instance, you may need to hire a second driver and a second loader, but the same mechanic may be able to service two trucks in less than twice the time it takes to service one truck. A full picture of how costs depend on the inputs to production becomes evident from the firm's production function.

production function: a relationship that shows the quantity of output for any given amount of input. (Ch. 6)

■ **The Production Function.**   Table 2 shows the number of hours of work required to move different numbers of pianos at Melodic Movements. It is Melodic Movements's short-run *production function*, showing how much output can be produced for each amount of labor input. You can calculate the variable costs at Melodic Movements, assuming a wage of $10 per hour, using the information in Table 2. To move 1 piano takes 15 hours of work; at $10 per hour, variable costs are $150. To move 10 pianos takes 166 hours of work; at $10 per hour, variable costs are $1,660. Similar calculations for all levels of output are shown in the third column of Table 2. Note that the variable costs in Table 2 are the same as those in Table 1. Thus, we have shown explicitly how the firm's costs depend on its production function.

TABLE 2
Using the Production Function to Compute Variable Costs

Quantity (pianos moved)	Hours of Work	Labor Costs at $10 Wage (variable costs)
0	0	0
1	15	150
2	27	270
3	37	370
4	48	480
5	60	600
6	74	740
7	90	900
8	109	1,090
9	134	1,340
10	166	1,660
11	216	2,160

Observe that increasing marginal product of labor exists at low levels of production; for example, it takes only 10 hours of labor to increase production [by 1 unit] from 2 to 3 units, whereas it takes 12 hours of labor to increase production [by 1 unit] from 1 to 2 units. At higher levels of production, decreasing marginal product of labor exists.

average product of labor: the quantity produced divided by the amount of labor input.

Recall from Chapter 6 that the *marginal product of labor* is the change in production that can be obtained with an additional unit of labor. Decreasing marginal product of labor is called *diminishing returns to labor*. Increasing marginal product of labor is called *increasing returns to labor*. The marginal product of labor is illustrated in Figure 3, which shows a graph of the production function from Table 2. Be sure to distinguish between the marginal product of labor and the average product of labor. The **average product of labor** is the quantity produced, or *total product*, divided by the amount of labor input. Thus, the average product of labor is Q/L, where Q is total product and L is labor input. On the other hand, the marginal product of labor is $\Delta Q/\Delta L$, where ΔQ is the change in the quantity produced and ΔL is the change in labor input.

You can see in Figure 3 that, for low levels of labor input, the marginal product of labor increases as labor input increases. This is akin to the previous example where you needed 1 driver, 1 loader, and 1 mechanic to move that first piano, but you needed only another driver and another loader (but not a second mechanic) to increase production to 2 piano moves. But you can also see that at high levels of labor input, the marginal product starts to decline as labor input increases: Diminishing returns set in. Adding a third loader or a third driver will not help the firm move more pianos unless it can expand its capital stock. In the short run, with a fixed capital stock, the marginal product (while falling initially) is likely to rise as production increases.

What this means is that initially, when the marginal product of labor is increasing, the marginal cost will be decreasing: Each additional unit of output requires fewer additional units of labor, and hence has a smaller additional cost. Subsequently, when the marginal product of labor is decreasing, the marginal cost will be increasing: Each additional unit of output requires more additional units of labor, and hence has a larger additional cost.

To summarize:

Increasing marginal product of labor → Decreasing marginal cost

Decreasing marginal product of labor → Increasing marginal cost

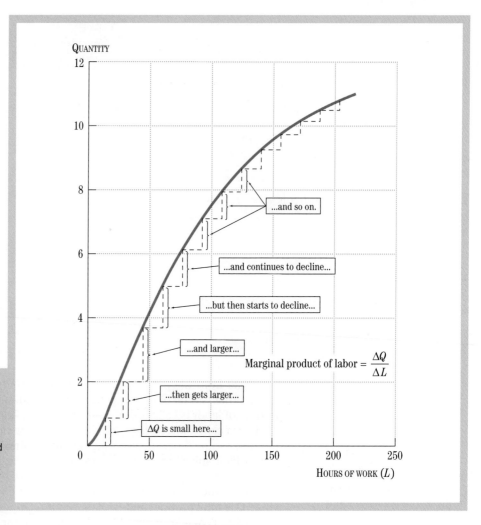

FIGURE 3
Melodic Movements'
Production Function

The curve shows the production function in which more labor input gives more output. Capital (trucks and terminals) is not changed. Observe that the marginal product of labor first increases and then decreases with more labor input.

R E V I E W

- The short run is the period of time in which it is not possible to change all inputs to production; only some inputs, such as labor, can be changed.

- The long run is the period of time in which the firm can vary all inputs to production, including capital.

- Total costs are the sum of all costs incurred by the firm in producing goods and services. Total costs can be written as the sum of fixed costs plus variable costs. Fixed costs are constant in the short run for all levels of production. Variable costs increase as more is produced.

- The marginal cost is the change in total costs as a result of producing one more unit of output. Marginal cost may rise or fall as production increases.

- The total cost per unit produced is called the average total cost. It can be separated into two parts: average variable cost, defined as variable costs divided by quantity, and average fixed cost, defined as fixed costs divided by quantity.

■ A firm's cost function depends on its production function. In the simple example we study, the firm's production function shows how many hours of labor are needed to produce a particular quantity of output, given a certain fixed level of capital.

■ When the marginal product of labor is increasing, it takes fewer workers to produce an additional unit of output; hence the additional cost of producing that unit of output (marginal cost) is decreasing. Conversely, when the marginal product of labor is decreasing, it takes more workers to produce an additional unit of output; hence the additional cost of producing that unit of output (marginal cost) is increasing.

COST CURVES

A portion of Table 1 can be turned into an informative graph, as shown in Figure 4. The vertical axis of Figure 4 shows the dollar cost, and the horizontal axis shows the quantity produced. The pairs of points from Table 1 are plotted as dots in Figure 4, and the dots have been connected to help visualize the curves. The curves are called the *marginal cost curve*, the *average total cost curve*, and the *average variable cost curve*. We label the curves *MC*, *ATC*, and *AVC*, respectively.

It is very clear from Figure 4 that marginal cost first decreases and then increases, as observed in Table 1. We now know the reason: The marginal product of each additional worker increases at lower levels of production and then decreases at higher levels of production. Figure 4 also makes it very clear that average total cost first declines and then increases. In other words, the average total cost curve is *U-shaped*.

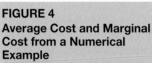

FIGURE 4
Average Cost and Marginal Cost from a Numerical Example
Average total cost first declines and then increases as more is produced. Marginal cost is below average total cost when average total cost is falling and above average total cost when average total cost is rising. This relationship also holds between average variable cost and marginal cost. These cost curves are plotted from the data given in Table 1.

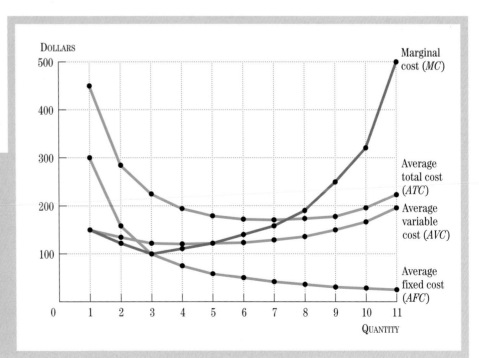

The relative positions of the average total cost curve and the marginal cost curve in Figure 4 are important and will come up repeatedly. Observe that whenever the marginal cost curve is below the average total cost curve, average total cost is declining. Whenever the marginal cost curve is above the average total cost curve, however, average total cost is increasing. This result also holds for average variable cost: If marginal cost is greater than average variable cost, then average variable cost is increasing; if marginal cost is less than average variable cost, then average variable cost is decreasing.

This implies a general and important result: *Marginal cost intersects average total cost at the lowest point of the average total cost curve. This has to be the case because whenever marginal cost is less than average total cost (to the left of the intersection point), average total cost is falling. Whenever marginal cost is more than average total cost (to the right of the intersection point), average total cost is risng.*

The same result holds between marginal cost and average variable cost. These relationships between the two average cost curves and the marginal cost curve are essential to the analysis that follows.

Marginal versus Average in the Classroom

The reason for the relationship between marginal cost and average total cost or average variable cost can be seen with an analogy. Consider another example of averages, say, your average grades on the weekly homework assignments in your economics class. Suppose that the average grade you have received on your first two assignments is 75. Now suppose that you get a 100 on your third homework assignment. The 100 you got on the third assignment was greater than the average grade of 75 you had before; in other words, your "marginal grade" of 100 is greater than your average grade of 75. What happens to your average homework grade? It will rise to 83.33. Now suppose that you had scored only a 60 on your third assignment. Then your "marginal grade" of 60 is less than the average grade of 75; hence, your average grade declines from 75 to 70.

This is a property of averaging, and it applies to grades, heights, weights, and so on, as well as to costs. When you add something into a group, an above-average contribution from the new addition increases the group average, while a below-average contribution decreases it.

Generic Cost Curves

The relationship between marginal and average allows us to sketch a *generic* cost curve diagram, the general properties of which characterize virtually all firms, not just Melodic Movements. Such a diagram is shown in Figure 5. Again, the vertical axis is the dollar cost and the horizontal axis is the quantity, but in a generic picture, we do not scale the axes because they apply to any firm, whether in textiles, moving, or electronics. Note that the marginal cost curve cuts both the average total cost curve and the average variable cost curve at the minimum point. If the marginal cost curve does not go through the lowest point of both the average total cost curve and the average variable cost curve, you have made an error in drawing a cost function.

There is another important relationship in Figure 5. The distance between the average total cost curve and the average variable cost curve gets smaller as production increases because fixed costs are a smaller and smaller proportion of total costs as production increases. Recall that fixed costs do not change as Q increases. The distance between the average total cost curve and the average variable cost curve is FC/Q, which declines as quantity increases. Hence, the distance between the

It's helpful to use the following checklist when you draw this graph:

1. Make sure the marginal cost curve cuts through the average total cost curve and the average variable cost curve at their minimum points, and understand the reason for this.

2. Make sure the distance between average total cost and average variable cost gets smaller as you increase the amount of production.

3. Put a small dip on the left-hand side of the marginal cost curve before the upward slope begins. This allows for the possibility of decreasing marginal cost at very low levels of production.

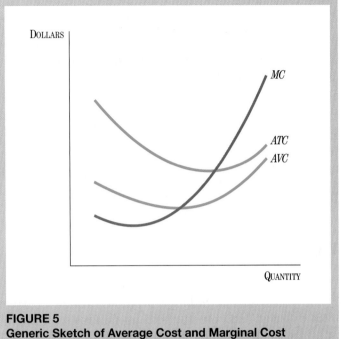

FIGURE 5
Generic Sketch of Average Cost and Marginal Cost
Every firm can be described by cost curves of the type drawn here. Compare these generic curves with the specific curves in Figure 4. Check these curves against the checklist in the margin.

ATC curve and the *AVC* curve grows smaller as you move to the right in the diagram. Any picture you draw should show this relationship.

Finally, observe that the marginal cost curve in the generic picture of Figure 5 has a region of declining marginal cost at low production levels. The graph allows for the possibility that at low production levels, the marginal product of labor increases and, therefore, marginal cost declines. This was true for Melodic Movements, which had increasing marginal product of labor initially, and we allow for it in the generic case.

You may have noticed that for the cost curves for Melodic Movements in Figure 4, the marginal cost curve and the average variable cost curve touch at 1 unit of output. This occurs because the marginal cost of producing 1 rather than zero units of output must equal the variable cost of producing 1 unit, and hence the average variable cost of producing 1 unit, as shown in Table 1. Thus, if the generic cost curve were drawn all the way over to 1 unit of output on the left of Figure 5, the marginal cost curve and the average variable cost curve would start at the same point. Because we do not usually draw generic cost curves that go all the way over to the vertical axis, we do not usually show them starting at the same point.

R E V I E W   ■ The marginal cost curve, the average total cost curve, and the average variable cost curve are closely related. In the region where the marginal cost is higher than the average total (or variable) cost, average total (or variable) cost is increasing, and vice versa.

- We can apply the lessons learned in the example of Melodic Movements to derive the generic shapes of a firm's cost curves. These curves should have the following attributes.

- The marginal cost (*MC*) curve should cut through both the average total cost (*ATC*) curve and the average variable cost (*AVC*) curve at their lowest points.

- The average fixed cost becomes very small as output increases. Therefore, the gap between average total cost and average variable cost gets smaller as more is produced.

- The marginal cost curve typically slopes downward at very low levels of output before sloping upward. The marginal cost and the average variable cost are also identical at 1 unit of output.

THE PRODUCTION DECISION IN THE SHORT RUN

As we saw in Chapter 6, a competitive firm takes the market price as given. If it is maximizing profits, it will choose a quantity to produce in the short run such that its marginal cost equals the market price (*P* = *MC*). But when the firm produces this quantity, are its profits positive? Or is the firm running a loss? If it is running a loss, should it shut down in the short run? To answer these questions, we need to use the cost curves to find the firm's profits.

The Profit or Loss Rectangle

The level of production for a competitive firm with the cost curves in Figure 5 is shown in Figure 6. The quantity produced is determined by the intersection of the marginal cost (*MC*) curve and the market price line (*P*). We draw a dashed vertical

FIGURE 6
Price Equals Marginal Cost
If a firm is maximizing profits, then it chooses a quantity (*Q*) such that price equals marginal cost. Thus, the quantity is determined by the intersection of the market price line and the marginal cost curve, as shown on the diagram. In this picture the *ATC* and *AVC* curves are a sideshow, but they enter the main act in Figure 7, when we look at the firm's level of profits.

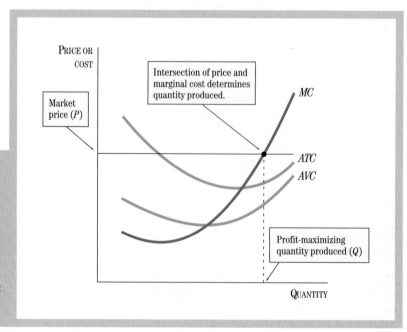

line to mark the quantity (Q) produced. Since profits equal total revenue minus total costs, we need to represent total revenue and total costs on the average cost diagram.

■ **The Total Revenue Area.**   Figure 6 shows a particular market price P and the corresponding level of production Q chosen by the firm. The total revenue that the firm gets is price P times quantity Q. Figure 7 shows that this total revenue can be represented by the area of a rectangle with width Q and height P. This rectangle is shown by the shaded area in Figure 7. The area of this rectangle, $P \times Q$, is total revenue.

■ **The Total Costs Area.**   Total costs can also be represented in Figure 7. First, observe the dashed vertical line in Figure 7 marking the profit-maximizing quantity produced. Next, observe the point where the average total cost curve intersects this dashed vertical line. This point tells us what the firm's average total cost is when it produces the profit-maximizing quantity. The area of the rectangle with the hash marks shows the firm's total costs. Why? Remember that average total cost is defined as total costs divided by quantity. If we take average total cost and multiply by quantity, we get total costs: $ATC \times Q = TC$. The quantity produced (Q) is the width of the rectangle, and average total cost (ATC) is the height of the rectangle. Hence, total costs are given by the area of the rectangle with the hash marks.

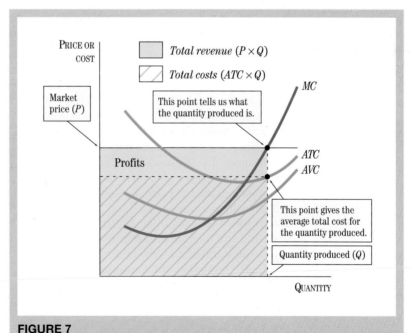

FIGURE 7
Showing Profits on the Cost Curve Diagram
The price and quantity produced are the same as those in Figure 6. The area of the shaded rectangle is total revenue. We use the *ATC* curve to find total costs in order to compute profits. First we mark where the *ATC* curve intersects the dashed vertical line showing the quantity produced. The area of the rectangle with the hash marks is total costs because the total costs (*TC*) equal average total cost (*ATC*) times quantity produced, *TC* = *ATC* × *Q*. The part of the shaded rectangle rising above the hash-marked area is profits.

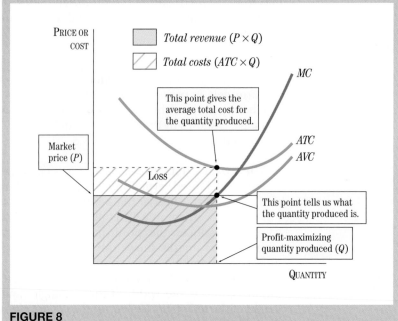

FIGURE 8
Showing a Loss on the Cost Curve Diagram
Here the market price is lower than in Figure 7. The market price line intersects the marginal cost curve at a point below the average total cost curve. Thus, the area of the total costs rectangle is larger than the area of the total revenue rectangle. Profits are less than zero, and the loss is shown in the diagram.

■ **Profits or Losses.** Since profits are total revenue less total costs, we compute profits by looking at the difference between the two rectangles. The difference is itself a rectangle, shown by the part of the revenue rectangle that rises above the total costs rectangle. *Profits are positive* in Figure 7 because total revenue is greater than total costs. But profits can also be negative, as shown in Figure 8.

Suppose that the market price is at a point where the intersection of the marginal cost curve and the market price line gives a quantity of production for which average total cost is *above* the price. This situation is shown in Figure 8. At this lower price, we still have the necessary condition for profit maximization. The firm will produce the quantity that equates price and marginal cost, as shown by the intersection of the price line and the marginal cost curve.

The amount of total revenue at this price is again price times quantity ($P \times Q$), or the shaded rectangle. Total costs are average total cost times the quantity produced, that is, $ATC \times Q$, or the area of the rectangle with the hash marks.

The difference between total revenue and total costs is profit, but in this case *profits are negative,* or there is a loss. Total revenue is less than total costs, as shown by the cost rectangle's extending above the revenue rectangle. The extent of cost overhang is the loss.

The Breakeven Point

If the intersection of price and marginal cost is at a quantity where price exceeds average total cost, the firm makes profits. If, on the other hand, the intersection of price and marginal cost is at a quantity where price is less than the average total cost,

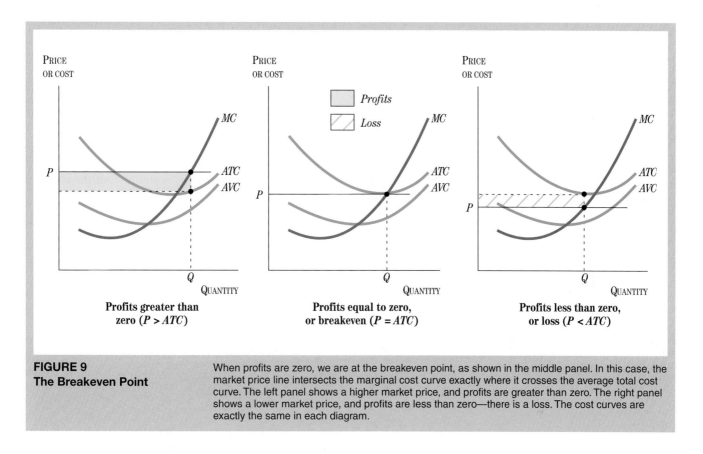

FIGURE 9
The Breakeven Point

When profits are zero, we are at the breakeven point, as shown in the middle panel. In this case, the market price line intersects the marginal cost curve exactly where it crosses the average total cost curve. The left panel shows a higher market price, and profits are greater than zero. The right panel shows a lower market price, and profits are less than zero—there is a loss. The cost curves are exactly the same in each diagram.

the firm loses money. Therefore, if the intersection of price and marginal cost is at a quantity where price is equal to average total cost, the firm is breaking even, neither making nor losing money.

This situation is shown in the middle panel of Figure 9. The market price is drawn through the point where the marginal cost curve intersects the average total cost curve, which as you recall is the minimum point on the average total cost curve. At that price, average total cost equals the price, so that the total revenue rectangle and the total cost rectangle are exactly the same. Thus, the difference between their areas is zero. At P = minimum ATC, the firm is at a **breakeven point** and economic profits are zero. The firm earns positive profits if the price is greater than the breakeven point (P > minimum ATC), as shown in the left panel. The firm has negative profits (a loss) if the price is lower than the breakeven point (P < minimum ATC), as shown in the right panel of Figure 9.

breakeven point: the point at which price equals the minimum of average total cost.

The Shutdown Point

The situation in the left panel of Figure 9 is not uncommon, every day we hear of businesses losing money. But many of these money-losing firms continue to stay in business. In 1993, Adidas, the running shoe company, lost $100 million. In 2001, Amazon.com lost over $1 billion, but the money-losing firm did not shut down in either case. Why does a firm with negative profits stay in business? At what point does it decide to shut down? Let's examine this more carefully.

The key concept to keep in mind is that in the short run, the fixed costs have to be paid even if the firm is shut down. So the firm should keep operating if it can minimize its losses by doing so, in other words, if the losses from shutting down exceed the losses from continuing to operate. Using our example of the piano-moving firm, Melodic Movements, it should keep producing as long as its revenue from moving pianos exceeds the cost of paying its workers to move the pianos, even if its revenue is insufficient to cover total costs, which include paying for the trucks and terminals in addition to paying the workers. If the firm shuts down, it will end up losing more because it will lose the entire fixed costs whereas if it keeps operating, it will earn enough to cover at least part of the fixed costs. On the other hand, if the price of moving pianos is so low that the revenue from moving the pianos is less than the workers are paid to move the pianos, it is best to shut down production and not move any pianos. The firm will lose the fixed costs for the trucks and the garage, but at least it will not lose any additional money.

We can make this analysis more formal by presenting it in terms of the cost curves shown in Figure 10. If the price is above minimum average variable cost ($P >$ minimum AVC), as shown in the left panel of Figure 10, the firm should not shut down, even if the price is below average total cost and profits are negative. Because total revenue is greater than variable costs, shutting down would eliminate this

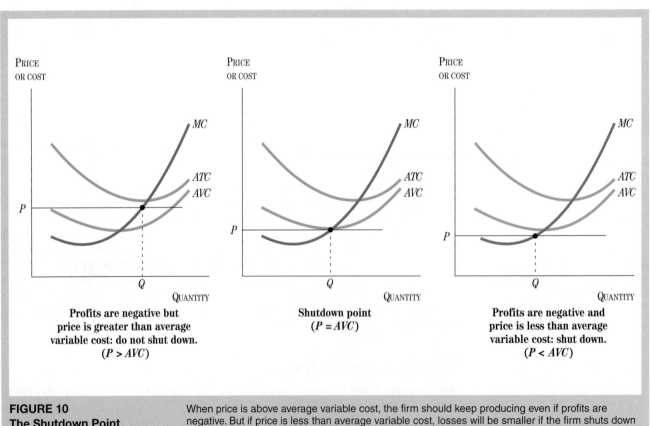

FIGURE 10
The Shutdown Point

When price is above average variable cost, the firm should keep producing even if profits are negative. But if price is less than average variable cost, losses will be smaller if the firm shuts down and stops producing. Hence, the shutdown point is when price equals average variable cost.

You can use some algebra to check the result that a firm should stop producing when the price is less than average variable cost: $P < AVC$. Note that

Profits = total revenue
−total costs

Because total costs equal variable costs plus fixed costs, we can replace total costs to get

Profits = $P \times Q - (VC + FC)$

Now, since

$VC = AVC \times Q$,

we have

Profits = $P \times Q - AVC \times Q - FC$

Rearranging this gives

Profits = $(P - AVC) \times Q - FC$

If $P < AVC$, the first term in this expression is negative unless $Q = 0$. Thus, if $P < AVC$, the best your firm can do is set $Q = 0$. This eliminates the negative drain on profits in the first term in the last expression. You minimize your loss by setting $Q = 0$.

shutdown point: the point at which price equals the minimum of average variable cost.

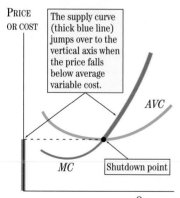

Two different points:
Shutdown point
     $P =$ minimum AVC
Breakeven point
     $P =$ minimum ATC

extra revenue. By continuing operations, the firm can minimize its losses, so it is better to keep producing in the short run. For example, Adidas did not shut down in 1993 because it had to pay fixed costs in the short run; with the price of running shoes greater than the average variable cost of producing them, the losses were less than if it had shut down.

The firm should shut down if the price falls below minimum average variable cost ($P <$ minimum AVC) and is not expected to rise again, as shown in the right panel of Figure 10. Because total revenue is less than variable costs, shutting down would eliminate the extra costs. By shutting down, the firm will have to pay its fixed costs in the short run but will not have the burden of any additional losses. Economists have developed the concept of sunk cost, which may help you understand and remember why a firm like Adidas would continue to operate in the short run even though it was reporting losses. A *sunk cost* is a cost that you have committed to pay and that you cannot recover. For example, if a firm signs a year's lease for factory space, it must make rental payments until the lease is up, whether the space is used or not. The important thing about a sunk cost is that once you commit to it, there is nothing you can do about it, so you might as well ignore it in your decisions. The firm cannot recover these costs by shutting down. All Adidas could do in the short run was reduce its losses, and it did so by continuing to produce (assuming that the revenue from each pair of shoes was greater than the variable cost of producing them).

Now, observe that the middle panel of Figure 10 shows the case where price exactly equals the minimum point of the average variable cost curve ($P =$ minimum AVC). This is called the **shutdown point;** it is the price at which total revenue exactly equals the firm's variable costs. If the price falls below the shutdown point, the firm should shut down. If the price is above the shutdown point, the firm should continue producing.

In thinking about the shutdown point, the time period is important. We are looking at the firm during the short run, when it is obligated to pay its fixed costs and cannot alter its capital. The question for Melodic Movements is what to do when it has already committed to paying for the trucks and terminals, but the price of moving pianos falls to such a low level that it does not cover variable costs. The shutdown rule says to stop in that situation. However, if profits are negative, but the price is greater than average variable cost, then it is best to keep producing.

The shutdown point can be incorporated into the firm's supply curve. Recall that the supply curve of a single firm tells us the quantity of a good that the firm will produce at different prices. As long as the price is above minimum average variable cost, the firm will produce a quantity such that marginal cost equals the price. Thus, for prices above minimum average variable cost, the marginal cost curve is the firm's supply curve, as shown in the figure in the margin. However, if the price falls below minimum average variable cost, then the firm will shut down; in other words, the quantity produced will equal zero ($Q = 0$). Thus, for prices below minimum average variable cost, the supply curve jumps over to the vertical axis, where $Q = 0$, as shown in the figure in the margin.

Be sure that you understand the difference between the shutdown point and the breakeven point. The shutdown point is where price equals the minimum average variable cost (Figure 10). The breakeven point is where price equals the minimum average total cost (Figure 9). If the price is between the minimum average total cost and the minimum average variable cost, then the firm is not breaking even; it is losing money. However, it does not make sense to shut down in the short run unless the price falls below the shutdown point.

A Dormant Mine Starts Up Again

By now you are familiar with the idea that the relationship between price and average cost is a critical one for a firm. When price is below average total cost but above average variable cost, a firm should continue operating in the short run even though it is losing money. If price falls below average variable cost, and is unlikely to rise above that level, then it should shut down. This article describes how an increase in the price of steel as a result of higher demand from China has revitalized the iron mines of Minnesota by raising price above average variable cost—and in some cases above average total cost.

The source of the rise in demand, which in turn leads to higher prices

When the price of steel fell in the 1980s and 1990s, while the costs of employing workers rose, many firms had to go out of business and lay off workers.

As price rises, the firms move away from the shutdown point and start producing at full capacity.

Surprise Revival for Iron Mines of Minnesota

AMANDA PAULSON, Staff writer of The Christian Science Monitor

EVELETH, MINN.—Spring comes slowly to Minnesota's Iron Range. It's home to the world's largest hockey stick, a place where the lakes are still frozen in late April and vowels roll slowly off people's tongues. For the past couple of decades, the region's economy has seemed frozen as well, its bedrock mining industry slowly dying.

In the past year, however, a new life has been blowing into these ochre hills from an unlikely place. You see it in the noise and dust that spews, 24 hours a day, from the recently dormant iron mine just above town, and in the guarded optimism of residents, used to bad news and silent cranes that claw at some of the world's largest open-pit mines.

In a weird twist on the typical globalization story, China is reviving a local economy that's been one of the most stubborn pockets of unemployment in the United States.

The Asian nation's insatiable appetite for steel fuels global demand for the metal and the ore used to make it. As steel-producing nations around the globe turn out more ingots and flat wire, mines here are once again producing some of the raw material—though most of it is not going directly to Beijing or Shanghai. In one case, a Chinese company helped buy and reopen the bankrupt mine here in Eveleth, sending its ore to Canada to replace raw material bound for China.

Whatever its circuitous route, the result is the same: At a time when many Americans lament the loss of manufacturing jobs to China, steel mills there are producing jobs for lunch-pail workers here whose families have worked the mines for generations.

"If you'd have said a year ago this would be happening, I'd never have believed it," says Joe Strlekar, president of local steelworkers 6860, whose workers were already training for new jobs after being laid off in May, only to get their jobs back when the mine reopened. "Instead of everything coming back into this country from China, it's good to have something going the other way."

This region was built on mining, in a very literal sense. Eveleth's location was moved in 1900, after iron was discovered beneath the town. Erie Mining created Hoyt Lakes from scratch, constructing houses, schools, streets, and shops. In Chisholm, the 81-foot statue of the "iron man"—a miner with pick and shovel, perched atop steel beams—stands guard over the carved-up red hills of the Mesabi Range, testament to a century of labor by the Finns, Serbs, Italians, and Slavs who settled this area.

Families here talk of uncles or grandparents blackballed for union work; oral histories in the Iron World Research Center tell of mine accidents and polka dancing, of 12-hour night shifts and using Sears Roebuck catalogues to teach new arrivals English.

Since then, the region has struggled to diversify. Forestry and mining still provide the most coveted jobs. But only 4,000 mining jobs remain, down from 16,000 in 1980, and many have wondered if Minnesota's iron ore days would become a relic. Thousands left during the mass layoffs of the 1980s, and in 2001 the LTV mine—Erie's successor—shut its doors for good, putting 1,400 people out of work.

So the news that the Eveleth mine was reopening in December came as a welcome surprise. With the dollar down and steel prices soaring, all six state mines are at full production for the first time in years. "It was a very nice Christmas here for a lot of people," says Paul Bachschneider, president of the area Chamber of Commerce.

Bill Matos, a blaster at United Taconite who's worked at that mine for 30 years, says the news was "bittersweet." He was pleased to get his job back, but rues the old company's bankruptcy, which froze his pension two months shy of retirement. "Now I'll have to work at least five more years," says Mr. Matos, in heavy boots and brown Carhartt overalls.

Matos always knew this was the work for him. His grandparents came here from Austria in 1904, and he's never wanted to leave. "If you want any pay, benefits, 40 hours a week," he says, "you'll be in the mines." Some fellow miners went back to school when they lost their jobs last summer, to learn masonry, carpentry, or nursing. But Matos figured he was too old.

"Maybe I would have worked as a bus driver," he says. "If I was younger, I could relocate, but I'm rooted in here pretty well."

These days, Matos says, miners are hopeful, though "even in good times, there's skepticism." He's happiest for the community. Schools, spinoff industries, even car dealerships benefit, he says. "I'd like to see it last another 20 years, for the people who work here, for the sake of the community. The schools are in bad shape. There's nothing for young people." ← *The spillover benefits of having mining jobs open up again*

How long the boom can last is an open question. According to Peter Clevenstine at the Minnesota Department of Natural Resources, the outlook is reasonably good. Demand may slow, he says, but "China's consumption will be there for a long time."

The steel market has always been largely determined by transportation costs. Iron ore is a relatively cheap commodity, and it doesn't pay to ship it long distances. So Minnesota and Michigan mines—which account for about 7 percent of the global production—typically ship only to mills near the Great Lakes. In recent years, the US has gotten more iron ore from big producers like Australia and Brazil, who've glutted the market and lowered demand for raw material.

Because of the ore transportation costs, "there's a limit to how far out you can go to be competitive," says Mr. Clevenstine. "But with the world's supply of iron ore going to China, we've moved out that radius."

Take US Steel's plant in Fairfield, Ala., which now gets its iron from a Minnesota mine. "A year ago, we wrote that off as being best supplied by foreign ore," says Clevenstine. "The economics have changed because of what the world ore price has done."

But experts are quick to recognize the industry's cyclical nature. The dollar could go up, and Brazil and Australia are increasing production to meet demand. "The momentary stability is a good thing," says Frank Ongaro, president of the Iron Mining Association of Minnesota. He estimates that the six mines will spend a couple hundred million dollars more on equipment and services this year than last year, which will benefit the area. "But whether it lasts one year or five years, eventually we are going to return to being entirely dependent on the lower Great Lakes marketplace." ← *Words of caution about the outlook for the future*

Long term, some state officials hope other developments—like a value-added process allowing mills to turn out nearly pure and more valuable "iron nuggets" to be used by popular minimills—will help the region compete. They're also hopeful about tapping copper, nickel, and palladium deposits.

At the newly reopened United Taconite mine, workers are moving the 75,000 tons of rock that get processed every 24 hours. Yellow trucks that can move 190 tons crisscross the massive open pit, a wasteland of gray rubble. . . .

But the prospect of retraining in a tight job market was far tougher, and Mr. Hartmann is glad to see his former workers back. "We rattle the town with our blasts," he says. "We make dust and noise. But I can't tell you how many townspeople were happy to feel those blasts again."

REVIEW

- Total revenue for a firm for a given price is represented by the area of the rectangle whose height is the price and whose width is the profit-maximizing quantity corresponding to that price. Total costs for a firm producing that quantity are represented by the area of the rectangle whose width is the quantity and whose height is the average total cost corresponding to that quantity.

- Profits can also be represented as a rectangle on the cost curve diagram. The profit or loss rectangle is the difference between the revenue rectangle and the loss rectangle.

- When $P >$ minimum ATC, total revenue exceeds total costs, so the firm is making profits. When $P <$ minimum ATC, total costs exceed total revenue, so the firm is losing money. When $P =$ minimum ATC, the firm is making zero profits; this is called the breakeven point.

- A firm that is losing money may continue to operate, or it may choose to shut down. That decision depends on the relationship between price and average variable cost, keeping in mind that fixed costs have already been incurred in the short run.

- If $P >$ minimum AVC, then the firm will continue to operate in the short run because it is earning enough to cover its variable costs and some, but not all, of its fixed costs. When $P <$ minimum AVC, profits are maximized by shutting down because continuing to operate will result in the firm losing even more than its fixed costs.

- The point where $P =$ minimum AVC is called the shutdown point. When price is in between the breakeven point and the shutdown point, the firm is losing money, but it is minimizing its losses in the short run by continuing to operate.

- The shutdown point can be incorporated into the supply curve. Since the firm will choose to stay in business only when $P >$ minimum AVC, the supply curve will be zero for prices below minimum AVC. Above minimum AVC, the marginal cost curve will be the supply curve.

COSTS AND PRODUCTION: THE LONG RUN

Thus far, we have focused our analysis on the short run. By definition, the short run is the period of time during which it is not possible for firms to adjust certain inputs to production. But what happens in the long run, when it *is* possible for firms to make such adjustments? For example, what happens to Melodic Movements when it opens new terminals or takes out a lease on a fleet of new trucks? To answer this question, we need to show how the firm can adjust its costs in the long run. All costs, fixed costs as well as variable costs, can be adjusted in the long run.

The Effect of Capital Expansion on Costs

First, consider what happens to fixed costs when the firm increases its capital. Suppose Melodic Movements increases the size of its fleet from 4 trucks to 8 trucks and raises the number of terminals from 2 to 4. Then its fixed costs would increase because more rent would have to be paid for 4 terminals and 8 trucks than for 2 terminals and 4 trucks. To obtain the increase in fixed costs, we need to use the price of capital. Suppose trucks cost $25 per day and a terminal costs $100 per day. Then 4 trucks and 2 terminals would cost $300 and 8 trucks and 4 terminals would cost $600. Fixed costs would rise from $300 to $600.

Second, consider what happens to variable costs when the firm increases its capital. An increase in capital increases the amount that each additional worker can produce. For example, according to Table 2, 166 worker-hours were required for Melodic Movements to move 10 pianos when there were 4 trucks and 2 terminals. With more capital (8 trucks and 4 terminals), it will take fewer hours of work to move the pianos. Assume, for example, that it takes only 120 worker-hours to deliver 10 pianos. In this scenario, with the wage equal to $10 per hour, the variable cost of moving 10 pianos falls from $1,660 to $1,200. In other words, variable costs decline as the firm expands its capital.

Now consider total costs. With fixed costs larger and variable costs smaller as a result of the increase in capital, what is the effect on total costs, which are the sum of fixed costs and variable costs? After the expansion, total costs will be higher at very low levels of output, where fixed costs dominate, but will be lower at high levels of output, where variable costs dominate.

Figure 11 illustrates this using the total cost curve. Figure 11 is essentially the same as Figure 2 except that the green curves show the old costs before the expansion of capital and the purple curves show the new costs with the additional capital.

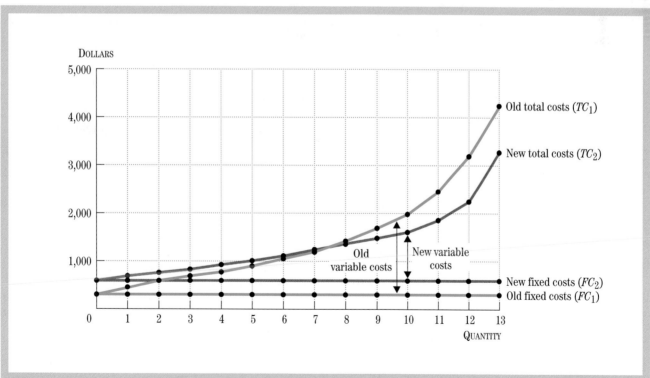

FIGURE 11
Shifts in Total Costs as a Firm Increases Its Capital in the Long Run

When a firm increases its capital, its fixed costs increase; as shown in the diagram, fixed costs rise from FC_1 to FC_2. However, its variable costs decrease, which is also shown. Thus, the new total costs curve (TC_2) will be above the old total costs curve (TC_1) for low-level output and below the old total costs curve (TC_1) for high-level output.

TABLE 3
Costs with More Capital (Compared with Table 1, fixed costs are higher and variable costs are lower in this table because capital is higher than in Table 1. Costs are measured in dollars.)

Quantity	Total Costs	Fixed Costs	Variable Costs	Average Total Cost
0	600	600	0	—
1	690	600	90	690
2	770	600	170	385
3	840	600	240	280
4	920	600	320	230
5	1,010	600	410	202
6	1,110	600	510	185
7	1,220	600	620	174
8	1,340	600	740	168
9	1,470	600	870	163
10	1,610	600	1,010	161
11	1,880	600	1,280	171
12	2,300	600	1,700	192

The diagram shows that the new fixed costs are higher and the new variable costs are lower. The new total cost curve (TC_2) is twisted relative to the old total cost curve (TC_1). The new total cost curve is above the old total cost curve at low levels of output and below the old total cost curve at high levels of output.

Table 3 provides the numerical information about the costs that appear in Figure 11. To see the effect of the firm's expansion on its costs, compare the fixed costs, variable costs, and total costs in Table 3 with those in Table 1. Observe that fixed costs are higher: $600 rather than $300. Variable costs are lower throughout the range of production. As a result, total costs are higher in Table 3 than in Table 1 for production of less than 8 units, and lower in Table 3 than in Table 1 for production of 8 units or more.

Our analysis of the effects of the firm's capital expansion on total costs can be used to derive the effects on average total cost. Remember, average total cost (ATC) is total costs (TC) divided by the quantity (Q). Thus, if total costs increase at a given quantity of output, so will average total cost. And if total costs decrease at a given level of output, so will average total cost.

This is illustrated in Figure 12. An average total cost curve, labeled ATC_1, corresponding to average total cost in Table 1 is plotted. Another average total cost curve, labeled ATC_2, corresponding to average total cost in Table 3 is also plotted. The new average total cost curve (ATC_2) is above the old average total cost curve (ATC_1) at low levels of output and below the old average total cost curve (ATC_1) at higher levels of output. Average total cost is higher for production of less than 8 units and lower for production of 8 units or more. This is precisely what is shown for total costs in Figure 11.

The Long-Run *ATC* Curve

Now that we have seen what happens at Melodic Movements when capital is expanded by a certain amount, we can see what happens when capital increases by even larger amounts. For example, suppose Melodic Movements expands throughout

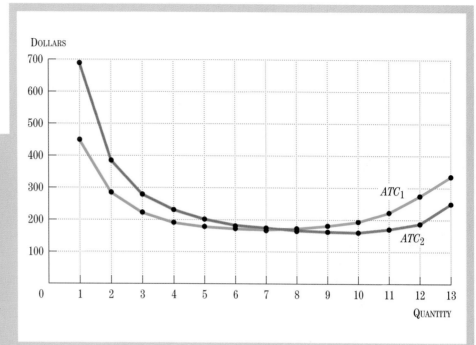

FIGURE 12

Shifts in Average Total Cost Curves When a Firm Expands Its Capital

The effects on average total cost follow directly from the effects on total costs in Figure 11. Here ATC_1 is the average total cost curve with a lower amount of capital, and ATC_2 is the average total cost curve with a higher amount of capital. To the left, at lower levels of output, higher fixed costs raise average total cost; to the right, at higher levels of output, lower variable costs tend to lower average total cost.

Houston and even beyond Houston by expanding the size of its fleet of trucks and the number of terminals to park and service the trucks.

Figure 13 shows four different average total cost curves. Each of the average total cost curves corresponds to increased capital expansion at Melodic Movements. The first two of these, ATC_1 and ATC_2, are the average total cost curves from Figure 12. Note that the second curve (ATC_2) is above the first (ATC_1) at low levels of output and below the first at high levels of output. The third and fourth curves are for even more trucks and terminals. The third average total cost curve (ATC_3) is above the second (ATC_2) at lower levels of output and below the second (ATC_2) at higher levels of output. The same is true of the fourth compared to the third.

The thick light green curve tracing out the bottoms of the four average total cost curves gives the lowest average total cost at any quantity produced. This thick line tells us what average total cost is when the firm can expand (or contract) its capital; in other words, this is the average total cost curve for the long run. For this reason, we call the curve that traces out the points on the lowest average total cost curves the **long-run average total cost curve.** The other average total cost curve that we have been discussing is called the *short-run average total cost curve*, or simply the average total cost curve.

The lack of smoothness in the long-run average total cost curve may seem strange. It occurs in Figure 13 because we have drawn only four short-run average total cost curves. If it is possible to expand capital in smaller amounts, then the curve will look smoother. For example, between the first and second short-run average total cost curves (ATC_1 and ATC_2) in Figure 13, there might be an average total cost curve for 6 trucks and 3 terminals. When we put in more and more short-run average total cost curves, the long-run average total cost curve gets smoother and smoother. But it still simply traces out the points of lowest cost for each level of output.

long-run average total cost curve: the curve that traces out the short-run average total cost curves, showing the lowest average total cost for each quantity produced as the firm expands in the long run.

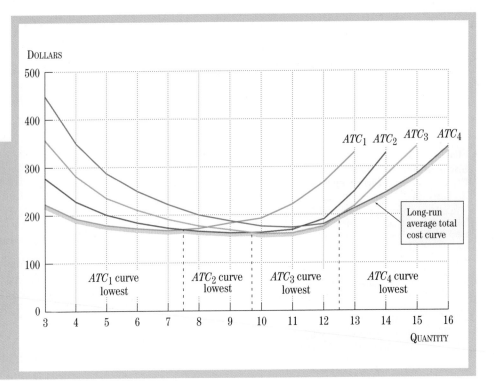

FIGURE 13
Long-Run versus Short-Run Average Total Cost

In the short run, it is not possible to change certain inputs, like the size of the factory or the number of machines. In the long run, these can be changed. For example, in the long run, Melodic Movements can build more terminals around town. This means that the ATC curve shifts. The diagram shows four different ATC curves for Melodic Movements; each new ATC curve represents more terminals, buildings, and machines than the ATC curve to its left. The long-run average total cost curve is shown by the thicker light green line.

Capital Expansion and Production in the Long Run

How does a firm like Melodic Movements decide whether to expand or contract its capital in the long run? How much does it produce in the long run? The decision is similar to the short-run decision about whether to hire more workers to move more pianos. Again, the firm sets the quantity produced to maximize profits. But now the quantity produced and profits can be affected by changes in capital as well as labor. At any level of capital and labor input, we can compute profits.

If the firm can increase its profits by expanding its capital and its output, then we predict that it will do so. If we find that the firm can increase its profits by reducing its capital and its output, then we predict that it will do so. In other words, the firm adjusts the amount of capital to maximize profits.

Furthermore, in the long run, the firm adjusts both its capital and its labor. What determines the mix of labor and capital when both are variable? The relative price of labor compared to capital will be the deciding factor.

In deriving the cost curves for Melodic Movements, we assumed that the cost of labor was $10 per hour and that the cost of capital, consisting of trucks and terminals, was $25 a day for trucks and $100 a day for terminals. If the cost of labor was higher, say, $20 per hour, then Melodic Movements would have the incentive to rent more trucks rather than hire more workers, at least to the extent that this was feasible.

However, if the cost of capital rose relative to that of labor, then the firm would have the incentive to hire more workers. In general, the firm will use more capital relative to labor if the cost of capital declines relative to that of labor. And conversely, the firm will use less capital relative to labor if the cost of capital rises relative to that of labor.

ECONOMICS IN ACTION

Expanding (and Shrinking) a Firm over Time

The first general-merchandise "five and dime" store was opened by Woolworth in 1879. By building new stores and merging with other firms over time, Woolworth expanded greatly in size. By 1919 it had 1,081 stores in the United States, France, England, and Germany. Through the development of discount stores (Woolco) and specialty stores (including the Lady Foot Locker shown here), this firm continued to expand. In 1999 the company dropped the name Woolworth and became Venator. The newly named firm sold many of its non-footwear businesses and eventually was renamed Foot Locker, Inc., in November 2001. By 2005, Foot Locker had over 4,000 specialty stores in Australia, Europe, New Zealand, and North America.

REVIEW

- In the long run, the firm can expand by increasing its capital. Fixed costs increase and variable costs decline at each level of production as the firm expands its capital.

- Thus, total costs, and average total cost, are higher at low levels of production and lower at high levels of production.

- The average total cost in the long run can be found by tracing out the lowest points of the short-run average total cost curves.

- In the long run, the firm adjusts the amount of capital to maximize profits. It will also choose the mix of labor and capital that maximizes profits, so that when the price of labor rises relative to capital, the firm will switch away from labor toward capital, and vice versa.

ECONOMIES OF SCALE

The long-run average total cost curve is one way in which economists study the behavior of a firm over time. Whether the long-run average total cost curve slopes up or down, and over what range, is crucial for understanding the nature of a firm, the industry in which it operates, and the role of government.

The long-run average total cost curve describes a situation in which the firm can expand all its inputs. When all inputs increase, we say that the *scale* of the firm increases. For example, if the number of workers at the firm doubles, the number of trucks doubles, the number of terminals doubles, and so on, then we say that the scale of the firm doubles. Thus, the long-run average total cost curve describes what happens to a firm's average total cost when its scale increases. There is some specialized terminology about different shapes of the long-run average total cost curve.

economies of scale: a situation in which long-run average total cost declines as the output of a firm increases.

diseconomies of scale: a situation in which long-run average total cost increases as the output of a firm increases.

constant returns to scale: a situation in which long-run average total cost is constant as the output of a firm changes.

We say that there are **economies of scale,** or *increasing returns to scale*, if long-run average total cost falls as the scale of the firm increases. We say that there are **diseconomies of scale,** or *decreasing returns to scale*, if long-run average total cost rises as the scale of the firm increases. The situation in the middle, where long-run average total cost neither rises nor falls, is called **constant returns to scale.** Figure 14 illustrates these three possible shapes for the long-run average total cost curve.

Determining Whether a Firm Has Economies or Diseconomies of Scale

Whether there are increasing, decreasing, or constant returns to scale depends on the type of firm and the type of product. Consider a firm like Melodic Movements. One can imagine that there would be economies of scale as the firm expanded the number of terminals around the city of Houston; with more terminals, trucks could be serviced at many different locations and would not have to be driven so far at the end of the day or towed so far in the event of a breakdown. With a larger work force, Melodic Movements could have workers who *specialize* in moving different types of pianos or who specialize in servicing different parts of the trucks. Some might specialize in moves to high-rise buildings. In other words, as the scale of a firm increases, the work can be divided into different tasks, and some members of the labor force can specialize in each task.

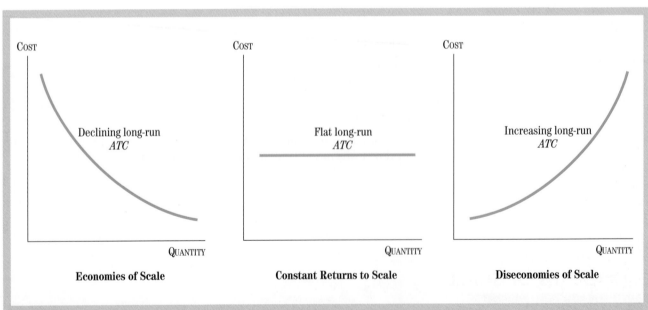

FIGURE 14
Economies and Diseconomies of Scale

If the long-run average total cost curve slopes downward, we say that there are economies of scale. If the long-run average total cost curve slopes upward, we say that there are diseconomies of scale. If the long-run average total cost curve is flat, we say that there are constant returns to scale, as shown in the middle panel.

Is there a limit to economies of scale? What about expanding beyond Houston to Galveston, Dallas, Tulsa, Mexico City, or even Lima, Peru? In the case of piano moving, returns to scale would probably begin to decline at some point. The extra administrative costs of organizing a large interstate or worldwide piano-moving firm would probably raise average total cost. Thus, one could imagine that the long-run average total cost curve for Melodic Movements would first decline and then increase as the firm grows in size.

Although no two firms are alike, the long-run average total cost curve for most firms probably declines at low levels of output, then remains flat, and finally begins to increase at high levels of output. As a firm gets very large, administrative expenses, as well as coordination and incentive problems, will begin to raise average total cost. The smallest scale of production for which long-run average total cost is at a minimum is called the **minimum efficient scale.** A typical long-run average cost curve and its minimum efficient scale are shown in Figure 15.

Mergers and Economies of Scope

An increase or decrease in the scale of a firm through capital expansion or contraction—as described in the previous two sections—is one kind of change in the firm over time. Firms can also change over time in other ways. They can grow through mergers between one firm and another firm. If the product lines of the two firms are similar, then such mergers may be a way to reduce costs, for example, by consolidating the number of executives or by reducing inefficient duplication of resources. That is one reason why large oil companies, such as Exxon and Mobil, merged in the 1990s.

Mergers are also a common way for firms to combine different skills or resources to develop new products. For example, America Online, an Internet firm, and Time Warner, a large firm producing movies, magazines, and CDs, merged in 2001. By bringing together distribution resources with content resources, this merger was intended to widen the scope of both firms and help them develop new products. The results did not turn out as expected, however, and in 2003 Time Warner dropped AOL

Gulliver and Economies of Scale
Like a firm expanding all its inputs—capital and labor—Gulliver found that he was bigger in *all* dimensions—arms and legs and head—than the Lilliputians. When economists consider economies of scale, they think of all the firm's inputs increasing, not just one. But when they consider diminishing returns to labor, they think of only one input (labor) increasing, which would be like Gulliver's finding that only his arms were bigger than the Lilliputians', with everything else the same size.

minimum efficient scale: the smallest scale of production for which long-run average total cost is at a minimum.

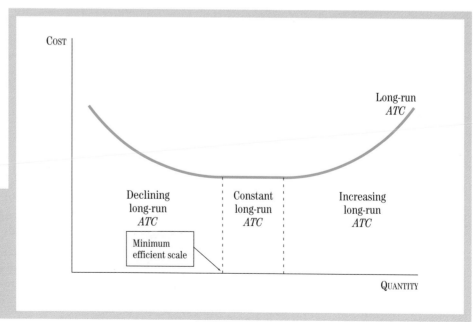

FIGURE 15
Typical Shape of the Long-Run Average Total Cost Curve

For many types of firms, the long-run *ATC* curve slopes down at low levels of output, then reaches a flat area, and finally begins to slope up at high levels. The minimum efficient scale is shown.

TABLE 4
Recent Big Mergers

Names Before Merger		Name After Merger	Primary Industry
Exxon	Mobil	ExxonMobil	Oil
BP	Amoco	BP Amoco (now BP)	Oil
J.P. Morgan	Chase Manhattan	JP Morgan Chase	Banking
Bank of America	Fleet Boston Financial	Bank of America Corp.	Banking
Chrysler	Daimler-Benz	DaimlerChrysler	Motor vehicles
WorldCom	MCI Communications	MCI WorldCom (now WorldCom)	Telecommunications
Walt Disney	Capital Cities/ABC	Walt Disney	Entertainment
America Online	Netscape	America Online	Internet
America Online	Time Warner	AOL Time Warner (now Time Warner)	Internet + entertainment

Most of these mergers are in the same industry and illustrate economies of scale except for the last, which may be due to expected economies of scope.

from its corporate name in an effort to demonstrate that the company still valued its "core" assets—magazines, books, cable (HBO, CNN), and movies. Combining different types of firms to reduce costs or create new products is sometimes called *economies of scope.* Table 4 lists some of the big mergers of recent years. Observe that most of those listed involve similar products.

When two firms merge into one firm, each of the original firms may become a division within the new firm. A merger of one firm with another means that the coordination of production moves from the market to within the organization. For example, the merger of the U.S. firm Chrysler with the German firm Daimler-Benz meant that the different makes of cars were produced in two divisions of the same firm. As with the AOL–Time Warner merger, Daimler and Chrysler found out that the merger did not bring the anticipated gains; they parted ways in 2007.

REVIEW

- Economies of scale are said to exist for a firm when the long-run average total cost curve declines as the scale of the firm increases. Economies of scale may occur because of the specialization that the division of labor in larger firms permits.

- Although economies of scale probably exist over some regions of production, the evidence indicates that as firms grow very large, diseconomies of scale set in.

- The smallest scale of production at which long-run average total cost is at a minimum is called the minimum efficient scale of the firm.

- Instead of changing by increasing the capital stock, firms sometimes change via mergers. Mergers between firms that produce similar products can result in lower costs and a higher minimum efficient scale of production.

- Mergers are also a common way for firms with different types of skills and expertise to combine that knowledge and widen the scope of what they jointly produce. Firms that have the ability to do this type of merger are said to have economies of scope.

ECONOMICS IN ACTION

Economist Finds Economies of Scale at Pin Factory

One way to get an intuitive feel for economies of scale is to visit a factory and watch people in action. If you look carefully, you can actually see economies of scale. Here is a short but wonderfully vivid description of workers at a pin-making factory. An economist wrote the description after a visit to the factory, and it illustrates how economists think. The workers are producing pins from metal wire.

> One man draws out the wire, another straightens it, a third cuts it, a fourth points it, a fifth grinds it at the top for receiving the head; to make the head requires two or three distinct operations; to put it on is a peculiar business, to whiten the pins is another . . . [T]en men only . . . could make upwards of forty eight thousand pins in a day. Each person, therefore, . . . might be considered as making four thousand eight hundred pins in a day.
>
> But if they had each wrought separately and independently they certainly could not each of them have made twenty, perhaps, not one pin in a day.
>
> That is certainly not the two hundred and fortieth, perhaps not the four thousand eight hundredth part of what they are at present capable of producing.

This story of the pin factory is not new. In what century do you think the economist watched this firm in action? And who do you think the economist was? (*Hint:* It was written up in a book called *Wealth of Nations*.) Whatever the answer, the story is as relevant now as it was when the account was written.

A more modern example of economies of scale involves Wal-Mart, the retail company founded by Sam Walton in 1962, now selling $312 billion and employing over 1.8 million employees. How did Wal-Mart grow to be the largest U.S. company in revenues in just forty years?

One of the keys to Wal-Mart's success is the use of economies of scale. With over 9,000 stores in the United States and over 2,500 additional stores in nine other countries, Wal-Mart uses central distribution points, a streamlined supply chain closely coordinated with its suppliers, lower inventories, centrally coordinated marketing, and its enormous buying power to lower its costs. Wal-Mart's focus on economies of scale, increased productivity, and cost reduction allowed it to charge lower prices and increase its

market share. A 2003 article in *BusinessWeek* magazine puts Wal-Mart's market share in groceries at 19%, pharmacies at 16%, and super-centers (large all-in-one retailers) at almost 80%. As an example of Wal-Mart's advantage over other general-merchandise retailers, its productivity measured by real sales per employee was 36% higher than its closest competitor in 1999. As a matter of fact, the economies of scale of the retail industry—particularly Wal-Mart—contributed greatly to the increase in U.S. productivity in the 1990s.

What similarities and differences do you see between Wal-Mart and the pin factory? What aspects other than economies of scale would you consider when measuring Wal-Mart's success and its impact on the economy?

The economist looks at what each worker does, and estimates that production each day at this ten-person firm equals 48,000 pins, or 4,800 per worker.

Now the economist imagines production at a much smaller firm consisting of one worker. Daily production is estimated at between 1 and 20 pins per worker.

Thus production per worker at the small firm is only 1/240 or 1/4,800 as much as at the large firm. That is big economies of scale.

CONCLUSION

In this chapter we have developed a model for studying why firms shut down, expand, or contract. This analysis of changes at firms over time is an extension of the analysis of a firm's short-run behavior in Chapter 6.

A centerpiece of the model is a graph (Figure 5) that shows the firm's average total cost and average variable cost. Using this graph, we can determine whether a firm will shut down in the short run. Using additional average total cost curves corresponding to alternative levels of capital, we can also determine whether the firm will expand or contract.

We showed how this model can be used to find the firm's long-run total cost and average cost curves. By looking at a firm's long-run average total cost curve (Figure 15), we can tell whether a firm has economies of scale. We will use the long-run average total cost curve extensively in the next several chapters of this book.

KEY POINTS

1. Firms start up, expand, contract, or shut down when conditions in the economy change.

2. The short run and the long run are two broad categories into which economists categorize time periods. The short run is the period of time during which it is not possible for the firm to change all the inputs to production; only some inputs, such as labor, can be changed. The long run is the minimum period of time in which the firm can vary all inputs to production, including capital.

3. Total costs are all the costs incurred by the firm in producing goods or services. Fixed costs are the portion of total costs that do not vary with the amount produced in the short run. Variable costs are the remaining portion of total costs that do vary as production changes.

4. Average total cost, or cost per unit, is widely used by economists, accountants, and investors to assess a firm's cost behavior. The profit made by the firm in the short run depends on the difference between the price and average total cost at the quantity corresponding to that price.

5. When the market price equals the minimum of average total cost, the firm breaks even. At higher prices, profits are positive. At lower prices, profits are negative.

6. The firm will keep producing, in some circumstances, even if profits are negative in the short run. This is because the fixed costs would have to be incurred regardless of whether or not any production is done. So if the price is enough to cover variable costs, the firm should keep producing so as to minimize its losses.

7. When the market price equals the minimum of average variable cost, the firm is just at the point of shutting down. If the price is below average variable cost, the firm should shut down.

8. The long-run average total cost curve describes how a firm's costs behave when the firm expands its capital.

9. If long-run average total cost declines, then there are economies of scale. For many firms, there is a range over which the long-run average total cost curve is flat, and we say that there are constant returns to scale over that range. When firms get very large, diseconomies of scale set in.

10. Firms can expand by merging with other firms. Such mergers can be motivated by either economies of scale or economies of scope.

KEY TERMS

short run

long run

average total cost (*ATC*)

average variable cost (*AVC*)

average fixed cost (*AFC*)

average product of labor

breakeven point

shutdown point

long-run average total cost curve

economies of scale

diseconomies of scale

constant returns to scale

minimum efficient scale

QUESTIONS FOR REVIEW

1. What is the difference between total costs, fixed costs, and variable costs?

2. How is marginal cost related to total cost?

3. Why does the marginal cost curve cut through the average total cost curve exactly at the minimum of the average total cost curve?

4. Why does the marginal cost curve cut through the average variable cost curve exactly at the minimum of the average variable cost curve?

5. What rectangles in the cost curve diagram depict total revenue, total costs, and profits?

6. What is the difference between the breakeven point and the shutdown point?

7. How is the long-run average total cost curve derived?

8. What is the minimum efficient scale of a firm?

9. What is the relationship between the shape of the long-run total cost curve and economies of scale?

10. What are economies of scope? How are mergers related to economies of scale and scope?

PROBLEMS

1. Consider the relationship between your average grade (GPA) and your marginal grade. Suppose you have taken 12 courses so far, and your average GPA is 3.25. Suppose the marginal grade is the grade you get in this course.
   a. If the grade you get in this class is an A (4.0), which is above your average, what will happen to your average GPA?
   b. If the grade you get in this class is a B (3.0), which is below your average, what will happen to your average GPA?
   c. What does this illustrate about the relationship between marginal and average curves in general?

2. Consider the age of the people working in the firm that you are doing an internship with this summer. Suppose the first person you meet is 40 years old, and the second and third are 33 and 27, respectively. Graph the average and marginal age of the three people in the firm, placing age on the vertical axis and quantity of people on the horizontal axis in the order in which you met them. What do you notice about the relationship between marginal and average age?

3. Fill out the entries in the table below.

Q	TC	FC	VC	ATC	AVC	MC
0	8					
1	12					
2	14					
3	20					
4	30					
5	50					

4. Fill out the entries in the table below.

Quantity	Total Cost	Fixed Cost	Variable Cost	Average Total Cost	Average Variable Cost	Marginal Cost
0						
1				$27.00		$9.00
2				$16.00		
3					$5.00	
4					$5.50	
5					$8.40	

5. Draw the typical average total cost, average variable cost, and marginal cost curves for a profit-maximizing, price-taking firm. For the case where price equals average total cost, show the rectangles that represent
   a. total costs and total revenues.
   b. fixed costs and variable costs.
   c. profits.
   d. In your diagram, show what happens to the size of these areas as the market price increases.

6. Consider the firm whose cost function was provided in Problem 3. Suppose that the firm is a price-taker, and that the market price is $15 per unit.
   a. What quantity will the firm produce?
   b. Will this firm be earning economic profits? If so, how much?
   c. What is the breakeven price?
   d. What is the shutdown price?

7. Consider the firm whose cost function was provided in Problem 4. Suppose that the firm is a price-taker, and that the market price is $13 per unit.

a. What quantity will this firm produce? Why?

b. At that quantity level, what profits or losses will this firm make?

c. In the short run, at what price would this firm break even? Explain briefly.

d. At what price would the firm shut down? Explain briefly.

8. Suppose the average total cost curves for a firm for three different amounts of capital are as follows:

Quantity	ATC_1	ATC_2	ATC_3
1	40	50	60
2	30	35	40
3	20	25	30
4	30	15	25
5	40	30	20
6	50	40	30

Plot the three average total cost curves in the same diagram. Then determine the long-run average total cost curve and show it in the same diagram.

9. Plot the following data on quantity of production and long-run average total cost for a firm. Show the areas of economies and diseconomies of scale and constant returns to scale. What is the minimum efficient scale?

Quantity	Long-Run ATC
1	33
2	27
3	25
4	25
5	30
6	38
7	50

10. Are there economies of scale to teaching an introductory economics course? What economies of scale are realized if class sizes increase? Is there a maximum class size beyond which diseconomies of scale are experienced?

Producer Theory with Isoquants

In this chapter we looked at how firms adjust their labor and capital inputs when the cost of these inputs changes over time. Here we give a graphical illustration of a firm's choice between labor and capital. The graphs are similar to the budget lines and indifference curves used to describe consumer choice in the appendix to Chapter 5. We use these graphs to show exactly how a firm's choice between labor and capital depends on the relative price of labor and capital.

Combining Capital and Labor

Consider an example of a firm with two inputs to production: capital and labor. Table A.1 shows the possible combinations of inputs available to the firm. For example, if

the firm has 2 units of capital and uses 24 hours of labor, it can produce 3 units of output. The hypothetical numbers in Table A.1 could represent a wide variety of firms producing different types of products, but observe that we have chosen the units in the table to be the same as those for the firm shown in Table 2. (To make a comparison between Table A.1 and Table 2, you can think of a "unit" of capital as corresponding to 4 trucks and 2 terminals with a cost of $300; 2 units of capital is 8 trucks and 4 terminals at a cost of $600.) Table A.1 could refer to a firm with any type of capital (computers, machine tools, telephones, or pizza ovens). To allow for all these possibilities, we refer to capital as a "unit" of capital.

The information in Table A.1 can be represented graphically, as shown in Figure A.1. Each column is

TABLE A.1
Production with Four Levels of Capital

| Quantity Produced | Labor Input (hours) | | | |
	With 1 Unit of Capital	With 2 Units of Capital	With 3 Units of Capital	With 4 Units of Capital
0	0	0	0	0
1	15	9	6	5
2	27	17	12	10
3	37	24	17	13
4	48	32	22	18
5	60	41	29	23
6	74	51	36	29
7	90	62	43	35
8	109	74	52	41
9	134	87	61	49
10	166	101	71	57
11	216	128	90	72
12	290	170	119	95
13	400	270	189	151
14	—	400	300	220
15	—	—	425	300
16	—	—	—	430

Note: The column showing labor input with 1 unit of capital corresponds to the production function for Melodic Movements discussed in Chapter 8 (see Table 2). The omitted entries in the table represent quantities of production that cannot be achieved without more capital.

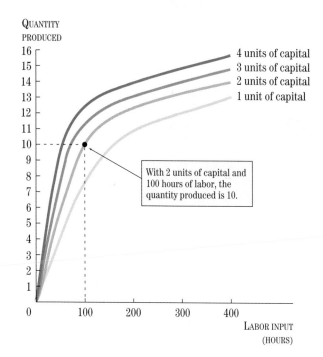

FIGURE A.1
The Production Function with Four Levels of Capital
As the amount of labor input increases, so does the amount of output. Each curve corresponds to a different level of capital. Higher curves represent higher levels of capital. The points on these four curves are obtained from the four columns of Table A.1.

plotted with labor input on the horizontal axis and the quantity produced on the vertical axis. Each column represents the production function for a given level of capital. Note that higher levels of capital increase the amount that can be produced with a given amount of labor. In other words, as we add more capital, the relationship between labor and output shifts up.

The information in Table A.1 and Figure A.1 can be displayed in another graph, Figure A.2, which provides a visual picture of how labor and capital jointly help a firm produce its product. Figure A.2 puts capital on the vertical axis and labor on the horizontal axis. We represent the quantity produced in Figure A.2 by writing a number in a circle equal to the amount produced with each amount of labor and capital. For example, with 1 unit of capital and 60 hours of labor, the firm can produce 5 units of output, according to Table A.1. Thus, we write the number 5 at the point in Figure A.2 that represents labor input equal to 60 and capital input equal to 1.

Isoquants

Observe in Figure A.2 that the same amount of output can be produced using different combinations of capital and labor. We illustrate this in the figure by connecting the circles with the same quantity by a curved line. Each curve gives the combinations of labor and capital that produce the same quantity of output. The curves in Figure A.2 are called *isoquants*, where *iso* means "the same" and *quant* stands for "quantity produced." Thus, an **isoquant** is a curve that shows all the possible combinations of labor and capital that result in the same quantity of production. Isoquants convey a lot of information visually. Higher isoquants—those up and to the right—represent higher levels of output. Each isoquant slopes down because as capital input declines, labor input must increase if the quantity produced is to remain the same. The slope of the isoquants tells us how much labor must be substituted for capital (or vice versa) to leave

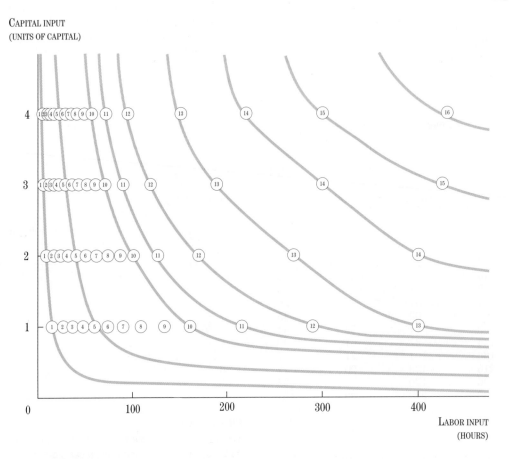

FIGURE A.2
Isoquants
Each circled number gives the quantity produced for the amounts of labor and capital on the axes at that point. The lines connecting equal quantities are called *isoquants*.

production unchanged. Thus, the isoquants are good for studying how firms substitute one input for another when the prices of the inputs change. The slope of the isoquant is called the **rate of technical substitution,** because it tells us how much capital needs to be substituted for labor to give the same amount of production when labor is reduced by 1 unit.

Remember that the points in Figure A.2 do not display any information that is not in Table A.1 or Figure A.1. The same information appears in a different and convenient way.

Isocost Lines

A firm's total costs can also be shown on a diagram like Figure A.2. In considering the choice between capital and labor, the firm needs to consider the price of both. Suppose that labor costs $10 per hour and capital costs $300 per unit. Then if the firm uses 1 unit of capital and 150 hours of labor, its total costs will be $1 \times \$300 + 150 \times \$10 = \$1,800$. For the same total costs, the firm can pay for other combinations of labor and capital. For example, 2 units of capital and 120 hours of labor also cost $1,800. Other combinations are as follows:

Hours of Labor	Units of Capital	Total Costs
180	0	$180 \times \$10 + 0 \times \$300 = \$1,800$
150	1	$150 \times \$10 + 1 \times \$300 = \$1,800$
120	2	$120 \times \$10 + 2 \times \$300 = \$1,800$
90	3	$90 \times \$10 + 3 \times \$300 = \$1,800$
60	4	$60 \times \$10 + 4 \times \$300 = \$1,800$
30	5	$30 \times \$10 + 5 \times \$300 = \$1,800$
0	6	$0 \times \$10 + 6 \times \$300 = \$1,800$

In other words, the $1,800 can be spent on any of these combinations of labor and capital. With $1,800, the firm can use 6 units of capital, but that would not permit the firm to hire any workers.

These different combinations of labor and capital that have total costs of $1,800 are plotted in Figure A.3. Each combination of labor and capital in the table is plotted, and the points are connected by a line. The line is called an **isocost line.** An isocost line shows the combinations of capital and labor that have the same total costs.

The position of the isocost line depends on the amount of total costs. Higher total costs are represented by higher isocost lines. This is shown in Figure A.4.

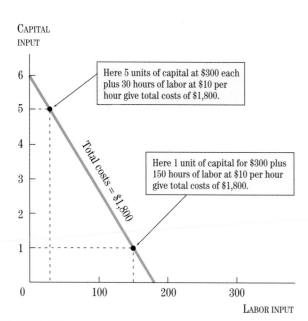

FIGURE A.3
An Isocost Line
Each isocost line shows all the combinations of labor and capital that give the same total costs. In this case, the price of capital is $300 per unit and the price of labor is $10 per hour. Total costs are $1,800. For example, if 1 unit of capital and 150 hours of labor are employed, total costs are $1,800 = (1 × $300) + (150 × $10).

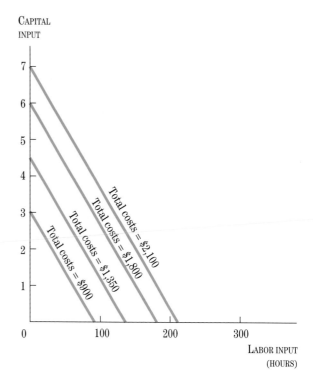

FIGURE A.4
Several Isocost Lines with Different Total Costs
Isocost lines with higher total costs are above and to the right of those with lower total costs. All the isocost lines in this diagram have a capital cost of $300 per unit and a labor cost of $10 per hour.

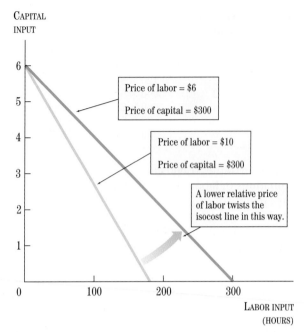

FIGURE A.5
Effect of a Change in Relative Prices on the Isocost Line
When the price of labor falls relative to the price of capital, the isocost line gets flatter, as in this diagram. In this case, the price of labor falls from $10 per hour to $6 per hour while the price of capital remains at $300 per unit. Total costs remain equal to $1,800 in this case.

Observe that the isocost line for total costs of $2,100 is above the one for total costs of $1,800.

The slope of the isocost line depends on the ratio of the price of labor to the price of capital. In particular, the slope equals −1 times the ratio of the price of labor to the price of capital. This is illustrated in Figure A.5 for the case where total costs equal $1,800. If the price of labor falls from $10 to $6, then the isocost line gets flatter. Thus, if the hourly wage were $6 instead of $10, the firm would be able to pay for 250 hours of work and 1 unit of capital, compared with only 150 hours and 1 unit of capital, and still have total costs of $1,800. Thus, as the price of labor (the wage) falls relative to the price of capital, the isocost line gets flatter.

Minimizing Costs for a Given Quantity

The isoquant and isocost lines can be used to determine the least-cost combination of capital and labor for any given quantity of production. Figure A.6 shows how. In Figure A.6 we show three isocost lines, along with an iso-

quant representing 11 units of output. For the isocost lines, the price of labor is $10 and the price of capital is $300. The point where the isocost line just touches the isoquant is a *tangency point*. It is labeled A.

Point A is where the firm minimizes the cost of producing 11 units of output. To see this, suppose you are at point A and you move to the left and up along the same isoquant to point B. This means that the firm increases capital and decreases hours of labor, keeping the quantity produced constant at 11 units; that is, the firm substitutes capital for labor. But such a substitution increases the firm's costs, as shown in the figure. The payment for the extra capital will be greater than the saving from the reduced labor. Thus, moving along the isoquant from A to B would increase the total costs to the firm.

A similar reasoning applies to moving from point A to point C. The firm uses fewer labor hours and less capital at point C, so that total costs are lower than at point A. But at point C the firm does not have enough inputs

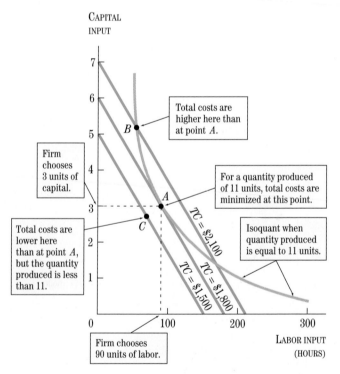

FIGURE A.6
Choosing Capital and Labor to Minimize Total Costs
The diagram illustrates how a firm chooses a mix of labor and capital to minimize total costs for a given level of output. Here the given level of output is 11 units, as shown by the single isoquant. Total costs are minimized by choosing the combination of labor and capital given by the tangency (point A) between the isocost line and the isoquant. For any other point on the isoquant, the quantity would be the same but total costs would be higher.

to produce 11 units of output. Thus, point *A* is the lowest-cost point at which the firm can produce 11 units of output. It is the point at which the lowest isocost line is touching the isoquant.

The Cost Minimization Rule

The rate of technical substitution of capital for labor and the ratio of the price of labor to the price of capital are equal at point *A*, because the slopes of the isoquant and of the isocost line are equal at point *A*. If the firm is minimizing its costs, then the rate of technical substitution must equal the input price ratio. The equality between the rate of technical substitution and the input price ratio is called the *cost minimization rule*.

Observe that isoquants are analogous to the indifference curves and the isocost lines are analogous to the budget line described in the appendix to Chapter 5. The cost minimization rule for a firm is much like the utility-maximizing rule for a consumer.

A Change in the Relative Price of Labor

Now we show how isoquants and isocost lines can be used to predict how a firm will adjust its mix of inputs when there is a change in input prices. For example, suppose that the hourly wage falls from $10 to $6 and the price of capital rises from $300 to $600. That is, labor becomes cheaper relative to capital. Originally, the ratio of the price of labor to the price of capital was 10/300 = .033; now it is 6/600 = .010. This is a big reduction, and we would expect the firm to adjust by changing capital and labor input. Figure A.7 shows how the firm would adjust the mix of capital and labor for a given quantity of output. Figure A.7 keeps the isoquant fixed but includes a new isocost line that reflects the lower relative price of labor and is tangent to the isoquant. Since the new isocost line is flatter, the point of tangency with the given isoquant no longer occurs at point *A*, where 3 units of capital are combined with 90 hours of labor. Now tangency occurs at point *D*, where there is a combination of 2 units of capital and 130 hours of labor. In other words, the firm has substituted labor for capital when the relative price of labor fell. At the new point *D*, the firm would use 1 less unit of capital and 40 more hours of labor.

In summary, common sense tells us that the firm will hire more labor and use less capital when the price of labor falls relative to the price of capital. The isoquants and isocost lines confirm this and tell us by exactly how much.

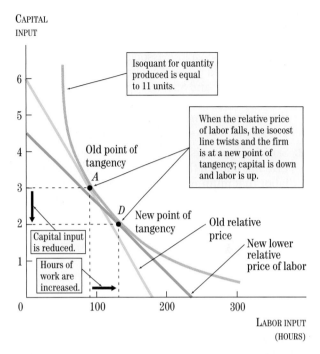

FIGURE A.7
Effect of a Lower Price of Labor Relative to Capital
The dark green isocost line has a lower price of labor relative to capital than the light green line. Hence, the amount of capital used by the firm decreases from 3 units to 2 units, and the amount of labor rises from 90 hours to 130 hours.

KEY TERMS AND DEFINITIONS

isoquant: a curve showing all the possible combinations of two inputs that yield the same quantity of output.

rate of technical substitution: the rate at which one input must be substituted for another input to maintain the same production; it is the slope of the isoquant.

isocost line: a line showing the combinations of two inputs that result in the same total costs.

QUESTIONS FOR REVIEW

1. Why does the isoquant slope downward?
2. Why does the isocost line slope downward?
3. What determines the slope of the isocost line?
4. Why does the firm minimize cost for a given level of output by choosing capital and labor at the point where the isocost line is tangent to the isoquant?

PROBLEMS

1. Graph the isocost line associated with a wage of $10 per hour and a price of capital of $50 for total costs of $200, $240, and $300. Suppose the wage rises to $15 and the price of capital stays at $50. Show how the isocost line moves for the case where total costs are $300.

2. Sketch a typical isocost line and isoquant where the firm has chosen the combination of capital and labor that minimizes total costs for a given quantity of output. Now suppose the price of capital rises and the wage does not change. What must the firm do to maintain the same level of output as before the increase in the price of capital and still minimize costs? Will it substitute away from capital?

3. Draw a diagram with an isocost line and an isoquant next to a diagram with a budget line and an indifference curve from the appendix to Chapter 5. List the similarities and differences. How are the isocost and budget lines analogous to each other? How are the isoquant and the indifference curve analogous to each other? What is the importance of the tangency point in each case?

Chapter 9

The Rise and Fall of Industries

Fred Smith's college term paper led to the birth of a new industry. In the paper, he described his idea for a new product: reliable overnight mail service. Although he got only a C on the paper, Fred Smith pursued his idea and became an entrepreneur. After graduating from college in 1973, he started a business firm that guaranteed next-day delivery of a letter or a package virtually anywhere in the United States. The firm, Federal Express, was an extraordinary success; its sales reached $1 billion by 1982, $4 billion by 1988, $8 billion by 1992, and over $29 billion by 2005.

Seeing the high profits earned by Federal Express, many other firms entered the express delivery industry. In the late 1970s, United Parcel Service (UPS) and DHL entered; in the early 1980s, the U.S. Postal Service entered; many small local firms you've probably never heard of also got into the act. The entire industry expanded along with Federal Express.

The express delivery industry is an example of an industry on the rise. Many other examples of fast-growing industries exist in the annals of economic history. Estée Lauder founded a cosmetics firm 50 years ago; it grew along with the cosmetics industry as a whole. Kemmons Wilson started the motel franchising industry when he saw the potential demand for clean, reliable rooms for travelers and opened his first Holiday Inn in Memphis in 1952; by 1968, there were 1,000 Holiday Inns, and now the industry includes other motel firms such as Days Inn and Motel 6.

Of course, industries do not always grow. The mainframe computer industry has declined as the personal computer industry has risen. The long-distance telephone industry has declined as the use of cellular phones has increased. The video rental store industry has shrunk as the DVD rental by mail industry and satellite and cable television companies have risen.

FedEx trucks are a common sight on roads today. Each day, they deliver millions of packages and documents to offices and residences all over the country.

The causes of the rise and fall of industries can be traced to new ideas such as overnight delivery, to new cost-reducing technologies such as the Internet or DVDs, or to changes in consumer tastes. This latter shift, for example, is one reason behind the widespread popularity of low-carb diets, which favor reducing the intake of foods like bread and pasta in favor of high-protein foods like meat and cheese, providing an unexpected boost for meat producers. Some industries have recurring ups and downs. The oil tanker shipping industry, for example, regularly expands when oil demand increases and declines when oil demand falls.

In this chapter, we develop a model to explain the behavior of whole industries over time. We examine how economic forces cause industries to adjust to new technologies and to shifts in consumer tastes. Changes in the industry then occur as firms either enter or exit the industry. The initial forces causing an industry to rise or fall are described by shifts in a cost curve or a demand curve. Our analysis assumes that the firms are operating in competitive markets. The central task of this chapter is to show how an industry grows or contracts as firms enter or exit the industry. Do profits of individual firms fall or rise as a result? Do the prices consumers pay increase or decrease?

MARKETS AND INDUSTRIES

industry: a group of firms producing a similar product.

We begin this analysis by providing a brief definition of what an industry is and by giving some examples of different industry types. An **industry** is a group of firms producing a similar product. The cosmetics industry, for example, refers to the firms producing cosmetics. The term *market* is sometimes used instead of industry. For example, the phrases "the firms in the cosmetics industry" and "the firms in the cosmetics market" typically mean the same thing. But the term *market* can also refer to the consumers who buy the goods and to the interaction of the producers and the consumers. Both firms and consumers are in the cosmetics market, but only firms are in the cosmetics industry.

Firms in an industry can produce *services* such as overnight delivery or overnight accommodations as well as manufactured goods. Many industries are global. Firms in the United States compete with firms in Japan, Europe, and elsewhere. Reduced transportation and communication costs in recent years have made many industries global. Until competition from Europe and Japan intensified 30 years ago, the automobile industry in the United States consisted mainly of three firms—General Motors, Ford, and Chrysler. Now the industry is truly global, with Honda, Toyota, Hyundai, and Nissan selling cars in the United States, and Ford and General Motors selling cars throughout the world.

THE LONG-RUN COMPETITIVE EQUILIBRIUM MODEL OF AN INDUSTRY

long-run competitive equilibrium model: a model of firms in an industry in which free entry and exit produce an equilibrium such that price equals the minimum of average total cost.

The model we develop to explain the behavior of industries assumes that firms in the industry maximize profits and that they are competitive. As in the competitive equilibrium model of Chapter 7, individual firms are price-takers; that is, they cannot affect the price. But in order to explain how the industry changes over time, in this chapter we add something new to the competitive equilibrium model: Over time, some firms will enter an industry and other firms will exit an industry. Because the entry and exit of firms takes time, we call this model the **long-run competitive equilibrium model.**

When we use the long-run competitive equilibrium model to explain the behavior of an actual industry, we do not necessarily expect that the industry exactly conforms to the assumptions of the model. A model is a means of explaining events in real-world industries; it is not the real world itself. In fact, some industries are very competitive, and some are not very competitive. But the model can work well as an approximation in many industries. In Chapters 10 and 11 we will develop alternative models of industry behavior that describe monopoly and the gray area between monopoly and competitive markets. But for this chapter, we focus on the competitive model. This model was one of the first developed by economists to explain the dynamic behavior of an industry; it has wide applicability, and it works well. Moreover, understanding the model will make it easier to understand the alternative models developed in later chapters.

Setting Up the Model with Graphs

Figure 1 illustrates the demand curve in a competitive market. The left graph views the market from the perspective of a single typical firm in an industry. The price is on the vertical axis, and the quantity produced by the single firm is on the horizontal axis. The assumption of a competitive firm implies that the firm faces a given price level, represented by a flat demand curve.

The market demand curve for the goods produced by the firms in the industry is shown in the right graph of Figure 1. The price is also on the vertical axis of the graph on the right, but the horizontal axis measures the *whole market or industry* production. Notice that even though the single firm takes the price as given, the market demand curve is downward-sloping because it refers to the whole market. If the price in the market rises, then the quantity demanded of the product will fall. If the market price increases, then the quantity demanded will decline.

free entry and exit: movement of firms into and out of an industry that is not blocked by regulation, other firms, or any other barriers.

■ **Entry and Exit.**   The new characteristic of competitive markets stressed in this chapter is the **free entry and exit** of firms in an industry. The question firms face is whether to *enter* an industry if they are not already in it or to *exit* from an industry they are in. The decisions are based on profits—total revenue less total costs. If profits are positive, there is incentive to enter the industry. If profits are negative, there is incentive to exit the industry. When profits are equal to zero, there is no incentive for either entry or exit.

When firms enter or exit an industry, the entire market or industry supply curve is affected. Recall that the market or industry supply curve is the sum of all the individual firms' supply curves. With more firms supplying goods, the total quantity of goods supplied increases at every price. Thus, more firms in the industry means that the market supply curve shifts to the right; fewer firms in the industry means that the market supply curve shifts to the left.

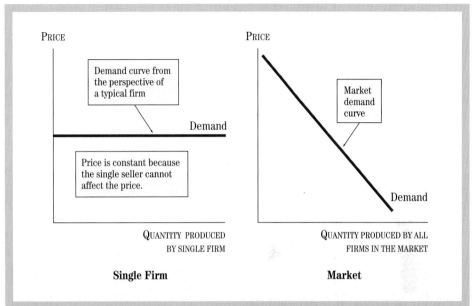

FIGURE 1
How a Competitive Firm Sees Demand in the Market
A competitive market is, by definition, one in which a single firm cannot affect the price. The firm takes the market price as given. Hence, the firm sees a flat demand curve, as shown in the graph on the left. Nevertheless, if all firms change production, the market price changes, as shown in the graph on the right. The two graphs are not alternatives. In a competitive market, they hold simultaneously. (In the graph on the right, a given length along the horizontal axis represents a much greater quantity than the same length in the graph on the left.)

■ **Long-Run Equilibrium.**   Figure 2 is a two-part diagram that shows the profit-maximizing behavior of a typical firm along with the market supply and demand curves. This diagram is generic; it could be drawn to correspond to the numerical specifications of the grape industry or any other industry. In the left graph are the cost curves of the typical firm in the industry with their typical positions: Marginal cost cuts through the average total cost curve at its lowest point. We did not draw in the average variable cost curve in order to keep the diagram from getting too cluttered.

The left and right graphs of Figure 2 are drawn with the same market price, and this price links the two graphs together. This market price, which the individual firm takes as given, is determined by the market supply and demand curves, which are shown to the right of the cost curve diagram in Figure 2. As in Figure 1, even though the vertical axis on each graph shows the same price, the horizontal axes have different units, with an inch on the horizontal axis of the right-hand diagram representing much more production than an inch on the horizontal axis in the left-hand diagram.

The graphs are set up so that the price that is at the intersection of the market supply and demand curves is at a level that touches the bottom of the average total cost curve on the left graph. We know from Chapter 8 that profits are zero when $P = ATC$. Because profits are zero, there is no incentive for firms to either enter or exit the industry. This situation, in which profits are zero and there is no incentive to enter or exit, is called a **long-run equilibrium.**

long-run equilibrium: a situation in which entry into and exit from an industry are complete and economic profits are zero, with price (P) equal to average total cost (ATC).

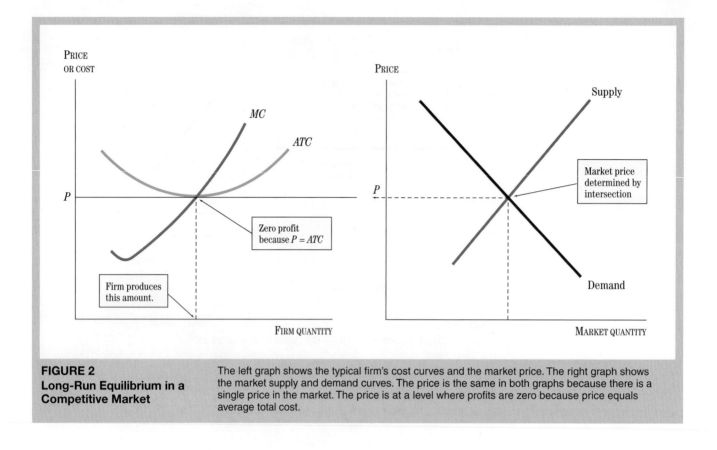

FIGURE 2
Long-Run Equilibrium in a Competitive Market

The left graph shows the typical firm's cost curves and the market price. The right graph shows the market supply and demand curves. The price is the same in both graphs because there is a single price in the market. The price is at a level where profits are zero because price equals average total cost.

An Increase in Demand

How does this long-run equilibrium come about? We can illustrate by examining what happens when there is a shift in demand—for example, suppose the demand for grapes increases. We show this increase in demand in the top right graph of Figure 3; the market demand curve shifts out from D to D'.

■ **Short-Run Effects.** Focus first on the top part of Figure 3, representing the short run. As the demand curve shifts out, we move up along the supply curve to a new intersection of the market supply curve and the market demand curve at a higher price, P'.

The implications of the rise in the market price for the individual firm are shown in the top left graph, where the price line is moved up from P to P'. A profit-maximizing firm that is already in the industry will produce more because the market price is higher. This is seen in the top left graph of Figure 3; the higher price intersects the marginal cost curve at a higher quantity of production. Note also—and this is crucial—that at this higher price and higher level of production, the typical firm is now earning profits, as shown by the shaded rectangle in the top left graph. Price is above average total cost, and so profits have risen above zero.

We have gone from a situation in which profits were zero for firms in the industry to a situation in which profits are positive. This shift has created a situation in the market in which there is a profit opportunity, encouraging new firms to enter the industry. Thus, we have moved away from a long-run equilibrium (which was

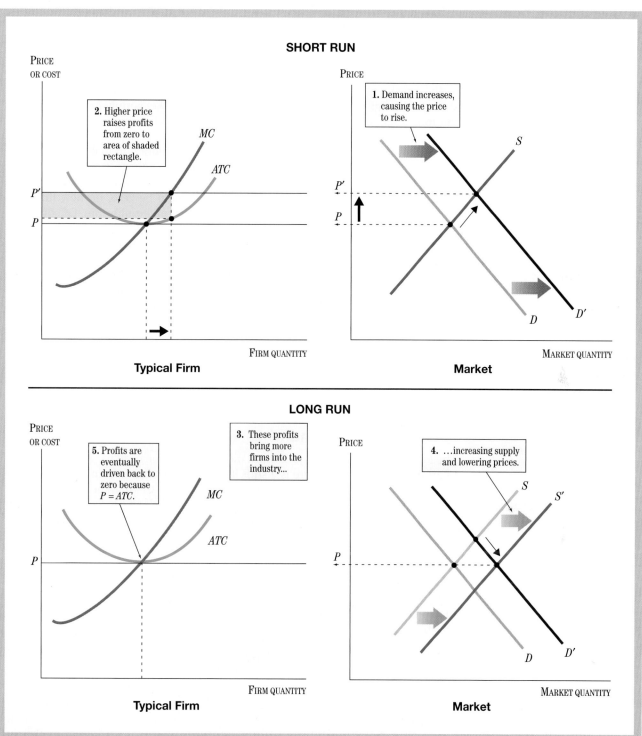

FIGURE 3
The Rise of an Industry After a Shift in Demand

The diagrams at the top show the short run. A shift in the demand curve to the right causes the price to rise from *P* to *P'*; each firm produces more, and profits rise. Higher profits cause firms to enter the industry. The diagrams at the bottom show the long run. As firms enter, the market supply curve shifts to the right, and the price falls back to *P*. New entry does not stop until profits return to zero in the long run.

defined as a situation in which profits are zero and there is no incentive to enter or exit) because of the disturbance that shifted the market demand curve.

■ **Toward a New Long-Run Equilibrium.**   Now focus on the two graphs in the bottom part of Figure 3, representing what happens in this industry in the long run. In the lower right-hand graph, the supply curve for the whole industry or market shifts to the right from S to S'. Why? Because the market supply curve is the sum of the individual supply curves, as more firms, attracted by higher profits, enter the industry, they add to supply.

The rightward shift in the supply curve causes a reduction in the price below P', where it was in the short run. The price will continue adjusting until the price line just touches the bottom of the average total cost curve, where average total cost equals marginal cost. At this point, profits will again be zero, no new firms have incentive to enter, and the industry will be in long-run equilibrium. Of course, this adjustment to a new long-run equilibrium takes time. It takes time for firms to decide whether or not to go into business, and it takes time to set up a firm once a decision is made.

The new long-run equilibrium for the typical firm is shown in the lower left graph. It may take several years for an industry to move from the top of Figure 3 to the bottom. In fact, it would be more accurate to draw several rows of diagrams between the top and the bottom, showing how the process occurs gradually over time. These additional rows could show more and more firms entering the industry with the price falling until eventually profits are zero again and the incentive to enter the market disappears. The market supply curve will shift to the right until the price comes back to the point where average total cost is at a minimum, where profits are zero, and where no firms will enter or exit the industry.

A Decrease in Demand

The long-run competitive equilibrium model can also be used to explain the decline of an industry. Suppose there is a shift in the demand curve from D to D', as illustrated in the top right graph in Figure 4. This causes the market price to fall. The lower market price (P') causes existing firms to cut back on production in the short run: At the new lower price, the individual firm depicted in the top left panel of Figure 4 is now running losses.

Over time, with profits less than zero, firms have an incentive to leave the industry. As they leave, the market supply curve shifts to the left from S to S', as shown in the bottom right graph of Figure 4. This causes the price to rise again. The end of the process is a new long-run equilibrium, as shown in the bottom left graph of Figure 4. In the long run, fewer firms are in the industry, total production in the industry is lower, and profits are back to zero.

■ **Economic Profits versus Accounting Profits.**   It is important at this point to emphasize that the economist's definition of profits is different from an accountant's definition. When you read about the profits of General Motors in the newspaper, it is the accountant's definition that is being reported. There is nothing wrong with the accountant's definition of profits, but it is different from the economist's definition. When an accountant calculates profits for a firm, the total costs do not include the opportunity cost of the owner's time or the owner's funds. Such opportunity costs are *implicit:* The wage that the owner could get elsewhere and the interest that could be earned on the funds if they were invested elsewhere are not explicitly paid, and the accountant therefore ignores them. When computing **accounting profits,** such implicit opportunity costs are *not* included in total costs.

accounting profits: total revenue minus total costs, where total costs exclude the implicit opportunity costs; this is the definition of profits usually reported by firms.

SHORT RUN

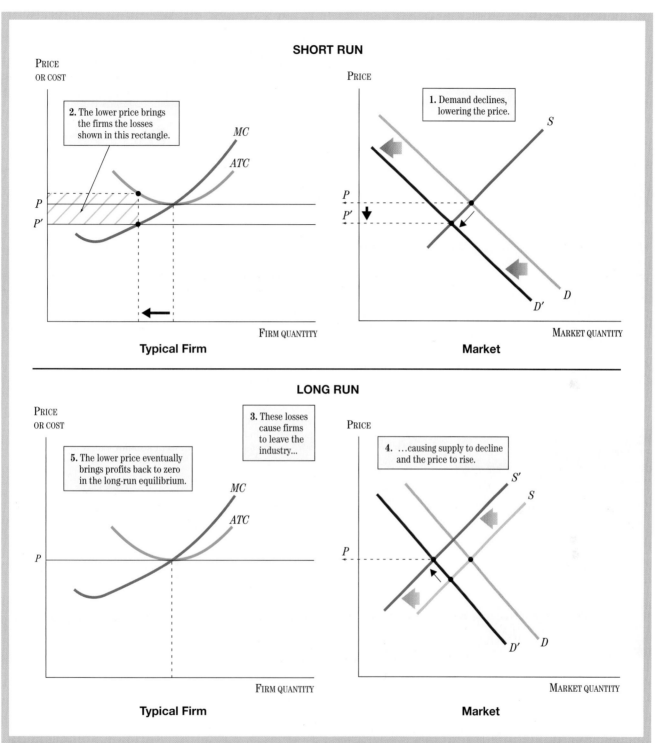

2. The lower price brings the firms the losses shown in this rectangle.

MC

ATC

PRICE OR COST

P

P'

FIRM QUANTITY

Typical Firm

1. Demand declines, lowering the price.

PRICE

S

P

P'

D

D'

MARKET QUANTITY

Market

LONG RUN

3. These losses cause firms to leave the industry...

5. The lower price eventually brings profits back to zero in the long-run equilibrium.

PRICE OR COST

MC

ATC

P

FIRM QUANTITY

Typical Firm

4. ...causing supply to decline and the price to rise.

PRICE

S'

S

P

D'

D

MARKET QUANTITY

Market

FIGURE 4
The Decline of an Industry After a Shift in Demand

In the short run, a reduction in demand lowers the price from *P* to *P'* and causes losses. Firms leave the industry, causing prices to rise back to *P*. In the long run, profits have returned to zero, the number of firms in the industry has declined, and the total quantity produced in the industry has fallen.

Entry and Exit in the DVD Rental Industry

One of the consequences of the rise in popularity of DVDs, and the resulting demise of the videotape, was the increased ease of shipping movies via the mail. An upstart company called Netflix changed the movie rental business for good when it entered the market with a new service that allowed consumers to rent movies by mail rather than having to go to the video store and browse a limited selection. Netflix's success led to the entry of other firms, most notably Blockbuster and Wal-Mart. The increased competition held down price increases but in the end proved to be too unprofitable for Wal-Mart, which left the market in 2005. This article reports on Wal-Mart's decision to exit the industry.

Wal-Mart announces its decision to leave the movie rental business.

Wal-Mart entered the industry last, and was also the first to exit the industry.

Wal-Mart's plan to integrate its movie rental business with its substantial "bricks-and-mortar" presence did not work.

Wal-Mart to Give Up DVD Rentals in Deal with Netflix

MICHAEL BARBARO | The Washington Post Staff Writer

Wal-Mart finally lost.

The nation's largest retailer, whose insatiable appetite for new business has plunged it into auto care, groceries, hair salons, check cashing, flower delivery and music downloads, said yesterday that it will scrap its online DVD rental service, conceding it has not kept pace with competitors.

The discount chain will encourage subscribers to switch to **Netflix** Inc., a seven-year-old Web-based firm with a bigger client list, a bigger movie library and bigger DVD rental revenue, in a partnership agreement.

The decision represented a rare defeat for a retailer used to being the biggest in everything. Wal-Mart Stores Inc., which is four times larger than its next-largest retail competitor, dominates sales of food, electronics, toys, even jewelry.

But after two years in the hyper-competitive online DVD rental business, Wal-Mart discovered just how hard it is to play catch-up. With fewer than 200,000 rental subscribers, Wal-Mart trailed far behind **Netflix,** with 3 million subscribers, and **Blockbuster** Inc., with 750,000, analysts and industry executives said.

It carried about half as many titles as **Netflix and Blockbuster,** and despite its claim of "always low prices," **Blockbuster** offered cheaper subscriptions.

"Wal-Mart did not get into this business with the same vim and vigor" as its competitors, said industry analyst Dennis B. McAlpine of McAlpine Associates.

Compounding its also-ran status in the new business, Bentonville, Ark.-based Wal-Mart found that its online rentals failed to translate into more frequent trips to the store—a key part of Wal-Mart's push into other online businesses.

Wal-Mart, whose Web site has 500,000 visitors a year, has aggressively expanded its range of online services, but always with an eye toward luring shoppers into its brick-and-mortar stores. The site's visitors can order tires, prescription drugs and prints of their digital photos—but they must pick them up at the store.

Not so with DVD rentals, which are mailed to customers. Wal-Mart had originally hoped online DVD renters would enjoy the convenience of the service and turn to Wal-Mart's stores when they needed a pair of winter gloves, a lawn mower, or a loaf of bread. The company even tucked advertisements for the rental service in DVD players sold in its thousands of stores. But the plan did not work, executives said.

The chain could not figure out "how you start online and end up in the store," John Fleming, Wal-Mart's chief marketing officer, said in an interview.

For **Netflix,** the Wal-Mart agreement is "just about the best deal that any online company can ever hope to happen: the big offline competitor giving up and partnering with you," Safa Rashtchy, an analyst at Piper Jaffray, wrote in a research note.

Wal-Mart is offering its existing DVD subscribers the chance to switch over to **Netflix** by June 17 for no extra charge, and it will advertise **Netflix** on its Web site. Wal-Mart rarely works with competitors, and **Netflix** chief executive Reed Hastings said it was a "unique thing to be promoted on **WalMart**.com."

In return, **Netflix** will advertise DVDs for sale inside Wal-Mart's stores. Financial terms of the deal were not disclosed.

Netflix, based in Los Gatos, Calif., revolutionized the movie rental industry, offering a broad selection of DVDs that are ordered online, delivered by mail and, conceivably, kept for as long as a customer wants, with no late fees. The service has an avid following, with sales soaring 86 percent in 2004 to $506.2 million. Its earnings were $20.8 million.

Part of that success has stemmed from **Netflix**'s investment in infrastructure. It has 34 distribution centers and 40,000 movie titles. Wal-Mart, by comparison, has 14 distribution centers and 16,000 movie titles.

McAlpine, the analyst, said Wal-Mart could easily beat **Netflix** if it wanted to spend the money. "Wal-Mart makes more money in a day than **Netflix** makes in a year," he said.

But as for the online DVD rental business, "it's not worth Wal-Mart's time," said Bernard Sosnick, a retail analyst at Oppenheimer & Co. He described the revenue lost by turning the business over to **Netflix** as "insignificant."

Fleming, the Wal-Mart executive, downplayed the idea that Wal-Mart had been defeated. "I would not characterize it as giving up," he said. He called it "reevaluating our priorities," adding, "We are not taking this service away from our customers. They will continue to get the service from the market leader."

Investor reaction to the announcement was fairly mild. **Netflix** shares rose 63 cents, or 4 percent, to close at $16.13, while shares of Wal-Mart fell 7 cents, or 0.2 percent, to close at $47.51.

Blockbuster, sensing opportunity, wasted little time trying to lure Wal-Mart's DVD rental subscribers. It offered a special deal to both Wal-Mart and **Netflix** customers, including two free months of service, plus a free DVD from one of its stores. **Blockbuster** shares fell 4 cents, or 0.4 percent, to $9.74.

"We see this as a definite opportunity for us to gain customers," said Shane Evangelist, senior vice president and general manager of **Blockbuster's** online division.

When one firm leaves the industry, other firms will typically get larger— both Netflix and Blockbuster are likely to gain as a result of Wal-Mart's departure.

economic profits: total revenue minus total costs, where total costs include opportunity costs, whether implicit or explicit.

When computing **economic profits**—the measure of profits economists use—implicit opportunity costs are included in total costs. Economic profits are equal to accounting profits less any opportunity costs that the accountants did not include when measuring total costs.

For example, suppose accounting profits for a movie rental store are $40,000 a year. Suppose the owner of the store could earn $35,000 a year running a bakery. Suppose also that the owner could sell the business for $50,000 and invest the money in a bank, where it would earn interest at 6 percent per year, or $3,000. Then the opportunity cost—which the accountant would not include in total costs—is $38,000 ($35,000 plus $3,000). To get economic profits, we have to subtract this opportunity cost from accounting profits. Thus, economic profits would be only $2,000.

Economic profits are used by economists because they measure the incentive that the owner of the firm has to stay in business rather than do something else. In this case, with $2,000 in economic profits, the owner has an incentive to stay in the business. But if the owner could earn $39,000 running a bakery, then economic profits for the movie rental store would be −$2,000 (40,000 − 39,000 − 3,000), and the owner would have an incentive to leave the movie rental store business, even though accounting profits at the store were $40,000. Thus, economic profits are a better measure of incentives than accounting profits. This is why when we refer to profits in this book, we mean economic profits because we are interested in the incentives that firms have to either enter or exit an industry.

Observe that if the store owner could earn exactly $37,000 at the bakery, then economic profits at the movie rental store would be zero. Then the owner would be indifferent on economic considerations alone between staying in the movie rental business or going to work for the bakery. The term **normal profits** refers to the amount of accounting profits that exist when economic profits are equal to zero. In this last case, normal profits would be $40,000.

normal profits: the amount of accounting profits when economic profits are equal to zero.

■ **The Equilibrium Number of Firms.** The long-run equilibrium model predicts that there will be a certain number of firms in the industry. The equilibrium number of firms will be such that there is no incentive for more firms to enter the industry or for others to leave. But how many firms is this? If the minimum point on the average cost curve of the typical firm represents production at a very small scale, then there will be many firms. That is, many firms will each produce a very small amount. If the minimum point represents production at a large scale, then there will be fewer firms; that is, a few firms will each produce a large amount.

To see this, consider the hypothetical case where all firms are identical. For example, if the minimum point on the average total cost curve for each firm in the grape industry occurs at 10,000 tons and the equilibrium quantity in the whole market is 100,000 tons, then the model predicts that there will be 10 firms in the industry. If the quantity where average total cost is at a minimum is 1,000 tons, then there will be 100 firms. If the demand for grapes increases and brings about a new long-run equilibrium of 130,000 tons, then the number of firms in the industry will rise from 100 to 130 (in the case where the minimum efficient scale was 1,000 tons) or from 10 to 13 (in the case where the minimum efficient scale was 10,000 tons).

■ **Entry or Exit Combined with Individual Firm Expansion or Contraction.** Thus far, we have described the growth or decline of an industry in terms of the increase or decrease in the number of firms. Recall from Chapter 8 that in the long run, a firm can expand its size by investing in new capital or reduce its size by getting rid of some of its capital. So the industry can grow or shrink as a result of changes in the size of existing firms.

In reality, industries usually grow by a combination of the expansion of existing firms and the entry of new firms. Similarly, industries can shrink either because of

Economics in Action

The Rise of Digital Cameras and the Death of Silver Halide Film

The long-run competitive equilibrium model is useful not only for explaining what happened to an industry in the past, but also for predicting what will happen to an industry in the future. Such predictions can help guide investment or career decisions.

The photographic film industry provides an interesting example of an industry that recently underwent dramatic changes. Photographic film, called silver halide film, was developed over 100 years ago and can give extremely high resolution and detail. The same technology is used for x-ray pictures, where detailed views are needed to detect hairline fractures and the like. This amazing film technology has brought enjoyment and better health to many millions of people.

But in the past decade, digital cameras rose in popularity among consumers, especially as the cost of digital cameras began to fall. Digital cameras now outsell cameras that use film, which is hardly surprising given how convenient they are for the average user. With a digital camera, you can take snapshots and load the images directly into a desktop computer. You can enlarge the images yourself, or have fun coloring your hair purple and e-mailing the image to your mother or father. Digital cameras are different from analog cameras in that they do not use film. As more people use digital cameras, the less film people will buy.

We can predict that the demand for photographic film and developing services will continue to decline in the future as digital cameras improve and become cheaper. The demand curve will shift to the left, profits will decline, and firms will exit the industry. In 2004, Kodak announced that it would no longer make nondigital cameras; in 2006, the camera manufacturers Konica and Minolta announced that they were getting out of the camera business altogether.

But all was not lost for silver halide film manufacturers. Film sales and film developing services may be declining rapidly, but many people still want to print their favorite images. And while some of the prints will be made on home inkjet printers, there is still a large demand for printing from retailers. These prints, whether they come from film or from a digital image, are produced on silver halide–based photographic paper. In fact, people may take and print more photographs with digital cameras than they did with film cameras (where each film roll yielded only a finite number of photographs). So the demand for photographic paper and printing services is likely to grow; the Silver Institute estimates that silver usage for these products will rise from 46.0 million troy ounces in 2000 to 60.1 million troy ounces in 2008.[1]

Naturally, other things could change. If the cost of printing high-quality photographs at home declines, fewer people might go outside to have their photos printed. The rise in popularity of online photo-sharing sites like Flickr and the increased popularity of cellphone cameras may lead to people sharing photographs in a way that is very different from the method of printing the photographs on paper and then sharing them with friends and family. Regardless of what happens, the economic model can help us determine the impact of changing technology and demand on industries in the economy.

---

[1] Don Franz, "The Global Silver Halide Photographic Market," *Silver News*, First Quarter 2004, www.silverinstitute.org.

exit of firms or because of a contraction in the size of existing firms. For example, when the expedited package express industry began to grow, it grew both because UPS and other firms entered and because Federal Express expanded.

The expansion of an existing firm can occur under one of two conditions. First, the original size of the firm may be smaller than the minimum efficient scale, so the firm may be able to lower its average costs while producing more units. Second, a change in technology or in the prices of inputs may change the cost function of the firm, pushing the minimum efficient scale to a larger number of units. Note that if the firm is already producing at the minimum long-run average total cost, then an increase in demand will not affect the size of the firm, and you will observe only entry of new firms into the industry.

Shifts in Cost Curves

Our analysis of the rise and fall of an industry thus far has centered around shifts in demand. But new technologies and ideas for new products that reduce costs can also cause an industry to change. The long-run competitive equilibrium model can also be used to explain these changes, as shown in Figure 5.

The case of cost-reducing technologies—as when Wal-Mart introduced checkout counter scanners—can be handled by shifting down the average total cost curve and the marginal cost curve, as shown in Figure 5. This will lead to a situation of positive profits because average total cost falls below the original market price P. If other firms that are already in the industry adopt similar cost-cutting strategies, the market price will fall to P', but profits will still be positive, as shown in Figure 5. With positive profits, other firms will have incentives to enter the industry with similar technologies. As more firms enter the industry, the market supply curve shifts out. The price falls further to P', and eventually competition brings economic profits back to zero.

If new entrants drive economic profits to zero in the long run, then what incentives do firms have to develop cost-cutting technologies? The answer is that the economic profits in the short run can be substantial. Wal-Mart may have made hundreds of millions of dollars in economic profits before the competition eroded the profits away. Hence, Wal-Mart benefited for a while from cost-cutting innovations. No idea will generate economic profits forever in a competitive market, but the short-run profits can still provide plenty of incentive.

■ **Average Total Cost Is Minimized.** In the long-run equilibrium, average total cost is as low as technology will permit. You can see this in Figures 2, 3, 4, and 5. In each case, the typical firm produces a quantity at which average total cost is at the *minimum point* of the firm's average total cost curve. This amount of production must occur in the long-run equilibrium because profits are zero. For profits to be zero, price must equal average total cost ($P = ATC$). The only place where $P = MC$ and $P = ATC$ is at the lowest point on the ATC curve. At this point, costs per unit are at a minimum.

That average total cost is at a minimum is an attractive feature of a competitive market where firms are free to enter and exit. It means that goods are produced at the lowest cost, with the price consumers pay being equal to that lowest cost. If firms could not enter and exit, this attractive feature would be lost.

■ **Efficient Allocation of Capital among Industries.** An efficient allocation of capital among industries is also achieved by entry and exit in competitive markets. Entry of firms into a booming industry, for example, means that more capital has gone into that industry, where it can better satisfy consumer tastes. In the case of a declining industry, capital moves out of the industry to other industries, where it is more efficiently used. Thus, the long-run competitive equilibrium has another

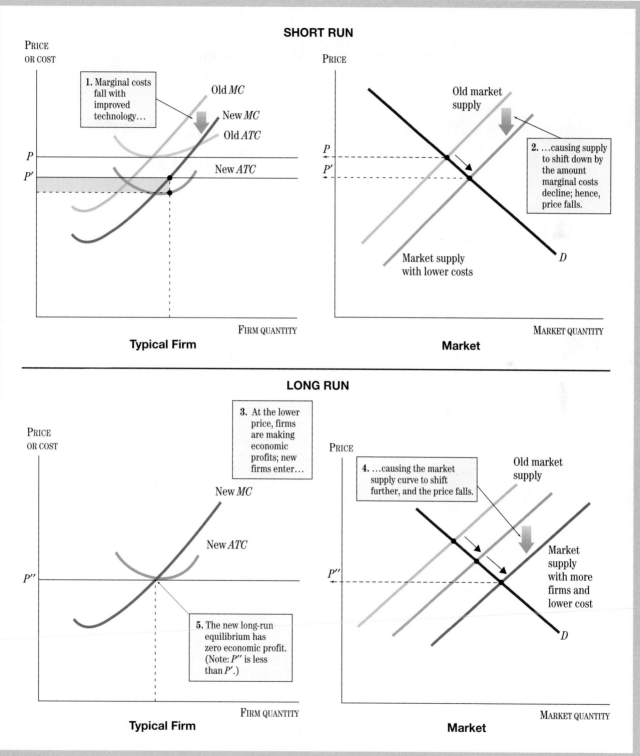

FIGURE 5
**Effect of a Reduction
in Costs**

A new technology reduces costs and shifts the typical firm's *ATC* and *MC* curves down. The market supply curve shifts down by the same amount as the shift in marginal cost if other firms in the industry adopt the new technology right away. But because there are economic profits, new firms have incentives to enter the industry. As shown in the lower left graph, in the long run, profits return to zero.

Cycles in the Grape Industry

This article discusses fluctuations in the California grape industry. It shows how a positive demand shock, in this case resulting from the discovery of potential health benefits of drinking wine, leads to improved profits for domestic wine producers, in turn leading more firms to enter into production. Over time, the increase in supply drove prices down and moved the wine industry toward long-run equilibrium. Recently, however, increases in wine imports from countries like South Africa, Chile, and Australia, as well as competition from other types of alcoholic beverages, have reduced the demand for domestic wine, causing prices to drop as the industry again moves toward long-run competitive equilibrium.

"What We Have Is Insufficient Demand for Wine Grape Supplies"

HARRY CLINE | westernfarmpress.com

February 4, 2003

California's wine grape industry is not going to heck in an oak barrel or a stainless steel tank.

"What we have is insufficient demand for the existing supplies," pronounced wine industry expert Barry Bedwell in explaining the current economic plight of California wine grapes in his best impersonation of actor Strother Martin. As you recall, Martin was immortalized for his famous line, "What we have here is a failure to communicate" from the movie Cool Hand Luke.

Bedwell, California wine broker coordinator for Joseph W. Ciatti Co. and Jon Fredrikson of Gomberg, Fredrikson and Associates avoided the G (glut) word like a glass of bad White Grenache when they reported on the status of the industry to a rapt crowd of more than 1,000 at the 9th annual United Wine and Grape Symposium recently in Sacramento, Calif.

Fredrikson and Bedwell are two of the most respected wine industry analysts. Bedwell's opening comment about "insufficient demand" was calculated to net a laugh from the audience, and it did.

However, it has not been a laughing matter for most wine grape growers and many wineries over at least the past two years as acreage coming into production has soared, creating an oversupply in many varietals and sending prices plummeting; imports taking an increasingly bigger share of the U.S. wine market and wine finding tough going in getting shelf space from beers and spirits.

No Wine Glut

However, there is no California wine glut, Bedwell said. There are oversupplies of some varietals like Cabernet Sauvignon, Pinot Noir and perhaps Syrah. However, supply and demand are getting closer to balances for Chardonnay, red Zinfandel, Sauvignon Blanc, Merlot and White Zinfandel.

The California wine industry is in a "down cycle," not in wine glut, according to Bedwell, after experiencing a decade of phenomenal growth following the 1991 French Paradox. That broadcast heralded the health benefits of moderate wine drinking. Sales have increased by 75 million cases since then.

"What I think Jon and I were trying to do in our industry assessments is counter the overwhelming negative publicity of the wine industry over the past few months that is ignoring the cyclical aspects of this industry," said Bedwell.

"This is a remarkably strong, $1.5 billion a year industry," Bedwell said.

"Is there an oversupply of wine grapes? Absolutely," said Bedwell, who said the value of wine grapes dropped $200 million last year and likely will drop another 7 percent to 10 percent this season as the industry works off oversupplies.

"The California situation is not a glut," echoed Fredrikson. "A glut is the wine lake in Europe where growers are producing wine that is not intended for sale as wine but to be used as gasohol as part of a social program."

Bedwell said the California wine industry has become notorious for overreacting. When things are good, new plantings quickly catch up with grape and wine demand and an oversupply situation is created, even with growing wine sales. When things go bad, growers become too aggressive with bulldozers in taking out vineyards.

attractive property: Capital is allocated to its most efficient use. Again, this property is due to the free entry and exit of firms. If entry and exit were limited or if the market were not competitive for some other reason, this advantage would be lost.

R E V I E W

- Industries grow and shrink over time, with existing firms expanding or contracting in size, new firms entering the industry and some existing firms going out of business. The long-run competitive equilibrium model explains how the entry and exit, expansion and contraction patterns evolve.

- The decision to enter or exit an industry is determined by profit potential. Positive economic profits will attract new firms. Negative economic profits will cause firms to exit the industry. A long-run competitive equilibrium is a situation where individual firms make zero profits ($P = ATC$) and there is no entry or exit of firms.

- If an industry that is in long-run competitive equilibrium experiences a demand increase, then market prices will rise. This increase in price will lead to positive profits for an individual firm in the short run because $P > ATC$. In response to the positive profit-making opportunity, new firms will enter, causing the market supply curve to shift to the right and causing price to come back down again until the profit-making opportunities are eroded away, and the economy is back in long-run competitive equilibrium.

- If a demand decrease causes market prices to fall, that decrease in price will lead to negative profits for an individual firm in the short run because $P < ATC$. The negative profits increase the incentive for firms to leave the industry, causing the market supply curve to shift to the left. This raises price and reduces the losses incurred by individual firms until the economy is back in long-run competitive equilibrium.

- Similar adjustments take place if changes in technology bring about a shift of the cost curves of individual firms in the economy.

- The industry can expand either because more firms enter the industry or because existing firms become larger. Similarly, the industry can shrink either because existing firms leave the industry or because they become smaller in size.

- How many firms are in an industry depends on the minimum efficient scale of the typical firm and the size of the industry. If firms are not operating at minimum efficient scale or if changes in technology make minimum efficient scale larger, then existing firms are likely to grow in size.

- When firms are allowed to freely enter and exit, another advantage is that average total cost is minimized. That goods are produced at the lowest possible cost is another advantage of competitive markets.

- Entry and exit also help to bring about an efficient allocation of capital. Booming industries will see entry of new firms and expansion of existing ones, which leads to more capital being allocated. Shrinking industries will see exit of firms and shrinking of firm size, which frees up capital for booming industries.

- Throughout this discussion, it is very important to keep in mind that the profits being discussed are economic profits rather than accounting profits. Economic profits differ from accounting profits because they take into account the opportunity costs of the owners of the firm.

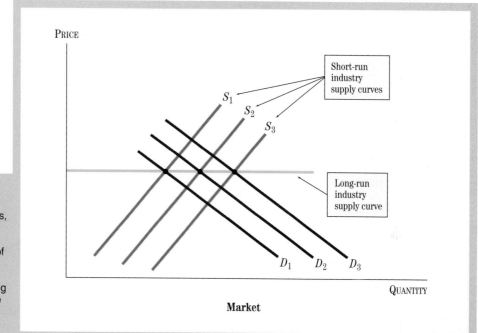

FIGURE 6
The Standard Assumption
As demand increases and price rises, more firms enter the industry, attracted by the prospect of higher profits. The increase in the number of firms pushes the supply curve out, lowering prices and reducing incentives for further entry. In the long run, the industry supply curve will be horizontal, at the price where profits for this typical firm are zero.

EXTERNAL ECONOMIES AND DISECONOMIES OF SCALE

In Chapter 8 we introduced the concept of economies and diseconomies of scale for a firm. A firm whose long-run average total cost declines as the firm expands has economies of scale. If long-run average total cost rises as the firm expands, there are diseconomies of scale. Economies and diseconomies of scale may exist for whole industries as well as for firms.

The Standard Assumption: A Flat Long-Run Industry Supply Curve

Look back to the graphs in the lower right-hand panels of Figures 3 and 4. You will see that the market price in the long-run equilibrium after the shift in demand is the same as that before the shift in demand. When demand increases, price rises, leading to higher profits for existing firms. The allure of positive profits brings new firms into the industry, pushing the supply curve out and lowering prices until profits are zero again. The intersections of the shifting demand and supply curves trace out the **long-run industry supply curve,** which, as you can see in Figure 6, is perfectly horizontal. The assumption of a flat long-run industry supply curve is the standard one economists use to study industries. Exceptions to this standard are examined below.

long-run industry supply curve: a curve traced out by the intersections of demand curves shifting to the right and the corresponding short-run supply curves.

External Diseconomies of Scale

When the number of firms in the grape industry increases, the demand for water for irrigation in grape-growing regions also increases, and this may raise the price of water in these regions. Even though no single firm's decision affects the price of water

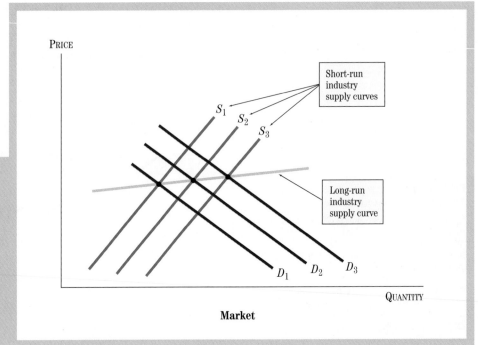

FIGURE 7
External Diseconomies of Scale

As demand increases and more firms enter the industry, each firm's costs increase, perhaps because the prices of inputs to production rise. The higher costs tend to limit the shift of the market supply curve to the right when new firms enter. The long-run industry supply curve slopes up, a phenomenon that is called external diseconomies of scale.

external diseconomies of scale: a situation in which growth in an industry causes average total cost for the individual firm to rise because of some factor external to the firm; it corresponds to an upward-sloping long-run industry supply curve.

external economies of scale: a situation in which growth in an industry causes average total cost for the individual firm to fall because of some factor external to the firm; it corresponds to a downward-sloping long-run industry supply curve.

for irrigation, the expansion of the industry does. If it does, then the cost of producing grapes increases for every firm. With the marginal cost of each grape producer increasing, the supply curve for each firm and for the industry or the market shifts up and to the left.

This is shown in the market supply and demand curves in Figure 7. Suppose there is a shift in the demand curve from D_1 to D_2. As the industry expands, more firms enter the industry, and the supply curve shifts to the right from S_1 to S_2. Because the marginal cost at each firm rises as the industry expands, the supply curve does not shift to the right by as much as the demand curve shifts. Thus, the long-run equilibrium—the intersection of the demand curve D_2 and the supply curve S_2—occurs at a higher price than the intersection of S_1 and D_1.

We could consider a further shift in demand to D_3, leading to a shift in supply to S_3. This would result in yet another long-run equilibrium at a higher price because average total cost is higher. Observe that as successive market demand curves intersect successive market supply curves, the price rises and quantity rises; an upward-sloping long-run industry supply curve is traced out. We call the phenomenon of an upward-sloping long-run industry supply curve **external diseconomies of scale.** The word *external* indicates that cost increases are external to the firm, due, for example, to a higher price for inputs (such as water) to production. In contrast, the diseconomies of scale considered in Chapter 8 were internal to the firm, due, for example, to increased costs of managing a larger firm; they can be called *internal diseconomies of scale* to distinguish them from the external case.

External Economies of Scale

External economies of scale are also possible. For example, an expansion of the domestic wine industry might make it worthwhile for students at agricultural schools to become specialists in wines made from domestic grapes. With a smaller

Internal economies or diseconomies of scale occur when a *single firm* expands (Chapter 8). *External* economies or diseconomies of scale occur when an *industry* expands (Chapter 9).

industry, such specialization would not have been worthwhile. The expertise that comes from that specialization could reduce the cost of grape production by more than the cost of hiring the specialist. Then as the industry expands, both the average total cost and the marginal cost for individual firms may decline.

Another example is the expansion of the personal computer industry, which allowed many small specialized firms servicing personal computer manufacturers to emerge. With a smaller-scale industry, this would not have been possible.

The case of external economies of scale is shown in Figure 8. Again, suppose there is a shift in the demand curve from D_1 to D_2. When the industry expands, the market supply curve shifts out from S_1 to S_2, or by *more* than the increase in demand, so that the price falls. The reason the market supply curve shifts more than the market demand curve is that marginal cost at each firm has declined as the number of firms in the industry has increased. This larger shift in supply compared to demand is shown in Figure 8. Thus, the price falls as the industry expands.

With additional shifts in demand from D_2 to D_3, the market demand curves intersect with successive market supply curves at lower prices, resulting in a long-run industry supply curve that is downward-sloping. Again, the word *external* is used to distinguish these economies that occur outside the firm from those that are internal to the firm.

Note the difference between internal and external economies of scale. The expansion of a single firm can generate internal economies of scale with the number of firms in the industry fixed because individuals within the firm can specialize. The expansion of an industry can generate external economies of scale even if the size of each firm in the industry does not increase. As an industry expands, firms might even split up into several specialized firms, each concentrating on one part of the specialized work.

FIGURE 8
External Economies of Scale
As demand expands and more firms enter the industry, each firm's costs decline, which causes the supply curve to shift to the right by even more than it would as a result of the increase in the number of firms. The long-run industry supply curve is thus downward-sloping, a phenomenon that is called external economies of scale.

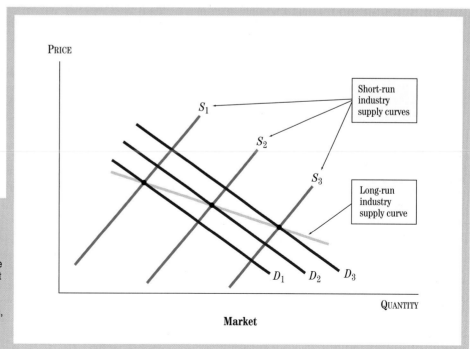

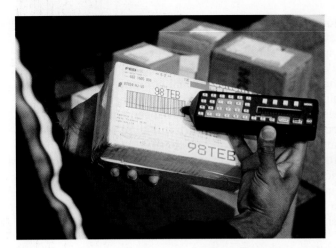

External Economies of Scale
As an industry expands in size, firms in other industries have incentives to develop new products to service the industry. These new products reduce average total cost in the industry, thereby giving rise to economies of scale, as illustrated by the development of special electronic scanners for use by the expanding express delivery service industry (left). The new ideas may in turn be used to reduce costs in other industries, as illustrated by the use of electronic scanners for self-service checkout in the retail food industry (right).

External and Internal Economies of Scale Together

In practice, it is possible for external and internal economies of scale to occur at the same time in one industry. When an industry grows in scale through the addition of new firms, it is common for the typical firm in the industry to expand its scale. Federal Express has grown in size at the same time that more firms have entered the industry. Through its larger size, Federal Express has achieved internal economies of scale (for example, by spreading the costs of its computer tracking system over more deliveries), and the larger industry as a whole has benefited from external economies of scale (as illustrated by the scanners shown in the photo).

R E V I E W

- The long-run industry supply curve is horizontal for the typical industry. When demand increases, raising prices and profits for existing firms, there is entry of new firms into the industry. This results in an increase in supply, pushing prices back down to the original level in the long run so that profits are zero again. The shifting demand and supply curves trace out a horizontal long-run industry supply curve.

- External diseconomies of scale occur when the expansion of an industry raises costs at individual firms, perhaps because of a rise in input prices. An increase in demand in such an industry will see a smaller shift out in supply because the marginal cost for each firm rises as the industry expands. This implies that the long-run industry supply curve is upward-sloping.

- External economies of scale arise when expansion of an industry lowers costs at individual firms in the industry. Opportunities for specialization for individuals and firms serving the industry are one reason for external economies of scale. An increase in demand in such an industry will see a larger shift out in supply because the marginal cost for each firm falls as the industry expands, bringing with it opportunities for specialization. This implies that the long-run industry supply curve is downward-sloping.

CONCLUSION

In this chapter, we have developed a model that can help explain why whole industries rise or fall over time. As consumer tastes change and new ideas are discovered, such changes are an ever-present phenomenon in modern economies around the world.

The model we have developed in this chapter to explain such changes extends the competitive equilibrium model we developed in Chapters 5 through 8 to allow for the entry or exit of firms into or out of an industry. Because such entry or exit usually takes time, we emphasize that this modification applies to the long run. Profits draw firms into the industry over time, whereas losses cause firms to leave. As firms enter, the industry expands. As firms leave, the industry declines. In the long-run equilibrium, profit opportunities have disappeared, and entry or exit stops.

In Chapters 10 and 11, we begin to leave the realm of the competitive market. We will develop models of the behavior of monopolies and other firms for which the assumption of a competitive market is not accurate. In the process, we will see that many of the results we have obtained with competitive markets in this chapter are no longer true.

However, many of the ideas and concepts developed in this and the previous few chapters on the competitive model will be used in these chapters. The cost curve diagram will reappear in the model of monopoly in Chapter 10; the idea of entry and exit will reappear in Chapter 11.

As we consider these new models and new results, we will use the models of this chapter as a basis of comparison. A central question will be: "How different are the results from those of the long-run competitive equilibrium model?" Keep that question in mind as you proceed to the following chapters.

KEY POINTS

1. Economic history is filled with stories about the rise and fall of industries. Industries grow rapidly when cost-reducing technologies are discovered or demand increases. They decline when demand decreases or when technological advances render an industry's product obsolete.

2. The long-run competitive equilibrium model assumes that firms will enter or exit an industry until economic profits are driven to zero. This model can be used to explain many facts about the rise and fall of industries over time.

3. When demand increases, the market price rises, leading to positive profits for individual firms in the short run. New firms will enter, causing the market supply curve to shift to the right and causing price to come back down again until the profit-making opportunities are eroded away.

4. When demand decreases, the market price falls, leading to losses for individual firms in the short run. Firms will exit the industry, causing the market supply curve to shift to the left, and causing price to rise until losses are eliminated and there is no further exit.

5. In discussing the condition of zero profits in long-run competitive equilibrium, you should keep in mind that it is economic profits, not accounting profits, that are being driven to zero. Economic profits are accounting profits less opportunity costs.

6. Entry and exit can also take place if changes in technology bring about a shift of the cost curves of individual firms in the economy.

7. An industry can expand either because more firms enter the industry or because existing firms become larger. An industry can shrink either because existing firms leave the industry or because they become smaller in size.

8. The number of firms in an industry depends on its size and the minimum efficient scale of the typical firm in the industry.

9. In the long run, the competitive equilibrium model implies that after entry and exit have taken place, average total costs are minimized and capital is allocated efficiently among industries.

10. The typical assumption is that the long-run industry supply curve is horizontal. However, industries may exhibit either external economies of scale, when the long-run industry supply curve slopes down, or external diseconomies of scale, when the long-run industry supply curve slopes up.

KEY TERMS

industry
long-run competitive equilibrium model
free entry and exit

long-run equilibrium
accounting profits
economic profits
normal profits

long-run industry supply curve
external diseconomies of scale

external economies of scale

QUESTIONS FOR REVIEW

1. What is the definition of an industry?

2. What are some possible sources of the rise of industries? Of the fall of industries?

3. What are the key characteristics of an economy that is in a long-run competitive equilibrium?

4. What happens to an industry in the long run when there is an increase in demand for the good produced by the industry?

5. What happens to an industry in the long run when there is a decrease in demand for the good produced by the industry?

6. What determines the number of firms in the economy?

7. When is it more likely for an increase in demand to lead to the entry of more firms in the economy rather than to existing firms becoming larger?

8. What is the difference between economic profits and accounting profits?

9. What are external economies of scale? How do they differ from internal economies of scale?

10. What are external diseconomies of scale? How do they differ from internal diseconomies of scale?

PROBLEMS

1. The data in the table is for a typical firm in a competitive industry (with identical firms). The firm can choose to have either 1 unit of capital or 2 units of capital in the long run. The two short-run average total cost curves (ATC_1 and ATC_2) and the two marginal cost curves (MC_1 and MC_2) are given in the table below.

Quantity	Costs with 1 Unit of Capital		Costs with 2 Units of Capital	
	ATC_1	MC_1	ATC_2	MC_2
1	7.0	5	10.0	6
2	5.5	4	7.5	5
3	4.7	3	6.3	4
4	4.5	4	5.5	3
5	4.6	5	5.0	3
6	4.8	6	4.8	4
7	5.1	7	4.9	5
8	5.5	8	5.0	6
9	5.9	9	5.2	7
10	6.3	10	5.5	8
11	6.7	11	5.8	9
12	7.2	12	6.2	10

a. Suppose the firm is currently producing with 2 units of capital. If the current price is $9 per unit, how much will the firm produce? How much are its profits?

b. Suppose the price falls to $7 per unit. How much will the firm produce now? How much are its profits?

c. What is the long-run ATC of the firm? Will the firm contract its output when it is able to change its capital?

d. What is the long-run industry equilibrium price and quantity for the typical firm? If there is a market demand of 4,000 units at that price, how many of these identical firms will there be in the industry?

2. Consider a typical office-cleaning firm that currently faces $24 in fixed costs and an $8 hourly wage for workers. The price the firm gets for each office cleaned in a large office building is $56 at the present equilibrium. The production function of the firm is shown in the following table.

Number of Offices Cleaned	Hours of Work
0	0
1	5
2	9
3	15
4	22
5	30

a. Find marginal costs and average total costs for the typical firm.

b. How many offices are cleaned by the typical firm at the present equilibrium price of $56? What are the firm's profits at this equilibrium?

c. What is the long-run equilibrium price level, assuming that the office-cleaning market is competitive?

d. How many offices are cleaned by the typical firm in long-run equilibrium?

3. Suppose corn farming in the United States can be represented by a competitive industry. Describe how this industry, currently in long-run equilibrium, would adjust to an increase in demand for corn. Explain your answer graphically, showing the cost curves for the typical farmer as well as the market supply and demand curves. Distinguish between the short run and the long run.

4. Consider developments in the airline industry. The old large airline firms relied on hubs to move passengers; passengers were flown to a hub airport, where they changed planes to continue their journeys. Southwest Airlines pioneered a new model of airline transportation that involved point-to-point transportation (with no stop at a hub), reliance on a single type of aircraft, and more flexible job descriptions that enabled planes to return to the air more rapidly after landing. These innovations reduced the costs per mile of transporting passengers. Describe the impact of this new model on the airline industry in the short run and in the long run.

5. Consider developments in the newspaper industry, which has been hit hard by the growth of the Internet. Many people have given up the habit of reading a newspaper daily and instead get their news from other sources. Explain what the impact of this change in people's preferences will be on the newspaper industry in the short run and in the long run.

6. Suppose the government imposes a sales tax on a good sold by firms in a competitive industry. Describe what happens to the price of the good in the short run and in the long run when firms are free to enter and exit. What happens to the number of firms in the industry and to total production in the industry?

7. Since there are zero profits in the long run for any firm in a competitive industry, what incentive is there for a firm in a competitive industry to pursue cost-cutting measures?

8. List some external economies of scale that might be realized by a computer manufacturing firm that locates in a high-tech industrial park. List some diseconomies of scale that might be realized by a computer programming firm that locates in an area of India that is attracting dozens of other such firms in search of software programmers. How do these economies or diseconomies of scale affect the shape of the long-run industry supply curve?

Chapter 10

Monopoly

In early 2007, France and several other European countries announced that they intended to take steps to ensure that songs that users purchased from the iTunes website could be used on music players other than the iPod, Apple's own iconic, and ubiquitous, player. According to news reports, Norwegian consumer advocate Erik Thon described this action as being needed because "It cannot be good for the music industry for [Apple] to lock music into one system." In response, Steve Jobs, the CEO of Apple, posted an item on Apple's website entitled "Thoughts on Music." Mr. Jobs argued that most of the music that is played on iPods comes from CDs that users were free to put on any music player they wanted, meaning that consumers had plenty of choices in terms of music players. Furthermore, he argued that the restrictions that Apple had to impose on songs downloaded from iTunes were required by the companies that owned the rights to the music in the first place; these companies imposed such restrictions to prevent their songs from being copied and made available for free over the Internet. According to Mr. Jobs's argument, any company that was able to come up with its own system for preventing illegal copying would be able to license and sell songs over the Internet. Apple had simply designed a very successful system in iTunes, a product that had given consumers access to more choices in how to listen to music instead of restricting their choices.

The iTunes case is the latest incident involving a situation where governments bring, or threaten to bring, action against a company because they believe that the company has effectively become a monopolist, a sole producer of a good. Monopolies operate very differently from firms in competitive markets. The biggest difference is that monopolies have the power to set the price in their markets. Consumers suffer because the monopolist restricts their choices, charges them higher prices, and supplies fewer goods than a competitive market would. Among the most notable cases in the past few decades were the breakup of AT&T in the

1980s and the decision in the early 2000s to split Microsoft into two (a decision that the Justice Department decided against carrying out).

The aim of this chapter is to develop a model of monopoly that can be used to understand how real-world monopolies operate. The model explains how a monopoly decides what price to charge its customers and what quantity to sell. We also use the model to explain some puzzling pricing behavior, such as why some airlines charge a lower fare to travelers who stay over a Saturday night. Monopolies and the reasons for their existence raise important public policy questions about the role of government in the economy. The model we develop shows that monopolies cause a loss to society when compared with firms providing goods in competitive markets; the model also provides a way to measure that loss. This loss that monopolies cause to society creates a potential role for government to step in to try and reduce this loss.

However, deciding when to, or whether to, intervene to break up a monopoly is an extremely complex task. As in the iTunes case or the Microsoft case, one often is faced with convincing arguments on both sides of the issue. Companies that are accused of being monopolists will argue that their products are simply superior to the competition and provide a service to consumers. Companies and governments will often disagree on what the appropriate definition of the "market" is. For instance, Apple could argue that consumers buy music from a variety of sources and play it on a variety of different devices; hence the iTunes-iPod combination, as popular as it is, could hardly be considered to be one that restricts consumer choice. In fact, even governments have a hard time agreeing. Shortly after the European action was announced, Thomas Barnett, a senior official in the Department of Justice's Antitrust Division, said in a speech that "consumers buy the expensive iPod device first, then have the option—not the obligation—to use the free iTunes software and buy the cheap iTunes songs."

Finally, it is important to keep in mind that in today's economy, monopolies frequently do not last very long. The increased use of the Internet and the decreased use of software that resides on one's own computer has greatly reduced concerns about Microsoft's monopoly; the rise of cellular phones makes us less concerned about local phone monopolies; satellite television provides competition to your cable television company's local monopoly; the technological advances made by chipmaker AMD erode concerns about Intel's once powerful role in the market for microprocessors. Similarly, as more music players and different music sales formats are introduced to the market, concerns about Apple may start to fade. Nevertheless, some monopolies do last a long time. De Beers is one of the most famous examples of a monopoly. It maintained its monopoly position from 1929 well into the 1980s, and even today it controls about half of the diamond market.

A MODEL OF MONOPOLY

monopoly: one firm in an industry selling a product for which there are no close substitutes.

barriers to entry: anything that prevents firms from entering a market.

A **monopoly** occurs when there is only one firm in an industry selling a product for which there are no close substitutes. Thus, implicit in the definition of monopoly are **barriers to entry**—other firms are not free to enter the industry. For example, De Beers created barriers to entry by maintaining exclusive rights to the diamonds in most of the world's diamond mines. Microsoft was accused of creating a barrier to entry in software production by bundling together its software with the Windows operating system that came preinstalled on computers. Sometimes the barriers to entry are artificially created by the government through systems of copyrights and patents that prevent other firms from duplicating a company's products. These patents and copyrights allow a company to earn revenue by licensing the right to produce the particular good that resulted from the company's innovation and creativity.

The economist's model of a monopoly assumes that the monopoly will choose a level of output that maximizes profits. In this respect, the model of a monopoly is like that of a competitive firm. If increasing production will increase a monopoly's profits, then the monopoly will raise production, just as a competitive firm would. If cutting production will increase a monopoly's profits, then the monopoly will cut its production, just as a competitive firm would.

market power: a firm's power to set its price without losing its entire share of the market.

price-maker: a firm that has the power to set its price, rather than taking the price set by the market.

The difference between a monopoly and a competitive firm is not what motivates the firm but rather how its actions affect the market price. The most important difference is that a monopoly has **market power.** That is, a monopoly has the power to set the price in the market, whereas a competitor does not. This is why a monopoly is called a **price-maker** rather than a *price-taker*, the term used to refer to a competitive firm.

The monopoly power of the salt industry has been illustrated throughout history. Salt monopolies have contributed to the rise of several state powers— from governments in ancient China to medieval Europe, where Venice's control of the salt monopoly helped finance its navy and allowed it to dominate world trade.

Getting an Intuitive Feel for the Market Power of a Monopoly

We can demonstrate the monopoly's power to affect the price in the market by looking at either what happens when the monopoly changes its price or what happens when the monopoly changes the quantity it produces. We consider the price decision first.

■ **There Is No One to Undercut the Monopolist's Price.** When there are several sellers competing with one another in a competitive market, one seller can try to sell at a higher price, but no one will buy at that price because there is always another seller nearby who will undercut that price. If a seller charges a higher price, everyone will ignore that seller; there is no effect on the market price.

The monopoly's situation is quite different. Instead of there being several sellers, there is only one seller. If the single seller sets a high price, it has no need to worry about being undercut by other sellers. There are no other sellers. Thus, the single seller—the monopoly—has the power to set a high price. True, the buyers will probably buy less at the higher price—that is, as the price rises, the quantity demanded declines—but because there are no other sellers, they will probably buy something from the lone seller.

■ **The Impact of Quantity Decisions on the Price.** Another way to see this important difference between a monopoly and a competitor is to examine what happens to the price when a firm changes the quantity it produces. Suppose that there are 100 firms competing in the bagel-baking market in a large city, each producing about the same quantity of bagels each day. Suppose that one of the firms—Bageloaf—decides to cut its production in half. Although this is a huge cut for one firm, it is a small cut compared to the whole market—only one-half a percent. *Thus the market price will rise very little.* Moreover, if this little price increase affects the behavior of the other 99 firms at all, it will motivate them to increase their production slightly. As they increase the quantity they supply, they partially offset the cut in supply by Bageloaf, and so the change in market price will be even smaller. Thus, by any measure, the overall impact on the price from the change in Bageloaf's production is negligible. Bageloaf has essentially no power to affect the price of bagels in the city.

But now suppose that Bageloaf and the 99 other firms are taken over by Bagelopoly, which then becomes the only bagel bakery in the city. Now, if Bagelopoly cuts production in half, the total quantity of bagels supplied to the whole market is cut in half, and *this will have a big effect on the price in the market.*

If Bagelopoly cut its production even further, the price would rise further. However, if Bagelopoly increased the quantity it produced, the price of bagels would fall. Thus, Bagelopoly has immense power to affect the price. Even if Bagelopoly does not know exactly what the price elasticity of demand for bagels is, it can adjust the quantity it will produce either up or down in order to change the price.

■ **Showing Market Power with a Graph.**   Figure 1 contrasts the market power of a monopoly with that of a competitive firm. The right-hand graph shows that the competitive firm views the market price as essentially out of its control. The market price is shown by the flat line and is thus the same regardless of how much the firm

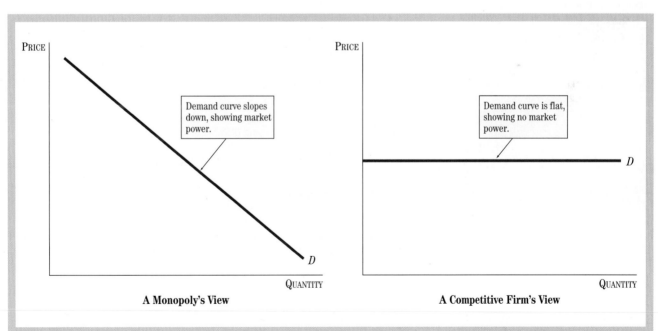

FIGURE 1
How the Market Power of a Monopoly and a Competitive Firm Differ

A monopoly is the only firm in the market. Thus, the market demand curve and the demand curve of the monopoly are the same. By raising the price, the monopoly sells less. In contrast, the competitive firm has no impact on the market price. If the competitive firm charges a higher price, its sales will drop to zero because there are many other sellers of identical products.

The Decline of the Diamond Monopolist

This article from *The Economist* magazine discusses how the diamond industry, once dominated by De Beers, has become more competitive in recent years as a result of government intervention, consumer advocacy, and the entry of new producers, especially from Russia.

Changing Facets

February 22, 2007 | JOHANNESBURG

The Economist print edition

An increased number of firms selling diamonds is a sign that the industry has become more competitive.

An industry once dominated by a cartel is starting to look like any other.

DIAMONDS are back on the big screen. The stones serenaded by Marilyn Monroe as a girl's best friend are now, however, portrayed by Hollywood as Africa's worst enemies. Leonardo DiCaprio may win an Academy Award for his performance in "Blood Diamond," as a mercenary hunting for the precious rocks during the war in Sierra Leone in the 1990s. But in reality, the shape of the industry—which produces an estimated $13 billion of rough stones and over $62 billion of diamond jewellery—has greatly changed since then.

Most of this transformation is due to the fact that De Beers, the company that once controlled much of the supply of rough diamonds, has loosened its grip, and a host of smaller producers are emerging. Regulators in Europe and America and governments in Africa have also promoted change, and "blood" diamonds have almost disappeared. As a result, the diamond trade is starting to look more like any other ordinary industry.

Some explanations for why the structure of the diamond industry has changed

The shift, says Gareth Penny, De Beers' managing director, has been "from a supply-controlled business to a demand-driven one." In the early 1990s the diamond giant was producing 45% of the world's rough diamonds, but selling about 80% of the total supply from its London marketing outfit, regulating the market through the careful management of a large stockpile. But sitting on a big inventory was not good for financial returns. At the same time regulators in America and Europe were calling for more competition and stories abounded about atrocities committed by diamond-financed rebels in Africa.

After new management arrived in the late 1990s, De Beers changed tack. Its main trading outfit stopped buying diamonds on the open market. The company delisted in 2001 and is now owned by Anglo American, the Oppenheimer family and the government of Botswana. It has settled its long-standing antitrust dispute with American regulators. And it has promised the European Union that it will stop buying diamonds from ALROSA, the state-owned Russian firm that extracts 20% or so of global production, by 2009 in order to promote competition. Today, De Beers sells about 45% of all rough diamonds, and its share of production is about 40%.

About half of what its market share was a decade and a half earlier

As the market becomes more dynamic, De Beers is investing heavily in exploration, developing four mines in Canada and South Africa and selling underperforming operations. The diamond giant has established a chain of jewellery shops in a joint venture with LVMH, a luxury-goods group. It now spends about $200m a year on marketing, which has helped to boost sales of diamonds, particularly in Asia. Marketing is also vital in persuading people to buy the real thing. Synthetic diamonds have captured 90% of the industrial market, but have made few inroads into jewellery, at least so far.

Technological advances that have provided substitutes for certain uses of diamonds have also helped break up the monopoly

Smaller firms such as Kimberley Diamond Group, Trans Hex and Gem Diamonds are racing to fill the gap between large producers and exploration juniors. Petra Diamonds, another small firm, has just bought one of De Beers' South African mines. Petra is confident that it can make money from the loss-making mine, unburdened by De Beers' costs. It is also about to start producing in Sierra Leone, and is optimistic about its exploration in Angola, where it is working with BHP Billiton. The company expects to produce 500,000 carats by 2010, up from 175,000 carats last year. But this is still tiny next to the record 51m carats De Beers produced in 2006.

Meanwhile Lev Leviev, a secretive diamond tycoon, has been setting up cutting and polishing facilities in Africa, buying some rough stones direct from governments and moving into production, putting further pressure on De Beers. "Leviev has been a driving force behind the revolution at De Beers," says Richard Chase of Ambrian Partners, an investment bank, though Mr. Penny shrugs this off.

What is certain is that Africa, which produces 60% of the world's diamonds, wants to do more than just supply rough stones. "De Beers has failed to properly appraise the aspirations of African governments," says Chaim Even-Zohar, a prominent diamond specialist. "Now it is payback time." Gone will be the days when African diamonds were shipped to London to be sorted and aggregated in lots before being sold.

In January the firm agreed with Namibia's government that all diamonds produced by their joint venture would be sorted at home, and about $300m worth of gems, just under half the output, would also be sold locally. Last week De Beers, which has already sold 26% of its South African arm to a black-owned consortium, said it would merge its Namaqualand mine with a state-owned diamond firm to create a new independent local producer. And by 2009, all De Beers stones from around the world will be sent to a swanky glass building in Botswana's capital to be aggregated. All this shows that mineral resources need not always be a curse.

African producers are also keen to cut and polish their own diamonds, which adds 50% or so to the value of rough stones, and even move into the jewellery business. Although it remains a big trading hub, Antwerp is no longer the world's cutting and polishing centre, and Israel has suffered as well. Almost all diamonds are now cut and polished in India or China, but African producers hope to get a share of the business.

And what of blood diamonds? Today, says Alex Yearsley of Global Witness, a pressure group, they make up a tiny fraction of world production. But Mr. DiCaprio's on-screen antics have raised awareness of the issue. Although it is a big step forward, the Kimberley process—a certification scheme set up in 2002 to ensure that diamonds are not paying for weapons—is not perfect, and dodgy diamonds can still find their way onto the market. De Beers says the film's release in America, just before the crucial Christmas season, did not dent jewellery sales. But more customers now want to know where their diamonds come from and want a guarantee that they are clean.

> Consumer interest in diamonds that did not come from conflict-ridden African countries greatly reduced entry barriers to producers from other countries who did not have the "blood diamond" spectre hanging over them.

This is good news for those producers that can demonstrate the provenance of their stones. Canada has developed a certification scheme for its diamonds, and since 2004 De Beers has been selling some stones in Asia with its Forevermark, a microscopic engraving that guarantees their origin. Small producers, such as Petra Diamonds, are following suit.

Even so, Global Witness says the industry is not much more transparent than it was a few years ago. Smuggling is rife, especially in countries like Angola and the Democratic Republic of Congo, and illegal diamonds still find their way to rich countries. Some 1m informal miners pan the rivers of Africa for alluvial diamonds, often in appalling conditions. The Kimberley process was designed to stem the flow of conflict diamonds, says Willie Nagel, an international diamond trader who was instrumental in setting it up, but "conflict-free diamonds should not be confused with ethical diamonds." Mining firms and voluntary groups are working to improve matters. Hollywood may not be looking to a Leonardo for its next portrayal of the industry—but it is by no means certain that it will be seeking a Marilyn either.

produces. If the competitive firm tried to charge a higher price, nobody would buy because there would be many competitors charging a lower price; so, effectively, the competitive firm cannot charge a higher price.

To a monopoly, on the other hand, things look quite different. Because the monopoly is the sole producer of the product, it represents the entire market. The monopoly—shown in the left-hand graph—sees a downward-sloping market demand curve for its product. *The downward-sloping demand curve seen by the monopoly is the same as the market demand curve.* If the monopoly charges a higher price, the quantity demanded declines along the demand curve. With a higher price, fewer people buy the item, but with no competitors to undercut that higher price, there is still some demand for the product.

The difference in the market power of a monopoly and a competitive firm—illustrated by the slope of the demand curve each faces—causes the difference in the behavior of the two types of firms.

The Effects of a Monopoly's Decision on Revenues

Now that we have seen how the monopoly can affect the price in its market by changing the quantity it produces, let's see how its revenues are affected by the quantity it produces.

Table 1 gives a specific numerical example of a monopoly. Depending on the units for measuring the quantity Q, the monopoly could be producing software, computer chips, or diamonds.

The two columns on the left represent the market demand curve, showing that there is a negative relationship between the price and the quantity sold: As the quantity sold rises from 3 to 4, for example, the price falls from $130 to $120 per unit.

TABLE 1
Revenue, Costs, and Profits for a Monopoly (price, revenue, and cost measured in dollars)

Market Demand

Quantity Produced and Sold (Q)	Price (P)	Total Revenue (TR)	Marginal Revenue (MR)	Total Costs (TC)	Marginal Cost (MC)	Profits
0	160	0	—	70	—	−70
1	150	150	150	79	9	71
2	140	280	130	84	5	196
3	130	390	110	94	10	296
4	120	480	90	114	20	366
5	110	550	70	148	34	402
6	100	600	50	196	48	404
7	90	630	30	261	65	369
8	80	640	10	351	90	289
9	70	630	−10	481	130	149
10	60	600	−30	656	175	−56

$TR = P \times Q$

$\dfrac{\text{Change in } TR}{\text{Change in } Q}$

$\dfrac{\text{Change in } TC}{\text{Change in } Q}$

$TR - TC$

■ Total Revenue and Marginal Revenue.

The third column of Table 1 shows what happens to the monopoly's *total revenue,* or price times quantity, as the quantity of output increases. Observe that at the beginning, when the monopoly increases the quantity produced, total revenue rises: When zero units are sold, total revenue is clearly zero; when 1 unit is sold, total revenue is 1 × $150, or $150; when 2 units are sold, total revenue is 2 × $140, or $280; and so on. However, as the quantity sold increases, total revenue rises by smaller and smaller amounts and eventually starts to fall. In Table 1, total revenue reaches a peak of $640 at 8 units sold and then starts to decline.

Marginal revenue, introduced in Chapter 6, is the change in total revenue from 1 more unit of output sold. For example, if total revenue increases from $480 to $550 as output rises by 1 unit, marginal revenue is $70 ($550 − $480 = $70). Marginal revenue for the monopolist in Table 1 is shown in the fourth column, next to total revenue. In addition, marginal revenue is plotted in the right-hand graph of Figure 2, where it is labeled *MR.*

The left-hand graph in Figure 2 shows how total revenue changes with the quantity of output for the example in Table 1. It shows that total revenue increases by a smaller and smaller amount, reaches a maximum, and then begins to decline. In other words, *marginal revenue declines as the quantity of output rises, and eventually becomes negative.* So, although a monopolist has the power to influence the price, this does not mean that it can get as high a level of total revenue as it wants.

Why does total revenue increase by smaller and smaller amounts and then decline as production increases? Because in order to sell more output, the monopolist must lower the price in order to get people to buy the increased output. As it raises output, it must lower the price more and more, and this causes the increase in total revenue to get smaller. As the price falls to very low levels, revenue actually declines.

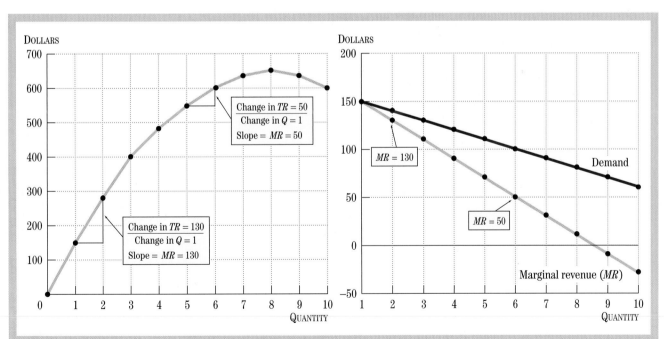

FIGURE 2
Total Revenue, Marginal Revenue, and Demand

The graph on the left plots total revenue for each level of output in Table 1. Total revenue first rises and then declines as the quantity of output increases. Marginal revenue is the change in total revenue for each additional increase in the quantity of output and is shown by the yellow curve at the right. Observe that the marginal revenue curve lies below the demand curve at each level of output except Q = 1.

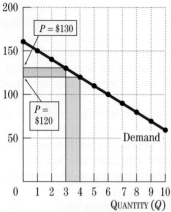

**Graph Showing the Two
Effects on Marginal Revenue**

When the monopoly raises output
from 3 units to 4 units, revenue
increases; that is, marginal revenue
is greater than zero. There is a
positive effect (blue rectangle)
because one more item is sold and
a negative effect (red rectangle)
because prices on the first 3 units
fall. Here the positive effect of the
sale of an extra unit at $120 (blue)
is greater than the negative effect of
selling each of the first 3 units at a
price that is $10 less than before
(red), so marginal revenue is
$120 − $30 = $90.

■ **Marginal Revenue Is Less than the Price.**   Another important relationship
between marginal revenue and price is that for every level of output, *marginal
revenue is less than the price* (except at the first unit of output, where it equals the
price). To observe this, compare the price (P) and marginal revenue (MR) in Table 1
or in the right-hand panel of Figure 2.

Note that the red line in Figure 2 showing the price and the quantity of output
demanded is simply the demand curve facing the monopolist. Thus, another way to
say that marginal revenue is less than the price at a given level of output is to say that
the *marginal revenue curve lies below the demand curve.*

Why is the marginal revenue curve below the demand curve? When the
monopolist increases output by 1 unit, there are two effects on total revenue: (1) a
positive effect, which equals the price P times the additional unit sold, and (2) a
negative effect, which equals the reduction in the price on all items previously sold
times the number of such items sold. For example, as the monopolist in Table 1
increases production from 4 to 5 units and the price falls from $120 to $110,
marginal revenue is $70; this $70 is equal to the increased revenue from the extra
unit produced, or $110, less the decreased revenue from the reduction in the price,
or $40 ($10 times the 4 units previously produced). Marginal revenue ($MR = $70) is
thus less than the price ($P = $110). The two effects on marginal revenue are
shown in the graph in the margin when quantity increases from 3 to 4. Because the
second effect—the reduction in revenue due to the lower price on the items
previously produced—is subtracted from the first, the price is always greater than
the marginal revenue.

■ **Marginal Revenue and Elasticity.**   Marginal revenue is negative when the
price elasticity of demand is less than 1. To see this, some algebra is helpful. Note
from the examples in the table below that the following equation holds.

$$MR = (P \times \Delta Q) - (\Delta P \times Q)$$

If $MR < 0$, then

$$P \times \Delta Q < \Delta P \times Q$$

which implies that

$$\frac{(\Delta Q/Q)}{(\Delta P/P)} < 1$$

Quantity Sold	Marginal Revenue (MR)		Price × (Change in Quantity)	−	(Change in Price) × (Previous Quantity Sold)
			P × (ΔQ)		(ΔP) × (Q)
1	150	=	$150 × 1	−	$10 × 0
2	130	=	$140 × 1	−	$10 × 1
3	110	=	$130 × 1	−	$10 × 2
4	90	=	$120 × 1	−	$10 × 3
5	70	=	$110 × 1	−	$10 × 4
6	50	=	$100 × 1	−	$10 × 5
7	30	=	$90 × 1	−	$10 × 6
8	10	=	$80 × 1	−	$10 × 7
9	−10	=	$70 × 1	−	$10 × 8
10	−30	=	$60 × 1	−	$10 × 9

or, in words, that the price elasticity of demand is less than 1. Since it would be crazy for a monopolist to produce so much that its marginal revenue was negative, we conclude that a monopoly would never produce a level of output where the price elasticity of demand is less than 1.

■ **Average Revenue.** We can also use average revenue to show that marginal revenue is less than the price. **Average revenue** is defined as total revenue divided by the quantity of output; that is, $AR = TR/Q$. Because total revenue (TR) equals price times quantity ($P \times Q$), we can write average revenue (AR) as ($P \times Q$)/Q or, simply, the price P. In other words, the demand curve—which shows price at each level of output—also shows average revenue for each level of output.

average revenue: total revenue divided by quantity.

Now recall from Chapter 8 that when the average of anything (costs, grades, heights, or revenues) declines, the marginal must be less than the average. Thus, because average revenues (prices) decline (that is, the demand curve slopes down), the marginal revenue curve must lie below the demand curve.

Finding Output to Maximize Profits at the Monopoly

Now that we have seen how a monopoly's revenues depend on the quantity it produces, let's see how its profits depend on the quantity it produces. Once we identify the relationship between profit and the quantity the monopoly will produce, we can determine the level of output that maximizes the monopoly's profits. Revenues alone can't determine how much a firm produces. For instance, we know that a monopolist will never produce a quantity where marginal revenue is negative. But that does not mean that it will produce until marginal revenue is zero. Even if each additional unit brings in extra revenue, the firm will have to look at the costs of producing that extra unit as well.

The last three columns of Table 1 show the costs and profits for the example monopoly. There are no new concepts about a monopoly's costs compared to a competitive firm's costs, so we can use the cost measures we developed in Chapters 7 to 9. The most important concepts are that total costs increase as more is produced and that marginal cost also increases, at least for high levels of output.

■ **Comparing Total Revenue and Total Costs.** The difference between total revenue and total costs is profits. Observe in Table 1 that as the quantity produced increases, both the total revenue from selling the product and the total costs of producing the product increase. However, at some level of production, total costs start to increase more than revenue increases, so that eventually profits must reach a maximum.

A quick glance at the profits column in Table 1 shows that this maximum level of profits is $404 and is reached when the monopoly produces 6 units of output. The price the monopoly must charge so that people will buy 6 units of output is $100, according to the second column of Table 1.

To help you visualize how profits change with quantity produced and to find the maximum level of profits, Figure 3 plots total costs, total revenue, and profits from Table 1. Profits are shown as the gap between total costs and total revenue. The gap reaches a maximum when output Q equals 6.

■ **Equating Marginal Cost and Marginal Revenue.** There is an alternative, more intuitive approach to finding the level of production that maximizes a monopolist's profits. This approach looks at marginal revenue and marginal cost and employs a rule that economists use extensively.

Consider producing different levels of output, starting with 1 unit and then rising unit by unit. Compare the marginal revenue from selling each additional unit of

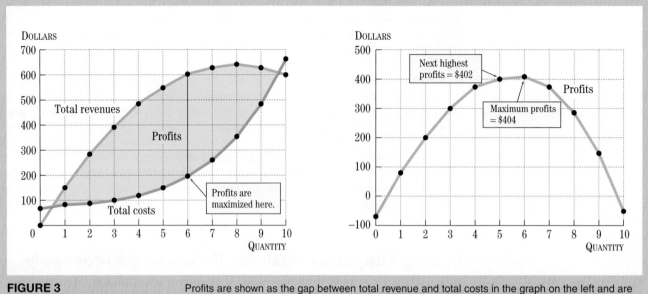

FIGURE 3
Finding a Quantity of Output to Maximize Profits

Profits are shown as the gap between total revenue and total costs in the graph on the left and are plotted on the graph on the right. Profits are at a maximum when the quantity of output is 6.

output with the marginal cost of producing it. If the marginal revenue is greater than the marginal cost of the additional unit, then profits will increase if the unit is produced. Thus, the unit should be produced, because total revenue rises by more than total costs. For example, in Table 1, the marginal revenue from producing 1 unit of output is $150 and the marginal cost is $9, so producing that unit increases profits by $141. Thus, at least 1 unit should be produced. What about 2 units? Then marginal revenue equals $130 and marginal cost equals $5, so that second unit adds $125 to profits, meaning that it makes sense to produce 2 units.

Continuing this way, the monopolist should increase its output as long as marginal revenue is greater than marginal cost. But because marginal revenue is decreasing, at some level of output marginal revenue will drop below marginal cost. The monopolist should not produce at that level. For example, in Table 1, the marginal revenue from selling 7 units of output is less than the marginal cost of producing it. Thus, the monopolist should not produce 7 units; instead, 6 units of production, with $MR = 50$ and $MC = 48$, is the profit-maximization level; this is the highest level of output for which marginal revenue is greater than marginal cost. Note that this level of output is exactly what we obtain by looking at the gap between total revenue and total costs.

Thus, *the monopolist should produce up to the level of production where marginal cost equals marginal revenue (MC = MR).* If the level of production cannot be adjusted so exactly that marginal revenue is precisely equal to marginal cost, then the firm should produce at the highest level of output for which marginal revenue exceeds marginal cost, as in Table 1. In most cases, the monopoly will be able to adjust its output by smaller fractional amounts (for example, pounds of diamonds rather than tons of diamonds), and therefore marginal revenue will equal marginal cost.

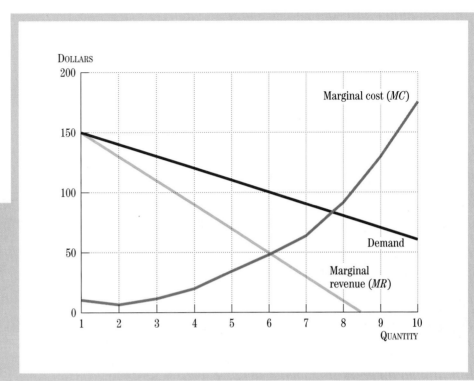

FIGURE 4
Marginal Revenue and Marginal Cost

The profit-maximizing monopoly will produce up to the point where marginal revenue equals marginal cost, as shown in the diagram. If fractional units cannot be produced, then the monopoly will produce at the highest level of output for which marginal revenue is greater than marginal cost. These curves are drawn for the monopoly in Table 1.

A picture of how this marginal revenue equals marginal cost rule works is shown in Figure 4. The marginal revenue curve is plotted, along with the marginal cost curve. As the quantity produced increases above very low levels, the marginal cost curve slopes up and the marginal revenue curve slopes down. Marginal revenue equals marginal cost at the level of output where the two curves intersect.

$MC = MR$ at a Monopoly versus $MC = P$ at a Competitive Firm

It is useful to compare the $MC = MR$ rule for the monopolist with the $MC = P$ rule for the competitive firm that we derived in Chapter 6.

■ **Marginal Revenue Equals the Price for a Price-Taker.** For a competitive firm, total revenue is equal to the quantity sold (Q) multiplied by the market price (P), but the competitive firm cannot affect the price. Thus, when the quantity sold is increased by 1 unit, revenue is increased by the price. In other words, for a competitive firm, marginal revenue equals the price; to say that a competitive firm sets its marginal cost equal to marginal revenue is to say that it sets its marginal cost equal to the price. Thus, the $MC = MR$ rule applies to both monopolies and competitive firms that maximize profits.

■ **A Graphical Comparison.** Figure 5 is a visual comparison of the two rules. A monopoly is shown on the right graph of Figure 5. This is the kind of graph we drew

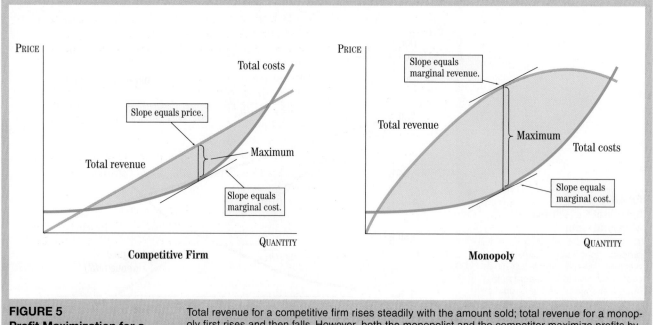

FIGURE 5
Profit Maximization for a Monopoly and a Competitive Firm

Total revenue for a competitive firm rises steadily with the amount sold; total revenue for a monopoly first rises and then falls. However, both the monopolist and the competitor maximize profits by making the gap between the total costs curve and the total revenue curve as large as possible or by setting the slope of the total revenue curve equal to the slope of the total costs curve. Thus, marginal revenue equals marginal cost. For the competitive firm, marginal revenue equals the price.

in Figure 3 except that it applies to any firm, so we do not show the units. A competitive firm is shown in the left graph of Figure 5. The scale on these two figures might be quite different; only the shapes are important for this comparison.

Look carefully at the shape of the total revenue curve for the monopoly and contrast it with the total revenue curve for the competitive firm. The total revenue curve for the monopoly starts to turn down at higher levels of output, whereas the total revenue curve for the competitive firm keeps rising in a straight line.

To illustrate the maximization of profits, we have put the same total costs curve on both graphs in Figure 5. Both types of firms maximize profits by setting production so that the gap between the total revenue curve and the total costs curve is as large as possible. That level of output, the profit-maximizing level, is shown for both firms. Higher or lower levels of output will reduce profits, as shown by the gaps between total revenue and total costs in the diagrams.

Observe that at the profit-maximizing level of output, the slope of the total costs curve is equal to the slope of the total revenue curve. Those of you who are mathematically inclined will notice that the slope of the total costs curve is how much total costs change when quantity is increased by 1 unit—that is, the marginal cost. Similarly, the slope of the total revenue curve is the marginal revenue—the increase in total revenue when output increases by 1 unit. Thus, we have another way of seeing that marginal revenue equals marginal cost for profit maximization.

For the competitive firm, marginal revenue is the price, which implies the condition of profit maximization at a competitive firm derived in Chapter 6: Marginal cost equals price. However, for the monopolist, marginal revenue and price are not the same thing.

R E V I E W

- When one firm is the sole producer of a product with no close substitutes, it is a monopoly. Most monopolies do not last forever. They come and go as technology changes. Barriers to the entry of new firms are needed to maintain a monopoly.

- A monopoly is like a competitive firm in that it tries to maximize profits. But unlike a competitive firm, a monopoly has market power; it can affect the market price. The demand curve that the monopoly faces is the same as the market demand curve.

- Marginal revenue is the change in total revenue as output increases by one unit. Marginal revenue declines as quantity sold increases and may even become negative at some level of output.

- Marginal revenue is less than the price at each level of output (except the first). This is because if we lower the price so as to increase the quantity sold by 1 unit, revenue increases by the amount of the sale price of the good, but revenue also decreases because the other units are now selling at a lower price.

- A monopolist will never produce at a quantity where marginal revenue is negative. But it also won't produce until marginal revenue equals zero. Even if an additional unit brings in extra revenue, the firm's decision to produce depends on how much it costs to produce that extra unit.

- The profit-maximizing quantity for a firm to produce is the quantity where marginal revenue equals marginal cost ($MR = MC$). As long as $MR > MC$, the firm should keep producing, and if $MR < MC$, the firm should not produce that additional unit.

- For a competitive firm, marginal revenue equals price, since the firm can't affect the price by increasing the quantity it sells. So marginal cost equals price, which in turn equals marginal revenue ($MR = MC = P$).

- For a monopoly, marginal revenue also equals marginal cost, but marginal revenue does not equal the price. Hence, for the monopolist, price is not necessarily equal to marginal cost.

THE GENERIC DIAGRAM OF A MONOPOLY AND ITS PROFITS

Look at Figure 6, which combines the monopoly's demand and marginal revenue curves with its average total cost curve and marginal cost curve. This diagram is the workhorse of the model of a monopoly, just as Chapter 8 Figure 6 on page 216 is the workhorse of the model of a competitive firm. As with the diagram for a competitive firm, you should be able to draw it in your sleep. It is a generic diagram that applies to any monopolist, not just the one in Table 1, so we do not put scales on the axes.

Observe that Figure 6 shows four curves: a downward-sloping demand curve (*D*), a marginal revenue curve (*MR*), an average total cost curve (*ATC*), and a marginal cost curve (*MC*). The position of these curves is very important. First, the marginal cost curve cuts through the average total cost curve at the lowest point on the average total cost curve. Second, the marginal revenue curve is below the demand

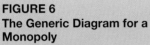

FIGURE 6
The Generic Diagram for a Monopoly

The marginal revenue and demand curves are superimposed on the monopoly's cost curves. The monopoly's production, price, and profits can be seen on the same diagram. Quantity is given by the intersection of the marginal revenue curve and the marginal cost curve. Price is given by the demand curve at the point corresponding to the quantity produced, and average total cost is given by the *ATC* curve at that quantity. Monopoly profits are given by the rectangle that is the difference between total revenue and total costs.

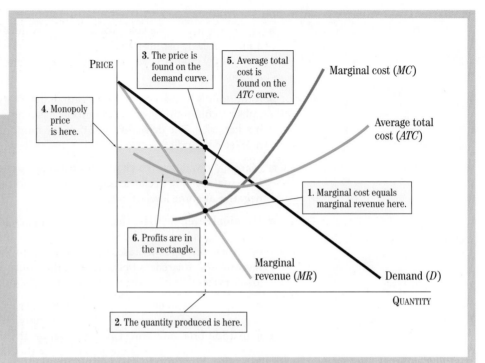

curve over the entire range of production (except at the vertical axis near 1, where they are equal).

We have already given the reasons for these two relationships (in Chapter 8 and in the previous section of this chapter), but it would be a good idea for you to practice sketching your own diagram like Figure 6 to make sure the positions of your curves meet these requirements.[1]

Determining Monopoly Output and Price on the Diagram

In Figure 6 we show how to calculate the monopoly output and price. First, find the point of intersection of the marginal revenue curve and the marginal cost curve. Second, draw a dashed vertical line through this point and look down the dashed line at the horizontal axis to see what the quantity produced is. Producing a larger quantity would lower marginal revenue below marginal cost. Producing a smaller quantity would raise marginal revenue above marginal cost. The quantity shown is the profit-maximizing level. It is the amount the monopolist produces.

What price will the monopolist charge? We again use Figure 6, but be careful: Unlike the quantity, the monopolist's price is *not* determined by the intersection of the marginal revenue curve and the marginal cost curve. The price has to be such

---

[1] When sketching diagrams, it is useful to know that when the demand curve is a straight line, the marginal revenue curve is always twice as steep as the demand curve and, if extended, would cut the horizontal axis exactly halfway between zero and the point where the demand curve would cut the horizontal axis.

that the quantity demanded is equal to the quantity that the monopolist decides to produce. To find the price, we need to look at the demand curve in Figure 6. The demand curve gives the relationship between price and quantity demanded. It tells how much the monopolist will charge for its product in order to sell the amount produced.

To calculate the price, extend the dashed vertical line upward from the point of intersection of the marginal cost curve and the marginal revenue curve until it intersects the demand curve. At the intersection of the demand curve and the vertical line, we find the price that will generate a quantity demanded equal to the quantity produced. Now draw a horizontal line over to the left from the point of intersection to mark the price on the vertical axis. This is the monopoly's price, about which we will have more to say later.

Determining the Monopoly's Profits

Profits can also be shown on the diagram in Figure 6. Profits are given by the difference between the area of two rectangles, a total revenue rectangle and a total costs rectangle. Total revenue is price times quantity and is thus equal to the area of the rectangle with height equal to the monopoly price and length equal to the quantity produced. Total costs are average total cost times quantity and are thus equal to the area of the rectangle with height equal to *ATC* and length equal to the quantity produced. Profits are then equal to the green-shaded area that is the difference between these two rectangles.

It is possible for a monopoly to have negative profits, or losses, as shown in Figure 7. In this case, the price is below average total cost, and therefore total revenue is less than total costs. Like a competitive firm, a monopolist with negative profits will shut down if the price is less than average variable cost. It will eventually exit the market if negative profits persist.

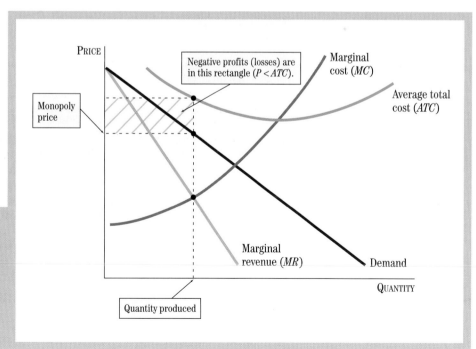

FIGURE 7
A Monopoly with Negative Profits

If a monopoly finds that average total cost is greater than the price at which marginal revenue equals marginal cost, then it runs losses. If price is also less than average variable cost, then the monopoly should shut down, just like a competitive firm.

R E V I E W

- A monopolist's profit-maximizing output and price can be determined graphically. The diagram shows four curves: the marginal revenue curve, the demand curve, the marginal cost curve, and the average total cost curve.

- The monopoly's production is determined at the point where marginal revenue equals marginal cost.

- The monopoly's price is determined from the demand curve at the point where the quantity produced equals the quantity demanded.

- The monopoly's profits are determined by subtracting the total costs rectangle from the total revenue rectangle. The total revenue rectangle is given by the price times the quantity produced. The total costs rectangle is given by the average total cost times the quantity produced.

COMPETITION, MONOPOLY, AND DEADWEIGHT LOSS

Are monopolies harmful to society? Do they reduce consumer surplus? Can we measure these effects? To answer these questions, economists compare the price and output of a monopoly with those of a competitive industry. First, observe in Figure 6 or Figure 7 that the monopoly does not operate at the minimum point on the average total cost curve even in the long run. Recall that firms in a competitive industry do operate at the lowest point on the average total cost curve in the long run.

To go further in our comparison, we use Figure 8, which is a repeat of Figure 6, except that the average total cost curve is removed to reduce the clutter. All the other curves are the same.

Comparison with Competition

Suppose that instead of there being only one firm in the market, there are now many competitive firms. For example, suppose Bagelopoly—a single firm producing bagels in a large city—is broken down into 100 different bagel bakeries like Bageloaf. The production point for the monopolistic firm and its price before the breakup are marked as "monopoly quantity" and "monopoly price" in Figure 8. What are production and price after the breakup?

The market supply curve for the new competitive industry would be Bagelopoly's old marginal cost curve because this is the sum of the marginal cost curves of all the newly created firms in the industry. Equilibrium in the competitive industry is where this market supply curve crosses the market demand curve. The amount of production at that point is marked by "competitive quantity" in Figure 8. The price at that equilibrium is marked by "competitive price" on the vertical axis.

Compare the quantity and price for the monopolist and the competitive industry. It is clear from the diagram in the margin that the quantity produced by the monopolist is less than the quantity produced by the competitive industry. It is also clear that the monopoly will charge a higher price than will emerge from a competitive industry. In sum, the monopoly produces less and charges a higher price than the competitive industry would.

This is a very important result. The monopoly exploits its market power by holding back on the quantity produced and causing the price to rise compared with the competitive equilibrium. This is always the case. Convince yourself by

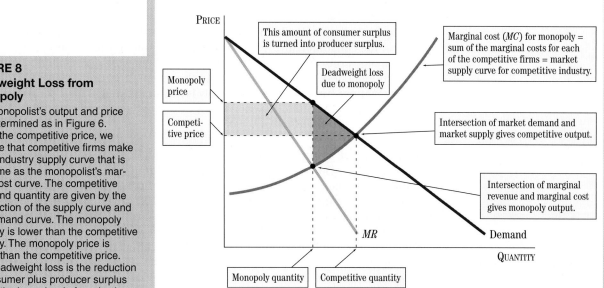

FIGURE 8
Deadweight Loss from Monopoly

The monopolist's output and price are determined as in Figure 6. To get the competitive price, we imagine that competitive firms make up an industry supply curve that is the same as the monopolist's marginal cost curve. The competitive price and quantity are given by the intersection of the supply curve and the demand curve. The monopoly quantity is lower than the competitive quantity. The monopoly price is higher than the competitive price. The deadweight loss is the reduction in consumer plus producer surplus due to the lower level of production by the monopolist.

drawing different diagrams. For example, when De Beers exercises its market power, it holds back production of diamonds, thereby raising the price and earning economic profits.

Note that even though the monopoly has the power to do so, it does not increase its price without limit. When the price is set very high, marginal cost rises above marginal revenue. That behavior is not profit maximizing.

Deadweight Loss from Monopoly

The economic harm caused by a monopoly occurs because it produces less than a competitive industry would. How harmful, then, is a monopoly?

■ **Consumer Surplus and Producer Surplus Again.** Economists measure the harm caused by monopolies by the decline in the sum of consumer surplus plus producer surplus. Recall that *consumer surplus* is the area above the market price line and below the demand curve, the demand curve being a measure of consumers' marginal benefit from consuming the good. The *producer surplus* is the area above the marginal cost curve and below the market price line. Consumer surplus plus producer surplus is thus the area between the demand curve and the marginal cost curve. It measures the sum of the marginal benefits to consumers of the good less the sum of the marginal costs to the producers of the good. A competitive market will maximize the sum of consumer plus producer surplus.

With a lower quantity produced by a monopoly, however, the sum of consumer surplus and producer surplus is reduced, as shown in Figure 8. This reduction in consumer plus producer surplus is called the *deadweight loss due to monopoly*. It is a quantitative measure of the harm a monopoly causes the economy. A numerical example is given in the margin.

How large is the deadweight loss in the U.S. economy? Using the method illustrated in Figure 8, empirical economists estimate that the loss is between .5 and

Numerical Example of Dead-weight Loss Calculation

The monopoly shown in the diagram above produces only 12 items, but a competitive industry would produce 18 items. For the 13th through 17th items, which are not produced by the monopoly, the marginal benefit is greater than the marginal cost by the amounts $5, $4, $3, $2, and $1, respectively, as shown by the areas between the demand curve and the supply curve for the competitive industry. Hence, the deadweight loss caused by the monopoly is the sum $5 + $4 + $3 + $2 + $1 = $15.

2 percent of GDP, or between $60 billion and $240 billion, per year. Of course, the deadweight loss is a larger percentage of production in industries where monopolies are a greater presence.

Figure 8 also shows that the monopoly takes, in the form of producer surplus, some of the consumer surplus that would have gone to the consumers in competitive markets. Consumer surplus is now the area below the demand curve and above the monopoly price, which is higher than the competitive price. However, this transfer of consumer surplus to the monopoly is not a deadweight loss, because what the consumers lose, the monopoly gains. This transfer affects the distribution of income, but it is not a net loss to society.

■ **Meaningful Comparisons.** In any given application, one needs to be careful that the comparison of monopoly and competition makes sense. Some industries cannot be broken up into many competitive firms without changing the cost structure of the industry. For instance, having 100 sewer companies laying down pipes to serve one local area would be very costly. Therefore, transforming a monopolistic sewer industry into a competitive sewer industry is unlikely to lead to greater societal benefits. Instead, we should try to affect the monopoly's decisions by government actions.

One should also be careful about concluding that a competitive industry of one type is preferable to a monopolistic industry of another type. History provides many such examples. Western settlers in the United States during the nineteenth century had a larger consumer surplus from railroads—in spite of the railroad monopolists' profits—than they did from competitive wagon trains. Modern-day users of the information highway—computers and telecommunications—reap a larger consumer surplus from Microsoft's software and Intel's computer chips, even if they are produced monopolistically, than they would from a competitive pocket calculator industry.

The Monopoly Price Is Greater than Marginal Cost

Another way to think about the loss to society from monopoly is to observe the difference between price and marginal cost. Figure 8, for example, shows that the monopoly price is well above the marginal cost at the quantity where the monopoly chooses to produce.

■ **Marginal Benefit Is More than Marginal Cost.** Because consumers will consume up to the point where the marginal benefit of a good equals its price, the excessive price means that the marginal benefit of a good is greater than the marginal cost. This is inefficient because producing more of the good would increase benefits to consumers by more than the cost of producing it.

The size of the difference between price and marginal cost depends on the elasticity of the monopoly's demand curve. If the demand curve is highly elastic (close to a competitive firm's view as shown in Figure 1), then the difference between price and marginal cost is small.

■ **The Price-Cost Margin.** A common measure of the difference between price and marginal cost is the **price-cost margin.** It is defined as

$$\frac{\text{Price minus marginal cost}}{\text{Price}}$$

For example, if the price is $4 and the marginal cost is $2, the price-cost margin is $(4 − 2)/4 = .5$. The price-cost margin for a competitive firm is zero because price equals marginal cost.

price-cost margin: the difference between price and marginal cost divided by the price. This index is an indicator of market power, where an index of 0 indicates no market power and a higher price-cost margin indicates greater market power.

Economists use a rule of thumb to show how the price-cost margin depends on the price elasticity of demand. The rule of thumb is shown in the equation below.

$$\text{Price-cost margin} = \frac{1}{\text{price elasticity of demand}}$$

For example, when the elasticity of demand is 2, the price-cost margin is .5. The flat demand curve has an infinite elasticity, in which case the price-cost margin is zero; in other words, price equals marginal cost.

REVIEW

- A monopoly creates a deadweight loss because it restricts output below what the competitive market would produce. The cost is measured by the deadweight loss, which is the reduction in the sum of consumer plus producer surplus.

- Sometimes the comparison between monopoly and competition is only hypothetical because it would either be impossible or make no sense to break up the monopoly into competitive firms.

- Another way to measure the impact of a monopoly is by the difference between price and marginal cost. Monopolies always charge a price higher than marginal cost. The difference—summarized in the price-cost margin—depends inversely on the elasticity of demand.

WHY MONOPOLIES EXIST

Given this demonstration that monopolies lead to high prices and a deadweight loss to society, you may be wondering why monopolies exist. In this section, we consider three reasons for the existence of monopolies.

Natural Monopolies

The nature of production is a key factor in determining the number of firms in the industry. If big firms are needed in order to produce at low cost, it may be natural for a few firms or only one firm to exist. In particular, *economies of scale*—a declining long-run average total cost curve over some range of production—can lead to a monopoly. Recall from Chapter 8 that the *minimum efficient scale* of a firm is the minimum size of the firm for which average total costs are lowest. If the minimum efficient scale is only a small fraction of the size of the market, then there will be many firms.

For example, suppose the minimum efficient scale for beauty salons in a city is a size that serves 30 customers a day at each salon. Suppose the quantity of hair stylings demanded in the city is 300 per day. We can then expect that there will be 10 beauty salons (300/30 = 10) in the city. But if the minimum efficient scale is larger (for example, 60 customers per day), then the number of firms in the industry will be smaller (for example, 300/60 = 5 salons). At the extreme case where the minimum efficient scale of the firm is as large as or larger than the size of the market (for example, 300 per day), there will probably be only one firm (300/300 = 1), which will be a monopoly.

natural monopoly: a single firm in an industry in which average total cost is declining over the entire range of production and the minimum efficient scale is larger than the size of the market.

A sewer company in a small town, for example, has a minimum efficient scale larger than the number of houses and businesses in the town. There are huge fixed costs to lay pipe down the street, but each house connection has a relatively low cost, so average total cost declines as more houses are connected. Other industries that usually have a very large minimum efficient scale are electricity and water service. In each of these industries, average total cost is lowest if one firm delivers the service. **Natural monopolies** exist when average total cost is declining and the minimum efficient scale is larger than the size of the market.

The prices charged by many natural monopolies are regulated by government. The purpose of the regulation is to keep the price below the monopoly price and closer to the competitive price. Such regulation can thereby reduce the deadweight loss from the monopoly. Alternative methods of regulating natural monopolies are discussed in Chapter 12. Water companies and electric companies are regulated by government.

A change in technology that changes the minimum efficient scale of firms can radically alter the number of firms in the industry. For example, AT&T used to be viewed as a natural monopoly in long-distance telephone service. Because laying copper wire across the United States required a huge cost, it made little sense to have more than one firm. The U.S. government regulated the prices that AT&T charged its customers, endeavoring to keep the price of calls below the monopoly price and closer to the competitive price. But when the technology for transmitting signals by microwave developed, it became easier for other firms also to provide services. Thus, MCI and Sprint, as well as AT&T, could provide services at least as cheaply as one firm. Because of this technological change, the government decided to end the AT&T monopoly by allowing MCI and Sprint to compete with AT&T. Nationwide telephone service is no longer a monopoly.

Patents and Copyrights

Another way monopolies arise is through the granting of patents and copyrights by the government. Intel's patent was the source of its monopoly on its computer chips. The U.S. Constitution and the laws of many other countries require that government grant patents to inventors. If a firm registers an invention with the U.S. government, it can be granted a monopoly in the production of that item for 20 years. In other words, the government prohibits other firms from producing the good without the permission of the patent holder. Patents are given for many inventions, including the discovery of new drugs. Pharmaceutical companies hold patents on many of their products, giving them a monopoly to produce and sell these products. Copyrights on computer software, chips, movies, and books also give firms the sole right to market the products. Thus, patents and copyrights can create monopolies.

The award of monopoly rights through patents and copyrights serves a useful purpose. It can stimulate innovation by rewarding the inventor. In other words, the chance to get a patent or copyright gives the inventor more incentive to devote time and resources to invent new products or to take a risk and try out new ideas. Pharmaceutical companies, for example, argue that their patents on drugs are a reward for inventing the drugs. The higher prices and deadweight loss caused by the patent can be viewed as the cost of the new ideas and products. By passing laws to control drug prices, government could lower the prices of drugs to today's sick people. This would be popular, but doing so would reduce the incentive for the firms to invent new drugs. Society—and, in particular, people in future years—could suffer a loss. When patents expire, we usually see a major shift toward competition. In general, when assessing the deadweight loss due to monopoly, one must consider the benefits of the research and the new products that monopoly profits may create.

As technology has advanced, patents and copyrights have had to become increasingly complex in order to prevent firms from getting around them. Nevertheless, patent and copyright protection does not always work in maintaining the monopoly. Many times potential competing firms get around copyrights on computer software and chips by "reverse engineering," in which specialists look carefully at how each part of a product works, starting with the final output. Elaborate mechanisms have been developed, such as "clean rooms," in which one group of scientists and programmers tells another group what each subfunction of the invention does but does not tell them how it is done. The other group then tries to invent an alternative way to perform the task. Because they cannot see how it is done, they avoid violating the copyright.

Licenses

Sometimes the government creates a monopoly by giving or selling to one firm a license to produce a product. The U.S. Postal Service is a government-sponsored monopoly. A law makes it illegal to use a firm other than the U.S. Postal Service for first-class mail. However, even this monopoly is diminishing with competition from overnight mail services and fax technology.

National parks sometimes grant or sell to single firms licenses to provide food and lodging services. The Curry Company, for example, was granted a monopoly to provide services in Yosemite National Park. For a long time the Pennsylvania Turnpike—a toll road running the width of the state—licensed a monopoly to Howard Johnson Company to provide food for travelers on the long stretches of the road. However, seeing the advantage of competition, the turnpike authorities eventually allowed several different fast-food chains to get licenses.

Attempts to Monopolize and Erect Barriers to Entry

Adam Smith warned that firms would try to create monopolies in order to raise their prices. One of the reasons Smith favored free trade between countries was that it would reduce the ability of firms in one country to form a monopoly; if they did form a monopoly and there were no restrictions on trade serving as barriers to entry for firms in other countries, then foreign firms would break the monopoly.

History shows us many examples of firms attempting to monopolize an industry by merging with other firms and then erecting barriers to entry. De Beers is one example of such a strategy apparently being successful on a global level. In the last part of the nineteenth century, several large firms were viewed as monopolies. Standard Oil, started by John D. Rockefeller in the 1880s, is a well-known example. The firm had control of most of the oil-refining capacity in the United States. Thus, Standard Oil was close to having a monopoly in oil refining. However, the federal government forced Standard Oil to break up into smaller firms. We will consider other examples of the government's breaking up monopolies or preventing them from forming in Chapter 12.

Barriers to entry allow a monopoly to persist, so for a firm to maintain a monopoly, it needs barriers to entry. In addition to the ways mentioned earlier, barriers to entry can also be created by professional certification. For example, economists have argued that the medical and legal professions in the United States erect barriers to the entry of new doctors and lawyers by having tough standards for admittance to medical school or to the bar and by restricting the types of services that can be performed by nurses or paralegals. Doctors' and lawyers' fees might be lower if there were lower barriers to entry and, therefore, more competition.

Simply observing that a firm has no competitors is not enough to prove that there are barriers to entry. Sometimes the threat of potential entry into a market may

ECONOMICS IN ACTION

How Best to Ensure Access to Clean Water in Developing Countries

Economists, unlike most other people in the world, tend to find strong associations between diamonds and water. The strength of this association dates back to Adam Smith's discussion of the diamond-water paradox, the idea that goods with great monetary value may have little practical usefulness and vice versa. As you read this chapter on monopolies, you may have noticed another, lesser-known association between water and diamonds—monopolies figure prominently in how both are provided to the market. In the case of diamonds, the monopoly was created by the control over the world's diamond supply exerted by De Beers. In many countries, cities, and towns, the monopoly over water exists not because one company controls the supply of water, but because of the potential existence of a natural monopoly for water—the minimum efficient scale exceeds the size of the market.

THE PROBLEM

The practical essentialness of water for human existence leads us to be more concerned about water monopolies than about diamond monopolies. In many countries the supply of water is considered to be a natural monopoly; entry by other providers is restricted, and the price of water is regulated by the government. If, however, the distribution of drinking water is in fact not a natural monopoly, then restrictions on entry may be keeping the supply of water artificially low and the price of water artificially high, thus restricting access to water by the poor. On the other hand, if the supply of water is a natural monopoly, but the government does not do an adequate job of regulating the price to keep it below the monopoly price, then there will be deadweight loss as the unregulated monopolist exerts its market power. Finally, some governments impose price ceilings on water that are so

[2] The 2006 Human Development Report, "Beyond Scarcity: Power, Poverty and the Global Water Crisis," freely available at http://hdr.undp.org/hdr2006/.

low that the monopoly provider has no incentive to install the pipes and taps needed to deliver water to those without access. Increasing access to clean water is one of the most important challenges of the twenty-first century, as discussed in the 2006 Human Development Report[2] issued by the United Nations. The Human Development Report eloquently lays out the problem

> In high income areas of cities in Asia, Latin America and Sub-Saharan Africa people enjoy access to several hundred liters of water delivered into their homes at low prices by public utilities. Meanwhile slum dwellers and poor households in rural areas of the same countries have access to much less than the 20 liters of water a day per person required to meet the most basic human needs. Women and young girls carry a double burden of disadvantage since they are the ones who sacrifice their time and their education to collect water.

Which type of industrial structure can best enhance access to clean water is an important challenge to economists. The theory of monopoly figures prominently in the search for a solution.

WHY ACCESS IS LIMITED

What are the main problems that limit access to water for the urban and rural poor? According to the Human Development Report, the cheapest source of water—water piped into the home by the public utility—often does not extend to rural areas and to urban slums. People living in these areas have to buy water from tankers or water vendors. Since these providers do not have the advantages of scale afforded to the public utility, poor people end up paying more for water than do their wealthier counterparts who are connected to utilities. Households that can't pay these high prices for water end up paying in time—a member of the household is often assigned the arduous task of bringing

contestable market: a market in which the threat of competition is enough to encourage firms to act like competitors.

be enough to get a monopolist to act like a competitive firm. For example, the possibility of a new bookstore's opening up off campus may put pressure on the campus bookstore to keep its prices low. When other firms, such as off-campus bookstores, can potentially and easily enter the market, they create what economists call a **contestable market.** In general, the threat of competition in contestable markets can induce monopolists to act like competitors.

water back from a river or a stream over a distance of several miles. A young woman adroitly balancing a large container of water on her head is a fairly common sight when one travels in rural Africa. The amount of time and effort (and lost productivity and wages) expended in collecting water is unfathomable to those of us who are used to turning on a tap and having all the water we could possibly need.

Why does the public utility not extend its infrastructure to cover these rural areas and urban slums? Often the utility lacks resources, as the government does not provide enough money for the public utility to invest in the infrastructure needed to deliver water. At the same time, governments often limit the ability of other providers to install a water delivery infrastructure so that the public utility can take advantage of the large minimum efficient scale. Many utilities are also hampered by bad management and corruption. To make up for the difficulties in issuing and collecting bills for the use of water, utilities often end up imposing extremely high connection costs for homes to connect to the water supply. Many poor households can't afford to pay these high connection costs because of credit and liquidity limitations; these households then end up paying private providers substantially more for each additional gallon of water they use.

Some governments have tried to tackle the problem of limited resources by privatizing water utilities, a controversial step in many countries. But privatization of an industry that very likely is a natural monopoly often results in the creation of a private monopoly provider who has little interest in expanding capacity or lowering prices. In order for privatization to be an improvement, the provision of water has to be handed over to a private provider with pockets deep enough to make the necessary infrastructure investments, while at the same time submitting that company to effective government regulation to make sure that the price it charges is less than the monopoly price. Unfortunately, in many poor countries, this type of effective regulation is not feasible. The private provider either gets away with charging monopoly prices that limit the access of the poor or does not invest its resources in expanding the system because it is forced to charge a price

that is even below the level needed to cover the fixed costs of connecting new customers to the system.

POTENTIAL SOLUTIONS

Solving this serious problem will require a multipronged approach. First, the public utility needs to be given enough resources to make the necessary investments in the infrastructure that is needed to connect people in rural areas and in slums to the water supply. This will allow the utility to take advantage of the decreasing average total costs and connect more people to the water supply. Second, governments need to either reduce or subsidize the cost of connections to the public utility so that the poor do not have to get their water from small-scale private providers who bear higher costs. Third, changes need to be made in countries where the government regulates the price of water to such a low level that it discourages further investment in expanding the number of connections. This is a perverse policy that provides a subsidy to those who can most afford to pay for water while denying access to those who can least afford to pay. Raising the price of water provided through the public utility while providing subsidies to the poor to pay for water will bring about a much more equitable outcome. Fourth, if privatization is deemed necessary because of the lack of public resources to invest in infrastructure, then effective regulation of the private provider is needed. Rich countries can help poor countries by providing the expertise needed to regulate a natural monopoly effectively. Finally, greater emphasis needs to be placed on protecting water supplies. In many countries, misguided policies and lax regulation lead to either water sources being polluted or large quantities of water being diverted for agricultural and industrial use at prices far below what consumers are charged for the substantially smaller quantities of water required for basic needs.

The issues discussed here have arisen in many developing countries, among the most prominent being China, India, Peru, Bolivia, and Mexico. You should be able to find plenty of interesting articles to read in newspapers and journals about the experience that these countries have had in expanding access to clean water.

R E V I E W   ■ Economies of scale, patents, copyrights, and licenses are some of the reasons monopolies exist.

■ Natural monopolies are frequently regulated by government.

■ Many large monopolies in the United States, such as Standard Oil and AT&T, have been broken apart by government action.

291

PRICE DISCRIMINATION

price discrimination: a situation in which different groups of consumers are charged different prices for the same good.

In the model of monopoly we have studied in this chapter, the monopolists charge a single price for the good they sell. In some cases, however, firms charge different people different prices for the same item. This is called **price discrimination.** Price discrimination is common and is likely to become more common in the future as firms become more sophisticated in their price setting. Everyday examples include senior citizen discounts at movie theaters and discounts on airline tickets for Saturday-night stayovers.

Some price discrimination is less noticeable because it occurs in geographically separated markets. Charging different prices in foreign markets and domestic markets is common. For example, Japanese cameras are less expensive in the United States than in Japan. In contrast, the price of luxury German cars in the United States is frequently higher than in Germany.

Volume or quantity discounts are another form of price discrimination. Higher prices are sometimes charged to customers who buy smaller amounts of an item. For example, electric utility firms sometimes charge more per kilowatt-hour to customers who use only a little electricity.

Consumers with Different Price Elasticities of Demand

Why is there price discrimination? Figure 9 shows a diagram of a monopoly that gives one explanation. Suppose the good being sold is airline travel between two remote islands, and suppose there is only one airline between the two islands. The two graphs in Figure 9 represent demand curves with different elasticities. On the left is

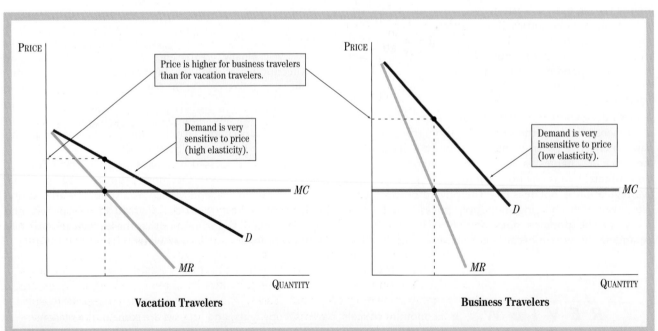

FIGURE 9
Price Discrimination Targeted at Different Groups

The monopolist has two groups of potential buyers for its travel services. For convenience, we assume the marginal cost curve is flat. The group on the left has a high price elasticity of demand. The group on the right has a low price elasticity of demand. If the monopolist can discriminate between the buyers, then it is optimal to charge a lower price to the high-elasticity group and a higher price to the low-elasticity group.

"Would it bother you to hear how little I paid for this flight?"

the demand for vacation air travel. Vacationers are frequently more price sensitive than businesspeople. They can be more flexible with their time; they can take a boat rather than a plane; they can stay home and paint the house. Hence, for vacationers, the price elasticity of demand is high. Business travelers, however, do not have much choice. As shown in Figure 9, they are less sensitive to price. An important business meeting may require a businessperson to fly to the other island with little advance notice. For business travel, the price elasticity of demand is low. Difference between price elasticities is a key reason for price discrimination.

In Figure 9, notice that both groups have downward-sloping demand curves and downward-sloping marginal revenue curves. For simplicity, marginal cost is constant and is shown with a straight line.

Figure 9 predicts that business travelers will be charged a higher price than vacationers. Why? Marginal revenue equals marginal cost at a higher price for business travelers than for vacationers. The model of monopoly predicts that the firm will charge a higher price to those with a lower elasticity and a lower price to those with a higher elasticity.

In fact, this is the type of price discrimination we see with airlines. But how can the airlines distinguish a business traveler from a vacation traveler? Clothing will not work: A business traveler could easily change from a suit to an aloha shirt and shorts to get the low fare. One device used by some airlines is the Saturday-night stayover. Business travelers prefer to work and travel during the week. They value being home with family or friends on a Saturday night. Vacationers frequently do not mind extending their travel by a day or two to include a Saturday night, and they may want to vacation over the weekend. Hence, there is a strong correlation between vacation travelers and those who do not mind staying over a Saturday night. A good way to price-discriminate, therefore, is to charge a lower price to people who stay at their destination on a Saturday night and to charge a higher price to those who are unwilling to do so.

Price discrimination based on different price elasticity of demand requires that the firm be able to prevent people who buy at a lower price from selling the item to other people. Thus, price discrimination is much more common in services than in manufactured goods.

Quantity Discounts

Another important form of price discrimination involves setting prices according to how much is purchased. If a business makes 100 telephone calls a day, it probably has to pay a higher fee per call than if it makes 1,000 calls a day. Telephone monopolies can increase their profits by such a price scheme, as shown in Figure 10.

The single-price monopoly is shown in the bottom graph of Figure 10. Two ways in which the monopoly can make higher profits by charging different prices are shown in the top two panels. In both cases, there is no difference in the price elasticity of demand for different consumers. To make it easy, assume that all consumers are identical. The demand curve is the sum of the marginal benefits of all the consumers in the market.

On the upper left, the firm sets a higher price for the first few items a consumer buys and a lower price for the remaining items. Frequent flier miles on airlines are an example of this kind of pricing. If you fly more than a certain number of miles, you get

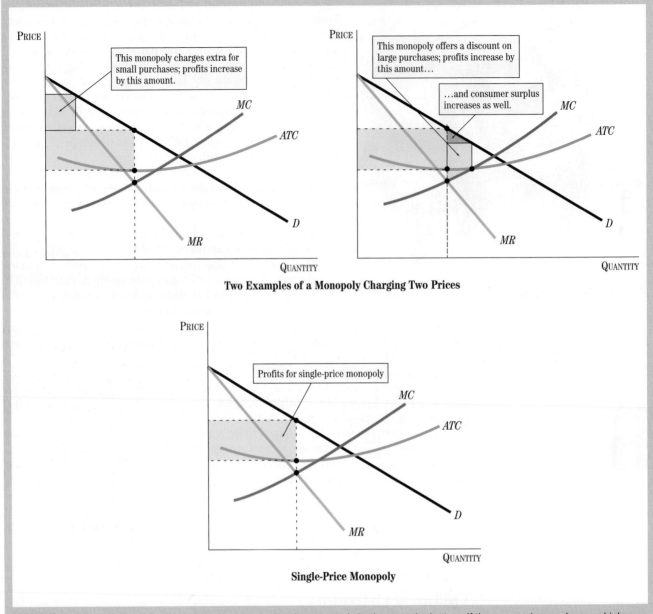

Two Examples of a Monopoly Charging Two Prices

Single-Price Monopoly

FIGURE 10
Price Discrimination Through Quantity Discounts or Premiums

The standard single-price monopoly is shown at the bottom. If the monopoly can charge a higher price to customers who buy only a little, profits can increase, as shown on the upper left. If the monopoly can give a discount to people who purchase a lot, it can also increase profits, as shown on the upper right. In this case, production increases.

a free ticket. Thus, the per-mile fare for 20,000 miles is less than the per-mile fare for 10,000 miles. As the diagram shows, profits for the firm are higher in such a situation. In the example at the left, the higher price is the fare without the discount.

On the upper right, we see how profits can be increased if the firm gives even deeper discounts to high-volume purchasers. As long as the high-volume purchasers cannot sell the product to the low-volume purchasers, there are extra profits to be made.

The upper right graph in Figure 10 illustrates an important benefit of price discrimination: It can reduce deadweight loss. With price discrimination, a monopoly actually produces more. For example, those who get a lower price because of frequent flier discounts may actually end up buying more. The result is that the airline has more flights. As already noted, the deadweight loss from a monopolist occurs because production is too low. If price discrimination allows more production, then it reduces deadweight loss.

R E V I E W
- Because a monopolist has market power, it can charge different prices to different consumers as long as it can prevent the consumers from reselling the good.
- Price discrimination explains telephone pricing as well as the complicated airfares on airlines.
- Deadweight loss is reduced by price discrimination.

CONCLUSION

The model of a monopoly that we developed in this chapter centers on a key diagram, Figure 6 on page 282. Learning how to work with this diagram of a monopoly is very important. In fact, economists use this same diagram to describe any firm that has some market power, not just monopolies, as we show in Chapter 11. Before proceeding, it is a good idea to practice sketching this generic diagram of a monopoly and finding output, price, and profits for different positions of the curve.

From the point of view of economic efficiency, the economic performance of monopolies is not nearly as good as that of competitive industries. Output is too low, marginal benefits are not equal to marginal costs, and consumer surplus plus producer surplus is diminished. But when assessing these losses, the fact that the expectation of monopoly profits—even if temporary—is the inducement for firms to do research and develop new products must also be considered.

Nevertheless, the deadweight loss caused by monopolies provides a potential opportunity for government to intervene in the economy. In fact, the U.S. government actively intervenes in the economy either to prevent monopolies from forming or to regulate monopolies when it is not appropriate to break them apart. We look further into government prevention or regulation of monopolies in Chapter 12.

KEY POINTS

1. A monopoly occurs when only one firm sells a product for which there are no close substitutes. Many local markets for water, sewage, electricity, and cable television are monopolies.

2. A monopolist possesses market power in the sense that it can lower the market price by producing more or raise the market price by producing less.

3. A monopoly's total revenue increases, but at a decreasing rate, as it increases production. This implies that its marginal revenue is initially positive but gradually becomes smaller.

4. Marginal revenue for a monopolist is always less than price. Even though the firm can increase its revenue by producing and selling an additional unit, it earns lower revenues on previously produced units because it had to lower its price in order to increase its sales.

5. The model of a monopoly assumes that the monopoly tries to maximize profits. In order to maximize profits, a monopolist chooses a quantity such that marginal revenue equals marginal cost.

6. A monopoly produces a smaller quantity and charges a higher price than a competitive industry; the lower production causes a deadweight loss.

7. Monopolies exist because of economies of scale that make the minimum efficient size of the firm larger than the market, or because of barriers to entry, including government patents and licenses.

8. Even though they create monopolies, patents and copyrights are useful to society because they provide incentives for creators of innovative products and works.

9. Many monopolies are short lived; technological change can rapidly change a firm from a monopoly to a competitive firm, as exemplified by the long-distance telephone market.

10. A price-discriminating monopoly charges different prices to different customers depending on how elastic their demand is. If price discrimination leads a monopolist to increase its production, then it can help reduce deadweight loss.

KEY TERMS

monopoly	price-maker	price-cost margin	contestable market
barriers to entry	average revenue	natural monopoly	price discrimination
market power			

QUESTIONS FOR REVIEW

1. What is a monopoly?
2. What market power does a monopoly have?
3. Why does marginal revenue decline as more is produced by a monopoly?
4. How does a monopoly choose its profit-maximizing output and price?
5. Why is the marginal revenue curve below the demand curve for a monopoly but not for a competitive firm?
6. Why does a monopolist produce less than a competitive industry?
7. What forces tend to cause monopolies?
8. What is the deadweight loss from a monopoly?
9. What is price discrimination?
10. How does price discrimination reduce deadweight loss?

PROBLEMS

1. The following table gives the total cost and total revenue schedule for a monopolist.

Quantity	Total Cost (in dollars)	Total Revenue (in dollars)
0	144	0
1	160	90
2	170	160
3	194	210
4	222	240
5	260	250
6	315	240
7	375	210

a. Calculate the marginal revenue and marginal cost

b. Determine the profit-maximizing price and quantity, and calculate the resulting profit.

c. Sketch the demand curve, the marginal revenue curve, and the marginal cost curve, and show how to derive the profit-maximizing quantity graphically.

2. Fill in the missing data on a monopolist, with fixed costs of $10, in the following table:

Quantity of Output	Price	Total Revenue	Marginal Revenue	Marginal Cost	Average Total Cost
1	11				18.00
2	10				11.00
3	9				7.67
4	8				7.00
5	7				6.60
6	6				7.00
7	5				8.00

a. At what quantity will the monopolist produce in order to maximize profits? What will be the price at this level of output? What will be the profits?

b. What quantity maximizes total revenue? Why is this not the profit-maximizing quantity?

c. Sketch the demand curve, the marginal revenue curve, the marginal cost curve, and the average total cost curve. Show how to derive the profit-maximizing quantity and the profits earned by the monopolist graphically.

3. Suppose you are an economic adviser to the president, and the president asks you to prepare an economic analysis of MonoTV, Inc., a firm that sells a patented device used in high-definition television sets. You have the following information about MonoTV, Inc.

Quantity (millions)	Price	Marginal Cost
1	10	4
2	9	5
3	8	6
4	7	7
5	6	8
6	5	9
7	4	10
8	3	11
9	2	12
10	1	13

a. Given the data in the table, graphically show all the elements necessary to represent the monopolist's profit maximization. *Note:* You do not need to draw the average total cost curve.

b. What level of output does MonoTV, Inc., produce? What price does it sell this output at?

c. Does MonoTV, Inc., produce at the socially optimal level? Why or why not? Show any inefficiency on your graph.

4. Consider the monopoly described in the following table.

Quantity	Price	Total Revenue	Marginal Revenue	Total Cost	Marginal Cost	Profit
0	320	0	—	140	—	−140
2	305	610	305	158	9	452
4	290	1,160	275	168	5	992
6	275	1,650	245	188	10	1,462
8	260	2,080	215	228	20	1,852
10	245	2,450	185	296	34	2,154
12	230	2,760	155	392	48	2,368
14	215	3,010	125	522	65	2,488
16	200	3,200	95	712	95	2,488
18	185	3,330	65	962	125	2,368
20	170	3,400	35	1,302	170	2,088
22	155	3,410	5	1,762	225	1,648
24	140	3,360	−25	2,322	280	1,038

a. What are the profit-maximizing quantity and price?

b. How much is the monopolist making in profits?

c. What would the equilibrium price and quantity have been if the market were competitive?

d. Calculate the deadweight loss caused by the monopolist.

5. Sketch the diagram for a monopoly with an upward-sloping marginal cost curve that is earning economic profits. Suppose the government imposes a tax on each item the monopoly sells. Draw the diagram corresponding to this situation. How does this tax affect the monopoly's production and price? Show what happens to the area of deadweight loss.

6. Why might a local electric company be a monopoly? Would your answer be the same for a local cable television company? How about your long-distance telephone company?

7. Under the Copyright Act of 1976, in the United States, authors and creators like Walt Disney were granted copyrights over their creations that would last for the life of the author plus 50 years. What are the tradeoffs involved in granting monopoly rights to an author? In 1998, the U.S. Congress decided to allow companies to extend copyrights that were reaching the end of their 50-year protected period and would be expiring by an additional 20 years. What do you think about the merits and demerits of that decision?

8. The following table gives the round-trip airfares from Los Angeles to New York offered by United Airlines.

Price	Advance Purchase	Minimum Stay	Cancellation Penalty
$418	14 days	Overnight on Saturday	100%
$683	3 days	Overnight on Saturday	100%
$1,900	None required	None required	None

Explain why United might want to charge different prices for the same route. Why are there minimum-stay requirements and cancellation penalties?

9. Why is it that firms need market power in order to price-discriminate? What other circumstances are required in order for a firm to price-discriminate? Give an example of a firm or industry that price-discriminates and explain how it is possible in that case.

10. Children, students, and senior citizens frequently are eligible for discounted tickets to movies. Is this an example of price discrimination? Explain the conditions necessary for price discrimination to occur and draw the graphs to describe this situation.

Chapter 11

Product Differentiation, Monopolistic Competition, and Oligopoly

When John Johnson launched his magazine business in 1942, he differentiated his products from existing products in a way that was valued by millions of African Americans. As a result, the new product lines, the magazines *Ebony* and *Jet*, were huge successes. Johnson became a multimillionaire, and his firm became the second largest black-owned firm in the United States. Similarly, when Liz Claiborne started her new clothing firm in 1976, she differentiated her products from existing products in a way that was valued by millions of American women. She offered stylish yet affordable clothes for working women, and she too was successful: Thirty years later, Liz Claiborne, Inc., was one of the largest producers of women's clothing in the world. Such stories of people finding ways to differentiate their products from existing products are told thousands of times a year, although not everyone is as successful as John Johnson and Liz Claiborne.

John Johnson's magazines and Liz Claiborne's suits and dresses were different in a way that was valued by consumers. Because their products were different from the products made by the many other firms in their industries—magazine publishing and women's clothing, respectively—they each had market power in the sense that they could charge a higher price for their products and not lose all their customers. Thus, neither Johnson Publishing nor Liz Claiborne, Inc., was just another firm entering a competitive industry in which every firm sold the same product. But Johnson Publishing and Liz Claiborne, Inc., were not monopolies either; there were other firms in their industries, and they could not prevent entry into the industries by even more firms. As is typical of many firms, they seemed to be hybrids between a competitive firm and a monopoly.

In this chapter, we develop a model that is widely used by economists to explain the behavior of such firms. It is called *the model of monopolistic competition*.

monopolistic competition: a market structure characterized by many firms selling differentiated products in an industry in which there is free entry and exit.

Monopolistic competition occurs in an industry with many firms and free entry, where the product of each firm is slightly differentiated from the product of every other firm. We contrast the predictions of this model with those of the models of competition and monopoly developed in previous chapters.

We also study another type of industry whose structure seems to fall between the models of monopoly and competition. In an **oligopoly,** there are very few firms in the industry. Because there are very few firms, each firm has market power—the actions of any one firm can significantly affect the market price. In an oligopoly, each firm needs to anticipate what the others will do and develop a strategy to respond. Neither the model of a competitive industry, where no one firm can affect the price, nor the model of monopoly, where one firm completely dominates the market, adequately describes such a situation. To develop a model of oligopoly, therefore, we need to extend our tools of economic analysis to deal with strategic behavior: how firms think about, anticipate, and react to other firms' moves.

oligopoly: an industry characterized by few firms selling the same product with limited entry of other firms.

Figure 1 compares the models of monopolistic competition, oligopoly, monopoly, and competition. Over time, an industry can change from being a monopoly to monopolistic competition, to oligopoly, to competition, and back again, as a result of changes in the number of firms or the degree of product differentiation.

In order to emphasize the distinction between the models of competition and monopolistic competition or between the models of monopoly and monopolistic competition, the terms *pure competition* and *pure monopoly* are sometimes used. In this book, we simply use the terms *competition* and *monopoly*.

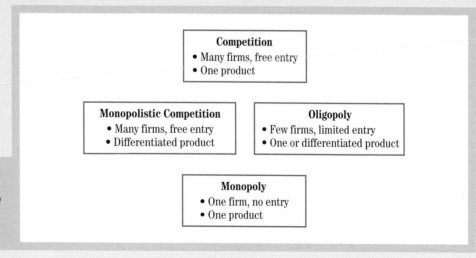

FIGURE 1
Four Types of Industries
Monopoly and competition are at the extreme ends. Monopolistic competition and oligopoly are in between.

PRODUCT DIFFERENTIATION

product differentiation: the effort by firms to produce goods that are slightly different from other types of goods.

The effort by firms to fashion products that are different from other firms' products in ways that people value is called **product differentiation.** Product differentiation is pervasive in market economies. It leads to a great variety of consumer goods and capital goods. Goods for which there is no product differentiation, such as aluminum ingots or gold bullion, are called *homogeneous products*, meaning that they are all exactly the same.

Variety of Goods in a Market Economy

Product differentiation is obvious from a casual examination of the wide variety of goods in a modern market economy. Table 1 gives an indication of this wide variety. If you like to run, you have a choice of 285 different types of running shoes. You can choose among 340 different types of cereals for breakfast and wear 70 different types of Levis' jeans.

The wide variety of products in a market economy contrasts starkly with the absence of such variety that existed in the centrally planned economies of Eastern Europe and the Soviet Union. Stores in Moscow or Warsaw would typically have only one type of each product—one type of wrench, for example—produced according to the specifications of the central planners. There was even relatively little variety in food and clothing. One of the first results of market economic reform in these countries has been an increase in the variety of goods available.

Product differentiation is a major activity of both existing firms and potential firms. Business schools teach managers that product differentiation ranks with cost cutting as one of the two basic ways in which a firm can improve its performance. An entrepreneur can enter an existing industry either by finding a cheaper way to produce an existing product or by introducing a product that is differentiated from existing products in a way that will appeal to consumers.

TABLE 1
Variety: An Illustration of Product Differentiation

Item	Number of Different Types	Item	Number of Different Types
Automobile models	260	National soft drink brands	87
Automobile styles	1,212	Bottled water brands	50
SUV models	38	Milk types	19
SUV styles	192	Colgate toothpastes	17
Personal computer models	400	Mouthwashes	66
Movie releases	458	Dental flosses	64
Magazine titles	790	Over-the-counter pain relievers	141
New book titles	77,446	Levis' jeans styles	70
Amusement parks	1,174	Running shoe styles	285
TV screen sizes	15	Women's hosiery styles	90
Frito-Lay chip varieties	78	Contact lens types	36
Breakfast cereals	340		

Source: 1998 Annual Report, Federal Reserve Bank of Dallas.

Product Differentiation versus Homogeneous Product
Even bottled water has become a highly differentiated product, more like breakfast cereal and soft drinks than like gold bullion, a homogeneous product for which there is no product differentiation.

Product differentiation usually means something less than inventing an entirely new product. Aspirin was an entirely new product when it was invented; wrapping aspirin in a special coating to make it easier to swallow is product differentiation. Coke, when it was invented in 1886, was a new product, whereas Pepsi, RC Cola, Jolt Cola, Yes Cola, and Mr. Cola, which followed over the years, are differentiated products.

Product differentiation also exists for capital goods—the machines and equipment used by firms to produce their products. The large earthmoving equipment produced by Caterpillar is different from that produced by other firms, such as Komatsu of Japan. One difference is the extensive spare parts and repair service that go along with Caterpillar equipment. Bulldozers and road graders frequently break down and need quick repairs; by stationing parts distributorships and knowledgeable mechanics all over the world, Caterpillar can offer quick repairs in the event of costly breakdowns. In other words, the products are differentiated on the basis of service and a worldwide network.

Puzzles Explained by Product Differentiation

Product differentiation explains certain facts about a market economy that could be puzzling if all goods were homogeneous.

■ **Intraindustry Trade.** Differentiated products lead to trade between countries of goods from the *same industry*, called **intraindustry trade.** Trade between countries of goods from *different industries*, called **interindustry trade,** can be explained by comparative advantage. Bananas are traded for wheat because one of these goods is grown better in warm climates and the other is grown better in cooler climates. But why should intraindustry trade take place? Why should the United States both buy beer from Canada and sell beer to Canada? Beer is produced in many different countries, but a beer company in one country will differentiate its beer from that of a beer company in another country. In order for people to benefit from the variety of beer, we might see beer produced in the United States (for example, Budweiser) being exported to Canada and, at the same time, see beer produced in

intraindustry trade: trade between countries in goods from the same or similar industries.

interindustry trade: trade between countries in goods from different industries.

Canada (for example, Molson) being exported to the United States. If all beer were exactly the same (a homogeneous commodity), such trade within the beer industry would make little sense, but it is easily understood when products are differentiated.

■ **Advertising.** Product differentiation also provides one explanation of why there appears to be so much advertising—the attempt by firms to tell consumers what is good about their products. If all products were homogeneous, then advertising would make little sense: A bar of gold bullion is a bar of gold bullion, no matter who sells it. But if a firm has a newly differentiated product in which it has invested millions of dollars, then it needs to advertise that product to prospective customers. You can have the greatest product in the world, but it will not sell if no one knows about it. Advertising is a way to provide information to consumers about how products differ.

Economists have debated the role of advertising in the economy for many years. Many have worried about the waste associated with advertising. For instance, the parent companies of Pepsi-Cola and Coca-Cola spend large sums of money on advertising for Aquafina and Dasani, their bottled water brands. It is hard to see how catchy phrases like "make your mouth water" and large advertising campaigns are providing useful information to consumers about a product that is essentially filtered tap water. One explanation is that the purpose of the advertising in these cases is to get people to try the product. If they like it, they will buy more; if they do not like it, they will not—but without the ad they might not ever try it. Whatever the reason, advertising will not sell an inferior product—at least, not for long. For example, despite heavy advertising, Federal Express failed miserably with Zapmail—a product that guaranteed delivery of high-quality faxes of documents around the country within hours—because of the superiority of inexpensive fax machines that even small businesses could buy. The Iridium satellite phone service was forced into bankruptcy in late 1999 because of the rapid spread of cell phone technology and networks all over the world.

Others say that advertising is wasteful partly because it is used to create a *perception* of product differentiation rather than genuine differences between products. For example, suppose Coke and Pepsi are homogeneous products (to some people's tastes, they are identical). Then advertising simply has the purpose of creating a perception in people's minds that the products are different. If this is the case, product differentiation may be providing a false benefit, and the advertising used to promote it is a waste of people's time and effort.

■ **Consumer Information Services.** The existence of magazines such as *Consumer Reports* is explained by product differentiation. These magazines would be of little use to consumers if all products were alike.

Such services may also help consumers sort through exaggerated claims in advertising or help them get a better perception of what the real differences between products are. It is hard to sell an expensive product that ends up last on a consumer-rating list, even with the most creative advertising.

How Are Products Differentiated?

Altering a product's *physical characteristics*—the sharpness of the knife, the calorie content of the sports drink, the mix of cotton and polyester in the shirt, and so on—is the most common method of product differentiation. JetBlue differentiated itself from other airlines by offering leather seats and satellite television on every seat on its airplanes. As the example of Caterpillar shows, products can also be differentiated on features other than the physical characteristics. Related features such as low installation costs, fast delivery, large inventory, and money-back guarantees also serve to differentiate products.

Location is another important way in which products are differentiated. A Blockbuster Video or a McDonald's down the block is a very different product for you from a Blockbuster Video or a McDonald's 100 miles away. Yet only the location differentiates the product.

Time is yet another way to differentiate products. An airline service with only one daily departure from Chicago to Dallas is different from a service with 12 departures a day. Adding more flights of exactly the same type of air service is a way to differentiate the product. A 24-hour supermarket provides a different service from one that is open only during the day.

Convenience is increasingly being used by firms to differentiate products. How could peanut butter and jelly sandwiches, a standard for lunch, be more convenient? You can buy frozen peanut butter and jelly sandwiches on white bread. Prepackaged salads containing greens, dressing, and croutons; yogurt in a tube; single-serving microwaveable soup containers—these are all products that have become very popular in recent times as people's lives have become busier and more hectic. Similarly, firms like Netflix and Blockbuster have eliminated the need to make a trip to the video store by making it possible for consumers to get movie rentals delivered to their homes.

The Optimal Amount of Product Differentiation at a Firm

Product differentiation is costly. Developing a new variety of spot remover that will remove mustard from wool (no existing product is any good at this) would require chemical research, marketing research, and sales effort. Opening another Lenscrafters (there are already hundreds in the United States) requires constructing a new store and equipping it with eyeglass equipment, trained personnel, and inventory.

But product differentiation can bring in additional revenue for a firm. The new spot remover will be valued by football fans who want to keep warm with woolen blankets or scarves but who also like mustard on their hot dogs. The people in the neighborhood where the new Lenscrafters opens will value it because they do not have to drive or walk as far.

The assumption of profit maximization implies that firms will undertake an activity if it increases profits. Thus, firms will attempt to differentiate their products if the additional revenue from product differentiation is greater than the additional costs. This is exactly the advice given to managers in business school courses. "Create the largest gap between buyer value . . . and the cost of uniqueness" is the way Harvard Business School professor Michael Porter puts it in his book *Competitive Advantage*.[1] If the additional revenue is greater than the additional cost, then business firms will undertake a product-differentiation activity.

For a given firm, therefore, there is an *optimal* amount of product differentiation that balances out the additional revenue and the additional cost of the product differentiation. This is illustrated in Figure 2, which shows the amount of product differentiation chosen by a firm. For a company that owns and operates a haunted house, the horizontal axis is the amount of gore and scary features in the haunted house. The additional revenue from adding more gore and scary features to a haunted house is shown by the downward-sloping line. While more gore and scary features attract additional customers, the additional revenue from increasing the

---

[1] Michael Porter, *Competitive Advantage* (New York: Free Press, 1985), p. 153.

ECONOMICS IN ACTION

What's the Future of Product Differentiation?

How many types of running shoes do you think will be available for people to buy 10 years from now? There are now about 285 different types, but the number has grown tremendously in the last 25 years—there were only 5 types in the 1970s. This large increase in product differentiation is not unique to running shoes; it has occurred in virtually all markets. Colgate now produces 17 different types of toothpaste, compared with only 2 types in the 1970s. But will this rapid increase in product differentiation continue?

To determine whether an economic trend will continue, we first need to explain the trend. According to the theory of the optimal amount of product differentiation at a firm (see Figure 2 on page 305), a possible explanation for the increase in product differentiation is a reduction in its cost. Shifting the curve showing the "additional cost of product differentiation" down in Figure 2 would lead to more differentiated products. In fact, there is evidence that the cost of product differentiation has been reduced; computerized machines used to produce shoes make it easier to change the settings and alter the shape, thickness, or treads of rubber soles.

So the model explains the recent trends very well, and if the costs of product differentiation continue to fall in the future, we can expect a greater variety of products.

There is already evidence that computer technology is continuing to lower the cost of product differentiation. For example, a company called Footmaxx uses computers to determine a person's individual foot shape and gait characteristics. As the customer walks on a sensitive pad, the foot shape and pressure are captured many times throughout the gait cycle, and the data are fed into a computer, which prescribes a custom orthotic insole, designed to fit the foot exactly and correct the individual's gait. Nike's iD division has been letting sneakerheads design their own shoes online for several years; in May 2005, it went one step further by inviting sneaker fans to use their cell phones to customize a pair of shoes that was displayed on a 22-story screen in the middle of Times Square in New York City. After a minute-long session designing their shoe, the consumer could then download the design as wallpaper for his or her mobile phone or go online and buy the newly designed sneakers. The interactive experience combined both design and technology innovations. Other companies are following suit. Converse recently launched its own "Design Your Own" service on its web site.

In principle, it will be possible to choose a shoe that is unique to the individual—not only in style and color, but also in the shape of the foot and the characteristics of the gait. One can imagine more than a thousand types of running shoes—perhaps millions, one for every runner! Similar ideas are being developed for clothing, where a person's body is scanned by a laser and a shirt comes out exactly in the person's size.

Of course, these projections for the future require the *ceteris paribus* assumption that other things will remain the same. How important do you think that assumption is in this case? In particular, do you think consumers might change their behavior in response to such an explosion of product types?

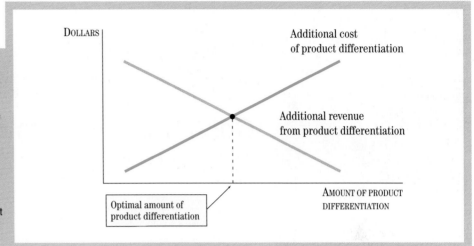

FIGURE 2
A Firm's Decision about Product Differentiation
Determining how much product differentiation a firm should undertake is a matter of equating the additional revenue from and additional cost of another differentiated product. (Note that these "additional cost" and "additional revenue" curves are analogous to marginal cost and marginal revenue curves except that they depend on the amount of product *differentiation* rather than the *quantity* of a particular product.)

amount of gore and scary features declines because there are only so many people who would consider visiting a haunted house in a given area. It is therefore increasingly difficult to attract additional customers. The additional cost of adding more gore and scary features to a haunted house is shown by the upward-sloping line. This additional cost increases because the cheapest effects that could be included for differentiation would be added first. The optimal amount of gore and scary features for a haunted-house operator is at the point where the additional revenue from more gore and scary features is just equal to the additional cost. Beyond that point, more gore and scary features would reduce profits, since the additional cost would exceed the additional revenue.

This is far from a trivial analysis for haunted-house owners. Theme parks are increasingly interested in attracting Halloween traffic, and more gore and scary features attract more customers. In some theme parks, Halloween is the largest event all year.

Using this analysis in practice is difficult because the revenue gains from product differentiation depend on what other firms do. The amount of additional revenue generated by additional gore and scary features in a haunted house depends on how much gore and how many scary features are included in other nearby haunted houses. In the next section, we will look at more formal models of industries with differentiated products.

R E V I E W

■ Product differentiation is evident in the variety of products we see every day, in the absence of such variety in centrally planned economies, and in the proliferation of such variety after market reforms.

■ Intraindustry trade, advertising, and consumer information are some of the facts that can be better explained by product differentiation.

■ Products can be differentiated by physical characteristics, location, time, and convenience, among other features.

■ Profit-maximizing firms will fashion a differentiated product if the additional revenue from doing so is greater than the additional cost.

The Deliciousness of Product Differentiation

In the last two decades, Americans stopped thinking about coffee as a homogenous beverage and began to pay attention to whether the coffee they drank came from Starbucks or Peet's, and whether it was brewed from beans grown in Sumatra or Kenya. In the past decade a similar transformation has occurred in the chocolate industry. This article, from the Associated Press, talks about how American consumers now care about who made their chocolate, whether the cacao beans came from Guatemala or Sao Tome, and how high the cacao count is.

Product differentiation has become a feature of all these industries in recent decades. People no longer consider coffee to be a homogeneous product; they have clear preferences for Starbucks or Peets or Caribou. Scharffenberger and Steinberg saw the opportunity to create a niche for their product.

Product differentiation for chocolate can come from the content of cacao and from the origins of the cacao bean. These days, many high-end chocolate wrappers display this information, much like a bottle of fine wine displays its appellation.

Product differentiation seems to have been successful in attracting chocolate connoisseurs to their product.

Calif. Chocolatiers Boost Premium Boom

By LISA LEFF

Americans' love of chocolate has become a dark and bittersweet affair, and it took a former vintner to make it so. John Scharffenberger and Robert Steinberg launched the first U.S. chocolate manufacturing company in half a century, drawing heavily on Scharffenberger's refined palate and his past as a maker of sparkling wines. Together, they set out to do for dark chocolate what fellow Californian Robert Mondavi had done for wine—demystify, democratize and domesticate it. Call it kismet, uncanny timing or creative chemistry, but in the 11 years since co-founding Scharffen Berger Chocolate Maker they have watched the public's appetite for gourmet chocolate expand from a Valentine's Day extravagance to an everyday indulgence.

"We've gone through a food revolution in this country," said Scharffenberger. Just as Americans have become more sophisticated about wine, whole-bean coffee, artisan cheeses and other products that once were the luxury of certified foodies have been mainstreamed to the masses. "The one thing that remained to be done was chocolate, and that's what we hit on," Scharffenberger said. Like the label of a fine wine, the wrapper on a Scharffen Berger chocolate tells you exactly what's inside. It was the first U.S. chocolatier to feature the cacao count prominently on its wrappers—the higher the number, the darker and more bitter the chocolate. And the source of the beans is also noted, for those who like knowing whether their chocolate got its start in Madagascar, Ecuador, Ghana or Peru. Scharffen Berger bars now are prominently displayed in the checkout lines of grocers like Trader Joe's, Andronico's and Whole Foods.

Yet venerable players like Reading, Pa.-based Godiva Chocolatier Inc., part of The Campbell Soup Co., and Ghirardelli Chocolate Co., now headquartered in San Leandro, Calif., jump-started the trend, said Marcia Mogelonsky, an analyst with the market research firm Mintel International. They popularized fancy chocolates with upscale, single-serving packaging, wider distribution and savvy marketing, she said. Even The Hershey Co., the name synonymous with American chocolate, has invested heavily in premium chocolate, showing it is more than a fad, she said. Besides buying Scharffen Berger 1 1/2 years ago, the company has introduced its own line of premium chocolate bars and late last year purchased Ashland, Ore.-based Dagoba Organic Chocolate.

Between 2003 and 2005, U.S. sales of premium chocolates went from $1.4 billion to $1.79 billion, according to Mogelonsky. While it still represents only a fraction of the overall $15.7 billion chocolate market, the growth rate for the good stuff has been much faster—28 percent over the three-year period compared to annual rates of 2 to 3 percent for the industry as a whole. "People were ready for a change," said Mogelonsky. She relates the trend to Americans' growing self-indulgence. "I can't afford a mink and a diamond, but I can afford a piece of really good chocolate," she said.

As with wine and coffee, the origin of premium chocolate has increasingly become a selling point. And consumers have also responded to manufacturers' efforts to tout their relationships with growers in the developing countries where cacao typically comes from, she said. The quality and quantity of cacao in a bar or bonbon is what distinguishes fine chocolate from the coating on a Snicker's, according to Scharffenberger, who personally oversees the blending of 30 varieties of beans that go into the company's products and visits the ranches in Guatemala, Madagascar and other countries where it secures supplies. "We aren't creating flavors that are earth-shattering, just delicious," he said. The Food and Drug Administration requires milk chocolate to contain at least 10 percent cacao, but Scharffen Berger's milk chocolate contains a whopping 41 percent. Its darkest dark chocolate, 82 percent.

Before Scharffenberger and Steinberg set up shop, California already was home to plenty of chocolate makers—both high-end and pedestrian. Besides Ghirardelli, they include Glendale-based Nestle USA, Guittard Chocolate Co. in Burlingame, Joseph Schmidt Confections, which also was bought out by Hershey's last year, and See's Candies in South San Francisco.

The growth has been steady enough that by 2000 California had edged out Pennsylvania, home of Hershey's, to become the nation's chocolate capital. In 2004, the last year for which figures were available, California had 136 companies churning out chocolate and cocoa products compared to Pennsylvania's 122, according to the U.S. Census Bureau.

Besides its reputation as a food snob's paradise, there is a practical reason the San Francisco Bay area, in particular, has emerged as the heart of chocolate activity: the consistent, moist climate, according to Scharffenberger. "It's a pain to make chocolate when it's hot," he said. Like a winery, the company offers tours of its Berkeley factory where participants—about 40,000 of them a year—receive morsels of chocolate trivia along with free samples. On a recent morning, a tour group learned, for example, that cacao beans are technically a fruit, that dark chocolate tastes better melted on the tongue instead of chewed, and that the actual ◄— cacao content of white chocolate is zero.

By offering tours, chocolate companies, like vineyards, can create future customers who appreciate their product.

Adrienne Newman, an aspiring chocolatier from Austin, Texas, was taking the tour for the third time after making chocolate "a full-time hobby." Over the holidays, she took her boyfriend to Switzerland so she could taste the local wares, and she mail orders chocolate from new companies whose products she wants to try. For a long time, she could still enjoy a Hershey's bar, Newman said, but no more.

"I'm beyond that," she said. "After three years of tasting exquisite stuff, there is no going back."

MONOPOLISTIC COMPETITION

The model of monopolistic competition, first developed by Edward Chamberlin of Harvard University in the 1930s, is designed to describe the behavior of firms operating in differentiated product markets. Monopolistic competition gets its name from the fact that it is a hybrid of monopoly and competition. Recall that monopoly has one seller facing a downward-sloping market demand curve with barriers to the entry of other firms. Competition has many sellers, each facing a horizontal demand curve with no barriers to entry and exit. Monopolistic competition, like competition, has many firms with free entry and exit, but, as in monopoly, each firm faces a downward-sloping demand curve for its product.

The monopolistically competitive firm's demand curve slopes downward because of product differentiation. When a monopolistically competitive firm raises its price, the quantity demanded of its product goes down but does not plummet to zero, as in the case of a competitive firm. For example, if Nike raises the price of its running shoes, it will lose some sales to Reebok, but it will still sell a considerable number of running shoes because some people prefer Nike shoes to other brands. Nike running shoes and Reebok running shoes are differentiated products to many consumers. On the other hand, a competitive firm selling a product like wheat, which is a much more homogeneous product, can expect to lose virtually all its customers to another firm if it raises its price above the market price.

As we will see, free entry and exit is an important property of monopolistic competition. Because of it, firms can come into the market if there is a profit to be made or leave the market if they are running losses.

A Typical Monopolistic Competitor

Figure 3 illustrates the key features of the model of monopolistic competition. Each graph in Figure 3 shows a typical monopolistically competitive firm. At first glance, the graphs look exactly like the graph for a monopoly, introduced in Chapter 10. They should, because both monopolistic and monopolistically competitive firms face downward-sloping demand curves. However, the demand curve facing a monopolistically competitive firm has a different interpretation because there are other firms in the industry. The demand curve is not the market demand curve; rather, it is the demand curve that is *specific* to a particular firm. When new firms enter the industry—for example, when Converse enters with Nike and Reebok—the demand curves specific to both Nike and Reebok shift to the left. When firms leave, the demand curves of the remaining firms shift to the right. The reason is that new firms take some of the quantity demanded away from existing firms, and when some firms exit, there is a greater quantity demanded for the remaining firms.

The difference between the graphs for a monopolist and a monopolistic competitor shows up when we move from the short run to the long run, that is, when firms enter and exit. This is illustrated in Figure 3. Note that the three graphs in the figure have exactly the same average total cost curve. The graphs differ from one another in that the location of the demand and marginal revenue curves relative to the average total cost curve is different in each. Graphs (a) and (b) represent the short run. Graph (c) represents the long run, after the entry and exit of firms in the industry.

Observe that the demand curve in graph (c) is drawn so that it just touches the average total cost curve. At this point, the profit-maximizing price equals average total cost. Thus, total revenue is equal to total costs, and profits are zero. On the other hand, in graphs (a) and (b), the demand curve is drawn so that there is either a positive profit or a negative profit (loss) because price is either greater than or less than average total cost.

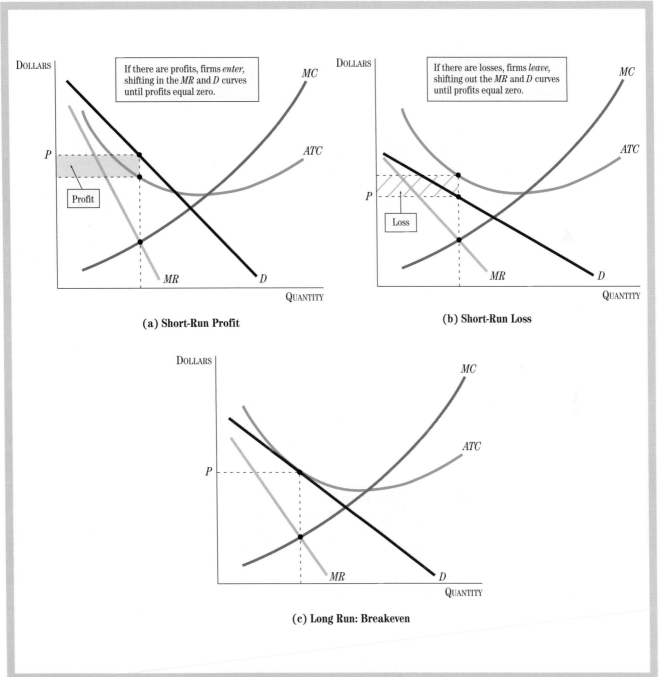

(a) Short-Run Profit

(b) Short-Run Loss

(c) Long Run: Breakeven

FIGURE 3
Monopolistic Competition

Each graph shows a typical firm in a monopolistically competitive industry. Firms enter the industry if there are profits, as in graph (a). This will shift the demand and marginal revenue curves to the left for the typical firm because some buyers will switch to the new firms. Firms leave if there are losses, as in graph (b). This will shift the demand and marginal revenue curves to the right because the firms that stay in the industry get more buyers. In the long run, profits are driven to zero, as in graph (c).

■ **The Short Run: Just Like a Monopoly.**   Consider the short-run situation, before firms either enter or exit the industry. The monopolistic competitor's profit-maximization decision is like that of the monopoly. To maximize profits, it sets its quantity where marginal revenue equals marginal cost. Because the monopolistically competitive firm faces a downward-sloping demand curve, its profit-maximizing price and quantity balance the increased revenue from a higher price with the lost customers brought on by the higher price. The marginal-revenue-equals-marginal-cost condition achieves this balance. The profit-maximizing quantity of production is shown by the dashed vertical lines in graphs (a) and (b) of Figure 3.

For example, ForEyes, Lenscrafters, and PearleVision are monopolistic competitors in many shopping areas in the United States. Each local eyeglass store has an optometrist, but each offers slightly different services. At a shopping area with several of these eyeglass stores, if one of them raises prices slightly, then fewer people will purchase glasses there. Some people will walk all the way to the other end of the mall to the store with the lower-priced glasses. Others, however, will be happy to stay with the store that raised its prices because they like the service and the location. These outlets are not monopolists, but the downward slope of their demand curves makes their pricing decision much like that of monopolists. The slope of the demand curve for a monopolistic competitor may be different from that for a monopolist, but the qualitative relationship between demand, revenue, and costs—and the firm's decisions in setting quantity and price—is the same.

■ **Entry and Exit: Just Like Competition.**   Now consider entry and exit, which can take place over time. In the model of long-run competitive equilibrium in Chapter 9, we showed that if there were economic profits to be made, new firms would enter the industry. If firms were running losses, then firms would exit the industry. Only when economic profits were zero would the industry be in long-run equilibrium, with no tendency for firms either to enter or to exit.

In monopolistic competition, the entry and exit decisions are driven by the same considerations. If profits are positive, as in graph (a) of Figure 3, firms have an incentive to enter the industry. Consider the market for skin care products. Beginning in the 1980s, liquid soap products, especially soaps scented with natural oils, were introduced by a few manufacturers and quickly caught on with consumers. Soon, virtually every manufacturer of soap and shampoo products began to offer liquid soap products fortified with vitamins and flavored by aromatics. In contrast, if profits are negative, as shown in graph (b) of Figure 3, firms have an incentive to exit the industry. During the dot-com boom of the late 1990s, several companies entered the business of home delivery of groceries. Perhaps the best known of these firms, Webvan, tried to differentiate its product by offering to deliver groceries within a 30-minute delivery window requested by the consumer. Despite a promising start, most of these new entrants were unable to make profits and left the industry. Webvan, for example, foundered after the costs of building its own warehousing and distribution network turned out to be far greater than the revenue it could earn from grocery sales.

As we move from the short run to the long run, the entry and exit of competing firms will tend to shift the demand curve for each of the firms remaining in the industry to the point at which the demand curve and the average total cost curve are tangent—that is, the point where the two curves just touch and have the same slope.

Entry into the industry will shift the demand curve of each existing firm to the left because the existing firms will be sharing their sales with the new firms. If Suave sells a new brand of shampoo similar to Pantene shampoo, then some consumers who had been buying Pantene will instead buy Suave's similar new shampoo. The demand for Pantene and other shampoos will therefore decline because of the availability of Suave's new product. Thus, the existing firms will see their demand curves shift to the left—each one will find that it sells less at each price. The differences in the positions of the demand (and marginal revenue) curves in the short run and the long run illustrate this shift. The shift in the demand curve causes each firm's profits to decline, and eventually profits decline to zero. (Recall that these are economic profits, not accounting profits, and are therefore a good measure of the incentive for firms to enter the industry.)

The case of negative profits and exit is similar. If demand is such that firms are running a loss, then some firms will exit the industry, leaving their share of sales to the surviving firms. This causes the demand curve facing the remaining firms to shift to the right until the losses (negative economic profits) are driven to zero. When Caribou Coffee closed in Ann Arbor, University of Michigan students bought coffee at other nearby coffee shops instead, increasing the demand for coffee at these nearby shops. This is illustrated by comparing graph (b) of Figure 3, where there are losses in the short run, with graph (c), where there are zero profits.

The Long-Run Monopolistically Competitive Equilibrium

There are two differences between monopolistically competitive firms and competitive firms in the long run. To see these differences, consider Figure 4, which replicates graph (c) of Figure 3, showing the position of the typical monopolistic competitor in long-run equilibrium, after entry and exit have taken place.

First, observe that price is greater than marginal cost for a monopolistically competitive firm. This was also true for the monopoly; it means that the market is not as efficient as a competitive market. Production is too low because the marginal benefit

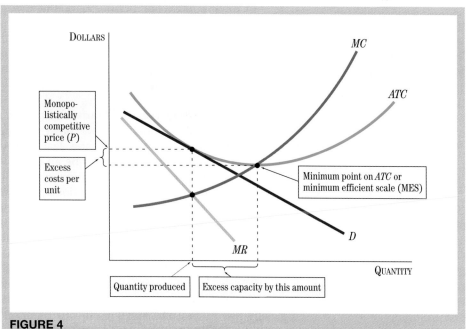

FIGURE 4
Excess Costs per Unit and Excess Capacity with Monopolistic Competition
In the long run, profits are zero for a monopolistically competitive firm, but the firm does not produce the quantity that minimizes average total cost. If the firm increases production, costs per unit will decline. In this sense, the firm operates at less than full capacity; it has excess capacity.

of additional production is greater than the marginal cost. Because each firm has some market power, it restricts output slightly and gets a higher price. The sum of producer plus consumer surplus is reduced relative to that in a competitive market. In other words, there is a loss of efficiency—a deadweight loss.

Second, as shown in Figure 4, the quantity produced is not at the minimum point on the average total cost curve, as it was for the competitive industry. That is, the quantity that the monopolistic competitor produces is at a higher-cost point than the quantity that the perfectly competetive firm would produce. Thus, monopolistically competitive firms operate in a situation of **excess costs.** If each firm expanded production and lowered its price, average total cost would decline. Each firm operates with some **excess capacity** in the sense that it could increase output and reduce average total cost. The firms choose not to do so because they have some market power to keep their prices a little higher and their output a little lower than that. Their market power comes from the downward-sloping demand curve that they face. For example, each coffee shop charges a little more and sells slightly fewer cups of coffee than it would in a perfectly competitive market.

excess costs: costs of production that are higher than the minimum average total cost.

excess capacity: a situation in which a firm produces below the level that gives the minimum average total cost.

■ Comparing Monopoly, Competition, and Monopolistic Competition.
Table 2 compares the different effects of competition, monopoly, and monopolistic competition.

A competitive firm will produce the quantity that equates price and marginal cost. A competitive market is efficient in that consumer surplus plus producer surplus is maximized and there is no deadweight loss. Average total cost is minimized.

In a monopoly, price is greater than marginal cost. A monopoly is inefficient because consumer surplus plus producer surplus is not maximized, so there is deadweight loss. Moreover, average total cost is not minimized. Economic profits remain positive because firms cannot enter the market.

In monopolistic competition, price is also greater than marginal cost. Thus, consumer surplus plus producer surplus is not maximized, and there is deadweight loss; average total cost is not minimized. However, profits are zero in the long-run equilibrium because of entry and exit. Monopolistic competition does not result in as efficient an outcome as competition. Monopolistic competition, as well as monopoly, is inefficient.

■ Product Variety versus Deadweight Loss.
When comparing monopolistic competition with competition, we must recognize—as with the comparison of monopoly and competition in the last chapter—that replacing monopolistic competition with competition may be an impossibility or require a loss to society. Remember that product differentiation is the key reason for monopolistic competition. We showed in the previous section that the variety of products that comes from product differentiation is usually something that consumers value. Some people like having both Pepsi and Coke. Roads and airports are better because

---

TABLE 2
A Comparison of Monopolistic Competition with Monopoly and Competition

Type of Model	Price	Deadweight Loss?	Average Total Cost Minimized?	Profit in Long Run?
Competition	$P = MC$	No	Yes	No
Monopolistic competition	$P > MC$	Yes	No	No
Monopoly	$P > MC$	Yes	No	Yes

of the different capabilities of earthmoving equipment sold by Caterpillar and Komatsu. Thus, eliminating monopolistic competition by having a single competitive product, whether Coksi or Catematsu, even if it were possible, would probably reduce consumer surplus by more than the gain that would come from competition over monopolistic competition.

More generally, product differentiation may be of sufficient value to consumers that it makes sense to have monopolistically competitive firms despite the deadweight loss. Or, to state it somewhat differently, the deadweight loss from monopolistic competition is part of the price consumers pay for the variety or the diversity of products.

R E V I E W

- The model of monopolistic competition is a hybrid of competition and monopoly. Entry and exit are possible, as in competition, but firms see a downward-sloping demand curve, as in monopoly, although there are many firms.

- The analysis of monopolistic competition in the short run is much like that of monopoly, but entry and exit lead to zero economic profits in the long run.

- Monopolistic competitors produce less than competitive firms and charge prices higher than marginal costs. Thus, there is a deadweight loss from monopolistic competition. In the long run, monopolistic competition produces less than the quantity that would minimize average total cost.

- The deadweight loss and excess costs can be viewed as the price of product variety.

OLIGOPOLY

Thus far, we have seen two situations in which firms have market power: monopoly and monopolistic competition. But those are not the only two. When there are *very few* producers in an industry—a situation termed *oligopoly*—each firm can have an influence on the market price even if the goods are homogeneous. For example, if Saudi Arabia—one of the major producers of crude oil in the world and a member of the Organization of Petroleum Exporting Countries (OPEC)—decides to cut its production of crude oil, a relatively homogeneous commodity, it can have a significant effect on the world price of oil. However, the effect on the price will depend on what other producers do. If the other producing countries—Iran, Kuwait, and so on—increase their production to offset the Saudi cuts, then the price will not change by much. Thus, Saudi Arabia, either through formal discussion with other oil-producing countries in OPEC or by guessing, must take account of what the other producers will do.

Such situations are not unusual. The managers of a firm in an industry with only a few other firms know that their firm has market power. But they also know that the other firms in the industry have market power too. If the managers of a firm make the right assessment about how other firms will react to any course of action they take, then their firm will profit. This awareness and consideration of the market power and the reactions of other firms in the industry is called **strategic behavior.** Strategic behavior also may exist when there is product differentiation, as in monopolistically competitive industries, but to study and explain strategic behavior, it is simpler to focus on oligopolies producing homogeneous products.

strategic behavior: firm behavior that takes into account the market power and reactions of other firms in the industry.

game theory: a branch of applied mathematics with many uses in economics, including the analysis of the interaction of firms that take each other's actions into account.

A common approach to the study of strategic behavior of firms is the use of **game theory,** an area of applied mathematics that studies games of strategy like poker or chess. Game theory has many applications in economics and the other behavioral sciences. Because oligopoly behavior has many of the features of games of strategy, game theory provides a precise framework to better understand oligopolies.

An Overview of Game Theory

Game theory, like the basic economic theory of the firm and consumer (described in Chapters 5 and 6 of this book), makes the assumption that people make purposeful choices with limited resources. More precisely, game theory assumes that the players in a game try to maximize their payoffs—the amount they win or lose in the game. Depending on the application, a payoff might be measured by utility, if the player is a person, or by profits, if the player is a firm.

However, game theory endeavors to go beyond basic economic theory in that each player takes explicit account of the actions of each and every other player. It asks questions like: "In a poker game, what should Mary do if Deborah sees her bet and raises her by $10?" The aims of game theory are to analyze the choices facing each player and to design utility-maximizing actions, or strategies, that respond to every action of the other players.

prisoner's dilemma: a game in which individual incentives lead to a nonoptimal (noncooperative) outcome. If the players can credibly commit to cooperate, then they achieve the best (cooperative) outcome.

payoff matrix: a table containing strategies and payoffs for two players in a game.

An important example in game theory is the game called the **prisoner's dilemma,** illustrated in Figure 5. The game is between Bonnie and Clyde, two prisoners who have been arrested for a crime that they committed. The **payoff matrix** shown in Figure 5 has two rows and two columns. The two columns for Bonnie show her options, which are labeled at the top "confess" and "remain silent." The two rows for Clyde show his options; these are also labeled "confess" and "remain silent." Inside the boxes, we see what happens to Bonnie and Clyde for each option, confess or remain silent. The top right of each box shows what happens to Bonnie. The bottom left of each box shows what happens to Clyde. Each year of prison sentence is considered to have a payoff of -1. Both Bonnie and Clyde would like to maximize their payoff, which means they would prefer a shorter sentence of 1 year (with a payoff of -1) to longer sentences of 5 years (with a payoff of -5) or 7 years (with a payoff of -7).

The police already have enough information to get a conviction for a lesser crime, for which Bonnie and Clyde would each get a 3-year jail sentence. Thus, if both Bonnie and Clyde remain silent, they are sent to jail for 3 years each, as shown in the lower right-hand corner of the table.

FIGURE 5
Two Prisoners Facing a Prisoner's Dilemma
Clyde and Bonnie are in separate jail cells, held for a crime they *did* commit. The punishment for each—in years in jail—is given in the appropriate box and depends on whether they both confess or they both remain silent or one confesses while the other remains silent. The top right of each box shows Bonnie's punishment; the bottom left of each box shows Clyde's punishment.

But Bonnie and Clyde each have the option of confessing to the more serious crime that they committed. If Bonnie confesses and Clyde does not, she gets a reward. If Clyde confesses and Bonnie does not, he gets a reward. The reward is a reduced penalty: The jail sentence is only 1 year—not as severe as the 3 years it would be if the prosecutor had no confession. However, the penalty for being convicted of the more serious crime in the absence of a confession is 7 years. Thus, if Bonnie confesses and Clyde does not, he gets a 7-year sentence. If both confess, they each get a 5-year sentence.

What should Clyde and Bonnie do? The answer depends on their judgment about what the other person will do. And this is the point of the example. Bonnie can either confess or remain silent. The consequences of her action depend on what Clyde does. If Bonnie confesses and Clyde confesses, she gets 5 years. If Bonnie confesses and Clyde remains silent, Bonnie gets 1 year. If Bonnie remains silent and Clyde remains silent, she gets 3 years. Finally, if Bonnie remains silent and Clyde confesses, she gets 7 years. Clyde is in the same situation as Bonnie.

Think about a strategy for Bonnie. Bonnie is better off confessing, regardless of what Clyde does. If Clyde confesses, then by confessing herself, Bonnie gets 5 years rather than the 7 years she would get by remaining silent. If, on the other hand, Clyde remains silent, then Bonnie is still better off by confessing because she only gets 1 year rather than the 3 years she would get by remaining silent. Hence, there is a great incentive for Bonnie to confess because she does better in either case.

Clyde is in the same situation. He can compare what his sentence would be whether Bonnie confesses or remains silent. In this case, Clyde is better off confessing regardless of whether Bonnie confesses or remains silent.

What this reasoning suggests is that both Bonnie and Clyde will confess. If they both had remained silent, they would have gone to jail for only 3 years, but the apparently sensible strategy is to confess and go to jail for 5 years. This is the prisoner's dilemma. The case where both remain silent is called the **cooperative outcome** of the game because to achieve this, they would somehow have to agree in advance not to confess and then keep their word. The case where both confess is called the **noncooperative outcome** of the game because Clyde and Bonnie follow an "everyone for himself or herself" strategy. Note that the cooperative outcome is preferred to the noncooperative outcome by both Clyde and Bonnie, yet both choose the option that results in the noncooperative outcome.

The mathematician and Nobel laureate in economics John Nash defined the noncooperative equilibrium—which economists call a **Nash equilibrium**—as a set of strategies from which no player would like to deviate unilaterally—that is, no player would see an increase in his or her payoff by changing his or her strategy while the other players keep their strategies constant.

cooperative outcome: an equilibrium in a game where the players agree to cooperate.

noncooperative outcome: an equilibrium in a game where the players cannot agree to cooperate and instead follow their individual incentives.

Nash equilibrium: a set of strategies from which no player would like to deviate unilaterally.

Applying Game Theory to Oligopolies

How do we apply game theory to determine the strategy of firms in an oligopoly? The easiest case is in an industry with only two firms. This is a particular type of oligopoly called *duopoly*. A prominent example of an industry characterized by a duopoly is the large commercial airplane manufacturing industry, where Boeing and Airbus have to plan their strategy taking the other's strategy into account. The competition between Netflix and Blockbuster in the mail-order DVD rental business is another example. In a duopoly, market supply is determined by the output of the two firms, so in deciding how much more to produce of a good, the firm has to consider its own additional costs of production, the change in the market price when it increases production, and how the other firm's subsequent response in terms of increasing or decreasing its production will affect the market price. A numerical example is worked out for you in the

ECONOMICS IN ACTION

A Duopoly Game

On October 10, the town of Pumpkinville will hold a farmer's market where folks can buy giant pumpkins to carve in time for Halloween. Jack and Jill are the only two producers of giant pumpkins in Pumpkinville—Jack has a farm 5 miles east of town, while his competitor, Jill, has a farm 5 miles west of town. Back in April, Jack and Jill planted the seeds; they cared for the pumpkins during the summer, and each now has 60 giant pumpkins ready to harvest. The day before the market, Jack and Jill have to decide how many pumpkins they should harvest and transport to the market. Both are profit maximizers who take costs and revenues into account. All the costs until today (seeds, fertilizer, water, labor, and so on) cannot be altered, and should not affect the decision of whether to send the pumpkins to market or let them rot on the ground. The only relevant cost is the $1 per pumpkin for harvest and transportation.

Jack and Jill also know that while the townsfolk love their pumpkins, they are not willing to pay *any* price. The market demand for giant pumpkins is Price = $241 − $2 × Quantity, where the quantity is the sum of what Jack and Jill independently and simultaneously bring to the market on October 10. For example, if Jack decides to harvest and transport 60 pumpkins, while Jill decides to send only 30, then the total quantity supplied to the market will be 90, and the market price for giant pumpkins will be $61 (241 − 2 × 90). As you can see, Jack's decision will influence the price that Jill receives for her pumpkins, and vice versa. This situation is perfect for game theoretic analysis.

To simplify our analysis, let's assume that Jack's and Jill's strategies are limited to three actions: They can bring either 30, 40, or 60 pumpkins to the market. With the information on cost, prices, and available strategies, Jack and Jill can build the payoff matrix in Figure 6.

The first step is to build the skeleton of the matrix. We know that there are two players—Jack and Jill—and three possible actions—30, 40, or 60 pumpkins. Thus, we build a three-by-three matrix with a total of nine blank boxes, one for each combination of Jack's and Jill's actions; the boxes are numbered for easy reference. Each of these boxes will be filled with the profits that Jack and Jill obtain given their actions. For example, in box 1, both Jack and Jill choose to harvest and transport only 30 pumpkins to the market. Let's calculate Jack's payoffs first. Total revenue will be the price of a pumpkin times the number of pumpkins sold by Jack. For this first box, Jack sells 30 pumpkins, while the market quantity is 60 pumpkins (30 from Jill's farm and 30 from Jack's), so the price is $121 (241 − 2 × 60) and total revenue is $3,630 ($121 times 30 pumpkins). Jack's relevant cost is $30 ($1 times 30 pumpkins). We subtract $30 from $3,630, and we get a payoff of $3,600 for Jack, which we write on the bottom left corner of the first box. The calculation for Jill is similar, and it also yields $3,600 (top right corner of the first box). The rest of the payoff matrix in Figure 6 is calculated in a similar way.

Jack and Jill are aware of the nine possible outcomes, and the question is how each of them is going to choose a quantity to deliver to the farmer's market. How many pumpkins each of them should harvest and bring to the market depends on how many the other person chooses to bring. So Jack and Jill engage in a mental exercise, each trying to figure out what the other will do.

Put yourself in Jill's shoes. She can easily see that her maximum payoff of $4,000 happens when she sends 40 pumpkins to the market while Jack sends only 30. However, Jill knows that Jack is a profit maximizer too, and if Jill sells 40 pumpkins, then Jack can increase his payoff from $3,000 to $3,200 by selling 40 instead of 30 pumpkins. So

accompanying Economics in Action feature. Economics and game theory predict that the outcome of the duopoly will be the Nash equilibrium of the game—the quantity levels at which neither firm has an incentive to deviate.

■ **Competition in Quantities versus Competition in Prices.** The model of oligopoly in which firms compete by choosing what quantities to produce, given the other firm's production decision, is called *Cournot competition* in honor of the French economist Augustin Cournot, who created the original version of this model in 1838 (Cournot did not use game theory and the concept of Nash equilibrium,

FIGURE 6
Payoff Matrix for Jack and Jill
The payoff matrix contains the profits for Jack and Jill for every possible combination of their actions. For example, in box 6, Jack sends 40 pumpkins to the market, while Jill delivers 60; the market quantity will be 100, and the price will be $41 (241 − 2 × 100). Jack's revenue will be $1,640 (40 × $41) and his cost will be $40 ($1 per pumpkin), and thus his payoff is $1,600 ($1,640 − $40). Jill receives the same price per pumpkin, but since she sold 60, her revenue will be higher ($2,460), with costs of $60 and a payoff of $2,400.

		Jill		
		30 pumpkins	40 pumpkins	60 pumpkins
Jack	30 pumpkins	1 $3,600 $3,600	2 $4,000 $3,000	3 $3,600 $1,800
	40 pumpkins	4 $3,000 $4,000	5 $3,200 $3,200	6 $2,400 $1,600
	60 pumpkins	7 $1,800 $3,600	8 $1,600 $2,400	9 $0 $0

box 2 cannot be a solution to Jill's and Jack's problem. Similarly, Jack's maximum payoff of $4,000 happens when he sends 40 pumpkins to the market while Jill sends only 30. But were he to do so, then Jill would be able to increase her payoff by selling 40 pumpkins instead of 30. So box 4 cannot be a solution.

Jack and Jill may soon independently realize that box 1 provides the highest combined payoff ($7,200). If they were to collude, then they could achieve this outcome, where each farmer produces 30 pumpkins and makes $3,600. This outcome is equivalent to the monopoly solution; by colluding, Jack and Jill are effectively acting like a single producer to maximize collective profits.

But they are unlikely to be able to sustain this collusive outcome. If Jill chooses to sell 30 pumpkins, once again Jack will have the incentive to increase his production and sell 40 pumpkins, leaving Jill with a lower profit. The same is true if Jack chooses to sell 30 pumpkins because Jill has the same incentive to sell 40 pumpkins, so box 1 does not work either.

At this point you can guess that we are looking for a combination of strategies from which neither player would like to deviate unilaterally—that is, a Nash equilibrium. By carefully exploring all the boxes and checking to see if either player has an incentive to deviate from that particular combination, we find that the only Nash equilibrium in this example is in box 5, where Jack and Jill sell 40 pumpkins each, for a payoff of $3,200 each. At that level, neither Jack nor Jill wants to produce more or less pumpkins, given the production of their competitor. That is the outcome of the duopoly situation.

which was not invented until 1950). Instead of competing in quantities, oligopolists can also compete in prices; this is called *Bertrand competition* for the French mathematician who reworked Cournot's model in terms of prices in 1883. We do not analyze the Bertrand model in this book, but it may be interesting to note that it predicts that with a homogeneous good, oligopolists will charge the same price and sell the same number of units as competitive firms would.

Comparison with Monopoly and Perfect Competition. How does the outcome for a duopoly compare to the outcomes for a perfectly competitive market and a monopoly? Figure 7 shows the demand and marginal cost curves for pumpkins in the case study involving the pumpkin duopoly. The intersection of demand and marginal cost represents the competitive equilibrium, where Jack and Jill each supply 60 pumpkins at a price of $1 and obtain zero profits. The maximum combined payoff is the monopoly solution, which occurs when each farmer sells 30 pumpkins at a price of $121 per pumpkin. The duopoly solution lies between the monopoly and competitive equilibria in terms of price, quantity, and profit.

explicit collusion: open cooperation of firms to make mutually beneficial pricing or production decisions.

■ **Collusion.**   Firms in an oligopoly know that their combined profits can be maximized if they act together as a monopolist. There are three ways in which firms might act together. The first is by **explicit collusion,** in which the managers communicate with each other and agree to fix prices or cut back on production. Although explicit collusion is illegal, it still happens. In the 1980s and 1990s, several firms in Florida and Texas were found guilty of agreeing to fix prices for milk sold to schools. In 1990, the Justice Department charged that several Ivy League universities colluded among themselves to offer similar financial aid packages to admitted students, thus depriving these students of the more generous aid packages that would have resulted from the schools competing with one another for the best students. The governments of many countries that produce oil routinely collude to cut back production and raise prices. A group of producers that coordinates its pricing and production decisions is called a **cartel.**

cartel: a group of producers in the same industry who coordinate pricing and production decisions.

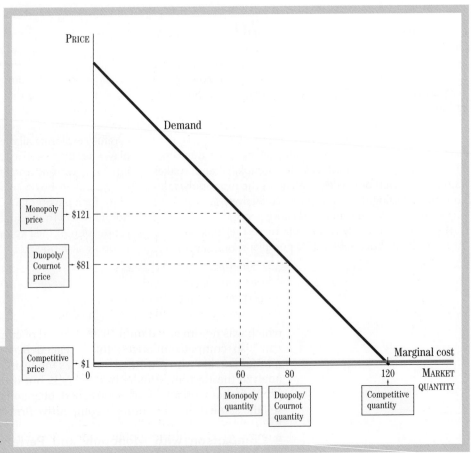

FIGURE 7
Comparison of Monopoly, Duopoly, and Competitive Equilibria
Prices and quantities for a Cournot duopoly lie between the equilibria for a monopoly and a competitive market.

tacit collusion: implicit or unstated cooperation of firms to make mutually beneficial pricing or production decisions.

price leader: the price-setting firm in a collusive industry in which other firms follow the leader.

Second, there might be **tacit collusion,** where there is no explicit communication between firms, but firms keep prices high by regularly following the behavior of one firm in the industry. The dominant firm is sometimes called a **price leader.** Third, the firms could merge and form a single entity.

■ **Incentives to Defect.** In oligopoly, game theory predicts that unless there is a way to bind each firm to cooperation, there is a tendency to defect. Since the defection results in a lower than monopoly price, consumers gain from the defection, and deadweight loss is reduced.

Incentives to Cooperate: Repeated Games

Although the prisoner's dilemma and the Cournot duopoly suggest that there is a tendency to the noncooperative outcome, there is a difference between the situation of the prisoners Bonnie and Clyde and the farmers Jack and Jill because Pumpkinville's farmer's market will probably be open for many years, allowing Jack and Jill to interact with each other in the future. Firms that interact with each other repeatedly may behave very differently from firms that interact only once. If the same game is to be played year after year—a repeated game—then the firms might be able to build up a reputation for not defecting.

Experimental economists have conducted experiments in which two people play the same prisoner's dilemma game over and over again. (The people in the experiments are given small monetary rewards rather than jail penalties!) These experiments indicate that people frequently end up using strategies that lead to a cooperative outcome. A typical strategy that people use is called "tit-for-tat." Using a tit-for-tat strategy, one player regularly matches, *in the next game,* the actions of the other player *in the current game.* For example, Clyde's tit-for-tat strategy would be to confess the next time the game is played if Bonnie confesses in the current game, and not to confess the next time the game is played if Bonnie does not confess in the current game. A tit-for-tat strategy gives the other player an incentive to follow the cooperative action—not confess—and thereby leads to a cooperative outcome. There are several other strategies that players can use to support a specific outcome in a repeated game.

■ **Secret Defections.** Even though reputational consequences may help firms better sustain a cooperative outcome, there are still incentives for firms to defect. The incentives for a firm to defect from an agreement will be greater if it is difficult for other firms to detect the defection. In the pumpkin example, it is impossible for Jack to increase his production without Jill's knowing it. This makes defection less likely. If one firm can secretly increase production or cut prices, enforcing the agreement will be more difficult. But it may be possible for a member of OPEC to sell oil to China under a secret agreement, or for a member of the world coffee cartel to ship coffee without being detected, at least for a while. The impact of such secret defections is much like the situation in boxes 2 and 4 in Figure 6. Profits to the defector increase, and profits to the other producers decrease. Consumers are better off because the quantity supplied to the market increases, helping to lower the price.

For a long time, Japanese construction firms operated a now well-known collusion scheme called *dango.* Firms took turns offering a slightly lower bid while all the other firms submitted high-priced bids to the government. This ensured that each construction firm would get periodic contracts that were very lucrative, without worrying about being undercut by its competitors. Ironically, and unfortunately for consumers, making the bids public made it harder for any firm to defect because firms in the agreement would know at once which firm had lowered its prices.

R E V I E W

- Game theory provides a framework for studying strategic behavior in an oligopoly. A game theory setting typically describes how the outcomes that a player can achieve by pursuing a particular strategy vary depending on the strategies pursued by the other players.

- A game theory setting can have a cooperative outcome, where the players agree to cooperate, or a noncooperative outcome, which is what results when players follow their individual incentives.

- The concept of a Nash equilibrium—a set of strategies from which no player wishes to unilaterally deviate—is used to identify the noncooperative solution.

- The prisoner's dilemma is a widely known example where the two parties will not be able to achieve the superior cooperative equilibrium, and instead have to settle for the inferior noncooperative equilibrium.

- Firms can compete with one another on the basis of quantity (Cournot) or price (Bertrand). The examples we look at in this chapter are for Cournot competition.

- Game theoretic concepts can illustrate why firms in an oligopoly will be tempted to defect from any agreement and not act like a monopolist. However, since there are only a few producers in the market, the outcome will not be the same as in the case of perfect competition. Prices and quantities for an oligopoly lie in between the solutions for a monopolist and for a competitive market.

- To the extent that a firm colludes, either explicitly or tacitly, it acts more like a monopolist and reduces economic efficiency by raising price above marginal cost.

- Repeated interactions among firms and the inability to defect secretly from an agreement make it more likely that collusive behavior among a group of firms is sustainable.

CONCLUSION

In this chapter, we have explored two different types of models—monopolistic competition and oligopoly—that lie in the complex terrain between competition and monopoly. The models were motivated by the need to explain how real-world firms—Johnson Publications, Liz Claiborne, Nike, and PepsiCo—and the members of OPEC operate in markets with differentiated products or with a small number of other firms or countries.

In the models introduced in this chapter, firms have market power in that they can affect the price of the good in their market. Market power enables a firm to charge a price higher than marginal cost. It is a source of deadweight loss. Observations of the behavior of actual firms show a wide variation in market power among firms.

The ideas about monopolistic competition and oligopoly discussed in this chapter are used by economists in government and businesses. Economists working in the U.S. Department of Justice use them to determine whether the government should intervene in certain industries, as we will explore in Chapter 12. Consultants to business use them to help firms decide how to differentiate their products from those of other firms.

Having concluded our discussion of the four basic types of models of markets in this chapter, it is useful to remember the important distinction between *models* and the *facts* that the models endeavor to explain or predict. None of the assumptions of these models—such as homogeneous products or free entry—hold exactly in reality. For example, when contrasted with the monopolistic competition model of this chapter, the model of competition, with its assumption of homogeneous goods, might seem not to apply to very many markets at all. Very few goods are exactly homogeneous. But when economists apply their models, they realize that these models are approximations of reality. How close an approximation comes to reality depends much on the application. The model of competition can be helpful in explaining the behavior of firms in industries that are approximately competitive, just as the model of monopoly can be helpful in explaining the behavior of firms in industries that are approximately monopolistic. Now we have a richer set of models that apply to situations far removed from competition or monopoly.

KEY POINTS

1. Firms that can differentiate their product and act strategically are in industries that fall between competition and monopoly.

2. Product differentiation—the effort by firms to create different products of value to consumers—is pervasive in a modern market economy. It helps explain intraindustry trade, advertising, and information services.

3. Monopolistic competition arises because of product differentiation. With monopolistic competition, firms have market power, but exit from and entry into the industry lead to a situation of zero profits in the long run.

4. With monopolistic competition, the firm sets the quantity produced so that price exceeds marginal cost. As a result, there is a deadweight loss, and average total cost is not minimized.

5. The deadweight loss and excess costs of monopolistic competition are part of the price paid for product variety.

6. Strategic behavior occurs in industries with a small number of firms because each firm has market power to affect the price, and each firm cannot ignore the response of other firms to its own actions.

7. The tools of game theory, such as Nash equilibrium, can help us identify the cooperative and noncooperative outcomes of strategic interaction by firms competing on the basis of quantity or price.

8. The price, quantity, and deadweight loss outcomes from an oligopoly are in between the outcomes from a monopoly and a competitive market.

9. Game theory suggests that collusive behavior will frequently break down, making noncooperative outcomes more likely.

10. Collusion is more likely when firms interact repeatedly in a market and secret defections can be prevented.

KEY TERMS

monopolistic competition	excess costs	payoff matrix	cartel
oligopoly	excess capacity	cooperative outcome	tacit collusion
product differentiation	strategic behavior	noncooperative outcome	price leader
intraindustry trade	game theory	Nash equilibrium	
interindustry trade	prisoner's dilemma	explicit collusion	

QUESTIONS FOR REVIEW

1. What is product differentiation?
2. What factors are relevant to the determination of optimal product differentiation?
3. Why is product differentiation an important reason for monopolistic competition?
4. What are two key differences between monopolistic competition and monopoly?
5. Why don't monopolistic competitors keep their average total cost at a minimum?

6. Why is the noncooperative outcome of a prisoner's dilemma game likely?
7. Why is duopoly like a prisoner's dilemma?
8. How does the market outcome for an oligopoly compare to the outcome for a monopoly? To the outcome for a competitive market?
9. What is the difference between explicit and tacit collusion?
10. Why are secret defections a problem for cartels?

PROBLEMS

1. Match the following characteristics with the appropriate models of firm behavior and explain the long-run efficiency (or inefficiency) of each.
   a. Many firms, differentiated product, free entry
   b. Patents, licenses, or barriers to entry; one firm
   c. Many firms, homogeneous product, free entry
   d. Few firms, strategic behavior

2. You are traveling by taxi in a South American city. When the taxi stops at a stoplight, you observe several people walking among the stopped cars offering apples for sale. Your taxi driver rolls down the window and purchases an apple from one of the vendors. You ask the taxi driver, "Why did you buy the apple from that vendor?" The driver replies, "I often buy from that vendor because the apple is always of excellent quality." In what market structure are the vendors operating at that site? Why?

3. Consider Al's gasoline station, which sells Texaco at a busy intersection along with three other stations selling Shell, Conoco, and Chevron.
   a. Draw the marginal cost, average total cost, demand, and marginal revenue curves for Al's station, assuming that the profit-maximizing price is greater than average total cost.
   b. Show Al's profits on the diagram.
   c. Explain what would happen in this situation to bring about a long-run equilibrium. Would more stations open, or would some leave?

4. Compare the long-run equilibrium of a competitive firm with that of a monopolistically competitive firm with the same cost structure. Why is the long-run price different in these two models? Which type of firm operates at a minimum cost? Draw a diagram and explain.

5. Suppose there are 10 monopolistically competitive restaurants in your town with identical costs. Given the following information, calculate the short-run price and quantity produced by each of the firms.

Each Firm's Demand		Each Firm's Costs	
Quantity	Price	Average Total Cost	Marginal Cost
1	10.00	12	—
2	8.00	9	6
3	6.00	8	6
4	4.00	9	12
5	2.00	10	14

   a. Would the price rise or fall at the typical firm in the long run? Explain.
   b. What would be the level of production if this industry were a competitive industry?
   c. If there is free entry and exit in both monopolistic competition and competition, why is there a difference in the quantity the typical firm produces?

6. Suppose the government places a sales tax on firms in a monopolistically competitive industry. Draw a diagram showing the short-run impact and the adjustment to the new long-run industry equilibrium. What happens to the equilibrium price and number of firms in the industry?

7. Which of the following conditions will tend to induce collusion among sellers in a market?
   a. The transactions are publicly announced.
   b. There are few sellers.
   c. Some sellers have lower costs than other sellers.
   d. The market is open for only one year.
   e. The sellers cannot meet one another.

8. How can firms in an oligopoly ensure that their industry earns the largest possible profit? Why is it likely that this outcome will not be reached? If this outcome is not reached, will there be a larger or a smaller deadweight loss in the market?

9. Two firms, Faster and Quicker, are the only two producers of sports cars on an island that has no contact with the outside world. The firms collude and agree to share the market equally. If neither firm cheats on the agreement, each firm makes $3 million in economic profits. If only one firm cheats, the cheater can increase its economic profit to $4.5 million, while the firm that abides by the agreement incurs an economic loss of $1 million. If both firms cheat, they earn zero economic profit. Neither firm has any way of policing the actions of the other.

a. What is the payoff matrix of the game if it is played just once?

b. What is the equilibrium if the game is played only once? Explain.

c. What do you think will happen if the game can be played many times? Why?

d. What do you think will happen if a third firm comes into the market? Will it be harder or easier to achieve cooperation among the three firms? Why?

10. Store A and Store B are the only two flower shops in a small town. The demand for a dozen roses is $P = 25 - Q$. Neither Store A nor Store B has any fixed costs, whereas the marginal cost of Store A is constant at $3, and the marginal cost of Store B is constant at $5. Each seller can sell either 5 dozen or 10 dozen roses, and they meet only once in this market.

a. Create the payoff matrix. Show your calculations and explain verbally as necessary.

b. Find the Nash equilibrium or equilibria. Explain verbally.

c. If there are multiple equilibria, which equilibrium do you think is most likely to occur and why?

Chapter 12

Antitrust Policy and Regulation

t was the biggest breakup that never happened. In April of 2000, a federal judge issued a ruling that software giant Microsoft should be broken up into two entities—one that sold operating systems and the other that sold its web browser, Internet Explorer, and the company's flagship Microsoft Office software. In issuing this ruling, the court concluded that "Microsoft maintained its monopoly power by anticompetitive means and attempted to monopolize the Web browser market, both in violation of [Section] 2 [of the Sherman Antitrust Act]." Subsequently, an appeals court overturned the ruling that Microsoft be broken up because certain actions of the judge who had issued the ruling had called his impartiality into question. The appeals court did, however, uphold the legal finding that Microsoft had a monopoly in the market for operating systems and was sustaining that monopoly by anticompetitive actions.

The U.S. government has been involved in many cases where it intervened to prevent a restriction of competition in an industry. When two office superstores, Staples and Office Depot, wanted to merge, the U.S. Federal Trade Commission objected and eventually succeeded in stopping the merger. When DIRECTV and Echostar, two competing satellite television providers, wanted to join together to form a single company, the Federal Communications Commission rejected the merger on the grounds that this would create a monopoly that would raise prices for satellite television customers.

The intent of the government in these cases was to promote competition, which we know is an essential ingredient of market efficiency. The models of monopoly and monopolistic competition that you studied in Chapters 10 and 11 showed that when firms have market power, they raise prices above marginal cost, reduce the quantity produced, and create a deadweight loss to society. In such cases, the government may be able to reduce the deadweight loss and increase economic efficiency by taking actions that can lead to increased competition.

In this chapter you will learn about some of the different ways the government can promote competition and regulate firms with market power. We consider two broad types of policy: (1) antitrust policy, which is concerned with preventing anticompetitive practices like price fixing and with limiting firms' market power by preventing mergers or breaking up existing firms, and (2) regulatory policy, in which the government requires firms that have a natural monopoly to set prices at prescribed levels. We will also talk about the limits and difficulties of government intervention. The government may step in and regulate markets even when there is no clear indication of anticompetitive behavior. In fact, because government agencies are susceptible to external influences, sometimes the regulators may end up limiting competition through their interventions. Understanding and appreciating the problems associated with both market failure and government failure is an important skill for an economist to possess.

ANTITRUST POLICY

antitrust policy: government actions designed to promote competition among firms in the economy; also called competition policy or antimonopoly policy.

Antitrust policy refers to the actions the government takes to promote competition among firms in the economy. Antitrust policy includes challenging and breaking up existing firms with significant market power, preventing mergers that would increase monopoly power significantly, prohibiting price fixing, and limiting anticompetitive arrangements between firms and their suppliers.

Attacking Existing Monopoly Power

Antitrust policy began in the United States more than 100 years ago in response to a massive wave of mergers and consolidations. Similar merger movements occurred in Europe at about the same time. These mergers were made possible by rapid innovations in transportation, communication, and management techniques. Railroads and telegraph lines expanded across the country, allowing large firms to place manufacturing facilities and sales offices in many different population centers. It was during this period that the Standard Oil Company grew rapidly, acquiring about 100 firms and gaining about 90 percent of U.S. oil refinery capacity. Similarly, the United States Steel Corporation was formed in 1901 by merging many smaller steel companies. It captured about 65 percent of the steel ingot market. These large firms were called *trusts*.

Sherman Antitrust Act: a law passed in 1890 in the United States to reduce anticompetitive behavior; Section 1 makes price fixing illegal, and Section 2 makes attempts to monopolize illegal.

The **Sherman Antitrust Act** of 1890 was passed in an effort to prevent these large companies from using their monopoly power. Section 2 of the act focused on the large existing firms. It stated, "Every person who shall monopolize, or attempt to monopolize . . . any part of the trade or commerce among the several states, or with foreign nations, shall be deemed guilty of a felony."

■ A Brief History: From Standard Oil to Microsoft.

It was on the basis of the Sherman Antitrust Act that Theodore Roosevelt's administration took action to break apart Standard Oil. After 10 years of litigation, the Supreme Court ruled in 1911 that Standard Oil monopolized the oil-refining industry illegally. To remedy the problem, the courts ordered that Standard Oil be broken into a number of separate entities. Standard Oil of New York became Mobil; Standard Oil of California became Chevron; Standard Oil of Indiana became Amoco; Standard Oil of New Jersey became Exxon. Competition among these companies was slow to develop, since their shares were still controlled by John D. Rockefeller. But as the shares were distributed to heirs and then sold, the companies began to compete against each other. Now the oil-refining companies have much less monopoly power. In fact, with the greater degree of competition, the Clinton administration allowed some of these firms to merge, although not into one single oil-refining firm. For example, on November 30, 1999, Exxon and Mobil merged to form a new firm called Exxon Mobil.

Soon after its success in splitting apart Standard Oil, the U.S. government took successful action under the Sherman Act against the tobacco trust, splitting up the American Tobacco Company into 16 different companies. It also broke up several monopolies in railroads, food processing, and chemicals. However, the government was not successful in using the Sherman Act against United States Steel. As part of the Standard Oil decision, the Supreme Court developed a **rule of reason** that required not only that a firm have monopoly power but also that it intend to use that power against other firms in a way that would restrict competition. Monopoly per se, in and of itself, was not enough, according to the Supreme Court in 1911. Since most competitors and customers of United States Steel said that the company's actions did not restrain competition, the Supreme Court, applying its rule of reason, decided in 1920 that United States Steel was not guilty under the Sherman Act.

Twenty-five years later, a 1945 Supreme Court decision that found Alcoa Aluminum guilty of monopolization refined the rule of reason to make it easier to prove guilt. Although a monopoly per se was still not enough, the intent to willingly acquire and maintain a monopoly—easier to prove than an intent to restrict competition—was enough to establish guilt.

In 1969 the U.S. government brought antitrust action against IBM because of its dominance in the mainframe computer market. After a number of years of litigation, the government dropped the case. One reason was rapid change in the computer market. Mainframes were facing competition from smaller computers. Firms such as Digital Equipment and Apple Computer were competing with IBM by 1982, when the government withdrew its case. Looking at the competition picture more broadly and recognizing that it had already spent millions, the government decided that antitrust action was no longer warranted.

The U.S. government took action against AT&T in the 1970s. It argued that AT&T, as the only significant supplier of telephone service in the nation, was restraining trade. As a result of that antitrust action, AT&T was broken apart and had to compete with MCI and Sprint in providing long-distance telephone service nationwide. This increase in competition lowered the cost of long-distance calls.

The most recent major case was brought against Microsoft. After several antitrust-related investigations, negotiations, and lawsuits in the 1990s, a federal judge found that Microsoft had monopoly power and used it to harm its competitors and consumers, and ordered the firm's breakup in June 2000. However, that order was reversed in 2001, and the federal government reached an agreement whereby the Justice Department proposed that Microsoft should instead permit computer manufacturers to install software from Microsoft's competitors and that Microsoft should make enough information about its operating system available so that other companies

rule of reason: an evolving standard by which antitrust cases are decided, requiring not only the existence of monopoly power but also the intent to restrict trade.

"This town isn't big enough for both of us— let's merge."

could write software that worked well with Microsoft's operating systems.

■ **Predatory Pricing.** Attempts by firms to monopolize by predatory pricing have also been challenged by the government and by other firms, though breakup is not usually the intended remedy. **Predatory pricing** refers to an attempt by a firm to charge a price below its shutdown point in order to drive its competitors out of business, after which it then forms a monopoly.

A 1986 Supreme Court decision, *Matsushita v. Zenith*, has made predatory pricing harder to prove. Matsushita and several other Japanese companies were accused by Zenith of predatory pricing of televisions in the U.S. market. After five years of litigation and appeals, the Court decided that there was not sufficient evidence for predatory pricing. The Court argued that the Japanese firms' share of the U.S. market was too small compared to Zenith's to make monopolization plausible. Moreover, the low price of the Japanese televisions seemed to be based on low production costs. Thus, the Court's majority opinion stated that this predatory pricing case appeared to make "no economic sense."

Predatory pricing is difficult to distinguish from vigorous competition, which is essential to a well-functioning market economy. For example, Wal-Mart has been accused of predatory pricing by smaller retailers, who find it is hard to compete with Wal-Mart's low prices. Yet, in many of these cases, it is likely that Wal-Mart is more efficient. Its lower prices are due to lower costs. In 1993, Northwest Airlines sued American Airlines for predatory pricing in Texas but lost. The jury decided that although American Airlines was charging prices below its shutdown point, it was not attempting to monopolize the market.

Merger Policy

There has been a decline in the frequency of government-forced breakups in recent years, which may be due to greater international competition or to the effectiveness of merger policy, which we now consider. For firms to occupy a huge share of the market, they must either grow internally or merge with other firms. If the government can implement a merger policy that manages to prevent the formation of firms with substantial market power, then there will be less need to break up firms because they have too much market power.

The Sherman Antitrust Act dealt with monopolies that were already in existence. The **Clayton Antitrust Act** of 1914 aimed to prevent the creation of monopolies and now provides the legal basis for preventing mergers that would significantly reduce competition. The **Federal Trade Commission (FTC)** was set up in 1914 to help enforce these acts along with the Justice Department.

To this day, the **Antitrust Division of the Justice Department** and the FTC have dual responsibility for competition policy in the United States. The Justice Department has more investigative power and can bring criminal charges, but for the most part, there is a dual responsibility.

How does the government decide whether a merger by firms reduces competition in the market? The economists and lawyers in the Justice Department and the FTC provide much of the analysis. They focus on the market power of the firm. The

predatory pricing: action on the part of one firm to set a price below its shutdown point in order to drive its competitors out of business.

Clayton Antitrust Act: a law passed in 1914 in the United States aimed at preventing monopolies from forming through mergers.

Federal Trade Commission (FTC): the government agency established to help enforce antitrust legislation in the United States; it shares this responsibility with the Antitrust Division of the Justice Department.

Antitrust Division of the Justice Department: the division of the Justice Department in the United States that enforces antitrust legislation, along with the Federal Trade Commission.

more concentrated the firms in an industry, the more likely it is that the firms have significant market power.

Herfindahl-Hirschman index (HHI): an index ranging in value from 0 to 10,000 indicating the concentration in an industry; it is calculated by summing the squares of the market shares of all the firms in the industry.

■ **The "Herf."** Concentration is usually measured by the **Herfindahl-Hirschman index (HHI).** This index is used so frequently to analyze the impact of mergers on the competitive structure of an industry that it has a nickname: the "Herf." The HHI is defined as the sum of the squares of the market shares of all the firms in the industry. The more concentrated the industry, the larger the shares and, therefore, the larger the HHI. For example, if there is one firm that controls the entire market, the HHI is $(100)^2 = 10,000$, the maximum value it can attain. If there are two firms, each with a 50 percent share, the HHI is $(50)^2 + (50)^2 = 5,000$. If there are 10 firms with equal shares, the HHI is 1,000. Values of the HHI for several hypothetical examples of firm shares in particular industries are listed in Table 1.

Observe that the HHI is not merely a measure of the number of firms that exist within an industry. The HHI tends to be lower when there are more firms in the industry but it also tends to be lower when all the firms' shares are more equal. Even when the number of firms in the industry is very large, the HHI can be large if one or two firms have a large share. For example, an industry with 20 firms in which one firm has 81 percent of the market and the others each have 1 percent has a very large HHI of 6,580, even greater than that of a two-firm industry with equal shares.

According to the *merger guidelines* put forth by the Justice Department and the FTC, mergers in industries with a postmerger HHI *above 1,800* are likely to be challenged if the HHI rises by 50 points or more. When the HHI is *below 1,000*, a challenge is unlikely. *Between 1,000 and 1,800*, a challenge is likely to occur if the HHI rises by 100 points or more.

Some examples are found in Table 1. Suppose that the two smallest firms in industry C in Table 1 merge and the industry thereby takes the form of industry B. Then the HHI rises by 32, from 3,376 to 3,408. Hence it is unlikely that the government would challenge this merger. In contrast, suppose that the two smallest firms in industry B merge. Then the HHI increases by 192, from 3,408 to 3,600, and the government would be likely to challenge the merger.

The HHI is used because it indicates how likely it is that firms in the industry after the merger will have enough market power to raise prices well above marginal cost, reduce the quantity produced, and cause economic inefficiency. For example, when the FTC blocked the merger of Office Depot and Staples in 1997, it stated that the "post-merger HHIs average over 3000" and that "increases in HHIs are on average over 800 points."[1]

contestable market: a market in which the threat of competition is enough to encourage firms to act like competitors. (Ch. 10)

The FTC or the Justice Department looks at other things in addition to concentration measures. Ease of entry of new firms into the industry is an important factor, as is the potential contestability of the market by other firms. Recall the idea of *contestable markets* discussed in Chapter 10: Even if firms are highly concentrated in

TABLE 1
Examples of the HHI in Different Industries

Industry Example	Number of Firms	Shares (percent)	HHI
A	3	40, 40, 20	3,600
B	4	40, 40, 12, 8	3,408
C	5	40, 40, 12, 4, 4	3,376

[1] Public Brief to D.C. District Court on *FTC v. Staples and Office Depot*, April 7, 1997.

TABLE 2
Price-Cost Margins in Several Industries

Industry	Price-Cost Margin
Food processing	.50
Coffee roasting	.04
Rubber	.05
Textiles	.07
Electrical machinery	.20
Tobacco	.65
Retail gasoline	.10
Standard automobiles	.10
Luxury automobiles	.34

Source: T. F. Bresnahan, "Empirical Studies of Industries with Market Power," *Handbook of Industrial Organization*, Vol. II, ed. R. Schmalensee and R. D. Willig (Amsterdam: Elsevier Science Publishers, 1989).

price-cost margin: the difference between price and marginal cost divided by the price. This index is an indicator of market power, where an index of 0 indicates no market power and a higher price-cost margin indicates greater market power. (Ch. 10)

market definition: demarcation of a geographic region and a category of goods or services in which firms compete.

an industry, potential entry by other firms provides competitive pressure on the industry. Thus, an industry with a high degree of concentration may, in fact, be acting competitively because of the threat of new firms coming into the business.

■ **Price-Cost Margins.** Another way of measuring market power is the *price-cost margin.* The greater the price (P) is above the marginal cost (MC), the more market power firms have. Table 2 gives some estimates of the price-cost margin [($P - MC$)/P] for firms in several different industries. The higher the price-cost margin, the more market power firms in the industry have. Observe in Table 2 that the price-cost margin is very small for coffee roasting, rubber, textiles, retail gasoline, and standard automobiles. The firms in these markets apparently have little market power. In contrast, the price-cost margin is very high for food processing and tobacco.

An interesting example is Anheuser-Busch, the producer of Budweiser beer. Before the introduction of Lite Beer by Miller, Anheuser-Busch had considerable market power; the price-cost margin was .3. After Lite Beer was introduced, the firm lost market power. The price-cost margin dropped to .03. Evidently Lite Beer made Miller a more visible player in the beer market and thus increased competition in the market in the sense that Anheuser-Busch's market power declined.

■ **Market Definition.** When measuring concentration in a market, the market definition is very important. A **market definition** is a demarcation of a geographic region and a category of goods and services in which firms compete. Table 3 shows the range of possibilities along the category dimension for market definition when considering the merger of soft drink producers. Should the market definition be narrow (carbonated soft drinks) or broad (all nonalcoholic beverages)? The market definition makes a big difference for concentration measures. In 1986, the FTC blocked a merger between Coca-Cola and Dr. Pepper that would have increased the HHI by 341 in the carbonated soft drink market. However, the HHI would have increased by only 74 if bottled water, powdered soft drinks, tea, juices, and coffee were also included in the market, along with carbonated soft drinks.

TABLE 3
Different Market Definitions in the Beverage Industry

						Milk
					Tea	Tea
				Coffee	Coffee	Coffee
			Juice drinks	Juice drinks	Juice drinks	Juice drinks
		Bottled water	Bottled water	Bottled water	Bottled water	Bottled water
	Powdered soft drinks	Powdered soft drinks	Powdered soft drinks	Powdered soft drinks	Powdered soft drinks	Powdered soft drinks
Carbonated soft drinks	Carbonated soft drinks	Carbonated soft drinks	Carbonated soft drinks	Carbonated soft drinks	Carbonated soft drinks	Carbonated soft drinks

Narrow Market Definition   **Medium Market Definition**   **Broad Market Definition**

ECONOMICS IN ACTION

The Issue: Are Mergers Good for the Economy?

The announcement of a potential merger between two large companies can send a shiver of anticipation rippling through the economy. Some of the anticipation is positive: The complicated financial and legal transactions involved imply a lot of work for investment bankers and lawyers, the shareholders of one or both companies may anticipate a sharp rise in the value of their holdings, and some consumers expect new and exciting products to emerge from the combined firm. But some of the anticipation will also be negative: Competitors are concerned about how the increased market power of the merged firm will affect their business, employees of the firms being merged worry that they will lose their jobs once the new firm begins eliminating duplicate positions, consumers worry that the new firm will raise prices, and government antitrust regulators worry about the impact of the merger on the degree of competition in the industry. Almost every merger that takes place in the economy will therefore have a constituency of supporters and a constituency of opponents.

The best way to understand the opportunities and concerns that arise when two firms decide to merge is to look at a specific example. The April 2004 merger between Fleet and Bank of America, a deal valued at $50 billion, concluded a process that began in October of 2003 when Bank of America announced its intention to buy Fleet. Shareholders of Fleet had to agree to the deal, and since the merger involved two banking companies, the Federal Reserve had to approve it before the two banks could join together. Over the next year, the new company (now called Bank of America) consolidated the two businesses and transformed Fleet bank branches into Bank of America branches.

SUPPORTERS: THE BANK OF AMERICA/FLEET MERGER IS GOOD FOR THE ECONOMY

Outside of Fleet and Bank of America's stockholders, no other entity's approval of the merger mattered more than the Federal Reserve's. In a detailed order issued on March 8, 2004, the Federal Reserve described why it thought the Fleet/Bank of America merger should be allowed to go ahead.[2] The Fed provided 60 days' notice for "interested parties" to submit their opinions on issues regarding the merger. Public meetings were held in San Francisco and Boston, and the Fed heard testimony from 180 interested parties and received written comments from more than 2,000 individuals and organizations. A large number of commenters supported the merger and commended the community development efforts of Fleet and Bank of America. But a large number of commenters opposed the proposed merger on the grounds that it would reduce lending to small businesses and in low- and middle-income areas; that it would reduce competition and increase industry concentration; and that job losses would result from branch closings and the elimination of Fleet's corporate headquarters in Boston. After considering how the merger would affect the HHIs in the New York and Florida markets, the Fed concluded that the merger would not result in the newly formed bank having too much market power.

Congress also held hearings on the merger. In testimony before the House Committee on Financial Services, Anne

---

[2] If you are feeling particularly inspired, you can read the entire report online at www.federalreserve.gov/boarddocs/press/orders/2004/200 40308/attachment.pdf.

Finucane, president of Northeast Bank of America, discussed the effects of the merger on employment and communities.[3] She concluded that:

- The impact of mergers on jobs depends critically on the type of merger. In an "in-market" merger, where two banks doing business in the same market join together, consolidation affects headquarters, back-office, and support operations as well as bank branches. But in "out-of-market" mergers, such as the proposed Fleet/Bank of America merger, only headquarters and back-office operations are affected. In fact, only two branches in Florida were closed as a result of the merger.

- The merged entity has cut almost 3,000 jobs in New England, but it plans to hire more employees, so that the overall reduction is around 1,800 jobs.

- Bank of America honored and exceeded all goals it had set for community lending in previous mergers. The same was true for Fleet when it merged with Bank Boston in 1999. The new entity could thus be trusted to be serious about fulfilling its pledge of $750 billion over 10 years.

CRITICS: THE BANK OF AMERICA/FLEET MERGER IS BAD FOR THE ECONOMY

There were many groups that strongly disapproved of the Bank of America merger on various grounds. Some of the strongest opposition came from the New England/Mid-Atlantic region, where politicians worried about the employment impact of layoffs and community advocates worried about what would happen to lending to local communities when a strong regional bank was replaced by a bank with a more national/international focus. Andrea Nuciforo, Jr., chair of the Massachusetts State Senate Committee on Banks and Banking, presented some of his concerns to Congress at the House Financial Services Committee hearings.[4]

- The history of bank mergers in Massachusetts has been one in which promises are made that jobs will not be cut, only to be followed by layoffs and replacements of full-time workers with part-time workers. When Fleet merged with Bank Boston in 1999, almost 4,000 jobs were cut. The *Boston Globe* reported that Bank of America intended to cut 12,500 jobs nationwide, including almost 850 in Massachusetts.

- While bank mergers are bad for many low-level employees who are laid off, they tend to be very lucrative for bank executives. This is true even for those executives who leave. Fleet's CEO received $20 million when Bank Boston and Fleet merged, the president of Fleet would get $17 million in the Bank of America merger, and two executives who left the company after the merger each received $20 to $25 million in severance packages.

Chris Cole, the regulatory counsel for the Independent Community Bankers of America (ICBA), a trade association representing community banks and smaller thrift institutions, also gave testimony before the House committee about the impact of bank mergers on smaller banks and bank competition.[5] ICBA was concerned about the concentration of banking in America and the effect that this concentration has on bank competition, consumers, small businesses, and communities. In his testimony, Cole reported that there is little evidence that mergers have benefited consumers through economies of scale. Large bank mergers often seem to result in higher prices to consumers. Fees charged to consumers by banks with a multistate presence tend to be significantly higher than the fees charged by banks with a single-state presence.

The ICBA recommended that large national banks like Bank of America be examined in the two years following the merger to see if they are indeed honoring their pledges and to compare their actual community spending with Fleet National Bank's programs prior to the merger.

---

[3] As with most nonclassified House committee hearings these days, you can find the testimony online at http://financialservices.house.gov/media/pdf/121404af.pdf.

[4] State Senator Nuciforo's testimony is available online at http://financialservices.house.gov/media/pdf/121404an.pdf.

[5] Mr. Cole's testimony can be read online at www.icba.org/advocacy/testimonydetail.cfm?ItemNumber=537&s n.ItemNumber=1699.

Defining the geographic area of a market is also a key aspect of defining the market for a good or service. In an integrated world economy, a significant amount of competition comes from firms in other countries. For example, in the automobile industry in the United States, there have been only three major producers. This is a highly concentrated industry. However, intense competition coming from Japanese, Korean, German, and other automobile companies increases the amount of competition. The rationale for challenging a merger is mitigated substantially by international competition.

■ **Horizontal versus Vertical Mergers.** Merger policy also distinguishes between **horizontal mergers,** in which two firms selling the same good or the same type of good merge, and **vertical mergers,** in which a firm merges with its supplier, as, for example, when a clothing manufacturer merges with a retail clothing store chain. The merger guidelines refer to horizontal mergers. Virtually all economists agree that horizontal mergers have the potential to increase market power, all else the same.

There is considerable disagreement among economists about the effects of vertical mergers, however. A vertical merger will seldom reduce competition if there are firms competing at each level of production. However, some feel that a vertical merger may aid in reducing competition at the retail store level.

horizontal merger: a combining of two firms that sell the same good or the same type of good.

vertical merger: a combining of two firms, one of which supplies goods to the other.

Price Fixing

In addition to breaking up firms and preventing firms with a great amount of market power from merging, antitrust policy prevents firms from conspiring to restrict competition. For example, when two or more firms conspire to fix prices, they engage in an illegal anticompetitive practice. **Price fixing** is a serious offense that is deemed to be illegal *per se* by Section 1 of the Sherman Antitrust Act.

Laws against price fixing are enforced by bringing lawsuits against the alleged price fixers. Suits can be brought both directly by the Justice Department and by individual firms that are harmed by price fixing; typically, the number of private suits greatly exceeds the number of government suits. Individual firms can collect **treble damages** (a provision included in the Clayton Act)—three times the actual damages. The treble damage penalty aims to deter price fixing.

price fixing: the situation in which firms conspire to set prices for goods sold in the same market.

treble damages: penalties awarded to the injured party equal to three times the value of the injury.

One of the most famous price-fixing cases in U.S. history occurred in the 1950s and involved Westinghouse and General Electric. Through an elaborate system of secret codes and secret meeting places, the executives of these two firms agreed together to set the price of electrical generators and other equipment that they were selling in the same market. Through this agreement, they set the price well above competitive levels, but they were discovered and found guilty of price fixing. Treble damages amounting to about $500 million were awarded, and criminal sentences were handed down; some executives went to prison.

A more recent price-fixing case involved the production of computer memory chips. Several firms, including the leading chipmaker Samsung, were fined $300 million for fixing prices for computer memory chips. Newspapers reported at the time that the fine was the second largest in U.S. history. Other notable cases included the 1996 suit filed by the Justice Department against the large agricultural firm Archer-Daniels-Midland (ADM) for fixing prices of animal feed and the 2001 settlement of a lawsuit brought against the legendary auction houses Sotheby's and Christie's by clients who had bought or sold items at auction. Both cases resulted in large fines: ADM paid over $100 million in fines, while Sotheby's and Christie's each paid over a quarter of a billion dollars in fines.

Vertical Restraints

The price-fixing arrangements just described are an effort to restrict trade in one horizontal market, such as the electrical machinery market or the market for computer memory chips. Such restraints of trade clearly raise prices, reduce the quantity produced, and cause deadweight loss. But there are also efforts by firms to restrain trade vertically by limiting the number of sellers of a particular product in a market. There are several ways in which trade in a product can be restrained vertically. For example, **exclusive territories** occur when a manufacturer of a product gives certain retailers or wholesalers exclusive rights to sell that product in a given area. This practice is common in soft drink and beer distribution. **Exclusive dealing** is the practice by which a manufacturer does not allow a retailer to sell goods made by a competitor. **Resale price maintenance** is the practice of a manufacturer's setting a list price for a good and then forbidding the retailer to offer a discount.

exclusive territories: the regions over which a manufacturer limits the distribution or selling of its products to one retailer or wholesaler.

exclusive dealing: a condition of a contract by which a manufacturer does not allow a retailer to sell goods made by a competing manufacturer.

resale price maintenance: the situation in which a producer sets a list price and does not allow the retailer to offer a discount to consumers.

Do vertical restraints reduce economic efficiency? There is considerable agreement among economists that manufacturers cannot increase their own market power by placing restraints on the firms to which they supply goods. A manufacturer's requirement that a retailer take a certain action with respect to the manufacturer's product does not give the manufacturer a greater ability to raise prices over competitors without losing sales. In addition, in some circumstances, such restraints may actually increase economic efficiency.

Consider resale price maintenance, for example. Suppose that low-price, low-service discount stores compete with high-price retail stores that provide lots of useful services to customers. If a discount store could offer the same product with little or no service, then people could go to the higher-price store, look the product over, get some useful advice from knowledgeable salespeople, and then buy at the discount store. In such a world, the high-service stores would disappear. Resale price maintenance can thus be viewed as a means of preserving stores that offer such service by preventing the discount store from charging a lower price.

Sometimes stores are able to maintain this high level of service by other means: High-end wedding dress stores will often remove the labels from wedding dresses so that prospective brides will not be able to try on dozens of dresses using the time and expertise of a knowledgeable store assistant, choose the perfect dress, and then go buy it for a much lower price from a discount store that provides no such service. But for most goods, resale price maintenance will ensure that there are more stores selling the product, some providing a high level of service for those who value that attribute over a lower price, and others offering a low level of service for those customers who value lower prices more than service. In 2007, the Supreme Court ruled that minimum resale price maintenance would no longer be illegal per se under the Sherman anti-trust act. Instead, such agreements would have to be examined on a case by case basis to determine if they were being used to reduce competition.

Similar arguments can be made for exclusive territories and for exclusive dealing. If McDonald's wants to allow only two franchises to serve a particular town, there is no reason why Wendy's or Burger King cannot open franchises in that town to cater to potential customers. If a producer wants to limit stores that carry its product from selling competitors' products, that would be no different from the case where a producer and a retailer are vertically integrated into one firm. For example, the Gap sells only its own products in its retail outlets. Why should a producer like Levi Strauss be treated differently and not be permitted to dictate that stores sell only Levis, were it to want to impose such a limitation?

Price Fixing in the Ivy League

This article is about a price-fixing case from the early 1990s, one that all college students can relate to. Almost two dozen leading colleges and universities were pooling information about students to make sure that schools had the "latest, most accurate assessment of students' financial needs." The Justice Department launched an investigation into whether the meeting constituted price fixing, in that the schools were limiting the ability to compete for students by offering them more financial aid (which would lower the price of college attendance).

Why the schools claimed they had the meeting

What the possible antitrust violation was

23 Colleges Won't Pool Fiscal Data

By SUSAN CHIRA

A continuing Federal investigation into possible antitrust violations by some of the nation's leading colleges has prompted them to cancel an annual information-sharing meeting in late March for the first time in more than 30 years.

The schools involved said they had agreed not to meet this year as "a sign of good faith" while discussions with the Justice Department continue, although they say the meetings are legal.

Since the 1950's, 23 of the most prestigious colleges in the United States have convened what they call "overlap" meetings to discuss financial aid for students who have applied to several of the schools. University officials say they have pooled information on students only to insure that each school has the latest, most accurate assessment of students' financial needs and to help insure that students choose a college based on academic and personal considerations.

But critics have said the meetings are part of a broader price-fixing enterprise, enabling colleges to reduce competition by setting similar tuitions and offering similar financial aid packages.

Disruption of Talks Feared

Although the Justice Department's antitrust investigation began in the summer of 1989, all but two schools attended last year's overlap meeting; Yale University and Barnard College did not.

The colleges decided to cancel the meeting this year because they feared disrupting discussions they have been holding with the Justice Department, according to Robert K. Durkee, Princeton University's vice president for public affairs.

"We know the department is concerned about overlap," Mr. Durkee said. "So, rather than divert the dicussion, it was decided that it was better as a sign of good faith not to go ahead, and to see if we couldn't keep pressing ahead with Justice."

Over the years, the 23 schools have met in two groups—one consisting of Ivy League schools and the Massachusetts Institute of Technology, and the second of other prestigious colleges in the Northeast. The original purpose, financial aid officers say, was to avoid bidding wars for talented students and to insure that students do not receive too much or too little aid.

How the Justice Department's interest in the case influenced the actions of the parties

"There may be government institutions that feel it makes sense to entice students with monetary awards, but I don't happen to share that point of view." said Jacqueline Foster, director of undergraduate financial aid at Yale.

Financial Analyses Compared

At the meetings, financial aid officials said, the participants usually compare their analyses of how much money a student's family can afford to contribute toward tuition.

For example, Ms. Foster said, a student might tell one university that a brother was also in college, but in another form sent later to another university the student might note that the brother had taken a semester off. The universities can then reduce the amount of financial aid offered.

Ms. Foster and Mr. Durkee said the colleges did not agree at the meeting on identical financial aid packages. But because most schools have similar aid allocation formulas, depending on a family's financial need, similar offers often emerge.

Now that the meeting no longer takes place, are schools competing more on financial aid? What was your experience when you applied to college?

Besides M.I.T. and Yale, the Ivy League members of the overlap group are Brown, Columbia, Cornell, Dartmouth, Harvard, Princeton and the University of Pennsylvania. The non-Ivy League members, besides Barnard, are Amherst, Bowdoin, Bryn Mawr, Colby, Middlebury, Mount Holyoke, Smith, Trinity, Tufts, Vassar, Wellesley, Wesleyan and Williams.

The list of schools involved

However, some argue that resale price maintenance is a way to reduce competition at the retail level. They see retailers having competitive pressure to keep prices low as more important than the possible loss of some retail customer services. In sum, there is more controversy among economists about the effect of vertical restraints than about horizontal restraints.

R E V I E W

- Breaking up monopolies, preventing mergers that would create too much market power, and enforcing laws against price fixing are the main government actions that constitute antitrust policy.

- These actions are backed by several important laws. Section 1 of the Sherman Antitrust Act outlaws price fixing, while Section 2 of the Sherman Antitrust Act allows the government to break up firms with monopoly power. The Clayton Antitrust Act provides the legal basis for merger policy.

- All these policies aim to increase competition and thus improve the efficiency of a market economy.

- The U.S. government has broken up several monopolies since the Sherman Act was passed, including Standard Oil, American Tobacco, and AT&T. In recent years the number of breakups of firms has decreased.

- The U.S. government also takes action to prevent mergers that can create too much market power. It uses tools like the Herfindahl-Hirschman Index (HHI) to gauge how competitive an industry is. The HHI tends to be lower, indicating more competition, when the market shares of firms are more equal and there are more such equal firms in the market.

- Both the U.S. government and private entities that have been harmed by higher prices can bring lawsuits against firms that conspire to fix prices. In recent years, several firms have been found guilty of price fixing and been fined hundreds of millions of dollars.

- Mergers and price restraints are differentiated into two types: vertical (suppliers, producers, manufacturers, and retailers of a particular product) and horizontal (firms selling the same product). Vertical mergers and vertical restraints on making markets are considered less likely to make markets anticompetitive than are horizontal mergers and horizontal restraints.

REGULATING NATURAL MONOPOLIES

The goal of antitrust policy is to increase competition and improve the efficiency of markets. Under some circumstances, however, using antitrust policy to break up a monopoly into several competing firms is not necessarily in the interest of efficiency. For example, to provide its services, a water company must dig up the streets, lay the water pipes, and maintain them. It would be inefficient to have two companies supply water because that would require two sets of pipes and would be a duplication of resources. Another example is electricity. It makes no sense to have two electric utility firms supply the same neighborhood with two sets of wires. A single supplier of electricity is more efficient.

Water and electricity are examples of *natural monopolies,* industries in which one firm can supply the entire market at a lower cost than two firms can. Recall from the discussion in Chapter 10 that the key characteristic of a natural monopoly is that the minimum efficient scale is larger than the size of the market; the average total

natural monopoly: a single firm in an industry in which average total cost is declining over the entire range of production and the minimum efficient scale is larger than the size of the market. (Ch. 10)

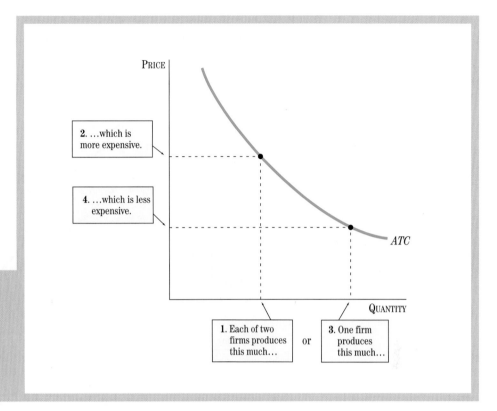

FIGURE 1
Natural Monopoly: Declining Average Total Cost

If two firms supply the market, dividing total production between them, costs are higher than if one firm supplies the market. The costs would be even greater if more than two firms split up the market.

cost curve is declining over the entire range of production. Average total cost declines as more is produced because fixed costs are very large compared to variable costs. Once the main line is laid for the water supply, it is relatively easy to hook up another house. Similarly, with electricity, once the main lines are installed, it is relatively easy to run wires into a house. A large initial outlay is necessary to lay the main water pipes or main electrical lines, but thereafter the cost is relatively low. The more houses that are hooked up, the less the average total cost is.

Figure 1 shows graphically why one firm can always produce more cheaply than two or more firms when the average total cost curve is downward-sloping. The figure shows quantity produced on the horizontal axis and dollars on the vertical axis; a downward-sloping average total cost curve is plotted. If two firms divide up the market (for example, if two water companies supply water to the neighborhood), then the average total cost is higher than if one firm produces for the entire market. It is more costly for two or more firms to produce a given quantity in the case of a declining average total cost curve than for one firm.

Methods of Regulating a Natural Monopoly

What is the best government policy toward a natural monopoly? On the one hand, having one firm in an industry will result in a lower average cost of production, but there will be inefficiencies associated with a monopoly: Price will be higher than marginal cost, and there will be a deadweight loss. On the other hand, breaking up the monopoly into two firms will result in more competition, but each firm will be saddled with a higher average cost of production and it will be inefficient to have both firms incur the high fixed costs. To get both the advantages of one firm producing at a lower average cost *and* a lower price, the government can regulate the firm.

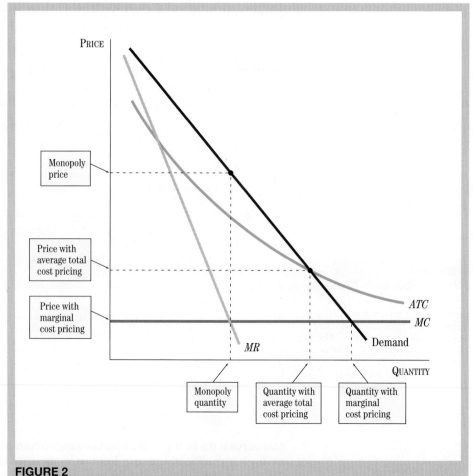

FIGURE 2
Monopoly Price versus Alternative Regulatory Schemes
Two alternatives, marginal cost pricing and average total cost pricing, are compared with the monopoly price. Marginal cost pricing gives the greatest quantity supplied, but since price is less than average total cost, the firm earns negative profits. Average total cost pricing results in a larger quantity supplied, and the firm earns zero economic profits.

The monopoly price and quantity of a natural monopoly with declining average total cost are illustrated in Figure 2. The monopoly quantity occurs where marginal revenue equals marginal cost, the profit-maximizing point for the monopolist. The monopoly price is above marginal cost. If the firm's price is regulated, then the government can require the firm to set a lower price, thereby raising output and eliminating some of the deadweight loss associated with the monopoly. There are three ways for the government to regulate the price: marginal cost pricing, average total cost pricing, and incentive regulation. We discuss each in turn.

■ **Marginal Cost Pricing.** We know that there is no deadweight loss with competition because firms choose a quantity of output such that marginal cost is equal to price. Hence, one possibility is for the government to require the monopoly to set its price equal to marginal cost. This method is called **marginal cost pricing.** However, with declining average total cost, the marginal cost is lower than average total cost. This is shown in Figure 2 for the case where marginal cost is constant.

marginal cost pricing: a regulatory method that stipulates that the firm charge a price that equals marginal cost.

Thus, if price were equal to marginal cost, *the price would be less than average total cost*, and the monopoly's profits would be negative (a loss). There would be no incentive for any firm to come into the market.

For example, if the regulators of an electrical utility use a pricing rule with price equal to marginal cost, there will be no incentive for the electrical utility to build a plant or produce electricity. Although the idea of mimicking a competitive firm by setting price equal to marginal cost might sound reasonable, it fails to work in practice.

▇ Average Total Cost Pricing. Another method of regulation would have the firm set the price equal to average total cost. This is called **average total cost pricing** or, sometimes, cost-of-service pricing. It is also illustrated in Figure 2. When price is equal to average total cost, we know that economic profits will be equal to zero. With the economic profits equal to zero, there will be enough to pay the managers and the investors in the firm their opportunity costs. Although price is still above marginal cost, it is less than the monopoly price; the deadweight loss will be smaller, and more electricity will be produced compared with the monopoly.

average total cost pricing: a regulatory method that stipulates that the firm charge a price that equals average total cost.

But there are some serious problems with average total cost pricing. Suppose the firm knows that whatever its average total cost is, it will be allowed to charge a price equal to average total cost. In that situation, there is no incentive to reduce costs. Sloppy work or less innovative management could increase costs. With the regulatory scheme in which the price equals average total cost, the price would rise to cover any increase in cost. Inefficiencies could occur with no penalty whatsoever. This approach provides neither an incentive to reduce costs nor a penalty for increasing costs at the regulated firm.

▇ Incentive Regulation. The third regulation method endeavors to deal with the problem that average total cost pricing provides too little incentive to keep costs low. The method is called **incentive regulation.** It is a relatively new idea, but it is quickly spreading, and most predict that it is the way of the future. The method projects a regulated price out over a number of years. That price can be based on an estimate of average total cost. The regulated firm is told that the projected price will not be revised upward or downward for a number of years. If the regulated firm achieves an average total cost that is lower than the price, it will be able to keep the profits, or perhaps pass on some of the profits to a worker who came up with the idea for the innovation. Similarly, if sloppy management causes average total cost to rise, then profits will fall because the regulatory agency will not revise the price.

incentive regulation: a regulatory method that sets prices for several years ahead and then allows the firm to keep any additional profits or suffer any losses over that period of time.

Thus, under incentive regulation, the regulated price is only imperfectly related to average total cost. The firm has a profit incentive to reduce costs. If a firm does poorly, it pays the penalty in terms of lower profits or losses.

Under incentive regulation, the incentives can be adjusted. For example, the California Public Utility Commission (the regulators of utility firms in California) has incentive schemes by which electrical utility firms and their customers share equally in the benefits of reduced costs and in the penalties from increased costs. This reduces the incentive to the firm in comparison to the case where the benefits and penalties are not shared.

Incentive regulation is sometimes made difficult by *asymmetric information*; that is, when one of the parties has access to more or better information. In this case, the regulated firm has more information than the regulator about its equipment, technology, and workers. Thus, the firm can mislead the regulator and say that its average total cost is higher than it actually is in order to get a higher price, as shown in Figure 3.

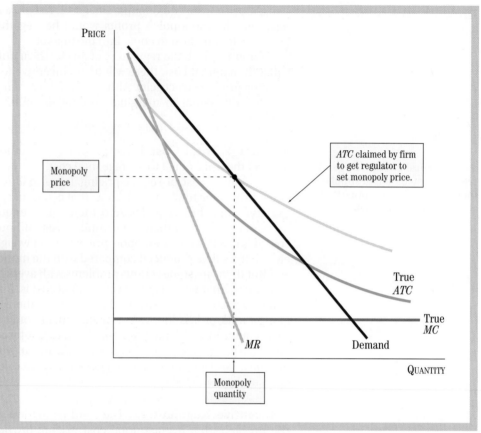

FIGURE 3
Asymmetric Information and Regulation

If a regulator uses average total cost pricing but does not have complete information about costs at the firm, the firm could give misleading information about its costs in order to get a higher price from the regulator. In an extreme case, shown in this figure, the firm could say its costs were so high that it could get the monopoly price.

R E V I E W

- A natural monopoly is said to exist when the minimum efficient scale is larger than the size of the market, implying that one firm can produce at a lower average total cost than two or more firms.

- A government may not want to allow a natural monopoly to exist unhindered, even though the single firm is producing at the lowest average total cost, because a monopoly creates deadweight loss. On the other hand, breaking up the natural monopoly can reduce deadweight loss but will also lead to inefficiently high costs of production.

- The solution is to allow a single firm to produce the output to take advantage of the declining average total cost, but regulate the firm so that it charges a price less than the monopoly price. There are several alternatives, including marginal cost pricing, average total cost pricing, and incentive regulation.

- If government regulates the monopoly by setting a price equal to marginal cost, the firm will run losses because for natural monopolies, average total cost tends to exceed marginal cost given the high level of fixed costs.

- If the government regulates the monopoly by setting a price equal to average total cost, it encourages firms to incur high costs because the price they are allowed to charge increases with costs.

- Incentive regulation is becoming the preferred method of regulation. By allowing firms to charge a price that is not revised up or down for a number of years, firms are encouraged to pursue strategies to lower costs and increase profits.

TO REGULATE OR NOT TO REGULATE

Our analysis thus far suggests that the government should regulate firms' prices in situations where natural monopolies exist. In practice, this requires deciding when a natural monopoly exists, which is frequently difficult.

There are many examples in American history of the government's regulating a firm's prices even when it is far-fetched to think of the firm as a natural monopoly. For example, for a long period of time, trucking was regulated by the federal government. Trucking regulation grew out of railroad regulation, which was originally justified when railroads were the only rapid form of transportation and thus were natural monopolies. Under trucking regulation, the federal government controlled which companies had permits to ship goods across state lines and also set uniform rates that the trucking firms could charge. Federal regulation of trucking was disbanded in the early 1980s. Studies have shown that trucking rates fell as a result.

Borderline Cases

Clearly, trucking is not a natural monopoly. The trucking industry is at the opposite end of the spectrum from water or electrical utility companies, which are almost always regulated.

But there are many borderline cases that are more controversial. Many of these arise in high-technology industries such as telecommunications and computing. An important example is cable television. In 1992, there was considerable debate about whether the federal government should regulate cable television. At first glance, it may appear that cable television is no different from electricity or water. Once a cable television company lays down the cable in a neighborhood, there is a fairly small cost to connect each individual house to it. On the other hand, there are alternatives to cable television for many homes. For example, over-the-air television channels do provide some competition to cable television. If one lives in an area where there are few over-the-air channels, there is little competition. However, if there are six, seven, or eight over-the-air channels, then there is more competition.

Until 1992, the Federal Communications Commission (FCC), the federal agency that regulates the telecommunications industry, measured competition by the number of over-the-air channels. At first, the commission decided that three over-the-air channels represented effective competition. It did not regulate cable television companies in areas where there were more than three over-the-air channels. Later on, when it noticed that prices of cable television were rising and consumers were complaining, the FCC raised the limit to six over-the-air channels. In 1992, Congress passed a law saying that it did not matter how many channels there were; the law required the FCC to regulate cable television firms in any case.

Over-the-air channels are not the only competition for cable television. People can use satellite dishes, which provide access to numerous channels at a price competitive with cable. Eventually, it may be possible to use the telephone wires to transmit television signals, in which case the telephone companies could compete with the cable television companies.

High-tech industries change quickly, and it is difficult for government regulators to keep up with the changes. Inflexible regulatory rules could slow innovation, but inadequate regulation could stifle competition. Recently, the FCC ruled that neither phone nor cable companies would be required to share their broadband connections with competitors like America Online. The FCC argued that such restrictions discouraged phone and cable companies from investing in high-speed Internet service. Critics of the FCC decision argued that this would reduce competition in the

Competition for Cable
Satellites provide customers in remote areas with a way of accessing television broadcasts. In more densely-populated areas, satellites provide competition to cable companies and help keep cable prices lower than they would be otherwise.

broadband market and limit high-speed Internet access. Both critics and supporters of the FCC decision argued that the action they advocated was what was needed to make sure that the United States does not fall further behind in broadband access compared to countries like South Korea.

The FCC often has to make decisions on issues like Voice over Internet Protocol (VoIP), a technology that allows people to make phone calls over the Internet, or Net Neutrality, a proposal to ensure that broadband providers would not be able to charge different rates to certain types of web sites, especially ones that provide telephone services or video and audio content. These issues involve technologies that were barely in existence a few years ago, and that will change and evolve very rapidly in the years immediately ahead.

Regulators as Captives of Industry

Government and government agencies are run by people who have their own motivations, such as being reelected or increasing their power, wealth, and influence, which may differ from doing what's best for society. Thus, despite the economic advice about what government regulatory agencies should do, the agencies may end up doing something else.

The railroad industry is an example of how regulators have sometimes ended up helping the industry at the expense of the consumer. Originally, railroads were considered to be a natural monopoly for moving goods across the country, and regulation was intended to reduce prices below the monopoly price. But as competition to the railroads from trucks and eventually airlines increased, the industry continued to be regulated. Eventually, the regulators were helping the industry; they kept prices from falling to prevent railroad firms from failing. Furthermore, to keep trucking firms from competing with the railroads, government authorities regulated trucking prices as well to keep them at a high level. The Teamsters Union, which represents truck drivers, was one of the strongest supporters of regulation because it knew that the regulations were keeping trucking prices high. In a sense, the regulators became captives of both the firms and the workers in the industry.

An economist, George Stigler, won the Nobel Prize for showing how regulatory agencies could become captive to the industry and therefore tend to thwart competition. The concern that regulators will become captives is one reason some economists worry about allowing the government to regulate a new industry, like broadband Internet. Eventually, the government may try to protect the broadband Internet operators in order to prevent them from failing. The government might limit competition in the future from DSL service or from fiber-optic lines laid by the telephone company or from wireless Internet providers.

The Deregulation Movement

deregulation movement:
begun in the late 1970s, the drive to reduce the government regulations controlling prices and entry in many industries.

Starting in the late 1970s under Jimmy Carter and continuing in the 1980s under Ronald Reagan, the **deregulation movement**—the lifting of price regulations—radically changed several key industries. The list of initiatives that constitute this deregulation movement is impressive. For example, air cargo was deregulated in 1977, air travel was deregulated in 1978, satellite transmissions were deregulated in 1979, trucking was deregulated in 1980, cable television was deregulated in 1980 (although regulation was reimposed in 1992), crude oil prices and refined petroleum products were deregulated in 1981, and radio was deregulated in 1981. There was also deregulation of prices in the financial industry. Prior to the 1980s, the price—that is, the interest rate on deposits—was controlled by the financial regulators. Regulation of brokerage fees was also eliminated. This deregulation of prices reduced deadweight loss. Airline prices have declined for many travelers, it is now cheaper to ship goods by truck or by rail, and both satellite television and satellite radio options are available for consumers.

But deregulation has its critics. Deregulation of the airline industry led to widespread fears that large airlines would dominate the industry because of their market power at the hubs. However, the large airlines are now so cost-heavy that smaller regional airlines have made significant headway in attracting even business travelers with their low-cost flights. Boston-based business travelers, for example, might be willing to suffer the inconvenience of traveling to Providence to take a cheaper Southwest Airlines flight rather than fly out of Boston on one of the large carriers. Also when price regulations are lifted, firms may figure out ways to price-discriminate. Price discrimination can be welfare-enhancing if it allows the firm to sell to a larger customer base, but clearly some groups will be unhappy. For instance, business travelers complain that they now have to pay more for air travel, although vacation travelers can pay less.

R E V I E W

- In many cases, determining whether or not a natural monopoly exists (and thus that price regulation is needed) is a challenge.

- There has frequently been price regulation where there is no natural monopoly, as in trucking. Continuing to regulate an industry long after it has ceased to be a natural monopoly will keep prices artificially high.

- With certain industries, such as cable television or broadband Internet access, it is much more difficult to definitively determine whether the industry is a natural monopoly. Fast-changing technology and the need to balance incentives for innovation with effective competition make the task of a regulator a challenging one.

- Regulators can also become captives of the industries they are assigned to regulate. If individuals are motivated more by personal gain than by societal benefit, they may use their regulatory power to protect the interests of the firms they regulate by thwarting competition rather than to protect the interests of consumers by enhancing competition.

- In response to economic analysis that showed that it is harmful to regulate the prices of firms that are not natural monopolies, many industries were deregulated in the 1970s and the 1980s. Trucking, airline, and railroad transportation prices are lower as a result of this deregulation.

- As with most economic changes, not everyone benefited, and not everyone agreed that all industries saw enhanced competition. Some industries, like cable television, were reregulated in the 1990s.

CONCLUSION

This chapter analyzed a key role of government in a market economy: maintaining competitive markets through antitrust policy or the regulation of firms. By reducing the deadweight loss due to monopoly, the government can reduce market failure and improve people's lives.

However, this analysis must be placed in the context of what in reality motivates government policymakers. The example of regulators becoming captives of industry reminds us that having an analysis of what should be done is very different from getting it done. Government failure is a problem that must be confronted just like market failure. Reducing government failure requires designing the institutions of government to give government decision-makers the proper incentives.

KEY POINTS

1. The government has an important role to play in maintaining competition in a market economy.

2. Part of antitrust policy is breaking apart firms with significant market power, although this technique is now used infrequently. Section 2 of the Sherman Antitrust Act provides the legal authority for challenging existing monopolies.

3. A more frequently used part of antitrust policy is preventing mergers that would cause significant market power. In the United States, the government must approve mergers.

4. Concentration measures such as the HHI are used to decide whether a merger should take place.

5. Price fixing is a serious antitrust offense in the United States, and the laws against it are enforced by allowing private firms to sue, providing for treble

damages, and allowing the government to ask for criminal penalties.

6. In the case of natural monopolies, the government can either run the firm or regulate a private firm. In the United States, the latter route is usually taken.

7. A natural monopoly can be regulated by using marginal cost pricing, average total cost pricing, or incentive regulation. Marginal cost pricing will discourage firms from making the investments needed to provide services, and average total cost pricing discourages firms from producing in a cost-efficient manner, so regulatory agencies have been using incentive regulation more frequently in order to give firms incentives to hold costs down.

8. Determining whether regulation is needed is a challenging task, especially in industries where technology changes very rapidly.

9. Even when regulation is needed, the regulator is vulnerable to regulatory capture—acting to protect the interests of the firms being regulated by thwarting competition instead of acting to protect the interests of consumers by enhancing competition.

10. In response to economic research showing that several industries were no longer natural monopolies and regulatory capture had taken place, many industries were deregulated in the 1970s and 1980s, including trucking and airlines.

KEY TERMS

antitrust policy
Sherman Antitrust Act
rule of reason
predatory pricing
Clayton Antitrust Act
Federal Trade Commission (FTC)

Antitrust Division of the Justice Department
Herfindahl-Hirschman index (HHI)
market definition
horizontal merger
vertical merger

price fixing
treble damages
exclusive territories
exclusive dealing
resale price maintenance
marginal cost pricing

average total cost pricing
incentive regulation
deregulation movement

QUESTIONS FOR REVIEW

1. What historical development gave the impetus to the original antitrust legislation in the United States?

2. What are the key laws that govern antitrust policy in the United States?

3. What are the different ways in which the government intervenes to promote competition in the economy?

4. What does the HHI measure? Under what type of market structure would the HHI be highest? When would it be lowest?

5. Why does the government allow firms affected by price fixing to file lawsuits and collect treble damages if they win?

6. Why are vertical mergers and price restraints considered less likely to be anticompetitive than horizontal mergers and price restraints?

7. Why would a government prefer a regulated natural monopoly to an unregulated natural monopoly or to breaking up the natural monopoly firm into several competing firms?

8. What are the different ways in which the government can regulate the price of a natural monopoly? Which of these methods is an improvement on the others?

9. What is regulatory capture? Why is it damaging for the economy?

10. Why is there more controversy about regulating industries where technology changes very rapidly?

PROBLEMS

1. Which legislation—Section 1 of the Sherman Act, Section 2 of the Sherman Act, or the Clayton Act—gives the government the authority to take action in each of the following areas: prosecuting price fixing, preventing proposed mergers, breaking up existing monopolies, suing for predatory pricing?

2. Consider an industry with 10 firms whose market shares are given in the following frequency table:

Market Share	Number of Firms
5 percent	2
10 percent	7
20 percent	1

a. Calculate the HHI for this industry.
b. Suppose one of the firms with a 5 percent market share announces a plan to buy the other firm with

a 5 percent market share. Is the U.S. Department of Justice likely to challenge the merger? Why or why not?

c. Suppose the firm with the 20 percent market share announces a plan to buy one of the firms with a 5 percent market share. Is the U.S. Department of Justice likely to challenge the merger? Why or why not?

d. Suppose one of the firms with a 10 percent market share announces a plan to buy the firm with the 20 percent market share. Is the U.S. Department of Justice likely to challenge the merger? Why or why not?

3. The following table shows the market shares of firms in three different industries.

Industry	Number of Firms	Shares	HHI
1	100	Each firm with 1 percent	
2	15	10 firms with 5 percent 5 firms with 10 percent	
3	3	1 firm with 60 percent 2 firms with 20 percent	

a. Complete the above table by calculating the Herfindahl-Hirschman index.
b. Will the FTC try to prevent a significant merger in industry 2? In industry 3? Why?

4. Compare the following two hypothetical cases of price fixing.
a. General Motors, Ford, and Chrysler are found to be coordinating their prices for Chevy Blazers, Ford Broncos, and Jeep Cherokees.
b. General Motors is coordinating with Chevy dealers around the country to set the price for Chevy Blazers.

Which is more likely to raise prices and cause a deadweight loss? Explain.

5. In 2007, the European Union sued Apple under its antitrust laws. Apple has established country-specific web sites for European customers of iTunes. The music inventory and prices vary among the different country-specific sites, and customers are prohibited from purchasing music from an iTunes site outside their country of residence. The European Union claims that this is an unlawful territorial sales restriction. Do you think Apple should be permitted to engage in this practice?

6. Why is it better to break up monopolies that are not natural monopolies rather than regulate them, even if it is possible to regulate them?

7. Sketch a graph of a natural monopoly with declining average total cost and constant marginal cost.
a. Show how the monopoly causes a deadweight loss.
b. Describe the pros and cons of three alternative ways to regulate the monopoly and reduce deadweight loss: marginal cost pricing, average total cost pricing, and incentive regulation.

8. The demand schedule and total costs for a natural monopoly are given in the following table.

Price	Quantity	Total Costs
16	6	82
15	7	87
14	8	92
13	9	97
12	10	102
11	11	107
10	12	112
9	13	117
8	14	122
7	15	127
6	16	132
5	17	137
4	18	142

a. Why is this firm a natural monopoly? What will the monopoly price be? Calculate profits.
b. Suppose the government sees that this is a natural monopoly and decides to regulate it. If the regulators use average total cost pricing, what will the price and quantity be? What should profits be when the regulators are using average total cost pricing?
c. If the regulators use marginal cost pricing, what will the price and quantity be? What are profits in this situation? Why is this policy difficult for regulators to pursue in practice?
d. Why might the government want to use incentive regulation?

9. Prior to 1982, AT&T had a monopoly on local telephone service throughout most of the United States. It also provided long-distance telephone service and did not give other companies access to its local telephone lines. As a result of the development of satellites, fiber-optic cable, and other technological advances, it became possible for other companies to provide long-distance service, but their lack of access to local lines seriously inhibited the development of this service. The Justice Department sued AT&T under the antitrust laws, and a 1982 settlement required AT&T to sell its local operating companies. In the years after 1982, the local operating companies gradually merged, and by 2006 almost all the local operating companies had merged together and rejoined with AT&T long distance. The U.S. Justice Department did not challenge the re-creation of the 1982 AT&T structure. What changes occurred between 1982 and 2006 that led to this lack of action by the Department of Justice?

10. In reflecting on a recent term of service, a former head of the Antitrust Division said, "I was convinced that a little bit of efficiency outweighs a whole lot of market power." Evaluate this statement by considering two sources of efficiency: decreasing average total cost and research and development. Describe how these should be balanced against the deadweight loss from market power.

Markets, Income Distribution, and Public Goods

Chapter 13

Labor Markets

After a long winter, many people wake up on March 1 with a sense of anticipation that spring is just around the corner. For many college seniors, however, the arrival of the month of March brings with it anxiety about life after graduation, rather than eager anticipation of the prospect of warm weather. When will they be able to find a job? How many more résumés and cover letters should they send out? What other networks of alumni and friends could they reach out to? Should they start looking for jobs in other cities? Would online sites like Monster.com be better than the job placement center at their university? These are all questions that run through many students' minds. The anxiety level only ratchets up as they hear about other friends who have found jobs, as they read articles about a possible recession looming for the U.S. economy, and as well-intentioned family and friends make the inevitable inquiries about how the college seniors are going to put their expensive education to use.

All these questions pertain to labor markets. If you asked yourself questions like "What occupation will offer the best jobs in the future?" and "What college major will provide the best chance of getting one of those jobs?" then you started thinking about the labor market long before you became a college senior. The odds are that you will be asking questions about the labor market long after you leave college as well. In your twenties, you will have to make decisions about moving to new locations and about leaving work temporarily to pursue graduate work or to raise a family; in your thirties, you will worry about having hit a ceiling in terms of your career progress and about whether it is too late to make a career switch; in your forties, you will worry about earning enough money at your job to pay for your kid's college or your own retirement; in your fifties, you will worry about whether you would be able to find a comparable job at your age were you to lose your job and about how you would cope without health insurance; and in your sixties, you will be trying to figure out how long to keep working and how to coordinate retirement decisions with your spouse. Labor markets are the most pervasive markets in the world, touching many more people directly than most markets do. For most people, income in the form of wages and salaries earned in the labor market is the largest source of lifetime earnings. Therefore, studying economics to develop a better understanding of how labor markets work is even more important than taking economics to learn more about how the stock market works.

For students of economics, the interest in labor markets is not confined to one's own experiences with it. There are many important economic policy issues related to labor markets that you may be interested in learning about. Why, for instance, do women earn less than men? Why do certain occupations that are vital to society, such as being a nurse, a firefighter, or a preschool teacher, pay less than other occupations that seem to have less of a beneficial social impact? What is the appropriate level of the minimum wage in the economy? What impact do labor unions have on wages and unemployment levels? These are all questions that can be answered only with an understanding of how labor markets operate.

In this chapter, we show how to use the standard supply and demand framework to study the labor market. As you might expect by now, the labor demand and supply model rests on the central economic idea that people make purposeful choices with limited resources and interact with other people when they make these choices. We will begin by reviewing some interesting facts about the labor market, and then explain how wages are determined and why wages change over time. This will help explain why there are gaps between the wages of skilled and unskilled workers, between the wages of women and men, and between the wages of union and nonunion workers. Even some of the problems caused by discrimination can be better understood using the standard tools of supply and demand.

THE MEASUREMENT OF WAGES

We begin our discussion of labor markets by defining what exactly is meant by "the wage" and showing how it is measured. We will also look at recent wage trends in the United States to see whether wages have been increasing or not, and if they were increasing, whether they were increasing more rapidly or more slowly than in the recent past.

Measuring Workers' Pay

When examining data on workers' pay, we must be specific about (1) what is included in the measure of pay, (2) whether inflation may be distorting the measure, and (3) the interval of time over which workers receive pay.

fringe benefits: compensation that a worker receives excluding direct money payments for time worked: insurance, retirement benefits, vacation time, and maternity and sick leave.

■ **Pay Includes Fringe Benefits.** Pay for work includes not only the direct payment to a worker—whether in the form of a payroll check, currency in a pay envelope, or a direct deposit into the worker's bank account—but also **fringe benefits.** Fringe benefits may consist of many different items: health or life insurance, when the employer buys part or all of the insurance for the employee; retirement benefits, where the employer puts aside funds for the employee's retirement; paid time off such as vacations and sick or maternity leave; and discounts on the company's products.

In recent years, fringe benefits have become an increasingly larger share of total compensation in the United States and many other countries. In the United States, fringe benefits are now about 30 percent of total pay; each worker costs about $27 an hour to employ, of which a little over $8 comes in the form of benefits. In 1960, fringe benefits were only about 8 percent of total pay.

wage: the price of labor defined over a period of time worked.

The term *wage* sometimes refers to the part of the payment for work that excludes fringe benefits. For example, a minimum wage of $5.15 per hour does not usually include fringe benefits. But in most economics textbooks, the term **wage** refers to the *total* amount a firm pays workers, *including* fringe benefits. This book uses the usual textbook terminology. Thus, the wage is the price of labor.

■ **Adjusting for Inflation: Real Wages versus Nominal Wages.** When comparing wages in different years, it is necessary to adjust for inflation, the general increase in prices over time. The term *nominal wage* is used to emphasize that a wage has not been corrected for inflation. The **real wage** is a measure of the wage that has been adjusted for changes in inflation. The real wage is computed by dividing the stated wage by a measure of the price of the goods and services. The most commonly used measure for this purpose is the consumer price index (CPI), which gives the price of a fixed collection, or market basket, of goods and services each year compared to some base year. For example, the CPI increased from 1 in the 1996 base year to 1.285 in 2006. This means that the same goods and services that cost $100 in 1996 cost $128.50 in 2006. Suppose the hourly wage for a truck driver increased from $10 to $20 from 1996 to 2006. The nominal wage increase would be 100 percent, but the real wage increased from $10 (= $10/1.00) to $15.56 (= $20/1.285), or an increase of 55.6 percent. Thus, because of the increase in prices, the real wage gain for the truck driver was less than the 100 percent stated wage gain would suggest. The real wage is the best way to compare wages in different years.

real wage: the wage or price of labor adjusted for inflation; in contrast, the nominal wage has not been adjusted for inflation.

■ **The Time Interval: Hourly versus Weekly Measures of Pay.** It is also important to distinguish between *hourly* and *weekly* measures of workers' pay. Weekly earnings are the total amount a worker earns during a week. Clearly, weekly earnings will be less for part-time work than for full-time work (usually 40 hours per week) if hourly earnings are the same. Because part-time work has increased and the average number of hours per week has declined in the last 30 years in the United States, weekly earnings for the average worker have increased less rapidly than hourly earnings.

Wage Trends

Having described how to measure wage trends, let's now look at what has happened to wages in the United States in recent years. Figure 1 shows average real hourly wages in the United States. In 2006, the average real wage was about $23.33 per hour (in year 2000 dollars), *including* a total of about $7.00 (in year 2000 dollars) in real fringe benefits.

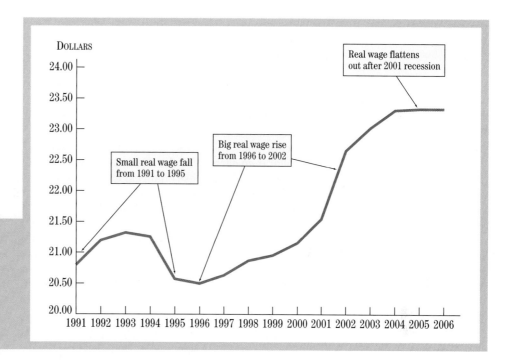

FIGURE 1
The Average Hourly Real Wage

In the United States, average real hourly wages (including fringe benefits) started to grow more rapidly in the mid-1990s before flattening out in the early 2005. (Wages are in year 2000 dollars.)

What is most noticeable in Figure 1 is that workers' pay began to rise more rapidly in the mid-1990s, after stagnating for several years. From 1996 to 2002, real wages rose by an average of 1.9 percent per year, a rate more than 6 times greater than the .3 percent average in the earlier years of the decade. Unfortunately, after 2002, real wages have become more stagnant again, growing at .75 percent a year. Later in this chapter we will provide an economic explanation for why real wages rose in the late 1990s after a period of stagnation and why they stagnated again.

Figure 1 shows the average real wage for all workers. What about the dispersion, or distribution, of wages across the population? Casual observation reveals large differences between the earnings of some people or groups and others. Sports celebrities and corporate executives are paid in the millions, many times the average wage in the United States. Workers with higher skills are paid more than workers with lower skills. College graduates earn more on average than those with a high school education or less. But there are other types of wage dispersions. For example, women on average earn less than men. Table 1 shows the differences in wages across some

TABLE 1
Hourly Real Wages, 2005

Management jobs	$38.59	Service jobs	$12.98
Goods sector	$25.86	Services sector	$22.81
Full-time	$24.84	Part-time	$11.90
Union	$29.68	Nonunion	$20.84
Workplace with less than 100 employees	$17.89	Workplace with over 500 employees	$30.50
Northeast	$24.54	South	$19.50
West	$23.13	Midwest	$21.58

categories of interest, including type of job, type of industry, size of employer, full- or part-time status, and geographic region.

The distribution of wages across workers has also changed substantially in recent years. One development that has received much attention from economists is that the pay gap between skilled and less skilled workers has increased. In the mid-1970s, college graduates earned about 45 percent more than high school graduates. In the 1990s, this was up to about 65 percent. Another change is in the wage difference between women and men, which, though still wide, has been narrowing in recent years. In the mid-1970s, women on average earned less than 60 cents for each dollar men earned. By the late 1990s, the gap had closed to around 76 cents.

What causes these changes? Can the economists' model of labor markets explain them? After developing the model in the next section, we will endeavor to answer these questions.

R E V I E W

- Workers' pay includes the direct payments of cash to the worker plus fringe benefits, which are about 30 percent of workers' pay in the United States.

- When you read about, or participate in, a discussion of wages, you should be clear as to whether it is about wages including benefits or wages without benefits, whether it is about the real wage or the nominal wage, and whether it is about an hourly wage or weekly earnings.

- Real hourly wages stagnated in the early 1990s, grew very rapidly from 1996 to 2002, then have slowed down again since then.

- Discussions about the average real wage in the economy must be accompanied by an understanding of how wages are dispersed by skill, gender, industry, occupation, size of firm, full- or part-time status, and geographic region.

- In recent times, the dispersion of wages between skilled and unskilled workers has increased, with college-educated workers gaining over those without a college education. The difference between the average wage of women and men is substantial, although it has narrowed in recent years.

THE LABOR MARKET

labor market: the market in which individuals supply their labor time to firms in exchange for wages and salaries.

The **labor market** consists of firms that have a demand for labor and people who supply the labor. In analyzing labor markets, economists stress their similarity to other markets; this enables economists to use the standard supply and demand model. To see the analogy, consider Figure 2, which illustrates a typical *labor market*. It shows a typical labor supply curve and a typical labor demand curve. On the vertical axis is the price of labor, or the wage. On the horizontal axis is the quantity of labor, either the number of workers or the number of hours worked. People work at many different types of jobs—physical therapists, accountants, mechanics, teachers, Web developers, judges, professional athletes—and there is a labor market for each type. The labor market diagram in Figure 2 could refer to any one of these particular types of labor.

The first thing to remember about the labor demand curve and the labor supply curve is that firms demand labor and people supply it. Labor—like other factors of

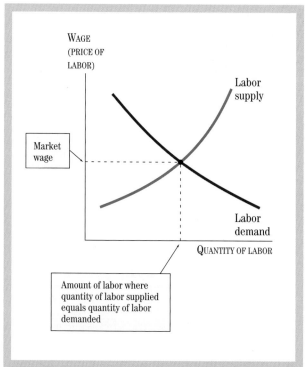

WAGE
(PRICE OF
LABOR)

Labor
supply

Market
wage

Labor
demand

QUANTITY OF LABOR

Amount of labor where
quantity of labor supplied
equals quantity of labor
demanded

FIGURE 2
Labor Demand Curve and Labor Supply Curve
The basic economic approach to the labor market is to make
an analogy with other markets. Labor is what is bought or sold
on the labor market. The demand curve shows how much
labor firms are willing to buy at a particular wage. The supply
curve shows how much labor workers are willing to sell at a
particular wage.

labor demand: the relationship
between the quantity of labor
demanded by firms and the wage.

labor supply: the relationship
between the quantity of labor
supplied by individuals and the
wage.

derived demand: demand for
an input derived from the demand
for the product produced with that
input.

production—is demanded by firms because it can be used to
produce goods and services; the labor demand curve tells us
the quantity of labor demanded by firms at each wage. The
labor supply curve tells us the quantity of labor supplied by
workers at each wage.

Note that the labor demand curve slopes downward and
the labor supply curve slopes upward, just like other demand
and supply curves. Thus, a higher wage reduces the quantity
of labor demanded by firms, and a higher wage increases the
quantity of labor supplied by people. Note also that the
curves intersect at a particular wage and a particular quantity of labor. As with any other market, this intersection predicts the quantity of something (in this case, labor) and its
price (in this case, the wage). Having defined the basics of
the labor supply and demand model, we will more closely
study how these curves are derived.

LABOR DEMAND

In this section, we look at **labor demand,** the relationship
between the quantity of labor demanded by firms and the
wage. In the next section, we look at **labor supply,** the relationship between the quantity of labor supplied by people
and the wage. We start with a single firm's demand for labor
and then sum up all the firms that are in the labor market to
get the market demand for labor.

In deriving a firm's labor demand, economists assume
that the firm's decision about how many workers to employ,
like its decision about how much of a good or service to pro-
duce, is based on profit maximization. The demand for labor is a **derived demand;** that
is, it is derived from the firm's decision about how many goods or services it can produce with the labor. The firm sells these goods and services to consumers in product
markets, which are distinct from the labor market. Labor and other factors of production are not directly demanded by consumers; the firm's demand for labor is derived
from consumers' demand for the firm's goods and services.

A Firm's Employment Decision

Recall how the idea of profit maximization was applied to a firm's decision about the
optimal quantity to produce: If producing another ton of steel will increase a steel
firm's profits—that is, if the marginal revenue from producing a ton is greater than
the marginal cost of producing that ton—then the firm will produce that ton of output. However, if producing another ton of steel reduces the firm's profits, then the
firm will not produce that ton.

The idea of profit maximization is applied in a very similar way to a firm's decision about how many workers to employ: If employing another worker increases the
firm's profits, then the firm will employ that worker. If employing another worker
reduces the firm's profits, then the firm will not employ the worker.

We have already seen that a firm produces a quantity that equates marginal revenue to marginal cost ($MR = MC$). The firm satisfies an analogous condition in
deciding how much labor to employ, as we discuss next.

TABLE 2
Labor Input and Marginal Revenue Product at a Competitive Firm

Workers Employed Each Week (L)	Quantity Produced (Q)	Marginal Product of Labor (MP)	Price of Output (dollars) (P)	Total Revenue (dollars) (TR)	Marginal Revenue Product of Labor (dollars) (MRP)
0	0	—	100	0	—
1	17	17	100	1,700	1,700
2	31	14	100	3,100	1,400
3	42	11	100	4,200	1,100
4	51	9	100	5,100	900
5	58	7	100	5,800	700
6	63	5	100	6,300	500
7	66	3	100	6,600	300
8	68	2	100	6,800	200
9	69	1	100	6,900	100

$\dfrac{\text{Change in } Q}{\text{Change in } L}$ P does not depend on Q. $P \times Q$ $\dfrac{\text{Change in } TR}{\text{Change in } L}$ or $P \times MP$

■ From Marginal Product to Marginal Revenue Product.

To determine a firm's demand curve for labor, we must examine how the firm uses labor to produce its output of goods and services. We start by assuming that the firm sells its output in a *competitive market*; that is, the firm is a *price-taker*. We also assume that the firm takes the wage as given in the labor market; in other words, the firm is hiring such a small proportion of the workers in the labor market that it cannot affect the market wage for those workers. Table 2 gives an example of such a competitive firm. It shows the weekly production and labor input of a firm called Getajob, which produces professional-looking job résumés in a college town. To produce a résumé, workers at Getajob talk to each of their clients—usually college seniors—give advice on what should go into the résumé, and then produce the résumé.

The first two columns of Table 2 show how Getajob can increase its production of résumés each week by employing more workers. This is the *production function* for the firm; it assumes that the firm has a certain amount of capital—word-processing equipment, a small office near the campus, and so on. We assume that labor is the only variable input to production in the short run, so that the cost of increasing the production of résumés depends only on the additional cost of employing more workers. Observe that the *marginal product (MP) of labor*—which we defined in Chapter 6 as the change in the quantity produced when one additional unit of labor is employed, holding other inputs fixed—declines as more workers are employed. In other words, there is a diminishing marginal product of labor, or diminishing return to labor: As more workers are hired with office space and equipment fixed, each additional worker adds less and less to production. For example, the first worker employed can produce 17 résumés a week, but if there are already 8 workers at Getajob, hiring a ninth worker will increase production by only 1 résumé.

Suppose that the market price for producing this type of résumé service is $100 per résumé, as shown in the fourth column of Table 2. Because Getajob is assumed to

marginal product of labor:
the change in production due to a one-unit increase in labor input, holding other inputs fixed. (Ch. 6)

be a *competitive firm*, it cannot affect this price. Then, the total revenue of the firm for each amount of labor employed can be computed by multiplying the price (P) times the quantity produced (Q) with each amount of labor (L). This is shown in the next-to-last column. For example, total revenue with $L = 3$ workers employed is $P =$ $100 times $Q = 42$, or $4,200.

The last column of Table 2 shows the **marginal revenue product (MRP) of labor.** *The marginal revenue product of labor is defined as the change in total revenue when one additional unit of labor is employed, holding all other inputs fixed.* For example, the marginal revenue product of labor from hiring a third worker is the total revenue with 3 workers ($4,200) minus the total revenue with 2 workers ($3,100), or $4,200 − $3,100 = $1,100. The marginal revenue product of labor is used to find the demand curve for labor, as we will soon see.

What is the difference between the marginal product (MP) and the marginal revenue product (MRP)? The marginal product is the increase in the *quantity produced* when labor is increased by one unit, holding other inputs fixed. The marginal revenue product is the increase in *total revenue* when labor is increased by one unit, holding other inputs fixed. For a *competitive firm* taking the market price as given, the marginal revenue product (MRP) can be calculated by multiplying the marginal product (MP) by the price of output (P). For example, the marginal product when the third worker is hired is 11 résumés; thus, the additional revenue that the third worker will generate for the firm is $100 per résumé times 11, or $1,100.

Observe in Table 2 that the marginal revenue product of labor declines as more workers are employed. This is because the marginal product of labor declines.

■ The Marginal Revenue Product of Labor Equals the Wage ($MRP = W$).

Now we are almost ready to derive the firm's demand curve for labor. Suppose first that the wage for workers with the type of skills Getajob needs in order to produce résumés is $600 per week (for example, $15 per hour for 40 hours). Then, hiring 1 worker certainly makes sense because the marginal revenue product of labor is $1,700, or much greater than the $600 wage cost of hiring the worker. How about 2 workers? The marginal revenue product from employing a second worker is $1,400, still greater than $600, so it makes sense to hire a second worker. Continuing this way,

marginal revenue product of labor: the change in total revenue due to a one-unit increase in labor input, holding other inputs fixed.

Wait: Before you read any further, make sure you can explain the difference between marginal product (MP) and marginal revenue product (MRP).

Looking for Work
These day workers are job hunting for construction cleanup work at a downtown street corner in Austin, Texas. The workers signal their availability by showing up at the street corner; labor contractors will come by and hire the number of workers they need that day.

we see that *the firm will hire a total of 5 workers when the wage is $600 per week*, because hiring a sixth worker would result in a marginal revenue product of only $500, less than the $600 per week wage.

Thus, if a firm maximizes profits, it will hire the largest number of workers for which the marginal revenue product of labor is greater than the wage; if fractional units of labor input (for example, hours rather than weeks of work) are possible, then the firm will keep hiring workers until the marginal revenue product of labor exactly equals the wage. Thus, we have derived a key rule of profit maximization: Firms will hire workers up to the point where *the marginal revenue product of labor equals the wage*.

The rule that the marginal revenue product of labor equals the wage can be written in symbols as *MRP* = *W*.

The Firm's Derived Demand for Labor

Now, to find the demand curve for labor, we need to determine how many workers the firm will hire at *different* wages. We know that Getajob will hire 5 workers if the wage is $600 per week. What if the wage is $800 per week? Then the firm will hire only 4 workers; the marginal revenue product of the fifth worker ($700) is now less than the wage ($800), so the firm will not be maximizing its profits if it hires 5 workers. Thus we have shown that a higher wage reduces the quantity of labor demanded by the firm. What if the wage is lower than $600? Suppose the wage is $250 a week, for example. Then the firm will hire 7 workers. Thus, a lower wage increases the quantity of labor demanded by the firm.

Figure 3 shows how to determine the entire demand curve for labor. It shows the wage on the vertical axis and the quantity of labor on the horizontal axis. The plotted points are the marginal revenue products from Table 2. To find the demand curve, we ask how much labor the firm would employ at each wage. Starting with a high wage,

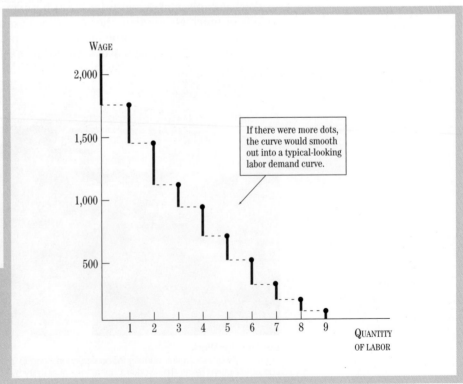

FIGURE 3
Determining a Firm's Demand Curve for Labor

The black dots are exactly the same as the marginal revenue product of labor in Table 2. The red line indicates the quantity of labor demanded at each wage.

we reduce the wage gradually, asking at each wage how much labor the firm would employ. At a weekly wage of $2,000, the marginal revenue product is less than the wage, so it does not make sense to hire any workers. Therefore, the quantity demanded is zero at wages above $2,000. At a weekly wage of $1,500, it makes sense to hire one worker, and so on. As the wage is gradually lowered, the quantity of labor demanded rises, as shown by the red line in Figure 3. The steplike downward-sloping curve is the labor demand curve. There would be more black dots and the curve would be very smooth if we measured work in fractions of a week rather than in whole weeks.

Observe in Figure 3 that a firm's demand curve for labor is completely determined by the firm's marginal revenue product of labor. We have shown why the demand curve for labor is downward-sloping: because the marginal revenue product of labor curve is downward-sloping. A higher wage will reduce the quantity of labor demanded, and a lower wage will increase the quantity of labor demanded, because workers with a marginal revenue product that is lower than the wage will not be hired. Changes in the quantity of labor demanded that result from changes in the wage are *movements along* the downward-sloping labor demand curve.

We also can explain why a firm's labor demand curve would *shift*. For example, if the price (P) of the good (résumés) rises—perhaps because the demand curve for résumés shifts outward—then the marginal revenue product of labor ($MRP = P \times MP$) will rise and the firm will be willing to employ more workers at any given wage level. This implies that the demand curve for labor will shift outward. Similarly, a rise in the marginal product of labor (MP) will also lead the firm to increase the quantity demanded of labor at each wage level, shifting the labor demand curve outward. On the other hand, a decline in the price (P) or a decline in the marginal product (MP) will shift the labor demand curve to the left.

■ **What If the Firm Has Market Power?** This approach to deriving the demand curve for labor works equally well for the case of a firm that is not a price-taker but is instead a monopoly or a monopolistic competitor. Table 3 shows an

TABLE 3
Labor Input and Marginal Revenue Product for a Firm with Power to Affect the Market Price

Workers Employed Each Week (L)	Quantity Produced (Q)	Marginal Product of Labor (MP)	Price of Output (dollars) (P)	Total Revenue (dollars) (TR)	Marginal Revenue Product of Labor (dollars) (MRP)
0	0	—	100	0	—
1	17	17	92	1,564	1,564
2	31	14	85	2,635	1,071
3	42	11	79	3,318	683
4	51	9	75	3,825	507
5	58	7	71	4,118	293
6	63	5	69	4,347	229
7	66	3	67	4,422	75
8	68	2	66	4,488	66
9	69	1	65	4,485	-3

Change in Q / Change in L · P declines with Q. · P × Q · Change in TR / Change in L

example of such a firm. The key difference between the firm in Table 2 and this firm is in the column for the price. Rather than facing a constant price for its output and thus a horizontal demand curve, this firm faces a downward-sloping demand curve: It can increase the quantity of résumés demanded by lowering its price. For example, if Getajob's résumés are slightly differentiated from those of other résumé producers in town, then the demand curve that Getajob faces when selling résumés may be downward-sloping.

Once we observe that the price and output are inversely related, we can continue just as we did with the competitive firm. Again, total revenue is equal to the price times the quantity, and marginal revenue product is the change in total revenue as 1 more worker is hired. Again, the marginal revenue product declines as more workers are hired, as shown in the last column of Table 3. However, now the marginal revenue product declines more sharply as more workers are employed, and it even turns negative. The reason is that as more workers are hired and more output is produced and sold, the price of output must fall. This cuts into revenue because all units, not just the last unit, are sold at the lower price. But the principle of labor demand is the same: Firms hire up to the point where the marginal revenue product of labor equals the wage. The marginal revenue product determines the labor demand curve.

In the case of a firm with market power, the simple relationship $MRP = P \times MP$ no longer holds, however, because the firm does not take the market price as given. Instead, we replace the price (P) by the more general marginal revenue (MR) in that relationship. This implies that the marginal revenue product is equal to the marginal revenue (MR) times the marginal product (MP). The relationship $MRP = MR \times MP$ holds for all firms, whether they have market power or not. Only for a competitive firm is $MR = P$.

■ **Market Demand for Labor.** To get the demand for labor in the market as a whole, we must add up the labor demand curves for all the firms demanding workers in the labor market. At each wage, we sum the total quantity of labor demanded by all firms in the market; this is illustrated in Figure 4 for the case of two firms producing résumés. The two curves on the left are the labor demand curves for two résumé-producing firms, Getajob and Careerpro. (The curves are smoothed out compared with that in Figure 3 so that they are easier to see.) The process of summing individual firms' demands for labor to get the market demand is analogous to summing individual demand curves for goods to get the market demand curve for goods. At each wage, we sum the labor demand at all the firms to get the market demand.

A Comparison of $MRP = W$ with $MC = P$

Note that a firm's decision to employ workers is closely tied to its decision about how much to produce. We have emphasized the former decision here and the latter decision in earlier chapters. To draw attention to this connection, we show in Table 4 the marginal cost when the wage is $600. Marginal cost is equal to the change in variable costs divided by the change in quantity produced. Variable costs are the wage times the amount of labor employed.

Now, consider the quantity of output the firm would produce if it compared price and marginal cost as discussed in earlier chapters. If the price of output is $100, the firm will produce 58 résumés, the highest level of output for which price is greater than marginal cost. This is exactly what we found using the $MRP = W$ rule, because 58 units of output require 5 workers. Recall that employing 5 workers is the profit-maximizing labor choice when the wage is $600.

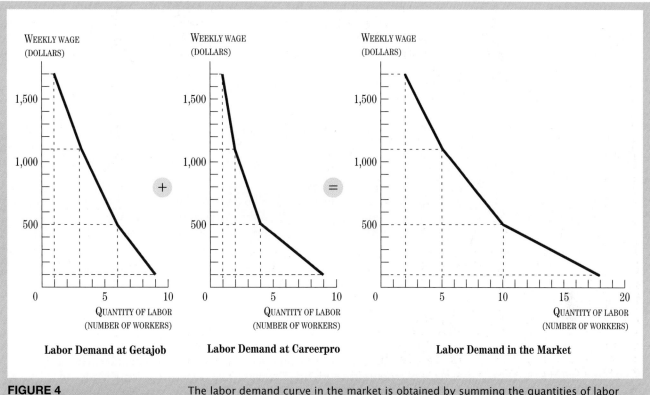

FIGURE 4
Summing Firms' Demands to Get the Labor Market Demand Curve

The labor demand curve in the market is obtained by summing the quantities of labor demanded by all the firms at each wage.

TABLE 4
Marginal Cost and the Production Decision at Getajob

Workers Employed Each Week (L)	Quantity Produced (Q)	Variable Costs (dollars) (VC)	Marginal Cost (dollars) (MC)
0	0	0	0
1	17	600	35
2	31	1,200	43
3	42	1,800	55
4	51	2,400	67
5	58	3,000	86
6	63	3,600	120
7	66	4,200	200
8	68	4,800	300
9	69	5,400	600

$600 wage × L

$$\frac{\text{Change in } VC}{\text{Change in } Q}$$

If the profit-maximizing firm could produce fractional units, then it would set marginal cost exactly equal to price ($MC = P$). The resulting production decision would be exactly the same as that implied by the rule that the marginal revenue product of labor equals the wage.

R E V I E W

- The demand for labor is a relationship between the quantity of labor a firm will employ and the wage, which is the price of labor

- The demand for labor is a derived demand because it is derived from the goods and services produced by labor.

- If the marginal revenue product of an additional worker exceeds the wage, the firm should employ that worker. If the marginal revenue product of an additional worker is less than the wage, the firm should not employ that worker.

- Accordingly, a profit-maximizing firm will hire workers until the marginal revenue product of labor equals the wage.

- When the wage rises, the quantity of labor demanded by firms declines. When the wage falls, the quantity of labor demanded increases. These are movements along the labor demand curve.

- When the marginal revenue product of labor rises, the demand curve for that type of labor shifts outward. The marginal revenue product of labor can increase if either the marginal product of labor rises or the price of the good produced using labor rises.

- The market demand for labor is obtained by adding up the labor demand curves of all firms looking for workers in the labor market.

LABOR SUPPLY

We now focus on *labor supply*. An individual's labor supply curve is derived from that person's decision about whether to work and how much to work, at different wage rates. The market labor supply curve is the sum of many people's individual labor supply curves. The decision about whether to work and how much to work depends very much on individual circumstances, so we begin by examining the individual's decision.

Work versus Two Alternatives: Home Work and Leisure

Consider a person deciding how much to work—either how many hours a week or how many weeks a year. As with any economic decision, we need to consider the alternative to work. Economists have traditionally called the alternative *leisure*, although many of the activities that make up the alternative to work are not normally thought of as leisure. These activities include "home work," like painting the house or caring for children at home, as well as pure leisure time, such as simply talking to friends on the telephone, going bowling, or hiking in the country. The price of leisure is the opportunity cost of not working, that is, the wage. If a person's marginal benefit from more leisure is greater than the wage, then the person will choose more leisure. The decision to consume more leisure is thus like the decision to consume more of any other good. This may seem strange, but the analogy works quite well in practice.

▓ **Effects of Wage Changes: Income and Substitution Effects.** Like the decision to consume a commodity, the decision to work can be analyzed with the concepts of the *substitution effect* and the *income effect*.

Recall that the *substitution effect* says that a higher price for a good will make that good less attractive to purchase relative to alternatives. In the case of the labor market, since the wage is the price of leisure (or home work), the higher the wage, the less attractive leisure (or home work) will seem relative to work. In other words, a higher wage makes work more rewarding compared to the alternatives. So even if you really enjoy your nonwork activities, including sleeping, watching movies, playing video games, or even studying, if the wage paid for part-time student employment triples from $10 an hour to $30 an hour, you would be more likely to sacrifice these nonwork activities and work an extra hour each day. The sacrifice—less time to study, sleep, watch TV, and so on—will be worth the higher wage. Therefore, the quantity of labor supplied tends to increase when the wage rises because of the substitution effect.

Recall also that the *income effect* reflects the fact that changes in the price of a good either reduce (if a price increase) or expand (if a price decrease) your ability to buy all goods, even ones whose prices have not changed, by changing your real income. In the case of the labor market, a higher wage will increase the real income of an individual and enable that individual to buy more of all goods, including leisure. For example, if you were working 10 hours a week at a wage of $10 an hour, you might decide that at a wage of $30 an hour, you would be happier working 5 hours a week and enjoying 5 more hours of leisure. Note that in this case, even after working fewer hours, you have more money to buy other goods. The income effect works in the opposite direction from the substitution effect: The quantity of labor supplied tends to decrease, rather than increase, when the wage rises because of the income effect.

▓ **The Shape of Supply Curves.** Because the substitution effect and the income effect work in opposite directions, the labor supply curve can slope either upward or downward. The supply curve slopes upward if the substitution effect dominates—as the wage rises, individuals work more because the price of leisure (the opportunity cost of not working) rises. The labor supply curve slopes downward if the income effect dominates—as the wage rises, individuals choose to work less because they can earn as much if not more money by working fewer hours. Several possibilities for the shape of a labor supply curve are illustrated in Figure 5.

Moreover, the same supply curve may slope upward for some range of wages and downward for another range. For example, at high wage levels—when people earn enough to take long vacations—the income effect may dominate. At lower wages, the substitution effect may be dominant. This would then result in a **backward-bending labor supply curve,** as shown in Figure 6.

This derivation of the labor supply curve may seem unrealistic. After all, the workweek is 40 hours for many jobs; you may not have much choice about the number of hours you work per week. In fact, the sensitivity of the quantity of labor supplied to the wage is probably small for many workers. But economists have shown that the effect is large for some workers, and therefore it is useful to distinguish one worker's supply curve from another's.

In a family with two adults and children, for example, one of the adults may already have a job and the other may be choosing between working at home and working outside the home. This decision may be very sensitive to the wage and perhaps the cost of child care or of consuming more prepared meals. In fact, the

backward-bending labor supply curve: the situation in which the income effect outweighs the substitution effect of an increase in the wage at higher levels of income, causing the labor supply curve to bend back and take on a negative slope.

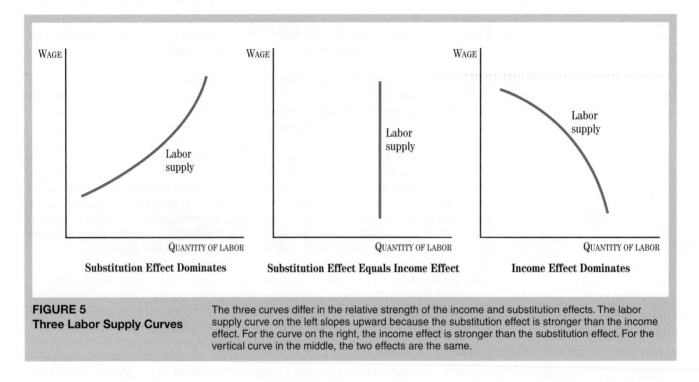

FIGURE 5
Three Labor Supply Curves

The three curves differ in the relative strength of the income and substitution effects. The labor supply curve on the left slopes upward because the substitution effect is stronger than the income effect. For the curve on the right, the income effect is stronger than the substitution effect. For the vertical curve in the middle, the two effects are the same.

increased number of women working outside the home may be due to the increased opportunities and wages for women. The increase in the wage induces workers to work more in the labor market. Economists have observed a fairly strong wage effect on the amount women work, as illustrated in the Economics in the News box on page 365.

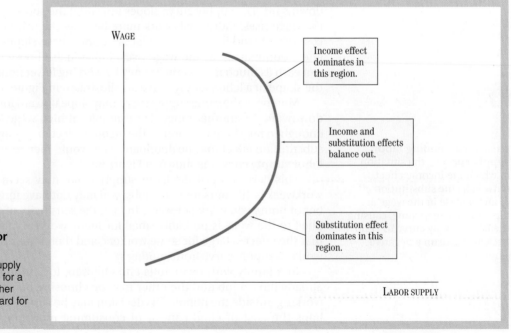

FIGURE 6
Backward-Bending Labor Supply Curve

A person may have a labor supply curve that is positively sloped for a low wage, is steeper for a higher wage, and then bends backward for a still higher wage.

Incentives to Work

As more and more families have two potential workers, the decision about labor supply has become a household decision. This newspaper article from the *San Jose Mercury News* (February 14, 1993) tells a story that pairs the human side of the decision with the economic side. According to the calculations in the table, the net earnings from work—after taxes and all other expenses—may be very small in some cases.

Many parents finally decide it doesn't pay to have two incomes any longer, once they account for the cost of child care and other work-related expenses. Here are budget comparisons for two hypothetical couples trying to decide if the lower-paid spouse should stay home with their one child—and the fiscal impact the decision will have on their current standard of living.

Does It Pay to Stay Home?

By MARK SCHWANHAUSSER
Mercury News staff writer

For Yolanda Achanzar, going to work was like listening to an old-fashioned cash register ring. She'd drop off her two toddlers with a sitter (*ka-ching*: $29 a day). She'd commute to the office in her Mercury Villager (*ka-ching*: $8). She'd dig into her purse for breakfast and lunch (*ka-ching*: $10). And she'd dress up for work (*ka-ching*: $5 a day, $8.50 if she snagged her hose, $12.50 if you include the dry-cleaning bills). "If you add all that up," she said, "it's just not worth it, vs. the time you could have spent with your children, loving them, rearing them, nurturing them."

And so, although she loved her job and co-workers, although her $25,000 paycheck accounted for nearly 40 percent of her family's total income, she chucked her job Friday to stay home with 27-month-old Marissa and 14-month-old Jordan. She felt she simply couldn't afford her job any longer.

Achanzar and her husband, Gil, are among the millions of American parents who agonize trying to discover the proper mix for a family's financial welfare, the children's care and the parents' careers. For them, money is an issue—and something has to give.

For many parents, the decision starts with a bottom-line analysis of dollars in and dollars out. But next comes the long-term equation that consists of nothing but variables. How much is it worth to stay home with the kids? What lifestyle will we have?

	Both spouses work	One stays home	Both spouses work	One stays home
Income				
Spouse A	$35,600	$35,600	$67,000	$67,000
Spouse B	24,000	0	35,000	0
Total Income	**59,600**	**35,600**	**102,000**	**67,000**
Taxes[1]				
Taxable income	46,700	22,700	89,100	54,100
Federal	7,949	2,929	19,900	10,091
State	1,938	383	5,866	2,564
Social Security	4,559	2,723	7,091	4,413
Total taxes	**14,446**	**6,035**	**32,857**	**17,068**
Work expenses[2]				
Child care	5,000	0	10,000	0
Transportation	1,500	0	2,250	0
Meals	1,250	0	2,000	0
Wardrobe	900	0	1,200	0
Dry cleaning	360	0	500	0
Total expenses	**9,010**	**0**	**15,950**	**0**
Total income	59,600	35,600	102,000	67,000
Total taxes	14,446	6,035	32,857	17,068
Total expenses	9,010	0	15,950	0
Left to spend	**$36,144**	**$29,565**	**$53,193**	**$49,932**
Decreases in spendable cash		**$6,579**		**$3,261**
Percentage change		**18%**		**6%**

[1] Includes $480 federal child-care credit and variable state credit.
[2] Work expenses are for the lower-paid spouse only. Although that spouse's work expenses would be erased by staying home, bills at home would rise and should be included in a full-cost analysis.
Source: San Jose Mercury News, February 14, 1993.

One also needs to distinguish between the effects of a temporary change in the wage and those of a more permanent change. Empirical studies show that the quantity of labor supplied rises more in response to a temporary increase in the wage than to a permanent increase. What's the explanation? Consider an example. If you have a special one-time opportunity tomorrow to earn $100 an hour rather than your usual $6 an hour, you are likely to put off some leisure for one day; the substitution effect dominates. But if you are lucky enough to land a lifetime job at $100 an hour rather than $6 an hour, you may decide to work fewer hours and have more leisure time; the income effect dominates.

This difference between temporary and permanent changes helps explain the dramatic decline in the average hours worked per week in the United States as wages have risen over the last century. These are more permanent changes, for which the income effect dominates.

Work versus Another Alternative: Getting Human Capital

The skills of a worker depend in part on how much schooling and training the worker has had. The decision to obtain these skills—to finish high school and attend a community college or obtain a four-year college degree—is much like the choice between work and leisure. In fact, an important decision for many young people is whether to go to work or to finish high school; if they have finished high school, the choice is whether to go to work or to go to college.

human capital: a person's accumulated knowledge and skills.

Economists view the education and training that raise skills and productivity as a form of *investment*, a decision to spend funds or time on something now because it pays off in the future. Continuing the analogy, an investment in a college education raises the amount of **human capital**—a person's knowledge and skills—in the same way that the investment in a factory or machine by a business firm raises physical capital. Figure 7 demonstrates the kind of difference this investment can make.

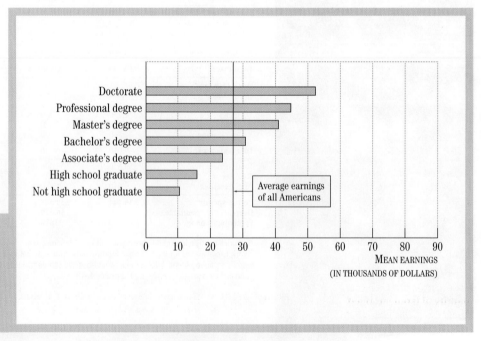

FIGURE 7
Higher Education and Economic Success
According to this chart, education pays off in terms of earnings, with doctorate degree holders earning the most, followed by workers with professional and master's degrees.

The decision to invest in human capital can be approached like any other economic choice. Suppose the decision is whether Angela should go to college or get a job. If she does not go to college, she saves on tuition and can begin earning an income right away. If she goes to college, she pays tuition and forgoes the opportunity to earn income at a full-time job. However, if Angela is like most people, college will improve her skills and land her a better job at higher pay. The returns on college education are the extra pay. Angela ought to go to college—invest in human capital—if the returns are greater than the cost.

on-the-job training: the building of the skills of a firm's employees while they work for the firm.

People can increase their skills at work as well as in school. In fact, **on-the-job training** is one of the most important ways in which workers' productivity increases. On-the-job training can be either *firm-specific*, where the skills are useful only at one firm, or *general-purpose*, where the skills are transferable to other jobs.

R E V I E W

- An individual's labor supply curve can be viewed as the outcome of the choice between work and some other activity, whether home work or leisure.

- Wages can be thought of as the price of that alternative activity, whether it be home work or leisure. This is because the opportunity cost of allocating an hour to that activity is the forgone wage that could have been earned from work.

- Changes in wages have both a substitution effect and an income effect on the labor supply. The substitution effect is that as wages rise, the cost of not working rises—there is an increased attractiveness of work relative to its alternatives. The income effect is that a rise in the wage increases the real income of an individual and enables that individual to enjoy more of all goods, including leisure.

- The income effect will tend to lower the incentive to work as the wage rises, while the substitution effect will increase the incentive to work. In some situations, the substitution effect dominates, leading to an increase in the quantity of labor supplied as the wage rises—an upward-sloping labor curve. In other situations, the income effect dominates, leading to a decrease in the quantity of labor supplied as the wage rises—a downward-sloping labor curve.

- Individuals also have to make decisions between working and acquiring human capital through education and training. Then the cost of acquiring human capital is the forgone wages, while the benefit of human capital is the extra wages one can earn using the knowledge and skills accumulated from going to school or receiving on-the-job training. If the returns are greater than the costs, then individuals should continue with their education.

EXPLAINING WAGE TRENDS AND DIFFERENCES

Labor Productivity

labor market equilibrium: the situation in which the quantity of labor supplied equals the quantity of labor demanded.

When we combine the labor demand and labor supply curves derived in the previous two sections, we get the model of the labor market summarized in Figure 2. The model predicts that the wage in the labor market will be at the intersection of the supply and demand curves. The point of intersection, where the quantity of labor supplied equals the quantity of labor demanded, is the **labor market equilibrium.**

ECONOMICS IN ACTION

Why It's Better Being an Economist

When you decided to study economics, you made a decision that was very wise, wiser than you may have thought at the time. The concepts and models that you learn in your study of economics are invaluable in making sense of what you observe in the world. Furthermore, as you take more economics courses, you will find yourself developing a range of skills, both quantitative and qualitative, that will help you do well in many other courses in different fields of study. But you will be really grateful that you chose to study economics when college graduation looms. The study of economics opens many doors and leaves you with an almost bewildering array of options for career paths to follow. You can continue on to graduate school and pursue graduate study in economics; you can take your quantitative skills to Wall Street and find a job with a leading investment bank; you can work at a consulting company, where you can apply your problem-solving skills and the knowledge you gained about how firms, industries, and countries work to help companies sort out business strategy options; you can take your experience working with data and program evaluation to a Federal Reserve Bank or a policy research firm, where you work with other economists on research projects and policy design; you can travel to another country and work for a nonprofit organization that is focused on international development issues like providing AIDS treatment to pregnant mothers or creating microcredit programs for the rural poor. These are but a few of the paths that lie on the other side of the doors that you have been able to open with the help of your economics knowledge.

The plethora of opportunities available for economists applies just as strongly to newly minted Ph.D.s in the field. Unfortunately, the job market for Ph.D.s in many other fields, including but not limited to anthropology, mathematics, and literature, is much more limited. An article by Richard Freeman that appeared in the *Journal of Economic Perspectives* in 1999[1] took a closer look at the reasons for the differences between the job markets for economists and the job markets for mathematicians and physicists. Freeman argues that the differential prospects are, somewhat ironically, best understood by applying a classic supply and demand analysis. In this box, we summarize Professor Freeman's article; if you are interested in more details, you will find that the article is very readable even for someone who has only taken Principles of Economics (see the citation below).

QUANTIFYING THE DISPARITIES

The following table, taken from Prof. Freeman's paper, lays out the disparities between economics and two important scientific disciplines: mathematics and physics. As you can see, Ph.D. economists are much more likely to be in a full-time job after obtaining their doctorate, while mathematicians and physicists are much more likely to be in postdoctoral positions or part-time academic positions. Economists earn more, in some cases substantially more, than graduates in the other two fields; this earnings gap exists across different employer types. What then are the explanations for why the job markets for these graduates are so different?

The Economist's Edge over Mathematics and Physics

	Economics	Mathematics	Physics
Percent of Ph.D. recipients			
In temporary job	19	46	57
In postdoctoral position	4	26	48
Median starting salary by area			
Education (9–10 months)	48,000	36,000	33,000
Business	73,500	60,000	62,000
Government	54,800	57,260	63,000
Postdoctoral	42,800	37,500	36,000
Median salary of PhDs, in universities and 4-year colleges	59,000	53,000	55,400
Percentage change in median salary, 1977–1995	179%	—	143%

Sources: Siegfried and Stock, *Journal of Economic Perspectives* (August 1999, Tables 7 and 8); Commission on Professionals in Science and Technology (1998a, 1998b); National Science Foundation (1995, Table 40).

THAT CAN'T BE IT!

Professor Freeman begins by ruling out certain potential explanations.

- Economists do not earn more because their discipline is more technically rigorous and hence accessible only to those who are especially intellectually gifted. He points out that, in fact, the opposite is true. Doctoral students in physics and mathematics tend to score higher on standardized tests than economics doctoral students do. Furthermore, many economics graduate programs would happily admit mathematics and physics doctoral students because of their technical expertise, whereas most mathematics and physics programs would not admit economics students because of their technical shortcomings.

- Physicists and other scientists, although perhaps not mathematicians, use millions of dollars worth of expensive laboratory equipment to fund their research, whereas most economists work with nothing more sophisticated than a personal computer. Typically, wages are higher for workers in countries or industries where they work with a lot of capital; this does not seem to be true for physicists.

- Artificial restrictions on supply are not the explanation because anyone can be an economist! The profession does not use licensure requirements to restrict how many people or who is allowed to work as an economist.

- The idea that economists are better at explaining their world than scientists are at explaining theirs is also easily rebutted. Economists study the actions of people making purposeful decisions with limited resources; the conclusions that they reach about how a particular policy would affect the economy by affecting that behavior are a far cry from the predictions that scientists can make about natural phenomena, drawing on the many immutable laws of natural and physical science.

FREEMAN'S CONJECTURES ABOUT "WHY IT'S BETTER BEING AN ECONOMIST"

Having dispatched some of the likely explanations for the disparity, Professor Freeman offers his conjectured reasons, drawing on the basic supply and demand framework. The reasons he comes up with are as follows:

- Many children grow up hearing about famous scientists like Newton, Darwin, and Einstein. A sizable fraction of these youngsters want to emulate their heroes and become scientists themselves. This results in a fairly inelastic labor supply curve for scientists—if you want to be the next Einstein, you are hardly likely to be derailed from your plans by financial obstacles. When labor demand fluctuates, say because of government funding changes, and when labor supply fluctuates, say because of the influx of mathematicians and physicists from the former Soviet Union, wages can fall quite dramatically.

- In stark contrast, almost no child grows up wanting to become a famous economist. The labor supply curve for economists is very elastic. If labor demand for economists were to fall, the equilibrium quantity of economists would fall much more than wages would—undergraduate economics majors would simply become actuaries, lawyers, or accountants instead.

- Economists have solved relatively few of the major unsolved mysteries related to the field. Because the existing stock of knowledge is low, the marginal product of additional research is much higher than in scientific fields, where there is a much greater base of knowledge and hence a lower marginal product of an additional hour of research.

- The corollary to this difference in the existing base of knowledge is that economists do not need as much specialized training as scientists do; hence they need to spend less time in postdoctoral research positions and can instead start doing their own research much earlier than scientists do. This would explain why so many science Ph.D.s take postdoctoral positions.

- Finally, economists have a much wider demand for their services. Business schools, law schools, medical schools, and public policy schools all want to hire economists because they all have to understand how people make purposeful decisions with limited resources. This ensures that the labor demand for the general skills that economists possess is higher than the labor demand for the specific skills that mathematicians and physicists possess.

The moral of the story is that you should be happy that you made the decision to embark on the process of becoming an economist. Not only can you achieve intellectual satisfaction through your studies, but you will find many different career paths awaiting you at the culmination of your undergraduate studies. This will hopefully provide some solace to you as you ponder why you were never inspired to become Darwin or Einstein and to others who may be plagued by a sense of inferiority that their roommate majoring in physics or mathematics is smarter. Paraphrasing the immortal words of the *Saturday Night Live* character, say to yourself:

I'm good enough, I'm smart enough, and doggone it, I am an economist.

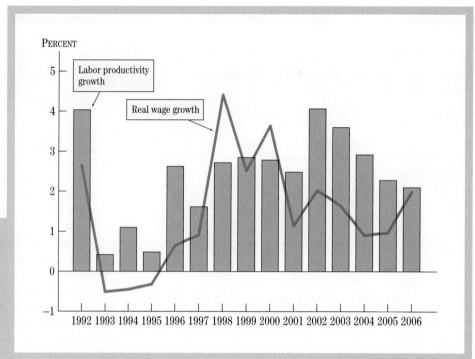

FIGURE 8
Labor Productivity Growth and Real Wage Growth
Prior to 2001, labor productivity growth was closely related to the growth of real wages, much as would be predicted by the labor supply and demand model. The relationship between these two variables has weakened in the past five years.

The model also predicts that the equilibrium wage equals the marginal revenue product. If the marginal product of labor employed at a firm increases, then the model predicts that the firm's labor demand curve will shift to the right, as the firm will be willing to hire more workers at any given wage. Suppose the marginal product of labor rises for the economy as a whole; then the labor demand curve for the economy should shift to the right and both the equilibrium quantity of labor and the equilibrium wage should also rise. Is this what occurs in reality?

■ **The Relationship Between Real Wages and Labor Productivity.** In Figure 8, the line graph shows the percentage by which real wages have increased each year since 1992. Note that real wages rose rapidly in the five years starting in 1996. After the 2001 recession, the growth rate of real wages slowed down somewhat. The bars in Figure 8 show output per hour of work in the same period. Output per hour of work is called **labor productivity** and is a good indication of trends in the marginal product of labor on average in the United States. Labor productivity growth in the United States has been very robust since the mid-1990s. The labor market model predicts that wages in the United States should increase when labor productivity increases. Do they?

Figure 8 shows a strong correlation between labor productivity and the real wage. Note that the change in the labor productivity trend occurred in the mid-1990s, at almost the same time as the change in the trend of real wage growth. The empirical association between wages and labor productivity has been less pronounced in the five years after 2001 than in the five years before 2001. Nevertheless, the data series shown in this chart suggests that labor productivity is a key explanation of changes in real wages over time.

labor productivity: output per hour of work.

Wage Dispersion and Productivity

Can labor productivity also explain wage differences between groups of people? As we saw earlier in this chapter, real wages vary across workers depending on their occupa-

ECONOMICS IN ACTION

Does Productivity or Compensating Differentials Explain the Academic Wage Gap?

People with Ph.D.'s who teach or do research at colleges and universities are paid 10 percent less than people with Ph.D.'s who work for government and 20 percent less than people with Ph.D.'s who work for business firms. Why does the academic wage gap exist?

There are two possibilities: (1) People with Ph.D.'s who work in business and government are more skilled and more productive, or (2) people with Ph.D.'s who work in business and government are paid a compensating wage differential because the job is less pleasant. (They don't have the pleasure of teaching students or the flexible academic hours.)

How can we tell which is the right explanation? Looking at what happens to people with Ph.D.'s when they move provides an answer. If their wages increase when they move to a nonacademic job, then compensating wage differentials rather than productivity differences is the correct explanation.

The following table shows the average salary increases between 1985 and 1987 of people with Ph.D.'s who either (1) did not move, (2) moved to another college or university, or (3) moved to business or government. The salary increases are largest for those who left academia. For example, the average salary increase for engineering Ph.D.'s nearly doubled when they moved from academia to work in a business firm or government. This indicates that the differences are due not to skill but to compensating wage differentials.

This is one of the rare cases in which economists have actually been able to obtain data that distinguish compensating wage differentials from productivity or other explanations for wage differences. But if the case is representative, compensating wage differentials may play a big part in wage dispersion.

> Largest increase for every type of Ph.D.

Increase in Salary (dollars)

	Did Not Move	Moved to Another College	Left Academia
Physical science	7,303	10,216	15,330
Mathematical science	6,523	9,716	15,727
Environmental science	6,292	4,688	11,333
Life science	5,870	6,710	8,115
Psychology	5,920	6,559	10,371
Social science	5,796	7,687	12,485
Engineering	7,294	6,724	14,025
Humanities	5,042	5,380	8,204

Source: Adapted from Albert Rees, "The Salaries of Ph.D.'s in Academia and Elsewhere," *Journal of Economic Perspectives,* Winter 1993. Reprinted with permission.

tion, the industry they work in, full- or part-time status, union status, and education, among other reasons. For instance, if the marginal product of labor increases with additional skills from investment in human capital, then, on average, wages for people with a college education should be higher than those for people without a college education. Hence, productivity differences are an explanation for the wage gap between workers who do not receive education beyond high school and those who are college educated.

Although human capital differences undoubtedly explain some of the dispersion of wages, some people have argued that the greater productivity of college-educated workers is due not to the skills learned in college, but to the fact that colleges screen applicants. For example, people who are not highly motivated or who have difficulty communicating have trouble getting into college. Hence, college graduates would earn higher wages even if they learned nothing in college. If this is so, a college degree *signals* to employers that the graduate is likely to be a productive worker.

Unfortunately, it is difficult to distinguish the skill-enhancing from the signaling effects of college. Certainly your grades and your major in college affect the kind of job you get and how much you earn, suggesting that more than signaling is important to employers. In reality, signaling and human capital both probably have a role to play in explaining the higher wages of college graduates.

Whether it is signaling or human capital that explains the higher wages of college graduates, labor productivity differences are still the underlying explanation for the wage differences. However, labor productivity does not explain everything about wages. Consider now some other factors.

■ **Compensating Wage Differentials.**   Not all jobs that require workers with the same level of skill and productivity are alike. Some jobs are more pleasant, less stressful, or safer than other jobs. For example, the skills necessary to be a deep-sea salvage diver and a lifeguard are similar—good at swimming, good judgment, and good health. But the risks—such as decompression sickness—for a deep-sea diver are greater and the opportunity for social interaction is less. If the pay for both jobs were the same, say, $10 per hour, most people would prefer the lifeguard job.

But this situation could not last. With many lifeguard applicants, the beach authorities would be unlikely to raise the wage above $10 and might even try to cut the wage if they faced budget cuts. With few applicants, the deep-sea salvage companies would have to raise the wage. After a while, it would not be surprising to see the equilibrium wage for lifeguards at $9 per hour and the equilibrium wage for deep-sea divers at $18 per hour. Thus, we would be in a situation where the skills of the workers were identical, but their wages were much different. The higher-risk job pays a higher wage than the lower-risk job.

High Wages for High Work
Compensating wage differentials are illustrated by the relatively high wages paid to someone for performing risky jobs such as window washing on a skyscraper.

Situations in which wages differ because of the characteristics of the job are widespread. Hazardous duty pay is common in the military. Wage data show that night-shift workers in manufacturing plants are paid wages that are about 3 percent higher on average than those of daytime workers, presumably to compensate for the inconvenience.

Such differences in wages are called **compensating wage differentials.** They are an important source of differences in wages that are not based on marginal product. With compensating differentials, workers may seek out riskier jobs in order to be paid more.

compensating wage differential: a difference in wages for people with similar skills based on some characteristic of the job, such as riskiness, discomfort, or inconvenience of the time schedule.

■ **Discrimination.** As noted earlier, there is a gap in earnings between women and men, even though that gap has been narrowing in recent years. Women now make close to 80 percent of the wages of men, whereas 50 years ago, women earned only about 50 percent of the wages of men. The gap between the wages of blacks and whites is also closing, although not quite as quickly. In the 1950s, the ratio of the wages of blacks to those of whites was about 60 percent; it has narrowed to about 70 percent since then. Wage differences between white and minority workers and between men and women are indications of discrimination if the wage differences cannot be explained by differences in marginal product or other factors unrelated to race or gender.

Some, but not all, of these differences may be attributed to differences in human capital. The wage gaps between blacks and whites and between men and women with comparable education and job experience are smaller than the ratios in the preceding paragraph. But a gap still exists.

Discrimination on the basis of race or gender prejudice can explain such differences. This is shown in Figure 9. *Discrimination* can be defined in the supply and

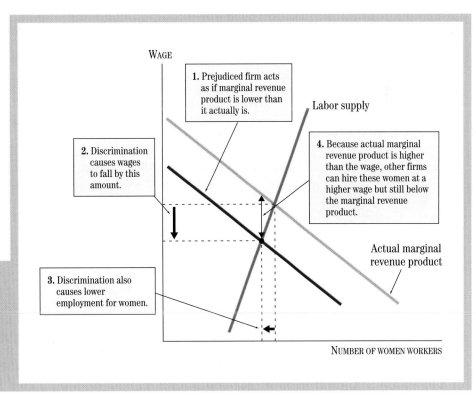

FIGURE 9
Discrimination in the Labor Market

Firms that discriminate against women pay them a wage that is less than their marginal product. But this gives other firms an opportunity to recruit workers from prejudiced firms by paying higher wages.

demand model as not hiring women or minority workers even though their marginal product is just as high as that of other workers, or paying a lower wage to such workers even though their marginal product is equal to that of other workers. Either way, discrimination can be interpreted as a leftward shift of the labor demand curve for women or minority workers. As shown in Figure 9, this reduces the wages and employment for those discriminated against.

An important implication of this supply and demand interpretation of the effects of discrimination is that competition among firms may reduce it. Why might competition reduce discrimination? Remember that a firm will increase profits if the wage is less than the marginal revenue product. If markets are competitive, then firms that discriminate against women or minorities will pay them a wage lower than their marginal revenue product, as shown in Figure 9. In this situation, any profit-maximizing firm will see that it can raise its profits by paying these workers a little more—but still less than their marginal revenue product—and hiring them away from firms that discriminate. Thus, firms in competitive markets that discriminate will lose out to firms that do not. Much like firms that do not keep their costs as low as other firms, they will eventually be driven out of the industry. This is an advantage of competitive markets that should be added to the advantages already mentioned. Furthermore, competition for workers will raise wages until the wages are eventually equal to the marginal products of labor.

This description of events relies on a market's being competitive. If firms have monopoly power or entry is limited, so that economic profits are not driven to zero, then discrimination can continue to exist. That discrimination effects on wages do persist may be a sign that there are market power and barriers to entry. In any case, there are laws against discrimination that give those who are discriminated against for race, gender, or other reasons the right to sue those who are discriminating.

Some laws have been proposed requiring that employers pay the same wage to workers with comparable skills. Such proposals are called *comparable worth proposals*. The intent of such proposals is to bring the wages of different groups into line. However, such laws might force wages to be the same in situations where wages are different for reasons other than discrimination, such as compensating wage differentials. This would lead to shortages or surpluses, much as price ceilings or price floors in any market do. In the lifeguard/deep-sea diver example, a law requiring employers to pay lifeguards and deep-sea divers the same wage would cause a surplus of lifeguards and a shortage of deep-sea divers. For example, suppose that with comparable worth legislation, the wage for both lifeguards and deep-sea divers was $10 per hour. Because the labor market equilibrium wage for lifeguards, $9 per hour, is less than $10 per hour, there would be a surplus of lifeguards: More people would be willing to be lifeguards than employers would be willing to hire. And because the labor market equilibrium wage for deep-sea divers, $18 per hour, is greater than $10, there would be a shortage of deep-sea divers: Firms would be willing to hire more deep-sea divers than the number of deep-sea divers willing to dive for the $10 per hour wage.

■ **Minimum Wage Laws.** Another example in which the wages received by a worker may not be connected to the worker's marginal product is when the government stipulates a wage floor, or a *minimum wage*, which must be paid to workers. Because wages differ due to skills, the impact of the minimum wage depends on the skills of the workers. Figure 10 shows what the supply and demand model predicts about the impact of the minimum wage on skilled and unskilled workers. A labor

THE FAR SIDE® By GARY LARSON

Hopeful parents

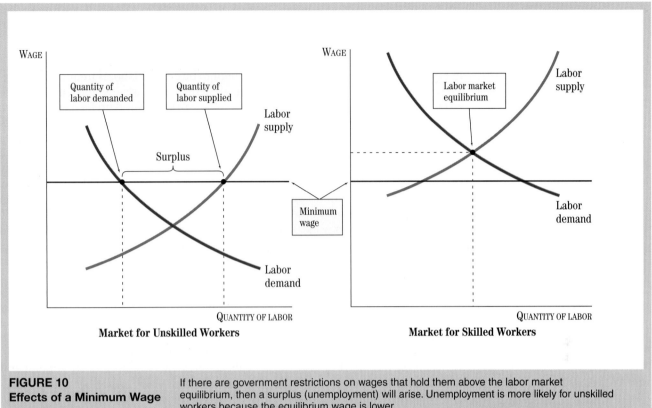

FIGURE 10
Effects of a Minimum Wage

If there are government restrictions on wages that hold them above the labor market equilibrium, then a surplus (unemployment) will arise. Unemployment is more likely for unskilled workers because the equilibrium wage is lower.

market for unskilled workers is shown on the left; the minimum wage is shown to be above the labor market equilibrium wage. There is thus a surplus, or unemployment: The quantity of labor demanded by firms at the minimum wage is less than the quantity of labor that workers are willing to supply at that wage. A labor market for skilled workers is shown on the right: The minimum wage is shown to be below the market equilibrium wage for skilled workers. Thus a minimum wage at the level shown in the graph would not cause unemployment among skilled workers.

Therefore, the labor supply and demand model predicts that the minimum wage is a cause of unemployment among less skilled or less experienced workers, and thereby ends up hurting some of the least well off in society. This is why many economists are concerned about the impact of minimum wage legislation.

In interpreting this result, remember that the supply and demand model is a *model* of reality, not reality itself. Although the model explains much about wages, its predictions about minimum wage laws should be verified like the predictions of any other economic model. In fact, labor economists have been trying to check the predictions of the model for the minimum wage for many years. Some economists, such as David Card of the University of California at Berkeley and Alan Krueger of Princeton University, have examined the effects of different minimum wage laws in different states on low-skilled fast-food workers and have not found evidence of the predicted impact on unemployment. Others, like David Neumark of Michigan State University and William Wascher of the

Federal Reserve, have disputed Card's and Krueger's data and have found that the minimum wage enacted in those same states did have a negative effect on employment.

■ **Fixed Wage Contracts.** The agreement to buy or sell labor is frequently a long-term one. Job-specific training and the difficulty of changing jobs make quick turnover costly for both firms and workers. Most workers would prefer a certain wage to an uncertain one; such workers will prefer a fixed wage that does not change every time the marginal revenue product changes. Long-term arrangements of this kind are quite common. A worker—a person working at Getajob, for example—is hired at a given weekly wage. If marginal revenue product declines because of a week of stormy winter weather with frequent power outages, Getajob will not reduce the weekly wage. On the other hand, when college graduation season arrives in May, the Getajob workers will have to work harder—their marginal revenue product will rise—but they will not be paid a higher wage. Thus, the weekly wage does not change with the actual week-to-week changes in the marginal revenue product of the worker. The wage reflects marginal revenue product over a longer period. Most workers in the United States are paid in this way.

An alternative wage payment arrangement endeavors to match productivity with the wage much more closely. Such contracts are used when the weekly or hourly wage does not provide sufficient *incentive* or where the manager cannot observe the worker carefully. Under a **piece-rate system,** the specific amount that workers are paid depends on how much they produce. Thus, if their marginal product drops off, for whatever reason, they are paid less. Piece rates are common in the apparel and agriculture industries.

> **piece-rate system:** a system by which workers are paid a specific amount per unit they produce.

Consider California lettuce growers, for example. The growers hire crews of workers to cut and pack the lettuce. A typical crew consists of two cutters and one packer, who split their earnings equally. The crew is paid a piece rate, about $1.20 for a box of lettuce that might contain two dozen heads. A three-person crew can pick and pack about 75 boxes an hour. Thus, each worker can earn about $30 an hour. But if they slack off, their wages decline rapidly.

On the same lettuce farms, the truck drivers, the workers who carry the boxes to the trucks, and the workers who wash the lettuce may be paid by the hour. Why the difference? Piece rates are used when it is difficult to monitor the quantity of a worker's effort. If you pay crews of lettuce workers in the field by the hour, then some of them will put in less effort and generate less output. Paying them according to the quantity of lettuce they pick ensures that those with the highest marginal revenue product earn the highest wages. This system would not work with the workers washing lettuce at the main building or the workers carrying the boxes to the trucks. The quality of their work (whether the lettuce was damaged by rough handling, whether all the dirt was properly washed out) cannot be measured as easily as with the lettuce pickers. These workers might sacrifice quality for speed under a piece-rate system.

■ **Deferred Wage Payments.** Yet another payment arrangement occurs when a firm pays workers less than their marginal revenue product when they are young and more than their marginal revenue product at a later time as a reward for working hard. Lawyers and accountants frequently work hard at their firms when they are young; if they do well, they make partner and are then paid much more than their marginal revenue product when they are older. Such contracts are called **deferred payment contracts.** Generous retirement plans are another form of deferred payment contract. A reward for staying at the firm and working hard is a nice retirement package.

> **deferred payment contract:** an agreement between a worker and an employer whereby the worker is paid less than the marginal revenue product when young, and subsequently paid more than the marginal revenue product when old.

R E V I E W

- The labor supply and demand model predicts that economywide increases in marginal product should lead to an increase in the real wage.

- Using labor productivity as a measure of marginal product for an economy, we can see that the growth rate of labor productivity is positively correlated with the growth rate of real wages. The relationship was especially strong in the mid-1990s.

- Differences in labor productivity are also an explanation for some of the differences in wages across groups, especially the differences between workers with different levels of education.

- However, there are other factors that bring about a disconnect between labor productivity and real wages. These include compensating wage differentials, discrimination, minimum wage laws, fixed wage contracts, and deferred wage payments.

- Compensating wage differentials occur because some jobs are more attractive than others. Workers with the same level of productivity will earn more in the sector that is less desirable to work in.

- Discrimination reduces the wages of those who are discriminated against below their marginal revenue product. Competition can be a force against the effects of discrimination because other firms can step in and hire the workers who are being discriminated against, offering to pay them a wage that is higher than what they are currently getting but still less than their marginal revenue product.

- Minimum wage laws can also lead to workers being paid a wage higher than their marginal revenue product. If the government imposes a minimum wage that is higher than the marginal revenue product of unskilled workers, it will cause some of these workers to lose their jobs, while the lucky ones earn a wage that is higher than what their marginal revenue product will indicate.

- Many labor market transactions are long term. Most employees receive a fixed hourly or weekly wage, even though their marginal revenue product fluctuates.

- In certain types of jobs, piece-rate contracts adjust the payment directly according to actual marginal product; they are a way to increase incentives to be more productive.

- Deferred compensation is another form of payment that aims at improving incentives and worker motivation.

LABOR UNIONS

labor union: a coalition of workers, organized to improve the wages and working conditions of the members.

industrial union: a union organized within a given industry, whose members come from a variety of occupations.

craft union: a union organized to represent a single occupation, whose members come from a variety of industries.

The model of labor supply and demand can also help us understand the impact of labor unions. **Labor unions** such as the United Auto Workers or the United Farm Workers are organizations with the stated aim of improving the wages and working conditions of their members. There are two types of unions: **Industrial unions** represent most of the workers in an industry—such as the rubber workers, farm workers, or steelworkers—regardless of their occupation; **craft unions** represent workers in a single occupation or group of occupations, such as printers or dockworkers. In the 1930s and 1940s, there were disputes between those organizing craft unions and industrial unions. John L. Lewis, a labor union leader, argued that craft unions were not suitable for large numbers of unskilled workers. Hence, he and other union leaders split in 1936 from the American Federation of Labor (AFL), a group representing many labor unions, and formed the Congress of Industrial Organizations (CIO). It was not until

The Collective Voice of Union Workers
The lockout of dock workers in West Coast ports in the fall of 2002 paralyzed billions of dollars' worth of cargo going in and out of the United States. At the heart of the conflict was the introduction of new technology that would eliminate 200 to 600 jobs.

1955 that the AFL and the CIO resolved their disputes and merged; one of the reasons behind their reconciliation was that union membership was beginning to decline.

But the decline continued. In 2005, there was a split within the AFL-CIO. Three large unions representing service workers, truck drivers, and food and commercial workers withdrew from the AFL-CIO, expressing their unhappiness over the decline of union membership. About 12.5 percent of the U.S. labor force is currently unionized, down from about 25 percent in the mid-1950s. The fraction is much higher in other countries.

Unions negotiate with firms on behalf of their members in a collective bargaining process. Federal law, including the National Labor Relations Act (1935), gives workers the right to organize into unions and bargain with employers. The National Labor Relations Board has been set up to make sure that firms do not illegally prevent workers from organizing and to monitor union elections of leaders.

In studying unions, it is important to distinguish between the union leaders who speak for the union members and the union members themselves. Like politicians, union leaders must be elected, and as with politicians, we can sometimes better understand the actions of union leaders by assuming that they are motivated by the desire to be elected or reelected.

Union/Nonunion Wage Differentials

Studies of the wages of union workers and nonunion workers have shown that union wages are about 15 percent higher than nonunion wages, even when workers' skills are the same. There are two different explanations of how unions raise wages.

■ **The Restricted Supply Explanation.** One theory is that unions raise wages by restricting supply. By restricting membership, for example, they shift the labor supply curve to the left, raising wages, just as a monopolist raises the price of the good it sells by restricting supply. But when a union restricts supply, workers outside the union in another industry get paid less.

This effect of unions is illustrated in Figure 11. The graph on the right is one industry; the graph on the left is another industry. Suppose both industries require workers of the same skill level. Imagine the situation before the union is formed. Then the wages for the workers on the left and on the right in Figure 11 would be the same.

Now suppose a union organizes the industry on the left. Wages rise in the industry on the left, but the quantity of labor demanded in the industry falls. The workers

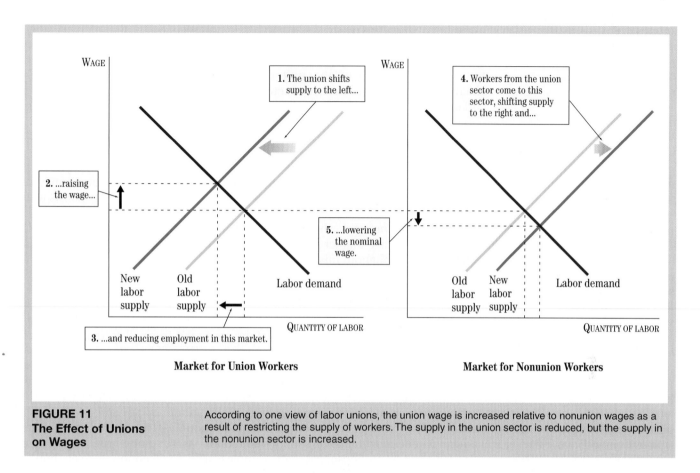

FIGURE 11
The Effect of Unions on Wages

According to one view of labor unions, the union wage is increased relative to nonunion wages as a result of restricting the supply of workers. The supply in the union sector is reduced, but the supply in the nonunion sector is increased.

in the industry on the left who become unemployed will probably move to the industry on the right. As they do so, the labor supply curve in the right-hand graph of Figure 11 shifts and the wage in that industry declines. Thus, a wage gap between the similarly skilled union and nonunion workers is created.

■ **The Increased Productivity Explanation.** Another theory, which was developed extensively in the book *What Do Unions Do?* by Richard Freeman and James Medoff of Harvard University, is that labor unions raise the wages of workers by increasing their marginal product. They do this by providing a channel of communication with management, motivating workers, and providing a democratic means of resolving disputes.

A worker who has a dispute with the management of a firm or who sees the opportunity to get a higher wage at another firm could, in principle, move. But such moves can have huge costs: The firm may have invested in job-specific training, and the worker might like the area where the firm is located. In situations where exit from a firm is costly, people find other ways to improve their situation without exiting. The economist Albert Hirschman, in a famous book called *Exit, Voice, and Loyalty*, has called this alternative "voice." Rather than exit or quit, the worker may try to show the firm that a raise is deserved. Or the worker can discuss with the employer how conditions can be changed. The choice between exit and voice arises in many contexts: Should you transfer to a new college or tell the dean how the teaching might be improved? Should parents send their children to a private school or work to improve the local public school?

In many situations, exercising your voice requires collective action. If you alone complain to the dean, nothing much will happen, but if you organize a "students against lousy teaching" group, you may see some changes. Those who emphasize this collective-voice role of labor unions argue that unions provide a means through which workers improve their productivity. This explains why the wages of union workers are higher than those of nonunion workers with the same skills and training.

Monopsony and Bilateral Monopoly

The analysis of labor unions in Figure 11 stresses the market power of unions as *sellers* of their members' labor in the labor market: By restricting supply, the union can raise the price of its members' wages, much as a monopolist or a group of oligopolists with market power can raise the price of the goods they sell.

monopsony: a situation in which there is a single buyer of a particular good or service in a given market.

However, the *buyers* in the labor market—that is, the firms that purchase the labor—may also have market power to affect the wage, contrary to the assumption we have made throughout this chapter that firms do not have such market power in the labor market. **Monopsony** is a situation in which there is only one buyer. By reducing its demand for the good (in this case, labor), a monopsony can reduce the price in the market (in this case, the wage). In fact, there are few examples of monopsony; for most types of workers—salesclerks, accountants, engineers—there are typically many potential employers. Exceptions are found in small towns, where, for example, there may be only one auto repair shop. Then, if auto mechanics do not want to move, the auto repair shop is effectively the only employer. Another exception is found in professional sports leagues, where team owners form agreements with one another restricting workers' (that is, the players') mobility between teams.

bilateral monopoly: the situation in which there is one buyer and one seller in a market.

The situation in which there is only one seller (a monopoly) and one buyer (a monopsony) in a market is called a **bilateral monopoly.** A labor market with one labor union deciding the labor supply (the monopolist) and one firm deciding the labor demand (the monopsonist) is an example of a bilateral monopoly. Even though we typically associate a monopolist with the creation of deadweight loss, the outcome of a bilateral monopoly is difficult to predict. Compared to a situation where a monopsony faces competitive sellers, however, the bilateral monopoly can lead to a more efficient outcome.

For instance, a firm with monopsony power over the labor market would choose to hire fewer workers, in order to drive down the wage, than would a group of competitive firms. By banding together in a labor union, the workers can confront this monopsony power with their own monopoly power. For example, they could refuse to work for less than the competitive wage. If their refusal is credible, they could take away the incentive for the monopsony to reduce labor demand because doing so would not reduce the wage. An example is in the arena of professional sports, where powerful players' unions have helped reduce the effects of the teams' monopsony power and led to players' salaries rising dramatically in recent years. They were aided in their cause by the erosion of teams' monopsony power through rulings that allowed for things like free agency in major league baseball.

R E V I E W

- Today, less than 15 percent of U.S. workers belong to labor unions, a significant decline from the mid-1950s, when about a quarter of workers belonged to unions.

- Workers who belong to unions are paid about 15 percent more on average than workers with the same skills who are not in unions.

- One explanation for this difference is that labor unions improve productivity by improving worker motivation and providing workers with a collective voice.

- Another view is that labor unions raise productivity by restricting supply, much as a monopolist would, rather than by increasing productivity.

- In certain situations where a single firm, a monopsonist, has market power in hiring workers, the creation of a labor union as a monopoly provider of labor services can actually increase the efficiency of the resulting market outcome.

CONCLUSION AND SOME ADVICE

In this chapter, we have shown that the labor supply and demand model is a powerful tool with many applications. In fact, the model may apply to you, so consider carefully what it implies.

First, increasing your own labor productivity is a good way to increase your earnings. Many of the large differences in wages across individuals and across time are due to differences in productivity. Productivity is enhanced by increases in human capital, whether obtained in school or on the job. Such human capital will also prove useful if your firm shuts down and you need to find another job.

Second, if you are choosing between two occupations that you like equally well, choose the one that is less popular with other students of your generation and for which it looks like demand will be increasing. Both the supply and the demand for labor affect the wage, and if the supply is expected to grow more rapidly than the demand in the occupation you are training for, wages will not be as high as in the occupation for which labor is in relatively short supply.

Third, be sure to think about the wage you receive or the raises you get in real terms, not nominal terms, and make sure you are aware of fringe benefits offered or not offered.

Fourth, think about your job in a longer-term perspective. Partly for incentive reasons, some jobs pay little at the start, with the promise of higher payments later.

KEY POINTS

1. When measuring workers' pay, it is important to consider fringe benefits in addition to the monetary portion, to adjust for inflation before comparing wages at different points in time, and to distinguish between hourly and weekly pay because of distinctions between full-time work and part-time work.

2. Wage growth in the United States, which is defined by the real hourly average pay (including fringe benefits), began increasing at a faster rate in the mid-1990s but has flattened out somewhat more recently. Wage dispersion has also increased.

3. The supply and demand framework can be applied to the labor market to gain insight into labor market trends. The demand for labor is a derived demand that comes from the profit-maximizing decisions of firms. Firms adjust their employment until the marginal revenue product of labor becomes equal to the wage.

4. The supply curve for labor can be explained by looking at the choices of individuals or households. A person will work more hours if the wage is greater than the marginal benefit of more leisure.

5. An increase in the wage will have both an income effect (real income rises, so the worker does not have to work as many hours as before to afford other goods and services) and a substitution effect (the opportunity cost of engaging in leisure or home work activities instead of working rises, increasing the incentive to work).

6. The substitution effect and the income effect work in opposite directions, so that the labor supply curve can be either upward-sloping, vertical, downward-sloping, or backward-bending.

7. Long-term trends in wages are closely correlated with changes in labor productivity, with the relationship being especially pronounced in the mid-1990s.

8. Labor productivity differences also explain some of the differences in wages paid to different people. However, differences in marginal productivity do not explain everything. Compensating wage differentials, discrimination, minimum wages, long-term contracts, and deferred compensation are all examples of why workers may not be paid a wage equivalent to their marginal revenue product.

9. The number of union workers in the United States has been declining, but union workers still earn more than nonunion workers who have the same skills. This occurs either because unions increase labor productivity or because they restrict the supply of workers in an industry.

10. Even though unions act like monopolists or oligopolists in the labor market in terms of selling the services of their members, they are not always associated with inefficient economic outcomes. In cases of bilateral monopoly, a monopoly seller of labor (such as a union) can counter a monopsony buyer of labor services and bring about more efficient economic outcomes.

KEY TERMS

fringe benefits
wage
real wage
labor market
labor demand
labor supply

derived demand
marginal revenue product of labor
backward-bending labor supply curve
human capital

on-the-job training
labor market equilibrium
labor productivity
compensating wage differential
piece-rate system

deferred payment contract
labor union
industrial union
craft union
monopsony
bilateral monopoly

QUESTIONS FOR REVIEW

1. What are fringe benefits? How significant a part of average pay are they in the United States?

2. Why is it important to distinguish between real wages and nominal wages? What about between hourly wages and weekly wages?

3. Why do we say that the demand for labor is a derived demand?

4. How does the relationship between marginal revenue product and the wage determine how many workers the firm should hire?

5. Why is the demand for labor downward-sloping?

6. Provide an intuitive explanation of the income and substitution effects. Then explain why the substitution effect and the income effect of a wage increase work in opposite directions on labor supply.

7. What is the empirical relationship between labor productivity and the real wage in the United States since 1990?

8. What factors can lead to workers being paid a wage that differs from their marginal revenue product of labor?

9. What are the two main views of labor unions?

10. Explain when a labor union will reduce economic efficiency. When could it increase economic efficiency?

PROBLEMS

1. Marcelo farms corn on 500 acres in a competitive industry, receiving $3 per bushel. The relationship between the number of workers Marcelo hires and his production of corn is shown below.

Number of Workers	Production (bushels per year)
1	30,000
2	43,000
3	51,000
4	55,000
5	57,000
6	58,000

   a. Calculate the marginal product and marginal revenue product of labor for Marcelo's farm.
   b. If the wage for farm workers is $8,000 per year, how many workers will Marcelo hire? Explain.
   c. Suppose the yearly wage for farm workers is $8,000, the fixed rent is $600/acre per year, and there are no other costs. Calculate Marcelo's profits or losses.
   d. Will there be entry into or exit from this industry?

2. Suppose a firm with some market power faces a downward-sloping demand curve for the product it produces. Using the information on demand given in the table below, complete the table and draw the resulting demand curve for labor. If the hourly wage is $30, how many workers will this firm hire?

3. Recently, there has been an increased demand for corn-based ethanol to substitute for gasoline in the United States. How will this affect the marginal product, marginal revenue product, and wages of farm workers on corn farms?

4. Use the definition of the demand for labor as the marginal revenue product to argue that the increasing wage dispersion between skilled and unskilled workers could come from (1) increases in the relative productivity of skilled workers and (2) increases in the demand for the products produced by skilled workers.

5. Since 1950, Americans have greatly reduced their home cooking in favor of eating at restaurants. What is the explanation for this? Do you expect it to continue in the next half century?

6. Analyze the labor supply schedules for Joshua and Scott below.

Wage	Hours Worked by Scott	Hours Worked by Joshua
$5	5	0
$8	10	8
$12	20	15
$15	30	25
$18	40	35
$20	45	33
$25	50	30

   a. Draw the labor supply schedules for Joshua and Scott.
   b. How does Scott's marginal benefit from more leisure compare with Joshua's?
   c. At what point does the income effect begin to outweigh the substitution effect for Joshua? Explain.

7. College professors are frequently paid less than others with equivalent skills working outside academia. Use the idea of compensating differentials to explain why professors' wages are relatively low.

Problem 2	Quantity of Labor	Quantity of Output	Marginal Product of Labor	Price of Output	Total Revenue	Marginal Revenue	Marginal Revenue Product of Labor
	10	100		9			
	20	180		8			
	30	240		7			
	40	280		6			
	50	300		5			
	60	310		4			

8. The government of Egalitariania wants to favor firms, and it is considering implementing a maximum wage. As an economic adviser to the government of Egalitariania, explain (verbally and graphically) the consequences of the maximum wage in the competitive labor market. Make sure your explanation includes the gains or losses to firms, workers, and the people of Egalitariania as a whole.

9. Draw a typical supply and demand for labor diagram to represent a labor market. Now suppose you are asked to modify this diagram to depict the market for doctors. In order to practice medicine in the United States, your medical education has to be certified, and you have to obtain a state license after completing a residency program. What impact does this restriction have on the wage rate for doctors in the economy? Will there be a shortage or a surplus of doctors at that wage rate? Should the government intervene and reduce these requirements to increase the supply of doctors? Would your answer change if the market (and the licensing requirement) were for lawyers? What about economists?

10. A toy manufacturing company is considering hiring sales representatives to market its new toys to retail stores. Under what circumstances should it pay a commission for every order of toys promoted by its sales representatives, and under what circumstances should it pay the sales representatives an hourly wage?

Chapter 14

Taxes, Transfers, and Income Distribution

The words of the chairman of the Federal Reserve are among the most closely scrutinized in the world. Whenever Ben Bernanke gives a speech, he knows that what he says will be reported in newspapers all over the country, even all over the world, and that dozens of analysts will be poring over his comments to glean some tidbits of useful information about what the Federal Reserve believes the primary challenges facing the economy are. So when Bernanke went before the Greater Omaha Chamber of Commerce in February of 2007, he was extremely aware of the import of his words. The title of Bernanke's speech was "The Level and Distribution of Economic Well-Being"[1]; in it he talked about three important ideas: (1) guaranteeing the equality of economic opportunity, an idea that he called a "bedrock American principle," (2) once equality of opportunity is guaranteed, not striving for equality of outcomes, and (3) ensuring that no one would slip too far down the economic ladder, especially for reasons beyond an individual's control.

He then proceeded to talk about the trends in income distribution in the United States. He argued that even though almost every level of the income distribution has gained in absolute terms from the U.S. economy, the top end of the income distribution has gained more than the lower end, resulting in a rising pattern of inequality, especially over the past three decades. In his words:

> In real terms, the earnings at the 50th percentile of the distribution (which I will refer to as the median wage) rose about 11-1/2 percent between 1979 and 2006. Over the same period, the wage at the 10th percentile, near the bottom of the wage distribution, rose just 4 percent, while the wage at the 90th percentile, close to the top of the distribution, rose 34 percent.

---

[1] You can read the full text of Bernanke's remarks at the website of the Board of Governors of the Federal Reserve, http://www.federalreserve.gov/boardDocs/Speeches/2007/20070206/default.htm.

The speeches and statements of Federal Reserve Chairman Ben Bernanke are closely followed by economic analysts, observers, and policymakers.

Bernanke's main point was that rising inequality, especially if outcomes were persistent, would threaten the dynamism of the U.S. economy because workers would be more resistant to change driven by technology and globalization. He was careful to point out that there is a wide range of individual opinion about the causes of income inequality and what government should do about it. But by speaking about it from his privileged vantage point, it was clear that Bernanke was signaling that policymakers in the United States would have to start paying attention to measures of income inequality, social safety nets, and income redistribution.

The purpose of this chapter is to provide an economic analysis of these issues. We begin by focusing on the system of taxes and transfers. Throughout the twentieth century, all the world's democracies chose to set up government-run redistribution systems aimed at either reducing income inequality or helping the poor; taxes and transfers lie at the heart of any government redistribution system. The aim is to make income distribution less unequal by taxing individuals who are relatively well off and making transfer payments to those who are relatively less well off. We begin the chapter with an analysis of the tax system, which is used to pay not only for transfer payments to the poor but also for government spending of all types—military, police, road building, schools. We then go on to consider transfers, such as welfare payments to the poor and social security payments to the elderly. After we examine the features of tax and transfer systems, and understand how they affect the incentives of individuals making purposeful choices with limited resources, we examine the actual distribution of income and discuss how it has been affected by the tax and transfer system in the United States.

This is an exciting time to study tax and income distribution policy. We are now observing some of the effects of the major welfare legislation enacted in the late 1990s. Passionate debates rage about whether the tax cuts implemented by President Bush in his first term of office should be extended when they expire beginning in 2009. Considerable debate exists about issues such as whether the estate tax should be abolished, whether the Earned Income Tax Credit program should be simplified so that more people can benefit from it, whether taxing capital income at a different rate from labor income is "fair," and whether social security and Medicare benefits should be available only on a means-tested basis for those below some income or wealth threshold. This chapter endeavors to provide you with some economic principles that will help you form and defend your opinions about these controversial matters.

THE TAX SYSTEM

We begin by considering the tax system. The first part of our analysis is descriptive, looking at the different types of taxes used in the United States. Then we move into a more analytical mode, and review the efficiency and distributional implications of the tax system. Finally, we draw on these analytical findings to look at some policy proposals for reforming the tax system and discuss their merits.

The major types of taxes that exist in the United States are the *personal income tax* on people's total income, the *payroll tax* on wage and salary income, the *corporate income tax* on corporate profit income, *excise/sales taxes* on goods and services purchased, *estate* and *gift taxes* on inheritances and gifts from one person to another, and *tariffs*, which are taxes on goods imported into the country. In addition, many local governments raise revenue through *property taxes*.

As shown in Figure 1, the personal income tax and the payroll tax are by far the largest sources of tax revenue for the federal government. Together they account for nearly 80 percent of federal tax revenue. Hence, we focus most of our attention on these two taxes in the following discussion.

The Personal Income Tax

personal income tax: a tax on all forms of income an individual or household receives.

taxable income: a household's income minus exemptions and deductions.

The **personal income tax** is a tax on all the income an individual or household receives, including wage and salary income, interest and dividend income, income from a small business, rents on property, royalties, and capital gains. (A *capital gain* is the increase in the value of an asset like a corporate stock. When the asset is sold, the capital gain—equal to the difference between the original purchase price and the selling price of the asset—is treated as income and is taxed.) The personal income tax was introduced in 1917 in the United States, soon after the ratification of the Sixteenth Amendment to the U.S. Constitution, which authorized income taxes. Most states have now followed the federal government and have enacted a personal income tax at the state level; we focus our attention on the personal income tax collected by the federal government.

■ **Computing the Personal Income Tax.** To explain the economic effects of the personal income tax, we must examine how the amount of tax a household owes is determined. The amount of tax owed by a household depends on the tax rate and the amount of taxable income. **Taxable income** is defined as a household's income minus certain exemptions and deductions. An *exemption* is a dollar amount that can be subtracted from income for each person in the household. *Deductions* are other expenditure items actually incurred—such as interest payments on a home mortgage, charitable contributions, and moving expenses—that can be subtracted from income before taxes are assessed.

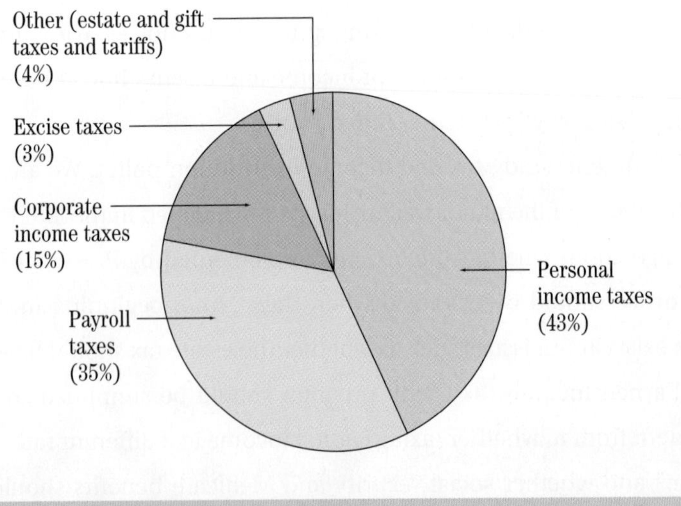

FIGURE 1
Taxes Paid to the Federal Government in 2006
Nearly 80 percent of federal taxes comes from the personal income tax and the payroll tax.

Pie chart labels:
- Other (estate and gift taxes and tariffs) (4%)
- Excise taxes (3%)
- Corporate income taxes (15%)
- Payroll taxes (35%)
- Personal income taxes (43%)

Consider, for example, the Lee family, which has four members: a wife, a husband, and two children. Suppose the Lees can subtract $3,300 as a personal exemption for each of the four people in the family, for a total of $13,200, and are entitled to a deduction of $10,300. Thus, they can subtract a total of $23,500 ($13,200 + $10,300) from their income. Suppose that the husband and wife together earn a total income of $80,000. Then their taxable income is $56,500 ($80,000 − $23,500).

Now let us see how we combine taxable income with the tax rate to compute the tax. Figure 2 shows two different tax rate schedules that appeared in a recent IRS 1040 form. The tax rate schedule labeled "Schedule X" in the figure is for a taxpayer who is single; the tax rate schedule labeled "Schedule Y-1" is for two married taxpayers who are paying their taxes together. The first two columns give a range for taxable income, or the "amount on Form 1040, line 37." The next two columns tell how to compute the tax. The percentages in the tax rate schedule are the tax rates.

Look first at Schedule Y-1; the 10 percent tax rate in the schedule applies to all taxable income up to $15,100, at which point any additional income up to $61,300 is taxed at 15 percent. Any additional income over $61,300 but less than $123,700 is taxed at 25 percent, and so on for tax rates of 28 percent, 33 percent, and 35 percent. Each of the rows in these schedules corresponds to a different tax rate; the range of taxable income in each row is called a **tax bracket.**

tax bracket: a range of taxable income that is taxed at the same rate.

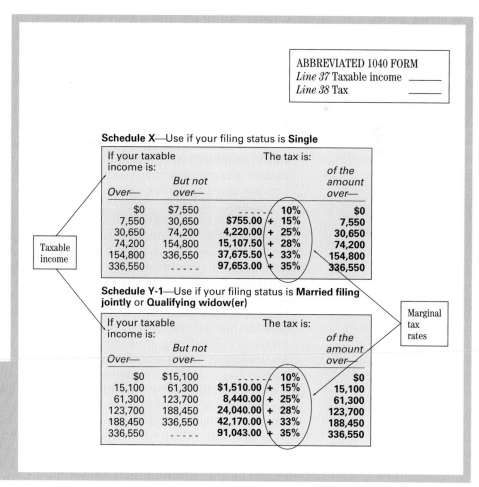

FIGURE 2
Two Tax Rate Schedules from the 1040 Form

The tables show how to compute the tax for each amount of taxable income. Observe how the marginal rates rise from one tax bracket to the next.

As an example, let us compute the Lees' tax. Recall that their taxable income is $56,500. They are married and filing jointly, so we look at Schedule Y-1. We go to the second line because $56,500 is between $15,100 and $61,300. In other words, the Lees are in the 15 percent tax bracket. We find that they must pay $1,510 plus 15 percent of the amount their income is over $15,100—that is, plus $.15 \times (\$56,500 - \$15,100) = \$6,210$. Thus, the amount of tax they must pay is $1,510 + $6,210 = $7,720.

■ **The Marginal Tax Rate.** Now consider what happens when the Lees' income changes. Suppose that one of the Lees decides to earn more income by working more hours and the Lees' income rises by $3,500. Thus, their taxable income rises from $56,500 to $60,000. Now what is their tax? Again looking at Schedule Y-1, we see that the tax is $1,510 + $.15 \times (\$60,000 - \$15,100) = \$1,510 + \$6,735 = \$8,245$. Thus, the Lees' tax has increased from $7,720 to $8,245, or by $525, as their income rose by $3,500. Observe that the tax rose by exactly 15 percent of the increase in income.

marginal tax rate: the change in total tax divided by the change in income.

The amount by which taxes change when one's income changes is the **marginal tax rate.** It is defined as the change in taxes divided by the change in income. In examining how the Lees compute their tax, we have discovered that their marginal tax rate is 15 percent. In other words, when their income increased, their taxes rose by 15 percent of the increase in income. As long as they stay within the 15 percent tax bracket, their marginal tax rate is 15 percent.

Observe that the marginal tax rate depends on one's income. The marginal rate varies from 10 percent for low incomes up to 35 percent for very high incomes. Suppose that one of the Lees did not work and that their taxable income was $12,500 rather than $56,500. Then they would be in the 10 percent bracket, and their marginal tax rate would be 10 percent.

average tax rate: the total tax paid divided by the total taxable income.

In contrast to the marginal tax rate, the **average tax rate** is the total tax paid divided by the total taxable income. For example, the Lees' average tax rate before we considered changes in their income was $\frac{\$7,720}{\$56,500} = .137$, or 13.7 percent, which is lower than the 15 percent marginal tax rate. In other words, the Lees pay 13.7 percent of their total taxable income in taxes but must pay 15 percent of any additional income in taxes. The average tax rate is less than the marginal tax rate because the Lees pay only 10 percent on the first $15,100 of taxable income.

Economists feel that the marginal rate is important for assessing the effects of taxes on individual behavior. Their reasoning can be illustrated with the Lees again. Suppose that the Lees' marginal tax rate was 10 percent rather than 15 percent. Then, if one of the Lees decided to work an additional half day a week, the family would be able to keep 90 cents of each extra dollar earned, sending 10 cents to the government. But with a marginal tax rate of 15 percent, the Lees could keep only 85 cents on the dollar. If the marginal tax rate for the Lees was 35 percent, then they could keep only 65 cents of each dollar earned. To take the example to an even greater extreme, suppose the marginal rate was 91 percent, which was the highest marginal rate before President Kennedy proposed reducing tax rates. Then, for each extra dollar earned, one could keep only 9 cents! Clearly, the marginal tax rate is going to influence people's choices about how much to work if they have a choice. The marginal tax rate has a significant effect on what people gain from working additional hours. This is why economists stress the marginal tax rate rather than the average tax rate when they look at the impact of the personal income tax on people's behavior.

Figure 3 provides a visual perspective on marginal tax rates. It plots the marginal tax rate from IRS Schedule Y-1 in Figure 2; the marginal tax rate is on the vertical axis, and taxable income is on the horizontal axis. Observe how the marginal tax rate rises with income.

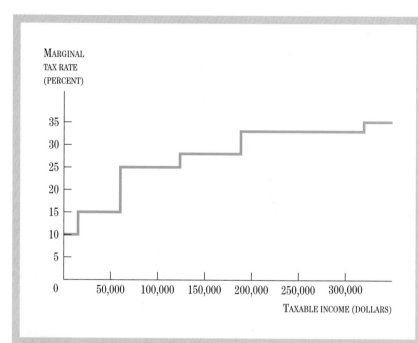

FIGURE 3
Marginal Tax Rates

As an example, the marginal tax rates from the IRS tax rate schedule Y-1 are plotted. The marginal tax rate is the change in the amount of tax paid for an extra dollar earned. The marginal tax rate increases with income. Each step takes the taxpayer to a higher tax bracket. Thus, higher-income people have a higher marginal tax rate than lower-income people. Under a flat tax, the marginal tax rate would be constant for all taxable income levels.

A tax is **progressive** *if the amount of the tax as a percentage of income rises as income increases.* If the marginal tax rate rises with income—in which case people with higher incomes pay a larger percentage of their income in taxes—then the tax is progressive. *A tax is* **regressive** *if the amount of the tax as a percentage of income falls as income rises.* An income tax would be regressive if the marginal tax rate declined as income rose, or if people with high incomes could use deductions or other schemes to reduce the tax they paid to a smaller percentage of income than people with lower incomes paid. *A tax is* **proportional** *if the amount of the tax as a percentage of income is constant as income rises.*

■ **Zero Tax on Low Incomes.** In assessing how progressive the income tax is, one needs to remember that the taxes are based on taxable income, which is less than the income a household actually receives. Taxable income can be zero even if a household's income is greater than zero. For example, if the Lee family earned only $23,500 for the year, then their taxable income would be zero, because $23,500 equals the sum of their exemptions and deductions. In general, the personal income tax is zero for household incomes up to the sum of the exemptions and deductions.

A **flat tax** occurs when the marginal tax rates are constant for all levels of taxable income, in which case the line in Figure 3 would become flat. Even a flat rate tax system would have a degree of progressivity: The tax paid would rise as a percentage of income from zero (for workers below the sum of exemptions and deductions) to a positive amount as income rises.

The Payroll Tax

The **payroll tax** is a tax on the wages and salaries of individuals; the payroll tax goes to finance social security benefits, Medicare, and unemployment insurance. Payroll taxes are submitted to the government by employers. For example, the Lees' employers must submit 15.3 percent of the Lees' wage and salary income to the federal government. Thus, the payroll tax on the Lees' wage and salary income of $80,000 would be $12,240 (that is, .153 × $80,000), almost 50 percent more than the total that the Lees would pay in personal income taxes!

The tax law says that half of the 15.3 percent payroll tax is to be paid by the worker and half is to be paid by the employer. Thus, the Lees would be notified of only half of the payroll tax, or $6,120, even though their employer sent $12,240 to the government. If a person is self-employed—a business consultant, say, or a free-lance editor—then the person pays the full 15.3 percent, because a self-employed person is both the employee and the employer. One of the most important things

progressive tax: a tax for which the amount of an individual's taxes rises as a proportion of income as the person's income increases.

regressive tax: a tax for which the amount of an individual's taxes falls as a proportion of income as the person's income increases.

proportional tax: a tax for which the amount of an individual's taxes as a percentage of income is constant as the person's income rises.

flat tax: a tax system in which there is a constant marginal tax rate for all levels of taxable income.

payroll tax: a tax on the wages and salaries of individuals.

The "Death Tax" Debate

Repeal of the federal estate tax has been a topic of frequent debate since it was included as part of the Bush tax cuts enacted in 2001. Under this legislation, the estate tax is to be gradually phased out until it is completely gone in 2010, but unless further measures are taken to repeal the tax permanently, the estate tax will return in 2011 under sunset provisions of that law. As with most tax policy, the estate tax issue is not simple or clear-cut, and it has, in fact, generated a great deal of heat, as described in this article.

White House Watch: Ann McFeatters / Send in the Spin
The "death tax" debate is alive and kicking in the Senate

Sunday, August 14, 2005

WASHINGTON—Once again, we are about to be hit with an emotional barrage of misleading "information" about the nation's urgent need to deal with the federal estate tax, which President Bush dubs the "death tax" and demands "must be repealed forever."

In an essay for The Wall Street Journal, Senate Majority Leader Bill Frist of Tennessee, one of the wealthiest members of the Senate, insists the "death tax is the cruelest, most unfair tax our government imposes." He said that in the first week after Labor Day he will call for a Senate vote to repeal it. "There will be no more hiding on the issue of permanent death-tax repeal," he warned.

The House voted April 13 to permanently repeal the estate tax. So Frist's vow sets up another all-out fight in the Senate. Republicans want to act now on repeal, even if they're defeated in their attempt, so they can use it as an issue against Democrats in next year's congressional elections. For their part, many Democrats intend to filibuster and charge Republicans with kowtowing to the rich.

The 2001 tax cut orchestrated by Bush gradually phases out the estate tax until it is gone completely in 2010. But in 2011, it comes back with a vengeance unless Congress permanently repeals the tax or lifts the amount exempted or otherwise changes the law.

So, what's the deal? Would the nation be better off without the grim-sounding "death tax"?

Those who shout "yes!" argue that the tax is duplicative because in some cases federal income taxes already have been imposed on assets accumulated. However, at the time of death, capital gains tax usually has not been paid on the vast block of stocks or bonds or property that have risen substantially in value.

Supporters of repeal say estate taxes are unfair to farm families and small businesses. But the Tax Policy Center estimates that last year estate taxes were paid on only 440 farms and small businesses out of the thousands of farms and small businesses left to heirs, and that taxes paid averaged less than 20 percent of the value of the estate. Also, there are special rules for estates with farms and businesses that reduce taxes owed.

Those who shout "no!" to repeal say the number of families actually subject to the estate tax is minuscule. The Congressional Research Service notes IRS figures that show that of the 2.4 million people who die in this country each year, only 1.3 percent of their estates owe any estate tax.

The "no" side makes the point that billions of dollars lost to the government by repeal would either mean cuts in federal programs or higher taxes elsewhere. The Congressional Budget Office estimates lost revenue from repealing the estate tax would be $380 billion over 10 years.

In a little-noticed irony, millions of American who pay no estate tax now could be hit with heavy new capital gains taxes on inheritances, depending on what Congress does. And the complications of determining how much capital gains would be due on property held for years by someone now deceased would be mind-boggling. Nobody in his or her right mind would want to be executor of a will.

The astonishing thing is that this would be so arduous, even for tax lawyers, and taxes could be so much higher that there would be a huge uproar at the same time Bush is promising, as he did this past week, to "develop a simpler [tax] code that's a fairer code and one that encourages economic growth."

Without any doubt, the coming debate will be mean and confusing. The argument of the American Conservative Union, for repeal, is: "Everything you have worked hard for your entire life, everything you wanted to leave to your children and grandchildren to keep your legacy alive, will again be taxed. And this time the tax rate will be that of a loan shark." FactCheck.org, which calls itself a nonpartisan, nonprofit, consumer advocate for voters and takes no stand on repeal, says nothing in that statement is true.

Supporters of keeping the estate tax argue that the true beneficiaries of repeal would be America's wealthiest families, those with many millions of dollars and flanks of lawyers able to figure out how to set up new tax shelters such as family limited partnerships and avoid capital gains taxes. Calling repeal the "Paris Hilton Relief Act," they claim the estate tax is one of the fairest, most progressive taxes, and that repeal would lower contributions to charity by 6 percent. But that's a highly debatable claim.

There is little doubt that the inordinately complex estate tax, at the least, needs an overhaul with higher exemptions. A million dollars ain't what it used to be.

But the vitriolic, misleading, partisan debate in the Senate we're about to have to endure will not do anyone any good.

to understand about the payroll tax is that, as we will soon prove, its economic effects do not depend on who is legally required to pay what share of the tax; only the total 15.3 percent matters.

Other Taxes

corporate income tax: a tax on the accounting profits of corporations.

excise tax: a tax paid on the value of goods at the time of purchase.

sales tax: a type of excise tax that applies to total expenditures on a broad group of goods.

property tax: a tax on the value of property owned.

All other federal taxes together amount to a little over one-fifth of total revenue. **Corporate income taxes** are taxes on the accounting profits of corporations. Currently the corporate tax rate ranges from 15 percent to 38 percent, depending on the level of earnings.

Excise taxes are taxes on goods that are paid when the goods are purchased. The federal government taxes several specific items, including gasoline, tobacco, beer, wine, and hard liquor. A **sales tax** is a type of excise tax that applies to total expenditures on a broad group of goods. For example, if your expenditures on many different goods at a retail store total $100 and the sales tax rate is 5 percent, then you pay $5 in sales tax. There is no national sales tax in the United States, but sales taxes are a major source of revenue for many state and local governments.

Finally, the federal government raises revenue by imposing tariffs on goods as they enter the United States. Until the Sixteenth Amendment was ratified and the personal income tax was introduced, tariffs were the major source of revenue for the U.S. government. Now revenue from tariffs is a minor portion of total revenue.

Local governments rely heavily on **property taxes**—taxes on residential homes and business real estate—to raise revenue. Recall that income taxes—both personal and corporate—are also used at the state level to raise revenue for state governments.

The Effects of Taxes

The purpose of most of the taxes just described is to raise revenue, but taxes can have significant effects on people's behavior. To examine these effects, let us start with a tax we looked at before in Chapter 7: a tax on a good or service.

■ **The Effect of a Tax on a Good.**   Recall that a tax on a good adds the amount of the tax to the marginal cost of the seller of the good. For example, a tax of $1 on a gallon of gasoline will shift the supply curve up by the amount of the tax, a result shown in Figure 9 in Chapter 7 on page 195. Once the supply curve shifts as a result of the tax, equilibrium price and quantity will also change. The ultimate impact on price and quantity will depend on the price elasticities of supply and demand.

The four panels of Figure 4 are designed to enable us to show how the price elasticity of demand and the price elasticity of supply determine the impact of the tax. In each of the four panels of the figure, the supply curve shifts up due to a tax of the same amount, shown by the blue arrow to the left of each vertical axis. As a result, in each of the four panels, the equilibrium price rises and the equilibrium quantity falls because of the tax. The decline in the equilibrium quantity creates a loss of consumer surplus plus producer surplus, which we have called the deadweight loss from the tax. The size of the deadweight loss and the relative size of the impact on the price and the quantity are different in each panel of Figure 4 because the supply curve and the demand curve have different price elasticities.

One key point illustrated in Figure 4 is that *when the price elasticity of demand or the price elasticity of supply is very low, the deadweight loss from the tax is small*. This is shown in the two graphs in the left part of Figure 4, which have either a low elasticity of demand (top left) or a low elasticity of supply (bottom left). In either case, the deadweight loss is small compared with that in the graphs at the right, which have higher elasticities.

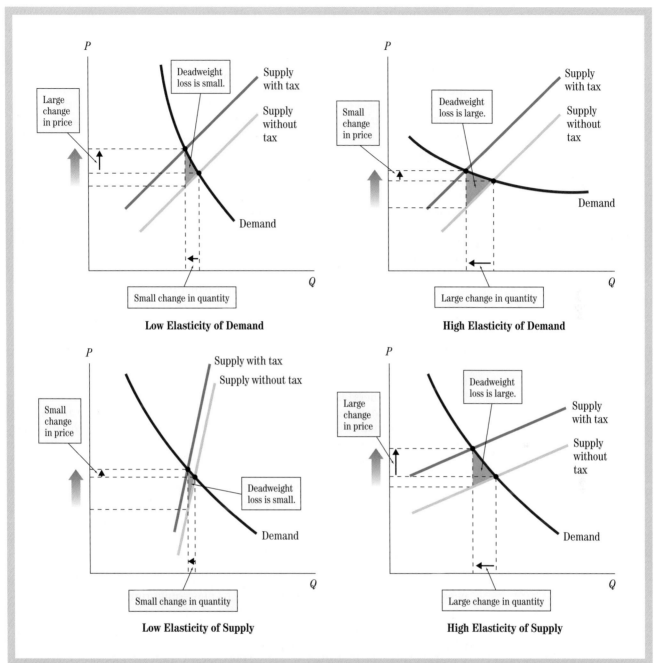

FIGURE 4
How Elasticities Determine the Effects of Taxes

(1) *Deadweight loss effects:* When price elasticities are low, as in the left graphs, the deadweight loss is small and the change in equilibrium quantity is small. When price elasticities are high, as in the right graphs, the deadweight loss is large and the change in equilibrium quantity is large.
(2) *Tax incidence and price effects:* When the price elasticity of demand is low or the price elasticity of supply is high, the tax is largely passed on to the consumer in the form of higher prices. In contrast, when the price elasticity of demand is high or the price elasticity of supply is low, the burden of the tax falls on the producer because there is little price change.

The intuitive reason why low elasticities result in small deadweight losses is that the quantity of the good does not change very much when the price changes. Recall that a low price elasticity of demand means that quantity demanded is not very sensitive to a change in the price, as, for example, in the case of a good like salt, which has few substitutes. A low elasticity of supply means that there is only a small change in the quantity supplied when the price changes. Thus, in the case of low elasticities, there is only a small difference between the efficient quantity of production and the quantity of production with the tax. There is little loss of efficiency. On the other hand, *when the price elasticity of demand or the price elasticity of supply is very high, the deadweight loss from the tax will be relatively large*. Here changes in price have big effects on either the quantity demanded or the quantity supplied, and the deadweight loss is large.

The price elasticities of supply and demand also affect how much the price changes in response to a tax. If the price rises by a large amount, then the tax is passed on to buyers in the form of higher prices, and the burden of the tax falls more on buyers. If the price rises little or not at all, then the seller absorbs the burden of the tax, and most of the tax is not passed on to buyers. **Tax incidence** refers to who actually bears the burden of the tax, the buyers or the sellers.

tax incidence: the allocation of the burden of the tax between buyer and seller.

By comparing the graphs in Figure 4, we see that *the smaller the price elasticity of demand and the larger the price elasticity of supply, the greater the rise in the price*. The intuitive reason for this result is somewhat more complicated than before. The price that the consumer has to pay increases immediately by the amount of the tax, reducing the quantity demanded; when demand is not very elastic, the quantity demanded will not decrease by very much in the face of this higher price. Furthermore, even though the price paid by consumers has increased by the amount of the tax, the price received by suppliers (and hence the quantity supplied) has not changed. This implies that there is a small excess supply in the aftermath of the tax, which needs to be cleared for the market to reach its new equilibrium. With a very elastic supply curve, the price does not have to fall by very much from its new level to clear the market. The market will reach equilibrium at a new price that is close in value to the original price plus the tax. In other words, buyers will end up paying the bulk of the tax.

The opposite will be true if the elasticity of demand is large and the elasticity of supply is small—the impact of the tax will raise the price by only a little. Once again the price that the consumer has to pay increases immediately by the amount of the tax, reducing the quantity demanded. Since demand is very elastic, the quantity demanded will decrease substantially in the face of this higher price. The quantity supplied does not immediately change because the price received by suppliers has not changed. This creates substantial excess supply in the aftermath of the tax, which needs to be cleared for the market to reach its new equilibrium. With a very inelastic supply curve, price has to fall considerably from its new level to clear the market. The market will reach equilibrium at a new price that is close in value to the original price. In other words, sellers will end up paying the bulk of the tax.

What this tells us is that taxing a good like cigarettes, with a low elasticity of demand, will result in the buyers of cigarettes bearing the tax. In contrast, taxing a good like land, which has a low elasticity of supply, will not affect the price very much, and the suppliers of the land will bear the burden of the tax.

■ **Effects of the Personal Income Tax.**   We can apply the results of this analysis to the personal income tax. The personal income tax is a tax on *labor* income (wages and salaries) as well as on *capital* income (interest, dividends, small business profits). However, labor income is by far the larger share of most people's income: For all 1040 forms filed, wages and salaries are over 75 percent of total income. Thus, we model the personal income tax as a tax on labor income.

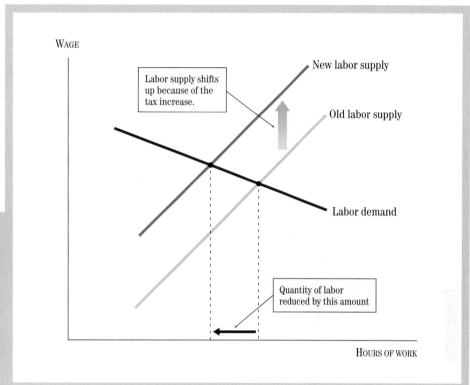

WAGE

Labor supply shifts up because of the tax increase.

New labor supply

Old labor supply

Labor demand

Quantity of labor reduced by this amount

HOURS OF WORK

FIGURE 5
Effects of a Higher Income Tax on Labor Supply
An income tax shifts the labor supply curve up by the amount of the tax on each extra hour of work because the worker must pay part of wage income to the government and thus receives less for each hour of work. Thus, the quantity of labor supplied declines. The decline in hours worked would be small if the supply curve had a low elasticity.

The analysis of the personal income tax is illustrated in Figure 5. Because the personal income tax is a tax on labor income, we need a model of the labor market to examine the effects of the tax. Figure 5 shows a labor demand curve and a labor supply curve. The wage paid to the worker is on the vertical axis, and the quantity of labor is on the horizontal axis. Figure 5 shows that the personal income tax shifts the labor supply curve up. The size of the upward shift depends on the marginal tax rate because the income received from work would be reduced by the marginal tax. If the person was in the 15 percent bracket, the income received from working would be 85 cents for each extra dollar earned working. Thus, to supply exactly the same quantity as without the tax, people require a higher wage. Because the wage paid to the worker is on the vertical axis, the labor supply curve shifts up to show this.

As the labor supply curve shifts up, the equilibrium quantity of labor declines. Thus, we predict that an income tax will reduce the amount of work. The reduced amount of work will cause a deadweight loss just like that caused by the tax on a commodity. The size of the decline in hours of work will depend on the labor supply and labor demand elasticities. The higher the labor supply elasticity, the greater the reduction in the quantity of labor supplied in response to the personal income tax.

Economists disagree about the size of the labor supply elasticity. One thing that is sure is that the elasticity is different for different people. For example, the labor supply elasticity appears to be quite high for second earners in a two-earner family such as the Lees. If elasticity is high, a high marginal tax rate can reduce hours of work and thereby income. But if the labor supply curve has a low elasticity, there is little effect on hours of work.

■ **The Effect of a Payroll Tax.**   We can use the same type of labor market diagram to analyze a payroll tax, as shown in Figure 6. Clearly, the payroll tax is a tax on labor in

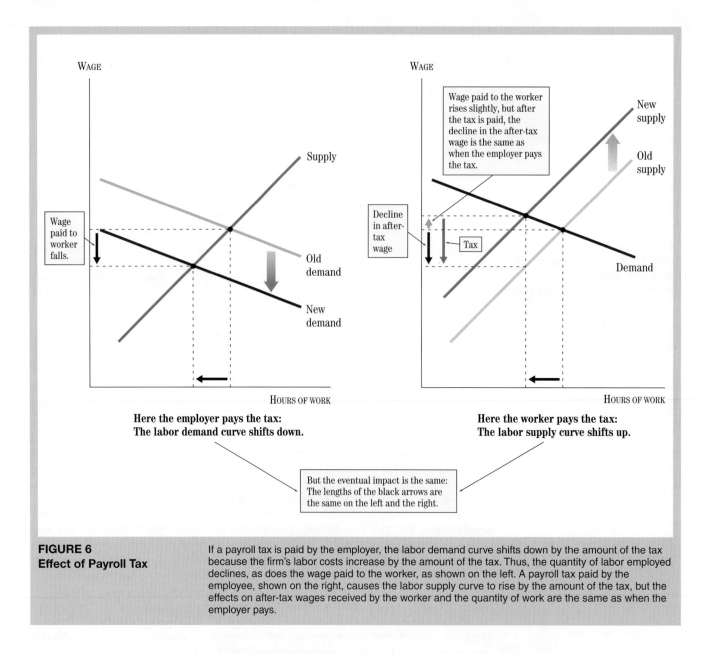

FIGURE 6
Effect of Payroll Tax

If a payroll tax is paid by the employer, the labor demand curve shifts down by the amount of the tax because the firm's labor costs increase by the amount of the tax. Thus, the quantity of labor employed declines, as does the wage paid to the worker, as shown on the left. A payroll tax paid by the employee, shown on the right, causes the labor supply curve to rise by the amount of the tax, but the effects on after-tax wages received by the worker and the quantity of work are the same as when the employer pays.

that it applies to wages and salaries. However, in the case of the payroll tax, we need to consider that the tax is paid by both the employer and the employee, as required by law. Figure 6 handles the two cases.

Suppose that the wage before the tax is $10 per hour and that the payroll tax is 10 percent, or $1 per hour. The case where the tax is paid by the employee is shown on the right of Figure 6. This picture looks much like Figure 5. The labor supply curve shifts up by the amount of the tax ($1) because the worker now has to pay a tax to the government for each hour worked. In other words, the worker will supply the same amount of work when the wage is $11 and the tax is $1 as when the wage is $10 and the tax is zero.

When the labor supply curve shifts up, we see in the right-hand panel of Figure 6 that the equilibrium quantity of labor employed declines. Observe that the wage paid

TABLE 1
Tax Rates and Tax Revenue: An Example

Tax Rate	Wage	Hours Worked	Tax Revenues
.50	$10/hour	2,000	$10,000
.75	$10/hour	1,500	$11,250
.90	$10/hour	500	$ 4,500

by the employer rises; this is because of the lower supply of labor. However, the "after-tax wage"—the wage less the tax—declines because the increase in the wage is less than the tax increase.

The case where the tax is paid by the employer is shown in the left graph of Figure 6. In this case, the labor demand curve shifts down by the amount of the tax ($1) because the firm has to pay an additional $1 for each hour of work. When the labor demand curve shifts down, the equilibrium quantity of labor employed declines and the wage falls. Observe that the impact of the payroll tax is the same in both cases: There is a new equilibrium in the labor market with a lower wage and a lower quantity of labor.

Thus, a payroll tax has both an employment-reduction effect and a wage-reduction effect. As with any tax, the size of the quantity change and the price (wage) change depends on the supply and demand elasticities. If we apply the results from Figure 4, we know that when the labor supply elasticity is low and the labor demand elasticity is high, there will be a small reduction in employment, but the wage will fall by a large amount. However, if the labor supply elasticity is high and the labor demand elasticity is low, there will be a large employment effect, but the wage effect will be small.

tax revenue: the tax rate times the amount subject to tax.

■ The Possibility of a Perverse Effect on Tax Revenue.   **Tax revenue** received by the government is equal to the tax rate times the amount that is subject to the tax. For example, in the case of a gasoline tax, the tax revenue is the tax per gallon times the number of gallons sold. As the tax rate increases, the amount subject to the tax will fall because the higher price due to the tax reduces the quantity demanded. If the quantity demanded falls sharply enough, then tax revenue could actually fall when the tax rate is increased.

The same possibility arises in the case of taxes on labor, either the payroll tax or the personal income tax. In the case of the payroll tax or the personal income tax for a worker, tax revenue is equal to the tax rate times the wage and salary income. As the tax rate rises, the amount of income subject to tax may fall if labor supply declines. Thus, in principle, it is possible that a higher tax rate could result in reduced tax revenue. For example, consider the high marginal tax rates shown in Table 1: 50 percent, 75 percent, and 90 percent. If labor supply declines with a higher tax rate, as assumed in the table, then tax revenue first increases as the tax rate goes from 50 to 75 percent but then declines as the tax rate goes from 75 to 90 percent.

The general relationship between tax rates and tax revenue is illustrated in Figure 7. As in the example of Table 1, tax revenue first rises and then falls as the tax rate increases. Figure 7 can apply to any tax on anything. At the two extremes of zero percent tax rate and 100 percent tax rate, tax revenue is zero. What happens between

FIGURE 7
The Tax Rate and Tax Revenue
As the tax rate increases from low levels, tax revenue rises. At some point, however, the high tax rate reduces the quantity of the item that is taxed and encourages so much tax avoidance that the amount of tax revenue declines. This curve is frequently called the *Laffer curve*. The particular tax rate at which the curve bends depends on the price elasticity of the item being taxed and is a subject of great debate among economists.

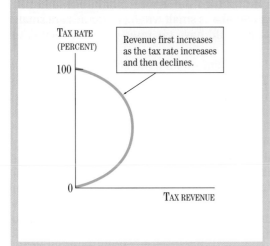

these two extremes depends on the elasticities. This relationship between the tax rate and tax revenue, now frequently called the Laffer curve after the economist Arthur Laffer, who made it popular in the 1980s, has long been known to economists. It implies that if the tax rate is so high that we are on the downward-sloping part of the curve, then reducing the tax rate may increase tax revenue. However, there is great debate among economists about the tax rate at which the curve bends around. Few economists believe that the curve bends at a rate that is as low as 35 percent, the current top marginal rate in the United States.

Other factors that influence tax revenue, especially when marginal tax rates get very high, are tax avoidance and tax evasion. *Tax avoidance* means finding legal ways to reduce taxes, such as buying a home rather than renting in order to have a deduction for interest payments on a mortgage. *Tax evasion* is an illegal means of reducing one's tax. For example, at high tax rates, people have incentives to evade the tax by not reporting income. Workers are tempted not to report tips. Or people resort to barter, which is difficult for the government to track down. For example, an employer may "pay" a little extra to a truck driver by allowing free use of the truck on weekends for fishing trips.

Tax Policy and the Tradeoff Between Efficiency and Equality

We have observed in our analysis of each tax that the equilibrium quantity of the item taxed declines when the tax rate rises. This is where the inefficiency of the tax comes from. If the tax rate is very high, or the elasticities are very high, the inefficiency can be so severe that it could thwart one of the purposes of raising the taxes: to provide income support in order to increase the well-being of the least well-off in the society. Why? Because the reduction in the quantity of labor supplied or goods produced could be so great that there would be less total income in the society. Thus, there would be less going to the poor even if they received a larger share of total income. In other words, there is a *tradeoff between equality and efficiency*. If one raises taxes too high for the purpose of making the income distribution more equal, the total amount of income may decline. In that event, there will be less available to redistribute.

Given these considerations, how should the tax system—the combination of all the taxes in society—be designed or improved?

First, in order to reduce deadweight loss to a minimum, the ideal tax system should tax items with small price elasticities of supply and demand rather than items with large elasticities. We know that the deadweight loss is small when elasticities are small. The optimal tax system would have tax rates inversely related to the elasticities.

Second, the ideal tax system would try to keep the marginal tax rates low and the amount that is subject to tax high. For example, we saw that deductions reduce the amount subject to personal income tax by lowering taxable income. Some deductions are put in the tax system to encourage certain activities: A deduction for research expenses may encourage firms to fund research, for example. However, the more deductions there are, the higher the tax rate has to be in order to get the same tax revenue. Economists use the term *broadening the tax base* to describe an increase in the amount of income subject to taxation by limiting or eliminating deductions and exemptions. With a broader tax base, a lower marginal tax rate can generate the same amount of revenue; the lower marginal tax rate has the additional advantage of reducing the inefficiency of the

"And do you promise to love, honor, and cherish each other, and pay the United States government more taxes as a married couple than you would have paid if you had just continued living together?"

tax. Most tax reform efforts have involved trying to broaden the tax base while lowering marginal tax rates. This was the idea behind the tax reform efforts in the 1960s under President Kennedy and in the 1980s under President Reagan. In the early 2000s, the marginal tax rates on all taxpayers were reduced substantially. However, many new deductions, exemptions, and credits were also introduced, so the tax base was not broadened.

Third, the ideal tax system should be as simple and as fair as possible. If a tax system is not simple, then valuable resources—people's time, computers, and so on—must be devoted to paying and processing taxes. A tax system is seen as unfair if it is regressive. Another view of fairness frequently used is the **ability-to-pay principle;** this view is that those with greater income should pay more in taxes than those with less income. The tax system is also viewed as unfair if people with the same incomes are taxed at different rates. For example, in the U.S. tax system, a married couple with each making $60,000 a year pays a higher tax than an unmarried couple with exactly the same income. This is viewed by some as unfair.

ability-to-pay principle: the view that those with greater income should pay more in taxes than those with less income.

REVIEW

- Taxes are a vital source of revenue for the government. In the United States, the personal income tax and the payroll tax are the largest source of tax revenue for the government. Other sources of tax revenue include corporate income taxes, excise taxes, and gift taxes.

- In analyzing how a tax system works, key variables to pay attention to include deductions and exemptions, tax brackets and the associated marginal tax rates, and how progressive the tax code is.

- Taxes cause inefficiencies in the form of reduced economic activity and deadweight loss. The deadweight loss associated with a tax is high when the price elasticities of supply and demand are high.

- Tax incidence identifies who bears the burden of paying the tax. When the elasticity of demand is low and the elasticity of supply is high, the burden of paying the tax falls largely on the consumer. Conversely, in situations where the elasticity of demand is high and the elasticity of supply is low, the burden of paying the tax is largely borne by the seller.

- The impact of higher taxes on tax revenue depends on the impact on equilibrium quantity. If the equilibrium quantity falls by a sufficiently large amount, then tax revenue could actually decline.

- This implies that there is a tradeoff between efficiency and equality in designing tax policy; raising taxes to reduce inequality may increase economic inefficiency and thereby reduce the amount of total income and tax revenue.

- To minimize the inefficiencies, items with low elasticities should be taxed more than items with high elasticities. Other methods of eliminating inefficiencies include policies that broaden the tax base while lowering the marginal tax rate, and keeping the tax system simple and fair so as to not to create incentives for tax evasion and tax avoidance.

- The criterion of "fairness" is also used to evaluate how ideal a tax system is. Principles of fairness include progressivity and treating people who have the same income identically—regardless of marital status, for example.

TRANSFER PAYMENTS

transfer payment: a grant of funds from the government to an individual.

Transfer payments, payments made by the government to an individual that are not in exchange for goods or services, have important implications for the alleviation of poverty and the distribution of income in the United States. Transfer payments can be either in cash or in kind, such as vouchers that can be used to buy food or housing.

There are two types of government transfer payments in the United States: **means-tested transfers,** which depend on the income (the means) of the recipient and focus on helping poor people, and **social insurance transfers,** which do not depend on the income of the recipient.

means-tested transfer: a transfer payment that depends on the income of the recipient.

social insurance transfer: a transfer payment, such as social security, that does not depend on the income of the recipient.

Means-Tested Transfer Programs

Means-tested transfer payments are made to millions of people in the United States each year. The major programs are listed in Table 2.

The 1996 federal welfare law (called the Personal Responsibility and Work Opportunity Reconciliation Act, or PRWORA) created the **Temporary Assistance to Needy Families (TANF) program,** replacing the Aid to Families with Dependent Children (AFDC), which was what people typically referred to as "welfare" in the United States. TANF is a transfer program that provides cash payments to eligible poor families with children. The federal government provides grants to the states, which then decide which poor families are eligible. Unlike AFDC, TANF assistance is limited in duration (there is a five-year lifetime limit) and requires that recipients work a certain number of hours per week.

Temporary Assistance to Needy Families (TANF) program: transfer programs through which the federal government makes grants to states to give cash to certain low-income families.

Medicaid is a health insurance program that is designed primarily to pay for health care for people with low incomes. Once income increases to a certain level, Medicaid support stops, so that the family must find another means of obtaining health insurance. **Supplemental security income (SSI)** is a program designed to help the neediest elderly as well as poor people who are disabled or blind. About 6.6 million people receive SSI assistance, including 4.6 million disabled and 2 million aged people.

Medicaid: a health insurance program designed primarily for families with low incomes.

supplemental security income (SSI): a means-tested transfer program designed primarily to help the poor who are disabled or blind.

TABLE 2
Means-Tested Transfer Programs in the United States (Each of these federal programs requires that the recipient's income or assets be below a certain amount in order to receive payment.)

Temporary Assistance to Needy Families (TANF)	Payments to poor families with children as determined by each state
Medicaid	Health insurance primarily for welfare recipients
SSI (Supplemental Security Income)	Payments to poor people who are old, disabled, or blind
Food Stamp Program	Coupons allowing low-income people to buy food
Head Start	Preschool education for low-income children
Housing Assistance	Rental subsidies and aid for construction

food stamp program: a government program that provides people with low incomes with coupons (food stamps) that they can use to buy food.

Head Start: a government transfer program that provides day care and nursery school training for poor children.

housing assistance programs: government programs that provide subsidies either to low-income families to rent housing or to contractors to build low-income housing.

earned income tax credit (EITC): a part of the personal income tax through which people with low income who work receive a payment from the government or a rebate on their taxes.

The **food stamp program** is a major means-tested transfer program; it makes payments to about 17 million people each year. Like Medicaid, food stamps are an in-kind payment. People are not supposed to use the coupons to buy anything but food. This is a popular program because the intent of the money is to provide nutrition and because the program is fairly inexpensive to run. The National School Lunch Program is similar to food stamps in that it aims to provide food to lower-income children. It provides school lunches for about 29 million children.

Head Start, another in-kind program, provides for preschool assistance to poor children to help them get a good start in school. It also is a popular program because there is evidence that it improves the performance, at least temporarily, of preschool children as they enter elementary school.

Housing assistance programs provide rental subsidies to people who cannot afford to buy a home. The programs sometimes provide aid to business firms that construct low-income housing. Many complain about waste and poor incentives in the housing programs and argue that these programs are in need of reform.

The **Earned Income Tax Credit (EITC)** program is a means-tested transfer payment program received by about 20 million working poor families. The EITC is actually part of the personal income tax, the form to obtain the transfer payment is sent to people by the IRS along with the 1040 form. Working people whose income is below a certain level, either because their wage is very low or because they work part time, get a refundable credit that raises their take-home pay. For example, consider the four-person Lee family again. We know that if the Lees earn less than $23,500, they pay no income tax. However, if the Lees earn between $0 and $11,350 in wages and salary and have no other income, then the EITC will pay 40 cents for each dollar they earn up to a maximum of $4,536 per year. To make sure that the EITC does not make payments to high-income people, the payments decline if the Lees make more than $16,850. For each dollar they earn above $16,850, they lose 22 cents of their $4,536 until the benefits run out (when their income reaches $38,348 with more than one qualifying child).

Observe that the EITC raises the incentive to work for incomes up to $11,350 and reduces the incentive to work for incomes greater than $16,850 and less than $38,348. With the EITC, the marginal tax rate is effectively *negative* 40 percent for income below $10,750; that is, you *get* 40 cents rather than *pay* 40 cents for each dollar you earn. But the EITC adds 22 percent to the marginal tax rate for incomes between $16,850 and $38,348.

Incentive Effects

The previous section describes a variety of government programs that aim to transfer funds to the poor. As we will see, evidence suggests that these programs do have an impact in reducing income inequality. However, some people feel that the programs may create a disincentive to work, since welfare payments are reduced when income from work rises.

The top panel of Figure 8 illustrates the first disincentive problem. The total income of an individual is plotted against the number of hours worked. Total income consists of wage income from work plus a welfare payment. The more steeply sloped solid black line shows the individual's wage income from work: The more hours worked, the more wage income the individual receives. This line intercepts the horizontal axis at zero income, so if there is no work and there is no welfare or charity, the person is in a state of extreme poverty.

The individual's total income is shown by the less steeply sloped dashed line in the top graph of Figure 8. It intercepts the vertical axis at an amount equal to the

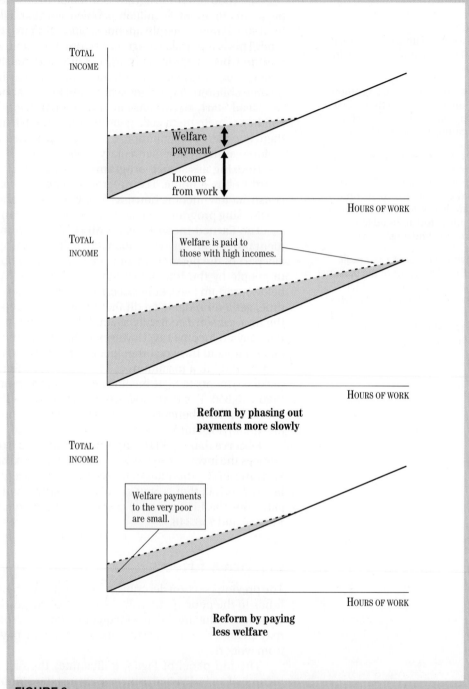

FIGURE 8
Welfare Reform to Improve Work Incentives
The top graph shows how welfare reduces the marginal earnings from working more hours because welfare payments are phased out. There are two basic approaches to reform: phasing out the payments more slowly (as in the middle graph) or lowering the welfare payment (as in the lower graph). Each has both advantages and disadvantages.

welfare payment the individual gets when he or she is not working at all. As the individual begins to work, the need for welfare declines, and so the welfare payment declines. Observe that the amount of the welfare payment, which is represented by the shaded gap between the steep line and the less steep line, diminishes as the hours of work increase, and finally, after a certain number of hours worked, the welfare payment disappears.

Because the welfare payment is reduced when the individual's income from work rises, it creates a disincentive. The flatter the dashed line, the greater the disincentive. For example, if someone decides to work 10 hours a week for a total of $50 per week, but the welfare payment is reduced by $30 per week, then effectively the marginal tax rate is 60 percent, high enough to discourage work.

Welfare reform endeavors to change the welfare system in order to reduce this disincentive. Looking at Figure 8, we see that there are two ways to make the dashed line steeper and thereby provide more incentive to work. One way is to reduce the amount of welfare paid at the zero income amount. Graphically, this is shown in the lower graph of Figure 8. This twists the dashed line because the intercept on the vertical axis is lower, but the intersection of the dashed line and the solid line is at the same number of hours of work as in the top graph. This will increase the slope of the dashed line and therefore provide more incentive to work. But the problem with this approach is that poor people get less welfare: The poverty rate could rise.

A second way to make the dashed line steeper is to raise the place at which it intersects the black solid line, as in the middle graph of Figure 8. But that might mean making welfare payments to people who do not need them at all, people who earn $50,000 or $60,000 annually.

The welfare reform act signed into law by President Clinton in 1996 left the decision as to which welfare reform approach to take up to the states. The states went off in different directions; some chose to cut welfare benefits for those who were not working, while others raised the amount that can be earned before welfare is reduced. Some states require adult welfare recipients to go to work immediately. Twenty-four states require that people work after two years on welfare. Other states require that a single parent finish high school in order to get the full welfare payment. These proposals are aimed at increasing the incentive to get off welfare and go to work. Have they worked? Supporters say emphatically, yes—welfare rolls have been dramatically reduced, employment levels of the very poor have risen, and poverty levels have declined. Critics argue that the poverty alleviation is the result of the health of the economy, not the welfare reform. They also note that many of those previous recipients of welfare are still struggling—they may be working, but they are not earning enough to raise themselves out of poverty. These critics contend that many of these people will have trouble keeping jobs unless they have adequate support services, such as health insurance and child care.

Social Insurance Programs

The largest transfer payment programs in the United States, social security, Medicare, and unemployment insurance, are not means-tested programs. These programs are called *social insurance* programs because they make payments to anyone—rich or poor—under certain specific circumstances. **Social security** is the system through which payments from the government are made to individuals when they retire or become disabled. **Medicare** is a health insurance program for older people. **Unemployment insurance** pays money to individuals who are laid off from work.

social security: the system through which individuals make payments to the government when they work and receive payments from the government when they retire or become disabled.

Medicare: a government health insurance program for the elderly.

unemployment insurance: a program that makes payments to people who lose their jobs.

Assessing the Success of the 1996 Welfare Reform a Decade Later

The 1996 welfare reform act was an important yet controversial piece of legislation. It imposed time limits and work requirements for welfare recipients. At the time, supporters argued that these limits would ensure that the plan was there to help those who were truly in need while still providing incentives for recepients to go find work instead of being dependent on welfare. Opponents argued that the reform would hurt welfare recepients, especially single mothers, who would have a hard time juggling full-time employment with child care requirements and expenses. As 2006 approached, there was a heightened interest in reassessing how the 1996 reform had affected the lives of welfare recepients. This article from the *New York Times* is one such piece.

Arguments that confirm the predictions of those who backed welfare reform

The criticism made by opponents that some single mothers have been left behind by the reform

Description of the reform enacted in 1996

A summary of what the outcomes have been

Reforming means-tested transfer programs has proven to be much easier than reforming social insurance programs. Can you explain why this may be?

A Decade After Welfare Overhaul, a Fundamental Shift in Policy and Perception — By ROBERT PEAR and ERIK ECKHOLM

WASHINGTON, Aug. 20—Ten years after a Republican Congress collaborated with a Democratic president to overhaul the nation's welfare system, the implications are still rippling through policy and politics. The law, which reversed six decades of social welfare policy and ended the idea of free cash handouts for the poor, was widely seen as a victory for conservative ideas. When it was passed, some opponents offered dire predictions that the law would make things worse for the poor. But the number of people on welfare has plunged to 4.4 million, down 60 percent. Employment of single mothers is up. Child support collections have nearly doubled.

"We have been vindicated by the results," said Representative E. Clay Shaw Jr., Republican of Florida and an architect of the 1996 law who was vilified at the time. "Welfare reform was one of the most successful policy changes in our nation's history." But critics say it has cut adrift some single mothers who seem unable to hold steady jobs and are not receiving cash assistance—women who have neither work nor welfare.

To help poor single mothers help themselves, officials used a combination of conservative and liberal policy tools. These included work requirements and time limits on public assistance, tax credits for low-income working parents, child-care subsidies and health insurance for people leaving welfare.

"We hardly ever make radical change in this country, but welfare reform was a radical change," said Prof. Richard P. Nathan, director of the Nelson A. Rockefeller Institute of Government at the State University of New York. "It sent a very strong signal to welfare recipients: We can help you, if you help yourself." In an interview, former President Bill Clinton said he was "more convinced than ever" that he had been right to sign the bill, after vetoing two earlier versions that he had seen as too harsh. "The bill has done far more good than harm," Mr. Clinton said. "Most of the people who got jobs are still working."

When the 1996 law was passed, Democrats like Senator Daniel Patrick Moynihan, liberal advocacy groups like the Children's Defense Fund and liberal academics predicted that it would increase child poverty, hunger and homelessness. The predictions were not fulfilled. But Republican hopes have not been completely realized either. While single mothers are more likely to work, many remain in poverty.

The 1996 law did not become a template for changes in other programs, nor did it portend a major ideological shift to the right. President Bush's efforts to curb the growth of larger entitlement programs and to create an "ownership society" have faltered. Congress authorized health savings accounts but rebuffed proposals for a nationwide program of school vouchers. Mr. Bush's campaign to overhaul Social Security, with the creation of personal retirement accounts, ended in a political fiasco for him and his party.

The law has largely neutralized welfare as a political issue. Welfare mothers are seen in a more favorable light now that most are required to work. Welfare has become "more supportable and acceptable, more defensible," said Professor Nathan, a moderate Republican who served as a welfare official in the Nixon administration. Democrats and Republicans fight over important details, like the amount of money available for child care or the number of hours that must be worked by welfare recipients. But hardly anyone advocates a return to the old system.

If the new system has been a success, much of the credit goes to state and local officials who changed the mission of welfare agencies to emphasize work over welfare. Governors, who lobbied for the 1996 law, have won new respect in Washington, and Congress is more willing to entrust them with power and discretion, as it did in Medicaid legislation passed this year. The old focus on the "social pathology" of welfare has given way to a broader debate over a more complicated challenge: how to enable not only single mothers, but all low-wage workers to earn more. "The problems of the working poor who came off welfare are mainly the problems that all low-wage earners in America have," Mr. Clinton said. "They are not unique to people who came off welfare."

Prof. Jeffrey T. Grogger, an economist at the University of Chicago, said, "The 1996 law was more successful in promoting work and reducing the rolls than anyone imagined." But, Professor Grogger said, the earnings of former welfare recipients often remain low. "We took people who used to be the welfare poor," he said, "and now they are the working poor."

While many people left welfare for jobs that paid progressively better wages, others have been on and off assistance. Chevaughn L. Stephens of Seattle, a 29-year-old mother of three, said: "The emphasis on work first did not help me at all. It kept me back. It kept me from getting the education and skills I needed." In the last decade, Ms. Stephens said, she has had jobs as a waitress, a taxi dispatcher and a telephone sales representative. She is taking courses to get a high school equivalency certificate, needed for better-paying jobs. Ronald T. Haskins, a welfare policy expert who worked on the legislation as an aide to House Republicans, said, "Surveys show that about 60 percent of the mothers who leave welfare are working at any given moment, and around 70 percent have held at least one job since leaving welfare." But Mr. Haskins, now a senior fellow at the Brookings Institution, said, "Some mothers at the bottom of the income distribution—perhaps 10 percent of single mothers who had been on welfare—are floundering and appear to be worse off now than before welfare reform." He said that federal data suggested "a disconcerting increase in the number of poor mothers with no obvious sources of income."

The 1996 law changed the psychology of welfare recipients and caseworkers. Mindful of time limits under the law, single mothers came to see welfare as temporary, short-term assistance. One of the most significant features of the 1996 law was the five-year limit on assistance for any family. Democrats feared it would cause immense hardship. To the surprise of welfare officials and policy analysts, most welfare recipients came nowhere near the limit. But the looming time limit may nevertheless have influenced the choices and behavior of welfare recipients. Professor Grogger said many people, aware of the deadline, left welfare after only a couple of years so they could "save the benefits for a rainy day."

Overhaul of the welfare system coincided with a booming economy, which created more jobs for single mothers surging into the work force. Many of the most positive trends slowed after 2001, suggesting that economic conditions might be just as important as program changes.

"Welfare" used to mean a monthly check that could be immediately converted to cash. But more than half of the money now goes into child care, education, training and other services—a huge shift since 1996.

Olivia A. Golden, a senior fellow at the Urban Institute who was a welfare official in the Clinton administration, said: "The next steps that will make a difference for low-income families are not primarily about welfare, which now serves a very small number of families. They are about supporting working families who left welfare or never went on it."

New battle lines are forming. Conservatives are pushing for stiffer work requirements and for more attention to marriage as an antidote to poverty. Many moderates and liberals want to broaden support for poor workers by providing more money for child care, more access to unemployment insurance and higher minimum wages. And many experts say the states have yet to come to grips with the group of single mothers whose lives are so troubled that they are unlikely to hold steady jobs.

The new challenge is how to improve the lives of those who work low-paying jobs. The incentive to leave welfare and enter the labor force would be much higher if these entry-level jobs were more attractive.

Without additional programs to deal with child care and education problems, single mothers will always be the ones who will have the most difficulty in meeting the conditions imposed by the welfare reform act.

The challenges that loom in the years ahead

These programs have effects on income distribution because they transfer income between different groups. Social security and Medicare payments are financed by payroll taxes from workers. But the payroll taxes paid by a currently working individual are only loosely related to the funds paid out to the same individual after he or she retires. In reality, each year the funds paid in by current workers are paid out to current retirees. In other words, social security and Medicare are, in effect, transfer programs from young people to older people.

Because the social insurance programs are not means-tested, they can end up transferring income from the current working poor to middle-income and even wealthy retirees. In other words, these programs are not well targeted at the lower-income groups. For this reason, many people have suggested that these programs be means-tested. The arguments for means testing have become stronger as the aging of the U.S. population increases the strain on these programs, especially on Medicare. In fact, recent legislation has effectively reduced social security benefits to higher-income older people by requiring that a major part of the benefits be included in taxable income; social security benefits were formerly excluded from taxable income.

Mandated Benefits

mandated benefits: benefits that a firm is required by law to provide to its employees.

Mandated benefits occur when a firm is required by the government to provide a benefit for its workers. For example, a federal law requires firms to give unpaid leave to employees to care for a newborn baby or a sick relative. Such benefits are a cost to the firm (for example, the cost of finding and training replacements or providing health insurance to the workers on leave). But, of course, they are a benefit to the

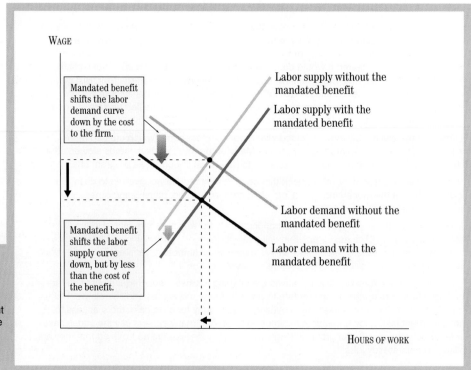

FIGURE 9
Effect of a Mandated Benefit
A mandated benefit is a cost to the firm; it shifts down the demand curve for labor just as a payroll tax does. But in the case of a mandated benefit, the labor supply curve shifts down too. Hence, the wage paid to the worker falls, as does employment.

WAGE

Mandated benefit shifts the labor demand curve down by the cost to the firm.

Labor supply without the mandated benefit

Labor supply with the mandated benefit

Labor demand without the mandated benefit

Mandated benefit shifts the labor supply curve down, but by less than the cost of the benefit.

Labor demand with the mandated benefit

HOURS OF WORK

workers. Another example of a mandated benefit is a proposal that would require firms to pay a portion of the health insurance costs of their workers.

The effects of mandated benefits can be analyzed using the supply and demand for labor diagram, much as we analyzed the effects of a payroll tax. As shown in Figure 9, the labor demand curve shifts down, as it did in Figure 6 for the employer-paid payroll tax—to hire a given quantity of labor, the wage that the firm will be willing to pay is lower because it also has to pay the mandated benefits. But the mandated benefits also shift the labor supply curve down—workers will be willing to work for a lower wage because they receive the mandated benefits by working. The labor supply curve will probably not shift down as much as the labor demand curve does because the workers probably will not value the benefit quite as much as its cost to the firm.

In any case, the new equilibrium in Figure 9 shows that the wage paid to the workers will fall as a result of the creation of the mandated benefit. In other words, despite the fact that the employer is the one supposedly "paying" for the mandated benefit, both the employer and the employee end up paying the benefit. There will also be a reduction in employment. If the workers value the benefit exactly as much as it costs the firm, then the wage will fall by the full amount of the benefit. In this case, employment will not fall at all.

REVIEW

- There are two major types of transfer payments: means-tested programs, which depend on the income of the recipient, and social insurance programs, which do not depend on the income of the recipient.

- The major means-tested transfer programs in the United States includes the TANF program, Medicaid, and the Earned Income Tax Credit program. All of these transfer programs target their benefits to the poor and reduce benefits as the income levels of individuals rise.

- As a result, means-tested transfer payments create disincentives for work. The loss of assistance from means-tested programs as one's labor income rises implies that these programs act as a tax on labor income.

- The purpose of welfare reform is to reduce those disincentives for the TANF program by imposing work requirements and time limits on payment of benefits to welfare recipients. The EITC program is also designed so that there is incentive for the very poor to work because their benefits initially rise with labor income.

- Social insurance programs like social security and Medicare are the largest transfer programs in the United States. These programs are not means-tested, which means that they transfer income from current workers to current retirees regardless of how poor the current worker is and how wealthy the current retiree is.

- As the number of elderly Americans rises and the cost of these transfer programs increases, economists and policymakers have advocated turning them into means-tested programs.

- Another way that the government can transfer money to individuals is through mandated benefits, such as family leave. If individuals do not value the benefit as much as it costs firms to provide it, then the workers' wages will fall by an amount less than the increase in the benefit. If the workers value the benefit at exactly the level that it costs the firm to provide it, then the wage will fall by the full amount of the benefit. In either case, the costs of the benefit are borne by both the firm and the worker, even if the firm is the one that technically pays for the benefit.

THE DISTRIBUTION OF INCOME IN THE UNITED STATES

Now that we have understood some important details about the tax and transfer system in the United States, we can take a closer look at how these have affected the distribution of income in the United States. We begin by examining what the distribution of income in the United States actually looks like, and how that distribution compares to the distribution in other countries. We then ask what changes there have been in income distribution over time, and how those changes are related to the tax and transfer policies adopted by the government.

The Personal Distribution of Income

To answer questions about income distribution in the United States, we first need to know what kinds of data are available and how we can construct a quantitative measure of income distribution using those data. Data about people's income in the United States are collected by the Census Bureau in a monthly survey of about 60,000 households called the **Current Population Survey.**

Current Population Survey: a monthly survey of a sample of U.S. households done by the U.S. Census Bureau; it measures employment, unemployment, the labor force, and other characteristics of the U.S. population.

Economists and statisticians usually study the income distribution of families or households rather than individuals. A *family* is defined by the Census Bureau as a group of two or more people related by birth, marriage, or adoption who live in the same housing unit. A *household* consists of all related family members and unrelated individuals who live in the same housing unit. Because the members of a family or a household typically share their income, it is usually more sensible to consider families or households rather than individuals. One would not say that a young child who earns nothing is poor if the child's mother or father earns $100,000 a year. In a family where one spouse works and the other remains at home, one would not say that the working spouse is rich and the nonworking spouse is poor.

quintiles: divisions or groupings of one-fifth of a population ordered by income, wealth, or some other statistic.

Because there are so many people in the population, it is necessary to have a simple way to summarize the income data. One way to do this is to arrange the population into a small number of groups ranging from the poorest to the richest. Most typically, the population is divided into fifths, called **quintiles,** with the same percentage of families or households in each quintile. For example, in Table 3, the 77 million families in the United States are divided into five quintiles, with 15.4 million families in each quintile. The first row shows the poorest 20 percent—the bottom quintile. The next several rows show the higher-income quintiles, with the last row showing the 20 percent with the highest incomes.

The second and third columns of Table 3 show how much income is earned by families in each of the five groups. The bottom 20 percent of families have incomes below $24,780, the families in the next quintile have incomes greater than $24,780

TABLE 3
Range of Annual Family Incomes for Five Quintiles

Quintile	Income Greater Than	Income Less Than
Bottom 20 percent	0	$24,780
Second 20 percent	$24,780	$43,400
Third 20 percent	$43,400	$65,832
Fourth 20 percent	$65,832	$100,000
Top 20 percent	$100,000	—

Source: Statistical Abstract of the United States, 2007, Table 678.

but less than $43,400, and so on. Note that the lower limit for families in the top 20 percent is $100,000. The lower limit for the top 5 percent (not shown in the table) is $173,640.

Inequality can be better measured by considering the total income in each quintile as a percentage of the total income in the country. Table 4 provides this information. The second column in Table 4 shows the income received by families in each quintile as a percentage of total income in the United States.

A quick look at Table 4 shows that the distribution of income is far from equal. Those in the lower 20 percent earn only 4.0 percent of total income. On the other hand, those in the top 20 percent earn 48 percent of total income. Thus, the amount of income earned by the richest quartile is twelve times the amount of income earned by the poorest quartile.

The Lorenz Curve and Gini Coefficient

The third column of Table 4 shows the cumulative portion of income earned by the different segments of the distribution. The bottom 20 percent earn 4.0 percent of the income, the bottom 40 percent earn 13.6 percent of the income, the bottom 60 percent earn 29.0 percent of the income, and the bottom 80 percent earn 52.0 percent of the income. The top 5 percent, not shown in Table 4, earn 20.9 percent of the aggregate income.

TABLE 4
Distribution of Family Income by Quintile

Quintile	Percentage of Income	Cumulative Percentage of Income
Bottom 20 percent	4.0	4.0
Second 20 percent	9.6	13.6
Third 20 percent	15.4	29.0
Fourth 20 percent	23.0	52.0
Top 20 percent	48.0	100.0

Source: Statistical Abstract of the United States, 2007, Table 678.

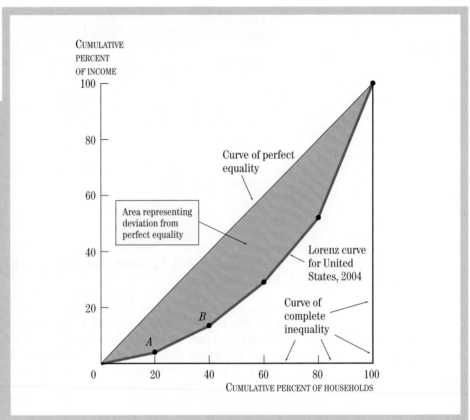

FIGURE 10
The Lorenz Curve for the United States

Each point on the Lorenz curve gives the percentage of income received by a percentage of households. The plotted points are for the United States. Point *A* shows that 4.0 percent of income is received by the lowest 20 percent of families. Point *B* shows that 13.6 percent of income is received by the lowest 40 percent of families. These two points and the others in the figure come from Table 4. In addition, the 45-degree line shows perfect equality, and the solid lines along the horizontal and right-hand vertical axes show perfect inequality. The shaded area between the 45-degree line and the Lorenz curve is a measure of inequality. The ratio of this area to the area of the triangle below the 45-degree line is the Gini coefficient. The Gini coefficient for 2007 is .406.

These data can be presented in a useful graphical form. Figure 10 shows the cumulative percentage of income from the third column of Table 4 on the vertical axis and the percentage representing each quintile from the first column on the horizontal axis. The five dots in the figure are the five pairs of observations from the table. For example, point *A* at the lower left corresponds to the 4 percent of income earned by the lowest 20 percent of people. Point *B* corresponds to the 13.6 percent of income earned by the lowest 40 percent of people. The other points are plotted the same way. The uppermost point is where 100 percent of the income is earned by 100 percent of the people.

If we connect these five points, we get a curve that is bowed out. This curve is called the **Lorenz curve.** To measure how bowed out the curve is, we draw the solid black 45-degree line. The 45-degree line is a line of perfect equality. On that line, the lowest 20 percent earn exactly 20 percent of the income, the lowest 40 percent earn exactly 40 percent of the income, and so on. Every household earns exactly the same amount.

The degree to which the Lorenz curve is bowed out from the 45-degree line provides a visual gauge of the inequality of income. The more bowed out the line is, the more unequal is the income distribution. The most unequal distribution possible would occur when only one person earns all the income. In that case, the curve could be so bowed out from the 45-degree line that it would consist of a straight line on the horizontal axis up to 100 and then a vertical line. For example, 99.9 percent of the households would earn zero percent of the income. Only when the richest person is included do we get 100 percent of the income.

Lorenz curve: a curve showing the relation between the cumulative percentage of the population and the proportion of total income earned by each cumulative percentage. It measures income inequality.

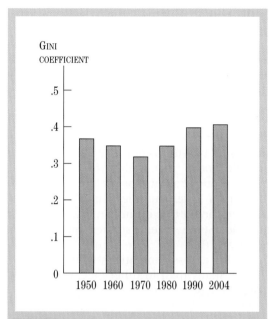

FIGURE 11

Changes in Income Inequality: The U.S. Gini Coefficient

The Gini coefficient is large when there is more inequality, as measured by the Lorenz curve in Figure 10. Thus, by this measure, inequality fell in the United States from 1950 to 1970 but increased from 1970 to 2004.

Gini coefficient: an index of income inequality ranging between 0 (for perfect equality) and 1 (for absolute inequality); it is defined as the ratio of the area between the Lorenz curve and the perfect equality line to the area between the lines of perfect equality and perfect inequality.

The **Gini coefficient** is a useful numerical measure of how bowed out the Lorenz curve is. It is defined as the ratio of the area of the gap between the 45-degree line and the Lorenz curve to the area between the lines of perfect equality and perfect inequality. The Gini coefficient can range between 0 and 1. It has a value of zero if the area between the diagonal line and the Lorenz curve is zero. Thus, when the Gini coefficient is zero, we have perfect equality. The Gini coefficient would be 1 if only one person earned all the income in the economy.

Figure 11 shows how the Gini coefficient has changed in the United States over the last 50 years. The Gini coefficient has varied within a narrow range, from .3 to slightly over .4. The most notable feature of the trend in the Gini coefficient in Figure 11 is the decline after World War II until around 1970 and the subsequent increase. It is clear that income inequality has increased in recent years. Higher earnings of skilled and educated workers relative to the less skilled and less educated may partly explain this change in income distribution. But the reason for these changes in income inequality is still a major unsettled question for economists.

It is important to note, however, that an increase in income inequality, as in Figure 11, does not necessarily mean that the rich got richer and the poor got poorer. For example, if one looks at average income in each quintile, one finds an increase for all groups from 1970 to 2004, even after adjusting for inflation. However, average income in the top quintile increased by a larger percentage amount than average income in the bottom quintile.

■ **Comparison with Other Countries.** Lorenz curves and Gini coefficients can be calculated for different countries or groups of countries. For most European countries, the Lorenz curve is closer to equality than it is for the United States. Canada, Australia, and the United Kingdom have Lorenz curves very similar to that of the United States. However, income distribution varies much more when we look beyond the developed countries. As Figure 12 shows, Bangladesh, a very poor country, has a more equal income distribution than the United States. Brazil, a middle-income country that is also much poorer than the United States, has a much less equal income distribution. Among individual countries, Bangladesh and Brazil are close to the extremes: 60 percent of the population receives 40 percent of the income in Bangladesh, 19 percent of the income in Brazil, and 29 percent in the United States.

Income distribution for the world as a whole is far more unequal than that for any one country because the very poor in some countries are combined with the very rich in other countries. For example, when West Germany united with East Germany to form one country, the income distribution became more unequal for the unified country as a whole than it had been for either country before unification. The Lorenz curve for the world as a whole—as illustrated in Figure 12—shows far greater inequality than the curve for any one country: 60 percent of the world's population receives only 5 percent of the income.

■ **Income Mobility.** In interpreting income distribution statistics, it is important to recognize that the quintiles do not refer to the same people as the years go by. In its 2003 Survey of Income and Program Participation, the U.S. Census Bureau reported that 38 percent of those households in the lowest-income quintile in 1996 were in a higher-income quintile in 1999. People who are in the top quintile in one year may be

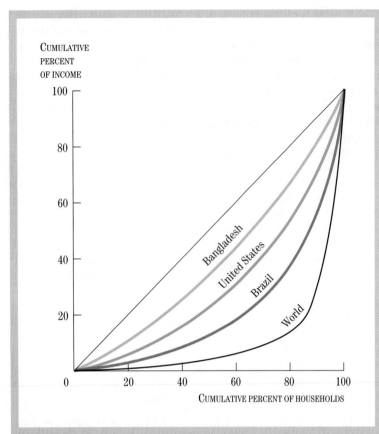

FIGURE 12
Income Distribution Around the World
Income distributions vary widely across the world. Bangladesh and Brazil are on either side of the United States. When we look at the world as a whole, income inequality is highest because we combine the very poor of sub-Saharan Africa with the very rich of the OECD.

Note: World curve computed from population data for low-, lower-middle-, upper-middle-, and high-income countries.

in the bottom quintile the next year (perhaps because they retired, or because they temporarily left the labor force). And people who are in the bottom quintile one year may be in the top quintile the next year (because they completed their MBA degree or because they re-entered the work force after a short absence).

How significant is income mobility? Economic research on the United States shows that about two-thirds of the people in any one quintile move to another over a 10-year period. About half of those in the top quintile move to a lower quintile, and about half of those in the bottom quintile move to a higher quintile. Some recent studies have shown, however, that the persistence of income inequality across generations is higher in the United States than in other OECD countries, like Germany.

■ **Longer-Term Income Inequality.** Distinguishing between income in any one year and income over several years is also important. In a typical life span, people usually earn less when they are young than when they are middle-aged. As they grow older and become more experienced, their wages and salaries increase. When people retire, their income usually declines again. Thus, even if everyone had the exact same lifetime income, one would see inequality in the income distribution every year. Middle-aged people would be relatively rich, while young and old people would be relatively poor.

■ **Changing Composition of Households.** The formation or splitting up of households can also affect the distribution of income. For example, if two individuals who were living separately form a household, the household income doubles. Households splitting apart can also alter the income distribution drastically. If one adult leaves the family, perhaps because of divorce or desertion, and the other one stays home with the children, the income of the household declines substantially. It appears that the splitting apart of households has had an impact on income distribution in the United States. According to some estimates, if household composition had not changed in the United States in the last 20 years, there would have been only half as great an increase in inequality as measured by the Gini coefficient.

■ **Distribution of Income versus Distribution of Wealth.** Another factor to keep in mind when interpreting data on the income distribution is the distinction between *income* and *wealth.* Your annual income is what you earn each year. Your wealth, or your net worth, is all you own minus what you owe others.

Wealth changes over a person's lifetime even more than income does as people save for retirement. For example, a young person who has just graduated and gotten a high-paying job may have a high income but little wealth or, with a college loan still to pay off, may even have negative net worth. Conversely, a diligent saver who has just retired from his job will have little income but may have a sizable retirement fund, and thus be relatively wealthy.

A survey of about 3,000 families in the United States in 2001 found that the top 10 percent of households held about 72 percent of the net worth in the United States. Although such surveys are not as accurate as the regular monthly surveys of 60,000 households on which our information about income distribution is based, it is clear that the distribution of wealth is less equal than the distribution of income. About one-third of the net worth in this survey was in the form of net worth held in small businesses.

Poverty and Measurement

Poverty can be observed virtually everywhere. The poor are visible in the blighted sections of cities and in remote rural areas. Almost everyone has seen the serious problems of the homeless in cities of the United States. CNN has brought the agony of poverty from faraway countries like Somalia and from nearby cities like New Orleans closer to us through our TV screens.

As with inequality, economists have developed quantitative measures of poverty. The **poverty rate** is the percentage of people who live in poverty. To calculate the poverty rate, one needs to define what it means to live in poverty. In the United States, poverty is usually quantitatively defined by a **poverty line,** an estimate of the minimal amount of annual income a family needs in order to avoid severe economic hardship. The poverty line in the United States is based on a survey showing that families spend, on average, one-third of their income on food. The poverty line is thus obtained by multiplying by 3 the Department of Agriculture's estimate of the amount of money needed to purchase a low-cost nutritionally adequate amount of food. In addition, adjustments are made for the size of the family. Table 5 shows the poverty line for several different family sizes. Since the 1960s, when it was first developed, the poverty line has been increased to adjust for inflation.

Using the poverty line and data on the income distribution, one can determine the number of people who live in poverty and the poverty rate. The overall poverty rates in the United States have varied over the last 50 years. The overall poverty rate for families declined sharply from 18 percent in 1960 to 8.8 percent in 1973, but has risen somewhat since then. In 2005 the poverty rate for families was 9.9 percent, while the poverty rate for all individuals was 12.6 percent, or 37 million people.

There are important trends in poverty for different groups in the population. For example, the percentage of children who live in poverty rose in the 1970s, 1980s, and early 1990s. During the same time period, the poverty rate for the elderly declined, and this held down the overall poverty rate. In 1993, when child poverty was at a peak, 22.7 percent of children were living in poverty; at the same time, the poverty rate for the elderly was 12.2 percent. The dramatic decline in the poverty rate for the elderly since the 1970s (from 24.6 percent in 1970) is largely attributed to the change in social security benefits during that time period—along with better retirement benefits.

The increase in poverty for children is troublesome, and it is difficult to explain. Some of it may have to do with the increase in single-headed households with children, which are usually poorer than two-adult households. Poverty rates in households

poverty rate: the percentage of people living below the poverty line.

poverty line: an estimate of the minimum amount of annual income required for a family to avoid severe economic hardship.

TABLE 5
The Poverty Line in the United States, 2004

Family Size	Poverty Line
Unrelated individuals	$ 9,827
Two persons	$12,649
Three persons	$14,776
Four persons	$19,484
Seven persons	$31,096

Source: U.S. Census Bureau.

ECONOMICS IN ACTION

Should We Be Concerned About Income Inequality?

Live 8, a historic musical event, took place on July 2, 2005. Ten concerts were held on the same day in the United States, Canada, France, Germany, Italy, Japan, Russia, and the United Kingdom (collectively known as the G8), and in South Africa as well. The goal of the Live 8 concert organizers was to raise awareness of poverty in Africa among citizens of the G8 nations. In turn, these citizens would put pressure on their leaders to forgive the debts of, and increase aid to, African countries. Musically and politically, the concerts seemed to be a success. A week after the concerts, the leaders of the G8 nations pledged to increase African aid to $25 billion. Given that there are 700 million people who live in sub-Saharan Africa, the increase in aid worked out to approximately $35 per person.

For those of us who live in the developed world, $35 will do very little to improve our lives. But there is a staggering amount of income inequality across countries in the world. In sub-Saharan Africa, where the 700 million people have an average per capita income of less than $500, even $35 a person can make a difference. In the poorest African countries, like Sierra Leone and Niger, per capita income is only about $200.[2] Almost 60 percent of the population in these countries live on less than $1 a day. In contrast, per capita income in the United States is $37,500, which means that the average income of someone living in America is almost 200 times as large as the average income of someone living in Niger.

Income inequality is also present within countries, not just across countries. Even in a rich country like the United States, 12.7 percent of the population, or more than 35 million people, live on an income below the poverty line. Economist Paul Krugman has pointed out[3] that the 13,000 richest families in the United States earn as much income as the 20 million poorest families. The average family in the United States earns 1/300th of the income that one of those 13,000 richest families earns. Krugman also points out that over the past 30 years, the average annual salary in America increased by about 10 percent in real terms, but the average real compensation of CEOs increased almost 30-fold. To put it another way, the average CEO salary went from about 40 times the pay of an average worker to about 1,000 times the pay of an average worker.

Should we be concerned about this level of income inequality? Keep in mind that the question is not "Should we be concerned about poverty?" There is a subtle yet important difference between these two questions. Suppose you were asked if you would approve of implementing an economic policy that would increase per capita income in Niger by 50 percent (from $200 to $300). You would probably approve of such a policy. Now suppose you found out that implementing that policy would also double per capita income in the United States, from $37,500 to $75,000. This would imply that per capita income in the United States would now be 250 times per capita income in Niger instead of less than 200 times. Would that information change your approval of the policy? In the U.S. example, you should ask yourself if your approval of a policy that would increase the real wage of the typical worker by 10 percent would be tempered by the knowledge that the same policy would increase CEOs' compensation by 20 percent.

The critical question being raised here is whether you are concerned about income inequality per se or you care about income inequality only because of your concern for the well-being of the poor.

FOCUS ON POVERTY, NOT ON INEQUALITY

Harvard University professor Martin Feldstein argues that the concern over rising income inequality is misplaced.[4] He does not believe that rising inequality per se warrants the creation of new redistributive policies that seek to reduce inequality. Instead, he argues, we should focus on reducing poverty and use redistributive policies only for alleviating poverty. Feldstein's reasoning can be summarized as follows:

- Economists use the Pareto principle to evaluate policies. If a policy makes someone better off without making others worse off, such a policy is generally thought of as being a good policy.[5] Therefore, changes that increase the earnings of high-income individuals without decreasing the earnings of lower-income individuals should be considered to be good policies.

- Applying the above principle to the changes that have taken place in the U.S. economy in recent years, the greater increase in the earnings of high-income individuals should not be a concern. These increases are driven by four factors: market forces rewarding individuals with advanced education; a rise in

---

[2] You can find a variety of interesting cross-country data series in the World Bank's *World Development Report.* Available online at http://econ.worldbank.org/wdr/.
[3] Paul Krugman, "For Richer," *New York Times Magazine*, Oct. 20, 2002. Available online at http://www.pkarchive.org/economy/ForRicher.html.

[4] Martin Feldstein, "Reducing Poverty, Not Inequality," *Public Interest,* no. 137, Fall 1999. Available at http://www.nber.org/feldstein/pi99.html.
[5] These are not the only good policies; policies that make some people worse off but others better off in a manner such that the gains outweigh the losses will also typically be regarded as being good policies.

entrepreneurial activity, resulting in a spurt of new business creation; the tendency of high-wage individuals like lawyers, doctors, and investment bankers to work long hours; and decreases in financial risk and the cost of capital that have translated into higher stock and bond prices. None of these changes hurt the poor, even though they helped the rich.

- Redistribution to alleviate poverty can easily be justified on the grounds that an extra $100 of income means less to a millionaire than it does to someone earning $10,000. However, that does not imply that we should prevent the millionaire from earning an extra $100, because that person still values the $100.

- Focusing on policies that can help the poor, such as improved education, better job training, and reducing incentives to stay on welfare instead of work, is the way to tackle "real and serious poverty" in the United States.

- Macroeconomists are concerned about the impact of inequality on economic growth. Work by Kristin Forbes, an economist at MIT, using data on income inequality gathered from a variety of countries, shows that in the short run, an increase in income inequality can actually lead to an increase in growth.[6]

FOCUS ON INEQUALITY, NOT JUST ON POVERTY

Branko Milanovic, an economist at the World Bank, strongly disagrees with Martin Feldstein's view that we should care only about poverty alleviation, not about inequality per se.[7] He argues that to be concerned only about poverty alleviation is to be internally intellectually inconsistent. Milanovic uses this example to make his point:

> Suppose a group of friends are in a room together and a benefactor (arbitrarily) gives $20,000 to one person and 25 cents to everyone else. Feldstein's argument would say that everyone is better off as a result and should therefore be happier. However, reality is likely to be very different. Many of the people who received 25 cents would think that they are worse off because someone else got $20,000. The reason for their feeling worse is that people compare themselves to their (perceived) peers. When a peer is treated better by society, individuals may feel as if they are being valued less by society. In other words, the income of others may enter into our own utility function, hence others doing better may affect our well-being.

Economist Nancy Birdsall points out that there has been a dramatic transformation in how economists think about inequality.[8] As recently as 1990, the World Bank's report on poverty made little or no mention of it, choosing instead to focus on poverty alleviation. Since then, Birdsall argues, many economists have changed their views about inequality. Inequality matters "not only because it affects growth or other economic variables but in and of itself." For one thing, Birdsall argues, recent research on the determinants of "happiness" has shown that people care about their relative standing (how their income compares to that of others in their community) and also about the expected change in their relative standing: They may be more willing to accept the fact that some people are better off than they are if they feel that in the future, they or their children can be the among the ones who are better off. In addition, inequality can undermine the political process. In countries where political institutions are weak, an unequal distribution of income and wealth can allow the better off to usurp the political process to maintain the status quo. This can lead to conflicts like civil war, which in turn adversely affect the economy.

The recent comments of Ben Bernanke, the chairman of the Federal Reserve, add more nuance to this discussion by arguing that we should care about inequality *of opportunity* per se, but not about inequality *of outcomes* per se. In other words, Mr. Bernanke would seem to come out on the "focus on poverty, not on inequality" side of the debate when it comes to how well people do, provided that everyone has equal opportunity to achieve those outcomes. But he also comes out on the "focus on inequality, not just on poverty" side of the issue when comparing the opportunities that the poor have to acquire the education, the skills, or the training needed to increase their economic well-being to the opportunities available to others. Without equality of opportunity, Mr. Bernanke argues, the dynamism of the U.S. economy is at risk because people who find their living standards stagnating will fight against economic changes related to trade, technology, and globalization. It is also important to understand what Mr. Bernanke means by "equality of opportunity." It does not mean that you or I should be allowed to play in the NBA or study nuclear physics at Cal-Tech. It just means that there should be no artificial barriers put up by society that prevent us from achieving the goal. In the end, the lack of a jump shot or the inability to solve multivariate differential equations will doom my chances, but that's okay.

---

[6] Kristin Forbes, "A Reassessment of the Relationship Between Inequality and Growth," *American Economic Review* 90(4), September 2000.
[7] Branko Milanovic, "Why We All Do Care About Inequality (but Are Loath to Admit It)." Available at www.worldbank.org/research/inequality/pdf/feldstein.pdf.

[8] Nancy Birdsall, "Why Global Inequality Matters," in Susan M. Collins and Carol Graham, eds., *Globalization, Poverty, and Inequality* (Washington, D.C.: Brookings Institution Press, 2004).

with a single head and at least one child have ranged between 35 and 40 percent in the last 20 years—three times the overall poverty rate. However, since 1993, the poverty rate for children has made some progress, declining from 22.7 percent to 16.2 percent in 2000. Since then, it has risen slightly to 17.6 percent in 2005.

Effects of Taxes and Transfers on Income Distribution and Poverty

Many believe that the main purpose of government redistribution of income through taxes and transfers is to help the poor. For this reason, the term *social safety net* is sometimes used for an income redistribution system; the idea is that these programs try to prevent those who were born poor or who have become poor from falling too far down in income and therefore in nutrition, health, and general well-being.

How successful has this redistribution effort been? Estimates by the U.S. Census Bureau indicate that the tax and transfer system reduces the poverty rate by about 10 percentage points: Without the tax and transfer system, the Census Bureau estimates that the poverty rate would be 20 percent rather than 10 percent. To be sure, these estimates ignore any of the incentive effects mentioned earlier, such as the reduced work incentives that might result from the tax and transfer system. And they ignore any possible response of private efforts to redistribute income—such as charities—that might occur as a result of changes in the government's role.

R E V I E W

- The distribution of income can be measured by the percentage of income earned by quintiles of households or families. In the United States in 2004, the bottom quintile earned about 4 percent of the income, while the top quintile earned about 48 percent.

- The Lorenz curve provides a graphical summary of the relationship between the cumulative quintiles (ordered from poorest to richest) and cumulative income. If income inequality is not very pronounced, the Lorenz curve will lie closer to the 45-degree "line of perfect equality."

- The Gini coefficient is a numerical measure of inequality—it captures how bowed out the Lorenz curve is from the 45-degree line. The higher the Gini coefficient, the more unequal the distribution of income is.

- Income inequality has risen in the United States since 1970. Part of the explanation may be the materialization of higher returns to educated and skilled workers in recent times, but this is by no means the only explanation.

- Before we worry about the magnitude of the Gini coefficient, we should recognize the possibility that people may be mobile across quintiles, that longer-term income inequality may paint a different picture from that provided by a study done at one point in time, that aging populations and changing compositions of households can affect income inequality measures without any changes in the earning patterns of different groups in the economy, and that the distribution of wealth is also an important measure of inequality.

- Taxes and transfers are widely used to combat poverty and reduce income inequality in the United States. Evaluating the success of these programs requires an understanding of how poverty is defined and measured.

- The poverty rate is a quantitative measure of the amount of poverty in the United States, it is defined as the percentage of people living below a poverty line. The poverty line for the United States is an estimate of how much money a family needs to avoid severe economic hardship.

- Over the last three decades, the poverty rate among children has increased while the poverty rate for the elderly has declined. Estimates indicate that the tax and transfer system currently makes the poverty rate lower than it would otherwise be. Nevertheless, the increase in poverty among children has raised serious concerns about the tax and transfer system in the United States.

CONCLUSION

In a democracy, the amount of government redistribution of income is decided by the people and their representatives. A majority seem to want some redistribution of income, but there is debate about how much the government should do. Why doesn't a democracy lead to much more redistribution? After all, 60 percent of the people, according to Table 4, receive only 29 percent of the income. Since 60 percent of the voting population is enough to win an election, this 60 percent could vote to redistribute income much further. Why hasn't it?

There are probably a number of reasons. First, there is the tradeoff between equality and efficiency stressed in this chapter. People realize that taking away incentives to work will reduce the size of the pie for everyone. Another reason is that most of us believe that people should be rewarded for their work. Just as we can think of a fair income distribution, we can think about a fair reward system. If some students want to work hard in high school so that they can attend college, why shouldn't they get the additional income that comes from that?

There is also the connection between personal freedom and economic freedom. Government involvement in income distribution means government involvement in people's lives. Those who cherish the idea of personal freedom worry about a system that takes a large amount of income from people who work.

Finally, much income redistribution occurs through the private sector—private charities and churches. The distribution of food and the provision of health care have long been supported by nongovernment organizations. In times of floods or earthquakes, it is common for people to volunteer to help those in distress. Private charity has certain advantages over government. Individuals become more personally involved if they perform a public service, whether volunteering at a soup kitchen or tutoring at an elementary school.

In recent years, the United States has experienced a rise in income inequality, which has raised concerns about the adequacy of the existing transfer and tax policies. Expanding the EITC program, means testing social insurance programs, and changing the progressivity of the income tax system are all proposals that have been suggested for dealing with the fact that the incomes of the poor have been growing much more slowly than have the incomes of the rich. Similar concerns have been raised about poverty, including the increase in poverty among children and the rising number of people without adequate health insurance programs, who could suffer a serious hit to their net worth if they were to fall ill.

If income inequality continues to rise, and more people begin to worry about its potential to have detrimental effects on the economy, the democratic system should bring about policies and policymakers that take a keen interest in the issues discussed in this chapter.

KEY POINTS

1. In modern democracies, the government plays a major role in trying to help the poor and in providing a more equal income distribution through the use of taxes and transfers.

2. Taxes are needed to pay for transfers and other government spending. In the United States, the personal income tax and the payroll tax are by far the most significant sources of tax revenue at the federal level. Sales taxes and property taxes play a significant role at the local level.

3. Taxes cause inefficiencies, as measured by deadweight loss, because taxes reduce the amount of the economic activity being taxed—whether it is the production of a good or the labor of workers.

4. The incidence of a tax depends on the price elasticity of supply and demand. The deadweight loss from taxes on goods with low price elasticities is relatively small.

5. Transfer payments are classified into means-tested programs—such as welfare and food stamps—and social insurance programs—such as social security and unemployment insurance.

6. Transfer payments can cause inefficiency as a result of disincentives to work or the incentive for families to split up.

7. There is a tradeoff between equality and efficiency. Tax reform and welfare reform try to improve incentives and reduce inefficiency.

8. The distribution of income has grown more unequal in recent years.

9. Poverty among children has increased, while poverty among the elderly has declined in recent years.

10. The tax and transfer system has reduced income inequality and lowered poverty rates, but there is much room for improvement and reform.

KEY TERMS

personal income tax	sales tax	supplemental security income (SSI)	Current Population Survey
taxable income	property tax	food stamp program	quintiles
tax bracket	tax incidence	Head Start	Lorenz curve
marginal tax rate	tax revenue	housing assistance programs	Gini coefficient
average tax rate	ability-to-pay principle	earned income tax credit (EITC)	poverty rate
progressive tax	transfer payment	social security	poverty line
regressive tax	means-tested transfer	Medicare	
proportional tax	social insurance transfer	unemployment insurance	
flat tax	Temporary Assistance to Needy Families (TANF) program	mandated benefits	
payroll tax	Medicaid		
corporate income tax			
excise tax			

QUESTIONS FOR REVIEW

1. Provide simple definitions of the following: tax bracket, marginal tax rate, average tax rate, deductions, exemptions.

2. Why is there a deadweight loss from the personal income tax? What factors can lead to the deadweight loss being large or small?

3. What do economists mean when they talk about "tax incidence"? How is the incidence of taxes related to the elasticities of demand and supply?

4. What are the impacts of an increase in the income tax on the labor market?

5. Intuitively explain why the effects of a payroll tax are the same whether the employer or the worker pays it.

6. What is the relationship between the tax rate and tax revenue? Explain under what circumstances a Laffer curve would emerge.

7. What are the major types of transfer programs in the United States? Provide examples of specific programs that fall under each type.

8. How do these transfer programs affect the incentives to work? Be sure to describe both positive and negative effects.

9. How is the distribution of income measured by the Lorenz curve and the Gini coefficient?

10. Why are income mobility and lifetime income important to consider in interpreting Gini coefficients and other income distribution statistics?

PROBLEMS

1. Consider the following 2006 personal income tax schedule obtained from the IRS web site. It applies to a taxpayer who is not married (single).

If Taxable Income Is Over	But Not Over	The Tax Is
$0	$7,550	10% of the amount over $0
$7,550	$30,650	$755 plus 15% of the amount over $7,550
$30,650	$74,200	$4,220 plus 25% of the amount over $30,650

a. What is the tax due on a taxable income of $25,000?
b. What is the tax due on a taxable income of $50,000?
c. Why does the tax more than double when the income doubles?
d. Is this tax system progressive?

2. Consider the following 2006 personal income tax schedule obtained from the IRS website. It applies to a married couple who are combining their incomes and filing jointly.

If Taxable Income Is Over	But Not Over	The Tax Is
$0	$15,100	10% of the amount over $0
$15,100	$61,300	$1,510 plus 15% of the amount over $15,100
$61,300	$123,700	$8,440 plus 25% of the amount over $61,300

a. What is the tax due for a couple where each spouse has a taxable income of $25,000?
b. Use the results from the preceding question to compare the tax the couple would have paid if they were not married (and filed as single persons) to the amount of tax they pay as a married couple (filing jointly).
c. What is the tax due for a couple where one spouse has a taxable income of $50,000 and the other spouse has no taxable income?
d. Does the tax system treat households making the same amount of income in an identical manner? Can it do so while remaining a progressive system?

3. Two popular programs for helping workers with very low incomes are to raise the minimum wage and to raise the earned income tax credit (EITC). Why do economists tend to favor the EITC?

4. California tried to impose a "snack" tax—one that applied only to what the legislators thought was junk food. Suppose snack food has a higher elasticity of demand than nonsnack food. Draw a supply and demand diagram to explain which tax— on snack food or on nonsnack food—will cause the price to rise more. Which will produce a greater deadweight loss?

5. Suppose the government decides to increase the payroll tax paid by employers. If the labor supply curve has a low elasticity, what will happen to the workers' wages? Who actually bears the burden of the tax, the workers or the firms? Would it be different if the labor supply had a high elasticity?

6. Suppose that the labor demand curve is perfectly flat. What is the impact on a typical worker's hourly wage if the government increases the payroll tax paid by employers by 10 percent of the wage? Show what happens in a labor supply and labor demand graph. Why does the slope of the labor supply curve not affect your answer?

7. The Family Leave Act is a federal law that requires employers to give employees unpaid leave to care for a newborn or a sick relative. Show how the Family Leave Act affects the supply and demand for labor. According to this model, what will happen to wages and employment compared to the situation before the law was passed?

8. The following table gives hours worked and the welfare payment received.

   a. Calculate the missing data in the table, given that the hourly wage is $5 and total income is the sum of the wage payment and the welfare payment.

Hours Worked	Wage Payment	Welfare Payment	Total Income
0		$10,000	
500		$8,000	
1,000		$6,000	
1,500		$4,000	
2,000		$2,000	

   b. Draw a graph that shows how much total income a worker earns with and without this welfare

program. Put the number of hours worked on the horizontal axis and total income on the vertical axis.

   c. What is the increase in total income for each additional hour worked without any welfare program? Compare it with the increase in total income for each additional hour worked under the welfare program.

   d. How could the welfare program be changed to increase the incentive to work without reducing total income for a full-time worker (40 hours per week, 50 weeks per year, $5 per hour) below $12,000, which is already below the poverty line for a family of four?

9. The following table gives the income distribution in Brazil and in Australia. Draw the Lorenz curve for each. Which country has the larger Gini coefficient?

Quintile	Percent of Income in Brazil	Percent of Income in Australia
Bottom 20 percent	2.4	4.4
Second 20 percent	5.7	11.1
Third 20 percent	10.7	17.5
Fourth 20 percent	18.6	24.8
Top 20 percent	62.6	42.2

10. Analyze the distribution of income, using the household incomes in the following table. Rank the families by income. Compute the percentage of total income going to the poorest 20 percent of the families, the second 20 percent, and the richest 20 percent. Draw a Lorenz curve for the income distribution of these 10 families. Is their distribution more equal or less equal than that of the population of the United States as a whole?

Family	Income
Jones	$ 12,000
Pavlov	$100,000
Cohen	$ 24,000
Baker	$ 87,000
Dixon	$ 66,000
Sun	$ 72,000
Tanaka	$ 18,000
Bernardo	$ 45,000
Smith	$ 28,000
Lopez	$ 33,000

Chapter 15

Public Goods, Externalities, and Government Behavior

Most economists aspire to use their knowledge to design economic policies that have an impact on the lives of others. In the United States, one of the most prominent positions from which an economist can influence public policy is at the President's Council of Economic Advisers (CEA) in Washington, D.C. Since 1946, more than 70 economists have served as members of the council, including two Nobel Prize winners—James Tobin and Joseph Stiglitz—and three future Federal Reserve chairmen—Arthur Burns, Alan Greenspan, and Ben Bernanke. Hundreds of other famous economists have served on the staff of the CEA, where they were given the task of using their knowledge of economics to help the government figure out what economic policies to implement.

The economists who worked at the CEA have left a legacy of important economic policy accomplishments, but the process by which they influence policy is often an unglamorous one. A classic description of the way in which economic policy in Washington is formed was provided by Robert Solow,[1] a member of President Kennedy's council who later went on to win a Nobel Prize in economics. Solow put it this way:

> On any given day in the executive branch, there are more meetings than Heinz has varieties. At a very large proportion of these meetings, the representative of some agency or some interest will be trying to sell a harebrained economic proposal. I am exaggerating a little. Not every one of these ideas is crazy. Most of them are just bad: either impractical, inefficient, excessively costly, likely to be accompanied by undesirable side effects, or just misguided—unlikely to accomplish their stated purpose. Someone has to knock those proposals down. . . . That is where the Council's comparative advantage lies." Solow emphasized that he had good people and good arguments to work with, but

---

[1] Robert M. Solow, "It Ain't the Things You Don't Know That Hurt You, It's the Things You Know That Ain't So," *American Economic Review*, May 1997, pp. 107–108.

that "does not mean that we won all the battles; we lost at least as many as we won. The race is not always won by the best arguments, not in political life anyway. But we always felt we had a chance and we kept trying.

The purpose of this chapter is to examine two important concepts—public goods and externalities—that economists on the president's council and elsewhere use to determine when government intervention in the economy is needed. Public goods are goods (or services) that would be underprovided by the private sector, creating a need for government to step in and provide the good. Externalities are situations where the production or consumption of a good or a service by a consumer or a firm in the private sector has a spillover effect on others in the economy. This often creates a situation where the government can step in to either increase (if the spillover is positive) or restrict (if the spillover is negative) production of the good.

Economists can play a vital role in advising policymakers when to intervene and when not to intervene in the economy. They also play an important role in identifying the costs and benefits of the different interventions that a government should take. We will discuss how to use cost-benefit analysis to compare different policy interventions. Finally, we examine different models of government behavior to understand why "in political life" the best economic arguments do not always win. We will show that politicians are influenced by incentives as much as anyone else, and do not always implement policies that enhance society's well-being.

PUBLIC GOODS

Table 1 shows the range of goods and services produced by all levels of government in the United States: the federal government, the 50 state governments, and more than 85,000 local governments (counties, cities, towns, and school districts). According to data from the Census Bureau, in terms of employment, the largest sector of government production in the United States is education at all levels, from elementary school to graduate school. Education is followed by health and hospital services, police, national defense, the postal service, corrections (prisons), and highways. (The figures for national defense include only civilian workers; if Table 1 included those serving in the armed forces, national defense would be second on the list.) The other categories, ranging from the judicial and legal system (federal, state, and county courts) to parks and recreation, are each significant but are small relative to the total.

Observe also the types of goods and services that are not on the list because they are produced by the private sector. Manufacturing, mining, retail trade, wholesale trade, hotel services, and motion picture production are some of the items that are largely left to the private sector. Note also that for all the goods and services on the list in Table 1, the private sector provides at least some of the production. There are 6 million workers in the private health-care sector, for example, compared to 2 million

TABLE 1
Types of Goods and Services Produced by Government in the United States

Type of Good or Service	Employment as a Percent of Total Government
Education	46
Health and hospitals	9
Police protection	6
National defense (civilian)	4
Postal service	4
Corrections (prisons)	4
Highways	3
Judicial and legal	2
Parks and recreation	2
Fire protection	2
All other	18

public good: a good or service that has two characteristics: nonrivalry in consumption and nonexcludability.

nonrivalry: the situation in which increased consumption of a good by one person does not decrease the amount available for consumption by others.

nonexcludability: the situation in which no one can be excluded from consuming a good.

free-rider problem: a problem arising in the case of public goods because those who do not contribute to the costs of providing the public good cannot be excluded from the benefits of the good.

in government health care. The private sector is also involved in mail delivery, education, garbage collection, and even fire protection (volunteer fire departments).

Why is the government involved in the production of police services and education services but not in the production of automobiles? Why are education and health services provided by both the private sector and the government sector while judicial services and national defense services are provided only by the government? In more general terms, why is it necessary for governments to produce *any* goods and services? The concept of a public good helps us answer the question.

Nonrivalry and Nonexcludability

A **public good** is a good or service that has two characteristics: *nonrivalry in consumption* and *nonexcludability*. **Nonrivalry** in consumption means that more consumption of a good by one person does not imply less consumption of it by another person. Clean air and national defense are examples of goods with nonrivalry. For example, if you were to take a walk outside and bask in the warm sunshine and breathe more clean air, you are not depriving another person of the opportunity to enjoy the sunshine or to breathe the clean air. Similarly, the sense of security that you get from a country's national defense—the military personnel, the strategic alliances, the missile defense system—is not reduced by the fact that your neighbor enjoys the same benefits of a national defense system.

In contrast, for most goods, there is rivalry in consumption. For example, if you purchase a ripe apple from the supermarket and eat it, then no one else can consume that apple. When you sit in the library and read this economics textbook, no one else can read this particular copy of the textbook. But for a good with nonrivalry in consumption, everybody can consume more if they want to. There is a collective aspect to the good, and the total benefit is the sum of the benefits to every person.

Nonexcludability means that one cannot exclude people from consuming the good. For example, the supermarket will not let you eat the apple unless you pay for it. The library will not let you check out the copy of the textbook unless you have a valid student ID card. These are excludable goods. On the other hand, no one can stop you from going outside, basking in the sunshine, and breathing clean air. The security provided by national defense is available to you, and no one can prevent you from benefiting from that security. A good or service that has nonrivalry in consumption and nonexcludability is a *public good*. In contrast, a *private good* has excludability and rivalry.

Free Riders: A Difficulty for the Private Sector

People can enjoy the consumption of a nonexcludable good or service without having to pay for it. Furthermore, if that good is also a nonrival good, then its use by nonpaying consumers does not reduce the ability of paying consumers to enjoy that good. Hence, instead of there being a clamor to deny use of the good to nonpaying consumers, you would see previously paying consumers also turn into nonpaying consumers. Pretty soon, the only consumers of the nonrival, nonexcludable good will be nonpaying ones, and hence there will be no incentive for anyone to provide that public good to the marketplace. We describe this situation as a **free-rider problem** associated with public goods: People who do not contribute to the costs of providing the good end up benefiting from the good because they cannot be excluded.

To better understand this concept, imagine that you bought a huge bus for the purpose of transporting students around the college town and collecting a little money for your service. But suppose the bus had a broken rear door that allowed

In the Wake of Hurricane Katrina
A Chinook helicopter drops sand bags to plug a canal levee break in the Gentilly neighborhood of New Orleans, Louisiana, on September 11, 2005. Levees are a public good, having characteristics of both nonrivalry and nonexcludability.

people to get on and off without paying and without interfering with other people's travel. In that situation, you would soon find that all your riders would be nonpaying ones. If you could not fix the door or do something else to exclude the free riders, you would not be in the transportation business long, because without fares, you would have losses.

National defense is like the huge bus with the broken rear door. You cannot exclude people from enjoying it, even if they do not pay—for instance, if there is an enemy aircraft that is intent on dropping bombs on a city, then shooting down that plane protects everyone's house, not just those of the people who paid for the antiaircraft missile. It is clear, then, that a private firm will have difficulty producing and selling national defense to the people of a country, since everyone will be hoping that someone else will pay for the antiaircraft missile that protects his or her house. Given the free-rider problem, the public good would have to be provided by the government. For instance, the government will be willing to provide national defense. Similar actions are taken with other public goods such as police protection, fire protection, and the judicial system. The government can broadly fund its provision of these public goods by assessing taxes on households.

Certain types of information also have the features of a public good. Everyone can benefit from information that a hurricane is on the way; there is no rivalry in consuming this information. Excluding people from consuming that information would also be difficult, since the most effective ways of notifying people quickly would involve radio and television broadcasts that are accessible to all. The U.S. Weather Service will therefore collect and distribute information about hurricanes and other adverse weather events. But you should keep in mind that not all information is nonexcludable. For example, if you want to analyze broad trends in the U.S. economy, you will find that much of the information you need is freely available through the Department of Commerce. However, if you want to analyze detailed information about companies trading on the New York Stock Exchange, you will have to pay a fee to a company before you can gain access to that information. Our focus here is on the type of information that has a public good feature associated with it.

The Classic Lighthouse Example
How can the free-rider problem be avoided without government providing the service?

Avoiding Free-Rider Problems

Even though we define public goods as being goods and services that are nonrival and nonexcludable, keep in mind that few goods are completely nonexcludable. Sometimes the private sector is able to find ways of making a good excludable to a degree sufficient to overcome the free-rider problem. A classic example used by economists to explore the nature of public goods is the lighthouse that warns ships of nearby rocks and prevents them from running aground. A lighthouse has the feature of nonrivalry. If one ship enjoys the benefit of the light and goes safely by, this does not mean that another ship cannot go by. Similarly, it is impossible to exclude ships from using the lighthouse because any ship can benefit from the light it projects.

However, lighthouse services are not always provided by the government. Early lighthouses were built by associations of shippers, who charged fees to the ships in nearby ports. This system worked well because the fees could be collected from most shippers as they entered nearby ports. So even if not every ship that used the lighthouse's services could be individually charged for that service (for instance, a ship that did not come into port but sailed by, using the lighthouse to gauge where land was, would not be charged for lighthouse services), many of those who benefited from the good were charged fees, thus alleviating the free-rider problem without government involvement.

Another example is over-the-air radio or television broadcasts. Such broadcasts have both characteristics of a public good. They are nonexcludable because anyone can tune in to the broadcast, regardless of whether they have paid to see or hear that particular show. They are nonrival because the use of an antenna or an aerial to capture a television or radio signal does not prevent anyone else from doing the same. Despite the public good characteristics of radio and television services, however, private firms have always provided the vast majority of such services in the United States. They are able to do so by using advertising to pay for the provision of the broadcast service, thus avoiding the free-rider problem.

user fee: a fee charged for the use of a good normally provided by the government.

Sometimes governments are able to charge people for the use of particular services that have a certain amount of excludability. This charge is called a **user fee.** In recent years, user fees have become more common in many government-provided services, including the national parks. The aim is to target the payments more closely to the users of the goods and services.

Some public goods and services have closely associated supplements that are privately provided. For instance, even though police services are almost always provided by a local government, businesses and wealthier families in a town may choose to avail themselves of security services provided by private firms to supplement the police services. In these cases, there is no free-rider problem because the private security service is excludable; it is targeted at a particular group, which will be charged for the use of that service.

Changes in Technology and Excludability

Modern technology is also constantly changing the degree to which certain goods are nonexcludable. A good example is the changing public good features of television. Cable TV and the ability to scramble signals for those who use satellites to obtain their television signals have reduced the problem of nonexcludability. If one does not pay a cable television bill, the service can be turned off. If one does not pay the satellite fee, the signals can be scrambled so that reception is impossible. Thus, it is now common to see cable television stations like HBO and Showtime delivering specialized programming to small audiences that pay extra for the special service. Such broadcasts may even have the luxury of being free of advertising because users can be directly charged for the services.

The Production of Goods by the Government

If we look at the types of goods produced by government in Table 1, we see many public goods, such as national defense, police protection, and the judicial and legal system. However, other goods in the list do not have features of public goods. Postal delivery, for example, is a service that has both rivalry in consumption and excludability. If you do not put a stamp on your letter, it is not delivered, and there is certainly rivalry in the consumption of a postal delivery worker's time. In principle, education also is characterized by rivalry in consumption and excludability. For a given-sized school, an additional student may reduce the education of other students, and it is technologically feasible to exclude a student who does not pay school fees or meet certain admissions criteria.

The mere production of a good by the government does not make that good a public good. In centrally planned economies, the government produces virtually everything, private goods as well as public goods. The economist's definition of a public good is specific and is useful for determining when the government should produce something and when it is better left to the market. If a good or service being produced by the government is not a public good, then it is important to find out the other reasons why the government is involved in the production of that good or service.

Cost-Benefit Analysis

Suppose the government decides that a particular good or service is a public good and that because of free-rider problems, the private sector will not get involved in the production of that good. Should the good be produced by the government? If so, how much of the good should be produced? Such decisions are ultimately made by voters and elected officials after much political debate. Economic analysis of the costs and benefits of providing the goods and services is critical if the participants in this debate are to make informed decisions. Balancing the costs and benefits of providing a good or service before making a decision is called **cost-benefit analysis.**

cost-benefit analysis: an appraisal of a project based on the costs and benefits derived from it.

■ **Marginal Cost and Marginal Benefit.** To determine the quantity of a government-provided service that should be produced, the marginal cost and marginal benefit of the service should be considered. In the case of police services, for example, a decision about whether to increase the size of the police force should consider both the marginal benefit to the people in the city—the reduction in the loss of life and property caused by crime, the increased enjoyment from a secure environment, and safer schools—and the marginal cost—the increased payroll for the police. If the marginal benefit of more police is greater than the marginal cost of more police, then the police force should be increased. The optimal size of the police force should be such that the marginal cost of more police is equal to the marginal benefit of more police.

Measuring the costs of producing government-provided services is not difficult because government workers' wages and materials used in production have explicit dollar values. But measuring the benefits of government-provided services is much more difficult. How do we measure how much people value greater security in their community? How do we value a reduction in violence at schools or a reduced murder rate? Public opinion polls in which people are asked how much they would be willing to pay are a possibility. For example, people can be asked in surveys how much they would be willing to pay for more police in an area. Such estimates of willingness to pay are called **contingent valuations** because they give the value contingent on the public good's existing and the person's having to pay for it. Some economists think that contingent valuation is not reliable if people do not actually have to pay for the good or service. People may not give a good estimate of their true willingness to pay.

contingent valuation: an estimation of the willingness to pay for a project on the part of consumers who may benefit from the project.

R E V I E W

- Public goods have two characteristics: nonrivalry, which means that more consumption of the good by one person does not mean that there would be less of the good available for someone else, and nonexcludability, which means that it is not possible to exclude those who do not pay for the good from consuming the good.

- These two characteristics lead public goods to have a free-rider problem—people who do not pay for the good can use it without interfering with the ability of those who paid for the good to use it. Instead of objecting to nonpayers' use of the good, the paying customers will soon stop paying. This means that private producers have little incentive to produce this good; thus, government production is frequently necessary.

- If the goods are not completely nonexcludable, the private sector may be able to come up with ways to charge at least some users of the good, enabling it to deal with the free-rider problem and produce goods in the market. Changes in technology can also help make previously nonexcludable goods and services at least partially excludable. Sometimes, even the government may levy user fees on users of some public goods that the government provides.

- In deciding how much of a public good should be provided, cost-benefit analysis can be used. The optimal quantity of the public good or service is the quantity at which the marginal benefit of the good or service equals its marginal cost.

- Even though the marginal cost of providing a public good can be fairly easily calculated, the marginal benefit is harder to calculate. Estimates of willingness to pay, known as contingent valuations, are a somewhat controversial measure of the marginal benefit of a public good.

EXTERNALITIES: FROM THE ENVIRONMENT TO EDUCATION

externality: the situation in which the costs of producing or the benefits of consuming a good spill over onto those who are not producing or consuming the good.

negative externality: the situation in which costs spill over onto someone who is not involved in producing or consuming the good.

positive externality: the situation in which benefits spill over onto someone who is not involved in producing or consuming the good.

We have seen that the existence of public goods provides an economic rationale for government involvement in the production of certain goods and services. Another rationale for government involvement in production is a market failure known as an externality. An **externality** occurs when the costs of producing a good or the benefits from consuming a good spill over onto individuals who are not producing or consuming the good. The production of goods that cause pollution is the classic example of an externality. For example, when a coal-fired electric utility plant produces energy, it emits smoke that contains carbon dioxide, sulfur dioxide, and other pollutants into the air. These pollutants can make life miserable for people breathing the air and cause serious health concerns. Similarly, people who smoke cigarettes pass on the health risks associated with secondhand smoke to those in their vicinity and reduce the quality of life for people who have negative reactions to the smell of cigarette smoke. These are examples of **negative externalities** because they have a negative effect—a cost—on the well-being of others. A **positive externality** occurs when a positive effect—a benefit—from producing or consuming a good spills over onto others. For example, you might benefit if your neighbor plants a beautiful garden that is visible from your house or apartment. Similarly, if you decide to get a flu shot, then not

Oil Spill: A Negative Externality
The oil spilled into the ocean by this sinking oil tanker is an example of a negative externality: The production of goods or services (transportation of oil) by a firm raises costs or reduces benefits to people (the oil spill).

only are you protected against the flu, but you will not pass on the flu to others you come into contact with. We will first look at the effects of negative externalities and then consider positive externalities.

Negative Externalities

In the case of negative externalities, a competitive market produces a quantity that exceeds the efficient amount of production. For example, companies may be too inclined to use air-polluting fossil fuels for generating energy instead of using a non-polluting source of energy like solar power. The reason is that producers do not take into account the external costs when they calculate their costs of production. If they did take these costs into account, they would produce less.

The reason why competitive markets are not efficient in the case of negative externalities can be illustrated using the supply and demand curves. For example, consider an example of a negative externality due to pollution caused by the production of electricity. This negative externality occurs because the production of electricity raises pollution costs to other firms and to individuals. The actual cost of producing electric power is greater than the costs perceived by the electrical utility. In other words, because of the externality, the marginal cost as perceived by the private firm, which we now call the **marginal private cost,** is less than the true marginal cost that is incurred by society, which we call the **marginal social cost.** Marginal social cost is the sum of the firm's marginal private cost and the marginal external cost, the increase in external costs to society as more is produced.

marginal private cost: the marginal cost of production as viewed by the private firm or individual.

marginal social cost: the marginal cost of production as viewed by society as a whole.

Marginal social cost = marginal private cost + marginal external cost

We illustrate this in Figure 1 by drawing a marginal private cost curve below the marginal social cost curve. We use the term *marginal private cost* to refer to what we have thus far called marginal cost in order to distinguish it from marginal social cost. Recall that adding up all the marginal (private) cost curves for the firms in a market gives the market supply curve, as labeled in the diagram.

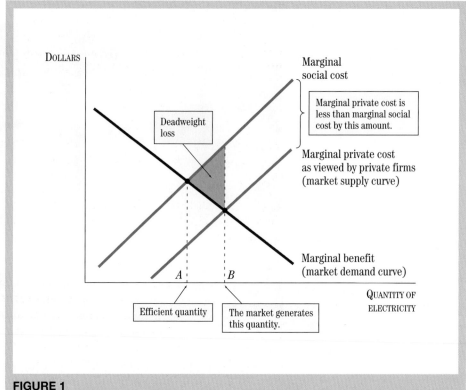

FIGURE 1
Illustration of a Typical Negative Externality
Because production of the good creates costs external to the firm, the marginal social cost is greater than the marginal private cost to the firm. Thus, the equilibrium quantity that emerges from a competitive market is too large: Marginal benefit is less than marginal social cost.

Figure 1 also shows the marginal benefit to consumers from using the product, in this case electrical energy. This is the market demand curve for electricity. According to the supply and demand model, the interaction of firms and consumers in the market will result in a situation in which the marginal cost of production—the marginal private cost—equals marginal benefit. This situation occurs at the market equilibrium, where the quantity supplied equals the quantity demanded. The resulting quantity produced is indicated by point *B* in Figure 1.

However, at this amount of production, the marginal benefit of production is less than the marginal *social* cost of production. Marginal benefit equals marginal private cost but is less than marginal social cost. Only at point *A* in the figure is marginal benefit equal to marginal social cost. Thus, point *A* represents the efficient level of production. Because of the externality, too much is produced. Firms produce too much because they do not incur the external costs.

Recall that we calculated how well off an economy is as a result of a particular outcome by adding up the values of consumer surplus and producer surplus. The sum of consumer and producer surplus is the area between the market supply curve and the market demand curve over the range of output produced. Another way to think about it is as the difference between marginal benefit (demand) and marginal cost (supply) over the range of output produced.

In the presence of a negative externality, how well off an economy is should really be measured as the difference between marginal benefit and the *marginal social cost* of production. You can see that for each additional unit that is produced above point *A* and below point *B*, the marginal benefit is *less* than the marginal social cost. Hence, the production of each additional unit is a net loss to society, and the overall deadweight loss from producing at the market equilibrium quantity of *B* is indicated by the shaded triangle in Figure 1.

Positive Externalities

A positive externality occurs when the activity of one person makes another person better off, either by reducing costs or by increasing benefits. For example, an individual who acquires additional education will obtain private benefits in the form of increased earnings. But the education also benefits society. Going to school and learning to read, write, and think makes people better citizens who will be able to teach their kids how to read and write, who will be able to pass on knowledge about discoveries they make to others, and who will be able to read about proper hygiene and health practices and thus put less of a burden on the public health system.

Another example of a good with a positive externality is research. Firms that engage in research get some of the benefits of that research through the products that they can sell—for instance, a new pharmaceutical to treat a particular disease. But the benefits from the research expenditures often go well beyond the individual or the company undertaking the research. The research spreads, and other people take advantage of it as well. An example is military research into global positioning systems (GPS), which spilled over into the private sector and found its way into devices such as navigation systems for automobiles.

Let us examine what happens when a positive externality raises social benefits above private benefits. To show how positive externalities affect the quantity produced in a competitive market, we need to look at the supply and demand curves. The externality makes the marginal benefit as perceived by the consumer, which we now call the **marginal private benefit**, less than the true benefit to society, which we call the **marginal social benefit**. With a positive externality, the marginal social benefit is greater than the marginal private benefit because there is a marginal external benefit from more consumption. That is,

> Marginal social benefit = marginal private benefit + marginal external benefit

We illustrate this in Figure 2 by drawing a marginal private benefit curve that lies below the marginal social benefit curve. We use the term *marginal private benefit* curve to refer to what we have thus far called marginal benefit or the market demand curve in order to distinguish it from marginal social benefit. Suppose that Figure 2 refers to the market for education. The market equilibrium is where the marginal private benefit curve (the market demand curve) intersects the marginal cost curve (the market supply curve). The resulting quantity produced is indicated by point *C* in Figure 2.

However, at this amount of production, the marginal *social* benefit of production exceeds the marginal cost of production. Only at point *D* in the figure is marginal social benefit equal to marginal cost. Thus, point *D* represents the efficient level of production. Because of the positive externality, too little is produced. Firms do not have the incentive to produce more because they do not gain directly from the benefits that are spilling over onto others.

In the presence of a positive externality, the sum of consumer and producer surplus should really be measured as the difference between the *marginal social benefit* and marginal cost. You can see that each additional unit that is not produced above point *C* and below point *D* results in forgone net benefit to society because the marginal social benefit exceeds the marginal cost of production. By not

marginal private benefit: the marginal benefit from consumption of a good as viewed by a private individual.

marginal social benefit: the marginal benefit from consumption of a good from the viewpoint of society as a whole.

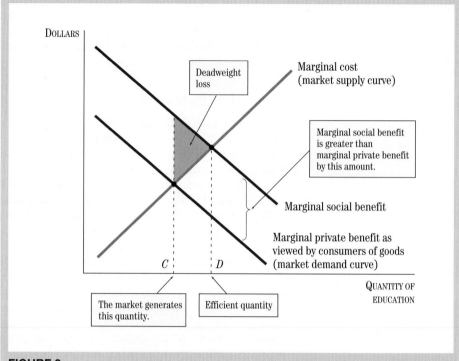

FIGURE 2
Illustration of a Typical Positive Externality
Because consumption of the good gives benefits to others, the marginal social benefit is greater than the marginal private benefit. Hence, the equilibrium quantity that emerges from a competitive market is too low.

increasing production from point *C* to point *D*, we incur a deadweight loss that is indicated by the shaded triangle in Figure 2.

Externalities Spread Across Borders

Externalities are by no means limited in their geographic impact. Sulfur dioxide emissions from electrical utility plants are an externality with international effects. The sulfur dioxide travels high into the air and is then dispersed by winds across long distances. Rainfall then brings the sulfur dioxide back to earth in the form of acid rain, which lands on forests and lakes hundreds of miles away. In some cases, the acid rain occurs in countries different from the country in which the sulfur dioxide was first emitted. In North America, acid rain that results from burning fuel in the Midwest industrial centers may fall in Canada or upstate New York.

Global warming is another example of an externality with international dimensions. When too much carbon dioxide accumulates in the earth's atmosphere, it prevents the sun's warmth from escaping out of the atmosphere, causing a greenhouse effect. Global warming is caused by the emission of carbon dioxide by firms and individuals but has effects all over the world.

The ease and prevalence of modern air travel also leads to negative spillover effects on other countries from a poor health-care system in one country. For instance, if patients in one country fall victim to an infection like the avian flu but go untreated, they can very easily spread that disease to many other countries as the people they come into contact with travel the world.

ECONOMICS IN ACTION

Excludability, Rivalry, and the Classification of Goods and Services

The following is a simple table that classifies goods and services on the rivalry/excludability dimensions. Goods in the bottom right corner are public goods that are nonrival and nonexcludable. The free-rider problems associated with these goods and services would lead to their underprovision by the private sector. On the other hand, goods in the top left corner are the rival and excludable goods that the private sector will do a good job of providing. But these are not the only two categories in which goods and services can be classified on the excludability/rivalry dimensions. Interesting economic issues arise with regard to goods that are nonexcludable but rival (the bottom left) and goods that are nonrival but excludable (top right). In this box, we will discuss some examples of goods that fall into these categories and learn a little more about the associated economic analysis.

	Rival	Nonrival
Excludable	An iPod, a pen, a banana	Satellite television, computer software code a new pharmaceutical treatment
Nonexcludable	Fish in the ocean, grazing land	Defense, clean air, an aerial fireworks display

NONRIVAL BUT EXCLUDABLE

Classic examples of nonrival but excludable goods are technological innovations: new discoveries or ideas that can be used to produce more output from inputs. Once discovered, ideas are nonrival, as multiple people can use an idea at the same time. If I were working out some calculus problems with a pencil, then you would not be able to use the pencil I was using (because the pencil is a rival good), but there is nothing stopping you from using the tools of calculus simultaneously (since the knowledge of calculus is nonrival). Some ideas, like calculus or basic scientific discoveries, are in fact nonrival *and* nonexcludable. They would fall into the public goods category. But other ideas, such as a new word-processing program, a new web-search algorithm, or a new pharmaceutical treatment of a disease, can be made excludable thanks to intellectual property laws such as patents and copyrights. This implies that some level of government intervention is necessary to set up the institutions that help make these discoveries excludable; however, once these protections are in place, the private sector can do the production without additional intervention by the government.

The challenge for the government is that the way to make the discovery excludable is to grant the inventor or researcher who made the discovery temporary monopoly rights over the product. For example, in the United States, when the Food and Drug Administration approves a new pharmaceutical for sale, and a patent is granted for the product, that patent protection will last 20 years—no other firm may sell that pharmaceutical product (or produce one with the identical chemical content) for 20 years. The government needs to balance the interests of the consumer (lower drug prices resulting from vigorously competitive markets) with the interests of the pharmaceutical company (monopoly power to recoup its research expenses and to provide incentives for future discoveries). Thus government intervention with these types of excludable, yet nonrival products can be either too much or too little.

Similar controversies erupt over creative content such as music or movies. Once a song is recorded or a movie is made, the content of that song or that movie is a nonrival good. So, for example, people in Sydney, Australia, can enjoy *Little Miss Sunshine* without in any way diminishing the enjoyment that the residents of Alaska derive from the movie. But in countries with strong copyright laws, the content is excludable—you have to pay if you want to watch the movie or listen to the song. Creators of movies and music often strongly protest when governments in some countries turn a blind eye to patent and copyright protection. In some Asian countries, it is not uncommon for pirated copies of the latest movies and music to be widely and cheaply available. If this lack of excludability becomes pervasive, then the resulting free-rider problems will lead to underprovision of creative content by the private sector.

NONEXCLUDABLE BUT RIVAL

Another interesting category of goods lies in the bottom left corner of the above table. These are goods that are nonexcludable, but rival. In other words, everyone technically can use the good, but the use of the good by one person detracts from the ability of others to enjoy the good. In economics, goods that exhibit the features of nonexcludability and rivalry are said to suffer from the *tragedy of the commons* problem. This term traces back to a classic article by Garrett Hardin that appeared in the magazine *Science* in 1968.[2] Hardin summarized the problem faced by goods with this combination of characteristics in the following, now famous, words.

> The tragedy of the commons develops in this way. Picture a pasture open to all. It is to be expected that each herdsman will try to keep as many cattle as possible on the commons. . . . As a rational being, each herdsman seeks to maximize his gain. Explicitly or implicitly, more or less consciously, he asks, "What is the utility to me of adding one more animal to my herd?" This utility has one negative and one positive component.
>
> 1. The positive component is a function of the increment of one animal. Since the herdsman receives all the proceeds from the sale of the additional animal, the positive utility is nearly +1.
> 2. The negative component is a function of the additional overgrazing created by one more animal. Since, however, the effects of overgrazing are shared by all the herdsmen, the negative utility for any particular decisionmaking herdsman is only a fraction of −1.
>
> Adding together the component partial utilities, the rational herdsman concludes that the only sensible course for him to pursue is to add another animal to his herd. And another. . . . But this is the conclusion reached by each and every rational herdsman sharing a commons. Therein is the tragedy. Each man is locked into a system that compels him to increase his herd without limit—in a world that is limited. Ruin is the destination toward which all men rush, each pursuing his own best interest in a society that believes in the freedom of the commons. Freedom in a commons brings ruin to all.

Because the good (in this case, the grazing pasture) is nonexcludable, each herder can graze his animals there. However, because the pasture is rival, more consumption by the animals of one herder means less pasture for the animals owned by other herders to graze on. In essence, what Hardin is describing is a situation in which the actions of a herdsman (adding one more animal to the flock) create an externality (less grazing for all the animals of other herdsmen). Furthermore, if individuals do not internalize this externality, the common resource, in this case the grazing land, gets depleted very quickly. Government intervention of some kind, either through regulation of access to the common resource or through assigning property rights over

the resource to some party or parties, can improve the outcomes generated by the private sector.

One of the most striking manifestations of the tragedy of the commons problem in recent times has been the decimation of fish stocks in the world's oceans. The incentive to catch one more fish is overwhelming because the benefit goes to the boat catching the fish, whereas the negative impact is diffused across all other fishing boats. But if everyone catches that extra fish (or 1,000 fish), then the world's fish stocks will begin to decrease rapidly. This is what has in fact occurred in some of the greatest fisheries in the world, including the cod fishery and the halibut fishery in the United States. Governments have intervened in various ways to stop the overuse of the commons. They have introduced fishing seasons, required fishing licenses, imposed catch quotas, and put in requirements that only fish with certain dimensions are allowed to be kept.

Another potential welfare-enhancing government intervention in a tragedy of the commons situation is to assign property rights over the resource. A fascinating article by John Tierney that appeared in the *New York Times* in the year 2000 looked at two fishing grounds—New England and Australia—to show why a tragedy of the commons problem manifested itself in the former but not the latter.[3] A New England fishermen interviewed by Tierney summarizes the factors that led to the decimation of the Northeast fisheries for cod, tuna, and swordfish:

> Right now, my only incentive is to go out and kill as many fish as I can," Sorlien said. "I have no incentive to conserve the fishery, because any fish I leave is just going to be picked by the next guy.

To overcome the problem of the tragedy of the commons, governments all over the world have taken several steps. Perhaps the most notable in the United States is the requirement that you have a permit before you can fish. For example, the state of Maine limits the number of commercial lobstering licenses that it issues, and anyone who wants to get into the commercial lobstering business has to either buy a firm that has a license or work his way through a student/apprentice process to obtain a license. By making the fishing excludable, the government is taking steps to fix the free-rider problem. Furthermore, those lobstermen

---

[2] Garrett Hardin, "The Tragedy of the Commons," *Science* 162 (1968), pp. 1243–1248.

[3] John Tierney, "A Tale of Two Fisheries," *New York Times*, August 27, 2000.

who have permits to catch lobsters have an incentive to protect the resource. Today, many of you may be familiar with "farmed salmon," which again are an attempt to move fisheries out of the open ocean (where the tragedy of the commons loomed) and into a more excludable setting in the form of a fish farm.

The tragedy of the commons appears in many contexts ranging from overusing a water source to too many providers cramming onto radio frequency spectrums. Now you should be able to think more creatively about solutions to these problems, which again have the theme of forcing users to internalize the externalities through the use of property rights and quotas.

REVIEW

- Externalities occur when the benefits or costs of producing and consuming spill over onto others. The spillovers can be negative, as in the case of air pollution, or positive, as in the case of vaccinations.

- Externalities are a cause of market failure. For goods with negative externalities, more than the efficient amount is produced because the marginal social cost exceeds the marginal private cost. Private firms produce until the marginal benefit equals the marginal private cost, even though the optimal level is lower—where the marginal benefit equals the marginal social cost.

- For goods with positive externalities, less than the efficient amount is produced because the marginal social benefit exceeds the marginal private benefit. Private firms will produce only until the marginal private benefit equals the marginal cost, even though the optimal level is higher—where the marginal social benefit equals the marginal cost.

- Both positive and negative externalities result in deadweight loss. In the case of negative externalities, this is because too many goods are being produced; these additional goods have a marginal social cost that exceeds the marginal benefit. In the case of positive externalities, it is because too few goods are being produced; the forgone goods have a marginal social benefit that exceeds the marginal cost.

- Externalities are not necessarily local in their impact. Air pollution and global warming are examples of externalities whose effects are not hemmed in by borders. Changes in technology also are increasingly making the impact of one country's policy on, say, public health issues have a spillover effect on other countries.

REMEDIES FOR EXTERNALITIES

As the previous section shows, competitive markets do not generate an efficient level of production when externalities exist. What are some of the ways in which a society can alleviate problems caused by these externalities? In some cases involving positive externalities, the solution has been for government to produce the good or service because the private sector will produce less than the socially efficient level of output. For instance, elementary education is provided by governments all over the world with requirements that children attend school through a certain age. But in most cases where externalities are present, production is left to the private sector, and government endeavors to influence the quantity produced.

How can production in the private sector be influenced by government so as to lead to a more efficient level of production of goods and services in the economy? We will see that the answer involves changing behavior so that the externalities are taken into account internally by firms and consumers. In other words, the challenge is to **internalize** the externalities.

internalize: the process of providing incentives so that externalities are taken into account internally by firms or consumers.

There are four alternative ways to bring about a more efficient level of production in the case of externalities. The first method we discuss, private remedies, does not require direct government intervention. The other three—command and control, taxes or subsidies, and tradable permits—do.

Private Remedies: Agreements Between the Affected Parties

private remedy: a procedure that eliminates or internalizes externalities without government action other than defining property rights.

In some cases, people, through **private remedies,** can eliminate externalities themselves without government assistance. A Nobel Prize winner in economics, Ronald Coase of the University of Chicago, pointed out this possibility in a famous paper published in 1960.

Consider the following simple example. Suppose that the externality relates to the production of two products: health care and candy. Suppose that a hospital is built next door to a large candy factory. Making candy requires noisy pounding and vibrating machinery. Unfortunately, the walls of the new hospital are thin. The loud candy machinery can be heard in the hospital. Thus, there is an externality that we might call noise pollution. It has a cost. It makes the hospital less effective; for example, it is difficult for the doctors to hear their patients' hearts through the stethoscopes.

What can be done? The city mayor could adopt a rule prohibiting loud noise near the hospital, but that would severely impinge on candy production in the city. Or, because the hospital was built after the candy factory, the mayor could say, "Too bad, doctors; candy is important too" and tell the hospital to relocate somewhere where the noise is not too great. Alternatively, it might be better for the candy workers and doctors to work this externality out themselves. The supervisor of the candy workers could negotiate with the doctors. Perhaps the candy workers could agree to use the loud machines only at designated hours during the afternoon, during which time the doctors would avoid scheduling procedures that are sensitive to noise. Or perhaps the hospital would be willing to pay for a more insulated wall between the candy company and the hospital so that the noise is dampened, especially since it is cheaper than relocation. Or perhaps the candy company will be willing to pay for newer, less noisy machinery because it is preferable to the risk of having to shut down because of the noise pollution.

Thus, it is possible to resolve the externality by negotiation between the two parties affected. The privately negotiated alternatives seem more efficient than the mayor's rulings because the production of both candy and health care continues. Note that in these alternatives, both parties alter their behavior. For example, the doctors change their scheduling of noise-sensitive procedures, and the candy factory limits loud noise to the afternoon. Thus, the parties find a solution in which the polluter does not make all the adjustments, as would be the case if the mayor adopted a "no loud noise" rule.

■ The Importance of Assigning Property Rights.

property rights: rights over the use, sale, and proceeds from a good or resource. (Ch. 1)

For a negotiation like this to work, however, it is essential that property rights be well defined. *Property rights* determine who has the right to pollute or infringe on whom. Who, for example, is being infringed on in the case of the noise pollution? Does the candy factory have the right to use loud machinery, or does the hospital have the right to peace and quiet? The mayor's ruling could establish who has the property right, but more likely the case would be taken to a court and the court would decide. After many such cases, precedent would establish who has the property rights in future cases.

The property rights will determine who actually pays for the adjustment that remedies the externality. If the candy factory has the right, then the workers can demand some compensation (perhaps free health-care services) from the hospital for limiting their noise in the afternoon or the candy company can demand that the hospital bear some of the cost of the new machinery. If the hospital has the right, then perhaps the hospital staff and patients can get compensated with free candy or the hospital can ask the candy company to pay for some of the cost of building a thicker wall. The **Coase theorem** states that no matter who is assigned the property rights, the negotiations will lead to an efficient outcome as described in the candy/health-care example. The assignment of the property rights determines who makes the compensation.

Coase theorem: the idea that private negotiations between people will lead to an efficient resolution of externalities regardless of who has the property rights as long as the property rights are defined.

■ Transaction Costs.

transaction costs: the costs of buying or selling in a market, including search, bargaining, and writing contracts.

Even if property rights are well defined, for a private agreement like this to occur, transaction costs associated with the agreement must be small compared to the costs of the externality itself. **Transaction costs** are the time and effort needed to reach an agreement. As Coase put it, "in order to carry out a market transaction, it is necessary to discover who it is that one wishes to deal with, to inform people that one wishes to deal and on what terms, to conduct negotiations leading up to a bargain, to draw up the contract, to undertake the inspection needed to make sure that the terms of the contract are being observed, and so on. These operations are often extremely costly."[4] Real-world negotiations are clearly time-consuming, requiring skilled and expensive lawyers in many cases. If these negotiation costs are large, then the private parties may not be able to reach an agreement. If the negotiation in the health-care/candy example took many years and had to be repeated many times, then it might be better to adopt a simple "no loud noise" rule or an "existing firms get precedence over new arrivals" rule.

■ The Free-Rider Problem Again.

Free-rider problems can also prevent a private agreement from taking place. For example, a free-rider problem might occur if the hospital was very large, say, 400 doctors. Suppose that the candy workers have the right to noise pollute, so that they require a payment in the form of health care. The hospital would need contributions from the doctors to provide the care. Thus, if each doctor worked in the hospital an extra day a year, this might be sufficient.

However, any one of the 400 doctors could refuse to work the extra day. Some of the doctors could say that they have other job opportunities where they do not have to work an extra day. In other words, doctors who did not pay could free-ride: work at

---

[4] Ronald Coase, "The Problem of Social Cost," *Journal of Law and Economics* 3 (October 1960): 15.

the hospital and still benefit from the agreement. Because of this free-rider problem, the hospital might find it hard to provide health care to the candy workers, and a private settlement might be impossible.

Thus, in the case where the transaction costs are high or free-rider problems exist, a private remedy may not be feasible. Then the role of government comes into play, much as it did in the case of public goods, where the free-rider problem was significant. Again as Coase put it, "Instead of instituting a legal system of rights which can be modified by transactions on the market, the government may impose regulations which state what people must or must not do and which have to be obeyed."[5]

Command and Control Remedies

command and control: the regulations and restrictions that the government uses to correct market imperfections.

When private remedies for externalities are not feasible, either because transaction costs are too high or because of free-rider problems, there is a role for government intervention. One form of government intervention to solve the problem of externalities is the placement of restrictions or regulations on individuals or firms, often referred to as **command and control.** Firms that do not heed these restrictions and regulations are fined for their violations. Command and control methods are used widely by agencies such as the Environmental Protection Agency (EPA), which has responsibility for federal environmental policy in the United States. For example, in the United States, the corporate average fleet efficiency (CAFE) standards require that the fleet of cars produced by an automobile manufacturer each year achieve a stated number of miles per gallon on the average. Another example is a government requirement that electrical utilities put "scrubbers" in their smokestacks to remove certain pollutants from the smoke they emit. Through *commands*, the government *controls* what the private sector does. The government's actions, in principle, make the externalities internal to the firm by requiring that the firm act as if it was taking the external costs into account.

There are many disadvantages to the use of command and control to reduce externalities, especially in the environmental area. The most significant disadvantage is that command and control does not allow firms to find other, cheaper ways to reduce pollution. For example, under command and control, electrical utilities have to install a scrubber to remove pollutants; they do not have the incentive to discover a cheaper alternative technology that might be more effective at reducing pollution. Similarly, CAFE standards can lead to inefficient production decisions—because firms have to produce smaller, more fuel-efficient cars that they did not want to produce simply to offset the production of the less fuel-efficient SUVs—or to more gasoline consumption because people find that the per-mile cost of driving has fallen because of the higher fuel efficiency, and hence drive more.

Big Brother Is Watching Your Car!
Closed circuit television cameras loom above traffic in central London to monitor the license plates of the estimated 250,000 cars entering the city each day. Drivers pay a "congestion charge" to drive in central London, making it more expensive to drive there, with the ultimate goal of reducing traffic backups.

Taxes and Subsidies

Because of the disadvantages associated with command and control, economists recommend alternative

---

[5] Ronald Coase, "The Problem of Social Cost," *Journal of Law and Economics* 3 (October 1960): 17.

techniques to reduce the inefficiencies that result from externalities. The use of taxes and subsidies is often recommended by economists, with goods and services that have negative externalities being taxed while goods and services that have positive externalities are subsidized.

For example, consider the negative externalities that are imposed by drivers. When there are many drivers in a city, roads become congested, leading to traffic backups and delays. Each driver contributes to the congestion, imposing external costs on the other drivers. In 2003, a new tax, called a congestion charge, was imposed on vehicles that drive in central London during the day. Drivers can pay £8 before they travel or £10 the day after they travel; cameras mounted above the roads check vehicle registration numbers to make sure that the taxes are paid. The idea was to internalize the externality of congestion in central London during rush hour by making drivers pay for the external congestion costs through the tax. If the demand for days of driving in central London is downward-sloping, the tax will bring about a cutback in driving in central London, lower the external costs imposed on drivers by reducing congestion, and create government revenue. In fact, the evidence suggests that traffic in central London fell by a third.

The way that taxes can be used to reduce negative externalities is illustrated graphically in Figure 3, which uses the same curves as Figure 1. Recall that the marginal social cost of production is greater than the marginal private cost, as viewed from the private firm, because of the negative externality, resulting in the equilibrium

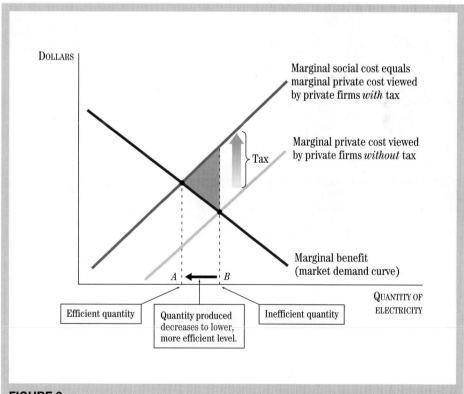

FIGURE 3
Using Taxes in the Case of a Negative Externality
A tax equal to the difference between the marginal private cost and the marginal social cost in Figure 1 shifts the supply curve up. This reduces the equilibrium quantity produced to the lower, more efficient level.

Realizing the Positive Externalities of a New Cancer Vaccine

In June of 2006, the Food and Drug Administration approved a vaccine that would prevent infection with and transmission of the human papillomavirus (HPV), a virus that has been associated with cervical cancer among women. Medical experts recommended that the vaccine be given to adolescent girls so that they would be protected against being infected by the HPV virus, and also so that they would not pass on the virus to anyone else after they became sexually active. The HPV vaccine is an example of a good with a positive externality, according to what we have learned thus far, the government should step in to ensure that the socially optimal level of vaccinations is carried out. State governments began the process of mandating the HPV vaccine and adding it to regular immunization schedules, while the federal government moved to add it to the Vaccines for Children program to ensure that young girls without insurance or coming from poor families would also be protected by the vaccine. But in this case, government intervention to increase consumption of a good with a positive externality created substantial debate. This article from the *Washington Post* highlights the challenges that governments face even when trying to intervene for a good with a positive externality.

The concern that the backlash against the HPV vaccine may lead to other vaccines with positive externalities not being consumed at the socially optimal level.

Parents Question HPV Vaccine; Push to Mandate Shots Rapidly Creates Backlash

SUSAN LEVINE, Washington Post Staff Writer

Description of the controversy over mandated immunizations

In barely nine months, the first cancer-specific vaccine to win federal approval has gone from licensing and the enthusiastic embrace of dozens of states to a widespread backlash against moves to mandate immunization for adolescent girls. Health experts are dismayed by the controversy over Merck's Gardasil, which protects against two common forms of the sexually transmitted virus that causes cervical cancer. But it has hardly surprised them. Never has compulsory use of a drug been pushed with such breakneck speed—with concerted lobbying by its manufacturer. Never have such efforts advanced largely through political and legislative channels instead of medical authorities and public education campaigns.

Votes to require the three-dose vaccine before students enter the sixth grade remain likely in the District and numerous jurisdictions. On Friday, Virginia Gov. Timothy M. Kaine (D) announced he would sign the first bill in the country to prescribe vaccination, albeit with an opt-out provision. However, doctors question whether there will be adequate funding and access to support these measures, and some fear that the opt-out clauses, included to counter opponents' concerns, could erode support for immunizations in general.

If parents are given broad opportunity to exempt their 11- and 12-year-old daughters from the vaccine for the human papillomavirus, or HPV, will they be less willing to have children of any age inoculated against other, more communicable diseases? "The message that we send to parents is exceedingly important," said Gary Freed, a professor of pediatrics and health policy at the University of Michigan and chairman of the federal government's National Vaccine Advisory Committee. "Are we going to be creating a culture of vaccine refusal that's not going to serve us well?"

Few people dispute the promise of the new vaccine, which clinical trials proved to be highly effective against two HPV strains that cause nearly three-quarters of the 10,000 annual cervical cancer cases in the United States. About 40 percent of women who receive the diagnosis die. Low-income and minority women are most affected, with African American mortality rates more than twice that of whites.

Still, for some parents those numbers might not be great enough to justify state intervention. Maureen Siegel of Manassas, who has a 10-year-old daughter, acknowledged she must learn more. "I don't know everything there is to know about the basics," she said. "I also don't know if cervical cancer is a big enough epidemic to make [vaccination] mandatory."

Questions about the extent of the positive externality

Because the virus is transmitted through intimate contact, the arguments for required vaccination differ from the rationale for enforcing shots against diseases easily spread in schools, such as measles. They are less about safeguarding the public and more about safeguarding individuals. "Why is this happening so fast? Why is there a mandate when this is such a different kind of disease?" asked Barbara Loe Fisher, president of the National Vaccine Information Center, a nonprofit consumer organization that opposes HPV legislation. Most states did not add the chickenpox vaccine to schoolchildren's immunization schedules until several years after its approval in the mid-1990s, she noted.

Yet the backlash is also about the age of children targeted. Although the government approved Gardasil for women up to 26, it recommended routine administration to girls 11 and 12 to ensure they be protected before they become sexually active. The vaccine is most effective when given before first sexual contact. Its duration is unclear. Some people argue that vaccination could encourage adolescents to be more promiscuous. More believe that parents' authority over their daughters' health care would be usurped. Others point out that cervical cancer will occur in only a fraction of the more than 7.5 million girls and young women estimated to be infected with the virus in this country.

The source of the controversy—is the government vaccinating the right age group? Supporters argue that the vaccine should be given before girls become sexually active. Opponents say that getting a vaccine like the HPV vaccine at a young age sends the wrong message about sexual behavior.

A Maryland state senator retreated quickly in January after being deluged by irate letters about her bill for mass HPV vaccination before middle school. Still pending is a second bill to create a task force of legislators, teachers and health professionals to study the issue through 2008. "I thought it was imperative to continue the conversation," explained Del. Joseline Peña-Melnyk (D-Prince George's), who introduced the study initiative. "People need to be educated on the issue in order to be able to support it."

In the District, a mandatory immunization bill could be voted out of the D.C. Council Health Committee as early as Friday. One sponsor, council member Mary Cheh (D-Ward 3), has heard mixed reaction from residents, with the positive responses coming "almost uniformly from women." "I really hope people don't lose sight of the fact that this is the first time we've ever had a vaccine against a cancer," Cheh said. "You seize and take advantage of it."

Local health experts urge more deliberate consideration. "There has to be a period of awareness," said Joseph Wright, executive director of the Child Health Advocacy Institute at Children's Hospital in Northwest Washington. The hospital has not decided its position on the council's pending bill. "Legislators would be wise to recognize the way the public winds are blowing and build in a very strong public education campaign before stressing the mandatory aspect."

Kim Koontz Bayliss, for one, was initially angered by the proposal, seeing it as an intrusion on her judgment of what is best for her 11-year-old, Nell. The Cleveland Park resident has come around some in the past month. After a television commercial on Gardasil prompted questions from her daughter, she read up on HPV and the vaccine. Nell is due soon for her annual checkup, and her mother plans to discuss it with the doctor.

The difficulties associated with enforcing a mandate

But, she added, "I'm not going to make a move until I talk to the pediatrician."

quantity produced by the market exceeding the efficient quantity. We know that taxes raise the marginal cost to the individual firm. They thereby shift up the market supply curve. If the tax is chosen to exactly equal the difference between the marginal social cost and the marginal private cost, then the quantity produced by the market will decline from the inefficient quantity shown at point *B* to the efficient quantity shown at point *A* in Figure 3.

There are many examples of taxes being used at least in part to reduce pollution. Gasoline taxes are widely viewed as being good for the environment because they reduce gasoline consumption, which pollutes the air. In the United States there is a federal tax of 18.4 cents per gallon and a variety of state taxes averaging an additional 23.6 cents per gallon. The big advantage of taxes or subsidies compared with command and control is that the market is still being used. Instead of restricting the ratio of SUVs to small, fuel-efficient cars that a producer can manufacture, the government simply raises the relative cost of driving an SUV versus driving a subcompact car by increasing the gasoline tax. If users of SUVs respond by switching over to smaller cars, then the car manufacturer has an incentive to produce smaller cars that consumers actually want to buy, or to research more fuel-efficient SUV engines.

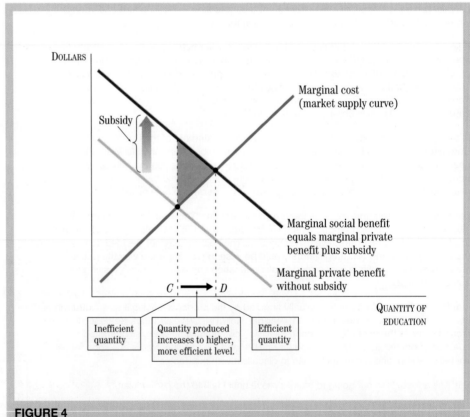

FIGURE 4
Using Subsidies in the Case of a Positive Externality
A subsidy equal to the difference between the marginal social benefit and the marginal private benefit of education or research shifts the demand curve up. This increases the equilibrium quantity produced to the higher, more efficient level and eliminates the deadweight loss due to the externality.

Next, we consider the use of subsidies for goods that have positive externalities. Recall that when a good has a positive externality, too little of it is produced in a competitive economy; a subsidy can be used to increase production and consumption of the good. The Vaccines for Children (VFC) program provides free vaccines for children who are poor and do not have access to health insurance. This program was implemented following an outbreak of measles that killed hundreds of children in the late 1980s. Vaccinations not only protect the child directly, but also produce a positive externality for others who will no longer risk being infected by that child. Government intervention to effectively drive the price of vaccinations to zero through the use of a subsidy will enable more children to be vaccinated and allow parents to internalize the positive externality of having their children vaccinated.

In Figure 4, which uses the same curves as Figure 2, we demonstrate how a subsidy can be used to encourage the production and consumption of a good with a positive externality. In this case, a subsidy to the user will raise the demand for the good. If the subsidy is chosen to be exactly the difference between the marginal private benefit and the marginal social benefit, then the quantity of the good that is produced and consumed will rise from the inefficient level (*C*) to the efficient level (*D*), as illustrated in Figure 4.

Another example of subsidizing positive externalities is the government's funding of research by providing grants to private firms and individuals. The National Science Foundation supports basic research, and the National Institutes of Health support medical research. In supporting research with a limited budget, it is important for the government to place more emphasis on research that has large positive externalities. Many view basic research as having larger positive externalities than applied research. The ideas in basic research, such as that on the structure of the atom, affect many parts of the economy. Applied research, such as that on a new lightweight metal for a bike, has more limited spillovers, and the products developed through applied research can usually be sold by the creator for profit. In fact, the federal government in the United States does spend more to subsidize basic research than applied research.

■ Emission Taxes. A more direct way to use taxes to deal with pollution externalities is to tax the firm based on the amount of pollution emitted rather than on the quantity of the potentially polluting good that is produced or consumed. For example, an electrical utility could be charged fees depending on how many particles of sulfur dioxide it emits, rather than on how much electricity it produces. Such charges are called **emission taxes.** They are much like taxes on the amount of the product sold, but they focus directly on the amount of pollution.

emission tax: a charge made to firms that pollute the environment based on the quantity of pollution that they emit.

Emission taxes have an advantage over taxes on production in that the firm can use technology to change the amount of pollution associated with its production. Thus, rather than producing less electricity, the firm can reduce the amount of pollution associated with a given amount of electricity if it can find a cheaper way to do so. Emission taxes have an even greater advantage over command and control than a tax on the product has.

■ Why Is Command and Control Used More Than Taxes? There is one feature of command and control that many people like: The total amount of pollution can be better controlled than with a tax. This may explain why command and control is used more than taxes. Suppose, for example, that a tax is used to equate marginal social cost with marginal benefit, as in Figure 3. Now suppose there is a sudden reduction in the private cost of producing electricity. The private marginal cost curve will shift down, and, with the tax unchanged, production (and pollution) will increase. A regulation that stipulates a certain quantity to produce would not have this problem.

The total amount of pollution would be fixed. Fortunately, in recent years, a new idea in pollution control has emerged that has both this advantage of command and control and the flexibility of the market. This new idea is tradable permits.

Tradable Permits

tradable permit: a governmentally granted license to pollute that can be bought and sold.

Tradable permits use the market to help achieve the standards set by the government. The way these permits work is as follows. The government decides what the limit it wants to impose on the overall level of a particular pollutant is. The government then issues a number of permits specifying permissible amounts of pollution. The total amount of pollution in the economy is equal to the total amount specified in the permits issued. If a firm plans to emit more pollutants than it has permits for, it will have to acquire additional permits from other firms. On the other hand, if a firm has more permits than the pollutants it plans to emit, it can sell its permits to another firm that wants them.

Firms now have an incentive to lower their emissions because they can sell the permits if they do not use them. Firms that can lower their emissions cheaply will choose to do so and benefit by selling their permits to other firms for which reducing the pollution is more costly. Tradable permits not only allow the market system to work, but also give firms an incentive to find the least costly form of pollution control. Rather than forcing individual firms to limit the quantity of the pollutant that they can release, tradable permits result in those firms that can reduce the emissions in the most cost-efficient manner doing the bulk of the emissions reduction. Firms that face a high cost of reducing pollution will cut back less on their pollution, but will have to internalize their pollution costs because of the need to buy permits. Those firms will also have an incentive to adopt technologies that will eventually emit fewer pollutants.

Tradable permits illustrate how important property rights are for resolving externalities. The role of government in this case is to create a market by defining certain rights to pollute and then allowing firms to buy and sell these rights. Once rights are assigned, the market can work and achieve efficiency.

Tradable permits are likely to be an increasingly common way to reduce pollution in the future. Perhaps the best known use of tradable permits in the United States has been to reduce emissions of sulfur dioxide. Other uses, past and present, of permits include reducing various types of air pollutants, the move to eliminate lead from gasoline in the United States, and the use of tradable permits to limit overfishing in the oceans. Tradable permits could also work in combating global warming. The amount of global warming depends on the total amount of carbon dioxide emissions in the world's atmosphere. It does not matter whether a firm in Los Angeles or in Shanghai emits the carbon dioxide. Tradable permits could control the total amount of pollution. The permits would let firms or individuals decide on the most cost-effective way for them to reduce the total amount of pollution.

Balancing the Costs and Benefits of Reducing Externalities

As with public goods, it is important to use cost-benefit analysis when considering how best to intervene in the economy to fix problems caused by externalities. There are clear benefits to reducing pollution, but there are associated costs in the form of lower production, lost jobs, administrative expenses, and so on. These costs should be compared to the associated benefits on a case-by-case basis before deciding on the appropriate intervention method.

For example, the Environmental Protection Agency introduced a new rule for stricter standards on the amount of sulfur allowed in diesel fuel in 2000.

Environmentalists saw a clear benefit from these new standards because they were concerned that diesel exhaust was causing accelerated cancer rates. On the other hand, trucking companies that use diesel fuel saw a clear cost because the effect of the stricter standards was to raise the price of the fuel needed to run their trucks. The Environmental Protection Agency estimated that the new, stricter standards would prevent 8,300 deaths and 360,000 asthma attacks, while increasing the price of diesel fuel by 4 to 5 cents per gallon. The oil industry reported that implementation of the stricter standards would cost $8 billion. Policymakers would have to do a cost-benefit analysis to determine whether the additional benefits coming from a stricter standard on sulfur justified the additional costs.

As the following two examples illustrate, sometimes the policymakers rule that the benefits justify the costs, whereas at other times they conclude that the costs outweigh the benefits. The first example was the regulation of carbon dioxide emissions, a policy that President George W. Bush had advocated during his 2000 campaign for the presidency. In 2001, President Bush changed his mind about regulating carbon dioxide emissions. A study by the Energy Department showed that this regulation would result in nearly a quadrupling of the cost of producing electricity from coal, causing large price increases for both electricity and natural gas. President Bush stated that the impact on utility prices made the cost of regulating carbon dioxide emissions too high.

The second example relates to stricter standards on the level of arsenic allowed in drinking water that President Clinton imposed shortly before leaving office. In March 2001, the Environmental Protection Agency rescinded the new, stricter standard and debated its merits. Scientific studies showed that higher levels of arsenic in drinking water lead to higher risks of fatal cancer, heart disease, and diabetes. The cost of the stricter standard for arsenic in drinking water was estimated to be billions of dollars because arsenic is a by-product in mining, is used as a wood preservative for lumber, and occurs naturally in water in some areas. After examining the evidence, the Bush administration decided to impose the stricter standard, convinced that the health benefits were worth the cost.

Some people object to the use of cost-benefit analysis for deciding whether or not environmental regulations should be implemented. They argue that environmental regulations can benefit rather than cost the economy, because requiring individuals to reduce pollution creates a demand for pollution-reducing devices and creates jobs in the pollution-reducing industry. But unless the pollution-reducing equipment is creating a benefit to society greater than the benefits of other goods, shifting more resources to pollution abatement will not be an efficient allocation of society's resources.

In recent years there has been significant concern about rising pollution levels in other parts of the world, especially in very fast growing economies like China, India, and Brazil. As more factories start producing goods and services, more forests are cleared to meet the space needs of expanding cities, more power generation is needed to meet the demands of newly electrified homes, and more vehicles enter the streets as people spend their rising incomes, air- and water-pollution problems in these countries become magnified. This poses a dilemma for policymakers because asking these countries to cut back on their rates of economic growth in order to reduce pollution clearly does not seem like a feasible plan. In fact, many people argue that the surest way to reduce pollution around the world is to make sure that the less-developed economies of the world increase their level of income. This will give them more resources to spend on pollution control.

Environmental economists and policymakers will continue to study these vexing cost-benefit analyses of how to reduce pollution at both local and global levels. What you have learned in this chapter about externalities, public goods, taxes, regulations, tradable permits, and private remedies will play an important role in their deliberations.

Environmental Economics

Economics has become a vital tool of environmentalists working to preserve the natural environment. Many have found that applying economic reasoning to issues that were once argued only on moral or ethical grounds can be a very effective way to persuade businesses and governments to consider environmental issues—and ultimately achieve the environmentalists' goals.

Green Groups See Potent Tool in Economics

By JESSICA E. VASCELLARO
Staff Reporter of The Wall Street Journal
August 23, 2005

Many economists dream of getting high-paying jobs on Wall Street, at prestigious think tanks and universities or at powerful government agencies like the Federal Reserve.

But a growing number are choosing to use their skills not to track inflation or interest rates but to rescue rivers and trees. These are the "green economists," more formally known as environmental economists, who use economic arguments and systems to persuade companies to clean up pollution and to help conserve natural areas.

Working at dozens of advocacy groups and a myriad of state and federal environmental agencies, they are helping to formulate the intellectual framework behind approaches to protecting endangered species, reducing pollution and preventing climate change. They also are becoming a link between left-leaning advocacy groups and the public and private sectors.

"In the past, many advocacy groups interpreted economics as how to make a profit or maximize income," says Lawrence Goulder, a professor of environmental and resource economics at Stanford University in Stanford, Calif. "More economists are realizing that it offers a framework for resource allocation where resources are not only labor and capital but natural resources as well."

Environmental economists are on the payroll of government agencies (the Environmental Protection Agency had about 164 on staff in 2004, up 36% from 1995) and groups like the Wilderness Society, a Washington-based conservation group, which has four of them to work on projects such as assessing the economic impact of building off-road driving trails. Environmental Defense, also based in Washington, was one of the first environmental-advocacy groups to hire economists and now has about eight, who do such things as develop market incentives to address environmental problems like climate change and water shortages.

"There used to be this idea that we shouldn't have to monetize the environment because it is invaluable," says Caroline Alkire, who in 1991 joined the Wilderness Society, an advocacy group in Washington, D.C., as one of the group's first economists. "But if we are going to engage in debate on the Hill about drilling in the Arctic we need to be able to combat the financial arguments. We have to play that card or we are going to lose."

The field of environmental economics began to take form in the 1960s when academics started to apply the tools of economics to the nascent green movement. The discipline grew more popular throughout the 1980s when the Environmental Protection Agency adopted a system of tradable permits for phasing out leaded gasoline. It wasn't until the 1990 amendment to the Clean Air Act, however, that most environmentalists started to take economics seriously.

The amendment implemented a system of tradable allowances for acid rain, a program pushed by Environmental Defense. Under the law, plants that can reduce their emissions more cost-effectively may sell their allowances to more heavy polluters. Today, the program has exceeded its goal of reducing the amount of acid rain to half its 1980 level and is celebrated as evidence that markets can help achieve environmental goals.

Its success has convinced its former critics, who at the time contended that environmental regulation was a matter of ethics, not economics, and favored installing expensive acid rain removal technology in all power plants instead.

Greenpeace, the international environmental giant, was one of the leading opponents of the 1990 amendment. But Kert Davies, research director for Greenpeace USA, said its success and the lack of any significant action on climate policy throughout early 1990s brought the organization around to the concept. "We now believe that [tradable permits] are the most straightforward system of reducing emissions and creating the incentives necessary for massive reductions."

Organizations are also applying economic reasoning toward saving wildlife. In response to arguments that undeveloped land hurts economic growth, Defenders of Wildlife founded a conservation-economics program in 1999 and recently oversaw a study of how much tourists would be willing to pay to visit a red-wolf reservation and educational center in Columbia, N.C. The finding that the center's $2 million price tag would be paid by tourism revenue in five to 10 years is helping raise money for the center and being used by advocacy groups attempting to reintroduce the population in the area.

Environmentalists have also come to recognize that if they can couch their arguments in economic terms, not only governments but also corporations are more likely to listen. Since 2001, the San Francisco-based Rainforest Action Network has persuaded J.P. Morgan Chase & Co., Citigroup Inc. and Bank of America Corp. to account for the cost of pollution in their loan-underwriting processes and, in some cases, to avoid investing in industrial logging companies.

"Companies are looking for certainty and stability," says Michael Brune, executive director of the Rainforest Action Network. "They can do that by investing in sustainable energy, where they don't run the risk of lawsuits or federal regulation or the reputation of being associated with environmentally controversial projects."

R E V I E W

■ There are four basic ways to improve the efficiency of markets in the presence of externalities: private remedies, command and control, taxes and subsidies, and tradable permits. In each of these approaches, the goal is to get firms to internalize the externality—to change their behavior to take into account the impact their actions have on others.

■ Private remedies do not require direct government intervention. The affected parties can negotiate among themselves and efficiently resolve the externalities. The Coase theorem states that as long as property rights are clearly defined, parties will come to an agreement. This also requires that transaction costs not be too high, and that free-rider problems associated with the settlement be minimized.

■ Command and control refers to direct rules and regulations imposed by the government to limit market imperfections. Examples include the imposition of fuel efficiency standards on auto manufacturers and requirements that coal-burning utilities install scrubbers.

■ Taxes and subsidies are considered by economists to be superior to command and control techniques because they use the market to internalize the externality. Taxes of an appropriate magnitude can help reduce the output of goods with negative externalities to the socially efficient level. Similarly, subsidies at an appropriate level can help increase the consumption and production of goods with positive externalities to the socially efficient level.

■ Tradable permits are a method of internalizing externalities that economists typically favor. The government can set strict limits on the production of a negative externality, such as a pollutant, by issuing a limited number of permits. However, by allowing the permits to be traded, the reduction in the pollutant can be done efficiently by allowing firms that are able to reduce it at the lowest cost to do the bulk of the reductions. Firms also have incentives to come up with new ways to reduce the externality because they can sell their permits to less efficient producers.

■ Regardless of which method is used to eliminate the impact of an externality, policymakers still have to do a cost-benefit analysis of the proposed intervention.

MODELS OF GOVERNMENT BEHAVIOR

The previous two sections outlined what government should do to correct market failure caused by public goods and externalities. Regardless of the reason that market failure occurs, the outcome is similar: Production may be too little or too much, and producer surplus plus consumer surplus is not maximized, resulting in deadweight loss. The role of government is to intervene in the economy to reduce this deadweight loss.

Using economics to explain the role of government in this way is considered a *normative* analysis of government policy. Normative economics is the study of what *should be* done. But there is another way to look at government policy. It falls into the area of *positive* economics and looks at what governments *actually do* rather than what they should do.

One of the reasons for studying what governments actually do is that governments sometimes fail because the normative recommendations are either ignored or poorly implemented. *Government failure* occurs when the government intervention fails to improve on the market or even makes things worse. One objective of positive analysis of government is to understand why there is success and failure in different situations.

government failure: the situation where the government fails to improve on the market or even makes things worse. (Ch. 1)

Public Choice Models

The government is run by people. Government behavior depends on the actions of voters, members of political parties, elected politicians, civil servants, and political appointees from judges to Cabinet officials. The work of government also depends on the large number of people who lobby and who participate in grassroots campaigns, from letter writing to e-mail messages to political protests. What motivates the behavior of all these people?

The motivations of politicians and government workers are complex and varied. Many people enter politics for genuine patriotic reasons and are motivated by a desire to improve the well-being of people in their city, state, or country, or even the world. Their motivations may be deeper than watching out for their own best interests, narrowly defined.

For example, Alexander Hamilton, the first secretary of the Treasury for the United States, worked hard to put the newly formed country on a firm economic foundation by having the federal government assume the debts of the states after the Revolutionary War. But in order to get the votes of the representatives from Virginia and Maryland for the federal government to assume the debts of the states, Hamilton agreed to vote to place the capital of the new country along the banks of the Potomac River between Maryland and Virginia, instead of selecting New York City, which was his home base.

At the same time, many other politicians are motivated by their own self-interest; the central idea of economics that people make purposeful choices with limited resources should apply to politics and government, as well as to consumers and firms. Economic models of government behavior are called **public choice models.** They start from the premise that politicians are motivated by increasing their chances of getting themselves or the members of their party elected or reelected. And without explicit incentives to the contrary, government workers are presumed to be motivated by increasing their power or prestige through increasing the size of their department or by getting promoted. By understanding this self-interest motivation, we can learn much about government, including the reasons for government failure and the reasons for government success.

public choice models: models of government behavior that assume that those in government take actions to maximize their own well-being, such as getting reelected.

The Voting Paradox

Let us first examine how voting is used to make economic policy decisions in a political environment. We will use the assumption of public choice models: that getting elected is the primary motivation of politicians.

▪ **Unanimity.** Let us start with the easiest case: There is only one economic policy decision to be made, and all the voters agree on what it should be. For example, suppose that the issue is spending on national defense, a public good where the government has a key role to play according to the normative economic analysis discussed earlier.

Suppose the specific issue is how much to spend on national defense now that the cold war is over. Some alternatives are shown in Table 2.

TABLE 2
Alternative Levels of National Defense Spending

National Defense as a Share of GDP	
1 percent	Japan's maximum
2 percent	U.S. in 1940
3 percent	U.S. in 2000
4 percent	Post–cold war
10 percent	U.S. in 1960
39 percent	U.S. in 1944

Suppose that everyone agrees that a level of national defense spending of around 4 percent of GDP in the United States is appropriate for the post–cold war period, in the absence of major world political changes such as the events of September 11, 2001. In reality, of course, opinions differ greatly about the appropriate level. But suppose that after looking at history or making international comparisons or listening to experts on defense and world politics, everyone agrees that 4 percent of GDP is the right amount to spend.

Under these circumstances, when there is only one issue on which all voters agree, voting will lead to the action that everyone prefers, that is, 4 percent, even if politicians are motivated by nothing other than getting elected. Suppose that one politician or political party runs for election on a plank of 39 percent defense spending and that the other argues in favor of 2 percent; clearly, the party with 2 percent will win because it is much closer to the people's views. But then the other politician or party will see the need to move toward the consensus and will run on a 5 percent spending platform; if the other party stays at 2 percent, then the higher-spending party will win. But clearly the other party will then try to get closer to 4 percent, and eventually 4 percent will be the winner.

This example shows that the political system yields the preferred outcome. Of course, after being elected, the politician might break the promise made during the campaign. But if such a change cannot be justified on the basis of a change in circumstances, that politician may have difficulty getting reelected.

■ **The Median Voter Theorem.**   What if people have different views? Suppose there is no unanimity about a 4 percent share of GDP for defense. Instead, the country consists of people with many different opinions. Some want more than 4 percent; some want less than 4 percent. Suppose that about half of the people want more than 4 percent and half want less than 4 percent; in other words, 4 percent is the desire of the *median* voter.

If there is only one issue, there will be convergence of the positions of the politicians or the parties toward the median voter's belief. For example, if one party or politician calls for 7 percent spending and the other party calls for 4 percent, then the party calling for 4 percent will attract more voters. The **median voter theorem** predicts that the politicians who run on what the median voter wants will be elected. The views of the people at the extremes will not matter at all.

■ **Convergence of Positions in a Two-Party System.**   An interesting corollary to the median voter theorem is that political parties or politicians will gravitate toward the center of opinion—toward the median voter. For example, in the case of national defense, it makes no sense for any politician to run on a 39 percent recommendation. The parties will gravitate toward the median voter. This **convergence of positions** may explain the tendency for Democrats and Republicans to take similar positions on many issues.

■ **Voting Paradoxes.**   When there are many different issues—defense, taxes, welfare, health-care reform—and people have different opinions and views about each issue, the outcome of voting becomes more complicated. Certain decision-making problems arise. The example of the **voting paradox** illustrates some of these problems.

Suppose three voters have different preferences on three different economic policy options—A, B, and C. Ali likes A best, B second best, and C the least; Betty likes B best, C second best, and A the least; and Camilla likes C best, A second best, and B the least. The three policy options could be three different levels of defense spending (high, medium, and low) or three different pollution control plans (emission taxes,

median voter theorem: a theorem stating that the median or middle of political preferences will be reflected in government decisions.

convergence of positions: the concentration of the stances of political parties around the center of citizens' opinions.

voting paradox: a situation where voting patterns will not consistently reflect citizens' preferences because of multiple issues on which people vote.

TABLE 3
Preferences That Generate a Voting Paradox

Ranking	Ali	Betty	Camilla
First	A	B	C
Second	B	C	A
Third	C	A	B

In voting on one option versus another, we get:

On A versus B: A wins 2 to 1

On B versus C: B wins 2 to 1

On A versus C: C wins 2 to 1

← Paradox because A wins over B and B wins over C, yet C wins over A

tradable permits, and command and control). Table 3 shows the three voters and their different preferences on each option.

Consider three different elections held at different points in time, each with one issue paired up against another. First, there is an election on A versus B, then on B versus C, and then on C versus A. The voting is by simple majority: The issue with the most votes wins. When the vote is on the alternatives A versus B, we see that A wins 2 to 1. That is, both Ali and Camilla like A better than B and vote for it, while only Betty likes B better than A and votes for B. When the vote is on B versus C, we see that B wins 2 to 1. Finally (this vote might be called for by a frustrated Camilla, who sees an opportunity), there is a vote on C versus A, and we see that now C wins 2 to 1. Although it looked like A was a winner over C—because A was preferred to B and B was preferred to C—we see that in the third vote, C is preferred to A; this is the paradox.

The voting paradox suggests that there might be instability in economic policies. Depending on how the votes were put together, the policy could shift from high defense to medium defense to low defense, or from one pollution control system to another, then to another, and then back again. Or taxes could be cut, then raised, and then raised again. All these changes could happen with nothing else in the world having changed. We could even imagine shifting between different economic systems involving different amounts of government intervention—from communism to capitalism to socialism to communism and back again!

This particular voting paradox has been known for two hundred years, but it is only relatively recently that we have come to know that the problem is not unique to this example. Kenneth Arrow showed that this type of paradox is common to any voting scheme. That no democratic voting scheme can avoid inefficiencies of the type described in the voting paradox is called the **Arrow impossibility theorem.**

The voting paradox suggests a certain inherent degree of instability in decisions made by government. Clearly, shifting between different tax systems frequently is a source of uncertainty and inefficiency. The voting paradox may be a reason for government failure in cases where the government takes on some activity such as correcting a market failure.

Arrow impossibility theorem: a theorem that says that no democratic voting scheme can avoid a voting paradox.

Special Interest Groups

The voting paradox is one reason for government failure. Special interest groups are another. It is not unusual for special interest groups to spend time and financial resources to influence legislation. They want policies that are good for them, even

ECONOMICS IN ACTION

Advising the Government to Auction Off the Spectrum

The U.S. government is responsible for distributing rights to use the radio-frequency spectrum in the United States. Each section, or band, of the spectrum is like a piece of property. Just as a farmer needs a piece of land to grow crops, a telecommunications firm needs a piece of the airwaves to send signals. And just as a piece of land has a price, so does a piece of the airwaves.

For many years, the U.S. government gave away the rights to use the spectrum in an arbitrary and inefficient manner. It was a classic example of elected officials and bureaucrats gaining influence or prestige by choosing who would get the rights. Economists had long recommended that government sell—auction off—the spectrum rather than give it away. They used models of government behavior to show why the traditional approach was inefficient and why it persisted. Finally, in 1993, Congress passed a bill giving the Federal Communications Commission (FCC) the authority to auction off the spectrum.

Auctioning off the airwaves is different from auctioning off art, however, because the value of a piece of the spectrum to firms depends on whether they also have adjacent parts of the spectrum—either adjacent geographically (like Florida and Georgia) or adjacent in frequency (with nearly the same megahertz number).

Because spectrum auctions were different, economists were called in to help design the spectrum auction. The

The first FCC auction

auction design chosen by the FCC was a novel one. In most auctions, goods are auctioned off *sequentially*—first one piece of art, then the next, and so on. In contrast, following the advice of economists, bands of spectrum were auctioned off *simultaneously* by the FCC. In other words, firms could bid on several bands at the same time. It would be as if ten works of art were auctioned off at the same time, with buyers able to offer different bids on each piece of art. Thus, if the bids on one piece were too high, a buyer could change the bid on another piece before the final sale was made. This simultaneous procedure dealt with the distinct characteristics of the spectrum, namely, that many buyers wanted adjacent bands rather than a single band.

Because such a simultaneous auction had never taken place before, economic experiments were used to try it out. For example, Charles Plott of the California Institute of Technology conducted experiments on simultaneous auction proposals made by Paul Milgrom and Robert Wilson of Stanford University. Partly because the proposal worked well in the experiments, the FCC decided to use this approach. The auction process has been heralded as a great success, and the FCC is expected to continue auctioning off the use of the spectrum. The Congressional Budget Office estimates that the revenue from these auctions over the past decade has been almost $50 billion.

if those policies are not necessarily good for the country as a whole. For example, the farming industry has a history of being able to successfully lobby for government intervention in the form of subsidies. If you look back at the reasons for government intervention—income distribution, public goods, externalities—you will see that they do not apply to the farm sector. Food does not fit the definition of a public good, farming does not have positive externalities, and many farmers who benefit from the intervention have higher incomes than other people in the society who do not benefit from such intervention. One can thus view the government regulation of agricultural markets as a form of government failure.

■ **Concentrated Benefits and Diffuse Costs.** One explanation for government failure in such situations is that special interest groups can have powerful effects on legislation that harms or benefits a small group of people a great deal but affects almost everyone else only a little. For example, the federal subsidy to the sugar growers in the United States costs taxpayers and consumers somewhere between $800 million and $2.5 billion per year, or about $3.20 to $10 per consumer per year. However, the gain from the subsidy amounts to about $136,000 per sugar grower. When a proposal to repeal the subsidy comes before Congress, almost no consumers are going to expend the resources to travel to Washington and support the legislation, or even to call up their representatives to encourage them to vote for the repeal; the $3 to $10 benefit is just not worth the time. However, the prospect of losing $136,000 is certainly worth the sugar growers' time and effort. They will travel to Washington, lobby representatives vigorously, and contribute to some political campaigns. Because the process of obtaining funds for election or getting support from the powerful interest groups is so critical for politicians' reelection chances, they will be much more likely to listen to those interest groups that have the incentive to lobby and work hard for the policy even if the majority of voters oppose it.

■ **Wasteful Lobbying.**   There is another economic harm from special interest lobbying. It is the waste of time and resources that the lobbying entails. Lobbyists are usually highly talented and skilled people, and millions of dollars in resources are spent on lobbying for legislation or other government actions. In many less-developed countries—where special interest lobbying is more prevalent than in the United States—such activity consumes a significant amount of scarce resources.

Incentive Problems in Government

In any large government, many of the services are provided by civil servants rather than by politicians and political appointees. In fact, it was to avoid the scandals of the spoils system—in which politicians would reward those who helped in a political campaign with jobs—that the civil service system set rules to protect workers against firing and established examinations and other criteria for qualifying workers for jobs.

But what motivates government managers and workers? Profit maximization as in the case of business firms is not a factor. Perhaps increasing the size of the agency or the department of government, rather than an efficient delivery of services, is the goal of managers. Profit motives and competition with other firms also give private firms an incentive to keep costs down and look for innovative production techniques and new products. These incentives do not automatically arise in government; thus, it is likely that a government service, whether a public good or a regulation, will not be provided as efficiently as a good provided by the private sector.

In recent years, there has been an effort to use incentives to improve the efficiency of government by using marketlike incentives such as more competition. Vouchers—including food stamps, housing vouchers, school vouchers, college tuition grants, and elementary school grants—have been suggested by economists as a way to add competition and improve government efficiency. The successes of these policies are often hotly debated, with both opponents and proponents being able to point to specific cases that bolster their side's arguments.

R E V I E W

- Public choice models of government behavior assume that politicians and government workers endeavor to improve their own well-being, much as models of firms and consumer behavior assume that firms and consumers do.

- In cases where there is consensus among voters, voting will bring about the consensus government policy. When there is no consensus, the median voter theorem shows that the center of opinion is what matters for decisions. However, the voting paradox points out that in more complex decisions with many options, the decisions can be unstable, leading to government failure.

- Other causes for government failure include special interest groups, especially where policies whose costs are greater but widely distributed while benefits are smaller but more narrowly concentrated are involved. By the use of campaign contributions and lobbying, special interest groups are able to influence politicians to implement policies that are inefficient and run contrary to the wishes of a majority of voters.

- Poor incentives in government also lead to government failure. Government employees may be more interested in enhancing their own power and influence than in carrying out policies that increase societal well-being.

- Economic models of government behavior suggest ways to reduce the likelihood of government failure and increase government efficiency through the use of incentives and competition. The success of these policies remains a hotly debated topic.

CONCLUSION

In this chapter, we have explored market failure due to public goods and to externalities. A competitive market provides too little in the way of public goods such as national defense and too little in the way of goods for which there are positive externalities, such as education and research. A competitive market results in too much production of goods for which there are negative externalities, such as goods that pollute the environment.

Most of the remedies for market failure involve the action of government. The provision of public goods by the government should require a careful cost-benefit analysis to make sure that the benefits are greater than the cost of producing a public good. Even though private parties can work out externalities by themselves, their ability to do so may be limited by transaction costs and free-rider problems. In that case, the government can intervene by using command and control policies, taxes and subsidies, or tradable permits. In these cases, the main role of the government is to ensure that firms internalize the externalities.

In addition to reaching normative conclusions about government intervention, it is very important to consider a positive analysis of government intervention. Doing so requires developing models of government behavior and recognizing the possibility of government failure. In reality, political considerations enter into the production of public goods. A member of Congress from one part of the country might push for a public works project in his or her local district in order to be reelected. Moreover, the externality argument emphasized in this chapter is frequently abused as a political device, providing justification for wasteful expenditures. Thus, finding ways to improve decision-making in government, such as through market-based incentives, is needed if government is to play its role in providing remedies for market failures.

KEY POINTS

1. Public goods are defined by two key characteristics, nonrivalry and nonexcludability. Nonrival goods are goods where increased use of the good by one person does not result in decreased use by another. Nonexcludable goods are goods whose use cannot be restricted to only those who have paid for them.

2. The nonexcludable and nonrival aspects of public goods result in the existence of free riders, people who use the good without paying for it. Free riding can explain why the private sector typically will not provide, or will underprovide, public goods. This creates a role for government intervention in the form of government supply of public goods like defense services.

3. Cost-benefit analysis is a technique for deciding how much of a public good should be produced. Measuring benefits is often difficult in the case of public goods. Furthermore, not all goods produced by the government are public goods. Examples in the United States include the postal service and education.

4. Externalities occur when the costs or benefits of a good spill over onto other parts of the economy. They create another potential role for government intervention because the private sector will supply less than the socially efficient quantity of goods with positive externalities, and more than the socially efficient quantity of goods with negative externalities.

5. In order to move the economy to the socially efficient outcome, producers and consumers of goods with externalities have to be made to internalize those externalities. This can be accomplished in certain cases by private agreements between the affected parties. In other cases, it will require government intervention in the form of regulations and restrictions, taxes and subsidies, or tradable permits.

6. Command and control, or regulations and restrictions imposed by the government on the economy, is the least flexible method of reducing externalities.

7. Taxes on goods with negative externalities and subsidies for goods with positive externalities can help to either restrict or expand output from the level provided by the market to the socially efficient level.

8. Tradable permits are favored by economists for reducing negative externalities because they allow the government to maintain a tight control on the quantity of the externality-causing good, while allowing the market to play a major role. Firms that can reduce pollution most effectively will do so, and will be rewarded for their actions by being able to sell permits to firms with a high cost of reducing pollution.

9. Even though public goods and externalities provide a normative theory for government intervention, you should also consider the positive theory of government intervention. Models of government behavior are based on the economic assumption that people try to improve their well-being. They can be used to explain why government failure occurs.

10. The voting paradox, the prominent role of special interest groups, and poor incentives for government employees are some of the other reasons for government failure. Marketlike incentives and competition are ways suggested by economists to reduce government failure.

KEY TERMS

public good	externality	internalize	public choice models
nonrivalry	negative externality	private remedy	median voter theorem
nonexcludability	positive externality	Coase theorem	convergence of positions
free-rider problem	marginal private cost	transaction costs	voting paradox
user fee	marginal social cost	command and control	Arrow impossibility
cost-benefit analysis	marginal private benefit	emission tax	theorem
contingent valuation	marginal social benefit	tradable permit	

QUESTIONS FOR REVIEW

1. What types of goods are produced or supplied by the government at the federal, state, and local levels?

2. Define the concepts of nonexcludability and nonrivalry, and provide examples of goods that are nonexcludable, nonrival, neither, and both.

3. Define the concept of free riding. How is it related to public goods?

4. What is the use of cost-benefit analysis for governments in deciding whether to supply public goods?

5. What is an externality? What is the difference between a positive externality and a negative externality?

6. What is the Coase theorem? How is it related to externalities?

7. What is the advantage of a system of taxes over command and control as a method of reducing the production of a good with a negative externality?

8. What are the advantages of using a system of tradable permits to reduce pollution?

9. What is government failure? How similar is it to market failure?

10. What are some explanations for why government failure occurs?

PROBLEMS

1. Suppose there is a neighborhood crime watch in which people volunteer to patrol the street where you live. If you do not participate in the patrol, but your neighborhood is safer because of the crime watch, are you a free rider? Why? What can your neighbors do to eliminate the free-rider problem?

2. The following table shows the marginal benefit per year (in dollars) to all the households in a small community from the hiring of additional firefighters. The table also shows the marginal cost per year (in dollars) of hiring additional firefighters.

Number of Firefighters	Marginal Benefit for for the Community	Marginal Cost
1	1,000,000	34,000
2	500,000	35,000
3	300,000	36,000
4	100,000	37,000
5	70,000	38,000
6	50,000	39,000
7	40,000	40,000
8	30,000	41,000
9	20,000	42,000
10	10,000	44,000

a. Is the service provided by the additional firefighters a public good?

b. Plot the marginal benefit and the marginal cost in a graph, with the number of firefighters on the horizontal axis.

c. What is the optimal amount of this public good (in terms of the number of firefighters)? Illustrate your answer on the graph in part (b).

d. Is this marginal benefit schedule the same as the town's demand curve for firefighters?

3. Suppose that there are only three households in the town in Problem 1. Each household's marginal benefit (in dollars) from additional firefighters is described in the following table:

Number of Firefighters	Household A	Household B	Household C
1	500,000	300,000	200,000
2	300,000	100,000	100,000
3	200,000	50,000	50,000
4	50,000	30,000	20,000
5	36,000	20,000	14,000
6	25,000	15,000	10,000
7	20,000	14,000	6,000
8	15,000	13,000	2,000
9	10,000	9,000	1,000
10	5,000	4,500	500

a. Plot each of the three marginal benefit schedules and the marginal benefit schedule for the whole town on the same graph, with the number of firefighters on the horizontal axis. (You will need a big vertical scale.) What is the relationship between the three household curves and the curve for the whole town?

b. Consider a system in which the town chooses the optimal amount of the public good and decides to pay for it by taxing each household the identical dollar amount. Which of the households would rather free-ride than pay the taxes, if it were possible to evade paying taxes?

4. Suppose that people value the continued existence of dolphins in the Pacific Ocean, but that tuna-fishing fleets kill large numbers of these mammals. Draw a graph showing the externality. Describe two alternative approaches to remedy the externality.

5. Is public education a public good? Does it have positive externalities? Explain what the implications are for whether public education should be provided by the government. Could the same outcomes be achieved if private education was subsidized by the government?

6. Consider two college roommates, one who smokes and one who does not. The smoker wishes to smoke in the room, and the nonsmoker dislikes smoking in the room. Suppose the smoker would be willing to pay $500 to be allowed to smoke in the room during the semester, and the nonsmoker would be willing to pay $600 to keep the room smoke-free.
   a. What would be the socially optimal outcome? Why is it optimal?
   b. How might this outcome be achieved by an agreement between the two roommates? What theorem does this illustrate?
   c. Suppose that the most the nonsmoker would be willing to pay was $200. Would this change the socially optimal outcome? Why or why not?

7. After September 11, the media paid closer attention to the potential use of shipped cargo containers to smuggle weapons and terrorists into the United States.
   a. Discuss why there may be a negative externality associated with the use of shipping containers.
   b. Graphically show the market for ship transportation of cargo. Make sure you include all the relevant aspects of this market, given your answer to part (a). Explain verbally as necessary.
   c. Graphically show any deadweight loss that occurs in this market.
   d. Discuss potential ways of reducing or eliminating deadweight loss in this market and the advantages and disadvantages of these remedies, including their impact on other markets.

8. The world's oceans are in trouble. Recently, experts have noted that stocks of fish are declining as the seas' resources are overused. Governments are increasingly becoming interested in ways of preserving fish stocks by limiting the catch. Consider the following four ways of doing so.
   • Assign property rights so that each shipping vessel is assigned a specific patch of ocean to catch fish in.
   • Tax fishing vessels heavily so as to reduce the number of such vessels that go out into the ocean.
   • Impose strict quotas on the amount of each species that a fishing vessel can catch.
   • Issue tradable permits to all fishing vessels such that the sum of the catch allowed by the permits is the desired catch limit.

   Which of these do you think is the best way to accomplish the conservation of the resource (fish in the ocean) efficiently? Explain.

9. Use the set of preferences for Ali, Betty, and Camilla shown in the following table to show that the paradox of voting does not always occur.

	Ali	Betty	Camilla
First	A	B	C
Second	B	A	A
Third	C	C	B

10. In recent years, we have heard much about the rise of extremely ideologically rigid attachments of segments of the population to particular political parties. Suppose that 25 percent of the population remains attached to Republicans, no matter what the party does, and a similar fraction stays attached to Democrats, no matter what the party does.
    a. Should this be a cause for concern in that the preferences of these voters will start driving public policy in the United States toward the fringes? Explain.
    b. Would your answer change if you were told that less than half of the U.S. population regularly votes in national elections and that the more ideologically attached voters have a higher likelihood of voting?

Chapter 16

Capital Markets

As gasoline prices rise seemingly inexorably upward, car buyers are increasingly purchasing hybrid vehicles like the Toyota Prius. Anyone who has ridden in a Prius immediately notices the technological improvements that differentiate it from other cars, including the whisper-quiet electric engine, the digital fuel efficiency gauge that is hard to look away from, and the ability to unlock doors and start the engine without ever removing the key from your pocket. Much less well-known is the fact that the factory in Japan where Toyota manufactures the Prius is equally distinguished from more traditional auto plants because of its technological and design advances. An article on the technology news website C|Net described some of those advances.[1]

> Robotic cars filled up with wiper blades and other parts amble along a track in the floor, taking parts from the procurement department to other ends of the factory. So that workers don't back into them, the robots emit an upbeat four-note ditty as they burble about. Overhead, chairlifts that look like they came from Disneyland's PeopleMover bring doors from one side of the factory, where they get removed from their cars, to another, where they get reunited with their parents after getting fitted with handles and interior panels. . . . Another concept you see on display on the floor is "jidoka," which roughly translates to "man and machine working together." In the vehicle assembly area, for instance, a dolly filled with parts and spare tools follows a worker as he walks from one end of his work area to another. (These are different from the motorized robots that scurry across the floor.) Following the worker cuts down on wasted movement. The dolly also has sensors that will detect whether bolts have been put on too tightly or loosely.

---

[1] Michael Kanellos, "Inside Toyota's Hybrid Factory," C|NET news.com, October 11, 2006, http://news.com/Inside+Toyotas+hybrid+factory/2100-11389_3-6124334.html.

From this description, it is clear that the process by which Toyota manufactures cars is a far more sophisticated version of Henry Ford's assembly-line production of motor cars. Workers are integrally involved in the production process, but as the description indicates, the production process quite intensively uses physical capital in the form of robots, chairlifts, tools, sensors, and an advanced factory building.

In this chapter, we extend our analysis of different types of markets to capital markets. We will first talk about physical capital markets, where things like houses, office buildings, construction equipment, and oil tankers are bought, sold, and rented. Millions of companies, almost all of which are smaller than Toyota, need physical capital for producing goods and services. Understanding what factors drive demand and supply in physical capital markets—for instance, why and when Toyota decides to build a new manufacturing plant, and what leads it to install robots that carry parts and tools around instead of hiring more workers—is important because firms are able to produce more output in the long run when they acquire more physical capital.

In order to purchase physical capital, companies need access to financial capital. Firms raise financial capital by issuing stocks and bonds. In this chapter, we also study markets for financial capital, paying particular attention to how the volatility of this market affects the demand for financial capital. According to the *Wall Street Journal*, "If a 25-year-old earning $30,000 invests 10% a year and realizes an annual return of 6%, he or she will accumulate about $1.1 million by age 65." Essentially, if you can put $10 a day into an investment account that pays a reasonable rate of return, your chances of becoming a millionaire are very high. But even though one can do very well over the long term by investing in stocks and other assets, stock prices do not always rise. In fact, stock prices did not rise much at all in the 1970s, and they fell sharply in the 1930s. Recently, there was a 30 percent decrease in the Dow Jones stock index in less than six months in 2002, and a more than 70 percent decrease in the Nasdaq stock index in less than three years. Stock prices are volatile, and thus stocks can be very risky.

We begin by defining physical and financial capital and describing how they are used by firms. We show that a firm's demand for physical capital can be analyzed in much the same way that we analyzed a firm's demand for labor in Chapter 13. We then go on to consider the specific markets for financial capital, stocks and bonds, while developing some new tools to handle risk and uncertainty.

THE DISTINCTION BETWEEN PHYSICAL CAPITAL AND FINANCIAL CAPITAL

depreciation: the decrease in an asset's value over time; for capital, it is the amount by which physical capital wears out over a given period of time.

Some basic terminology about physical and financial capital is useful in studying capital markets. *Physical capital* refers to all the machines, factories, oil tankers, office buildings, and other physical resources used in the production of goods or services. In previous chapters on the behavior of firms, we simply used the term *capital* when referring to "physical capital" because we were not contrasting it with financial capital. Firms combine physical capital with labor inputs to produce goods and services. They obtain physical capital by either building it, buying it, or renting it. For example, McDonald's might hire a construction firm to build a new facility near a highway, a local school district might purchase several hundred computers for use in classrooms, and a real estate developer might rent a construction crane for a year to help move building materials onto the site of a large apartment building project.

An important characteristic of physical capital is that it provides productive services for a number of years. Residential housing—single-family homes, apartments, trailers—is also a form of physical capital. It provides productive services in the form of living space that people can enjoy year after year. Government-owned roads, schools, and military equipment are also physical capital. It is useful to think of government capital as helping to produce services, whether transportation services, educational services, or national security.

Another important characteristic of physical capital is that it does not remain in new condition permanently. The gradual decline in the productive usefulness of capital is called **depreciation.** Trucks, trailers, roads, machines, and even buildings wear out and must eventually be either replaced or refurbished.

In order to purchase, rent, or build capital, a firm needs to obtain funds. These funds are an example of *financial capital*. Firms can obtain financial capital in two different ways: by issuing debt (borrowing) and by issuing equity (selling an ownership stake in the firm).

When a firm wants to borrow money, it can take out a bank loan. When a firm takes out a loan, it agrees to pay back the amount it borrowed plus interest at a future date. The amount of interest is determined by the *interest rate*. If the amount borrowed is $10,000 and is due in one year and the interest rate is 10 percent per year, then the borrower pays the lender $11,000 at the end of the year. The $11,000 includes the *principal* on the loan ($10,000) plus the *interest payment* ($1,000 = .1 times $10,000). Larger firms can also issue *corporate bonds*. A bond is an agreement by the issuer to make a specified number of payments in the future in exchange for a sum of money today. Both loans and bonds are a type of contract called a **debt contract** in which the lender agrees to provide funds today in exchange for a promise that the borrower will pay back the funds at a future date with interest.

debt contract: a contract in which a lender agrees to provide funds today in exchange for a promise from the borrower, who will repay that amount plus interest at some point in the future.

Firms are not the only entities that take out debt contracts. Most people who buy a house get a *mortgage*, which is a loan of funds to purchase real estate. In addition, many people get loans from banks to buy cars and consumer appliances. The biggest single issuer of bonds in the United States is the federal government. The federal government borrows funds by selling *government bonds*. State and local governments also issue bonds to finance physical capital investments like building a new public school, fixing a highway, or building a tunnel.

equity contract: shares of ownership in a firm; payments to the owners of the shares depend on the firm's profits.

Firms also can obtain financial capital by issuing *stock*, or shares of ownership in the firm. Shares of ownership are a type of contract called an **equity contract.** The purchaser of an equity contract acquires an ownership share in the firm that is typically proportional to the size of the equity contract. In contrast to a debt contract, where the payment by the firm (the interest payment) does not depend on the profits of the firm, in an equity contract the payment by the firm does depend on the firm's profits. Firms that make lots of profits will pay out more in *dividends* to their shareholders. Shareholders can also benefit if the firm increases in value because their shares will be worth more when they are sold.

Once bonds or stocks have been issued, they can be exchanged or traded. There are highly organized financial markets for trading stocks and bonds. The government and corporate bond markets are located in New York City, London, Tokyo, and other large financial centers. The stock markets include the New York Stock Exchange, the Nasdaq, several regional stock exchanges in the United States, and many stock exchanges in other countries.

Having defined some key terms, we now proceed to discuss the different types of capital markets. We begin with markets for physical capital.

REVIEW

- Physical capital and financial capital are distinct but closely related. Physical capital refers to the machines, buildings, and physical resources needed to produce output. To expand their physical capital, firms need to raise funds in some way. These funds are known as financial capital.

- Firms can buy, build, or rent physical capital. They can acquire financial capital by means of debt contracts or equity contracts.

- Debt contracts, such as bonds or loans, allow borrowers access to a sum of money today in exchange for a promise to repay that sum of money plus interest in the future. Equity contracts allow firms to obtain money today in exchange for handing over an ownership stake in the firm.

- The bonds or stocks that firms issue can be traded. Organized markets for trading bonds and stocks are found in all the world's financial centers.

MARKETS FOR PHYSICAL CAPITAL

The demand for physical capital is a relationship between the quantity of capital demanded by firms and the price of this capital. The demand for capital is a *derived demand* in the same sense that the demand for labor is a derived demand; that is, the demand for capital derives from the goods and services that firms produce with capital. In this section we show that just as the quantity of labor that the firm employs depends on the marginal revenue product of labor, the quantity of capital that the firm employs depends on the marginal revenue product of capital.

Rental Markets

The firm's capital decision is best understood if we first assume that the firm *rents* capital in a competitive rental market. In fact, it is common for firms to rent capital; for many types of equipment, there is a rental market in which many rental firms specialize in renting the equipment to other firms. For example, a construction firm can rent a dump truck; a clothing store can rent a storefront at a mall; an airline can lease an airplane. The price in the rental market is called the **rental price of capital.** It is the amount that a rental firm charges for the use of capital equipment for a specified period of time, such as a month.

Consider a hypothetical construction company, called Lofts-R-Us, deciding whether to rent a dump truck from a rental company called Acme Rental. To show how

rental price of capital: the amount that a rental company charges for the use of capital equipment for a specified period of time.

A Rental Market
Capital used by firms is frequently rented, as illustrated by this advertisement for equipment rentals. The rental price is determined by supply and demand in the rental market.

marginal revenue product of capital: the change in total revenue due to a one-unit increase in capital.

much capital a firm like Lofts-R-Us would rent, we need to consider the effect of this capital on the firm's profits. The marginal revenue product of capital can be used to assess this effect on profits. The **marginal revenue product of capital** is defined as the change in total revenue as the firm increases its capital by one unit. We assume that the marginal revenue product of capital declines as more capital is employed at the firm. For example, suppose the marginal revenue product of capital is $3,000 as capital rises from zero trucks to 1 truck, $1,500 as capital rises from 1 truck to 2 trucks, and $500 as capital rises from 2 trucks to 3 trucks.

Suppose the rental price of a dump truck is $1,000 a month. This is what Acme Rental charges, and all other rental firms in the area charge essentially the same price. Because the rental market is competitive, neither Acme Rental nor Lofts-R-Us has enough market power to affect the rental price. How many dump trucks would Lofts-R-Us use? With the marginal revenue product of capital from 1 dump truck equal to $3,000 a month, the firm will employ at least 1 dump truck. In other words, if the firm's total revenue increases by $3,000 and the rental price for the truck is $1,000, then it makes sense to rent the dump truck. With the marginal revenue product of capital from a second dump truck equal to $1,500, the firm will employ a second dump truck; by doing so, it can increase its profits by $500. However, with the marginal revenue product of capital from a third dump truck equal to only $500, the firm will lower its profits if it rents a third dump truck. Hence, if the rental price of the dump truck is $1,000, the firm will employ exactly 2 dump trucks. The firm rents the largest amount of capital for which the marginal revenue product of capital is greater than the rental price; if fractional units of capital were possible, then the firm would keep renting more capital until *the marginal revenue product of capital was exactly equal to the rental price.*

■ **The Demand Curve for Capital.** To derive the demand curve for capital, we must determine the quantity of capital demanded by the firm as the rental price of capital changes. For example, if the rental price of dump trucks declines to $400, then the quantity of dump trucks demanded by the firm will increase; a third dump truck will be rented because the price is now below the marginal revenue product of capital. In other words, as the rental price of capital falls, the quantity of capital demanded increases. Similarly, as the rental price of capital rises, the quantity of capital demanded decreases.

Figure 1 illustrates this general principle. It shows the marginal revenue product of capital for any firm. As more capital is employed, the marginal revenue product

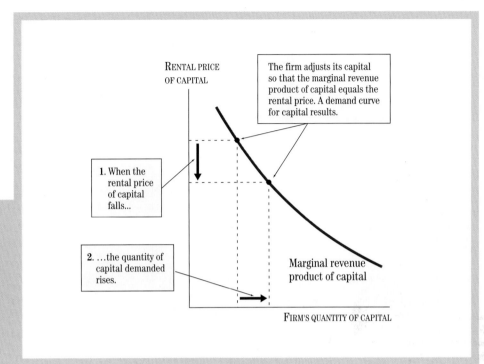

RENTAL PRICE
OF CAPITAL

The firm adjusts its capital so that the marginal revenue product of capital equals the rental price. A demand curve for capital results.

1. When the rental price of capital falls...

2. ...the quantity of capital demanded rises.

Marginal revenue product of capital

FIRM'S QUANTITY OF CAPITAL

FIGURE 1
Demand for Physical Capital by One Firm

A profit-maximizing firm chooses a quantity of capital that gives a marginal revenue product of capital equal to the rental price. Because the marginal revenue product of capital declines as more capital is used, a lower rental price of capital results in a larger quantity of capital demanded.

declines. For profit maximization, the firm will rent capital to the point where the marginal revenue product of capital equals the rental price. Thus, as we lower the rental price, the quantity of capital demanded increases. In other words, the demand curve for capital is downward-sloping.

The demand curve for capital is determined by the marginal revenue product of capital. If the marginal revenue product changes, the demand curve for capital will shift. For example, if the marginal product of dump trucks rises, the demand for dump trucks by Lofts-R-Us will shift outward.

■ **Demand for Factors of Production in General.**   Observe how similar this description of the demand for capital is to the description of the demand for labor in Chapter 13, in which we showed that the marginal revenue product of labor equals the wage. Here we showed that the marginal revenue product of capital equals the rental price. This same principle applies to any factor of production for which the market in that factor is competitive. *For any input to production, a profit-maximizing firm will choose a quantity of that input such that the marginal revenue product equals the price of that input.*

■ **The Market Demand and Supply.**   The market demand for physical capital is found by adding up the demand for physical capital by many firms. Figure 2 shows such a market demand curve.

On the same diagram, we show the market supply curve. It is the sum of the supply curves for all the firms in the industry providing capital for rent, such as Acme Rental. The higher the rental price of capital, the more likely Acme Rental is to buy new dump trucks and offer them as rentals to firms like Lofts-R-Us. If other rental firms behave the way that Acme Rental does, then the market supply of rental capital will be increasing with rental prices.

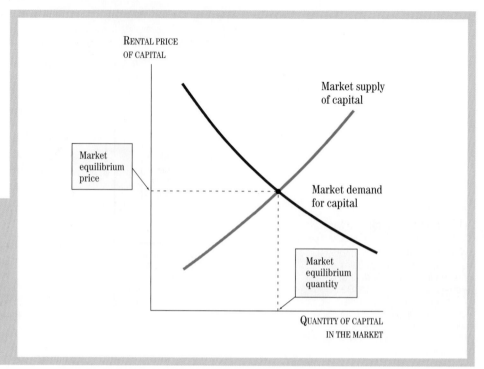

FIGURE 2
Market Supply and Demand for Physical Capital
The market demand for capital is the sum of the demands of the individual firms that use the equipment. The market supply is the sum of the supplies at the individual firms that provide the equipment. Market equilibrium occurs where the quantity of capital demanded equals the quantity of capital supplied.

The equilibrium rental price and the equilibrium quantity of capital rented are shown in the diagram. The supply and demand model for capital illustrated in Figure 2 can then be used to predict the effects of tax changes or other changes in the capital market in much the same way as any other supply and demand model. For example, if the government places a tax on construction firms like Lofts-R-Us proportional to the quantity of trucks they rent, perhaps because the heavy trucks damage city roads more than cars do, then the marginal revenue product of capital will decline and the demand curve for capital will shift down, or to the left. This will lower the equilibrium rental price received by Acme and reduce the quantity of capital rented. Alternatively, if the city government is eager to have new apartment buildings in the city, it may offer a subsidy on the rental of capital by construction firms. This would shift the demand curve for capital up, or to the right, and increase the quantity of capital rented.

■ **The Case of Fixed Supply: Economic Rents.** An important special case of a market for physical capital occurs when the supply of physical capital is completely fixed. Alfred Marshall gave the following famous example of physical capital with a completely fixed supply: "Let us suppose that a meteoric shower of a few thousand large stones harder than diamonds fell all in one place, so that they were all picked up at once, and no amount of search could find any more. These stones, able to cut every material, would revolutionize many branches of industry. . . ."[2]

The important thing about Marshall's stones is that their supply cannot be increased or decreased regardless of the price of the stones. In other words, the supply curve for Marshall's stones is perfectly vertical, or perfectly inelastic, as shown in Figure 3.

---

[2] Alfred Marshall, *Principles of Economics*, 8th ed. (New York: Macmillan, 1920), p. 415.

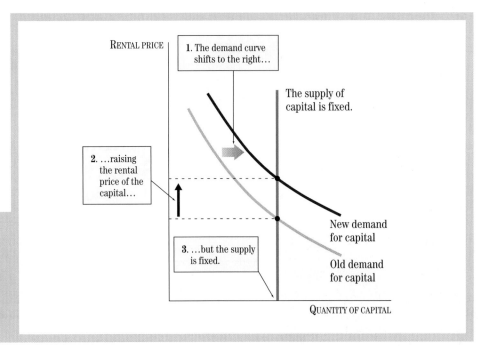

FIGURE 3
The Case of a Fixed Supply of Capital
When the supply of capital is perfectly inelastic, a shift in demand changes the rental price but not the quantity supplied. Marshall's stones are a hypothetical example of capital with a perfectly inelastic supply.

economic rent: the price of something that has a fixed supply.

Figure 3 shows what happens when there is a shift in demand for capital that is in fixed supply, such as Marshall's stones. A change in demand will change the price, but it will not change the quantity. Demand completely determines the price in this case because the quantity supplied cannot change.

Economists have a special terminology for the price in this circumstance: **Economic rent** is the price of anything that has a fixed supply. Economic rent is also sometimes called *pure rent*. Economic rent is a significant concept in economics precisely because the quantity supplied does not depend on the price. Thus, a tax on economic rents would not change the amount supplied; it would not affect economic efficiency or cause a deadweight loss. For example, if the government passed a tax (even a 99.9 percent tax) on the rental payments charged by the lucky owners of Marshall's stones, there would be no change in the quantity of stones supplied.

Marshall's stones are of course a hypothetical example. In practice, certain types of land may come close to being an item in fixed supply, but it is always possible to improve land or clear land and thereby change its supply to some degree. The perfectly inelastic supply of Marshall's stones or the near perfectly inelastic supply of certain types of land is in sharp contrast to the higher elasticity of supply of most capital goods. The supply of dump trucks, apartment buildings, and other types of capital is sensitive to changes in the price. Increases in the price provide an incentive to increase the quantity supplied, and decreases in the price provide an incentive to decrease the quantity supplied. In reality, therefore, taxes on capital would be expected to change the quantity of capital supplied.

The Ownership of Physical Capital

Rental markets for capital are common, but they are not the only way in which firms obtain capital. The same construction firm that rents dump trucks might choose to purchase and own a dump truck rather than rent one, especially if it expects to continually be engaged in projects for which a truck is required. The firm may also own

Physical Capital Accumulation of Google

Physical capital is an important part of the production process for many companies. Surprisingly, this is even true for a company like Google, whose primary product is essentially search engine services provided over the Internet. But as this article points out, providing search services efficiently requires a substantial amount of physical capital in the form of tens of thousands of computer servers.

The factory in this case is a giant building containing thousands of computers, which need to be cooled because of the heat they generate.

Like other businesses, Google locates where the main inputs (land and electricity) are cheap and available.

The computers and hard drives are also part of the physical capital.

Hiding in Plain Sight, Google Seeks More Power

By JOHN MARKOFF and SAUL HANSELL

THE DALLES, Ore., June 8—On the banks of the windswept Columbia River, Google is working on a secret weapon in its quest to dominate the next generation of Internet computing. But it is hard to keep a secret when it is a computing center as big as two football fields, with twin cooling plants protruding four stories into the sky.

The complex, sprawling like an information-age factory, heralds a substantial expansion of a worldwide computing network handling billions of search queries a day and a growing repertory of other Internet services.

And odd as it may seem, the barren desert land surrounding the Columbia along the Oregon-Washington border—at the intersection of cheap electricity and readily accessible data networking—is the backdrop for a multibillion-dollar face-off among Google, Microsoft and Yahoo that will determine dominance in the online world in the years ahead.

Microsoft and Yahoo have announced that they are building big data centers upstream in Wenatchee and Quincy, Wash., 130 miles to the north. But it is a race in which they are playing catch-up. Google remains far ahead in the global data-center race, and the scale of its complex here is evidence of its extraordinary ambition.

Even before the Oregon center comes online, Google has lashed together a global network of computers—known in the industry as the Googleplex—that is a singular achievement. "Google has constructed the biggest computer in the world, and it's a hidden asset," said Danny Hillis, a supercomputing pioneer and a founder of Applied Minds, a technology consulting firm, referring to the Googleplex.

The design and even the nature of the Google center in this industrial and agricultural outpost 80 miles east of Portland has been a closely guarded corporate secret. "Companies are historically sensitive about where their operational infrastructure is," acknowledged Urs Holzle, Google's senior vice president for operations.

Behind the curtain of secrecy, the two buildings here—and a third that Google has a permit to build—will probably house tens of thousands of inexpensive processors and disks, held together with Velcro tape in a Google practice that makes for easy swapping of components. The cooling plants are essential because of the searing heat produced by so much computing power.

The complex will tap into the region's large surplus of fiber optic networking, a legacy of the dot-com boom.

The fact that Google is behind the data center, referred to locally as Project 02, has been reported in the local press. But many officials in The Dalles, including the city attorney and the city manager, said they could not comment on the project because they signed confidentiality agreements with Google last year.

"No one says the 'G' word," said Diane Sherwood, executive director of the Port of Klickitat, Wash., directly across the river from The Dalles, who is not bound by such agreements. "It's a little bit like He-Who-Must-Not-Be-Named in Harry Potter."

Local residents are at once enthusiastic and puzzled about their affluent but secretive new neighbor, a successor to the aluminum manufacturers that once came seeking the cheap power that flows from the dams holding back the powerful Columbia. The project has created hundreds of construction jobs, caused local real estate prices to jump 40 percent and is expected to create 60 to 200 permanent jobs in a town of 12,000 people when the center opens later this year.

"We're trying to organize our chamber ambassadors to have a ribbon-cutting ceremony, and they're trying to keep us all away," said Susan Huntington, executive director of The Dalles Area Chamber of Commerce. "Our two cultures aren't matching very well."

Culture clashes may be an inevitable byproduct of the urgency with which the search engine war is being waged.

Google, Microsoft and Yahoo are spending vast sums of capital to build out their computing capabilities to run both search engines and a variety of Web services that encompass e-mail, video and music downloads and online commerce. ◄———

> *They are adding more capital to expand the scale of output and to enter into new markets.*

Microsoft stunned analysts last quarter when it announced that it would spend an unanticipated $2 billion next year, much of it in an effort to catch up with Google. Google said its own capital expenditures would run to at least $1.5 billion. Its center here, whose cost is undisclosed, shows what that money is meant to buy.

Google is known to the world as a search engine, but in many ways it is foremost an effort to build a network of supercomputers, using the latest academic research, that can process more data—faster and cheaper—than its rivals.

"Google wants to raise the barriers to entry by competitors by making the baseline service very expensive," said Brian Reid, a former Google executive who is now director of engineering at the Internet Systems Consortium in Redwood City, Calif.

The rate at which the Google computing system has grown is as remarkable as its size. In March 2001, when the company was serving about 70 million Web pages daily, it had 8,000 computers, according to a Microsoft researcher granted anonymity to talk about a detailed tour he was given at one of Google's Silicon Valley computing centers. By 2003 the number had grown to 100,000. ◄———

> *Expanding its physical capital has enabled Google to greatly expand the output it produces, which is how many web pages it searches.*

Today even the closest Google watchers have lost precise count of how big the system is. The best guess is that Google now has more than 450,000 servers spread over at least 25 locations around the world. The company has major operations in Ireland, and a big computing center has recently been completed in Atlanta. Connecting these centers is a high-capacity fiber optic network that the company has assembled over the last few years.

Google has found that for search engines, every millisecond longer it takes to give users their results leads to lower satisfaction. So the speed of light ends up being a constraint, and the ◄——— company wants to put significant processing power close to all of its users.

> *Capital also helps to improve the quality of output—in this case, the speed of the searches.*

the warehouse where it stores its building materials and the office where it keeps its books and meets prospective customers. Although there are legal and tax differences between renting and ownership, the economic principles are similar. In fact, even though owners of physical capital do not pay a rental price, economic considerations indicate that they pay an *implicit* rental price.

When a firm buys equipment, it must either borrow funds to pay for the equipment or use its own funds, funds that it could have put in an interest-earning account at a bank. If it borrows the funds, the monthly interest payment on the loan is like a rental payment. If it uses its own funds, the interest it would have received at the bank is an opportunity cost and is considered to be similar to a rental payment. In addition to these payments, the firm that owns the equipment must factor in the wear and tear, or depreciation, on the equipment. The amount by which the firm's equipment deteriorates is also a cost.

implicit rental price: the cost of the funds used to buy the capital plus the depreciation of the capital over a given period of time.

In sum, for a firm that chooses to purchase and own capital, the **implicit rental price** of capital for a year equals the interest payments for the year plus the amount of depreciation during the year. For example, suppose the interest rate is 10 percent, the purchase price of a dump truck is $40,000, and the dump truck depreciates $8,000 per year. Then the implicit rental price is $12,000 per year (.10 times $40,000, plus $8,000), or $1,000 a month, the same as the rental price in our dump truck example. It is important to note that the implicit rental price depends on the interest rate. The higher the interest rate, the higher the interest payments during the year, and thus the higher the implicit rental price. When the interest rate rises, the implicit rental price rises. When the interest rate falls, the implicit rental price falls.

The concept of the implicit rental price makes the firm's decision to buy a dump truck, or any other piece of capital, analogous to the decision to rent. The demand curve looks the same as that in Figure 1, except that it is the implicit rental price rather than the actual rental price that is on the vertical axis.

REVIEW

- The demand for physical capital at a firm is a derived demand. What firms are willing to pay for capital depends on the value of the goods and services they can produce with that capital.

- Firms that rent capital will choose to rent capital up to the point where the marginal revenue product of capital equals the rental price of capital.

- The marginal revenue product of capital decreases as the quantity of capital used by the firm increases. So when the rental price goes down, the firm will want to add extra machines until the marginal revenue product of capital equals the rental price.

- If capital is purchased rather than rented, the firm still faces an implicit rental price. The implicit rental price for a year is equal to the yearly interest payment on the loan to buy the equipment plus the amount of depreciation on the equipment during the year.

- The demand curve for purchased capital, then, looks very similar to the demand curve for rental capital; the demand curve is downward-sloping in the (implicit) rental price.

- Taxes imposed on the use of capital equipment by firms will lower the equilibrium rental price and quantity of capital. Subsidies that encourage the use of capital by firms will raise the equilibrium price and quantity of capital.

MARKETS FOR FINANCIAL CAPITAL

return: the income received from the ownership of an asset; for a stock, the return is the dividend plus the capital gain.

capital gain: the increase in the value of an asset through an increase in its price.

capital loss: the decrease in the value of an asset through a decrease in its price.

dividend yield: the dividend stated as a percentage of the price of the stock.

rate of return: the return on an asset stated as a percentage of the price of the asset.

> **Check the result.**
> The dividend was $.32. The closing price was $41.36. Dividing .32 by 41.36 gives .008, or 0.8 percent.

earnings: the accounting profits of a firm.

price-earnings ratio: the price of a stock divided by its annual earnings per share.

coupon: the fixed amount that a borrower agrees to pay to the bondholder each year.

maturity date: the date when the principal on a loan is to be paid back.

face value: the principal that will be paid back when a bond matures.

Having seen how markets for physical capital work, let us turn to the examination of markets for financial capital. As we discussed earlier, firms that want to acquire physical capital need to obtain financial capital. They can obtain financial capital by issuing stocks and bonds. Stocks and bonds are traded on financial markets. Their prices are determined by the actions of buyers and sellers, like prices in any other market. Understanding what drives the equilibrium prices of stocks and bonds is important for determining firms' ability to acquire financial capital. The ease of acquiring financial capital will in turn help determine how much physical capital firms can acquire and how much output they can produce.

Stock Prices and Rates of Return

Prices of the stocks of most large firms can be found in daily newspapers. Investors are interested in buying those stocks whose prices are likely to rise and that are more likely to pay back their profits to shareholders in the form of dividends. We can define the annual **return** from holding a stock as the *dividend* plus the *capital gain* during the year. The **capital gain** during the year is the increase in the price of the stock during the year. A **capital loss** is a negative capital gain: a decrease in the price. When comparing dividends across companies, we typically look at the **dividend yield,** the dividend stated as a percentage of the price. Similarly, in comparing returns across companies, we typically look at the **rate of return,** the return stated as a percentage of the price of the stock.

A simple example can illustrate these terms. For example, the dividend for Hewlett-Packard in 2006 was $.32 per year. At its year-end stock price of $41.36, the dividend yield was 0.8 percent. In 2006, the price of Hewlett-Packard stock rose from $29.28 to $41.36, a capital gain of $12.08. Combined with the dividend, the total return was $12.40, a rate of return of 42.3 percent. In this example, the capital gain is a much bigger portion of the rate of return than the dividend; this is a defining characteristic of "growth stocks," of which Hewlett-Packard is an example.

You can also figure out which firms are the most profitable, and hence more likely to generate a high rate of return for their shareholders, by looking at the firms' accounting profits, also known as **earnings.** Firms pay out some of their profits as dividends; the rest of the profits are retained and invested in physical capital or research. Stock tables also list the **price-earnings ratio:** the price of the stock divided by the annual earnings per share. The price-earnings ratio for Hewlett-Packard in 2006 was 17.1. With the price of the stock at $41.36, this means that earnings for the year were $2.4187 per share ($41.36/$2.4187 = 17.1). A firm's earnings ultimately influence the return on the firm's stock, so the price-earnings ratio is closely watched.

Bond Prices and Rates of Return

Bond prices for both corporate and government bonds can also be found in the financial pages of the newspaper. The "Economics in Action" box in this chapter shows you how to read the prices of different types of bonds.

There are four key characteristics of a bond: *coupon, maturity date, face value,* and *yield*. The **coupon** is the fixed amount that the borrower agrees to pay the bondholder each year. The **maturity date** is the time when the coupon payments end and the principal is paid back. The **face value** is the amount of principal that will be paid back when the bond matures. The bond boldfaced in the box has a maturity date of February 2037 and a coupon equal to 4.75 percent of the face value of the bond. That is, 4.75 percent, or $47.50, a year on a bond with a face value of

ECONOMICS IN ACTION

Understanding Stock and Bond Price Listings in Newspapers

Newspaper stock tables, such as this one from the *Financial Times* (March 1, 2007), summarize information about firms and the stocks that they issue. The table here is part of a much bigger table in which all the stocks traded on the New York Stock Exchange are listed in alphabetical order. Other tables provide information about stocks traded on other stock exchanges, such as the Nasdaq or the London Stock Exchange, in exactly the same way.

To understand how to read this table, focus on one company, such as the computer firm Hewlett-Packard, which was started in a garage by David Packard and William Hewlett in the 1930s. The information in the table pertains to a single day, February 28, 2007 (which was why the data were reported on March 1, the following day). According to the table, the price of Hewlett-Packard stock decreased by 45 cents to 38.93 on that day. Key terms introduced in this chapter—such as dividend yield and price-earnings ratio—are highlighted. To check your understanding, see if you can find out each of the critical pieces of information for one of the other firms in the table, such as Hershey, the maker of Hershey's Kisses.

| 52 weeks | | | | | | | |
Hi	Lo	Stock	Yld %	PE	Vol 1000s	Close	Net Chg
21.84	19.26	HealthMgmt	1.2	26.3	18476	19.87	−.09
47.69	37.35	Heinz	3.1	25.1	1406	45.67	−.20
57.00	49.34	Hershey	2.0	22.6	1146	52.99	+.11
56.02	38.50	Hess Cp	0.8	8.7	2378	53.19	+.14
43.53	**29.79**	**Hew.-Pack**	**0.8**	**17.1**	**10833**	**38.93**	**−.45**
37.53	23.00	HiltonHotl	0.5	25.4	2900	34.90	−.40
43.81	33.13	HomeDep	2.3	14.2	10254	39.45	−.15

High and low for previous year		Stock name	Dividend as a percent of price	Price-earnings ratio	Number of shares traded (in 1000s)	Closing price	Change in price from previous day

| 52 weeks | | | | | | | |
Hi	Lo	Stock	Yld %	PE	Vol 1000s	Close	Net Chg
43.53	29.79	Hew.-Pack	0.8	17.1	10833	38.93	−.45

$1,000, will be paid until 2037, and in February 2037, the $1,000 face value will be paid back. (The coupon is called a "rate" because it is measured as a percentage of the face value.)

Once bonds have been issued by the government, they can be sold or bought in the bond market. In the bond market, there are bond traders who make a living buying and selling bonds. The bond traders will *bid* a certain price at which they will buy, and they will *ask* a certain price at which they will sell. The bid price is slightly lower than the ask price, which enables the bond traders to earn a profit by buying at a price that is slightly lower than the price at which they sell.

yield: the annual rate of return on a bond if the bond were held to maturity.

The **yield,** or yield to maturity, is defined as the annual rate of return on the bond if the bond were bought at the current price and held to maturity. When people refer to the current interest rate on bonds, they are referring to the yield on the bond. Observe that the yield on the boldfaced bond maturing in February 2037 was 4.68 percent on March 1, 2007, slightly below the 4.75 percent coupon rate.

Why are bond yields different from the coupon rate? There is an inverse, or negative, relationship between the yield and the price. Why is there an inverse relationship?

The *Financial Times* also reports the prices of bonds, which, once they have been issued by a firm or by a government, are actively traded in bond markets. The table below reports information on government-issued bonds from the United Kingdom and the United States. Focus on the highlighted bond; it has a coupon rate of 4.75 percent and matures in February 2037. Thus, in February 2007, there were 30 years left to maturity on this newly issued bond. Sometimes bond price tables report the price that is *bid* for bonds by bond traders and the price that is *asked* for bonds by the traders. Only the bid price is given in this table, but the bid and ask are very close to each other. (There is enough of a difference to give the traders some profit; note that the price asked by the trader is always greater than the price bid.)

Notice that the reported yield is different from the coupon rate for all the bonds listed. Also notice that this difference is especially pronounced for some of the U.K. bonds.

Mar 1	Redemption date	Coupon	Bid price	Bid yield	Day chg yield	Wk chg yield	Month chg yield	Year chg yield
UK	12/07	7.25	101.3200	5.45	−0.01	−0.07	−0.16	+1.07
	03/12	5.00	99.7300	5.06	−0.09	−0.19	−0.30	+0.78
	08/17	8.75	132.7290	4.75	−0.05	−0.19	−0.25	+0.58
	03/36	4.25	100.1500	4.24	−0.01	−0.15	−0.17	+0.40
US	02/09	4.75	100.2344	4.63	−0.01	−0.24	−0.33	−0.08
	02/12	4.63	100.5391	4.50	−0.01	−0.23	−0.34	−0.13
	02/17	4.63	100.5313	4.56	—	−0.17	−0.28	−0.03
	02/37	**4.75**	**101.1406**	**4.68**	**+0.01**	**−0.15**	**−0.25**	**+0.12**

Source: Reuters.

| Date bond matures | Coupon as a percent of the face value | Bid price | Yield to maturity | Changes over time |

This is because the payments of the bond are fixed—the borrower (bond issuer) agrees to pay back the lender (bondholder) the principal on the maturity date and make coupon payments in the interim—regardless of what the buyer paid for the bond. The higher the price you pay today to get this fixed stream of interest and principal payments in the future, the lower the rate of return (yield) you earn. So unlike the coupon rate, which stays fixed, the yield will fluctuate with price. Furthermore, as the price rises, the yield will fall, and vice versa.

Why do bond yields fluctuate? Consider a simple example. Suppose you just bought a 1-year bond for $100 that says that the government will pay 5 percent of the face value, or $5, plus $100 at the end of the 1-year period. Now suppose that just after you bought the bond, interest rates on bank deposits suddenly jumped to 10 percent. Your bond says that you earn 5 percent per year, so if you hold it for the entire year, your rate of return is less than you could get on a bank deposit. Suddenly the bond looks much less attractive. You would probably want to sell it, but everyone else knows the bond is less attractive, also. You would not be able to get $100 for the bond. The price would decline until the rate of return on the bond

Here is a typical quote on bond yields:

"The price of the 30-year Treasury bond rose less than 1/8 point, or less than $1.25 for a bond with $1,000 face value, to 84 4/32. Its yield, which moves in the opposite direction of its price, dropped to 7.60% from 7.61% on Thursday."

was close to the interest rate at the bank. For example, if the price fell to $95.45, then the payment of $105 at the end of the year would result in a 10 percent rate of return [that is, .10 = (105 − 95.45)/95.45]. In other words, the yield on the bond would rise until it reached a value closer to 10 percent than to 5 percent.

If you look at the U.K. government bonds in the box, you will notice a bond maturing in 2017 with a coupon rate of 8.75 percent and a yield of 4.75. This bond must have been issued at a time when market interest rates were closer to 8.75 percent. As interest rates in the United Kingdom fell, people found that holding the bond was a more attractive proposition than keeping money in the bank, so they bid up the price of the bond, driving down the yield until it approached the new market interest rates in the United Kingdom. This implies that periods of falling interest rates are good for bondholders and bond issuers because the prices of their bonds rise, while periods of rising interest rates are bad for both bondholders and bond issuers.

Based on these considerations, there is a formula that gives the relationship between the price and the yield for bonds of any maturity. Let P be the price of the bond. Let R be the coupon. Let F be the face value. Let i be the yield. The formula relating to the price and the yield in the case of a 1-year bond is indicated in the first row of Table 1.

For a 1-year bond, a coupon payment of R is paid at the end of 1 year together with the face value of the bond. The price P is what you would be willing to pay *now, in the present*, for these future payments. It is the *present discounted value* of the coupon payment plus the face value at the end of the year. By looking at the formula in the first row of Table 1, you can see the negative relationship between the price (P) of the bond and the yield (i) on the bond. The higher the yield, the lower the price; and conversely, the lower the yield, the higher the price.

A 2-year-maturity bond is similar. You get R at the end of the first year and R plus the face value at the end of the second year. Now you want to divide the first-year payment by $1 + i$ and the second-year payment by $(1 + i)^2$. The formula still shows the inverse relationship between the yield and the price. A bond with a 3-year or longer maturity is similar. Computers do the calculation for the news reports, so even 30-year bond yields can easily be found from their price.

There is a convenient and simple approximation method for determining the price or yield on bonds with very long maturity dates. It says that the price is equal to the coupon divided by the yield: $P = R/i$. This is the easiest way to remember the inverse relationship between the price and the yield. It is a close approximation for long-term bonds like the 30-year bond.

TABLE 1
Bond Price Formula

One-year maturity:
$$P = \frac{R}{1 + i} + \frac{F}{1 + i}$$

Two-year maturity:
$$P = \frac{R}{1 + i} + \frac{R}{(1 + i)^2} + \frac{F}{(1 + i)^2}$$

Three-year maturity:
$$P = \frac{R}{1 + i} + \frac{R}{(1 + i)^2} + \frac{R}{(1 + i)^3} + \frac{F}{(1 + i)^3}$$

For very long term:
$$P = \frac{R}{i}$$

P = price of bond
R = coupon
F = face value
i = yield

R E V I E W
- Firms that want to purchase physical capital need financial capital to do so. They obtain financial capital by issuing stocks and bonds. Stocks and bonds are traded on financial markets.

- The return from holding stock is the dividend plus the change in the price. The rate of return is equal to the return measured as a percentage of the price of the stock.

- The return from holding bonds to maturity is the yield of the bond. Bond yields and bond prices move in opposite directions.

- Periods of falling interest rates are good for bondholders and bond issuers because the prices of bonds rise, while periods of rising interest rates are bad for both bondholders and bond issuers.

THE TRADEOFF BETWEEN RISK AND RETURN

One of the hallmarks of financial markets is volatility. The prices of individual stocks and bonds rise and fall over time. Over the long run, stock prices show a positive trend, but there are periods of significant decline from time to time, and the prices of individual stocks traded in the financial markets are very volatile. Similarly, even though you can always earn a rate of return equivalent to the yield by holding a bond issued by the U.S. government to maturity, in the interim the price of the bond will vary.

In the example discussed earlier, the price of a share of Hewlett-Packard increased by over 42 percent in 2006, but in 2000, the price fell by over 80 percent. For individual stocks, a change in price of 5 or 10 percent in one day is not uncommon. Because of such variability, buying stocks is a risky activity. The price of bonds can also change by a large amount. For example, from mid-1996 to mid-1997, the price of government bonds rose by nearly 20 percent, but from mid-1993 to mid-1994, the price of government bonds *fell* by nearly 20 percent! Thus, government bonds are also a risky investment.

In this section we show that the riskiness of stocks and bonds affects the decision of people to trade in financial markets. To do so, we first examine how individuals behave when they face risk.

Behavior Under Uncertainty

Most people do not like uncertainty. They are *risk averse* in most of their activities. Given a choice between two jobs that pay the same wage, most people will be averse to choosing the riskier job where there is a good chance of being laid off. Similarly, given a choice between two investments that pay the same return, people will choose the less risky one.

Let us examine this idea of risk aversion further. To be more precise, suppose that Melissa has a choice between the two alternatives shown in Table 2. She must decide what to do with her life savings of $10,000 for the next year. At the end of the year, she plans to buy a house, and she will need some money for a down payment. She can put her $10,000 in a bank account, where the interest rate is 5 percent, or she can buy $10,000 worth of a stock that pays a dividend of 5 percent and will incur either a capital gain or a capital loss. In the bank, the value of her savings is safe, but if she buys the stock, there is a 50 percent chance that the price of the stock will fall

TABLE 2	
Two Options: Different Risks, Same Expected Return	
Low-Risk Option	**High-Risk Option**
A bank deposit with	*A corporate stock with either*
5 percent interest (return = $500)	a. A 5 percent dividend and a 30 percent price decline ($500 − $3,000 = −$2,500)
	b. A 5 percent dividend and a 30 percent price increase ($500 + $3,000 = $3,500)

by 30 percent and a 50 percent chance that the price of the stock will rise by 30 percent. In other words, the risky stock will leave Melissa with the possibility of a return of −$2,500 (a loss) or a return of $3,500 (a gain). The bank account leaves her with a guaranteed $500 return.

expected return: the return on an uncertain investment calculated by weighting the gains or losses by the probability that they will occur.

Both the options in Table 2 have the same **expected return.** The expected return on an investment weights the different gains or losses according to how probable they are. In the case of the safe bank account, there is a 100 percent chance that the return is $500, so the expected return is $500. In the case of the stock, the expected return would be −$2,500 times the probability of this loss (1/2) plus $3,500 times the probability of this gain (also 1/2). Thus, the expected return is $500 (−2,500/2 + 3,500/2 = −1,250 + 1,750 = 500), the same as the return on the bank account.

The expected return is one way to measure how attractive an investment is. The word *expected* may appear misleading, since in the risky option $500 is not "expected" in the everyday use of the word. You do not expect $500; you expect either a loss of $2,500 or a gain of $3,500. If the term is confusing, think of the expected return as the average return that Melissa would get if she could take the second option year after year for many years. The losses of $2,500 and gains of $3,500 would average out to $500 per year after many years. (The term *expected return* has been carried over by economists and investment analysts from probability and statistics, where the term *expected value* is used to describe the mean, or the average, of a random variable.)

Given that the expected returns are the same, if Melissa is a risk-averse person (i.e., if she would dread a capital loss more than she would cherish a capital gain of a similar magnitude), she will choose the less risky of these two options. Although it is clear that Melissa would choose the less risky of the two options in Table 2, perhaps there is some compensation that Melissa would accept to offset her risk aversion. Although most people are averse to risk, they are willing to take on some risk if they are compensated for it. In the case of a risky financial investment, the compensation for higher risk could take the form of a higher expected return.

How could we make Melissa's expected return higher in the risky investment? Suppose Melissa had the choice between the same safe option as in Table 2 and a high-risk stock that paid a dividend of 20 percent. This new choice is shown in Table 3; the difference is that the risky stock now offers a dividend of 20 percent, much greater than the 5 percent in the first example and much greater than the 5 percent on the bank account. With the greater chance of a higher return on the stock, Melissa might be willing to buy the stock. Even in the worst situation, she loses just $1,000, which may still leave her with enough for the down payment on her new house. The expected return for the high-risk option is now $2,000, much greater than the $500 for the bank account (−1,000/2 + 5,000/2 = −500 + 2,500 = 2,000).

In other words, Melissa would probably be willing to take on the risky investment. And if the 20 percent dividend in the example is not enough for her, some higher divi-

TABLE 3
Two Options: Different Risks, Different Expected Returns

Low-Risk Option	High-Risk Option
A bank deposit with	*A corporate stock with either*
5 percent interest (return = $500)	a. A 20 percent dividend and a 30 percent price decline ($2,000 − $3,000 = −$1,000)
	b. A 20 percent dividend and a 30 percent price increase ($2,000 + $3,000 = $5,000)

Playing It Safe?
Most people are risk-averse when it come to large sums, but many are risk lovers when the stakes are low or when they can limit their potential losses—such as at casinos where people can choose to gamble a set amount or combine gambling with entertainment.

dend (25 percent? 30 percent?) would be. This example illustrates the general point that risk-averse people are willing to take risks if they are paid for it.

Before we develop the implication of our analysis of individual behavior under uncertainty, we should pause to ask about the possibility that some people might be risk lovers rather than risk avoiders. The billions of dollars that are bet in state lotteries in the United States and in private gambling casinos in Las Vegas, Atlantic City, and Monte Carlo indicate that some people enjoy risk. However, with few exceptions, most of the gambling on lotteries, slot machines, and even roulette wheels represents a small portion of the income or wealth of the gambler. Thus, you might be willing to spend $.50 or even $5 on lottery tickets or a slot machine for the chance of winning big, even if the odds are against you. Many people get enjoyment out of such wagers; but if the stakes are large compared to one's income or wealth, then few people want to play. For small sums, some people are risk lovers, but for large sums, virtually everybody becomes a risk avoider to some degree or another.

Risk and Rates of Return in Theory

What are the implications of our conclusion that investors will be willing to take risks if they are compensated with a higher return on the stock or bond? In the stock market, the prices of individual stocks are determined by the bidding of buyers and sellers. Suppose a stock, AOK, had a price that gave it the same expected rate of return as a bank account. Now AOK, being a common stock, clearly has more risk than a bank account because its price can change. Hence, no risk-averse investor will want to buy AOK. Just as Melissa will prefer to put her funds in a bank account in the example in Table 2 rather than into the risky option, investors will put their funds in a bank rather than buy AOK. People who own shares of AOK will sell and put their funds into a bank. With everybody wanting to sell AOK and no one wanting to buy it, the price of AOK will start to fall.

Now, the price and the expected rate of return are inversely related—recall that for a stock, the rate of return is the return divided by the price. Thus, if the price falls and the dividend does not change, the rate of return will rise. This fall in the price will drive up the expected rate of return on AOK. As the expected rate of return increases, it will eventually reach a point where it is high enough to compensate risk-averse investors. In other words, when the expected rate of return rises far enough above the bank account

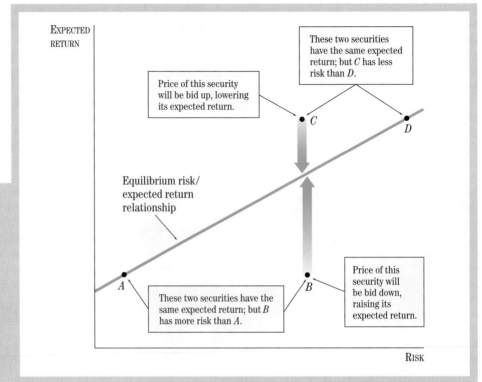

FIGURE 4
The Equilibrium Relationship Between Return and Risk
More risky securities tend to have higher returns on average over the long term. For example, bank deposits are low risk and have a low expected return. Corporate stocks are higher risk—their price fluctuates—but on average over the long term have a higher return. The higher return is like a compensating wage differential in the labor market. It compensates those who take on more risk.

equilibrium risk-return relationship: the positive relationship between the risk and the expected rate of return on an asset, derived from the fact that, on average, risk-averse investors who take on more risk must be compensated with a higher return.

rate to compensate people for the risk, the price fall will stop. We will have an equilibrium where the expected rate of return on the stock is higher than the interest rate on the safe bank account. The higher rate of return will be associated with the higher risk.

Now some stocks are more risky than others. For example, the risk on the stocks of small firms tends to be higher than the risk on the stocks of larger firms, because small firms tend to be those that are just starting up. Not having yet proved themselves, small firms have a higher risk. People like Melissa will sell the more risky stocks of smaller companies until the expected rate of return on those stocks is high enough compared with the less risky stocks of larger companies.

In equilibrium, we therefore expect to see a positive relationship between risk and the expected rate of return on securities. Securities with higher risks will have higher returns than securities with lower risks. Figure 4 shows the resulting **equilibrium risk-return relationship.**

There is probably no more important lesson about capital markets than this relationship. Individual investors should know it well. It says that to get a higher rate of return *on average over the long run,* you have to accept a higher risk. Again, the market forces at work are the same as the ones that led to the compensating wage differentials in the labor market. In the labor market, the higher wage in some jobs is the price that workers accept to take on the greater risk, or, more generally, the less pleasant aspects of the job.

Risk and Return in Reality

How well does this theoretical relationship work in reality? Very well. A tremendous amount of data over long periods of time on the financial markets support it. Table 4 presents data on the average return over 75 years for the four important types of securities we have mentioned in the theoretical discussion. The most risky of the four—the stocks of small firms—has the highest rate of return. Next highest in risk

TABLE 4		
Average Rates of Return for Different Risks, 1926–2001		
	Average Rate of Return per Year (percent)	Risk (average size of price fluctuations)
U.S. Treasury bills	3.8	3.2
Long-term corporate bonds	5.8	8.6
Large-company stocks	10.7	20.2
Small-company stocks	12.5	33.2

Note: These rates of return are not adjusted for inflation. The average rate of inflation was about 3 percent, which can be subtracted from each of the average returns to get the real return. The risk is the "standard deviation," a measure of volatility commonly used in probability and statistics.

Source: Data from Ibbotson Associates, *Stocks, Bonds, Bills and Inflation,* 2004 yearbook, Table 6–7.

are the common stocks of large firms. The least risky—short-term Treasury bills that are as safe as bank deposits—has the smallest rate of return. Long-term bonds, where price changes can be large, have a rate of return greater than that of Treasury bills. Although the relative risks of these four types of securities may seem obvious, a measure of the differences in the sizes of their price volatility is shown in the second column and confirms the intuitive risk rankings.

In general, Table 4 is a striking confirmation of this fundamental result of financial markets that higher expected rates of return are associated with higher risk.

Diversification Reduces Risk

The familiar saying "Don't put all your eggs in one basket" is particularly relevant to stock markets. Rather than a basket of eggs, you have a portfolio of stocks. A *portfolio* is a collection of stocks. Putting your funds into a portfolio of two or more stocks, whose prices do not always move in the same direction, rather than one stock is called **portfolio diversification.** The risks from holding a single stock can be reduced significantly by putting half your funds in one stock and half in another. If one stock falls in price, the other stock may fall less, may not fall at all, or may even rise.

portfolio diversification: spreading the collection of assets owned in order to limit exposure to risk.

Holding two stocks in equal amounts is the most elementary form of diversification. With thousands of stocks to choose from, however, diversification is not limited to two. Figure 5 shows how sharply risk declines with diversification. By holding 10 different stocks rather than 1, you can reduce your risk to about 30 percent of what it would be with 1 stock. If you hold some international stocks, whose behavior will be even more different from that of any one U.S. stock, you can reduce the risk even further. Mutual fund companies provide a way for an investor with only limited funds to diversify by holding 500 or even 5,000 stocks along with other investors. Some mutual funds—called *index funds*—consist of all the stocks in an index like the Standard & Poor's (S&P) 500 Index, a weighted average of the stocks of 500 major companies.

Efficient Market Theory

The shares of firms' stock on the market can be traded quickly at any time of day. For most large and medium-sized companies, some people are always willing to buy and sell. If people hear that Intel has made a discovery that is expected to raise its profits, they rush to buy Intel stock. If people suddenly learn about a decline in a company's profits or about losses, then people rush to sell that company's stock. This rush to buy and sell changes prices instantaneously, so that the price adjusts rapidly to good news or bad news. The rapid adjustment means that there are rarely any unexploited profit opportunities for regular investors without inside information or a special

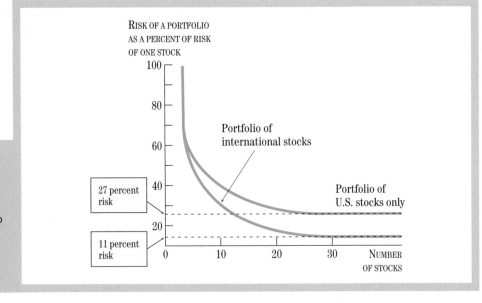

FIGURE 5
Risk Declines Sharply with Diversification
By holding more than one stock, the risk can be reduced. By holding 10 U.S. securities, the risk is reduced to 30 percent of the risk of holding 1 security. Diversifying internationally permits one to reduce risk further. (The risk is measured by the standard deviation.)

efficient market hypothesis: the idea that markets adjust rapidly enough to eliminate profit opportunities immediately.

ability to anticipate news, whether good or bad. The **efficient market hypothesis** states that there is an elimination of profit opportunities in financial markets as stock prices adjust quickly to new information. Rates of return greater than those due to the price of risk disappear soon after any good news about a stock appears.

Many tests over the years have found the efficient market hypothesis to be a close approximation of security price determination. It has led to the growth in popularity of index funds, where investors do not pay advisers to tell them when to buy and sell stock. They simply invest in a fund that includes a large number of stocks.

CORPORATE GOVERNANCE PROBLEMS

When corporations issue stock to buy physical capital or start up operations, a separation between the owners of the corporation—the stockholders—and the managers of the corporation is created. This separation leads to incentive problems—the manager might not act in the interest of the shareholder. Here we show how these problems can be analyzed with a theory called *asymmetric information theory.*

Consider a start-up firm. When an entrepreneur at a start-up firm obtains financial capital by issuing stock, a special relationship is formed. Those who supplied the financial capital by buying the stock relationship is formed. Those who supplied the financial capital by buying the stock become owners or at least part owners of the company. If the entrepreneur does well and the company is a success, they reap large returns.

Asymmetric Information: Moral Hazard and Adverse Selection

Shareholders of a firm have less information than the managers about how the firm is doing even though the shareholders put a considerable amount of funds in the firm. These differences in information, called **asymmetric information,** can cause several problems. First, the manager might not act in the interest of the owners. Taking unnecessary business trips on the company's aircraft to exotic areas or not working hard to find the right employees is harmful to the shareholders' interests.

asymmetric information: different levels of information available to different people in an economic interaction or exchange.

moral hazard: in insurance markets, a situation in which a person buys insurance against some risk and subsequently takes actions that increase the risk; analogous situations arise when there is asymmetric information in other markets.

adverse selection: in insurance markets, a situation in which the people who choose to buy insurance will be the riskiest group in the population; analogous situations apply in other markets.

profit sharing: programs in which managers and employees receive a share of profits earned by the firm.

Such actions are against the interest of the shareholders. They are called **moral hazards,** a term borrowed from research on the insurance industry, where asymmetric information is also a problem. Moral hazards in insurance occur when people are less careful about trying to prevent fires after they get fire insurance. In the case of the firm, the manager may be less careful about the firm after the shareholders' or investors' funds have been obtained.

Another problem is that those entrepreneurs who have more risky projects would seek equity financing—where dividend payments to shareholders would be optional—rather than debt financing, where interest payments are required. This is called **adverse selection,** another term borrowed from insurance. In insurance, adverse selection occurs when people who are unhealthy select health insurance while healthy people do not. In this case, managers who have more risky projects elect equity financing more than those who have less risky projects. This makes potential shareholders or investors less willing to supply funds to equity markets. Finding ways to write contracts between principals—the owners or shareholders and agents (the managers)—to reduce the problems of moral hazard or adverse selection requires paying attention to incentives.

Incentives to Overcome Adverse Selection and Moral Hazard Problems

Severe adverse selection and moral hazard problems can prevent the formation of business relationships between principals and agents. For example, people may be unwilling to buy stock in a firm because they believe that managers may use that money for their own benefit rather than for the company's interests. One of the more egregious cases of recent times was the indictment of Dennis Kozlowski, who was sentenced to 8 to 25 years in prison for misappropriating hundreds of millions of dollars. Similarly, investors may worry that firms that are interested in obtaining equity financing from the public precisely because they have been able to borrow from other lenders.

One way in which problems of moral hazard and adverse selection can be limited is through the use of **profit sharing** agreements, whereby managers and employees are given a share of the profits earned by the firm. That way the agents of the firms have a financial stake in the firm's success, and hence have their interests aligned with the principals—agents gain when the principal gains and the agent loses when the principal loses. In recent years many U.S. airlines have implemented profit sharing plans for their employees.

Another way to overcome the problems caused by moral hazard and adverse selection is to join with a group of investors and take over a company so that the problematic management team can be replaced. The mere threat of such a takeover can be an incentive for management to act in shareholder's interest rather than their own. Perhaps the most well-known takeover case in recent time was the purchase of RJR Nabisco for over $30 billion by KKR, a firm specializing in takeovers. In the last few years, there has been a rise to prominence of *private equity* firms like the Blackstone Group, which specialize in buying

A Shareholder Meeting: Principals, Agents, Asymmetric Information
Theories of corporate governance view a firm's shareholders (shown in the crowd) as the *principals* and the managers (shown on the stage) as the agents. Management incentive plans such as profit sharing are seen as ways of fostering good management performance when the principals have little information about what the *agents* actually do—a situation called *asymmetric information.*

Corporate Greed

Dennis Kozlowski, the former CEO of Tyco International, became the symbolic figure of corporate managers wasting, and in Kozlowski's case defrauding, shareholder money. The article points out other high profile cases and discusses the impact that the Kozlowski case might have on other corporate executives, with designs on stealing shareholder funds. It's important to realize that criminal charges cannot be brought for bad business decisions, so that most problems related to moral hazard will not be solved via the legal system.

Some of the more lavish uses of shareholder funds

Other examples of corporate executives who were convicted of stealing corporate funds and committing financial fraud

The punishment meted out to Kozlowski and Swartz indicates the severity of their crimes.

Ex-Tyco Officers Sentenced
Pair Get Up to 25 Years in Prison, Must Pay Almost $240 Million

By BEN WHITE | Washington Post Staff Writer

NEW YORK, Sept. 19— A state judge on Monday sentenced former Tyco International Ltd. executives L. Dennis Kozlowski and Mark H. Swartz to 8 1/3 to 25 years in prison for looting the company of hundreds of millions of dollars to pay for lavish parties, luxurious homes and extravagances such as a $6,000 shower curtain.

In a case that came to symbolize corporate greed, state Supreme Court Judge Michael J. Obus also ordered Kozlowski and Swartz to pay nearly $240 million in fines and restitution. Kozlowski and Swartz were immediately taken into custody and led from a packed courtroom in handcuffs as family members of both men sobbed. The men are likely to serve at least part of their sentences in one of New York's 16 maximum-security state prisons.

The sentences for Kozlowski and Swartz follow lengthy terms meted out to other white-collar defendants convicted in a wave of criminal cases that followed the collapse of the Internet bubble and multibillion-dollar frauds at companies such as WorldCom Inc. and Enron Corp.

Former WorldCom chairman Bernard J. Ebbers, 64, was sentenced to 25 years in prison for orchestrating an $11 billion accounting fraud at his company. Because of Ebbers's age, that could amount to a life sentence. John J. Rigas, the 80-year-old founder of Adelphia Communications Corp., received 15 years in prison for stealing millions from the cable company for personal extravagances, hiding more than $2.3 billion in debt and lying to investors. Rigas's son and former Adelphia chief financial officer Timothy J. Rigas was given 20 years in prison for his role in the scheme.

Prosecutors and many shareholder groups say long sentences are necessary to deter future abuses and restore investor confidence. But some defense lawyers question the extent to which a few high-profile cases will deter bad behavior at smaller public companies that present less tempting targets for prosecutors. "Officers and directors of major corporations, multinational corporations, clearly get the message," said defense attorney Jacob S. Frenkel. "The question is whether the message has been conveyed thoroughly to officers and directors at small and mid-size companies."

Kozlowski and Swartz will be able to cut one-sixth off of their 8 1/3 -year minimum sentence if they behave well and take part in prison programs, said Linda Foglia, a spokeswoman for the state Department of Correctional Services. That would reduce the point at which they can be paroled to six years and 11 months. Inmates are eligible to apply for work release two years before their first possible parole date, and parole officials will decide how much of the 8 1/3 to 25 years the former executives must serve. Several legal experts said it was unlikely either man would serve more than 10 years in total.

There is no parole in the federal system, under which many other white-collar defendants have been tried and sentenced. Though their sentences may be cut shorter than other executives', the time Kozlowski and Swartz spend behind bars may be in a harsher environment. Obus did not specify where the two former executives will serve their terms. He said that decision would be made by state corrections officials. But he said he did not view either man as a security risk, indicating he would not object if they are sent to a lower-security facility.

Former prosecutor David Gourevitch, however, said there were no facilities in the state system comparable to federal minimum-security prisons such as the one where entrepreneur Martha Stewart spent her five-month sentence. "In the federal system, outside of maximum-security places, generally people are physically safe. I don't think anybody would say that about New York state prison," Gourevitch said. "And from a state perspective, this is one of the longest sentences in a corporate fraud case that I can recall."

Foglia said that in most cases, defendants sentenced to more than six years are sent to maximum-security prisons. She said it would be several weeks before the state decides where to send Kozlowski and Swartz. In the meantime, they will stay at a holding facility known as the Tombs in Lower Manhattan and then be sent to Rikers Island, the temporary jail for New York City inmates before they are sent to state prisons.

In June, a jury found former Tyco chief executive Kozlowski, 58, and former chief financial officer Swartz, 45, guilty of criminal counts of grand larceny, conspiracy, securities fraud and eight of nine counts of falsifying business records.

Obus imposed the same prison sentence on both men. He ordered Kozlowski to pay a $70 million fine and Swartz to pay a $35 million fine. He ordered both men to repay Tyco a combined $134.4 million in restitution of illegal bonuses and other illicit payments.

Kozlowski and Swartz each made brief statements in court Monday, asking Obus to be lenient. Lawyers for each also pleaded with the court to recognize the former executives' charitable works and the scores of letters sent on their behalf by friends and family.

Prosecutors, by contrast, asked Obus to send a message that corporate theft will be treated the same as grand larceny committed with a handgun. They asked for the maximum term of 15 to 30 years for both men.

In imposing the sentence, Obus said, "The heart of this case is basic larceny" and described the charges as "extremely serious." He expressed befuddlement at Kozlowski's and Swartz's plights, at one point asking, "how the defendants, with all they had going for them, managed to get themselves into this disastrous position."

Attorneys for Kozlowski and Swartz said they would seek to have their clients released on bail pending appeal of their convictions. At the sentencing hearing on Monday, state prosecutors said the Securities and Exchange Commission staff had recommended that the agency bring an accounting fraud case against Tyco. Tyco has said it expects to settle the SEC suit and has set aside $50 million for that purpose. The SEC often simultaneously files and settles accounting cases.

shares of a public company and taking it private, so that they can replace the existing management with managers who presumably can improve the firm's performance.

However, such takeovers have also been criticized. Some say that the threat of being bought out by a hostile takeover firm or a private equity firm leads management to adopt a more short-sighted attitude toward the operation of the company's affairs than is ideal. Companies also expend considerable resources constructing "takeover defenses," which attempt to make it more difficult for outsiders to use a hostile takeover to take control of the firm.

R E V I E W

- Financial markets are very volatile; both stock prices and bond prices tend to rise and fall over time. The riskiness of bonds and stocks affects the willingness of people to buy and sell these financial assets, and hence affects their return.

- We can calculate the expected return of a risky asset by weighting the possible gains and losses by the probability that these gains or losses will occur. Given the choice between a risky asset and a safe asset that have the same expected return, an individual who is risk averse will always choose the safe asset.

- Risk-averse investors will hold risky assets only if they are compensated in the form of a higher expected return. Thus, when buyers and sellers trade stocks or bonds in the market, a relationship between return and risk emerges: Higher risk is associated with higher returns.

- Investors can reduce risk by diversifying their portfolio, that is, by holding many different stocks. Mutual funds and index funds offer diversification opportunities even to investors who have very little money to put into the stock market.

- Earning stock returns in excess of those justified by the greater level of associated risk is difficult. The efficient market hypothesis predicts that stock prices adjust quickly to eliminate such lucrative return opportunities.

CONCLUSION

In this chapter we have seen how to employ some basic economic tools to analyze capital markets. In reviewing the lessons learned, it is helpful to see how they may apply to you personally.

First, by diversifying a portfolio of stocks, you can reduce risk substantially. Conversely, by holding an undiversified portfolio, you are needlessly incurring risk.

Second, be aware of the efficient market hypothesis that profit opportunity disappears quickly in financial markets. Instead of buying and selling securities frequently, investors may be better off investing in a mutual fund—like an index fund.

Third, if you do try to pick your own portfolio rather than use a mutual fund, concentrate on areas you are familiar with. If you go into a medical career, you may know more than even the best investors about the promise of a new medical device or drug.

Fourth, over the short run, holding corporate stocks is more risky than putting your funds in a bank account, but over the long term, the higher rate of return on stocks outweighs the risks for most people. However, if you need money in the short term—to pay next year's tuition, for example—stocks may not be worth the risk.

KEY POINTS

1. Physical capital refers to the physical resources used to produce goods and services.

2. Financial capital, which include stocks and bonds, is used by firms to obtain funds to invest in physical capital.

3. A firm's demand for physical capital is a derived demand. A firm will use capital up to the point where the marginal revenue product of capital equals the rental price.

4. The supply and demand for capital determines the rental price or the implicit rental price. Tax and subsidy policies that affect the demand for capital goods will affect both the equilibrium rental price of capital and the equilibrium quantity of capital used by firms.

5. Firms raise money for investing in physical capital by issuing stocks and bonds. Once issued, the stocks and bonds trade on financial markets.

6. The rate of return on stocks is equal to the dividend plus the change in the price as a percentage of the price. The rate of return on bonds held to maturity is the yield of the bond.

7. The rate of return on stocks tends to rise when firms have higher earnings, which are either paid out in the form of dividends or reinvested in the company. The rate of return on bonds tends to rise in periods when market interest rates are falling.

8. Stock markets and bond markets tend to be extremely volatile. To understand how the riskiness of these assets affects their return, we need to understand how investors behave. Risk-averse investors will buy more risky stocks or bonds only if the expected rate of return is higher.

9. In market equilibrium, there is a positive relationship between risk and rate of return. If you want to get a higher rate of return, you have to accept higher risk.

10. Diversification helps reduce risk. Even individuals with limited resources can diversify their portfolios by investing in mutual funds.

KEY TERMS

depreciation	return	coupon	portfolio diversification
debt contract	capital gain	maturity date	efficient market hypothesis
equity contract	capital loss	face value	asymmetric information
rental price of capital	dividend yield	yield	moral hazard
marginal revenue product of capital	rate of return	expected return	adverse selection
economic rent	earnings	equilibrium risk-return relationship	profit sharing
implicit rental price	price-earnings ratio		

QUESTIONS FOR REVIEW

1. What is the difference between physical capital and financial capital?

2. How is the relationship between the marginal revenue product of capital and the rental price related to the firm's decision to rent additional units of physical capital?

3. Why is the quantity of physical capital demanded negatively related to the rental price of capital?

4. How does the implicit rental price of capital depend on the interest rate and depreciation?

5. What is the difference between a stock and a bond?

6. What determines the rate of return on stocks? On bonds?

7. What does it mean for an individual to be risk averse?

8. How do the actions of risk-averse individuals influence the relationship between risk and return in financial markets?

9. What is diversification? How does it affect risk?

10. What do economists mean when they say that financial markets are efficient?

PROBLEMS

1. Which of the following are physical capital, and which are financial capital?
   a. A Toyota Camry at Avis Car Rental
   b. A loan you take out to start a newspaper business
   c. New desktop publishing equipment
   d. A bond issued by the U.S. government
   e. A pizza oven at Pizza Hut

2. Suppose that Marshall's stones were dropped all over the earth and finding them was difficult. Would the supply curve for capital still be perfectly inelastic? Would there be economic rent?

3. Suppose a company owns a computer that costs $5,000 and depreciates $1,000 per year. If the interest rate is 5 percent, what is the implicit rental price of the computer? Explain why the implicit rental price depends on the interest rate.

4. The U.S. government issues a 1-year bond with a face value of $1,000 and a zero coupon. If the yield is 10 percent, what will the market price of the bond be? Now suppose you observe that the bond price falls by 5 percent. What happens to its yield?

5. Suppose a 2-year bond has a 5 percent coupon and a $1,000 face value, and the current market interest rate is 5 percent. What is the price of the bond? Now suppose that you believe that the interest rate will remain 5 percent this year, but next year will fall to 3 percent. How much are you willing to pay for the 2-year bond today? Why?

6. Consider the following possibilities for your stock market investment portfolio.

	Good Market	Bad Market	Disastrous Market
Probability	.50	.30	.20
Rate of return	.25	.10	−.25

   a. What is the expected return of this stock market investment portfolio?
   b. Would you choose this expected return or take a safe return of 7 percent from a savings deposit in your bank? Why?

   c. Suppose your teacher chooses the safe return from the bank. Is your teacher risk averse? How can you tell?

7. You are considering the purchase of stocks of two firms: a biotechnology corporation and a supermarket chain. Because of the uncertainty in the biotechnology industry, you estimate that there is a 50–50 chance of your either earning an 80 percent return on your investment or losing 80 percent of your investment within a year. The food industry is more stable, so you estimate that you have a 50–50 chance of either earning 10 percent or losing 10 percent. Which stock would you buy if you were a risk-averse individual? Why? What do you think other investors (most of whom are risk averse) would do? What would be the effect of these actions on the relative prices of the two stocks?

8. Graph the data on risk and expected return (in percent) for the following securities.

Asset	Expected Rate of Return	Risk
Bank deposit	3	0
U.S. Treasury bills	4	3
Goodcorp bonds	9	10
ABC stock	11	24
XYZ stock	13	24
Riskyco stock	16	39

   Draw an equilibrium risk-return line through the points. Which two assets should have changes in their prices in the near future? In which direction will their prices change?

9. Suppose a study indicated that stock prices were usually lower during the Christmas season than during the rest of the year. What would be the likely reaction of the market?

10. Suppose you have $10,000 and must choose between investing in your own human capital or investing in physical or financial capital. What factors will enter into your decision-making process? How much risk will be involved with each investment? What would you do? Why?

Present Discounted Value

A dollar in the future is worth less than a dollar today. This principle underlies all economic decisions involving actions over time. Whether you put some dollars under the mattress to be spent next summer, borrow money from a friend or family member to be paid back next year, or are a sophisticated investor in stocks, bonds, or real estate, that same principle is essential to making good decisions. Here we explain why the principle is essential and derive a formula for determining exactly *how much* less a dollar in the future is worth than a dollar today. The formula is called the *present discounted value formula.*

Discounting the Future

First let's answer the question, why is the value of a dollar in the future less than the value of a dollar today? The simplest answer is that a dollar can earn interest over time. Suppose a person you trust completely to pay off a debt gives you an IOU promising to pay you $100 in one year; how much is that IOU worth to you today? How much would you be willing to pay for the IOU today? It would be less than $100, because you could put an amount less than $100 in a bank and get $100 at the end of a year. The exact amount depends on the interest rate. If the interest rate is 10 percent, the $100 should be worth $90.91 because, if you put $90.91 in a bank earning 10 percent per year, at the end of the year you will have exactly $100. That is, $90.91 plus interest payments of $9.09 ($90.91 times .1 rounded to the nearest penny) equals $100.

The process of translating a future payment into a value in the present is called **discounting.** The value in the present of a future payment is called the **present discounted value.** The interest rate used to do the discounting is called the **discount rate.** In the preceding example, a future payment of $100 has a present discounted value of $90.91, and the discount rate is 10 percent. If the discount rate were 20 percent, the present discounted value would be $83.33 (because if you put $83.33 in a bank for a year at a 20 percent interest rate, you would have, rounding to the nearest penny, $100 at the end of the year). The term *discount* is used because the value in the present is

less than the future payment; in other words, the payment is "discounted," much as a $100 bicycle on sale might be "discounted" to $83.33.

Finding the Present Discounted Value

The previous examples suggest that there is a formula for calculating present value, and indeed there is. Let

> the present discounted value be *PDV*
> the discount rate be *i*
> the future payment be *F*

The symbol *i* is measured as a decimal, but we speak of the discount rate in percentage terms; thus we would say "the discount rate is 10 percent" and write "$i = .1$."

Now, the present discounted value *PDV* is the amount for which, if you put it in a bank today at an interest rate *i*, you would get an amount in the future equal to the future payment *F*. For example, if the future date is one year from now, then if you put the amount *PDV* in a bank for one year, you would get *PDV* times $(1 + i)$ at the end of the year. Thus, the *PDV* should be such that

$$PDV \times (1 + i) = F$$

Now divide both sides by $(1 + i)$; you get

$$PDV = \frac{F}{1 + i}$$

which is the formula for the present discounted value in the case of a payment made one year in the future. That is,

$$\text{Present discounted value} = \frac{\text{payment in one year}}{(1 + \text{the discount rate})}$$

For example, if the payment in one year is $100 and the discount rate $i = .1$, then the present discounted value is $90.91 [$100/(1 + .1)], just as we reasoned previously.

To obtain the formula for the case where the payment is made more than one year in the future, we must recognize that the amount in the present can be put in a bank and earn interest at the discount rate for more than one year. For example, if the interest rate is 10 percent, we could get $100 at the end of 2 years by investing $82.64 today. That is, putting $82.64 in the bank would give $82.64 times (1.1) at the end of one year; keeping all this in the bank for another year would give $82.64 times (1.1) times (1.1), or $82.64 times 1.21, or $100.00, again rounding off. Thus, in the case of a future payment in 2 years, we would have

$$PDV = \frac{F}{(1 + i)^2}$$

Analogous reasoning implies that the present discounted value of a payment made N years in the future would be

$$PDV = \frac{F}{(1 + i)^N}$$

For example, the present discounted value of a $100 payment to be made 20 years in the future is $14.86 if the discount rate is 10 percent. In other words, if you put $14.86 in the bank today at an interest rate of 10 percent, you would have about $100 at the end of 20 years. What is the present discounted value of a $100 payment to be made 100 years in the future? The above formula tells us that the PDV is only $.00726, less than a penny! All of these examples indicate that the higher the discount rate or the further in the future the payment is to be received, the lower the present discounted value of a future payment.

In many cases, we need to find the present discounted value of a *series* of payments made in several different years. We can do this by combining the previous formulas. The present discounted value of payments F_1 made in 1 year and F_2 made in 2 years would be

$$PDV = \frac{F_1}{(1 + i)} + \frac{F_2}{(1 + i)^2}$$

For example, the present discounted value of $100 paid in one year and $100 paid in 2 years would be $90.91 plus $82.64, or $173.55. In general, the present discounted value of a series of future payments $F_1, F_2, \ldots, F_N$ over N years is

$$PDV = \frac{F_1}{(1 + i)} + \frac{F_2}{(1 + i)^2} + \cdots + \frac{F_N}{(1 + i)^N}$$

KEY POINTS

1. A dollar to be paid in the future is worth less than a dollar today.

2. The present discounted value of a future payment is the amount you would have to put in a bank today to get that same payment in the future.

3. The higher the discount rate, the lower the present discounted value of a future payment.

KEY TERMS AND DEFINITIONS

discounting: the process of translating a future payment into a value in the present.

present discounted value: the value in the present of future payments.

discount rate: an interest rate used to discount a future payment when computing present discounted value.

QUESTIONS FOR REVIEW

1. Why is the present discounted value of a future payment of $1 less than $1?

2. What is the relationship between the discount rate and the interest rate?

3. What happens to the present discounted value of a future payment as the payment date stretches into the future?

4. Why is discounting important for decisions involving actions at different dates?

PROBLEMS

1. Find the present discounted value of
   a. $100 to be paid at the end of 3 years.
   b. $1,000 to be paid at the end of 1 year plus $1,000 to be paid at the end of 2 years.
   c. $10 to be paid at the end of 1 year, $10 at the end of 2 years, and $100 at the end of 3 years.

2. Suppose you win $1,000,000 in a lottery and your winnings are scheduled to be paid as follows: $300,000 at the end of 1 year, $300,000 at the end of 2 years, and $400,000 at the end of 3 years. If the interest rate is 10 percent, what is the present discounted value of your winnings?

3. You are considering two job offers. You expect to work for the employer for five years. For simplicity, we assume that you will be paid at the end of each year. The two offers are summarized in the following table.

Year	Offer 1	Offer 2
1	$30,000	$40,000
2	$33,000	$30,000
3	$36,000	$33,000
4	$39,000	$36,000
5	$42,000	$39,000

The primary difference between the two offers is a signing bonus of $10,000 paid under Offer 2. The annual salary paid in years 2 through 5 is higher under Offer 1 than under Offer 2. If the interest rate is 5 percent, which is the better offer? If the interest rate is 10 percent, which is better?

Trade and Global Markets

Chapter 17

The Gains from International Trade

Bangalore, an Indian city of about 6 million people, has undergone a remarkable economic transformation in recent times. Bangalore is now one of the leading cities in the production of computer software; according to India's National Association of Software and Service Companies, the value of software produced in Bangalore has increased 750-fold in the last 15 years. The rapid increase in jobs in the software and information technology industry has brought prosperity to an increasing number of workers in Bangalore. An article that appeared in *USA Today* on March 22, 2004, describes the transformation of the lives of Bangalore's software workers, who earn a salary doing work outsourced by U.S. companies and then spend their earnings on IBM computers, Hyundai cars, Domino's Pizza, and Stairmasters (to work off the pizza!).

Similar stories can be told about U.S. trade with many countries in the world. Every day, people in countries like China, Germany, Korea, Japan, and Sri Lanka buy American products: Caterpillar tractors, Motorola cellular phones, Microsoft software, Boeing 747s, and Merck pharmaceuticals. At the same time, Americans drive cars made in Germany and Japan, listen to CDs and MP3s on electronic equipment made in China and Malaysia, play tennis wearing Nike shoes made in Korea, or go swimming in Ocean Pacific swimsuits made in Sri Lanka.

These stories about firms selling their products around the world and people consuming goods made in other countries illustrate reasons why people benefit from international trade. First, international trade allows firms such as Merck access to a very large world market, enabling them to invest heavily in research and reduce costs by concentrating production. Second, international trade allows different countries to specialize in what they are relatively efficient at producing, such as pharmaceuticals in the United States or electronic equipment in Malaysia.

gains from trade:
improvements in income,
production, or satisfaction owing
to the exchange of goods or
services. (Ch. 1)

This chapter explores the reasons for these *gains from trade* and develops two models that can be used to measure the actual size of these gains. We begin, however, with a brief look at recent trends in international trade.

RECENT TRENDS IN INTERNATIONAL TRADE

international trade: the
exchange of goods and services
between people or firms in
different nations. (Ch. 1)

tariff: a tax on imports.

quota: a governmental limit on
the quantity of a good that may be
imported or sold.

commerce clause: the clause
in the U.S. Constitution that
prohibits restraint of trade
between states.

International trade is trade between people or firms in different countries. Trade between people in Detroit and Ottawa, Canada, is international trade, whereas trade between Detroit and Chicago is trade within a country. Thus, international trade is just another kind of economic interaction; it is subject to the same basic economic principles as trade between people in the same country.

International trade differs from trade in domestic markets, however, because national governments frequently place restrictions, such as **tariffs** or **quotas,** on trade between countries that they do not place on trade within countries. For example, the Texas legislature cannot limit or put a tariff on the import of Florida oranges into Texas. The **commerce clause** of the U.S. Constitution forbids such restraint of trade between states. But the United States can restrict the import of oranges from Brazil. Similarly, Japan can restrict the import of rice from the United States, and Australia can restrict the import of Japanese automobiles.

International trade has grown much faster than trade within countries in recent years. Figure 1 shows the exports for all countries in the world as a percentage of the world GDP. International trade has doubled as a proportion of the world GDP during the last 30 or so years. Why has international trade grown so rapidly? What economic or technological forces have led to this increase in globalization?

FIGURE 1
World Exports as a Share of GDP

The faster growth of exports compared to GDP is probably due to the reduction in trade restrictions and the lower cost of transportation, both characteristics of greater globalization.

Source: Angus Maddison, *The World Economy: A Millenial Perspective,* (OECD, 2001), Table F-5.

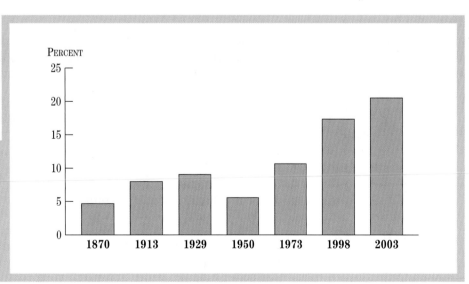

One reason is that the cost of transportation and communication has been reduced dramatically. The cost of air travel fell to 9.5 cents per mile in 2000 from 87 cents per mile in 1930, while the cost of a three-minute phone call from New York to London fell to $.24 in 2002 from $315 in 1930 (adjusting the 1930 prices for general inflation). E-mail and the Internet, unheard of in 1930, reduce costs even further.

However, the most important reason that trade has expanded so rapidly is that government restrictions on trade between countries have come down. Western European countries are integrating into a single market. Canada, Mexico, and the United States have agreed to integrate their economies into a free trade area, where the term *free* indicates the elimination of restrictions on trade. Previously closed economies have opened themselves to world trade through major political and economic reforms. The formerly closed economies in Eastern Europe, Russia, and, especially, China have joined the world trading system. Export-oriented countries in Asia are growing rapidly, and governments in South America such as Argentina and Chile are opening their economies to competition and foreign trade.

These countries are making these changes in an effort to help people. But how do people gain from international trade? Let's now consider that question.

R E V I E W

- The basic principles of economics apply to international trade between people in different countries.

- There is a greater tendency for governments to interfere with trade between countries than with trade within their own country.

- International trade has grown rapidly in recent years because of reduced transportation and communication costs and, especially, lower government barriers to trade.

COMPARATIVE ADVANTAGE

comparative advantage: a situation in which a person or country can produce one good at a lower opportunity cost than another person or country. (Ch. 1)

According to the theory of *comparative advantage*, a country can improve the income of its citizens by allowing them to trade with people in other countries, even if the people of the country are less efficient at producing all items.

Getting a Gut Feeling for Comparative Advantage

First, consider a parable that conveys the essence of comparative advantage. Rose is a highly skilled computer programmer who writes computer-assisted drawing programs. Rose owns a small firm that sells her programs to architects. She has hired an experienced salesman, Sam, to contact the architects and sell her software. Thus, Rose specializes in programming, and Sam specializes in sales.

absolute advantage: a situation in which a person or country is more efficient at producing a good in comparison with another person or country.

You need to know a little more about Rose. Rose is a friendly, outgoing person, and because she knows her product better than Sam does, she is better than Sam at sales. We say that Rose has an **absolute advantage** over Sam in both programming and sales because she is better at both jobs. But it still makes sense for Rose to hire Sam because her efficiency at programming compared to Sam's is greater than her efficiency at sales compared to Sam's. We say that Rose has a *comparative advantage* over Sam in programming rather than in sales. If Rose sold her programs, then she would have to sacrifice her programming time, and her profits would fall. Thus, even though Rose is better at both programming and sales, she hires Sam to do the selling so that she can program full time.

All this seems sensible. However, there is one additional part of the terminology that may at first seem confusing but is important. We said that Rose has the comparative advantage in programming, not in sales. But who does have the comparative advantage in sales? Sam does. Even though Sam is less efficient at both sales and programming, we say that he has a comparative advantage in sales because, compared with Rose, he does relatively better at sales than he does at programming. A person cannot have a comparative advantage in both of only two activities.

■ **Opportunity Cost, Relative Efficiency, and Comparative Advantage.** The idea of comparative advantage can also be explained in terms of *opportunity cost*. The opportunity cost of Rose or Sam spending more time selling is that she or he can produce fewer programs. Similarly, the opportunity cost of Rose or Sam spending more time writing programs is that she or he can make fewer sales.

opportunity cost: the value of the next-best forgone alternative that was not chosen because something else was chosen. (Ch. 1)

Observe that, in the example, Sam has a lower opportunity cost of spending his time selling than Rose does; thus, it makes sense for Sam to do the selling rather than Rose. In contrast, Rose has a lower opportunity cost of spending her time writing computer programs than Sam does; thus, it makes sense for Rose to write computer programs rather than Sam.

Opportunity costs give us a way to define comparative advantage. A person with a lower opportunity cost of producing a good than another person has a comparative advantage in that good. Thus, Rose has a comparative advantage in computer programming, and Sam has a comparative advantage in sales.

Comparative advantage can also be explained in terms of relative efficiency. A person who is relatively more efficient at producing good X than good Y compared to another person has a comparative advantage in good X. Thus, again, we see that Rose has a comparative advantage in computer programming because she is relatively more efficient at producing computer programs than at making sales compared to Sam.

■ **From People to Countries.** Why is this story about Rose and Sam a parable? Because we can think of Rose and Sam as two countries that differ in efficiency at producing one product versus another. In the parable, Rose has a comparative advantage over Sam in programming, and Sam has a comparative advantage over Rose in sales. In general, *country A has a comparative advantage over country B in the production of a good if the opportunity cost of producing the good in country A is less than in country B*, or, alternatively but equivalently stated, *if country A can produce the good relatively more efficiently than other goods compared to country B*. Thus, if you understand the Rose and Sam story, you should have no problem understanding comparative advantage in two countries, which we now examine in more detail.

Productivity in Two Countries

Consider the following two goods: (1) vaccines and (2) TV sets. Different skills are required for the production of vaccines and TV sets. Vaccine production requires knowledge of chemistry and biology, and the marketing of products where doctors make most of the choices. Producing TV sets requires knowledge of electrical engineering and microcircuitry, and the marketing of goods where consumers make most of the choices.

The Economic Impact of Outsourcing

Perhaps no trend in international trade has attracted as much recent attention as the increase in global outsourcing, whereby a U.S.-based company uses a foreign company to perform a portion of the work involved in producing a good or a service. This article, which appeared in the *New York Times* on June 19, 2005, discusses why some of the fears associated with outsourcing may be a little misplaced.

True or False: Outsourcing Is a Crisis

By EDUARDO PORTER

June 19, 2005, Late Edition Final

If you read only the headlines, the future of globalization may seem scary, indeed. American jobs have already been heading abroad. And as telecommunications and more powerful computers enable companies to take even more jobs overseas, the service sector, which accounts for about 85 percent of the United States work force, will be increasingly vulnerable to competition from the cheap labor pools of the developing world.

So the question looms: Is America on the verge of losing oodles of white-collar jobs? Probably not. The threat of global outsourcing is easily overstated. The debate over the global competition for jobs is awash in dire projections. All those legal assistants in New York and Washington, for example, could be replaced with smart young graduates from Hyderabad. Office support occupations—jobs like data entry assistant, file clerk and the entire payroll department—could also be carried out in remote locations. "We are really at the beginning stages of this, and it is accelerating rapidly," said Ron Hira, assistant professor of public policy at the Rochester Institute of Technology.

In a study published this year, two economists at the Organization for Economic Cooperation and Development in Brussels estimated that 20 percent of the developed world's employment could be "potentially affected" by global outsourcing. That could include all American librarians, statisticians, chemical engineers and air traffic controllers, the study said. What does "potentially affected" mean? Even if offshoring didn't drain away all these jobs, global competition for employment—including workers in developing countries who earn so little by comparison—could severely dent the livelihoods of American workers. "It isn't going to hurt in terms of jobs," said William J. Baumol, an economics professor at New York University who has studied the costs of globalization. "It is going to hurt in terms of wages."

But even if millions of tasks can be done by cheaper labor on the other side of the planet, businesses won't rush to move every job they can to wherever the cost is lowest. The labor market isn't quite that global, and it's unlikely to be anytime soon. In a new set of reports, the McKinsey Global Institute, a research group known for its unabashedly favorable view of globalization, argued that 160 million service jobs—about 10 percent of total worldwide employment—could be moved to remote sites because these job functions

Describes what outsourcing is

Identifies occupations most likely to be affected

Potential number of jobs affected

don't require customer contact, local knowledge or complex interactions with the rest of a business.

Yet after surveying dozens of companies in eight sectors, from pharmaceutical companies to insurers, it concluded that only a small fraction of these jobs would actually be sent away. The report estimates that by 2008, multinational companies in the entire developed world will have located only 4.1 million service jobs in low-wage countries, up from about 1.5 million in 2003. The figure is equivalent to only 1 percent of the total number of service jobs in developed countries.

The number of jobs that may actually be outsourced

Some sectors, like retail and health care, are likely to put very few jobs in poor countries. McKinsey estimated that less than 0.07 percent of health care jobs in 2008 would be outsourced to low-wage countries. But even designers of packaged software, whose work can easily be done abroad, will outsource only 18 percent of their jobs, the report said.

Moving tasks to faraway sites isn't simple. According to McKinsey's study, many business processes are difficult to separate into discrete chunks that can be sent away. Many insurance companies use information technology systems that have been cobbled together over time and would be difficult to manage remotely. Managers can be unwilling or unprepared to work overseas. And sometimes the tasks that can be sent offshore are too small to make the move worthwhile.

Limitations on outsourcing

To top it off, there aren't that many suitable cheap workers available. Human-resources managers interviewed for the McKinsey study said that for reasons ranging from poor language skills to second-rate education systems, only about 13 percent of the young, college-educated professionals in the big developing countries are suitable to work for multinationals. And competition from local companies reduces this pool.

Sure, there are a billion Indians, but only a tiny percentage of the Indian work force have the appropriate qualifications. "Only a fraction have English as a medium of instruction, and only a fraction of those speak English that you or I can understand," said Jagdish N. Bhagwati, a professor of economics at Columbia University.

Of course, many of these obstacles can be overcome with time. The pool of adequate workers in poorer countries will grow, and companies will eventually iron out many of the logistical complications.

But that is likely to take a while. "The rate at which companies are willing and able is much slower than you would realize," said Diana Farrell, director of the McKinsey Global Institute. "We see this as being evolutionary, continuous but measured change."

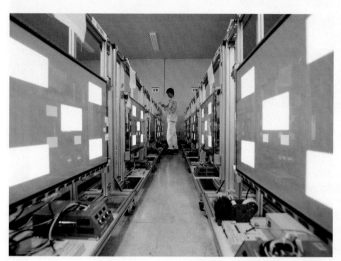 

Electronics versus Pharmaceuticals
In the example used in this chapter, Korea has a comparative advantage in an electronic good (TV sets), and the United States has a comparative advantage in a pharmaceutical (vaccines). Thus, with trade, the electronic good will be produced in Korea, as shown in the left-hand photo, and the pharmaceutical good will be produced in the United States, as shown in the right-hand photo.

Table 1 provides an example of productivity differences in the production of vaccines and TV sets in two different countries, the United States and Korea. Productivity is measured by the amount of each good that can be produced by a worker per day of work. To be specific, let us suppose that the vaccines are measured in vials, that the TVs are measured in numbers of TV sets, and that labor is the only factor of production in making vaccines and TV sets. The theory of comparative advantage does not depend on any of these assumptions, but they make the exposition much easier.

According to Table 1, in the United States it takes a worker one day of work to produce 6 vials of vaccine or 3 TV sets. In Korea, one worker can produce 1 vial of vaccine or 2 TV sets. Thus, the United States is more productive than Korea in producing both vaccines and TV sets. We say that a country has an *absolute advantage* over another country in the production of a good if it is more efficient at producing that good. In this example, the United States has an absolute advantage in both vaccine and TV set production.

However, the United States has a comparative advantage over Korea in the production of vaccines rather than TV sets. To see this, note that a worker in the United States can produce 6 times as many vials of vaccine as a worker in Korea but only 1.5 times as many TV sets. In other words, the United States is relatively more efficient in vaccines than in TV sets compared with Korea. Korea, being able to produce TV sets

TABLE 1
Example of Productivity in the United States and Korea

	Output per Day of Work	
	Vials of Vaccine	Number of TV Sets
United States	6	3
Korea	1	2

relatively more efficiently than vaccines compared to the United States, has a comparative advantage in TV sets.

Observe also how opportunity costs determine who has the comparative advantage. To produce 3 more TV sets, the United States must sacrifice 6 vials of vaccine; in other words, *in the United States, the opportunity cost of 1 more TV set is 2 vials of vaccine.* In Korea, to produce 2 more TV sets, the Koreans must sacrifice 1 vial of vaccine; in other words, *in Korea, the opportunity cost of 1 more TV set is only 1/2 vial of vaccine.* Thus, we see that the opportunity cost of producing TV sets in Korea is lower than in the United States. By examining opportunity costs, we again see that Korea has a comparative advantage in TV sets.

■ **An American Worker's View.** Because labor productivity in both goods is higher in the United States than in Korea, wages are higher in the United States than in Korea in the example. Now think about the situation from the point of view of American workers who are paid more than Korean workers. They might wonder how they can compete with Korea. The Korean workers' wages seem very low compared to theirs. It doesn't seem fair. But as we will see, comparative advantage implies that American workers can gain from trade with the Koreans.

■ **A Korean Worker's View.** It is useful to think about Table 1 from the perspective of a Korean worker as well as that of a U.S. worker. From the Korean perspective, it might be noted that Korean workers are less productive in both goods. Korean workers might wonder how they can ever compete with the United States, which looks like a productive powerhouse. Again, it doesn't seem fair. As we will see, however, the Koreans can also gain from trade with the Americans.

Finding the Relative Price

To measure how much the Koreans and Americans can gain from trade, we need to consider the *relative price* of vaccines and TVs in Korea and the United States. The relative price determines how much vaccine can be traded for TVs and, therefore, how much each country can gain from trade. For example, suppose the price of a TV set is $200 and the price of a vial of vaccine is $100. Then 2 vials of vaccine cost the same as 1 TV set; we say the relative price is 2 vials of vaccine per TV set. The next few paragraphs show how to determine the relative price from data on the costs of production.

> **Another example of relative prices may be helpful:**
> Price of U2 concert = $45
> Price of U2 T-shirt = $15
> Relative price = 3 T-shirts per concert

■ **Relative Price Without Trade.** First, let us find the relative price with no trade between the countries. The relative price of two goods should depend on the relative costs of production. A good for which the cost of producing an additional quantity is relatively low will have a relatively low price.

Consider the United States. In this example, a day of work can produce either 6 vials of vaccine or 3 TV sets. With labor as the only factor of production, 6 vials of vaccine cost the same to produce as 3 TV sets; that is, 2 vials of vaccine cost the same to produce as 1 TV set. Therefore, the relative price should be 2 vials of vaccine per TV set.

Now consider Korea. Electronic goods should have a relatively low price in Korea because they are relatively cheap to produce. A day of work can produce either 1 vial of vaccine or 2 TV sets; thus 1 vial of vaccine costs the same to produce as 2 TV sets in Korea. Therefore, the relative price is 1/2 vial of vaccine per TV set.

■ **Relative Price with Trade.** Now consider what happens when the two countries trade without government restrictions. If transportation costs are negligible and markets are competitive, then the price of a good must be the same in the United States and Korea. Why? Because any difference in price would quickly be eliminated by trade; if the price of TV sets is much less in Korea than in the United States, then traders will buy TV sets in Korea and sell them in the United States and make a profit; by doing so, however, they reduce the supply of TV sets in Korea and increase the supply in the United States. This will drive up the price in Korea and drive down the price in the United States until the price of TV sets in the two countries is the same. Thus, with trade, the price of vaccines and the price of TV sets will converge to the same levels in both countries. The relative price will therefore converge to the same value in both countries.

If the relative price is going to be the same in both countries, then we know the price must be somewhere between the prices in the two countries before trade. That is, the price must be between 2 vials of vaccine per TV set (the U.S. relative price) and 1/2 vial of vaccine per TV set (the Korean relative price). We do not know exactly where the price will fall between 1/2 and 2. It depends on the *demand* for vaccines and TV sets in Korea and the United States. *Let us assume that the relative price is 1 vial of vaccine per TV set after trade*, which is between 1/2 and 2 and is a nice, easy number for making computations. The calculation of the price with trade is summarized in Table 2.

Measuring the Gains from Trade

How large are the *gains from trade* due to comparative advantage? First, consider some examples.

■ **One Country's Gain.** Suppose that 10 American workers move out of electronics production and begin producing pharmaceuticals. We know from Table 1 that these 10 American workers can produce 60 vials of vaccine per day. Formerly, the 10 American workers were producing 30 TV sets per day. But their 60 vials of vaccine can be traded for TV sets produced in Korea. With the relative price of 1 vial per TV set, Americans will be able to exchange these 60 vials of vaccine for 60 TV sets. Thus, Americans gain 30 more TV sets by moving 10 more workers into vaccine production. This gain from trade is summarized in Table 3.

■ **The Other Country's Gain.** The same thing can happen in Korea. A Korean manufacturer can now hire 30 workers who were formerly working in vaccine production to produce TV sets. Vaccine production declines by 30 vials, but TV production increases by 60 TV sets. These 60 TV sets can be traded with Americans for 60 vials of vaccine. The reduction in the production of vaccine of 30 vials results in

TABLE 2
The Relative Price (The relative price—vials of vaccine per TV set—must be the same in both countries with trade.)

	United States	Korea
Relative price before trade:	2 vials of vaccine per TV set	1/2 vial of vaccine per TV set
Relative price range after trade:	Between 1/2 and 2	Between 1/2 and 2
Relative price assumption:	1	1

TABLE 3
Changing Production and Gaining from Trade in the United States and Korea

	United States (10 workers)		
	Change in Production	Amount Traded	Net Gain from Trade
Vaccines	Up 60 vials	Export 60 vials	0
TV sets	Down 30 sets	Import 60 sets	30 sets

	Korea (30 workers)		
	Change in Production	Amount Traded	Net Gain from Trade
Vaccines	Down 30 vials	Import 60 vials	30 vials
TV sets	Up 60 sets	Export 60 sets	0

an import of vaccine of 60 vials; thus, the gain from trade is 30 vials of vaccine. The Koreans, by moving workers out of vaccine production and into TV set production, are getting more vaccine. This gain from trade for Korea is summarized in Table 3. Observe that the exports of TV sets from Korea equal the imports of TV sets to the United States.

■ **Just Like a New Discovery.**   International trade is like the discovery of a new idea or technique that makes workers more productive. It is as if workers in the United States figured out how to produce more TV sets with the same amount of effort. Their trick is that they actually produce vaccines, which are then traded for the TV sets. Like any other new technique, international trade improves the well-being of Americans. International trade also improves the well-being of the Koreans; it is as if they discovered a new technique, too.

A Graphical Measure of the Gains from Trade

The gains from trade due to comparative advantage can also be found graphically with production possibilities curves, as shown in Figure 2. There are two graphs in the figure—one for the United States and the other for Korea. In both graphs, the horizontal axis has the number of TV sets and the vertical axis has the number of vials of vaccine produced.

■ **Production Possibilities Curves Without Trade.**   The solid lines in the two graphs show the production possibilities curves for vaccines and TV sets in the United States and in Korea before trade. To derive them, we assume, for illustrative purposes, that there are 10,000 workers in the United States and 30,000 workers in Korea who can make either vaccines or TV sets.

If all the available workers in the United States produce vaccines, then total production will be 60,000 vials of vaccine (6 × 10,000) and zero TV sets. Alternatively, if 5,000 workers produce vaccines in the United States and 5,000 workers produce TV sets, then total production will be 30,000 vials of vaccine (6 × 5,000) and 15,000 TV sets (3 × 5,000). The solid line in the graph on the left of Figure 2 shows these possibilities and all other possibilities for producing vaccines and TV sets. It is the production possibilities curve without trade.

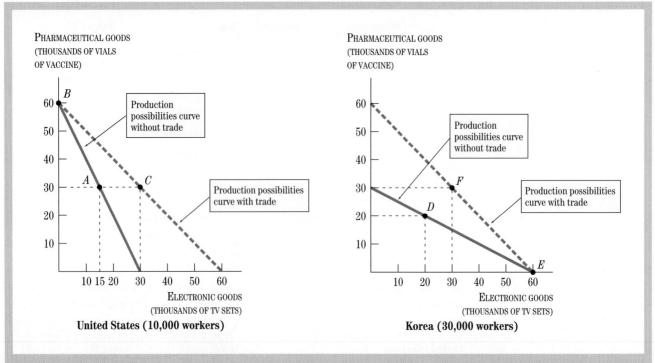

FIGURE 2
Comparative Advantage

On the left, Americans are better off with trade because the production possibilities curve shifts out with trade; thus, with trade, Americans reach a point like *C* rather than *A*. The gains from trade due to comparative advantage are equal to the distance between the two production possibilities curves—one with trade and the other without trade. On the right, Koreans are also better off because their production possibilities curve also shifts out; thus, Koreans can reach point *F*, which is better than point *D*. To reach this outcome, Americans specialize in producing at point *B* and Koreans specialize in producing at point *E*.

Korea's production possibilities curve without trade is shown by the solid line in the graph on the right of Figure 2. For example, if all 30,000 Korean workers produce TV sets, a total of 60,000 TV sets can be produced ($2 \times 30,000$). This and other possibilities are on the curve.

The slopes of the two production possibilities curves without trade in Figure 2 show how many vials of vaccine can be transformed into TV sets in Korea and the United States. The production possibilities curve for the United States is steeper than that for Korea because an increase in production of 1 TV set reduces vaccine production by 2 vials in the United States but by only 1/2 vial in Korea. The slope of the production possibilities curve is the opportunity cost; the opportunity cost of producing TV sets in the United States is higher than it is in Korea.

■ **Production Possibilities Curves with Trade.** The dashed lines in the two graphs in Figure 2 show the different combinations of vaccine and TV sets available in Korea and the United States when there is trade between the two countries at a relative price of 1 vial of vaccine for 1 TV set. These dashed lines are labeled "production possibilities curve with trade" to contrast them with the "production possibilities curve without trade" label on the solid line. The diagram shows that the production possibilities curves with trade are shifted out compared with the curves without trade.

ECONOMICS IN ACTION

Doing Politics and Economics

David Ricardo was a man of action. He went to work as a stockbroker at age 14 and eventually accumulated a vast fortune, including a beautiful country estate. He then became one of the most influential economists of all time. He also ran for and won a seat in the British Parliament from which to argue his economic position.

As an economist, Ricardo continued the tradition of Adam Smith. In fact, he got interested in economics after reading Smith's *Wealth of Nations* during a vacation. But Ricardo greatly extended and improved on Smith's theories and made them more precise. Along with Smith and Thomas Robert Malthus—who was Ricardo's close friend but frequent intellectual opponent—Ricardo is considered by historians to be in the classical school, which argued for laissez-faire, free trade, and competitive markets in eighteenth- and nineteenth-century Britain.

Ricardo grappled with three of the most important policy issues in economics: inflation, taxes, and international trade. But Ricardo's most famous contribution is to international trade—in particular, his theory of comparative advantage. Ricardo used this theory when he was in Parliament to argue for repeal of the restrictions on agricultural imports known as the corn laws.

Ricardo's theory of comparative advantage is a good example of how he improved on the work of Adam Smith.

Smith used commonsense analogies to illustrate the gains from trade; one of his examples was "The tailor does not attempt to make his own shoes, but buys them from the shoemaker." As with this tailor and shoemaker example, Smith focused on cases in which one person had an absolute advantage in one good and the other person had an absolute advantage in the other good. But Ricardo showed how there were gains from trade even if one person was better at producing both goods. Here is how Ricardo put it way back in 1817:

Two men can both make shoes and hats, and one is superior to the other in both employments; but in making hats, he can only exceed his competitor by one-fifth or 20 per cent., and in making shoes he can excel him by one-third or 33 per cent.;—will it not be for the interest of both that the superior man should employ himself exclusively in making shoes, and the inferior man in making hats?

DAVID RICARDO, 1772–1823

Born: London, 1772

Education: Never attended college

Jobs:
Stockbroker, 1786–1815
Member of Parliament, 1819–1823

Major Publications:
The High Price of Bullion, 1810
On the Principles of Political Economy and Taxation, 1817
A Plan for a National Bank, 1824

To see how the production possibilities curve with trade is derived, consider how the United States could move from point *A* to point *C* in Figure 2. At point *A*, without trade, Americans produce and consume 15,000 TV sets and 30,000 vials of vaccine by having 5,000 workers in each industry. Now suppose all U.S. workers move out of TV set production into vaccine production, shifting U.S. production to zero TV sets and 60,000 vials of vaccine, as shown by point *B*. Then by trading some of the vaccine, Americans can obtain TV sets. As they trade more vaccine away, they move down the production possibilities curve with trade: 1 less vial of vaccine means 1 more TV set along the curve. If they move to point *C* in the diagram, they have traded 30,000 vials of vaccine for 30,000 TV sets. Americans now have 30,000 TV sets and are left with 30,000 vials of vaccine. By producing more vaccine, the Americans get to purchase more TV sets. The distance from point *A* (before trade) to point *C* (after trade) in Figure 2 is the gain from trade: 15,000 more TV sets.

It would be possible, of course, to choose any other point on the production possibilities curve with trade. If Americans prefer more TV sets and fewer vials of vaccine, they can move down along that dashed line, trading more of their vaccine for more TV sets. In general, the production possibilities curve *with* trade is further out than the production possibilities curve *without* trade, indicating the gain from trade.

Observe that the slope of the production possibilities curve with trade is given by the relative price: the number of vials of vaccine that can be obtained for a TV set. When the relative price is 1 vial per TV set, the slope is -1 because 1 less vial gives 1 more TV set. If the relative price were 1/2 vial per TV set, then the production possibilities curve with trade would be flatter.

The gains to Korea from trade are illustrated in the right-hand graph of Figure 2. For example, at point *D*, without trade, Koreans produce 20,000 TV sets with 10,000 workers and, with the remaining 20,000 workers, produce 20,000 vials of vaccine. With trade, they shift all production into TV sets, as at point *E* on the right graph. Then they trade the TV sets for vaccine. Such trade allows more consumption of vaccine in Korea. At point *F* in the right diagram, the Koreans could consume 30,000 vials of vaccine and 30,000 TV sets, which is 10,000 more of each than before trade at point *D*. As in the case of the United States, the production possibilities curve shifts out with trade, and the size of the shift represents the gain from trade.

This example of Americans and Koreans consuming more than they were before trade illustrates the *principle of comparative advantage: By specializing in producing products in which they have a comparative advantage, countries can increase the amount of goods available for consumption.* Trade increases the amount of production in the world; it shifts out the production possibilities curves.

■ **Increasing Opportunity Costs: Incomplete Specialization.** One of the special assumptions in the example we have used in Table 2 and Figure 2 to illustrate the theory of comparative advantage is that opportunity costs are constant rather than increasing. It is because of this assumption that the production possibilities curves without trade in Figure 2 are straight lines rather than the bowed-out lines that we studied in Chapter 1. With increasing opportunity costs, the curves would be bowed out.

The straight-line production possibilities curves are the reason for *complete* specialization, with Korea producing no vaccines and the United States producing no TV sets. If there were increasing opportunity costs, as in the more typical example of the production possibilities curve, then complete specialization would not occur. Why? With increasing opportunity costs, as more and more workers are moved into the production of vaccine in the United States, the opportunity cost of producing more vaccine will rise. And as workers are moved out of vaccine production in Korea, the opportunity cost of vaccine production in Korea will fall. At some point, the U.S. opportunity cost of vaccine production may rise to equal Korea's, at which point further specialization in vaccine production would cease in the United States. Thus, with increasing opportunity costs and bowed-out production possibilities curves, there will most likely be incomplete specialization. But the principle of comparative advantage is not changed by increasing opportunity costs. By specializing to some degree in the goods they have a comparative advantage in, countries can increase world production. There are still substantial gains from trade, whether between Rose and Sam or between America and Korea.

> *REVIEW*
> - Comparative advantage shows that a country can gain from trade even if it is more efficient at producing every product than another country. A country has a comparative advantage in a product if it is relatively more efficient at producing that product than the other country.
>
> - The theory of comparative advantage predicts that there are gains from trade from increasing production of the good a country has a comparative advantage in and reducing production of the other good. By exporting the good it has a comparative advantage in, a country can increase consumption of both goods.
>
> - Comparative advantage is like a new technology in which the country effectively produces more by having some goods produced in another country.

REASONS FOR COMPARATIVE ADVANTAGE

What determines a country's comparative advantage? There are some obvious answers. For example, Central America has a comparative advantage over North America in producing tropical fruit because of weather conditions: Bananas will not grow in Kansas or Nebraska outside of greenhouses.

In most cases, however, comparative advantage does not result from differences in climate and natural resources. More frequently, comparative advantage is due to decisions by individuals, by firms, or by the government in a given country. For example, a comparative advantage of the United States in pharmaceuticals might be due to investment in research and in physical and human capital in the areas of chemistry and biology. An enormous amount of research goes into developing technological know-how to produce pharmaceutical products.

In Korea, on the other hand, there may be less capital available for such huge expenditures on research in the pharmaceutical area. A Korean comparative advantage in electronic goods might be due to a large, well-trained work force that is well suited to electronics and small-scale assembly. For example, the excellent math and technical training in Korean high schools may provide a large labor force for the electronics industry.

Comparative advantages can change over time. In fact, the United States did have a comparative advantage in TV sets in the 1950s and early 1960s, before the countries of East Asia developed skills and knowledge in these areas. A country may have a comparative advantage in a good it has recently developed, but then the technology spreads to other countries, which develop a comparative advantage, and the first country goes on to something else.

Perhaps the United States's comparative advantage in pharmaceuticals will go to other countries in the future, and the United States will develop a comparative advantage in other, yet unforeseen areas. The term *dynamic* comparative advantage describes changes in comparative advantage over time because of investment in physical and human capital and in technology.

Labor versus Capital Resources

To illustrate the importance of capital for comparative advantage, imagine a world in which all comparative advantage can be explained through differences between countries in the amount of physical capital that workers have to work with. It is such

capital abundant: a higher level of capital per worker in one country relative to another.

labor abundant: a lower level of capital per worker in one country relative to another.

capital intensive: production that uses a relatively high level of capital per worker.

labor intensive: production that uses a relatively low level of capital per worker.

a world that is described by the Heckscher-Ohlin model, named after the two Swedish economists, Eli Heckscher and Bertil Ohlin, who developed it. Ohlin won a Nobel Prize for his work in international economics. The Heckscher-Ohlin model provides a particular explanation for comparative advantage.

Here is how comparative advantage develops in such a model. Suppose America has a higher level of capital per worker than Korea. In other words, America is **capital abundant** compared to Korea, and—what amounts to the same thing—Korea is **labor abundant** compared to America. Pharmaceutical production uses more capital per worker than electronics production; in other words, pharmaceutical production is relatively **capital intensive,** while electronics production is relatively **labor intensive.** Hence, it makes sense that the United States has a comparative advantage in pharmaceuticals: The United States is relatively capital abundant, and pharmaceuticals are relatively capital intensive. On the other hand, Korea has a comparative advantage in electronics because Korea is relatively labor abundant, and electronics are relatively labor intensive. Thus, the Heckscher-Ohlin model predicts that if a country has a relative abundance of a factor (labor or capital), it will have a comparative advantage in those goods that require a greater amount of that factor.

The Effect of Trade on Wages

An important implication of the Heckscher-Ohlin model is that trade will tend to bring factor prices (the price of labor and the price of capital) in different countries into equality. In other words, if the comparative advantage between Korea and the United States was due only to differences in relative capital and labor abundance, then trade would tend to increase real wages in Korea and lower real wages in the United States.

More generally, trade tends to increase demand for the factor that is relatively abundant in a country and decrease demand for the factor that is relatively scarce. This raises the price of the relatively abundant factor and lowers the price of the relatively scarce factor. Suppose the United States is more capital abundant than Korea and has a comparative advantage in pharmaceuticals, which are more capital intensive than electronics. Then with trade, the price of capital will rise relative to the price of labor in the United States. The intuition behind this prediction—which is called **factor-price equalization**—is that demand for labor (the relatively scarce factor) shifts down with trade as the United States increases production of pharmaceuticals and reduces its production of electronic goods. On the other hand, the demand for capital (the relatively abundant factor) shifts up with trade. Although there is no immigration, it is as if foreign workers competed with workers in the labor-scarce country and bid down the wage.

Because technology also influences wages and productivity, it has been hard to detect such movements in wages due to factor-price equalization. Wages of workers in the developed world with high productivity due to high levels of technology remain well above wages of workers in the less-developed world with low productivity due to low levels of technology.

In other words, changes in technology can offset the effects of factor-price equalization on wages. If trade raises technological know-how sufficiently, then no one has to suffer from greater trade. In our example of comparative advantage, American workers are paid more than Korean workers both before and after trade; that is because their overall level of productivity is higher. Workers with higher productivity will be paid more than workers with lower productivity even in countries that trade.

Factor-price equalization can explain another phenomenon: growing wage disparity in the United States during the past 25 years, in which the wages of high-skilled workers have risen relative to the wages of less-skilled workers. The United States is

factor-price equalization: the equalization of the price of labor and the price of capital across countries when they are engaging in free trade.

relatively abundant in high-skilled workers, and developing countries are relatively abundant in low-skilled workers. Thus, high-skilled workers' wages should rise and low-skilled workers' wages should fall in the United States, according to factor-price equalization. In this application of factor-price equalization, the two factors are high-skilled workers and low-skilled workers.

In the next section, we show that there are gains in efficiency and lower cost from trade that can benefit all workers.

R E V I E W

- Comparative advantage changes over time and depends on the actions of individuals in a country. Thus, comparative advantage is a dynamic concept.

- International trade will tend to equalize wages in different countries. Technological differences, however, can keep wages high in high-productivity countries.

GAINS FROM EXPANDED MARKETS

In the introduction to this chapter, we mentioned the gains from trade that come from larger-sized markets. Having discussed the principle of comparative advantage, we now examine this other source of the gains from trade.

An Example of Gains from Trade Through Expanded Markets

Let us start with a simple example. Consider two countries that are similar in resources, capital, and skilled labor, such as the United States and Germany. Suppose there is a market in Germany and the United States for two medical diagnostic products—magnetic resonance imaging (MRI) machines and ultrasound scanners. Suppose the technology for producing each type of diagnostic device is the same in each country. We assume that the technology is identical because we want to show that trade will take place without differences between the countries.

Figure 3 illustrates the situation. Without trade, Germany and the United States each produce 1,000 MRIs and 1,000 ultrasound scanners. This amount of production meets the demand in the two separate markets. The cost per unit of producing each MRI machine is $300,000, while the cost per unit of producing each ultrasound scanner is $200,000. Again, these costs are the same in each country.

■ **Effects of a Larger Market.** Now suppose that the two countries trade. Observe in Figure 3—and this is very important—that the *cost per unit* of producing MRIs and ultrasound scanners *declines as more are produced*. Trade increases the size of the market for each product. In this example, the market is twice as large with trade as without it: 2,000 MRIs rather than 1,000 and 2,000 ultrasound scanners rather than 1,000. The production of MRIs in the United States can expand, and the production of ultrasound scanners in the United States can contract. Similarly, the production of ultrasound scanners in Germany can expand, and the production of MRIs in Germany can contract. With the United States specializing in production of MRIs, the cost per unit of MRIs declines to $150,000. Similarly, the cost per unit of ultrasound scanners declines to $150,000. The United States exports MRIs to Germany so that the number of MRIs in Germany can be the same as without trade,

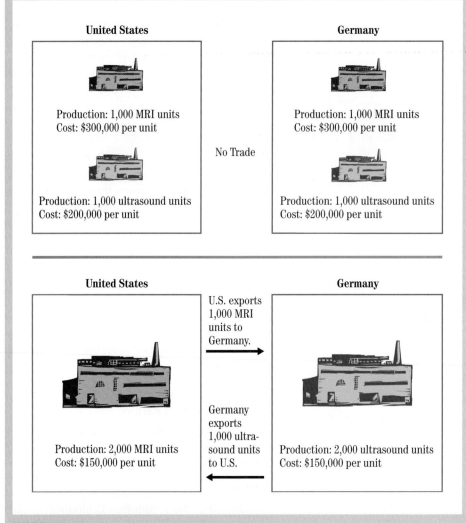

FIGURE 3
Gains from Global Markets
In this example, the technology for producing magnetic resonance imaging (MRI) machines and ultrasound scanners is assumed to be the same in the United States and Germany. In the top panel, with no trade between the United States and Germany, the quantity produced in each country is low and the cost per unit is high. With trade, the U.S. firm increases its production of MRIs and exports to Germany; the German firm increases its production of ultrasound scanners and exports to the United States. As a result, cost per unit comes down significantly.

and Germany exports ultrasound scanners to the United States. The gain from trade is the reduction in cost per unit. This gain from trade has occurred without any differences in the efficiency of production between the two countries.

Note that we could have set up the example differently. We could have had Germany specializing in MRIs and the United States specializing in ultrasound scanner production. Then the United States would have exported ultrasound scanners, and Germany would have exported MRIs. But the gains from trade would have been exactly the same. Unlike the comparative advantage motive for trade, the expanded markets motive alone cannot predict what the direction of trade will be.

intraindustry trade: trade between countries in goods from the same or similar industries. (Ch. 11)

interindustry trade: trade between countries in goods from different industries. (Ch. 11)

▪ **Intraindustry Trade versus Interindustry Trade.** MRIs and ultrasound scanners are similar products; they are considered to be in the same industry, the medical diagnostic equipment industry. Thus, the trade between Germany and the United States in MRIs and ultrasound scanners is called *intraindustry trade*, which means trade in goods in the same industry.

In contrast, the trade that took place in the example of comparative advantage was *interindustry trade*, because vaccines and TV sets are in different industries. In that example, exports of vaccines from the United States greatly exceed imports of vaccines, producing a U.S. industry trade surplus in vaccines. Imports of TV sets into the United States are much greater than exports of TV sets, producing a U.S. industry trade deficit in TV sets.

These examples convey an important message about international trade: Trade due to comparative advantage tends to be interindustry, and trade due to expanded markets tends to be intraindustry. In reality, a huge amount of international trade is intraindustry trade. This indicates that creating larger markets is an important motive for trade.

Measuring the Gains from Expanded Markets

The medical equipment example illustrates how larger markets can reduce costs. To fully describe the gains from trade resulting from larger markets, we need to consider a model.

▪ **A Relationship Between Cost per Unit and the Number of Firms.** Let us examine the idea that *as the number of firms in a market of a given size increases, the cost per unit at each firm increases*. The two graphs in Figure 4 are useful for this purpose. In each graph, the downward-sloping line shows how cost per unit (or average total cost) at a firm decreases as the quantity produced at that firm increases. Cost per unit measured in dollars is on the vertical axis, and the quantity produced and sold is on the horizontal axis. Observe that cost per unit declines through the whole range shown in the graph. Cost per unit declines because the larger quantity of production allows a firm to achieve a greater division of labor and more specialization.

Focus first on the graph on the left. The total size of the market (determined by the number of customers in the market) is shown by the bracket on the horizontal axis. We assume that the firms in the market have equal shares of the market. For example, if there are 4 firms in the market, then each firm will produce 1/4 of the market. Suppose that there are 4 firms; then, according to Figure 4, the cost per unit at each firm will be $30. This is the cost per unit for the quantity labeled by the box "1 of 4," which means that this is the quantity produced by each 1 of the 4 firms.

Now, suppose that there are 3 firms in the market and each firm produces 1/3 of the market. The cost per unit at each firm will be $25, as shown by the box labeled "1 of 3" in Figure 4. Cost per unit at each firm is lower with 3 firms than with 4 firms in the market because each firm is producing more—that is, 1/3 of the market is more than 1/4 of the market. Continuing in this way, we see that with 2 firms in the market, the cost per unit is $20. And with 1 firm in the market, the cost per unit is $10. In sum, as we decreased the number of firms in the market, each firm produced more and cost per unit decreased. If the number of firms in the market increased, then cost per unit at each firm would increase.

▪ **The Effect of the Size of the Market.** Now compare the graph on the left of Figure 4 with the graph on the right. The important difference is that the graph on the right represents a larger market than the graph on the left. The bracket in the right-hand graph is bigger to show the larger market.

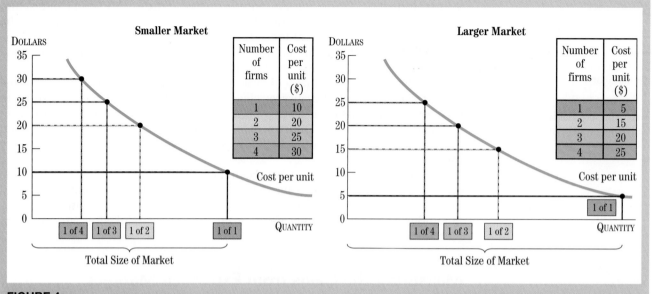

FIGURE 4
Cost per Unit: The Number of Firms and Market Size
(1) The market on the right is larger than the market on the left. Hence, cost per unit is lower on the right with the larger market.
(2) Regardless of the size of the market, cost per unit declines as the number of firms declines.

By comparing the graph on the left in Figure 4 (smaller market) with that on the right (larger market), we see that an increase in the size of the market reduces cost per unit at each firm, holding the number of firms in the industry constant. For example, when there is 1 firm in the market, cost per unit is $5 for the larger market compared with $10 for the smaller market. Or with 4 firms, cost per unit is $25 for the larger market compared with $30 for the smaller market. Compare the little tables in Figure 4. As the market increases in size, each firm produces at a lower cost per unit.

Figure 5 summarizes the information in Figure 4. It shows the positive relationship between the number of firms in the market, shown on the horizontal axis, and the cost per unit at each firm. As the figure indicates, more firms mean a higher cost per unit at each firm. (Be careful to note that the horizontal axis in Figure 5 is the *number* of firms in a given *market*, not the quantity produced by a given firm.) When the size of the market increases, the relationship between the number of firms in the market and the cost per unit shifts down, as shown in Figure 5. In other words, as the market increases in size, cost per unit declines at each firm if the number of firms does not change.

■ **A Relationship Between the Price and the Number of Firms.** A general feature of most markets is that as the number of firms in the market increases, the price at each firm declines. More firms make the market more competitive. Thus, there is a relationship between the price and the number of firms, as shown in Figure 6. As in Figure 5, the number of firms is on the horizontal axis. The curve in Figure 6 is downward-sloping because a greater number of firms means a lower price.

■ **Equilibrium Price and Number of Firms.** In the long run, as firms either enter or exit an industry, price will tend to equal cost per unit. If the price for each unit were greater than the cost per unit, then there would be a profit opportunity for

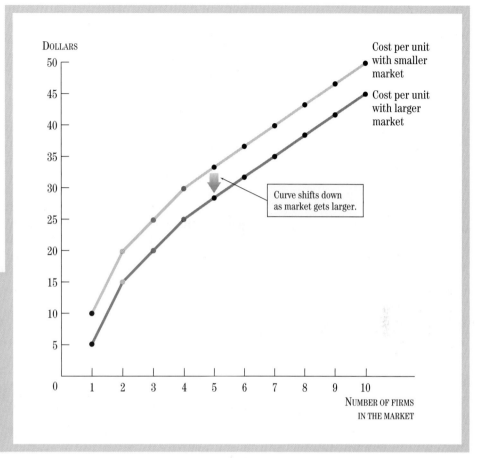

Cost per unit with smaller market

Cost per unit with larger market

Curve shifts down as market gets larger.

FIGURE 5
The Relationship Between Cost per Unit and the Number of Firms

The first four points on each curve are plotted from the two tables in Figure 4 for 1 to 4 firms; the other points can be similarly obtained. Each curve shows how cost per unit at each firm rises as the number of firms increases in a market of a given size. The curve shifts down when the size of the market increases.

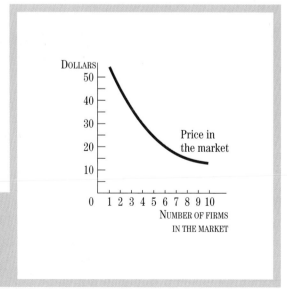

Price in the market

FIGURE 6
The Relationship Between the Price and the Number of Firms

As the number of firms increases, the market price declines. This curve summarizes this relationship.

new firms, and the number of firms in the industry would rise. If the price were less than the cost per unit, then firms would exit the industry. Only when price equals cost per unit is there a long-run equilibrium. Because price equals cost per unit, the curves in Figure 5 and 6 can be combined to determine the price and the number of firms in long-run equilibrium. As shown in Figure 7, there is a long-run equilibrium in the industry when the downward-sloping line for Figure 6 intersects the upward-sloping line (for the smaller market) from Figure 5. At this point, price equals cost per unit.

Corresponding to this long-run equilibrium is an equilibrium number of firms. More firms would lower the price below cost per unit, causing firms to leave the industry; fewer firms would raise the price above cost per unit, attracting new firms to the industry. Figure 7 shows how the possibility of entry and exit results in a long-run equilibrium with price equal to cost per unit.

■ **Increasing the Size of the Market.** Now let us see how the industry equilibrium changes when the size of the market increases due to international trade. In Figure 8, we show how an increase in the size of the market, due perhaps to the creation of a free trade area, reduces the price and increases the number of firms.

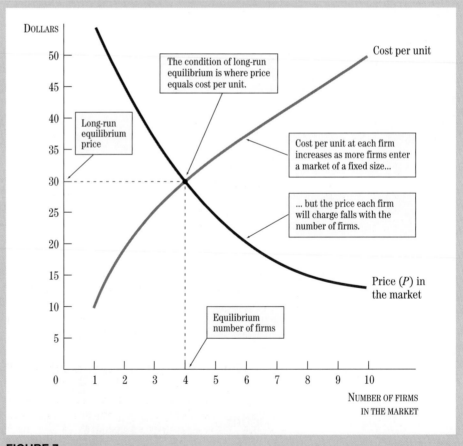

FIGURE 7
Long-Run Equilibrium Number of Firms and Cost per Unit
A condition for long-run equilibrium is that price equals cost per unit. In this diagram, this condition is shown at the intersection of the two curves.

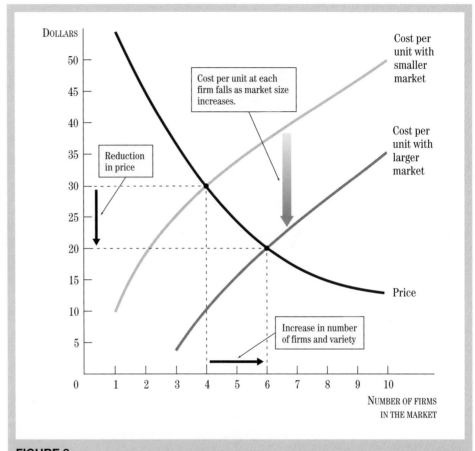

FIGURE 8
Gains from Trade Due to Larger Markets
When trade occurs, the market increases from the size of the market in one country to the combined size of the market in two or more countries. This larger market shifts the upward-sloping line down because cost per unit for each firm is lower when the market is bigger. In the long-run equilibrium at the intersection of the two new curves, the price is lower and there are more firms. With more firms, there is more variety. Lower price and more variety are the gains from trade.

The curve showing the cost per unit of each firm shifts down and out as the market expands; that is, for each number of firms, the cost per unit declines for each firm. This brings about a new intersection and a long-run equilibrium at a lower price. Moreover, the increase in the number of firms suggests that there will be more product variety, which is another part of the gains from trade.

■ **The North American Automobile Market.** The gains from trade due to larger markets arise in many real-world examples. Trade in cars between Canada and the United States now occurs even though neither country has an obvious comparative advantage. Before 1964, trade in cars between Canada and the United States was restricted. Canadian factories thus had to limit their production to the Canadian market. This kept cost per unit high. When free trade in cars was permitted, the production in Canadian factories increased, and the Canadian factories began to export cars to the United States. With more cars produced, cost per unit declined.

R E V I E W
- Lowering cost per unit through the division of labor requires large markets. International trade creates large markets.

- A graphical model can be used to explain the gains from international trade; the model shows that a larger market reduces prices.

CONCLUSION

In this chapter, we have focused on the economic gains to the citizens of a country from international trade. We have mentioned two reasons for such gains: comparative advantage and larger markets that reduce cost per unit. Both reasons apply to trade within a country as well as to international trade. Most of the chapter was spent showing how to measure the gains due to comparative advantage and larger markets.

In concluding this chapter, it is important to point out that the benefits of international trade go well beyond economic gains.

International trade sometimes puts competitive pressure on governments to deliver better policies. Within the United States, competition between states can make regulatory and tax policies more efficient. Similarly, competition can make regulatory policies in countries more efficient.

International trade can also improve international relations. Trade enables Americans to learn more about Southeast Asians or Europeans or Latin Americans. This improves understanding and reduces the possibilities for international conflict. Developing international trade with Russia and the other countries of the former Soviet Union might even reduce the possibility of another cold war or new international conflict in the future. If many people have an economic stake in a relationship, they will not like a military action that threatens that relationship.

KEY POINTS

1. The principles of economics can be used to analyze international trade just as they can be used to analyze trade within a country.

2. International trade is different from within-country trade because national governments can place restrictions on the trade of goods and services between countries and on immigration.

3. According to the principle of comparative advantage, countries that specialize in producing goods that they have a comparative advantage in can increase world production and raise consumption in their own country.

4. The gains from trade due to comparative advantage can be shown graphically by shifting out the production possibilities curve.

5. The relative price of two goods with trade is between the relative prices in the two countries without trade.

6. Comparative advantage is a dynamic concept. If people in one country improve their skills or develop low-cost production methods through research, they will alter the comparative advantage.

7. If differences in the relative abundance of capital and labor are the reason for differences in comparative advantage, then international trade will tend to equalize real wages.

8. Lower cost per unit in larger markets is another key reason for gains in trade.

9. When the size of the market increases, the price declines, there are more firms, and there is greater variety of products.

KEY TERMS

tariff
quota
commerce clause

absolute advantage
capital abundant

labor abundant
capital intensive

labor intensive
factor-price equalization

QUESTIONS FOR REVIEW

1. Why has international trade grown so rapidly in recent years?

2. What is the difference between absolute advantage and comparative advantage?

3. If the relative price of two goods is 4 in one country and 6 in another country before trade, in what range will the relative price be after trade?

4. What is the difference between the production possibilities curve before trade and after trade?

5. In what sense is comparative advantage a dynamic concept?

6. Why does trade take place even if one country does not have an absolute advantage over another?

7. What is the difference between capital abundant and capital intensive?

8. Why might costs per unit decline when the market increases in size?

9. What is the difference between interindustry trade and intraindustry trade?

PROBLEMS

1. Suppose France has 250 units of labor and Belgium has 100 units of labor. In France, 1 unit of labor can produce 1 box of chocolates or 3 bottles of wine. In Belgium, 1 unit of labor can produce 2 boxes of chocolates or 4 bottles of wine.
   a. Draw the production possibilities curve for each country.
   b. Which country has an absolute advantage in wine production? In chocolate production?
   c. Which country has a comparative advantage in wine production? In chocolate production?

2. Bill and Hillary are two very smart lawyers who also have an active interest in public policy. Bill can write a law paper in 3 months or a policy paper in 1 month. Hillary can write a law paper or a policy paper in 1 month. Bill and Hillary like each other a lot and would like to get married. However, since the marriage of two lawyers is often fraught with difficulty, they decide that one of them should write law papers while the other writes policy papers.
   a. Draw a production possibilities curve for Bill and one for Hillary.
   b. Who has an absolute advantage in writing law papers? In writing policy papers?
   c. Who has a comparative advantage in writing law papers? In writing policy papers?
   d. Explain how to reconcile your answers to (b) and (c).

3. Suppose that the United States has 200 million units of labor and Mexico has 100 million units, and that the production of wheat and strawberries per unit of labor in the United States and Mexico is as follows:

	Wheat	Strawberries
Mexico	1 bushel	3 pints
United States	2 bushels	3 pints

   a. What is the shape of the production possibilities curves for each country? What does this shape imply about the nature of the tradeoff between wheat and strawberries? Is this a realistic assumption? Explain.
   b. Which country has a comparative advantage in wheat production? Why?
   c. With free trade between the United States and Mexico, is it possible that 1 bushel of wheat will trade for 1 pint of strawberries? Why or why not?
   d. Suppose the free trade price is 1 bushel of wheat for 2 pints of strawberries. Draw a diagram indicating the production possibilities curve with and without trade.

4. Suppose there are two goods, wheat and clothing, and two countries, the United States and Brazil, in the world. The production of wheat and clothing requires only labor. In the United States, it takes 1

unit of labor to produce 4 bushels of wheat and 1 unit of labor to produce 2 items of clothing. In Brazil, it takes 1 unit of labor to produce 1 bushel of wheat and 1 unit of labor to produce 1 item of clothing. Suppose the United States has 100 units of labor and Brazil has 120.

a. Draw the production possibilities curve for each country without trade. Which country has the absolute advantage in each good? Indicate each country's comparative advantage.

b. In what range will the world trading price ratio lie when these countries open up to free trade? Will both countries be better off? Why? Show this on your diagram.

5. "Developing countries should exploit their own comparative advantage and quit trying to invest in physical and human capital to develop high-tech industries." Comment.

6. Suppose you found that exports from the United States to China were mainly goods, such as airplanes, that require much capital compared to labor, and that exports from China to the United States were mainly goods, such as toys, that require much labor compared to capital. Are these patterns consistent with comparative advantage?

7. "Comparative advantage suggests that high-skilled workers in developed economies and low-skilled workers in developing countries will be more supportive of free trade than low-skilled workers in developed economies and high-skilled workers in developing countries will be." Comment.

8. Comparative advantage explains interindustry trade in different goods between countries. How do economists explain intraindustry trade, that is, trade in the same industry between countries? Why might people in the United States want to buy German cars, and Germans want to buy cars from the United States?

9. Suppose that each firm in an industry has the total costs shown below.

Quantity of Output	Total Costs (dollars)
1	50
2	54
3	60
4	68
5	80
6	90
7	105
8	112

a. Suppose that the quantity demanded in the market is fixed at 4. Calculate the average total

cost for each firm when there are 1, 2, and 4 firms in the industry. Draw a diagram indicating the relationship between average total cost and number of firms.

b. Suppose the quantity demanded in the market expands because of an opening of trade and is now fixed at 8. Draw a diagram similar to the one in part (a) indicating the relationship between average total cost and the number of firms. Why does the opening of trade cause this shift in the curve?

10. The following relationship between price, cost per unit, and the number of firms describes an industry in an economy.

Number of Firms	Cost per Unit ($)	Price ($)
1	10	90
2	20	80
3	30	70
4	40	60
5	50	50
6	60	46
7	70	43
8	80	40
9	90	38
10	100	36

a. Graph (1) the relationship between cost per unit and number of firms and (2) the relationship between price and number of firms. Why does one slope up and the other slope down?

b. Find the long-run equilibrium price and number of firms.

c. Now suppose the country opens its borders to trade with other countries; as a result, the relationship between cost per unit and the number of firms becomes as follows:

Number of Firms	Cost per Unit ($)
1	5
2	10
3	15
4	20
5	25
6	30
7	35
8	40
9	45
10	50

Find the long-run equilibrium price and number of firms.

d. What are the gains from expanding the market through the reduction in trade barriers?

Chapter 18

International Trade Policy

In a democracy, there is a big difference between having an economic idea and implementing the idea in practice. Even if you have the greatest economic idea in the world, you have to spread the word, convince people, debate those in opposition, and even compromise if the idea is to be voted on favorably, signed into law, or serve as the basis for an international agreement.

We started this book with the central idea of economics—that people make purposeful choices with scarce resources and interact with other people when they make these choices. We have now seen that this central idea spawns many other powerful ideas—from the opportunity costs facing Tiger Woods to comparative advantage in international trade between countries.

Indeed, there is no better illustration of the difference between ideas and their implementation than the difference between the international trade *theory* of the previous chapter and international trade *policy*, which we take up now. From David Ricardo working in the British parliament to repeal protectionist trade laws 150 years ago to the present-day economists testifying in Congress in favor of a new trade agreement, the goal is the same: to achieve the economic gains from trade in practice in a democracy. It is not easy, but it is fascinating to watch or to participate in, and it is a fitting capstone to a book about economics.

We begin by examining the economic impact of the trade barriers that currently exist, reviewing the political history of past trade barriers in the United States, and considering the political-economic arguments given in favor of trade barriers. We discuss some of the arguments made by those protesting free trade agreements. We then go on to evaluate alternative political mechanisms in terms of their effectiveness in reducing trade barriers.

TARIFFS AND QUOTAS

Governments use many methods to restrict international trade. Policies that restrict trade are called *protectionist policies* because the restrictions usually protect industries from foreign imports.

Examining the economic impact of trade restrictions helps you understand why some industries lobby for protectionist policies. As you delve into the economic analysis, think about whether a protectionist policy would help or hurt you. If the United States restricts trade in clothing, how would this restriction affect U.S. clothing producers, foreign clothing producers, U.S. retailers that sell clothing, and U.S. consumers who buy clothing? How would the restriction affect U.S. employment in clothing production and the price of clothing? We'll see that there are winners and losers as a result of trade restrictions, but that the gains for the winners will be smaller than the losses of the losers. That is, the losses from trade restrictions outweigh the gains, creating deadweight loss.

As you learn the impact of a new trade restriction, check your understanding by considering the removal of an existing trade restriction. Again, there will be winners and losers as a result of removing trade restrictions, but the gains for the winners will be larger than the losses of the losers. Removing trade restrictions therefore eliminates deadweight loss.

Tariffs

ad valorem tariff: a tax on imports evaluated as a percentage of the value of the import.

specific tariff: a tax on imports that is proportional to the number of units or items imported.

The oldest and most common method by which a government restricts trade is the *tariff,* a tax on goods imported into a country. The higher the tariff, the more trade is restricted. An **ad valorem tariff** is a tax equal to a certain percentage of the value of the good. For example, a 15 percent tariff on the value of goods imported is an ad valorem tariff. If $100,000 worth of goods are imported, the tariff revenue is $15,000. A **specific tariff** is a tax on the quantity sold, such as 50 cents for each kilogram of zinc.

The economic effects of a tariff are illustrated in Figure 1. We consider a particular good—automobiles, for example—that is exported from one country (Japan, for example) and imported by another country (the United States, for example). An

Seattle, 1999
The goal of the WTO is to reduce trade barriers. But not everyone agrees with the goal, as the protest against the WTO meeting in Seattle reminds us. Though large antitrade protests have been less common in recent years, protectionist or isolationist sentiments continue to build as people worry about competition from China and other developing countries.

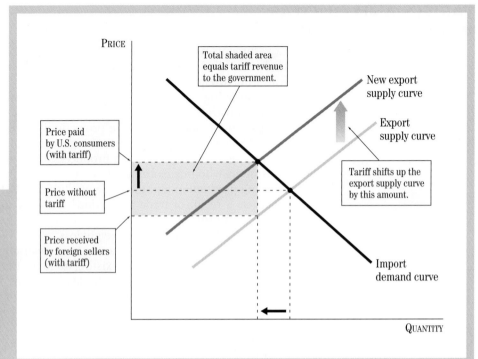

FIGURE 1
The Effects of a Tariff

A tariff shifts the export supply curve up by the amount of the tariff. Thus, the price paid for imports by consumers rises and the quantity imported declines. The price increase (upward-pointing black arrow) is less than the tariff (upward-pointing blue arrow). The revenue to the government is shown by the shaded area; it is the tariff times the amount imported.

import demand curve and an *export supply curve* are shown in Figure 1. The *import demand curve* gives the quantity of imported goods that will be demanded at each price. It shows that a higher price for imported goods will reduce the quantity of the goods demanded. A higher price for Nissans and Toyotas, for example, will lead to a smaller quantity of Nissans and Toyotas demanded by Americans. Like the standard demand curve, the import demand curve is downward-sloping.

The *export supply curve* gives the quantity of exports that foreign firms are willing to sell at each price. In the case of Nissans and Toyotas, the export supply curve gives the quantity of Nissans and Toyotas that Japanese producers are willing to sell in the United States. The supply curve is upward-sloping, just like any other supply curve, because foreign producers are willing to supply more cars when the price is higher.

In equilibrium, for any single type of good, the quantity of exports supplied must equal the quantity of imports demanded. Thus, the intersection of the export supply curve and the import demand curve gives the amount imported into the country and the price.

When the government imposes a tariff, the supply curve shifts up, as shown in Figure 1. The tariff increases the marginal cost of supplying cars to the United States. The amount of the tariff in dollars is the amount by which the supply curve shifts up; it is given by the length of the blue arrow in Figure 1.

The tariff changes the intersection of the export supply curve and the import demand curve. At the new equilibrium, a lower quantity is imported at a higher price. The price paid for cars by consumers rises, but the increase in the price is less than the tariff. In Figure 1, the upward-pointing black arrow shows the price increase. The blue arrow, which shows the tariff increase, is longer than the black arrow along the vertical axis. The size of the price increase depends on the slopes of the demand curve and the supply curve.

ECONOMICS IN ACTION

From Steel to Shrimp: The Same Old Tariff Story

Consider the case for and against a tariff to protect two different industries—steel and shrimp. In 2002, an increasing amount of steel in the United States was being imported, and steel prices were low. Many U.S. steel-producing companies were in debt, and in the past five years, 30 steelmakers had sought bankruptcy protection. To avoid additional bankruptcies and loss of jobs, the steel industry lobbied for protection from imported steel. In March 2002, President Bush imposed tariffs on steel imports. The tariffs were as high as 30 percent and were to last three years.

We would predict that a tariff on steel would increase the price of steel in the United States, increasing the profits of steelmakers and hurting steel consumers. As predicted, steel prices increased, steelmakers profited, and the steel-consuming industry was hurt by the higher prices. Some manufacturers claimed that the tariffs jeopardized more jobs in the steel-consuming industry than they saved in the steel-producing industry. Steelmakers in the rest of the world filed complaints with the World Trade Organization. The WTO ruled that the U.S. tariffs on steel were illegal. In December 2003, President Bush reversed this protectionist policy, removing the tariffs on steel. If you were determin-ing trade policy, how would you view the tradeoff between U.S. steel jobs and the effects of the higher price of steel on the U.S. manufacturing industry?

Between 2000 and 2004, shrimp imports in the United States increased 70 percent. This increase in the supply of shrimp caused the price of shrimp to tumble. U.S. shrimp fishermen lobbied for tariffs on imported shrimp, claiming that foreign shrimp was being dumped on the U.S. market at prices below production costs. In July 2004, the United States proposed tariffs on shrimp imported from some countries.

U.S. consumers benefit from the increase in shrimp imports and the tumble in shrimp prices. Foreign shrimp producers profit from their sale of shrimp in the United States. U.S. shrimp producers are requesting protection from these low shrimp prices. With tariffs we would expect profits for U.S. shrimp producers to increase, imports to fall, the price of shrimp to increase, and foreign producers' profits to fall. If you were determining trade policy, how would you view this tradeoff between the health of the U.S. shrimp-producing industry and the price of shrimp for U.S. consumers? Does your answer to these questions about tradeoffs depend on whether the protected industry is steel or shrimp?

The price received by suppliers equals the price paid by consumers less the tariff that must be paid to the government. Observe that the price received by the sellers declines as a result of the tariff.

The amount of revenue that the government collects is given by the quantity imported times the tariff, which is indicated by the shaded rectangle in Figure 1. For example, if the tariff is $1,000 per car and 1 million cars are imported, the revenue is $1 billion. Tariff revenues are called *duties* and are collected by customs.

The tariff also has an effect on U.S. car producers. Because the tariff reduces imports from abroad and raises their price, the demand for cars produced by import-competing companies in the United States—General Motors or Ford—increases. This increase in demand will raise the price of U.S. cars. Thus, consumers pay more for both imported cars and domestically produced cars.

Quotas

Another method of government restriction of international trade is the *quota*. A quota sets a limit, a maximum, on the amount of a given good that can be imported. The United States has quotas on the import of ice cream, sugar, cotton, peanuts, and other commodities. Foreigners can supply only a limited amount of these goods to the United States.

The economic effect of a quota is illustrated in Figure 2. The export supply curve and the import demand curve are identical to those in Figure 1. The quota, the maximum that foreign firms can export to the United States, is indicated in Figure 2 by the solid purple vertical line labeled "quota." Exporters cannot supply more goods than the quota, and, therefore, American consumers cannot buy more than this amount. We have chosen the quota amount to equal the quantity imported with the tariff in Figure 1. This shows that if it wants to, the government can achieve the same effects on the quantity imported using either a quota or a tariff. Moreover, the price increase in Figure 2, represented by the black arrow along the vertical axis, is the same as the price increase in Figure 1. Viewed from the domestic market, therefore, a quota and a tariff are equivalent. If the quota is set to allow in the same quantity of imports as the tariff, then the price increase will be the same. Consumers will pay more for imports in both cases, and the demand for domestically produced goods that are substitutes for imports will increase. The price of domestically produced cars will also increase if there is a quota on foreign cars.

Then what is the difference in the effects of a tariff and a quota? Unlike the situation with a tariff, no revenue goes to the government with a quota. The difference between the price that the foreign suppliers get and the higher price that the consumers pay goes to the holders of the quota—the ones who are allowed to import into the country. Frequently foreign countries hold the quotas. The revenue the quota holders get is indicated by the shaded rectangle in Figure 2. It is equal to the quantity imported times the difference between the price paid by the consumers and the price received by the producers. The size of that rectangle is identical to the size of the rectangle showing the revenue paid to the government in the case of the tariff in Figure 1.

On January 1, 2005, the 1973 Multi-Fiber Agreement, a set of quotas on textiles and apparel, expired. This system of global quotas restricting imports added an estimated 20 percent to the cost of clothing, while benefiting companies in places like the Philippines that specialized in supplying clothing under this quota system. The lifting of the quotas created widespread fears among U.S. and European Union clothing manufacturers about the flood of cheap Chinese apparel into these markets.

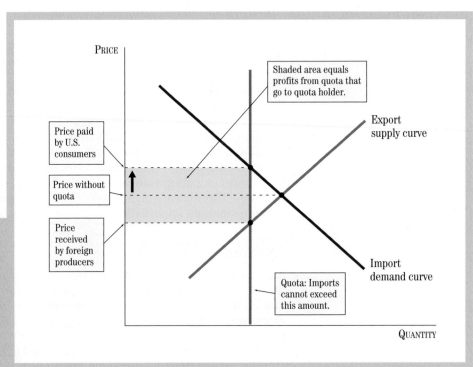

FIGURE 2
The Effects of a Quota

A quota can be set to allow the same quantity of imports as a tariff. The quota in this figure and the tariff in Figure 1 allow the same quantity of imports into the country. The price increase is the same for the quota and the tariff. But, in the case of a quota, the revenue goes to quota holders, not to the U.S. government.

The End of the Multi-Fiber Agreement

This news story from the Associated Press discusses the economic impact of the termination of the Multi-Fiber Agreement (MFA) on the economy of Sri Lanka. In this particular case, the cost to Sri Lanka is the loss of the quota rents that the country had earned under the Multi-Fiber agreement. The winners will be the lower-cost producers in countries like Mexico, who will no longer be shut out of the U.S. market, as well as consumers in the U.S. market.

The expiration of the MFA by the end of 2004

Impact on Sri Lanka

Sri Lanka's Revenue from Garment Exports to America Set to Drop 20 Percent as Trade Agreement Expires

November 15, 2004—*Associated Press*
Colombo, Sri Lanka

Benefits to U.S. consumers

SRI LANKA's revenue from garment and textile exports to the United States, its biggest customer, is expected to fall about 20 percent next year following the expiration of a preferential trade agreement, an industry official said Monday. The United States has purchased an annual average of about US$2.5 billion (€1.9 billion) garments and textiles from Sri Lanka since the two countries signed the Multi-Fiber Agreement in 1974. But the agreement is set to expire next month.

Tuli Cooray, who heads a committee of Sri Lankan business and government officials advising the industry, said American buyers will probably switch to lower cost manufacturers in China, Mexico and elsewhere in South Asia. As a result, he said Sri Lanka's shipments of garments and textiles to the United States will likely fall about 20 percent to about US$2 billion (€1.5 billion), in 2005.

Cooray said most small and medium garment manufacturers may need to downsize to stay in business, but added that the industry will bounce back by focussing on markets closer to home, such as India and Japan. "We don't envisage any serious shocks," Cooray told Dow Jones Newswires. "We have already initiated talks with Indian partners amid efforts to obtain a piece of that market," he said.

Overseas shipments of textiles and garments comprise 50 percent of Sri Lanka's total export earnings, and the United States has been the largest buyer of garments from Sri Lanka.

A coalition of U.S. producers claimed that 650,000 jobs were at risk. Since then, the European Union and the United States have both struggled to find a solution that will work for China and for domestic manufacturers, retailers, and consumers.

Since the expiration of the quotas, exports from China have surged, adding to downward pressure on prices of clothing in the United States. In contrast, exports from countries like the Philippines and Sri Lanka, that previously had quotas, have suffered. The surge in exports from China has caused U.S. clothing producers to lobby for new quotas though U.S. clothing retailers are opposed to them. If you were determining trade policy, how would you view this tradeoff between U.S. clothing prices and U.S. clothing production?

The Costs of Trade Restrictions

Trade barriers such as tariffs and quotas distort prices and reduce the quantity consumed, benefiting domestic producers at the expense of domestic consumers and foreign producers. For example, the United States imposes quotas on sugar to increase the price of domestic sugar beets and sugar cane. Producers receive $1 billion a year in additional surplus as a result of higher prices, but U.S. consumers lose $1.9 billion, for a net loss of $.9 billion to the United States.

The Multi-Fiber Agreement, which ended in January 2005, was another trade restriction that had substantial implications for U.S. consumers. The estimated loss to U.S. consumers was $24 billion a year, and the cost to the U.S. economy was around $10 billion a year.

R E V I E W

- The most common ways for government to restrict foreign trade are tariffs and quotas. Each has the same effect on price and quantity.

- With a tariff, the revenue from the tariff goes to the government. With a quota, that revenue goes to quota holders.

- Trade restrictions alter the allocation of resources in the economy and are significant sources of deadweight loss.

THE HISTORY OF TRADE RESTRICTIONS

revenue tariff: an import tax whose main purpose is to provide revenue to the government.

As stated earlier, tariffs are the oldest form of trade restriction. Throughout history, governments have used tariffs to raise revenue. **Revenue tariffs,** whose main purpose is raising revenue, were by far the most significant source of federal revenue in the United States before the income tax was made constitutional by the Sixteenth Amendment to the U.S. Constitution in 1913 (see Figure 3). Revenue tariffs are still common in less-developed countries because they are easy for the government to collect as the goods come through a port or one of a few checkpoints.

U.S. Tariffs

Tariffs are a big part of U.S. history. Even before the United States was a country, a tariff on tea imported into the colonies led to the Boston Tea Party. One of the first acts of the U.S. Congress placed tariffs on imports. Figure 4 summarizes the history of tariffs in the United States since the early 1800s.

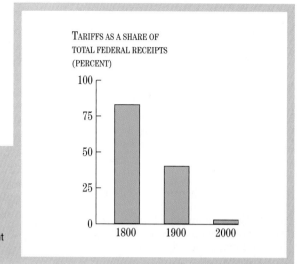

FIGURE 3
Tariffs as a Share of Total Federal Revenue
The first tariff, passed in 1789, represented nearly all of the federal government's revenue; 200 years later, tariff revenues were only about 1 percent of the total.

■ **From the Tariff of Abominations to Smoot-Hawley.** Tariffs were high throughout much of U.S. history, rarely going below 20 percent in the nineteenth century. In addition to raising revenue, these tariffs had the purpose of reducing imports of manufactured goods. The tariffs offered protection to manufacturers in the North but raised prices for consumers. Since the South was mainly agricultural and a consumer of manufactured goods, there was a constant dispute between the North and the South over these tariffs.

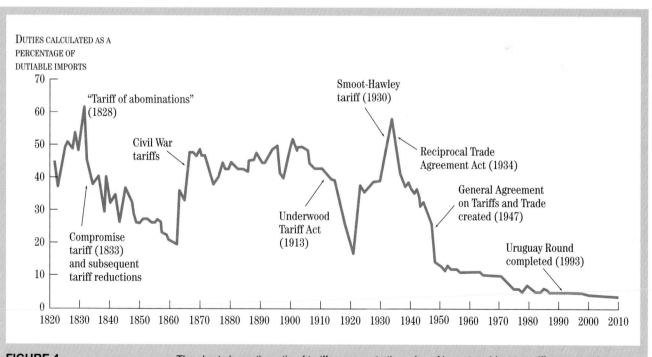

FIGURE 4
History of Tariffs in the United States

The chart shows the ratio of tariff revenues to the value of imports subject to tariffs measured as a percentage. This percentage is a measure of the average tariff excluding goods not subject to any tariff.

Smoot-Hawley tariff: a set of tariffs imposed in 1930 that raised the average tariff level to 59 percent by 1932.

trade war: a conflict among nations over trade policies caused by imposition of protectionist policies on the part of one country and subsequent retaliatory actions by other countries.

The highest of these tariffs was nicknamed the "tariff of abominations." This tariff, passed in 1828, brought the average tariff level in the United States to over 60 percent. The tariff made purchases of farm equipment much more expensive in the southern states. It almost led to a civil war before the actual Civil War, as the southern states threatened to secede. However, because the tariff was so high, it was soon repealed, and for the next 10 years tariffs were relatively low by nineteenth-century standards.

The most devastating increase in tariffs in U.S. history occurred during the Great Depression. The **Smoot-Hawley tariff** of 1930 raised average tariffs to 59 percent. Congress and President Hoover apparently hoped that raising tariffs would help stimulate U.S. production and offset the Great Depression. But the increase had precisely the opposite effect. Other countries retaliated by raising their tariffs on U.S. goods. Each country tried to beat the others with higher tariffs, a phenomenon known as a **trade war.** The Smoot-Hawley tariff had terrible consequences. Figure 5 is a dramatic illustration of the decline in trade that occurred at the time of these tariff increases during the Great Depression. The Smoot-Hawley tariff made the Great Depression worse than it would have otherwise been.

■ **From the Reciprocal Trade Agreement Act to the WTO.** The only good thing about the Smoot-Hawley tariff was that it demonstrated to the whole world how harmful tariffs can be. In order to achieve lower tariffs, the Congress passed and President Roosevelt signed the *Reciprocal Trade Agreement Act* in 1934. This act was probably the most significant event in the history of U.S. trade policy. It authorized the president to cut U.S. tariffs by up to 50 percent if other countries would cut their tariffs on a reciprocating basis. The reciprocal trade agreements resulted in a remarkable

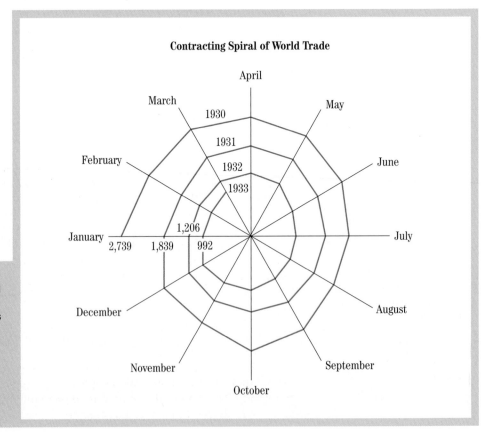

FIGURE 5
Decline in World Trade During the Great Depression
This circular graph, used by Charles Kindleberger of MIT, illustrates how world trade collapsed after tariffs increased during the Great Depression. The distance from the middle of the graph to the point on each spoke is the amount of trade (in millions of dollars) during each month.

reduction in tariffs. By the end of World War II, the average tariff level was down from a peak of 59 percent under Smoot-Hawley to 25 percent. The successful approach to tariff reduction under the Reciprocal Trade Agreement Act was made permanent in 1947 with the creation of a new international organization, the *General Agreement on Tariffs and Trade (GATT)*. GATT was set up to continue the process of tariff reduction. During the half-century since the end of World War II, tariffs have continued to decline on a reciprocating basis. By 1992, the average U.S. tariff level was down to 5.2 percent.

World Trade Organization (WTO): an international organization that can mediate trade disputes.

In 1993, GATT was transformed into the **World Trade Organization (WTO)**, which continues to promote reciprocal reductions in tariffs and other trade barriers. But the WTO also has authority to resolve trade disputes between countries. For example, if the United States complains that Europe is violating a trade agreement by restricting U.S. beef imports in some way, then the WTO determines whether the complaint has merit and what sanctions should be imposed on Europe. This dispute resolution authority has led to complaints, such as those made by the protesters in Seattle in 1999, that the WTO represents a loss of sovereignty for individual countries. On the other side of the argument, by resolving disputes, the WTO can avoid misunderstandings that otherwise can lead to trade wars between countries when trade disputes occur.

■ Antidumping Duties. No history of U.S. tariffs would be complete without a discussion of antidumping duties. **Antidumping duties** are tariffs put on foreign firms as a penalty for dumping. When a firm sells products in another country at prices below average cost or below the price in the home country, it is called *dumping*. Dumping can occur for many reasons. For example, the firm might want to sell at a lower price in the foreign market than in the home market because the demand in the foreign market is more elastic. If so, consumers in the foreign market benefit. But some people argue that dumping is a way for firms in other countries to drive domestic firms out of business and thereby gain market share and market power. In any case, in the United States and other countries, dumping is illegal; the penalty is a high tariff—the antidumping duty—on the good that is being dumped. Steel is one of the industries protected with antidumping duties in the United States, at a cost to consumers of as much as $732,000 per job protected, about 10 times what a steelworker earns. President Bush's increase in steel tariffs in 2002 provoked retaliation by the European Union and Japan, adding to the deadweight loss caused by trade barriers.

antidumping duty: a tariff imposed on a country as a penalty for dumping goods.

Many economists are concerned that antidumping duties, or even the threat of such duties, are serious restrictions on trade. They reduce imports and raise consumer prices. Moreover, they are frequently used for protectionist purposes. Firms in industries that desire additional protection can file dumping charges and request that tariffs be raised. Frequently, they are successful. Thus, an important issue for the future is how to reduce the use of antidumping duties for restricting trade.

■ The Rise of Nontariff Barriers. As tariffs were being reduced in the post–World War II period, a conflicting trend began to emerge. Some of the other methods of restricting trade—called **nontariff barriers** to trade—grew in popularity. Nontariff barriers include anything from quotas to quality standards aimed at reducing the import of foreign products. Nontariff barriers may have arisen as a replacement for tariffs in response to political pressure for protection of certain industries.

nontariff barrier: any government action other than a tariff that reduces imports, such as a quota or a standard.

Quality and performance standards are sometimes nothing more than barriers to trade. Some standards may have a good purpose, such as safety or compatibility with other products, but others do not. Consider the Canadian plywood standards for building construction, which keep out U.S. plywood. The Canadians argue that the standards are needed to satisfy building requirements in Canada, but Americans argue that plywood that does not meet the Canadian standards works just as well. A safety restriction against American-made baseball bats in Japan during the 1980s is another example. Most Americans viewed the bats as perfectly safe and viewed the Japanese safety standard as a restriction on trade.

Quality and performance standards, therefore, are a tricky problem because governments can argue that they are for the purpose of improving economic conditions in their own country. The U.S. Food and Drug Administration does not allow untested drugs into the United States even though foreign governments deem them safe. The FDA argues that the restriction is necessary to protect consumers, but foreign governments view it as a trade restriction. Such a standard does seem like a trade barrier, but in reality it is a matter of dispute.

REVIEW

- Tariffs were used by governments to raise revenue long before income taxes were invented.

- Tariffs have also been used for protectionist purposes in several important instances in U.S. history. Manufacturing firms in the North were protected by tariffs at the expense of consumers of manufactured goods, many of whom were in the South.

- The Smoot-Hawley tariff of the 1930s was one of the most harmful in U.S. history. It led to a trade war in which other countries raised tariffs in retaliation.

- Tariffs have come down since the 1930s. However, in recent years, nontariff barriers to trade have gone up.

ARGUMENTS FOR TRADE BARRIERS

Are there any good economic arguments for trade barriers? Let's examine some of the arguments that are typically made.

High Transition Costs

When an industry shrinks as a result of the removal of restrictions on trade, the cost of adjustment in the short run may be quite large, even if other industries grow. Those who lose their jobs in the protected industry, even temporarily, suffer. In the short run, it is difficult to retrain workers. Workers who are laid off as the industry shrinks cannot move easily to another industry. Many have to retire early. Retraining is possible, but it takes time and is difficult for older workers.

■ **Phaseout of Trade Restrictions.**   Some people argue that these costs are so high that we should not reduce trade barriers. But there is a better approach. These costs of adjustment are a reason for a slow phaseout of trade barriers. *Phaseout* means that trade barriers are reduced a little bit each year. A slow phaseout of trade barriers was part of the North American Free Trade Agreement (NAFTA) between Canada, Mexico, and the United States. This agreement called for a phaseout period of 10 to 15 years, depending on the product. For example, some tariffs were scheduled to be cut by 25 percent in the first year, 50 percent after 5 years, and 100 percent after 10 years. The purpose of the slow phaseout was to allow production to shift from one industry to another slowly. The intention was to adjust the work force through attrition as workers normally retired.

■ **Trade Adjustment Assistance.** Another approach is to use *trade adjustment assistance*, which refers to transfer payments to workers who happen to be hurt because of a move to free trade. Unemployment insurance and other existing transfer programs may go a long way toward providing such assistance. However, because society as a whole benefits from free trade, some increased resources can be used to help the workers who bear the brunt of the adjustment. In other words, the extra income that can be obtained by trade may be used to ease the adjustment.

Transition costs are not a reason to avoid free trade. They are a reason to phase out the restrictions on trade gradually and to provide trade adjustment assistance to workers as needed.

The Infant Industry Argument

infant industry argument: the view that a new industry may be helped by protectionist policies.

One of the earliest statements of the **infant industry argument** in favor of trade restrictions was put forth by Alexander Hamilton in 1791 in his *Report on Manufactures*. Hamilton argued that manufacturing firms in the newly created United States should be protected from imports. Once the industries were established, they could compete with foreign imports. But as they got started, they needed protection until they reached a certain scale.

A danger with the infant industry argument is that the protection may last long after it was initially justified. In Latin America, for example, infant industry arguments were used to justify import protection in the 1950s. However, these barriers to trade lasted long after any kind of reasonable infant industry argument could be made.

The National Security Argument

A nation's security is another argument for trade restrictions. The national security argument is that there are certain goods, such as special metals, computers, ships, or aircraft, that the country needs to be able to produce in time of war. If it does not have an industry that produces them, it could be at a severe disadvantage.

However, national security arguments can be used by firms seeking protection from foreign imports. Japanese rice farmers, for example, made national security arguments for protection from rice imports. In fact, the rice restriction has little to do with national security because rice can be imported from many different countries. In the United States, the textile industry has argued on national security grounds that it needs protection because it provides military uniforms made from U.S. textiles.

It is important to examine whether there are alternatives to trade restrictions before applying the national security argument and restricting trade. For example, rather than restricting rice imports, the Japanese could store a large amount of rice in case of a war emergency. Or the United States could store millions of extra uniforms rather than restrict textile imports if it was really thought that uniforms were a national security issue. In fact, the United States does have stockpiles of many rare minerals and metals needed for national defense production.

The Retaliation Argument

Threatening other countries or retaliating against them when they have trade restrictions is another possible reason to deviate from free trade. If the United States threatens the Japanese by saying that it will close U.S. markets, this may encourage Japan to open its markets to the United States. Thus, by retaliating or threatening, there is a possibility of increasing international trade around the world.

However, the retaliation argument can also be used by those seeking protection. Those in the United States who are most vocal about retaliation against other countries are frequently those who want to protect an industry. Many economists worry about threats of retaliation because they fear that other countries will respond with further retaliation, and a trade war will occur.

The Foreign Subsidies Argument

If foreign governments subsidize their firms' exports, does this justify U.S. government subsidies to U.S. firms to help them compete against the foreign firms?

Foreign subsidies to foreign producers are a particularly difficult issue. If foreign subsidies lower the price of U.S. imports, then U.S. consumers benefit. If Europe wants to use taxpayer funds to subsidize aircraft manufacturers, then why not enjoy the lower-cost aircraft? However, foreign subsidies enable industries to thrive more for political reasons than for economic ones. From a global perspective, such government intervention should be avoided, since it hurts consumers by encouraging less economically efficient production and, ultimately, higher prices.

Environment and Labor Standards Arguments

During the 1990s, a new type of argument against reducing trade barriers emerged: that tariffs or quotas should not be removed against countries with weak or poorly enforced environmental protection laws and labor standards, such as child labor laws and workplace safety laws. Because such laws and standards are generally weaker in developing countries than in developed countries, this argument frequently opposes reducing trade barriers to the imports of goods from relatively poor countries. For example, this argument is made by people who are against reducing tariffs on imports of Brazilian oranges into the United States.

Environmental and labor standard arguments are of two main types. First, some argue that holding back on the reduction of trade barriers until countries change their environmental and labor policies is a good way to persuade these countries to change. However, there is an important counterargument: Low trade barriers themselves lead to improvements in environmental and working conditions. History has shown that as their income grows, people become more concerned with the environment and their working conditions; people in deep poverty do not have the time or resources to deal with such issues. Thus, by raising income per capita, lower trade barriers can improve the environment and the workplace. Moreover, more effective and cheaper technologies to improve the environment or increase safety become available through trade.

A second type of argument is that it is difficult for workers and firms in the advanced countries to compete with those in less-developed countries who do not have to pay the costs of complying with environmental protection laws. However, by keeping trade barriers high, income growth may not be sufficient to address the environmental problems in developing countries, so the differences in the law will persist.

The Political Economy of Protection

Firms seek protection from foreign competition simply because the protection raises their profits. But the firms may use any of the above arguments to justify their case. In a famous satire of firms seeking protection from foreign competitors, a French economist, Frédéric Bastiat, wrote more than 150 years ago about candlemakers complaining about a foreign rival—the sun! The candlemakers in Bastiat's satire petitioned French legislators to pass a law requiring the closing of all shutters, curtains, and blinds during the day to protect them from this competition. The behavior Bastiat described seems to apply to many modern producers who seek protection from competition.

One reason that firms seeking protection are frequently successful is that they spend a lot more time and money lobbying the Congress than do the people who would be hurt by the protection. Even though consumers *as a whole* benefit more from reducing trade barriers than firms in the protected industry are harmed, each consumer benefits relatively little, so spending a lot of time and money lobbying is not worthwhile. It is difficult to get enough votes to remove trade barriers when a few firms each have a lot to lose, even though millions of consumers have something to gain.

R E V I E W

- Transition costs, environmental and labor standards, national security, infant industry, and retaliation are some of the arguments in favor of trade restrictions. Each has the possibility of being used by protectionists.

- Although many arguments in favor of trade barriers have been put forth over the years, in each case there are better ways to deal with the problems raised. The case for free trade holds up well in the debates when the economic rationale for the gains from trade is applied correctly and understood.

HOW TO REDUCE TRADE BARRIERS

Viewed in their entirety, the economic arguments against trade restrictions seem to overwhelm the economic arguments in favor of trade restrictions. The economic arguments in favor of free trade have been in existence for over 200 years. The recommendation of early economists such as Adam Smith and David Ricardo was simple: Reduce trade barriers.

However, it was not until many years after Smith and Ricardo wrote that their recommendations were translated into a practical trade policy. Then, as now, political pressures favoring protection made the repeal of trade barriers difficult. Hence, a carefully formulated trade policy is needed in order to reduce trade barriers. There are a variety of approaches.

Unilateral Disarmament

One approach to removing trade barriers in a country is simply to remove them unilaterally. Making an analogy with the arms race, we call this policy *unilateral disarmament*. When a country unilaterally reduces its arms, it does so without getting anything in arms reduction from other countries. With unilateral disarmament in trade policy, a country reduces its trade barriers without other countries also reducing their trade barriers. Unilateral disarmament is what Smith and Ricardo recommended for England.

The problem with unilateral disarmament is that some individuals are hurt, if only temporarily, and it is hard to compensate them. Of those who gain, each gains only a little. Of those who lose, each loses a lot. The political pressures that the losers exert are significant. As a result, unilateral disarmament is rarely successful in the developed countries today as a means of reducing trade barriers.

Multilateral Negotiations

multilateral negotiations: simultaneous tariff reductions on the part of many countries.

An alternative to unilateral disarmament is **multilateral negotiations,** which involve simultaneous tariff reductions by many countries. With multilateral negotiations, opposing political interests can cancel each other out. For example, import-competing domestic industries that will be hurt by the reduction of trade barriers, such as textiles in the United States or agriculture in Europe and Japan, can be countered by export interests that will gain from the reduction in trade barriers. Since consumers will gain, they are also a potential counter to protectionism, but they are too diffuse to make a difference, as we just discussed. With multilateral negotiations, interested exporters who gain from the reduction in barriers will push the political process to get the reductions.

Multilateral negotiations also balance international interests. For example, to get less-developed countries to remove their barriers to imports of financial and telecommunications services, the United States had to agree to remove agricultural trade barriers in the United States.

■ **The Uruguay Round.** Multilateral trade negotiations have taken place in a series of negotiating rounds, each of which has lasted several years. During each round, the countries try to come to agreement on a list of tariff reductions and the removal of other trade restrictions. There have been eight rounds of negotiations since 1947. The most recent was the **Uruguay Round,** named after the country where the first negotiations occurred in 1986. The Uruguay Round negotiations ended in 1993. Since 2002, the United States has been involved in negotiations for another global trade round, called the **Doha Development Round.** As with all such multilateral negotiations, this round is proving to be long and difficult and is still not finished.

The reduction in tariffs through multilateral negotiations under GATT has been dramatic. Tariffs have declined to below 3 percent on average in the United States with the implementation of the Uruguay Round agreement. Recall that this compares with nearly 60 percent in the mid-1930s.

■ **Most-Favored-Nation Policy.** Multilateral negotiations are almost always conducted on a *most-favored-nation* (*MFN*) basis. MFN means that when the United States or any other country reduces its tariffs as part of a multilateral trade agreement, it reduces them for everyone. Since the late 1990s, the term *normal trade relations* (*NTR*) has frequently been used in place of MFN because it is a more accurate description of the policy. Today, if a country is not granted MFN or NTR status, the United States imposes very high tariffs on the country. For example, concern about human rights in China has led some to argue that the United States should not grant MFN or NTR status to China. Without MFN or NTR, tariffs on Chinese imports to the United States would be about 60 percent.

Regional Trading Areas

Creating regional trading areas is an increasingly popular approach to reducing trade barriers. For example, NAFTA, the free trade agreement between the United States, Canada, and Mexico, removes all trade restrictions among those countries. An even wider free trade area covering the whole Western Hemisphere has been proposed.

Regional trading areas have some advantages over multilateral approaches. First, fewer countries are involved, so the negotiations are easier. Second, regional political factors can help offset protectionist pressures. For example, the political goal of European unity helped establish grassroots support to reduce trade barriers among the countries of Europe.

■ **Trade Diversion versus Trade Creation.** But there are disadvantages to regional trading areas in comparison with multilateral reductions in trade barriers under GATT. **Trade diversion** is one disadvantage. Trade is diverted when low-cost firms from countries outside the trading area are replaced by high-cost firms within

---

Uruguay Round: a most recent round of multilateral negotiations, opened in 1986 and completed in 1993.

Doha Development Round: the latest round of multilateral negotiations, opened in November 2001 in Doha, Qatar.

trade diversion: the shifting of trade away from the low-cost producer toward a higher-cost producer because of a reduction in trade barriers with the country of the higher-cost producer.

ECONOMICS IN ACTION

Ending the Corn Laws

Corn laws, recorded as far back as the twelfth century, restricted imports of grains, including wheat, rye, and barley, into England. Adam Smith devoted an entire chapter of his 1776 *Wealth of Nations* to the corn laws, arguing that "the praises which have been bestowed upon the law . . . are altogether unmerited."* But legislation introduced in 1791 raised the grain import tariff even further. The corn laws were unpopular with everyone except landowners and farmers.

The Anti-Corn League, founded in 1839 by Richard Cobden, was the most significant pressure group in nineteenth-century England. The Anti-Corn League used the economic arguments of Smith and Ricardo that the corn laws were an economic disaster and a moral tragedy: The laws impoverished and even starved the working class, constrained the growth of manufacturing, and provided government support to the wealthy. The catalyst was the Irish potato famine of 1845, which raised agricultural prices even further.

Robert Peel was the Tory prime minister from 1841 to 1846. Until 1845, he was against repeal of the corn laws, primarily because of strong support for them from landowners in the Tory party. But under pressure from Cobden and the Anti-Corn League, he changed his position after the potato famine and argued for the repeal of the corn laws.

In February 1846, Peel introduced a package of measures abolishing duties on imported corn over a three-year period. Only a minority of his party supported him, but the package passed. The split in the Tory party ended Peel's career, and the party did not win another election until 1868.

Thus, Peel paid a high political price for his policy of reducing trade protection, a policy that many feel helped make the British economy strong for the rest of the nineteenth century. How do you think he would have fared had he used one of the other methods (such as multilateral negotiations) to reduce protection rather than "unilaterally disarming"?

---

*Adam Smith, *Wealth of Nations* (New York: Modern Library, 1994), p. 560.

---

the trading area. For example, as a result of NAFTA, producers of electronic equipment in Southeast Asia have to pay a U.S. tariff, while producers of the same equipment in Mexico do not have to pay the tariff. As a result, some production will shift from Southeast Asia to Mexico; that is viewed as trade diversion from what might otherwise be a low-cost producer. The hope is that **trade creation**—the increase in trade due to the lower tariffs between the countries—will outweigh trade diversion.

trade creation: the increase in trade due to a decrease in trade barriers.

■ **Free Trade Areas versus Customs Unions.** There is an important difference between two types of regional trading areas: **free trade areas (FTAs)** and **customs unions.** In both, barriers to trade between countries in the area or the union are removed. But external tariffs are treated differently: Under a customs union, such as the European Union (EU), external tariffs are the same for all countries. For example, semiconductor tariffs are exactly the same in France, Germany, and the other members of the EU. Under a free trade area, external tariffs can differ for the different countries in the free trade area. For example, the United States's external tariffs on textiles are higher than Mexico's. These differences in external tariffs under an FTA cause complications because a good can be shipped into the country with the low tariff and then moved within the FTA to the country with the high tariff. To prevent such external tariff avoidance, *domestic content restrictions* must be incorporated into the agreement. These restrictions say that in order for a product to qualify for the zero tariffs between the countries, a certain fraction of the product must be made within the FTA. For example, under NAFTA, the majority of parts in television sets and automobiles must be manufactured in Canada, Mexico, or the United States in order for the television or car to qualify for a zero tariff.

free trade area (FTA): an area that has no trade barriers between the countries in the area.

customs union: a free trade area with a common external tariff.

531

R E V I E W

- There are many different approaches to removing restrictions on international trade, including unilateral disarmament, multilateral negotiations, and regional trading areas—FTAs and customs unions.

- Of all these approaches, unilateral disarmament is the most difficult politically. Multilateral and regional approaches are both more common and more successful in lowering trade barriers and keeping them low.

CONCLUSION

Very few economists disagree with the proposition that tariffs, quotas, and other trade barriers reduce the economic well-being of a society. In fact, polls of economists show that they disagree less on this proposition than on virtually any other in economics. This unanimity among economists was reflected in the debate over the North American Free Trade Agreement in the United States. Every living Nobel Prize–winning economist endorsed the agreement to eliminate tariffs and quotas among Canada, Mexico, and the United States.

This chapter has shown that despite this unanimity, many restrictions on international trade still exist. There is continued political pressure to erect new trade barriers or prevent the existing ones from being removed.

Thus, the need for good trade policies to reduce trade barriers is likely to increase rather than decrease in the future. The challenge is to develop a means for conducting international trade policy in a world with many sovereign governments, each of which is free to formulate its own policy.

KEY POINTS

1. Despite the economic arguments put forth in support of free trade, there are still plenty of restrictions on trade in the world.

2. Tariffs and quotas are the two main methods of restricting international trade. They are equivalent in their effects on prices and imports.

3. Tariffs were originally a major source of government revenue but are relatively insignificant sources of revenue today.

4. Quotas do not generate any revenue for the government. The quota holders get all the revenue.

5. National security and infant industry are two of the main arguments frequently put forth in support

of trade barriers. In most cases, they are overwhelmed by the arguments in favor of reduced trade barriers.

6. Eliminating restrictions on trade unilaterally is difficult because of the harm done to those who are protected by the restrictions.

7. Regional trading areas and multilateral tariff reductions endeavor to reduce trade barriers by balancing export interests against import-competing interests.

8. Free trade areas and customs unions both create trade and divert trade.

KEY TERMS

ad valorem tariff	trade war	infant industry argument	trade diversion
specific tariff	World Trade Organization (WTO)	multilateral negotiations	trade creation
revenue tariff		Uruguay Round	free trade area (FTA)
Smoot-Hawley tariff	antidumping duty	Doha Development Round	customs union
	nontariff barrier		

QUESTIONS FOR REVIEW

1. In what sense are a tariff and a quota equivalent?

2. Why might a tariff raise the price of the imported product by less than the amount of the tariff?

3. What are some examples of quality standards being used as trade barriers?

4. Why is unilateral disarmament a difficult way to reduce trade barriers?

5. How do multilateral negotiations or regional trading areas make the reduction of trade barriers easier politically?

6. Why might a regional trade agreement cause trade diversion?

7. What is the infant industry argument in favor of trade protection?

8. What are the disadvantages of using retaliation in trade policy?

PROBLEMS

1. Suppose French wine suddenly becomes popular in the United States. How does this affect the price and quantity of imports of French wine? Suppose the U.S. wine industry lobbies for protection. If the government imposes a tariff in order to restore the original quantity of imports, what will happen to the price of French wine in the United States? Show how much tariff revenue the government will collect.

2. Use a supply and demand diagram to show what happens to the price and quantity of sugar in the United States when the quotas on sugar are removed.

3. India has a 70 percent tariff on imported chocolate.
   a. Sketch a diagram to show the impact of this tariff on the price of imported chocolate in India.
   b. Suppose India cuts the tariff to zero but imposes a quota that results in the same high price for imported chocolate. Show this in a diagram.
   c. From the government's perspective, is it better off with a tariff or with a quota? Explain.

4. Suppose that in order to encourage tourism, a Caribbean country subsidizes hotel construction. What impact will this have on the United States? Be sure to identify who the winners and losers will be in the United States as a result of this decision by the Caribbean country.

5. Suppose the president of a nation proposes a switch from a system of import quotas to a system of tariffs, with the idea that the switch will not affect the quantity of goods imported. Who will be in favor of the switch? Who will oppose it?

6. The United States has a very generous system of farm subsidies that supports growers of crops such as corn, soybeans, and peanuts. Explain why countries like Brazil and Ghana, which are large producers of these crops, consider these subsidies to be a form of trade barrier.

7. Suppose the U.S. government has decided that for national security reasons, it must protect the machine tools industry. Name two ways in which the government can accomplish this goal. Which policy would you recommend? Why?

8. Suppose the North American Free Trade Agreement causes the United States to import lumber from Canada instead of from Finland, even though Finland is a lower-cost producer than Canada. Identify and explain this phenomenon.

9. Suppose the United States decides to withdraw most-favored-nation treatment from China. What will happen to the price and quantity of U.S. imports from China? Use a diagram to explain your answer.

10. Assume that several hundred independent farmers in Argentina are the only producers of a rare plant that is used for medicinal purposes around the world. Imagine that you are an economic adviser to the Argentine government. The president asks you to find a way to capture some of the economic rents from the production of this rare plant, so that more profits stay in Argentina. Your job is to design a trade policy that accomplishes the president's goal. Explain verbally what your trade policy would be, how it would affect quantity and price in the market, and how it would affect all the players in this market.

Glossary

ability-to-pay principle the view that those with greater income should pay more in taxes than those with less income. (14)

absolute advantage a situation in which a person or country is more efficient at producing a good in comparison with another person or country. (17)

accounting profits total revenue minus total costs, where total costs exclude the implicit opportunity costs; this is the definition of profits usually reported by firms. (9)

ad valorem tariff a tax on imports evaluated as a percentage of the value of the import. (18)

adverse selection in insurance markets, a situation in which the people who choose to buy insurance will be the riskiest group in the population; analogous situations apply in other markets. (16)

Antitrust Division of the Justice Department the division of the Justice Department in the United States that enforces antitrust legislation, along with the Federal Trade Commission. (12)

antidumping duty a tariff imposed on a country as a penalty for dumping goods. (18)

antitrust policy government actions designed to promote competition among firms in the economy; also called competition policy or antimonopoly policy. (12)

Arrow impossibility theorem a theorem that says that no democratic voting scheme can avoid a voting paradox. (15)

asymmetric information different levels of information available to different people in an economic interaction or exchange. (16)

average fixed cost (*AFC*) fixed costs divided by the quantity produced. (8)

average product of labor the quantity produced divided by the amount of labor input. (8)

average revenue total revenue divided by quantity. (10)

average tax rate the total tax paid divided by the total taxable income. (14)

average total cost (*ATC*) total costs of production divided by the quantity produced (also called cost per unit). (8)

average total cost pricing a regulatory method that stipulates that the firm charge a price that equals average total cost. (12)

average variable cost (*AVC*) variable costs divided by the quantity produced. (8)

backward-bending labor supply curve the situation in which the income effect outweighs the substitution effect of an increase in the wage at higher levels of income, causing the labor supply curve to bend back and take on a negative slope. (13)

barriers to entry anything that prevents firms from entering a market. (10)

bilateral monopoly the situation in which there is one buyer and one seller in a market. (13)

breakeven point the point at which price equals the minimum of average total cost. (8)

budget constraint an income limitation on a person's expenditure on goods and services. (5)

budget line a line showing the maximum combinations of two goods that it is possible for a consumer to buy, given a budget constraint and the market prices of the two goods. (5A)

capital abundant a higher level of capital per worker in one country relative to another. (17)

capital gain the increase in the value of an asset through an increase in its price. (16)

capital intensive production that uses a relatively high level of capital per worker. (17)

capital loss the decrease in the value of an asset through a decrease in its price. (16)

capitalism an economic system based on a market economy in which capital is individually owned, and production and employment decisions are decentralized. (2)

cartel a group of producers in the same industry who coordinate pricing and production decisions. (11)

Cartesian coordinate system a graphing system in which ordered pairs of numbers are represented on a plane by the distances from a point to two perpendicular lines, called axes. (2A)

ceteris paribus "all other things being equal"; refers to holding all other variables constant or keeping all other things the same when one variable is changed. (2)

choice a selection among alternative goods, services, or actions. (1)

Clayton Antitrust Act a law passed in 1914 in the United States aimed at preventing monopolies from forming through mergers. (12)

Coase theorem the idea that private negotiations between people will lead to an efficient resolution of externalities regardless of who has the property rights as long as the property rights are defined. (15)

command and control the regulations and restrictions that the government uses to correct market imperfections. (15)

command economy an economy in which the government determines prices and production; also called a centrally planned economy. (1)

commerce clause the clause in the U.S. Constitution that prohibits restraint of trade between states. (17)

comparative advantage a situation in which a group or country can produce one good at a lower opportunity cost than another person or country. (1, 17)

compensating wage differential a difference in wages for people with similar skills based on some characteristic of the job, such as riskiness, discomfort, or convenience of the time schedule. (13)

competitive equilibrium model   a model that assumes utility maximization on the part of consumers and profit maximization on the part of firms, along with competitive markets and freely determined prices. (7)

competitive market   a market in which no firm has the power to affect the market price of a good. (6)

complement   a good that is usually consumed or used together with another good. (3)

constant returns to scale   a situation in which long-run average total cost is constant as the output of a firm changes. (8)

consumer surplus   the difference between what a person is willing to pay for an additional unit of a good—the marginal benefit—and the market price of the good; for the market as a whole, it is the sum of all the individual consumer surpluses, or the area below the market demand curve and above the market price. (5)

contestable market   a market in which the threat of competition is enough to encourage firms to act like competitors. (10, 12)

contingent valuation   an estimation of the willingness to pay for a project on the part of consumers who may benefit from the project. (15)

controlled experiments   empirical tests of theories in a controlled setting in which particular effects can be isolated. (2)

convergence of positions   the concentration of the stances of political parties around the center of citizens' opinions. (15)

cooperative outcome   an equilibrium in a game where the players agree to cooperate. (11)

corporate income tax   a tax on the accounting profits of corporations. (14)

cost-benefit analysis   an appraisal of a project based on the costs and benefits derived from it. (15)

Council of Economic Advisers   a three-member group of economists appointed by the president of the United States to analyze the economy and make recommendations about economic policy. (2)

coupon   the fixed amount that a borrower agrees to pay to the bondholder each year. (16)

craft union   a union organized to represent a single occupation, whose members come from a variety of industries. (13)

cross-price elasticity of demand   the percentage change in the quantity demanded of one good divided by the percentage change in the price of another good. (4)

Current Population Survey   a monthly survey of a sample of U.S. households done by the U.S. Census Bureau; it measures employment, unemployment, the labor force, and other characteristics of the U.S. population. (14)

customs union   a free trade area with a common external tariff. (18)

deadweight loss   the loss in producer and consumer surplus due to an inefficient level of production. (7)

debt contract   a contract in which a lender agrees to provide funds today in exchange for a promise from the borrower, who will repay that amount plus interest at some point in the future. (16)

deferred payment contract   an agreement between a worker and an employer whereby the worker is paid less than the marginal revenue product when young, and subsequently paid more than the marginal revenue product when old. (13)

demand   a relationship between price and quantity demanded. (3)

demand curve   a graph of demand showing the downward-sloping relationship between price and quantity demanded. (3)

demand schedule   a tabular presentation of demand showing the price and quantity demanded for a particular good, all else being equal. (3)

depreciation   the decrease in an asset's value over time; for capital, it is the amount by which physical capital wears out over a given period of time. (16)

deregulation movement   begun in the late 1970s, the drive to reduce the government regulations controlling prices and entry in many industries. (12)

derived demand   demand for an input derived from the demand for the product produced with that input. (13)

diminishing marginal utility   the tendency for a consumer to derive less additional benefit from adding to the consumption of a good as her consumption of that good increases. (5)

diminishing returns to labor   a situation in which the increase in output due to a unit increase in labor declines with increasing labor input; a decreasing marginal product of labor. (6)

discount rate   an interest rate used to discount a future payment when computing present discounted value. (16A)

discounting   the process of translating a future payment into a value in the present. (16A)

diseconomies of scale   a situation in which long-run average total cost increases as the output of a firm increases. (8)

dividend yield   the dividend stated as a percentage of the price of the stock. (16)

division of labor   the division of production into various parts in which different groups of workers specialize. (1)

Doha Development Round   the latest round of multilateral negotiations, opened in November 2001 in Doha, Qatar. (18)

dual scale   a graph that uses time on the horizontal axis and different scales on the left and right vertical axes to compare the movements of two variables over time. (2A)

earned income tax credit (EITC)   a part of the personal income tax through which people with low income who work receive a payment from the government or a rebate on their taxes. (14)

earnings   the accounting profits of a firm. (16)

economic interaction   exchanges of goods and services between people. (1)

economic model   an explanation of how the economy or part of the economy works. (2)

economic profits   total revenue minus total costs, where total costs include opportunity costs, whether implicit or explicit. (9)

economic rent   the price of something that has a fixed supply. (16)

economic variable any economic measure that can vary over a range of values. (2)

economics the study of how people deal with scarcity. (1)

economies of scale a situation in which long-run average total cost declines as the output of a firm increases. (8)

efficient market hypothesis the idea that markets adjust rapidly enough to eliminate profit opportunities immediately. (16)

elastic demand demand for which the price elasticity is greater than 1. (4)

emission tax a charge made to firms that pollute the environment based on the quantity of pollution they emit. (15)

equilibrium price the price at which quantity supplied equals quantity demanded. (3, 7)

equilibrium quantity the quantity traded at the equilibrium price. (3)

equilibrium risk-return relationship the positive relationship between the risk and the expected rate of return on an asset, derived from the fact that, on average, risk-averse investors who take on more risk must be compensated with a higher return. (16)

equity contract shares of ownership in a firm; payments to the owners of the shares depend on the firm's profits. (16)

excess capacity a situation in which a firm produces below the level that gives the minimum average total cost. (11)

excess costs costs of production that are higher than the minimum average total cost. (11)

excise tax a tax paid on the value of goods at the time of purchase. (14)

exclusive dealing a condition of a contract by which a manufacturer does not allow a retailer to sell goods made by a competing manufacturer. (12)

exclusive territories the regions over which a manufacturer limits the distribution or selling of its products to one retailer or wholesaler. (12)

expected return the return on an uncertain investment calculated by weighting the gains or losses by the probability that they will occur. (16)

experimental economics a branch of economics that uses laboratory experiments to analyze economic behavior. (2)

explicit collusion open cooperation of firms to make mutually beneficial pricing or production decisions. (11)

external diseconomies of scale a situation in which growth in an industry causes average total cost for the individual firms to rise because of some factor external to the firm; it corresponds to an upward-sloping long-run industry supply curve. (9)

external economies of scale a situation in which growth in an industry causes average total cost for the individual firm to fall because of some factor external to the firm; it corresponds to a downward-sloping long-run industry supply curve. (9)

externality the situation in which the costs of producing or the benefits of consuming a good spill over onto those who are not producing or consuming the good. (15)

face value the principal that will be paid back when a bond matures. (16)

factor-price equalization the equalization of the price of labor and the price of capital across countries when they are engaging in free trade. (17)

Federal Trade Commission (FTC) the government agency established to help enforce antitrust legislation in the United States; it shares this responsibility with the Antitrust Division of the Justice Department. (12)

firm an organization that produces goods or services. (6)

first theorem of welfare economics the conclusion that a competitive market results in an efficient outcome; sometimes called the "invisible hand theorem"; the definition of efficiency used in the theorem is Pareto efficiency. (7)

fixed costs costs of production that do not depend on the quantity of production. (6, 8)

flat tax a tax system in which there is a constant marginal tax rate for all levels of taxable income. (14)

food stamp program a government program that provides people with low incomes with coupons (food stamps) that they can use to buy food. (14)

free entry and exit movement of firms into and out of an industry that is not blocked by regulation, other firms, or any other barriers. (9)

free trade area (FTA) an area that has no trade barriers between the countries in the area. (18)

free-rider problem a problem arising in the case of public goods because those who do not contribute to the costs of providing the public good cannot be excluded from the benefits of the good. (15)

freely determined price a price that is determined by the individuals and firms interacting in markets. (1)

fringe benefits compensation that a worker receives excluding direct money payments for time worked: insurance, retirement benefits, vacation time, and maternity and sick leave. (13)

gains from trade improvements in income, production, or satisfaction owing to the exchange of goods or services. (1, 17)

game theory a branch of applied mathematics with many uses in economics, including the analysis of the interaction of firms that take each other's actions into account. (11)

Gini coefficient an index of income inequality ranging between 0 (for perfect equality) and 1 (for absolute inequality); it is defined as the ratio of the area between the Lorenz curve and the perfect equality line to the area between the lines of perfect equality and perfect inequality. (14)

government failure a situation in which the government makes things worse than the market, even though there may be market failure. (1, 15)

gross domestic product (GDP) a measure of the value of all the goods and services newly produced in an economy during a specified period of time. (2)

Head Start a government transfer program that provides day care and nursery school training for poor children. (14)

Herfindahl-Hirschman index (HHI) an index ranging in value from 0 to 10,000 indicating the concentration in an industry; it is calculated by summing the squares of the market shares of all the firms in the industry. (12)

horizontal merger a combining of two firms that sell the same good or the same type of good. (12)

housing assistance programs government programs that provide subsidies either to low-income families to rent housing or to contractors to build low-income housing. (14)

human capital a person's accumulated knowledge and skills. (13)

implicit rental price the cost of the funds used to buy the capital plus the depreciation of the capital over a given period of time. (16)

incentive a device that motivates people to take action, usually so as to increase economic efficiency. (1)

incentive regulation a regulatory method that sets prices for several years ahead and then allows the firm to keep any additional profits or suffer any losses over that period of time. (12)

income elasticity of demand the percentage change in quantity demanded of one good divided by the percentage change in income. (4)

income effect the amount by which the quantity demanded falls because of the decline in real income from a price increase. (5)

income inequality disparity in levels of income among individuals in the economy. (7)

increasing opportunity cost a situation in which producing more of one good requires giving up an increasing amount of production of another good. (1)

indifference curve a curve showing the combinations of two goods that leave the consumer with the same level of utility. (5A)

individual demand curve a curve showing the relationship between quantity demanded of a good by an individual and the price of the good. (5)

industrial union a union organized within a given industry, whose members come from a variety of occupations. (13)

industry a group of firms producing a similar product. (9)

inelastic demand demand for which the price elasticity is less than 1. (4)

infant industry argument the view that a new industry may be helped by protectionist policies. (18)

inferior good a good for which demand decreases when income rises and increases when income falls. (3)

interindustry trade trade between countries in goods from different industries. (11, 17)

internalize the process of providing incentives so that externalities are taken into account internally by firms or consumers. (15)

international trade the exchange of goods and services between people or firms in different nations. (1, 17)

intraindustry trade trade between countries in goods from the same or similar industries. (11, 17)

invisible hand the idea that the free interaction of people in a market economy leads to a desirable social outcome; the term was coined by Adam Smith. (7)

isocost line a line showing the combinations of two inputs that result in the same total costs. (8A)

isoquant a curve showing all the possible combinations of two inputs that yield the same quantity of output. (8A)

labor abundant a lower level of capital per worker in one country relative to another. (17)

labor demand the relationship between the quantity of labor demanded by firms and the wage. (13)

labor intensive production that uses a relatively low level of capital per worker. (17)

labor market the market in which individuals supply their labor time to firms in exchange for wages and salaries. (13)

labor market equilibrium the situation in which the quantity supplied of labor equals the quantity demanded of labor. (13)

labor productivity output per hour of work. (13)

labor supply the relationship between the quantity of labor supplied by individuals and the wage. (13)

labor union a coalition of workers, organized to improve the wages and working conditions of the members. (13)

law of demand the tendency for the quantity demanded of a good in a market to decline as its price rises. (3)

law of supply the tendency for the quantity supplied of a good in a market to increase as its price rises. (3)

linear a situation in which a curve is straight, with a constant slope. (2A)

long run the minimum period of time during which all inputs to production can be changed. (8)

long-run average total cost curve the curve that traces out the short-run average total cost curves, showing the lowest average total cost for each quantity produced as the firm expands in the long run. (8)

long-run competitive equilibrium model a model of firms in an industry in which free entry and exit produce an equilibrium such that price equals the minimum of average total cost. (9)

long-run equilibrium a situation in which entry into and exit from an industry are complete and economic profits are zero, with price (P) equal to average total cost (ATC). (9)

long-run industry supply curve a curve traced out by the intersections of demand curves shifting to the right and the corresponding short-run supply curves. (9)

Lorenz curve a curve showing the relation between the cumulative percentage of the population and the proportion of total income earned by each cumulative percentage. It measures income inequality. (14)

macroeconomics the branch of economics that examines the workings and problems of the economy as a whole—GDP growth and unemployment. (2)

mandated benefits benefits that a firm is required by law to provide to its employees. (14)

marginal benefit the increase in the benefit from, or the willingness to pay for, one more unit of a good. (5)

marginal cost the change in total costs due to a one-unit change in quantity produced. (6, 8)

marginal cost pricing a regulatory method that stipulates that the firm charge a price that equals marginal cost. (12)

marginal private benefit the marginal benefit from consumption of a good as viewed by a private individual. (15)

marginal private cost the marginal cost of production as viewed by the private firm or individual. (15)

marginal product of labor the change in production due to a one-unit increase in labor input, holding other inputs fixed. (6, 13)

marginal rate of substitution the amount of one good for which the consumer is willing to trade one unit of another good and still have the same utility. (5A)

marginal revenue the change in total revenue due to a one-unit increase in quantity sold. (6)

marginal revenue product of capital the change in total revenue due to a one-unit increase in capital. (16)

marginal revenue product of labor the change in total revenue due to a one-unit increase in labor input, holding other inputs fixed. (13)

marginal social benefit the marginal benefit from consumption of a good from the viewpoint of society as a whole. (15)

marginal social cost the marginal cost of production as viewed by society as a whole. (15)

marginal tax rate the change in total tax divided by the change in income. (14)

marginal utility the increase in utility when consumption of a good increases by one unit. (5, 5A)

market an arrangement by which economic exchanges between people take place. (1)

market definition demarcation of a geographic region and a category of goods or services in which firms compete. (12)

market demand curve the horizontal summation of all the individual demand curves for a good; also simply called the demand curve. (5)

market economy an economy characterized by freely determined prices and the free exchange of goods and services in markets. (1)

market equilibrium the situation in which the price is equal to the equilibrium price and the quantity traded equals the equilibrium quantity. (3)

market failure any situation in which the market does not lead to an efficient economic outcome and in which there is a potential role for government. (1)

market power a firm's power to set its price without losing its entire share of the market. (10)

maturity date the date when the principal on a loan is to be paid back. (16)

means-tested transfer a transfer payment that depends on the income of the recipient. (14)

median voter theorem a theorem stating that the median or middle of political preferences will be reflected in government decisions. (15)

Medicaid a health insurance program designed primarily for families with low incomes. (14)

Medicare a government health insurance program for the elderly. (14)

microeconomics the branch of economics that examines individual decision-making at firms and households and the way they interact in specific industries and markets. (2)

minimum efficient scale the smallest scale of production for which long-run average total cost is at a minimum. (8)

minimum wage a wage per hour below which it is illegal to pay workers. (4)

mixed economy a market economy in which the government plays a very large role. (2)

moral hazard in insurance markets, a situation in which a person buys insurance against some risk and subsequently takes actions that increase the risks; analogous situations arise when there is asymmetric information in other markets. (16)

monopolistic competition a market structure characterized by many firms selling differentiated products in an industry in which there is free entry and exit. (11)

monopoly one firm in an industry selling a product for which there are no close substitutes. (10)

monopsony a situation in which there is a single buyer of a particular good or service in a given market. (13)

movement along the curve a situation in which a change in the variable on one axis causes a change in the variable on the other axis, but the position of the curve is maintained. (2A)

multilateral negotiation simultaneous tariff reductions on the part of many countries. (18)

Nash equilibrium a set of strategies from which no player would like to deviate unilaterally. (11)

natural monopoly a single firm in an industry in which average total cost is declining over the entire range of production and the minimum efficient scale is larger than the size of the market. (10, 12)

negative externality the situation in which *costs* spill over onto someone not involved in producing or consuming the good. (15)

negative slope a slope of a curve that is less than zero, representing a negative or inverse relationship between two variables. (2A)

negatively related a situation in which an increase in one variable is associated with a decrease in another variable; also called *inversely related*. (2)

nonexcludability the situation in which no one can be excluded from consuming a good. (15)

noncooperative outcome an equilibrium in a game where the players cannot agree to cooperate and instead follow their individual incentives. (11)

nonrivalry the situation in which increased consumption of a good by one person does not decrease the amount available for consumption by others. (15)

nontariff barrier any government action other than a tariff that reduces imports, such as a quota or a standard. (18)

normal good a good for which demand increases when income rises and decreases when income falls. (3)

normal profits the amount of accounting profits when economic profits are equal to zero. (9)

normative economics economic analysis that makes recommendations about economic policy. (2)

oligopoly an industry characterized by few firms selling the same product with limited entry of other firms. (11)

on-the-job training the building of the skills of a firm's employees while they work for the firm. (13)

opportunity cost the value of the next-best forgone alternative that was not chosen because something else was chosen. (1, 17)

Pareto efficient a situation in which it is not possible to make someone better off without making someone else worse off. (7)

payoff matrix a table containing strategies and payoffs for two players in a game. (11)

payroll tax a tax on the wages and salaries of individuals. (14)

perfectly elastic demand demand for which the price elasticity is infinite, indicating an infinite response to a change in the price and therefore a horizontal demand curve. (4)

perfectly elastic supply supply for which the price elasticity is infinite, indicating an infinite response of quantity supplied to a change in price and thereby a horizontal supply curve. (4)

perfectly inelastic demand demand for which the price elasticity is zero, indicating no response to a change in price and therefore a vertical demand curve. (4)

perfectly inelastic supply supply for which the price elasticity is zero, indicating no response of quantity supplied to a change in price and thereby a vertical supply curve. (4)

personal income tax a tax on all forms of income an individual or household receives. (14)

piece-rate system a system by which workers are paid a specific amount per unit they produce. (13)

portfolio diversification spreading the collection of assets owned in order to limit exposure to risk. (16)

positive economics economic analysis that explains what happens in the economy and why, without making recommendations about economic policy. (2)

positive externality the situation in which *benefits* spill over onto someone not involved in producing or consuming the good. (15)

positive slope a slope of a curve that is greater than zero, representing a positive or direct relationship between two variables. (2A)

positively related a situation in which an increase in one variable is associated with an increase in another variable; also called *directly related*. (2)

poverty line an estimate of the minimum amount of annual income required for a family to avoid severe economic hardship. (14)

poverty rate the percentage of people living below the poverty line. (14)

predatory pricing action on the part of one firm to set a price below its shutdown point in order to drive its competitors out of business. (12)

present discounted value the value in the present of future payments. (16A)

price the amount of money or other goods that one must pay to obtain the good. (3)

price ceiling a government price control that sets the maximum allowable price for a good. (4)

price control a government law or regulation that sets or limits the price to be charged for a particular good. (4)

price discrimination a situation in which different groups of consumers are charged different prices for the same good. (10)

price elasticity of demand the percentage change in the quantity demanded of a good divided by the percentage change in the price of that good. (4)

price elasticity of supply the percentage change in quantity supplied divided by the percentage change in price. (4)

price fixing the situation in which firms conspire to set prices for goods sold in the same market. (12)

price floor a government price control that sets the minimum allowable price for a good. (4)

price leader the price-setting firm in a collusive industry in which other firms follow the leader. (11)

price-earnings ratio the price of a stock divided by its annual earnings per share. (16)

price-cost margin the difference between price and marginal cost divided by the price. This index is an indicator of market power, where an index of 0 indicates no market power and a higher price-cost margin indicates greater market power. (10)

price-maker a firm that has the power to set its price, rather than taking the price set by the market. (10)

price-taker any firm that takes the market price as given; this firm cannot affect the market price because the market is competitive. (6)

prisoner's dilemma a game in which individual incentives lead to a nonoptimal (noncooperative) outcome. If the players can credibly commit to cooperate, then they achieve the best (cooperative) outcome. (11)

private remedy a procedure that eliminates or internalizes externalities without government action other than defining property rights. (15)

product differentiation the effort by firms to produce goods that are slightly different from other types of goods. (11)

producer surplus the difference between the price received by a firm for an additional item sold and the marginal cost of the item's production; for the market as a whole, it is the sum of all the individual firms' producer surpluses, or the area above the market supply curve and below the market price. (6)

production function a relationship that shows the quantity of output for any given amount of input. (6, 8)

production possibilities alternative combinations of production of various goods that are possible, given the economy's resources. (1)

production possibilities curve a curve showing the maximum combinations of production of two goods that are possible, given the economy's resources. (1)

profit maximization an assumption that firms try to achieve the highest possible level of profits—total revenue minus total costs—given their production function. (6)

profit sharing programs in which managers and employees receive a share of profits earned by the firm. (16)

profits total revenue received from selling the product minus the total costs of producing the product. (6)

progressive tax a tax for which the amount of an individual's taxes rises as a proportion of income as the person's income increases. (14)

property rights rights over the use, sale, and proceeds from a good or resource. (1, 15)

property tax   a tax on the value of property owned. (14)

proportional tax   a tax for which the amount of an individual's taxes as a percentage of income is constant as the person's income rises. (14)

public choice models   models of government behavior that assume that those in government take actions to maximize their own well-being, such as getting reelected. (15)

public good   a good or service that has two characteristics: nonrivalry in consumption and nonexcludability. (15)

quantity demanded   the quantity of a good that people want to buy at a given price during a specific time period. (3)

quantity supplied   the quantity of a good that firms are willing to sell at a given price. (3)

quintiles   divisions or groupings of one-fifth of a population ordered by income, wealth, or some other statistic. (14)

quota   a governmental limit on the quantity of a good that may be imported or sold. (17)

rate of return   the return on an asset stated as a percentage of the price of the asset. (16)

rate of technical substitution   the rate at which one input must be substituted for another input to maintain the same production; it is the slope of the isoquant. (8A)

real wage   the wage or price of labor adjusted for inflation; in contrast, the nominal wage has not been adjusted for inflation. (13)

regressive tax   a tax for which the amount of an individual's taxes falls as a proportion of income as the person's income increases. (14)

relative price   the price of a particular good compared to the price of other things. (2)

rent control   a government price control that sets the maximum allowable rent on a house or apartment. (4)

rental price of capital   the amount that a rental company charges for the use of capital equipment for a specified period of time. (16)

resale price maintenance   the situation in which a producer sets a list price and does not allow the retailer to offer a discount to consumers. (12)

return   the income received from the ownership of an asset; for a stock, the return is the dividend plus the capital gain. (16)

revenue tariff   an import tax whose main purpose is to provide revenue to the government. (18)

rule of reason   an evolving standard by which antitrust cases are decided, requiring not only the existence of monopoly power but also the intent to restrict trade. (12)

sales tax   a type of excise tax that applies to total expenditures on a broad group of goods. (14)

scarcity   the situation in which the quantity of resources is insufficient to meet all wants. (1)

scatter plot   a graph in which points in a Cartesian coordinate system represent the values of two variables. (2A)

Sherman Antitrust Act   a law passed in 1890 in the United States to reduce anticompetitive behavior; Section 1 makes price fixing illegal, and Section 2 makes attempts to monopolize illegal. (12)

shift of the curve   a change in the position of a curve, usually caused by a change in a variable not represented on either axis. (2A)

short run   the period of time during which it is not possible to change all inputs to production; only some inputs, such as labor, can be changed. (8)

shortage (excess demand)   the situation in which quantity demanded is greater than quantity supplied. (3, 7)

shutdown point   the point at which price equals the minimum of average variable cost. (8)

slope   a characteristic of a curve that is defined as the change in the variable on the vertical axis divided by the change in the variable on the horizontal axis. (2A)

Smoot-Hawley tariff   a set of tariffs imposed in 1930 that raised the average tariff level to 59 percent by 1932. (18)

social insurance transfer   a transfer payment, such as social security, that does not depend on the income of the recipient. (14)

social security   the system through which individuals make payments to the government when they work and receive payments from the government when they retire or become disabled. (14)

socialism   an economic system in which the government owns and controls all the capital and makes decisions about prices and quantities as part of a central plan. (2)

specialization   a concentration of production effort into a single specific task. (1)

specific tariff   a tax on imports that is proportional to the number of units or items imported. (18)

strategic behavior   firm behavior that takes into account the market power and reactions of other firms in the industry. (11)

substitute   a good that has many of the same characteristics as and can be used in place of another good. (3)

substitution effect   the amount by which quantity demanded falls when the price rises, exclusive of the income effect. (5)

supplemental security income (SSI)   a means-tested transfer program designed primarily to help the poor who are disabled or blind. (14)

supply   a relationship between price and quantity supplied. (3)

supply curve   a graph of supply showing the upward-sloping relationship between price and quantity supplied. (3)

supply schedule   a tabular presentation of supply showing the price and quantity supplied of a particular good, all else being equal. (3)

surplus (excess supply)   the situation in which quantity supplied is greater than quantity demanded. (3, 7)

tacit collusion   implicit or unstated cooperation of firms to make mutually beneficial pricing or production decisions. (11)

tangency point   the only point in common for two curves; the point where the two curves just touch. (5A)

tariff   a tax on imports. (17)

tax bracket   a range of taxable income that is taxed at the same rate. (14)

tax incidence   the allocation of the burden of the tax between buyer and seller. (14)

tax revenue   the tax rate times the amount subject to tax. (14)

taxable income   a household's income minus exemptions and deductions. (14)

Temporary Assistance to Needy Families (TANF) program transfer programs through which the federal government makes grants to states to give cash to certain low-income families. (14)

time-series graph   a graph that plots a variable over time, usually with time on the horizontal axis. (2A)

total costs   the sum of all costs incurred by producing goods or services. (6, 8)

total revenue   the price per unit times the quantity the firm sells. (6)

tradable permit   a governmentally granted license to pollute that can be bought and sold. (15)

trade creation   the increase in trade due to a decrease in trade barriers. (18)

trade diversion   the shifting of trade away from the low-cost producer toward a higher-cost producer because of a reduction in trade barriers with the country of the higher-cost producer. (18)

trade war   a conflict among nations over trade policies caused by imposition of protectionist policies on the part of one country and subsequent retaliatory actions by other countries. (18)

transaction cost   the cost of buying or selling in a market, including search, bargaining, and writing contracts. (15)

transfer payment   a grant of funds from the government to an individual. (14)

treble damages   penalties awarded to the injured party equal to three times the value of the injury. (12)

unemployment insurance   a program that makes payments to people who lose their jobs. (14)

unit-free measure   a measure that does not depend on a unit of measurement. (4)

Uruguay Round   the most recent round of multilateral negotiations, completed in 1993. (18)

user fee   a fee charged for the use of a good normally provided by the government. (15)

utility   a numerical indicator of a person's preferences in which higher levels of utility indicate a greater preference. (5)

utility maximization   an assumption that people try to achieve the highest level of utility given their budget constraint. (5)

variable costs   costs of production that vary with the quantity of production. (6, 8)

vertical merger   a combining of two firms, one of which supplies goods to the other. (12)

voting paradox   a situation where voting patterns will not consistently reflect citizens' preferences because of multiple issues on which people vote. (15)

wage   the price of labor defined over a period of time worked. (13)

World Trade Organization (WTO)   an international organization that can mediate trade disputes. (18)

yield   the annual rate of return on a bond if the bond were held to maturity. (16)

Index

Credits

Correspondence of David Ricardo, ed. Piero Sraffa (Cambridge University Press, 1962).

Chapter 18: p. 521, source of feature box material: "Sri Lanka's Revenue from Garment Exports to America Set to Drop 20% as Trade Agreement Expires" from the Associated Press, November 15, 2004. Reprinted by permission of the Associated Press; p. 523, Figure 3 source: Historical Statistics of the United States, Colonial Times to 1957, series Y, 259–260, and Budget of the U.S. Government, 2000; p. 523, Figure 4 source: Historical Statistics of the United States, Colonial Times to 1970, and Statistical Abstract of the United States, 1999; p. 524, Figure 5 source: "Contracting Spiral of World Trade," from Kindleberger, Charles, The World of Depression 1929–39 (Berkeley, California: University of California Press, 1973). Data reprinted by permission from League of Nations, Monthly Bulletin of Statistics, February 1934.